# Integrating Generative AI in Education to Achieve Sustainable Development Goals

Ruchi Doshi
*Universidad Azteca, Mexico*

Manish Dadhich
*Sir Padampat Singhania University, India*

Sandeep Poddar
*Lincoln University College, Malaysia*

Kamal Kant Hiran
*Aalborg University, Denmark*

IGI Global
PUBLISHER of TIMELY KNOWLEDGE

A volume in the Advances in Educational Technologies and Instructional Design (AETID) Book Series

Published in the United States of America by
IGI Global
Information Science Reference (an imprint of IGI Global)
701 E. Chocolate Avenue
Hershey PA, USA 17033
Tel: 717-533-8845
Fax: 717-533-8661
E-mail: cust@igi-global.com
Web site: http://www.igi-global.com



Library of Congress Cataloging-in-Publication Data

Names: Doshi, Ruchi, editor.
Title: Integrating generative AI in education to achieve sustainable development goals / edited by Ruchi Doshi, Manish Dadhich, Sandeep Poddar, Kamal Hiran.
Description: Hershey, PA : Information Science Reference, 2024. | Includes bibliographical references and index. | Summary: "This book investigates how Sustainable Development Goals could be advanced and how education might alter due to Generative Artificial Intelligence (AI)"-- Provided by publisher.
Identifiers: LCCN 2024002233 (print) | LCCN 2024002234 (ebook) | ISBN 9798369324400 (hardcover) | ISBN 9798369324417 (ebook)
Subjects: LCSH: Artificial intelligence--Educational applications. | Sustainable Development Goals.
Classification: LCC LB1028.43 .I5863 2024 (print) | LCC LB1028.43 (ebook) | DDC 371.33/4028563--dc23/eng/20240212
LC record available at https://lccn.loc.gov/2024002233
LC ebook record available at https://lccn.loc.gov/2024002234

This book is published in the IGI Global book series Advances in Educational Technologies and Instructional Design (AE-TID) (ISSN: 2326-8905; eISSN: 2326-8913)

British Cataloguing in Publication Data
A Cataloguing in Publication record for this book is available from the British Library.

All work contributed to this book is new, previously-unpublished material. The views expressed in this book are those of the authors, but not necessarily of the publisher.

For electronic access to this publication, please contact: eresources@igi-global.com.

# Advances in Educational Technologies and Instructional Design (AETID) Book Series

Lawrence A. Tomei
Robert Morris University, USA

ISSN:2326-8905
EISSN:2326-8913

## Mission

Education has undergone, and continues to undergo, immense changes in the way it is enacted and distributed to both child and adult learners. In modern education, the traditional classroom learning experience has evolved to include technological resources and to provide online classroom opportunities to students of all ages regardless of their geographical locations. From distance education, Massive-Open-Online-Courses (MOOCs), and electronic tablets in the classroom, technology is now an integral part of learning and is also affecting the way educators communicate information to students.

The **Advances in Educational Technologies & Instructional Design (AETID) Book Series** explores new research and theories for facilitating learning and improving educational performance utilizing technological processes and resources. The series examines technologies that can be integrated into K-12 classrooms to improve skills and learning abilities in all subjects including STEM education and language learning. Additionally, it studies the emergence of fully online classrooms for young and adult learners alike, and the communication and accountability challenges that can arise. Trending topics that are covered include adaptive learning, game-based learning, virtual school environments, and social media effects. School administrators, educators, academicians, researchers, and students will find this series to be an excellent resource for the effective design and implementation of learning technologies in their classes.

## Coverage

- Adaptive Learning
- Web 2.0 and Education
- E-Learning
- Instructional Design
- K-12 Educational Technologies
- Virtual School Environments
- Hybrid Learning
- Educational Telecommunications
- Higher Education Technologies
- Digital Divide in Education



The Advances in Educational Technologies and Instructional Design (AETID) Book Series (ISSN 2326-8905) is published by IGI Global, 701 E. Chocolate Avenue, Hershey, PA 17033-1240, USA, www.igi-global.com. This series is composed of titles available for purchase individually; each title is edited to be contextually exclusive from any other title within the series. For pricing and ordering information please visit http://www.igi-global.com/book-series/advances-educational-technologies-instructional-design/73678. Postmaster: Send all address changes to above address. 

## Titles in this Series

*For a list of additional titles in this series, please visit: http://www.igi-global.com/book-series/advances-educational-technologies-instructional-design/73678*

*Comprehensive Sexuality Education for Gender-Based Violence Prevention*
Mariana Buenestado-Fernández (University of Cantabria, Spain) Azahara Jiménez-Millán (University of Córdoba, Spain) and Francisco Javier Palacios-Hidalgo (University of Córdoba, Spain)
Information Science Reference • copyright 2024 • 342pp • H/C (ISBN: 9798369320532) • US $245.00 (our price)

*Enhancing Curricula with Service Learning Models*
Sharon Valarmathi (Christ University, India) Jacqueline Kareem (Christ University, India) Veerta Tantia (Christ University, India) Kishore Selva Babu (Christ University, India) and Patrick Jude Lucas (Christ University, India)
Information Science Reference • copyright 2024 • 328pp • H/C (ISBN: 9798369359334) • US $265.00 (our price)

*Encouraging Transnational Learning Through Virtual Exchange in Global Teacher Education*
Alina Slapac (University of Missouri-St. Louis, USA) and Cristina A. Huertas-Abril (University of Córdoba, Spain)
Information Science Reference • copyright 2024 • 424pp • H/C (ISBN: 9781668478134) • US $215.00 (our price)

*Utilizing Visuals and Information Technology in Mathematics Classrooms*
Hiroto Namihira (Otsuma Women's University, Japan)
Information Science Reference • copyright 2024 • 264pp • H/C (ISBN: 9781668499870) • US $220.00 (our price)

*Reshaping Learning with Next Generation Educational Technologies*
James Braman (Community College of Baltimore County, USA) Alexis Brown (Community College of Baltimore County, USA) and Mary Jo Richards (Community College of Baltimore County, USA)
Information Science Reference • copyright 2024 • 242pp • H/C (ISBN: 9798369313107) • US $235.00 (our price)

*Utilizing AI for Assessment, Grading, and Feedback in Higher Education*
Nasser Hamed Al Harrasi (University of Technology and Applied Science, Oman) and Mohamed Salah El Din (Majan University College, Oman)
Information Science Reference • copyright 2024 • 376pp • H/C (ISBN: 9798369321454) • US $255.00 (our price)

*Applied Linguistics and Language Education Research Methods Fundamentals and Innovations*
Hung Phu Bui (University of Economics, Ho Chi Minh City, Vietnam)
Information Science Reference • copyright 2024 • 281pp • H/C (ISBN: 9798369326039) • US $245.00 (our price)

*Utilizing AI Tools in Academic Research Writing*

IGI Global
PUBLISHER of TIMELY KNOWLEDGE

701 East Chocolate Avenue, Hershey, PA 17033, USA
Tel: 717-533-8845 x100 • Fax: 717-533-8661
E-Mail: cust@igi-global.com • www.igi-global.com

# Table of Contents

# Detailed Table of Contents



The year 2030 marks a significant juncture in the evolution of education, where Generative Artificial Intelligence (AI) tools are poised to revolutionize the learning experience. In education society, the importance of generative AI is to improve the accessibility of learning at the global level so that personalized learning experiences can be provided to every learner as per their needs. This chapter explores the multifaceted role of generative AI tools in reshaping educational practices, envisioning a future where these tools foster personalized, adaptive, and engaging learning environments. Generative AI tools, characterized by their ability to create and adapt content autonomously, are instrumental in tailoring educational materials to individual learner needs. This chapter surveys the landscape of generative AI applications in education, including content generation, interactive simulations, intelligent tutoring systems, and dynamic learning pathways. These tools aim to provide adaptive, context-aware learning experiences that cater to diverse learning styles and preferences. The adaptability of generative AI tools extends to the creation of personalized learning pathways. By leveraging data analytics and machine learning algorithms, these tools dynamically adjust content delivery, pacing, and complexity, ensuring that each learner's educational journey is optimized for their unique requirements. The discussion encompasses the potential of generative AI tools to support both formal and informal learning settings. Generative AI tools also play a crucial role in promoting inclusivity in education. By generating diverse and culturally relevant content, these tools contribute to breaking down barriers and addressing disparities in access to quality education. This chapter explores how generative AI can be leveraged to create content that resonates with learners from different backgrounds, fostering a more inclusive educational landscape.

Online proctoring tools and techniques have gained significant attention in recent years due to the increasing popularity of online learning platforms and online assessments. This chapter provides an in-depth analysis of different online proctoring techniques and tools that are commonly used to maintain the integrity of online exams. The chapter begins by highlighting the importance of online proctoring in ensuring fair evaluation and preventing cheating. It then explores various types of online proctoring techniques such as live proctoring, automated proctoring, and recorded proctoring. The advantages and limitations of each technique are discussed, providing a comprehensive understanding of when and how to use them effectively. Overall, this chapter aims to empower educators and administrators with the knowledge and information needed to implement effective online proctoring methods. By understanding the various techniques and tools available, they can enhance the credibility and security of their online assessments, ensuring a fair and reliable evaluation process.



This research study explores the rapidly growing area of AI-powered adaptive learning systems and how they are influencing individualised education. The purpose of this research is to examine these systems' capacities to improve education for students from a variety of backgrounds, as well as their limitations and opportunities. Adaptive learning, which includes data analytics, machine learning models, and algorithms driven by artificial intelligence, is the focus of this review. Learners' requirements and preferences are taken into account as these technologies adapt the delivery of content, tempo, and evaluation methods to each individual. The study also looks at how adaptive learning platforms driven by AI affect students' motivation, grades, and ability to remember what they've learned. Additionally, the authors look into ethical concerns related to data privacy, algorithmic biases, and fair access to technology.

The term "forensics" refers to a broad range of activities that involve gathering, analyzing, and presenting evidence that is admissible in a court of law and are intended to investigate potential entities. In particular, network and computer forensics examine a wide range of data in order to find evidence that can be used in court. During the forensic process, the examination and auditing of computer and network data is essential for gathering data, identifying breaches, and presenting legal evidence. In computer and network forensics, evidence relating to cybercrime is identified, acquired, extracted, examined, analyzed, interpreted, documented, and presented using a methodical, scientific approach. The field of network and computer forensics is constantly expanding, and as crimes move beyond computers and into networks, clouds, and social networks, it is essential to stay current with the newest tools and techniques. The goal of this chapter is to study and explore the methods and tools used in network and computer forensics.



This chapter's primary focus is to investigate the multifaceted nature of variables that influence the enrollment procedure in private educational institutions. A comprehensive analysis of various elements, including teaching faculty, curriculum quality, and infrastructure, reveals their significant impact on students' choices when choosing a college or university. However, with the rapid proliferation of digital technologies, online marketing has become a crucial factor in attracting potential students. As such, this study seeks to identify and evaluate these factors to enable higher education administrators to design tailored strategies and enhance their institutional competitiveness. This chapter also delves deeper into predictive analytics and how they assist in crafting personalized learning experiences. Additionally, this book chapter discusses strategies for student retention and the important discusses strategies for student retention and the importance of continuous improvement. Ethical considerations in data usage will be a central theme throughout the chapter.

descriptions. Its versatility in video generation, interpolation, and prediction marks a paradigm shift in educational content development. DreamPose, an advanced AI system leveraging stable diffusion, translates textual descriptions into visually stunning fashion videos. Its user-friendly design caters to diverse fashion styles, making it an ideal tool for educators seeking visually engaging content across disciplines. Fast Vid2Vid, a deep learning model, takes the spotlight for efficiently generating high-quality videos from a single image. Recognized for its realism, it holds promise in dynamic visualizations for educational purposes, spanning virtual and augmented reality experiences. Practical insights and implementation strategies empower educators to seamlessly integrate these models into educational settings, offering a comprehensive guide from planning and scripting to interactive element incorporation. This chapter lays the foundation for educators and content creators to elevate the educational experience through innovative visual storytelling and AI-driven technologies.



This chapter is all about an advanced system by which the speech without sound will be recognized, and the equivalent script will be generated automatically. All the relevant stakeholders, i.e. students, instructors, then collect script and study insight. To develop the proposed system, it is planned to use one of the most prominent and popular datasets called synthetic-speech-commands-dataset-SSCD, which is freely available. The outcome of this research will provide an opportunity to develop community/reason-based database which will be a potential contribution in the field of conventional education, AI based education and bioinformatics for the research community.



The consequence of Covid-19 has affected the traditional higher education system. Acknowledging the significant role of online education in national development for accessibility and quality education, countries around the world have understood its importance in current digital era. Indian policymakers have been giving due importance to enhancing the education quality, however the progress made by the country in higher education is not adequate. Amidst all the inadequacies of traditional education system, artificial intelligence (AI) technologies are bringing new ray of hope to democratize education system. This chapter is subjected to identify the challenges in online education and suggest specific ways to address each of them. The challenges are categorized into internal and external challenges/barriers. These challenges have been modeled with the expertise of educationalist's opinions and interpretive structural modeling to create a hierarchy of the barriers using MICMAC analysis and categorize these barriers into four clusters.

The chapter explores the evolution of AI, distinguishing it from generative AI, and examines its current applications in education, spanning from primary to higher education levels. Unveiling the multifaceted landscape of AI technologies, such as machine learning, deep learning, and natural language processing, the narrative delves into personalized learning, smart tutoring systems, and administrative efficiency. The chapter anticipates a future where AI collaborates seamlessly with educators, offering hyper-personalized learning journeys, immersive experiences through augmented and virtual reality, and fostering collaborative and project-based learning. Challenges, including ethical concerns, digital inclusion, and teacher training, are acknowledged, emphasizing the importance of addressing these issues for an inclusive and equitable AI-augmented educational future. As we stand at the brink of this transformative era, the chapter envisions a harmonious fusion of technology and human ingenuity shaping the minds of tomorrow.



Rapid technical breakthroughs and economic upheavals in the modern labour market require constantly evolving workforce capabilities. This change is sparked by AI, which introduces individualised learning paths and transforms conventional training methods. This study explores how artificial intelligence (AI) uses machine learning algorithms and natural language processing to create personalised training programmes and identify skill gaps.Analysing AI's capacity to deliver customised learning experiences, the abstract probes how AI systems adjust to different learners' preferences for speed, style, and degree of expertise. It explores intelligent tutoring systems, AI-powered recommendation engines, and adaptive learning systems, emphasising their function in selecting tailored information according to student performance and preferences. Case examples from the real world demonstrate how AI can improve worker training programmes in various sectors and how scalable and flexible it can be in huge organisations and small and medium-sized businesses.



It is known that individuals with autism spectrum disorder enjoy interacting with technological tools and enjoying being engaged with them. Because these interactions happen in a trustworthy and safe environment for them. Therefore, this chapter presents how chatbots can help children with autism spectrum disorder, and reviews the advantages and disadvantages of chatbots. In addition, the challenges that limit the use of chatbots and various ethical problems raised by the use of chatbots are reviewed. Finally, future research directions in this domain are presented.

# Foreword

Education becomes paramount as we stand at the intersection of unprecedented technological advancement and the urgent need for sustainable development. It is within the realms of education that we cultivate the minds and skills necessary to navigate the complexities of our modern world, and it is through education that we sow the seeds of progress and sustainability for generations to come. With great pleasure and anticipation, I introduce this remarkable volume, *Integrating Generative AI in Education to Achieve Sustainable Development Goals*. As a professor deeply committed to the intersection of technology and education, I am continually inspired by the innovative ways in which AI is transforming teaching and learning worldwide. In this book, esteemed editors and contributors explore the profound implications of integrating generative AI into educational practices, specifically focusing on its potential to advance the quality of education and Sustainable Development Goals (SDGs). The SDGs represent a global agenda for creating a more sustainable, equitable, and prosperous world by 2030, and education lies at the heart of this endeavor.

Moreover, this book serves as a call to action for stakeholders across academia, industry, and policy-making realms to collaborate and shape the future of AI-enabled education with sustainability at its core. By fostering interdisciplinary dialogue and cooperation, we can harness the full potential of generative AI to empower learners, educators, and communities worldwide in their quest for a more equitable, inclusive, and sustainable future.

As we navigate the complexities of the digital age, we must approach the integration of AI in education with a deep sense of responsibility, ethics, and equity. This book explores the exciting possibilities of AI-enhanced education and critically examines the ethical considerations, challenges, and opportunities inherent in this rapidly evolving landscape.

I commend the editors and contributors for their dedication to advancing knowledge and understanding in this crucial area of inquiry. I sincerely hope this volume will serve as a catalyst for further exploration, dialogue, and action towards harnessing the power of generative AI to achieve sustainable development goals and create a brighter future for all.

*Ahmed Antwi-Boampong*
*Aalborg University, Copenhagen, Denmark*

# Preface

As editors, we are thrilled to present this edited reference book, *Integrating Generative AI in Education to Achieve Sustainable Development Goals.* Quality education stands at the forefront of achieving the Sustainable Development Goals (SDGs), serving as a potent tool in reducing inequalities and fostering gender equality. In this rapidly evolving landscape, technology plays an increasingly pivotal role, yet it is essential to acknowledge that technological advancements, including Generative AI, are not inherently neutral but rather shaped by prevailing ideologies and worldviews.

This book delves into the intersection of Generative AI and education, exploring its potential to revolutionize teaching and learning while also posing profound questions about the future of education. How will educators adapt to the widespread adoption of AI technologies? What changes will AI bring to assessment practices? What new skills and competencies will be essential for navigating a world where human and machine intelligence intertwine?

Our aim in assembling this book is twofold: to underscore the importance of integrating Generative AI in education to advance the SDGs and to provide a comprehensive resource for academics, researchers, practitioners, and policymakers interested in this burgeoning field. Divided into three parts, each section delves into different facets of the intersection between Generative AI and education.

The first part delves into the technical aspects of Generative AI-powered innovations, exploring its potential in designing curricula and personalized instruction. The second part showcases multidisciplinary applications that enhance educational content and learning experiences through AI technologies. Finally, the third part addresses the imperative of fostering inclusive education through AI-driven solutions while also examining the ethical considerations inherent in deploying AI in educational settings.

For academicians, independent researchers, research scholars, students, scientists, libraries, and industry experts alike, this book offers a roadmap for navigating the evolving landscape of education in an AI-driven world. We believe that by harnessing the power of Generative AI, education can become more accessible, individualized, and effective, ultimately serving as a catalyst for progress toward achieving the SDGs.

We extend our gratitude to all the contributors who have shared their insights and expertise, making this book a valuable resource for anyone interested in the transformative potential of Generative AI in education.

## Chapter 1: An Introduction to Generative AI Tools for Education 2030

Written by academics from various Indian universities, this chapter offers a comprehensive overview of generative AI tools and their applications in shaping the future of education. By surveying the landscape of generative AI applications, including content generation and intelligent tutoring systems, the authors envision a paradigm shift towards personalized and adaptive learning experiences. The chapter underscores the potential of generative AI to cater to diverse learning styles and foster inclusivity in education.

## Chapter 2: AI-Powered Language Translation for Multilingual Classrooms

Authored by a scholar from Abu Dhabi University, United Arab Emirates, this chapter explores the transformative impact of AI-powered language translation technologies on multilingual classrooms. From historical perspectives to real-world case studies, the chapter elucidates the evolution and deployment of AI translation tools in educational settings. Emphasizing inclusivity and accessibility, the authors highlight how AI translation fosters a conducive learning environment for students of diverse linguistic backgrounds.

## Chapter 3: Augmented Intelligence for Knowledge Management and Green Education in the Post Covid-19 Era

Authored by scholars from Malaysia and Bangladesh, this chapter explores the integration of augmented intelligence into knowledge management and education in the post-COVID-19 era. By leveraging advanced hybrid platforms, such as Holographic Labs and Bionic Lenses, the authors advocate for the adoption of augmented intelligence to enhance virtual learning and training experiences. The chapter underscores the role of augmented intelligence in elevating educational standards and promoting sustainability.

## Chapter 4: Demystifying the Dynamic Determinants of Generative Artificial Intelligence (AI) Literacy for Adaptable Sustainable Education: Multistage Structure Equation Remodeling

Authored by academics from India and Malaysia, this chapter employs Multistage Structural Equation Modeling to elucidate the dynamic determinants of generative AI literacy for adaptable sustainable education. By analyzing relationships among variables such as AI literacy, digital split, and cognitive inclusion, the study offers insights into teacher perceptions and technological proficiency. The chapter underscores the importance of AI literacy in achieving adaptable and sustainable education outcomes.

## Chapter 5: Ethical Considerations and Data Privacy in Artificial Intelligence

Authored by academics from Indian universities, this chapter delves into the ethical dimensions of artificial intelligence, particularly focusing on data privacy concerns. By examining the intricate relationship between privacy and ethics in AI technologies, the authors underscore the need for robust frameworks to safeguard individual rights. The chapter offers insights into potential risks and promising solutions for creating a responsible and transparent AI ecosystem.

## Chapter 6: Empowering Healthcare Professionals Through AI-Powered Lifelong Learning for Improving Patient Care

Presented by scholars from India and Malaysia, this chapter explores the intersection of artificial intelligence and healthcare education. Highlighting AI's potential to revolutionize medical education and improve patient care, the authors advocate for integrating AI and technology-enhanced learning into medical curricula. By preparing healthcare professionals to embrace AI-enabled technologies, the chapter envisions a future healthcare system driven by innovation and compassion.

## Chapter 7: Exploring AI-Assisted Students Online Proctoring System: A Study

Written by researchers from Presidency University, India, and United Arab Emirates University, this chapter provides a comprehensive analysis of online proctoring techniques and tools. From live proctoring to automated solutions, the authors examine the advantages and limitations of various online proctoring methods. By empowering educators with knowledge and information, the chapter aims to enhance the credibility and security of online assessments.

## Chapter 8: Exploring the Efficacy of Adaptive Learning Platforms Enhanced by Artificial Intelligence

Presented by researchers from Indian universities, this chapter examines the efficacy of AI-powered adaptive learning platforms in individualized education. By leveraging data analytics and machine learning, the authors explore how these platforms tailor content delivery and assessment methods to each student's needs. The chapter also addresses ethical concerns related to data privacy and algorithmic biases, emphasizing the importance of fair access to technology.

## Chapter 9: Exploring the Implications of Emerging Artificial Intelligence Technologies at Edge Computing in Higher Education

Authored by scholars from Mexico, India, and Nigeria, this chapter investigates the implications of AI technologies at edge computing in higher education. By decentralizing computing and leveraging AI at the edge, the authors advocate for intelligent and personalized services for instructors and students. The chapter underscores the advantages of edge computing in enhancing student engagement and learning outcomes while addressing challenges related to data privacy and security.

## Chapter 10: Exploring the Role of Artificial Intelligence in Advancing Higher Education for Sustainable Development: A Bibliometric Study

Written by academics from Indian universities, this chapter analyzes the role of artificial intelligence in advancing higher education for sustainable development. Through a bibliometric study, the authors evaluate existing knowledge and identify trends, opportunities, and challenges in the field. By synthesizing research findings, the chapter provides valuable insights for further exploration and innovation in integrating AI into higher education for sustainable development.

## Chapter 11: AI-Based Career Counseling Chatbot for Secondary Level Students

Presented by researchers from Vishwakarma Institute of Information Technology, Pune, India, this chapter addresses the challenges students face in making informed career decisions. The authors propose a paradigm shift in career counseling through the adoption of an AI-driven chatbot system tailored to the needs of secondary school students. By leveraging machine learning algorithms and real-time job market data, the chatbot offers personalized career recommendations and guidance, empowering students to navigate their career paths effectively.

## Chapter 12: Advancing Digital Forensics Education With Generative AI for Sustainable Development Goals

Authored by a team of experts from various institutions in India, this chapter delves into the critical realm of digital forensics, particularly focusing on network and computer forensics. The authors underscore the dynamic nature of cybercrimes and the necessity for staying abreast of the latest methodologies and tools in the field. Through meticulous examination, the chapter aims to elucidate the methods and tools integral to network and computer forensics, essential for ensuring cybersecurity and upholding legal standards.

## Chapter 13: Market Segmentation In Higher Education: Enhancing Personalization in Education Using Market Segmentation

Authored by a team from KIET Group of Institutions, India, this chapter delves into the intricate variables influencing enrollment procedures in private educational institutions. By analyzing factors like teaching faculty quality, curriculum standards, and infrastructure, the chapter uncovers their profound impact on students' college choices. Moreover, in the digital age, online marketing emerges as a pivotal factor in attracting prospective students. Through a comprehensive investigation, the authors aim to equip higher education administrators with insights to tailor strategies and boost institutional competitiveness. The chapter also explores predictive analytics and its role in crafting personalized learning experiences, alongside strategies for student retention and continuous improvement, with a central theme of ethical considerations in data usage running throughout the narrative.

## Chapter 14: Revolutionizing Pedagogy Exploring AI Coaching in Enhancing Teacher Professionalism

Conducted by scholars from Lincoln University College, Malaysia, and NRS Govt College, India, this chapter investigates how AI coaching systems can elevate Malaysian teacher professionalism. Employing mixed-method research, the study examines AI coaching's impact on teaching, self-reflection, and career development through qualitative interviews, quantitative assessments, and observational analysis. Highlighting AI's potential to provide personalized feedback and enhance instructor development, the chapter advocates for AI coaching as an engine of educational innovation. By showcasing how AI augments digital educators' professionalism, learning, and stakeholder comprehension, the study underscores AI's transformative role in teacher professional development and educational practices.

## Chapter 15: Revolutionizing Workforce Education-A Conceptual Framework for AI-driven Skilling, Upskilling, and Reskilling

Authored by scholars from CMS Business School, Jain Deemed-to-be University, Bengaluru, India, this chapter presents a conceptual analysis of AI's role in skilling, upskilling, and reskilling the workforce. Arguing that AI fundamentally reshapes the workforce landscape, the authors explore its impact on employee skill development. Through a synthesis of existing literature, the chapter identifies trends, challenges, and opportunities in utilizing AI for workforce development. By informing decision-making and policy formulation in labor and employment realms, the chapter emphasizes AI's potential to redefine future work and requisite skill sets in an increasingly digitized world.

## Chapter 16: Role of AI In Skilling, Upskilling, and Reskilling the Workforce

Authored by researchers from Arya College of Engineering & I.T., India, and Manipal University Jaipur, India, this chapter investigates the latest advancements in AI and its application in transforming professional skills. By exploring AI's potential to automate tasks and alleviate cognitive burdens, the chapter emphasizes the need for organizational strategies to integrate AI effectively. Addressing the skills gap in the workplace, the authors advocate for mapping employee competencies and implementing policies supporting AI-enabled training and development. The chapter underscores the importance of fostering an organizational culture conducive to AI adoption and preparing the workforce for the evolving labor market.

## Chapter 17: Role of Generative Artificial Intelligence (AI) in Accountability, Transparency, and Governance in Higher Education—A Comprehensive Study

Conducted by scholars from Sir Padampat Singhania University, Udaipur, India, and All India Institute of Medical Sciences, Johdpur, India, this study investigates the impact of Generative AI on accountability, transparency, and governance in higher education. Through quantitative analysis, the chapter explores the relationships between AI and institutional governance variables, underscoring AI's transformative potential in higher education. By offering policy implications for responsible AI practices, the study aims to maximize AI's benefits in governance, transparency, and accountability realms.

## Chapter 18: Beyond the Classroom—AI's Impact on the Future of Education: BTC

Presented by researchers from universities in India, this chapter examines the transformative impact of artificial intelligence on education beyond traditional classroom settings. From adaptive learning platforms to AI-powered tutoring, the authors explore the diverse applications of AI in education. Emphasizing global collaboration and equitable access, the chapter envisions a future where AI revolutionizes higher education, fostering creativity and knowledge dissemination.

## Chapter 19: Role of Video Content Generation in Education System Using Generative AI

Authored by researchers from MNNIT ALLAHABAD, India, and BENNETT UNIVERSITY, India, this chapter explores the transformative potential of AI-driven models in reshaping educational video content creation. Through an examination of advanced AI systems like DreamPose and Fast Vid2Vid, the chapter highlights their versatility in generating visually engaging educational content. From fashion videos to dynamic visualizations, these AI-driven technologies offer innovative solutions for educators and content creators, paving the way for immersive educational experiences and enhanced storytelling.

## Chapter 20: Script Generation for Silent Speech in E-learning

This chapter, authored by scholars from the University of Nizwa, Oman, presents an advanced system for recognizing speech without sound and generating corresponding scripts automatically. By leveraging prominent datasets and cutting-edge technologies, the chapter aims to develop a community-based database that contributes to conventional and AI-based education and bioinformatics research. Through a collaborative approach involving stakeholders like students and instructors, the research endeavors to advance the field of silent speech recognition and script generation in e-learning.

## Chapter 21: Exploring Challenges in Online Higher Education for AI Integration Using MICMAC Analysis

Authored by scholars from various Indian universities, this chapter identifies challenges in online higher education and proposes specific strategies to address them. Through Interpretive Structural Modeling and MICMAC analysis, the authors categorize challenges into internal and external barriers, offering a hierarchical framework for mitigating obstacles. By understanding and addressing these challenges, the chapter advocates for harnessing AI's potential to democratize and improve education accessibility.

## Chapter 22: Shaping Tomorrow's Minds the Future of Education in an AI (Artificial Intelligence)-Augmented World

Authored by a scholar from KIET Group of Institutions, India, this chapter examines the evolution of AI and its current applications in education, spanning from primary to higher education levels. By exploring AI technologies like machine learning and deep learning, the chapter envisions a future where AI collaborates seamlessly with educators to offer personalized learning journeys and immersive experiences. However, it also acknowledges challenges such as ethical concerns and digital inclusion, emphasizing the need for inclusive and equitable AI-augmented educational practices.

## Chapter 23: The Role of AI in Skilling, Upskilling, and Reskilling the Workforce

Authored by a researcher from Abu Dhabi University, United Arab Emirates, this chapter explores how AI transforms workforce capabilities through personalized training programs and skill identification. By analyzing AI's capacity to deliver customized learning experiences, the chapter showcases intelligent tutoring systems and recommendation engines' role in enhancing worker training across various sectors. Through real-world case examples, the study demonstrates AI's scalability and flexibility in addressing skill gaps and improving training programs for organizations of all sizes.

## Chapter 24: Use of Chatbots to Support the Inclusion of People With Autism Spectrum Disorder

Authored by a scholar from Trakya University, Turkey, this chapter explores how chatbots can assist individuals with Autism Spectrum Disorder (ASD) and reviews the benefits, challenges, and ethical considerations associated with their use. By highlighting chatbots' potential in providing a safe and engaging environment for individuals with ASD, the chapter offers insights into future research directions in this domain. Through a comprehensive examination of chatbots' role in supporting ASD inclusion, the research aims to contribute to the field of assistive technology and special education.

## Chapter 25: Impact of Generative AI in Education 2030

Authored by scholars from Indian universities, this chapter explores the impact of generative AI on education in the year 2030. From large language models to reinforcement learning, the authors delve into the working processes and applications of generative AI in educational policy making, infrastructure development, and content generation. While acknowledging the transformative potential of AI, the chapter emphasizes the crucial role of human guidance in shaping AI-enabled educational experiences.

## Chapter 26: Bridging Data-Driven Learning and Generative AI—A Framework for Sustainable Education through Metacognitive Resource Utilization

Written by scholars from Sir Padampat Singhania University, India, this chapter proposes a framework for sustainable education by integrating data-driven learning and generative AI. Through a synthesis of educational theory and emerging technologies, the authors advocate for innovative pedagogical strategies that empower students to address global challenges. Despite acknowledged challenges, the framework represents a significant step towards fostering critical thinking and responsible citizenship among learners.

In concluding this edited reference book, *Integrating Generative AI in Education to Achieve Sustainable Development Goals*, we reflect on the multifaceted exploration of the intersection between Generative AI and education presented within its pages. From the technical intricacies of AI-powered innovations to the ethical considerations surrounding their deployment, each chapter contributes to a comprehensive understanding of how AI is reshaping the educational landscape.

As editors, we recognize the pivotal role that education plays in advancing the Sustainable Development Goals (SDGs), serving as a catalyst for social progress and economic prosperity. In this context, the integration of Generative AI presents both opportunities and challenges. While AI has the potential to revolutionize teaching and learning, it also raises important questions about equity, access, and ethical responsibility.

Throughout this book, contributors have examined diverse applications of Generative AI in education, from personalized learning platforms to AI-driven content creation tools. They have explored how AI can enhance student engagement, facilitate adaptive instruction, and promote inclusivity in educational settings. Moreover, they have grappled with the ethical implications of AI technologies, considering issues such as data privacy, algorithmic bias, and digital divide.

Looking ahead, the future of education in an AI-augmented world holds immense promise. By harnessing the power of Generative AI, educators can create more personalized, interactive, and effective learning experiences for students. However, realizing this vision requires a concerted effort to address challenges such as digital inequality, ethical dilemmas, and the need for continuous professional development.

As we conclude this book, we extend our gratitude to all the contributors who have shared their expertise and insights. It is our hope that this collection serves as a valuable resource for academics, researchers, practitioners, and policymakers navigating the complex intersection of Generative AI and education. By working together to leverage the transformative potential of AI responsibly, we can build a more equitable, inclusive, and sustainable future for education worldwide.

*Ruchi Doshi*
*Universidad Azteca, Mexico*

*Manish Dadhich*
*Sir Padampat Singhania University, India*

*Sandeep Poddar*
*Lincoln University College, Malaysia*

*Kamal Kant Hiran*
*Sir Padampat Singhania University, India & Lincoln University College, Malaysia*

# Acknowledgments

Recognizing the invaluable assistance and continuous input provided by numerous individuals is paramount in bringing this project to fruition. The realization of this book owes much to the invaluable support of IGI Global, USA. The team at IGI Global, including Melissa Wagner, Elizabeth Barrantes, Kaylee Renfrew, and Jocelynn Hessler, deserve sincere appreciation for generously offering this remarkable opportunity and demonstrating steadfast collaboration since the conception of this book. Their unique contributions, guidance, expertise, and persistent efforts have brought this book to fruition.

We extend our heartfelt gratitude to the individuals whose unwavering support, expertise, and guidance have been instrumental in creating this edited volume on integrating Generative AI in Education to Achieve Sustainable Development Goals.

First and foremost, we sincerely thank Prof. (Dr.) Prithvi Yadav, President, Sir Padampat Singhania University, Udaipur, India for his visionary leadership and invaluable insights throughout the editorial process. His extensive experience in educational leadership and his passion for leveraging technology for social good has been a constant source of inspiration. We deeply thank Col. (Dr.) Sanjay Sinha, Head of Education, JK Cement Education Vertical, India, for his astute guidance and unwavering encouragement in promoting a dynamic research environment.

We also extend our thanks to Prof. (Dr.) Amiya Bhaumik, President, Lincoln University College, Malaysia, for his motivation. His expertise in educational psychology and SDGs has provided invaluable insights into the potential impact of Generative AI on learning outcomes. Furthermore, we would like to thank Prof. (Dr.) Prasun Chakrabarti for his insightful contributions and intellectual support. His deep understanding of curriculum design and pedagogical approaches has been instrumental in shaping the practical applications of AI in educational settings explored in this book.

We extend our heartfelt thanks to esteemed institutions: Sir Padampat Singhania University, Udaipur, India; Lincoln University College, Malaysia; University of Nizwa, Oman; Trakya University, Turkey; Abu Dhabi University, UAE; Baghdad College of Economic Sciences University, Iraq; College of Education, Oju, Nigeria; Universidad Azteca, Mexico. These institutions provided a nurturing scholarly and research setting throughout this journey.

In addition to our esteemed colleagues, we would like to acknowledge the contributions of our dedicated team of researchers, editors, and support staff, who have worked tirelessly behind the scenes to bring this project to fruition. We are indebted to these distinguished individuals and teams for their generosity, expertise, and unwavering commitment to advancing knowledge and innovation in education. Their collective contributions have not only enriched this volume but also have the potential to catalyze positive change in educational practices worldwide. We extend our gratitude to all the contributors whose scholarly insights and research findings have contributed to the richness and diversity of perspectives presented in this volume. Their dedication to advancing the frontiers of knowledge in the intersection of generative AI and education is truly commendable.

Finally, the accomplishment of this book would have been unattainable without the assistance and backing from our family, friends, and colleagues. Their invaluable support is deeply appreciated, and we thank them for their contributions.

Warm Regards,

Editors:

*Ruchi Doshi*
*Universidad Azteca, Chalo, Mexico*

*Manish Dadhich*
*Sir Padampat Singhania University, Udaipur, Rajasthan, India*

*Sandeep Poddar*
*Lincoln University College, Malaysia*

*Kamal Kant Hiran*
*Sir Padampat Singhania University, Udaipur, Rajasthan, India*

# Chapter 1
# An Introduction to Generative AI Tools for Education 2030

**Ramandeep Sandhu**
https://orcid.org/0000-0003-2595-4030
*Lovely Professional University, India*

**Harpreet Kaur Channi**
*Chandigarh University, India*

**Deepika Ghai**
*Lovely Professional University, India*

**Gagandeep Singh Cheema**
*Lovely Professional University, India*

**Mandeep Kaur**
https://orcid.org/0000-0001-8054-1605
*Chitkara University, India*

## ABSTRACT

*The year 2030 marks a significant juncture in the evolution of education, where Generative Artificial Intelligence (AI) tools are poised to revolutionize the learning experience. In education society, the importance of generative AI is to improve the accessibility of learning at the global level so that personalized learning experiences can be provided to every learner as per their needs. This chapter explores the multifaceted role of generative AI tools in reshaping educational practices, envisioning a future where these tools foster personalized, adaptive, and engaging learning environments. Generative AI tools, characterized by their ability to create and adapt content autonomously, are instrumental in tailoring educational materials to individual learner needs. This chapter surveys the landscape of generative AI applications in education, including content generation, interactive simulations, intelligent tutoring systems, and dynamic learning pathways. These tools aim to provide adaptive, context-aware learning experiences that cater to diverse learning styles and preferences. The adaptability of generative AI tools extends to the creation of personalized learning pathways. By leveraging data analytics and machine learning algorithms, these tools dynamically adjust content delivery, pacing, and complexity, ensuring that each learner's educational journey is optimized for their unique requirements. The discussion encompasses the potential of generative AI tools to support both formal and informal learning settings. Generative AI tools also play a crucial role in promoting inclusivity in education. By generating diverse and culturally relevant content, these tools contribute to breaking down barriers and addressing disparities in access to quality education. This chapter explores how generative AI can be leveraged to create content that resonates with learners from different backgrounds, fostering a more inclusive educational landscape.*

DOI: 10.4018/979-8-3693-2440-0.ch001

## INTRODUCTION

In the not-so-distant future of 2030, the landscape of education is undergoing a profound metamorphosis, fuelled by the transformative power of Generative AI tools. As we stand at the intersection of technological innovation and pedagogical evolution, integrating Artificial Intelligence (AI) into educational frameworks promises a revolution in how we teach and learn. Generative AI is projected to alter the way we learn and teach today, with students having virtual teachers available 24 hours a day who provide massive quantities of information and examples, and teachers able to assess their pupils and provide feedback using innovative methods. This chapter delves into the exciting realm where cutting-edge Generative AI is reshaping the very fabric of education, propelling us into an era where personalized, immersive, and intelligent learning experiences are not just a vision but a tangible reality. The journey towards AI-powered education is rooted in the historical trajectory of educational technologies. From the advent of computers in classrooms to the rise of online learning platforms, each technological wave has left an indelible mark on the educational landscape. The present moment, however, marks a pivotal juncture, as Generative AI tools promise a level of adaptability and intelligence that transcends previous capabilities (Abdullah, M., Madain, A., & Jararweh, Y., 2022). This chapter seeks to unravel the potential of Generative AI in shaping education by exploring its current applications, envisioning future possibilities, and addressing the challenges and AI ethical considerations that come with this technological frontier. By examining case studies, discussing the evolving role of educators, and navigating the policy frameworks that will govern this transformation, we aim to provide a comprehensive roadmap for educators, policymakers, and stakeholders navigating the dynamic intersection of AI and education (Akgun, S., & Greenhow, C., 2022). Before embarking on this exploration, it is crucial to establish a foundational understanding of Generative AI. This section will offer a primer on the core concepts and technologies driving the Generative AI revolution, setting the stage for a deeper dive into its applications and implications in the educational sphere (Yu, H., & Guo, Y., 2023).

## THE EVOLUTION OF EDUCATION TECHNOLOGIES

The evolution of education technologies represents a dynamic journey marked by continuous innovation and adaptation. Commencing with traditional tools like chalkboards and projectors, education has witnessed transformative shifts driven by advancements in technology. The introduction of computers into classrooms heralded a new era, providing students with unprecedented access to information and interactive learning experiences. The proliferation of the internet further democratized knowledge, transcending geographical boundaries and fostering global connectivity in education (Baidoo-Anu, D., & Ansah, L.O., 2023). As we progressed into the digital age, interactive whiteboards, e-learning platforms, and learning management systems became ubiquitous, reshaping the educational landscape. Today, the current state of education technology reflects a mosaic of digital tools, encompassing cloud-based collaboration, augmented and virtual reality, and data-driven insights through learning analytics. This consolidation has given rise to a more personalized and interactive learning environment. Looking ahead, emerging trends, including Artificial Intelligence (AI) and Machine Learning (ML), are poised to be the vanguards of the next wave, promising to redefine education in ways yet to be fully realized. In exploring the evolution of education technologies, we discern a narrative of innovation that has profoundly influenced how knowledge is acquired and disseminated (Castelli, M., & Manzoni, L., 2022)

## Historical Perspectives of Education Technologies

The historical trajectory of education technologies unveils a captivating narrative of adaptation and advancement. In the early stages, the classroom landscape was characterized by traditional tools such as chalkboards and projectors, where educators linearly conveyed information. **Figure 1** provides the evolution of education technologies from 2020 till today's world. The advent of computers in the mid-20th century marked a transformative moment, introducing interactive learning experiences and paving the way for the integration of technology into educational settings. As we progressed through subsequent decades, the educational realm witnessed a paradigm shift with the emergence of the Internet. This revolutionary development democratized access to information, enabling students and educators to transcend the constraints of physical classrooms. The digital age brought forth interactive whiteboards, e-learning platforms, and learning management systems, providing a glimpse into the potential of technology to enhance pedagogy. The evolution of education technologies reflects a continuous quest for more effective and engaging teaching methods. The integration of multimedia resources and digital platforms not only expanded the scope of educational content but also diversified learning modalities. This historical perspective invites us to appreciate the transformative impact of technology on education, underscoring its role as a catalyst for innovation and inclusivity in the learning process (Dai, J., Wang, J., Huang, W., Shi, J., & Zhu, Z., 2020). As we delve into the historical roots, we gain insights into the foundations that have shaped the contemporary landscape of education technology (Doroudi, S., 2023).

## Current State of Education Technologies

In the present educational landscape, technology stands as a cornerstone, shaping the dynamics of teaching and learning. The current state of education technology is a multifaceted tapestry, interwoven with digital innovations designed to enhance the educational experience. Cloud-based collaboration tools have facilitated seamless communication and information sharing among students and educators, transcending geographical constraints and fostering global connectivity. Augmented Reality (AR) and Virtual Real-

*Figure 1. Evolution of education technologies from 2020 to 2020-present century*

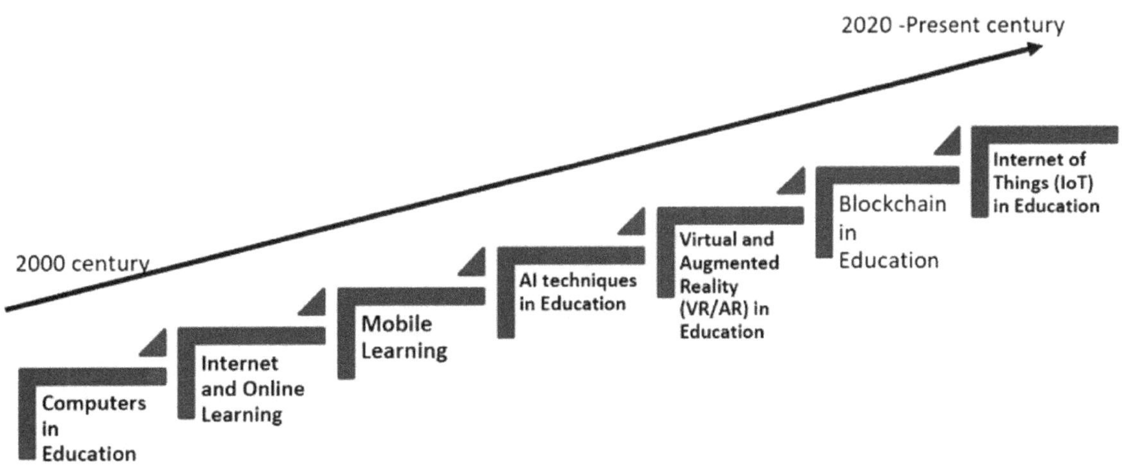

ity (VR) technologies have emerged as transformative forces, bringing immersive experiences into the classroom. These tools transport learners beyond the confines of traditional textbooks, offering interactive simulations and virtual field trips. Learning Management Systems (LMS) have become integral, providing a centralized hub for course materials, assessments, and collaborative spaces, streamlining the educational workflow. Moreover, learning analytics and big data have ushered in a data-driven era in education. Educators can now collect insights into student performance, track learning trends, and tailor instructional approaches to individual needs. The current technological landscape reflects a shift towards personalized and adaptive learning, where technology plays a pivotal role in catering to diverse learning styles and preferences. As we navigate the current state of education technology, it becomes evident that classrooms are no longer confined by physical boundaries. The integration of digital tools has created a dynamic and interactive learning environment, empowering educators and learners alike to engage with content in innovative ways (Furey, H., & Martin, F., 2019). This section serves as a snapshot of the contemporary educational technological arsenal, setting the stage for a deeper exploration of emerging trends and their potential impact on the future of education (Gao, P., Li, J., & Liu, S., 2021; Huang, X., 2021).

## Emerging Trends of Education Technologies

Looking forward to the educational landscape of the future, a constellation of emerging trends is poised to redefine the way we teach and learn. These nascent technologies offer a glimpse into the next chapter of the evolution of education (Hughes, R.T., Zhu, L., & Bednarz, T., 2021).

### Artificial Intelligence and Machine Learning

The convergence of AI and ML is a new trend (Faiz, M., Sandhu, R., Akbar, M., Shaikh, A.A., Bhasin, C., & Fatima, N., 2023). Technology like this can change the way schools work by making lessons more tailored to each student, streamlining paperwork, and revealing patterns in how well students are doing. Artificial Intelligence (AI) is changing the face of education by making room for new, more flexible ways of instruction (Humble, N., & Mozelius, P., 2022).

Gamification and Immersive Learning

Gamification and immersive learning experiences are gaining traction as powerful tools to enhance engagement and knowledge retention. By incorporating game elements into educational content and leveraging virtual and augmented reality, educators can create interactive and captivating learning environments. These approaches break away from traditional models, fostering a more participatory and dynamic educational experience (Eglash, R., Bennett, A., Babbitt, W., Lachney, M., Reinhardt, M., & Hammond-Sowah, D., 2020).

Blockchain in Education

Blockchain technology is emerging as a disruptor in the education sector, offering solutions for secure and transparent credentialing, verification, and record-keeping. This trend has the potential to reshape the way academic achievements are recorded, validated, and shared, providing a decentralized and tamper-proof system for educational credentials (De Oliveira Silva, A., & Dos Santos Janes, D., 2020).

Robotics and Coding Education

As the importance of digital literacy grows, there is a surge in interest in robotics and coding education. These initiatives aim to equip students with essential skills for the future job market, fostering creativity, problem-solving, and critical thinking. Robotics, in particular, is not only a learning tool but also a pathway to introduce students to engineering and technology principles (Megahed, F. M., Chen, Y.J., Ferris, J.A., Knoth, S., & Jones-Farmer, L.A., 2024).

Adaptive Learning Platforms

Adaptive learning platforms leverage data and analytics to tailor educational content to the individual needs of each learner. These platforms assess a student's progress in real-time and adjust the difficulty and content of lessons accordingly. This trend represents a move towards a more personalized and responsive educational experience, catering to the diverse needs of students. Exploring these emerging trends unveils a landscape where technology is not just a tool but a transformative force, shaping the future of education. As we delve into these advancements, we anticipate a dynamic educational ecosystem that adapts to the needs of learners in unprecedented ways, ushering in a new era in the evolution of education technologies (Santos, R.P.D., 2023).

## RELATED WORK ON GENERATIVE AI TOOLS FOR EDUCATION

A lot of research works has been done on Generative AI tools for education. When discussing the teaching and learning of STEM subjects from a decolonial viewpoint, (Eglash, R., Bennett, A., Babbitt, W., Lachney, M., Reinhardt, M., & Hammond-Sowah, D., 2020) framed their analysis within the framework of STEM education and its practical applications. demonstrate that the Indigenous material agency paradigm within generative STEM aligns more closely with decolonial goals and provides a more revolutionary outlook on the possible contribution of STEM to the shift from an extractive to a generative economic model. There has been a lot of buzz about how Artificial Intelligence (AI) is changing the way people learn and how schools operate. In their extensive analysis of AI's many effects on the field of education, (De Oliveira Silva, A., & Dos Santos Janes, D., 2020) covered all the bases, including how the technology may improve teaching techniques, tailor students' educational journeys, and disrupt existing pedagogical practices. To sum up, the use of AI in the classroom might revolutionize teaching and learning by making lessons more relevant and engaging for each student. The field of Statistical Process Control (SPC) stands to benefit greatly from the introduction of generative AI models like OpenAI's ChatGPT. A synopsis of Generative AI's history was provided by (Megahed, F. M., Chen, Y.J., Ferris, J.A., Knoth, S., & Jones-Farmer, L.A., 2024). According to (Santos, R.P.D., 2023), who used a constructionist theoretical framework, GenAIbots like ChatGPT and Bing Chat might be useful tools for chemistry teachers. Students' detailed interaction records with both AI systems in simulated Chemistry learning sessions were analyzed using a single-case research technique. Using four major social media sites, (Mogavi, R.H., Deng, C., Kim, J.J., Zhou, P., Kwon, Y.D., Metwally, A.H.S., et al., 2023) analyzed the material qualitatively. For teachers and students thinking about using ChatGPT or comparable generative AI technologies in the classroom, the study contributes to the current conversation by offering crowdsourced ideas. Existing literature on AI's potential for code creation and how users feel about tools that employ AI to aid in coding is few. To study how well generative big language models generate code from a variety of viewpoints across various social media platforms, (Feng, Y., Vanam, S., Cherukupally, M., Zheng, W., Qiu, M., & Chen, H., 2023) proposed a scalable crowdsourcing data-driven system. The introduction of new tools to the educational environment via Artificial Intelligence (AI) has the potential to revolutionize traditional methods of teaching and learning. An extensive review of Artificial Intelligence (AI) technologies, their possible uses in the classroom, and the challenges associated with them was provided by (Adıgüzel, T., Kaya, M.H., & Cansu, F.K., 2023). The findings from a set of semi-structured interviews with twelve students and six teachers addressing their knowledge, background, and preferences for the use of generative AI tools in computer science courses were published by (Zastudil, C., Rogalska, M., Kapp, C., Vaughn, J., & MacNeil, S., 2023). According to the findings, GAI tools will become more important in computer science classes. The boundaries between the actual and virtual worlds are becoming more porous, and we are all affected by the potential negative uses of GenAI. In addition to providing a comprehensive review of the literature on the dangers of GenAI and LLM abuse, (Ferrara, E. 2024) offers a fascinating glimpse into the future of GenAI, outlining the many dangerous uses for the technology and offering advice on how to be ready for them. Therefore, even partial and careless use of this technology in DR education runs the danger of sustaining digital coloniality. Consequently, overall advocates for AI-assisted educational reform while critically examining the potential reproduction of digital colonialism by AI-driven solutions such as ChatGPT in the Dominican Republic (DR) school system (Ovalle, A., 2023).

## GENERATIVE AI IN EDUCATION: A PRIMER

Generative Artificial Intelligence (AI), a frontier in technological innovation, is poised to redefine the landscape of education in profound ways. At its essence, Generative AI represents a paradigm shift from conventional AI systems by possessing the ability to create content autonomously. This content generation spans various formats, including text, images, and interactive simulations, driven by the system's capacity to discern patterns and information gleaned from its training data.

In the realm of education, Generative AI introduces a revolutionary approach to personalized learning. Unlike traditional AI, which often relies on predefined rules, Generative AI is inherently creative. It adapts dynamically to individual learners, crafting tailored content that aligns with their distinct preferences and learning styles. This primer aims to demystify the intricacies of Generative AI, elucidating its fundamental concepts and key technologies. From intelligent chatbots engaging students in natural language conversations to the development of dynamic and personalized learning paths, Generative AI promises a seismic shift in the educational paradigm. Throughout this primer, we will explore its multifaceted applications, elucidate the potential benefits it offers to both educators and learners, and delve into the considerations that accompany the integration of this transformative technology into educational frameworks. As we explore Generative AI in education, the overarching objective is to provide a foundational understanding of its capabilities and implications. By doing so, we seek to illuminate the path toward a future where education is not just an imparting of knowledge but a dynamic, adaptive, and personalized journey facilitated by the creative capacities of Generative AI.

### Understanding Generative AI

Generative Artificial Intelligence (AI) stands at the forefront of technological innovation, representing a category of AI systems with the remarkable ability to autonomously create content. Unlike traditional AI models that often follow predefined rules and patterns, generative models can produce novel outputs, including text, images, and more, based on the patterns and information they have learned from extensive training datasets. At the heart of Generative AI is the concept of neural networks, particularly generative models like Generative Adversarial Networks (GANs) and Variational Autoencoders (VAEs). These models leverage complex algorithms to understand and replicate patterns, enabling them to generate content that closely resembles the data they were trained on. In practical terms, understanding Generative AI involves grasping its capacity to create content that is not explicitly programmed. This ability has transformative implications for various fields, including education. In education, Generative AI can be employed to develop personalized learning materials, dynamically adapt content to individual students, and even create interactive simulations that enhance the learning experience. Despite its incredible potential, Generative AI also presents challenges, such as the ethical considerations surrounding content generation, potential biases in training data, and the need for robust regulation to ensure responsible and fair use. This section aims to illuminate the core concepts of Generative AI, providing readers with a foundational understanding of its mechanisms, applications, and the broader implications it holds for the future of technology and education (Karras, T., Laine, S., & Aila, T., 2019).

## Key Concepts and Technologies Used for Generative AI

In the fascinating domain of Generative Artificial Intelligence (AI) for education, several key concepts and technologies lay the foundation for transformative advancements. Central to this landscape are generative models, such as Generative Adversarial Networks (GANs) and Variational Autoencoders (VAEs), which employ sophisticated algorithms to learn patterns from extensive datasets and autonomously generate diverse and realistic content. Neural networks, emulating the structure of the human brain, play a pivotal role in processing information and facilitating the creation of content that mirrors the intricacies of the input data. For text-based applications, Natural Language Processing (NLP) empowers Generative AI to comprehend and generate human-like text, enabling the development of intelligent chatbots and educational content. Computer Vision technologies come into play for image and video content, allowing machines to interpret visual data and create realistic visualizations and simulations. Transfer learning facilitates the adaptation of knowledge gained in one context to excel in another, providing a foundation for personalized learning experiences. Finally, the principles of explainability and interpretability ensure transparency in AI decision-making processes, fostering trust and understanding in educational applications (Kingma, D.P., & Welling, M., 2019). As we explore these key concepts and technologies, it becomes evident that Generative AI holds the potential to revolutionize education by personalizing content creation and delivery in unprecedented ways. Navigating the realm of Generative Artificial Intelligence (AI) in education involves understanding key concepts and the underlying technologies that power its transformative capabilities.

### Generative Models

At the heart of Generative AI are sophisticated algorithms known as generative models. Notable examples include Generative Adversarial Networks (GANs) and Variational Autoencoders (VAEs) (Laupichler, M.C., Aster, A., Schirch, J., & Raupach, T., 2022). These models are designed to learn patterns from vast datasets and generate new, realistic content based on that learning. In education, these models can be employed to create diverse learning materials and simulations (Lehmann, F., & Buschek, D., 2021)

### Neural Networks

Generative AI heavily relies on neural networks, mimicking the structure and function of the human brain (Lim, W.M., Gunasekara, A., Pallant, J.L., Pallant, J.I., & Pechenkina, E., 2023). Neural Networks (NNs) process information in layers, learning intricate patterns and relationships. The application of neural networks enables generative models to understand and replicate complex data, making them adept at creating content that mirrors the input they've been trained on.

### Natural Language Processing

For text-based content generation, Natural Language Processing (NLP) plays a crucial role. NLP algorithms empower Generative AI to comprehend, interpret, and generate human-like text. This capability is instrumental in developing intelligent chatbots, generating educational content, and facilitating interactive conversations with learners.

### Computer Vision

In scenarios involving image and video content, Generative AI leverages Computer Vision technologies. These technologies enable machines to interpret and understand visual data, allowing for the creation of realistic images, interactive visualizations, and simulations that enhance the educational experience.

### Transfer Learning

Transfer learning is a key concept in Generative AI, allowing models to leverage knowledge gained from one task to excel in another. This enables quicker adaptation to new educational contexts, facilitating the creation of personalized content and learning experiences tailored to the unique needs of individual students (Macpherson, T., Churchland, A., Sejnowski, T., DiCarlo, J., Kamitani, Y., Takahashi, H., & Hikida, T., 2021).

### Explainability and Interpretability

Understanding and trusting AI-generated content in an educational setting necessitates explainability and interpretability. These concepts refer to the ability to understand how and why an AI system makes specific decisions. Ensuring transparency in Generative AI processes is vital for educators and learners alike.

As we delve into the key concepts and technologies of Generative AI in education, it becomes clear that these advancements hold significant potential for reshaping the way we create, deliver, and experience educational content. Balancing innovation with ethical considerations and transparency will be pivotal in harnessing the full benefits of Generative AI in the educational landscape.

## Applications of Generative AI in Educational Landscape

In the ever-evolving landscape of education, Generative Artificial Intelligence (AI) emerges as a transformative force, introducing a spectrum of applications that redefine traditional teaching paradigms. One of its primary contributions lies in the realm of personalized learning materials. Generative AI analyzes individual student data, including learning preferences and performance metrics, to dynamically craft tailored content, ensuring a customized educational experience. Intelligent chatbots, another application, facilitate real-time interaction, answering queries and offering personalized support to students. Dynamic learning paths, shaped by Generative AI, adapt in response to student progress, optimizing the curriculum for each learner. Beyond these, Generative AI enhances content creation and augmentation, generating diverse educational materials and providing interactive elements to enrich lessons. In language education, it assists learners by generating contextually relevant exercises and immersive language experiences. The technology extends into the sciences with the creation of virtual laboratories and simulations, fostering hands-on learning. Additionally, Generative AI contributes to creative writing by offering suggestions and co-creating narratives, acting as a collaborative tool. As Generative AI applications in education burgeon, they collectively pave the way for a more personalized, interactive, and adaptive learning environment, propelling education into a new era of innovation and individualization. As shown in **Figure 2**, Generative Artificial Intelligence (AI) introduces a myriad of innovative applications in the educational realm, reshaping the way content is created, delivered, and personalized for learners. Various innovative Apps of Generative AI used for education are enlisted as follows:

## Personalized Learning Materials

Generative AI enables the creation of personalized learning materials tailored to individual student needs. By analyzing student preferences, learning styles, and performance data, the technology generates customized content that optimally aligns with each learner's strengths and weaknesses.

*Figure 2. Innovative apps of generative AI in education*

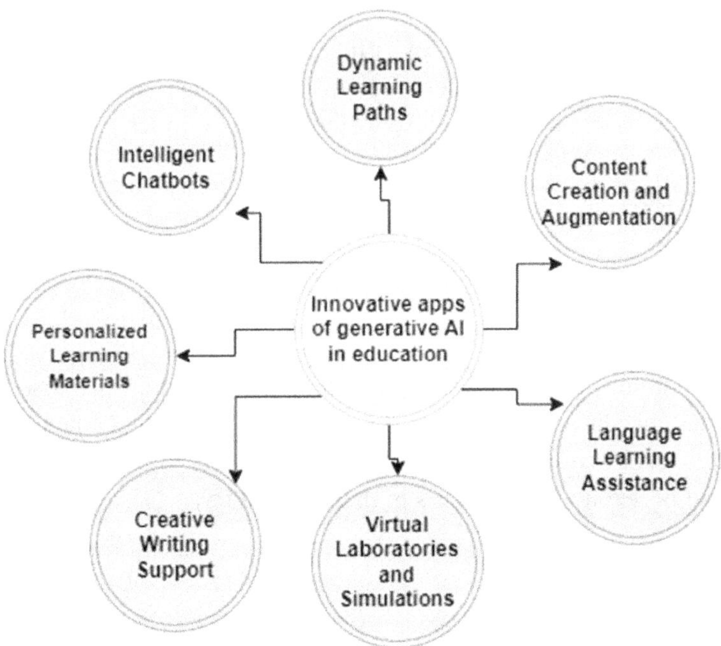

## Intelligent Chatbots for Support

Intelligent chatbots powered by Generative AI facilitate interactive and dynamic communication between students and educational platforms. These chatbots can provide real-time assistance, answer queries, and offer personalized guidance, fostering a more responsive and supportive learning environment.

## Dynamic Learning Paths

Generative AI contributes to the development of dynamic learning paths that adapt in real-time based on student progress. These adaptive learning systems identify areas where students excel or struggle, adjusting the curriculum to ensure a tailored educational journey that maximizes understanding and retention.

## Content Creation and Augmentation

Educational content creation is enhanced by Generative AI, which can generate diverse materials, including quizzes, assessments, and simulations. Additionally, it can augment existing content by providing alternative perspectives, additional examples, and interactive elements to enrich the learning experience (Zhang, Y., & Wang, H., 2022).

## Language Learning Assistance

In language education, Generative AI assists learners by generating contextually relevant language exercises, conversations, and immersive language experiences. This application aids in language acquisition by providing interactive and engaging content that adapts to the learner's proficiency level.

## Virtual Laboratories and Simulations

Generative AI contributes to the development of virtual laboratories and simulations, offering students practical and immersive learning experiences in fields like science and engineering. This not only supplements traditional learning methods but also fosters a deeper understanding of complex concepts.

## Creative Writing Support

Generative AI can assist students in creative writing endeavors by offering suggestions, generating prompts, and even co-creating narratives. This application serves as a collaborative tool, inspiring creativity and honing writing skills through AI-generated insights.

As Generative AI continues to evolve, its applications in education promise to revolutionize the learning experience, making education more personalized, interactive, and adaptive. These applications not only enhance traditional teaching methods but also open doors to innovative approaches that cater to the diverse needs and preferences of learners in the 21st century.

## Generative AI Techniques to Find the Grading System of Students

Generative AI techniques offer innovative solutions for redefining the grading systems of students, introducing a range of sophisticated methods to enhance efficiency and fairness. Automated grading algorithms, powered by Generative AI, streamline the evaluation process by autonomously assessing assignments and exams. By training on diverse datasets, these algorithms learn to recognize patterns in correct and incorrect responses, providing quick and consistent feedback. Natural Language Processing (NLP) within Generative AI becomes instrumental in essay grading, analyzing the quality and coherence of written responses against predefined criteria. Additionally, Generative Adversarial Networks (GANs) contribute by generating synthetic datasets that augment real-world grading datasets, improving the models' ability to assess a wide spectrum of student work. Personalized learning pathways, driven by Generative AI, tailor educational content to individual student performance, ensuring a customized and adaptive learning experience. These systems also extend beyond traditional assessments to analyze behavioral data, incorporating factors like student participation and engagement for a more holistic evaluation. Ethical considerations are paramount, and Generative AI can play a role in addressing bias by incorporating fairness metrics during training and striving for transparency and equity in the grading process. In essence, the integration of Generative AI techniques into grading systems marks a transformative step toward more efficient, personalized, and ethically grounded approaches to student assessment in education. As shown in **Figure 3**, Generative AI techniques can be employed in various ways to assist in the development and improvement of grading systems for students. Generative AI techniques offer a transformative approach to identifying and catering to the learning needs of both slow and fast learners within educational settings. Adaptive learning systems, powered by Generative AI, stand out as key tools in this endeavor. These systems continually analyze individual student performance, understanding the nuances of their learning pace, and dynamically adapting educational content. By providing additional resources and targeted exercises for slow learners and more advanced materials for fast learners, adaptive learning systems foster a customized and responsive learning experience (Terwiesch, C., 2023).

Behavioral analytics, facilitated by Generative AI, delve into patterns within student interactions, completion times, and engagement levels. This allows educators to discern indicators of different learning speeds, identifying those who may require additional support or challenges. Natural Language Processing (NLP) techniques contribute by assessing the speed and accuracy of written responses, shedding light on the comprehension rates of students, and pinpointing areas where additional assistance may be beneficial. Time series analysis, another technique, examines individual learning trajectories over time, revealing trends that signify diverse learning speeds. Predictive analytics utilize historical data to forecast future academic performance, aiding in the early identification of both slow and fast learners. This enables educators to implement targeted interventions, such as personalized tutoring for slow learners or enrichment programs for fast learners. Interactive learning platforms benefit from Generative AI by adapting content dynamically to individual learning paces. Slow learners receive additional explanations and examples, while fast learners are presented with more challenging problems. Feedback generation, driven by Generative AI, ensures personalized feedback for both groups. For slow learners, the feedback emphasizes areas for improvement and provides supplementary resources, while for fast learners, it acknowledges proficiency and offers advanced challenges. In summary, Generative AI techniques empower educators to recognize and address the diverse learning speeds of individual students through adaptive, data-driven, and personalized interventions. This approach fosters an inclusive and effective educational environment that caters to the unique needs of all learners (Salas-Pilco, S.Z., & Yang, Y., 2022).

*Figure 3. Generative AI techniques for education system*

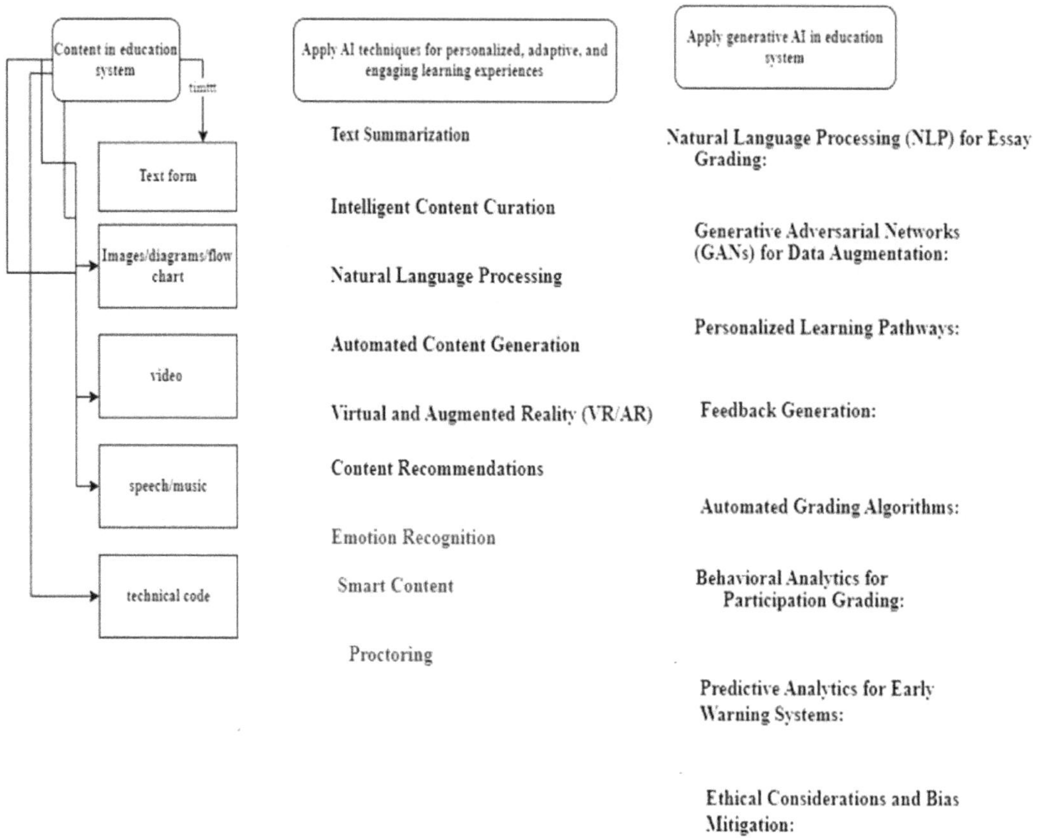


Various Generative AI techniques for the education system are explained as follows:

*a)* ***Automated Grading Algorithms:*** Generative AI can be used to create automated grading algorithms capable of evaluating assignments, quizzes, and exams. By training on a diverse set of sample answers, the model can learn to assess the quality and correctness of student responses, providing quick and consistent feedback.

*b)* ***Natural Language Processing (NLP) for Essay Grading:*** NLP algorithms within Generative AI can be applied to assess essays and written assignments. These models can analyze the structure, coherence, and content of written responses, assigning grades based on predefined criteria or learned patterns from a dataset of graded essays.

*c)* ***Generative Adversarial Networks (GANs) for Data Augmentation:*** GANs can be utilized to generate synthetic datasets that mimic the distribution of real student work. This synthetic data can then be combined with existing datasets to augment the training process of grading models, enhancing their ability to generalize and accurately assess a wide range of responses.

*d)* ***Personalized Learning Pathways:*** Generative AI can contribute to adaptive learning systems that tailor educational content based on individual student performance. By continuously generating and updating personalized learning paths, the system ensures that students receive assignments and assessments that match their current proficiency levels (Zhai, X., Chu, X., Chai, C. S., Jong, M. S. Y., Istenic, A., Spector, M., Liu, J.B., Yuan, J., & Li, Y., 2021)

*e)* ***Feedback Generation:*** Using generative models, AI can generate detailed and constructive feedback for students. By understanding common mistakes and providing targeted suggestions for improvement, these systems can support students in understanding their errors and guide them toward academic progress (Ghai, D., Tripathi, S. L., Saxena, S., Chanda, M., & Alazab, M., 2022).

*f)* ***Behavioral Analytics for Participation Grading:*** Beyond traditional assessments, Generative AI can analyze behavioral data, such as student participation in online forums, collaborative projects, or virtual classrooms. This information can be integrated into grading systems to provide a more holistic evaluation of a student's engagement and contributions.

*g)* ***Predictive Analytics for Early Warning Systems:*** Generative AI models can predict students at risk of academic challenges by analyzing various factors such as attendance, assignment completion, and quiz performance. Early warning systems can then trigger interventions to support struggling students and improve overall retention rates.

*h)* ***Ethical Considerations and Bias Mitigation:*** Generative AI can also play a role in mitigating bias in grading systems. By incorporating ethical considerations and fairness metrics during the model training phase, AI developers can strive to create grading systems that are objective, transparent, and free from discriminatory outcomes.

## Latest Generative AI Tools Shaping Education

Generative AI tools have been instrumental in shaping education by providing innovative solutions for content creation, personalization, and interactive learning experiences. OpenAI's GPT-3 remains a prominent player, showcasing its prowess in generating coherent and contextually relevant text, making it valuable for developing educational content and interactive applications (Terwiesch, C., 2023). The Hugging Face Transformers library continues to be a go-to resource for natural language processing models, facilitating tasks such as summarization and question-answering in an educational context. TensorFlow and PyTorch, being comprehensive machine learning frameworks, are widely used for building and training generative models, empowering educators and researchers to delve into advanced AI applications. Google Colab, with its access to free GPU resources, provides an accessible platform for collaborative experimentation with Generative AI. While specific educational tools might continue to evolve, these frameworks and platforms underline the ongoing impact of Generative AI on shaping dynamic and personalized learning experiences in the educational landscape. For the latest developments, it is recommended to check the most recent resources and updates in the field. Here, some latest Generative AI tools shaping education are explained as follows:

*a)* ***OpenAI's GPT-3 (Generative Pre-trained Transformer 3):*** OpenAI's GPT-3 is a state-of-the-art language model that has been used in various applications, including education. Its ability to generate coherent and contextually relevant text has made it valuable for creating educational content, generating quiz questions, and assisting with natural language understanding.

*b)* ***Hugging Face Transformers:*** Hugging Face provides a platform and library for natural language processing models, including various Generative AI models. Their Transformers library includes pre-trained models that can be fine-tuned for specific educational tasks, such as language understanding, summarization, and question-answering.

c) ***TensorFlow and PyTorch:*** TensorFlow and PyTorch are comprehensive machine-learning frameworks that include tools for building and training generative models. These frameworks are widely used in the research and development of Generative AI applications, and many educational projects leverage these libraries.
d) ***Google Colab:*** Google Colab is a cloud-based platform that provides free access to GPUs. It's a popular environment for experimenting with Generative AI models, allowing educators and students to run code collaboratively and explore AI projects without the need for extensive computational resources.
e) ***Jupyter Notebooks:*** Jupyter Notebooks are widely used for creating and sharing documents that contain live code, equations, visualizations, and narrative text. They are often used in educational settings to teach and explore Generative AI concepts collaboratively.
f) ***AI Dungeon:*** AI Dungeon is an interactive text-based adventure game that uses GPT-3 to generate dynamic and imaginative stories based on user input. While it's more of a recreational tool, it showcases the capabilities of large-scale language models and can be used to inspire creative writing or storytelling in educational contexts.
g) ***DeepArt:*** DeepArt is an AI-powered tool that uses neural style transfer to transform images into artwork. While it may not be directly educational, it demonstrates the creative potential of Generative AI and can be used in art-related educational projects.
h) ***Deep Dream Generator:*** A tool that uses neural networks to generate unique and abstract visualizations from images.
i) ***ChatGPT:*** A sibling model to GPT-3 specifically fine-tuned for conversational applications, which can be utilized for interactive educational chatbots.
j) ***Snorkel AI:*** A platform for building and managing training data for machine learning models, assisting in creating labeled datasets for education-related tasks.
k) ***Clara Train SDK:*** NVIDIA's toolkit for medical imaging, providing tools for creating AI models in healthcare education.
l) ***Runway ML:*** A creative toolkit that enables artists and educators to use and experiment with various AI models, including Generative AI.
m) ***DeepArt.io:*** An online platform using deep neural networks for transforming photographs into artwork, offering creative applications in art education.
n) ***Spell:*** A platform for machine learning and deep learning experimentation, offering cloud-based resources for model development in education.
o) ***Artbreeder:*** A tool that uses Generative Adversarial Networks (GANs) for creating and manipulating images, allowing for artistic exploration and expression.
p) ***Microsoft Azure Cognitive Services:*** Offers various AI services, including natural language processing and computer vision, applicable in educational contexts.
q) ***IBM Watson Studio:*** A platform that provides tools for data scientists and educators to build and deploy AI models.
r) ***Speechmatics:*** An automatic speech recognition (ASR) tool that can be applied in language learning and linguistics education.
s) ***AnkiDroid:*** An open-source flashcard app that can be enhanced with AI-powered language models for language learning.

*t)* ***Unity3D with ML-Agents:*** Integrates machine learning into the Unity game development engine, allowing for educational projects that involve AI agents in virtual environments.
*u)* ***Cognii:*** An AI-driven virtual tutor that provides personalized feedback on student essays, contributing to language learning and writing skills.
*v)* ***Keras:*** A high-level neural networks API, often used in conjunction with TensorFlow, is suitable for educational projects in deep learning.
*w)* ***Educative Platforms:*** Platforms like Coursera, edX, and Udacity leverage machine learning algorithms to provide personalized learning experiences for students.
*x)* ***AI-Generated Content Platforms:*** Platforms that use Generative AI to create educational content, such as lesson plans, quizzes, and interactive materials.

These tools showcase the diverse applications of Generative AI in education, from natural language processing to creative expression and beyond. The latest Generative AI tools in education are shown in **Table 1**.

## GENERATIVE AI TO HELP TEACHERS

Generative AI presents a range of opportunities to significantly aid and empower teachers in various aspects of their roles. One key advantage is in content creation and augmentation, where AI can assist educators in generating quizzes, assignments, and educational materials, alleviating the time burden associated with manual content development. Moreover, generative AI contributes to personalized learning experiences by analyzing individual student data and creating tailored learning materials, allowing teachers to address the diverse needs and learning styles within their classrooms. Automated grading powered by generative AI streamlines assessment processes, providing quick and consistent feedback, thereby enabling teachers to focus more on refining their instructional strategies and engaging with students. The development of adaptive learning systems ensures that students receive content aligned with their proficiency levels, fostering a more customized and effective learning environment. Additionally, generative AI supports teachers in creating virtual laboratories and simulations, enriching hands-on learning experiences. The technology's ability to generate detailed and constructive feedback enhances the quality of assessments and aids in student comprehension. By providing data-driven insights into student performance and learning patterns, generative AI equips teachers with valuable information to make informed instructional decisions. Overall, the integration of generative AI in education holds the promise of streamlining administrative tasks, personalizing learning, and offering valuable support to educators, ultimately enhancing the overall educational experience for both teachers and students. Generative AI offers several ways to assist and enhance the work of teachers, providing tools and capabilities that can streamline various aspects of the teaching process. Here are some ways in which generative AI can benefit teachers:

*a)* ***Content Creation and Augmentation:*** Generative AI can assist teachers in creating and augmenting educational content. It can generate quizzes, assignments, and other materials, saving time for educators and allowing them to focus on personalized interactions with students.

*Table 1. Latest generative AI tools used for education*

| Tools | Primary use case | Key features | Framework/ Library | Ease of use | Community support | License |
|---|---|---|---|---|---|---|
| OpenAI GPT-3 | Natural Language Processing | Advanced language modeling, versatile applications | OpenAI | Moderate | Strong | Commercial |
| Hugging Face Transformers | Natural Language Processing | Library with pre-trained NLP models | Transformers (PyTorch) | Moderate | Strong | MIT License |
| TensorFlow | General Machine Learning | Comprehensive ML framework | TensorFlow | Moderate | Strong | Apache 2.0 |
| PyTorch | General Machine Learning | Dynamic computational graphs, popular for research | PyTorch | Moderate | Strong | BSD |
| Google Colab | Cloud-Based Notebooks | Free GPU access, collaborative coding | TensorFlow, PyTorch | Easy | Strong | Free |
| Jupyter Notebooks | Interactive Coding Environments | Live code, visualizations, and narrative text | Multiple (Python, R, etc.) | Easy | Strong | BSD |
| AI Dungeon | Interactive Storytelling | Text-based adventure game powered by GPT-3 | OpenAI | Easy | Strong | Commercial |
| DeepArt | Neural Style Transfer | Transforming images into artwork using neural networks | Proprietary | Easy | Moderate | Free |
| ChatGPT | Conversational AI | GPT-3 model fine-tuned for interactive conversations | OpenAI | Easy | Strong | Commercial |
| DeepArt.io | Image Transformation | Deep neural networks for transforming photos into art | Proprietary | Easy | Moderate | Free |
| Deep Dream Generator | Image Generation | Using neural networks for abstract image visualizations | Proprietary | Easy | Moderate | Free |
| Spell | Machine Learning Platform | Cloud-based resources for machine learning experimentation | TensorFlow, PyTorch | Easy | Moderate | Freemium |
| Clara Train SDK | Medical Imaging | NVIDIA toolkit for medical imaging AI | NVIDIA | Moderate | Strong | Proprietary |
| Runway ML | Creative Toolkit | Toolkit for artists and educators to experiment with AI | Various | Easy | Moderate | Commercial |
| DeepArt.io | Image Transformation | Neural style transfer for transforming photos into art | Proprietary | Easy | Moderate | Free |
| Microsoft Azure Cognitive Services | Various AI Services | Wide range of AI services including NLP and computer vision | Proprietary | Moderate | Strong | Commercial |
| IBM Watson Studio | AI Development Platform | Tools for building and deploying AI models | Proprietary | Moderate | Strong | Commercial |
| Speechmatics | Automatic Speech Recognition | ASR tool for language learning and linguistics education | Proprietary | Moderate | Moderate | Commercial |
| AnkiDroid | Flashcard App | Open-source flashcard app with AI-powered language models | Proprietary | Easy | Moderate | Open Source |
| Unity3D with ML-Agents | Game Development with ML-Agents | Integrating machine learning into Unity game development | Unity | Moderate | Strong | Commercial |
| Cognii | Virtual Tutor for Essays | AI-driven virtual tutor providing feedback on student essays | Proprietary | Moderate | Moderate | Commercial |
| Keras | High-Level Neural Networks API | High-level neural networks API, often used with TensorFlow | TensorFlow | Easy | Strong | MIT License |
| Coursera, edX, Udacity | Online Learning Platforms | Leveraging machine learning algorithms for personalized learning | Proprietary | Easy | Strong | Commercial |

*b)* ***Personalized Learning Materials:*** By analyzing individual student data, generative AI can help teachers create personalized learning materials tailored to the specific needs and learning styles of each student. This enables more effective and targeted teaching strategies.

*c)* ***Adaptive Learning Paths:*** Generative AI can contribute to the development of adaptive learning systems that adjust the learning path based on individual student progress. This ensures that each student receives content at an appropriate level of difficulty, optimizing the learning experience.

*d)* ***Automated Grading:*** Generative AI can automate the grading process for assignments and assessments, providing quick and consistent feedback to students. This helps teachers save time on administrative tasks and focus more on addressing students' individual learning needs.

*e)* ***Intelligent Tutoring Systems:*** AI-powered tutoring systems can assist teachers by providing additional support to students outside of regular classroom hours. These systems can offer personalized guidance and practice, reinforcing classroom learning.

*f)* ***Language Translation and Accessibility:*** Generative AI tools that support language translation can be valuable for teachers working in multilingual environments. These tools facilitate effective communication with students and parents who speak different languages, promoting inclusivity.

*g)* ***Virtual Laboratories and Simulations:*** Generative AI can be used to create virtual laboratories and simulations, allowing students to engage in hands-on learning experiences in subjects like science and engineering. Teachers can use these tools to supplement theoretical lessons and make learning more interactive.

*h)* ***Feedback Generation:*** AI-generated feedback can assist teachers in providing detailed and constructive comments on student work. This personalized feedback helps students understand their strengths and areas for improvement, contributing to a more effective learning process.

*i)* ***Data-Driven Insights:*** Generative AI can analyze large sets of educational data to provide teachers with valuable insights into student performance, learning patterns, and areas that may need additional attention. This data-driven approach can inform instructional decisions.

*j)* ***Professional Development:*** Generative AI can assist in creating personalized professional development plans for teachers. By analyzing their teaching styles, strengths, and areas for growth, AI systems can recommend targeted training resources to enhance teaching skills.

While generative AI holds significant potential for supporting teachers, it's crucial to approach its implementation with careful consideration of ethical considerations, data privacy, and the need for ongoing human oversight. The collaboration between AI tools and human educators has the potential to create a more personalized, efficient, and inclusive educational environment.

## Top Ten Strategic Predictions in Education

Top strategic predictions in education are explained as follows:

*a)* ***Hybrid Learning Models:*** Education will continue to embrace hybrid learning models that combine in-person and online experiences. This flexibility accommodates diverse learning styles and preferences.

*b)* ***AI-Powered Personalization:*** AI will play a crucial role in tailoring education to individual needs. Adaptive learning platforms will use AI to customize content, pacing, and assessments for each student, enhancing personalized learning experiences.

c) ***Rise of Virtual Classrooms:*** Virtual classrooms and online learning platforms will become integral components of education. Augmented and virtual reality technologies will further enrich virtual learning environments, providing immersive educational experiences.
d) ***Skills-Based and Lifelong Learning:*** There will be a shift towards skills-based education and lifelong learning. Educational institutions and employers will collaborate to offer continuous learning opportunities to adapt to the evolving demands of the workforce.
e) ***Global Collaboration and Connectivity:*** Enhanced connectivity and digital platforms will facilitate global collaboration among students, educators, and institutions. Cross-cultural exchanges, collaborative projects, and shared resources will become commonplace.
f) ***Assessment Transformation:*** Traditional assessment methods will evolve to incorporate more authentic and competency-based assessments. AI and analytics will provide insights into students' skills, allowing for more comprehensive evaluations.
g) ***Focus on Well-Being and Mental Health:*** Education will prioritize the well-being and mental health of students and educators. Social-emotional learning (SEL) programs will be integrated into curricula, fostering emotional intelligence and resilience.
h) ***Blockchain for Credentialing:*** Blockchain technology will be increasingly used for secure and transparent credentialing. Digital credentials and micro-credentials will gain acceptance as valid indicators of skills and qualifications.
i) ***Innovations in EdTech:*** Continued innovations in educational technology will bring forth new tools and platforms, including AI-driven tutors, immersive learning simulations, and collaborative virtual environments.
j) ***Emphasis on Diversity, Equity, and Inclusion:*** Education will place a heightened emphasis on fostering diversity, equity, and inclusion. Curricula will be designed to reflect diverse perspectives, and efforts will be made to eliminate educational disparities.

## Adoption Strategies for Educational Institutions

Adopting new strategies and technologies in educational institutions requires a holistic and well-considered approach to ensure successful implementation and sustained impact. A crucial initial step is conducting a comprehensive needs assessment, identifying specific challenges and opportunities within the institution. Inclusivity is paramount; involving all stakeholders, including teachers, students, administrators, and parents, ensures that the adopted strategies align with the community's diverse needs. Professional development is a linchpin, with tailored training programs providing educators with the skills and confidence to integrate new technologies effectively. Implementing pilot programs on a smaller scale allows for real-world testing, feedback gathering, and adjustments before full-scale adoption. Infrastructure readiness is foundational, requiring investments in reliable internet connectivity, hardware, and software. Prioritizing data security and privacy considerations is essential, aligning practices with relevant regulations. Customized training resources, community engagement, and continuous evaluation foster a collaborative and supportive environment. Scalability and sustainability considerations, along with partnerships, contribute to long-term success. Cultivating a culture of innovation encourages experimentation and creativity, while regular reviews and a commitment to continuous improvement ensure that adopted strategies evolve to meet the evolving needs of educational institutions. Here are some key adoption strategies for educational institutions:

*a)* ***Needs Assessment:*** Conduct a thorough needs assessment to identify the specific challenges and opportunities within the educational institution. Understand the goals, requirements, and expectations of educators, students, and administrators.

*b)* ***Stakeholder Involvement:*** Involve all stakeholders, including teachers, students, administrators, and parents, in the decision-making process. Gather feedback and insights to ensure that the adopted strategies align with the community's diverse needs.

*c)* ***Professional Development:*** Provide comprehensive professional development programs for educators to build their skills and confidence in using new technologies. This includes training sessions, workshops, and ongoing support to ensure a smooth transition.

*d)* ***Pilot Programs:*** Implement pilot programs to test new technologies or strategies on a smaller scale before full-scale adoption. This allows for the identification of potential challenges and adjustments to be made based on real-world feedback.

*e)* ***Infrastructure Readiness:*** Ensure that the necessary infrastructure, such as robust internet connectivity, hardware, and software, is in place to support the adopted technologies. Conduct a technology audit to address any gaps and invest in necessary upgrades.

*f)* ***Data Security and Privacy:*** Prioritize data security and privacy considerations. Implement robust cybersecurity measures and communicate transparently about how data will be handled and protected, ensuring compliance with relevant regulations.

*g)* ***Customized Training Resources:*** Develop customized training resources and documentation for educators and staff. This may include video tutorials, user guides, and FAQs to support ongoing learning and troubleshooting.

*h)* ***Community Engagement:*** Foster community engagement by communicating the benefits of the adopted strategies to parents, students, and the broader community. Encourage involvement in school activities and initiatives related to the new technologies.

*i)* ***Continuous Evaluation and Feedback:*** Establish a system for continuous evaluation and feedback. Regularly assess the impact of the adopted strategies on teaching and learning outcomes, and make adjustments based on feedback from educators, students, and other stakeholders.

*j)* ***Scalability and Sustainability:*** Consider the scalability and long-term sustainability of the adopted strategies. Ensure that the chosen technologies and approaches can grow with the institution and adapt to future changes in educational practices and technology trends.

*k)* ***Partnerships and Collaboration:*** Explore partnerships with industry leaders, educational organizations, and technology providers. Collaborate with external experts to bring in fresh perspectives, resources, and support for effective implementation.

*l)* ***Cultivate a Culture of Innovation:*** Foster a culture of innovation within the educational institution. Encourage experimentation, creativity, and a willingness to explore new ideas among educators and students.

*m)* ***Regular Review and Iteration:*** Regularly review the effectiveness of the adopted strategies and be open to iterative improvements. Embrace a culture of continuous improvement, where lessons learned from implementation inform future decisions.

## ROLE OF EDUCATORS IN AI-ENHANCED CLASSROOM

In the AI-enhanced classroom, educators assume a multifaceted role that extends beyond traditional teaching responsibilities. They become orchestrators of a dynamic and technology-infused learning environment. Instead of being replaced by artificial intelligence, educators leverage these technologies to enrich the educational experience. They design and integrate AI into the curriculum, aligning learning objectives with innovative tools. As facilitators of learning, they guide students in navigating AI-driven resources and foster an environment of curiosity and critical thinking. Educators advocate for personalized learning, utilizing AI's analytical capabilities to tailor content and assessments to individual student needs. Furthermore, they take on the responsibility of teaching ethical AI use, ensuring students develop a nuanced understanding of societal implications. Educators continuously adapt their instructional strategies based on AI-generated insights, leveraging technology to monitor student progress and provide targeted support. By embracing technology integration and participating in continuous professional development, educators not only stay proficient in using AI tools but also contribute valuable insights to AI developers, ensuring that these technologies align with educational goals. Ultimately, their role evolves into that of mentors and guides, cultivating a generation of learners who are technologically fluent, ethically responsible, and critical thinkers in the AI-driven era. Educators play a pivotal role in shaping the AI-enhanced classroom, where artificial intelligence technologies complement and enhance traditional teaching methods. Here are key aspects of their role in this evolving educational landscape:

### Facilitators of Learning

Educators become facilitators of learning, guiding students in navigating AI-driven tools and resources. They create an environment that encourages curiosity, critical thinking, and exploration while leveraging AI to enrich the learning experience.

*a)* ***Curriculum Design and Integration:*** Educators design and integrate AI into the curriculum, identifying opportunities to infuse AI concepts and applications across various subjects. They align learning objectives with AI-driven tools to ensure a cohesive educational experience.

### Personalized Learning Advocates

With AI's capability to analyze individual learning styles and preferences, educators advocate for personalized learning. They use AI tools to tailor content, assessments, and feedback, addressing the unique needs of each student and fostering a more inclusive educational environment.

*a)* ***Quillionz:*** Quillionz is an AI tool that generates questions and answers from textual input. While not specifically designed for grading, it can be used to assess the understanding and depth of students' written responses.

*b)* ***SAS Writing Reviser:*** SAS Writing Reviser is an AI tool designed to assist with writing improvement. It can analyze text for various writing conventions and help students enhance their writing skills.

c) ***Squirrel AI:*** Squirrel AI is an adaptive learning platform that uses AI algorithms to personalize education for individual students. It assesses students' performance and tailors learning materials to their specific needs.

d) ***DreamBox:*** DreamBox is an adaptive math program for students. It uses AI to personalize math lessons based on each student's strengths and weaknesses, providing a customized learning experience.

e) ***Knewton:*** Knewton is an adaptive learning platform that uses AI to analyze students' performance data and deliver personalized learning recommendations. It is used in various educational settings, including K-12 and higher education.

f) ***SMART Learning Suite:*** SMART Learning Suite includes AI features for educational purposes. It offers tools for lesson creation, student engagement, and assessment. The platform uses AI to provide insights into student progress.

g) ***Cognii:*** Cognii is an AI tool designed for educational assessment, particularly in the area of assessing written responses to open-ended questions. It uses NLP to analyze and evaluate students' written answers to open-ended questions, providing feedback on content and writing style. While the specific details of Cognii's architecture and algorithms are proprietary, we can provide a general overview of how similar tools typically work:

- *Input Analysis:* Students provide written responses to open-ended questions. These responses are typically in natural language and can cover various subjects and topics.
- *Natural Language Processing (NLP):* Cognii employs NLP techniques to understand the semantic meaning of the written responses. This involves breaking down the text into its constituent parts, analyzing the structure of sentences, and identifying keywords and concepts.
- *Semantic Analysis:* Cognii assesses the semantic content of the responses to understand whether the student has correctly addressed the question, demonstrated a conceptual understanding, and communicated ideas effectively.
- *Feedback Generation:* Based on the analysis, Cognii generates personalized feedback for each student. This feedback may highlight strengths and weaknesses in the response, suggest improvements, and guide how to enhance the quality of the answer.
- *Grading and Scoring:* Cognii assigns a grade or score to each response based on predefined criteria. This could involve assessing the accuracy of information, the depth of understanding, the coherence of the response, and adherence to specific guidelines.
- *Adaptability:* Some AI assessment tools, including Cognii, may have adaptive capabilities. This means that the system learns from the data it processes and improves its ability to assess student responses over time. It can adapt its feedback based on patterns observed in a large dataset of responses.
- *Integration with Learning Management Systems (LMS):* Cognii can integrate with existing learning management systems used by educational institutions. This allows teachers and administrators to seamlessly incorporate AI-based assessment into their workflow.
- *Continuous Improvement:* Cognii and similar tools often have mechanisms for continuous improvement. This involves incorporating user feedback, refining algorithms, and updating the system to ensure that it remains effective in assessing a wide range of responses. **Figure 4** shows various models for continuous improvement.

Various approaches for continuous improvement are explained as follows:

*Figure 4. Continuous improvement*

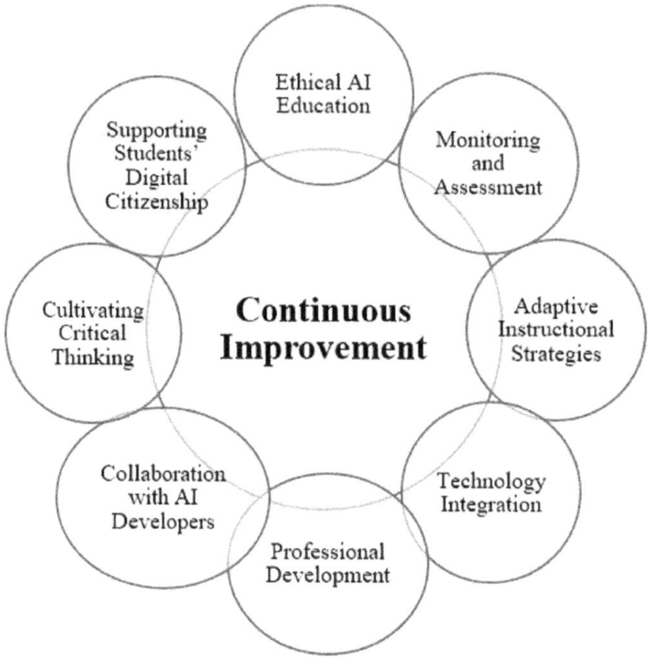


a) ***Ethical AI Education:*** Educators take on the responsibility of teaching students about the ethical use of AI. They discuss topics such as bias in algorithms, data privacy, and the societal impact of AI, fostering a critical awareness of the ethical considerations associated with these technologies.
b) ***Monitoring and Assessment:*** Educators leverage AI to monitor student progress and assess their performance. AI-driven analytics provide valuable insights into individual strengths and weaknesses, allowing educators to tailor interventions and support for each student's academic journey.
c) ***Adaptive Instructional Strategies:*** Educators adapt their instructional strategies based on AI-generated insights. They use data-driven recommendations to modify teaching approaches, ensuring that students receive targeted support and a more effective learning experience.
d) ***Technology Integration:*** Educators embrace technology integration by incorporating AI tools seamlessly into their teaching methods. They stay updated on the latest advancements, experimenting with new tools and platforms to enhance engagement and effectiveness in the classroom.
e) ***Professional Development:*** Continuous professional development becomes essential as educators hone their AI literacy and pedagogical skills. Training programs and workshops help them stay proficient in using AI tools, fostering a dynamic and adaptive teaching environment.
f) ***Collaboration with AI Developers:*** Collaboration between educators and AI developers is crucial. Educators provide insights into the practical needs of the classroom, offering feedback on the usability and effectiveness of AI tools This collaboration ensures that AI applications align with educational objectives.
g) ***Cultivating Critical Thinking:*** Educators emphasize the development of critical thinking skills alongside AI integration. They guide students in questioning, analyzing, and interpreting infor-

mation generated by AI, fostering a mindset that combines technological fluency with a nuanced understanding of content.

h) ***Supporting Students' Digital Citizenship:*** Educators nurture students' digital citizenship skills, helping them navigate the online world responsibly and ethically. This includes teaching them how to engage with AI-driven technologies while being mindful of their digital footprint and online behavior.

## Global Perspectives on AI in Education

Global perspectives on AI in education vary, reflecting diverse approaches, challenges, and opportunities in different regions. Globally, attitudes toward AI in education are characterized by a shared enthusiasm for its potential benefits and a collective emphasis on responsible implementation. In North America, Europe, and Asia-Pacific, there's a growing integration of AI to enhance personalized learning, address language barriers, and prepare students for the future workforce. The Middle East, Africa, and Latin America see AI as a tool to overcome educational disparities. Ethical considerations, digital inclusion efforts, and a focus on comprehensive teacher professional development are universal concerns. As nations collaborate in research and innovation hubs, a nuanced global perspective emerges, recognizing both the opportunities and challenges in leveraging AI for transformative education. Here are some key insights into how AI is perceived and utilized in education on a global scale:

a) ***North America:*** In North America, particularly in the United States and Canada, AI in education is embraced for its potential to enhance personalized learning experiences. EdTech companies and educational institutions explore AI applications in adaptive learning platforms, intelligent tutoring systems, and data analytics to improve student outcomes.

b) ***Europe:*** European countries are increasingly integrating AI into their educational systems. The focus includes leveraging AI for language learning, teacher professional development, and adaptive learning platforms. Ethical considerations and data privacy are central concerns, leading to efforts to establish clear guidelines and regulations.

c) ***Asia-Pacific:*** Countries in the Asia-Pacific region, including China, Japan, and South Korea, are at the forefront of AI adoption in education. AI is applied to improve language learning, assist with grading, and provide personalized feedback. These countries also emphasize AI skills development to prepare students for the future workforce.

d) ***Middle East and Africa:*** In the Middle East, countries like the United Arab Emirates are investing in AI for education, with a focus on smart learning environments and AI-driven tools. In Africa, AI is seen as a potential tool to address educational disparities and improve access to quality education, although challenges related to infrastructure and funding persist.

f) ***Latin America:*** Latin American countries are exploring AI applications in education to address challenges related to accessibility and quality. Initiatives include using AI for language learning, teacher training, and personalized learning experiences. Collaboration with AI developers and international organizations is growing.

g) ***Global Collaboration:*** There is a growing emphasis on global collaboration in AI research and education. Organizations, governments, and educational institutions collaborate to share best practices, research findings, and insights on effective AI integration in diverse cultural and educational contexts.

*h)* ***Ethical Considerations:*** Globally, there is a shared concern about the ethical implications of AI in education. The responsible and ethical use of AI, including addressing bias in algorithms, ensuring data privacy, and promoting transparency, is a common theme in discussions and initiatives worldwide.

*i)* ***Digital Inclusion:*** The global perspective on AI in education includes a focus on digital inclusion. Efforts are made to bridge the digital divide, ensuring that AI-enhanced educational resources are accessible to students across socioeconomic and geographic boundaries.

*j)* ***Teacher Professional Development:*** Recognizing the importance of educators in the AI-enhanced classroom, global perspectives emphasize the need for comprehensive teacher professional development. Training programs focus on AI literacy, pedagogical skills, and the effective integration of technology into teaching practices.

*k)* ***Innovation Hubs and Initiatives:*** Various regions host innovation hubs and initiatives that bring together educators, policymakers, and technology experts to explore and implement AI in education. These collaborative efforts contribute to the development of global best practices and frameworks.

## Case Studies on Generative AI Tools for Education

Some case studies on Generative AI tools for education are explained as follows:

*a)* ***Global Collaborative Learning Platform:*** A multinational consortium of educational institutions implements a collaborative learning platform driven by generative AI. This platform facilitates cross-cultural collaboration, content generation, and language translation, providing students worldwide with a diverse and inclusive learning experience. The case study explores the impact on global knowledge exchange, cultural understanding, and educational outcomes.

*b)* ***AI-Driven Inclusive Curriculum:*** An international organization adopts generative AI to develop an inclusive curriculum that caters to various cultural contexts and learning preferences. The case study investigates how the AI tool ensures cultural relevance, adapts to regional educational standards, and fosters a sense of global citizenship among students.

*c)* ***Remote Learning Revolution:*** In response to global challenges such as the COVID-19 pandemic, a coalition of countries utilizes generative AI tools to revolutionize remote learning. The case study assesses how AI-powered platforms enhance the effectiveness of virtual classrooms, provide personalized learning experiences, and bridge educational gaps on a global scale.

*d)* ***Multilingual AI Tutoring Network:*** An international network of schools implements a multilingual AI tutoring system to support students globally. The case study examines how the AI tool adapts to diverse linguistic needs, provides real-time tutoring in multiple languages, and contributes to improved academic performance across different cultural and linguistic backgrounds.

*e)* ***AI-Enhanced Teacher Training Program:*** A global educational foundation launches a generative AI-powered teacher training program accessible to educators worldwide. The case study evaluates how the program improves pedagogical skills, incorporates cultural nuances, and fosters a global community of educators committed to leveraging AI for enhanced learning outcomes.

f) ***Open Educational Resources (OER) Platform:*** A collaborative effort among nations establishes a generative AI-driven OER platform. This platform generates and curates educational content in multiple languages, making quality resources accessible to students and educators globally. The case study explores the impact on resource equality, collaborative content creation, and knowledge dissemination.

g) ***AI-Enhanced Credentialing System:*** A global initiative that implements a blockchain-based credentialing system powered by generative AI. This system ensures secure and universally recognized digital credentials, allowing students to seamlessly transition across international educational institutions. The case study assesses the efficiency, security, and global acceptance of the AI-driven credentialing system.

These hypothetical case studies illustrate the potential of generative AI tools to shape education on a global scale as shown in **Table 2**. As AI continues to advance and education evolves, real-world examples will emerge, showcasing the transformative impact of these technologies worldwide.

## CONCLUSION

In envisioning the educational landscape of 2030, the transformative potential of generative AI tools emerges as a catalyst for profound changes in teaching and learning. As we peer into this future, it becomes evident that these tools, driven by artificial intelligence, are poised to revolutionize education by fostering personalized, inclusive, and technologically advanced learning ecosystems. The case studies presented illustrate a broad spectrum of applications, showcasing how generative AI seamlessly integrates into various educational facets. From adaptive learning platforms tailoring content to individual student needs to multilingual AI tutoring systems breaking down language barriers, the transformative impact on education is palpable. In 2030, education is not a one-size-fits-all model; rather, it is a dynamic and personalized journey where AI tools empower both educators and learners. The adaptability

*Table 2. Different case studies on generative AI tools for education*

| Case Study Title | Description |
|---|---|
| Adaptive Learning Success at XYZ School | • Implementation of an adaptive learning platform powered by AI at XYZ School.<br>• Improved student engagement and performance through personalized learning paths. |
| Squirrel AI in Rural Education | • Deployment of Squirrel AI in a rural education setting to provide personalized tutoring.<br>• Impact assessment on student outcomes and bridging educational gaps. |
| AI-Enhanced Teacher Training at Government Schools | • Diksha platform utilized for AI-driven teacher training in government schools.<br>• Analysis of the effectiveness of AI tools in enhancing pedagogical skills. |
| Tech-Driven Language Learning at a Multilingual Institute | • Integration of language processing tools for multilingual education at ABC Institute.<br>• Assessment of AI's role in overcoming language barriers and fostering inclusivity |
| IBM Watson Analytics in Higher Education | • Adoption of IBM Watson for data analytics in a higher education institution.<br>• Examination of how AI analytics influence decision-making and student outcomes |
| BYJU'S Adaptive Learning App Impact Study | • Evaluation of the BYJU'S app impact on student learning outcomes<br>• Analysis of AI algorithms in adapting content delivery to individual learning styles |
| Yellowdig Social Learning in Universities | • Implementation of Yellowdig for social learning in university courses.<br>• Exploration of AI's role in enhancing collaborative learning experiences. |
| Skill Development with Simplilearn | • Case study on the use of Simplilearn for AI-driven skill development.<br>• Assessment of adaptive content delivery and its impact on skill acquisition. |

of generative AI to diverse cultural contexts and learning preferences stands out. Collaborative learning platforms facilitate global knowledge exchange, transcending geographical boundaries. The inclusive curriculum, informed by generative AI, respects cultural nuances and adapts to regional educational standards, fostering a sense of global citizenship among students. However, amidst the promise lies a set of challenges. Ethical considerations, data privacy concerns, and the imperative for continuous professional development emerge as critical factors. Responsible implementation of AI in education requires careful navigation of these challenges to ensure that the transformative potential is harnessed ethically and sustainably. Looking ahead, the synergy between education and generative AI represents a paradigm shift. It is a shift towards an education ecosystem that is not only responsive to individual learning needs but also anticipates and adapts to the evolving demands of the future. As we approach 2030, the collaboration between educators, technologists, and policymakers becomes pivotal. Together, they shape an educational landscape where generative AI tools are not just tools; they are the architects of a future where knowledge is dynamic, accessible, and tailored to every learner's unique journey. In this future, education becomes a transformative force, propelled by the limitless possibilities of generative AI.

## REFERENCES

Abdullah, M., Madain, A., & Jararweh, Y. (2022). ChatGPT: Fundamentals, applications & social impacts. In *2022 Ninth International Conference on Social Networks Analysis, Management & Security (SNAMS)*. IEEE.

Adıgüzel, T., Kaya, M. H., & Cansu, F. K. (2023). Revolutionizing education with AI: Exploring the transformative potential of ChatGPT. *Contemporary Educational Technology*, *15*(3), ep429. doi:10.30935/cedtech/13152

Akgun, S., & Greenhow, C. (2022). Artificial intelligence in education: Addressing ethical challenges in K-12 settings. *AI and Ethics*, *2*(3), 431–440. doi:10.1007/s43681-021-00096-7 PMID:34790956

Baidoo-Anu, D., & Ansah, L. O. (2023). Education in the era of generative artificial intelligence (AI): Understanding the potential benefits of ChatGPT in promoting teaching and learning. *Journal of AI*, *7*(1), 52–62. doi:10.61969/jai.1337500

Castelli, M., & Manzoni, L. (2022). Generative models in artificial intelligence and their applications. *Applied Sciences (Basel, Switzerland)*, *12*(9), 4127. doi:10.3390/app12094127

Dai, J., Wang, J., Huang, W., Shi, J., & Zhu, Z. (2020). Machinery health monitoring based on unsupervised feature learning via generative adversarial networks. *IEEE/ASME Transactions on Mechatronics*, *25*(5), 2252–2263. doi:10.1109/TMECH.2020.3012179

De Oliveira Silva, A., & Dos Santos Janes, D. (2020). Exploring the Role of Artificial Intelligence in Education: A Comprehensive Perspective. *Review of Artificial Intelligence in Education*, *1*(00), e05–e05. doi:10.37497/rev.artif.intell.education.v1i00.5

Doroudi, S. (2023). The intertwined histories of artificial intelligence and education. *International Journal of Artificial Intelligence in Education*, *33*(4), 885–928. doi:10.1007/s40593-022-00313-2

Eglash, R., Bennett, A., Babbitt, W., Lachney, M., Reinhardt, M., & Hammond-Sowah, D. (2020). Decolonizing posthumanism: Indigenous material agency in generative STEM. *British Journal of Educational Technology*, *51*(4), 1334–1353. doi:10.1111/bjet.12963

Faiz, M., Sandhu, R., Akbar, M., Shaikh, A. A., Bhasin, C., & Fatima, N. (2023). Machine Learning Techniques in Wireless Sensor Networks: Algorithms, Strategies, and Applications. *International Journal of Intelligent Systems and Applications in Engineering*, *11*(9s), 685–694.

Feng, Y., Vanam, S., Cherukupally, M., Zheng, W., Qiu, M., & Chen, H. (2023). Investigating code generation performance of ChatGPT with crowdsourcing social data. In *2023 IEEE 47th Annual Computers, Software, and Applications Conference (COMPSAC)* (pp. 876-885). IEEE. 10.1109/COMPSAC57700.2023.00117

Ferrara, E. (2024). GenAI against humanity: Nefarious applications of generative artificial intelligence and large language models. *Journal of Computational Social Science*, 1–21. doi:10.1007/s42001-024-00250-1

Furey, H., & Martin, F. (2019). AI education matters: A modular approach to AI ethics education. *AI Matters*, *4*(4), 13–15. doi:10.1145/3299758.3299764

Gao, P., Li, J., & Liu, S. (2021). An introduction to key technology in artificial intelligence and big data driven e-learning and e-education. *Mobile Networks and Applications*, *26*(5), 2123–2126. doi:10.1007/s11036-021-01777-7

Ghai, D., Tripathi, S. L., Saxena, S., Chanda, M., & Alazab, M. (Eds.). (2022). *Machine Learning Algorithms for Signal and Image Processing*. John Wiley & Sons. doi:10.1002/9781119861850

Huang, X. (2021). Aims for cultivating students' key competencies based on artificial intelligence education in China. *Education and Information Technologies*, *26*(5), 5127–5147. doi:10.1007/s10639-021-10530-2

Hughes, R. T., Zhu, L., & Bednarz, T. (2021). Generative adversarial networks–enabled human–artificial intelligence collaborative applications for creative and design industries: A systematic review of current approaches and trends. *Frontiers in Artificial Intelligence*, *4*, 604234. doi:10.3389/frai.2021.604234 PMID:33997773

Humble, N., & Mozelius, P. (2022). The threat, hype, and promise of artificial intelligence in education. *Discover Artificial Intelligence*, *2*(1), 22. doi:10.1007/s44163-022-00039-z

Karras, T., Laine, S., & Aila, T. (2019). A style-based generator architecture for generative adversarial networks. In *Proceedings of the IEEE/CVF conference on computer vision and pattern recognition* (pp. 4401-4410). IEEE. 10.1109/CVPR.2019.00453

Kingma, D.P., & Welling, M. (2019). An introduction to variational autoencoders. *Foundations and Trends® in Machine Learning, 12*(4), 307-392.

Laupichler, M. C., Aster, A., Schirch, J., & Raupach, T. (2022). Artificial intelligence literacy in higher and adult education: A scoping literature review. *Computers and Education: Artificial Intelligence*, *3*, 100101. doi:10.1016/j.caeai.2022.100101

Lehmann, F., & Buschek, D. (2021). Examining autocompletion as a basic concept for interaction with generative AI. *i-com, 19*(3), 251-264.

Lim, W. M., Gunasekara, A., Pallant, J. L., Pallant, J. I., & Pechenkina, E. (2023). Generative AI and the future of education: Ragnarök or reformation? A paradoxical perspective from management educators. *International Journal of Management Education, 21*(2), 100790. doi:10.1016/j.ijme.2023.100790

Macpherson, T., Churchland, A., Sejnowski, T., DiCarlo, J., Kamitani, Y., Takahashi, H., & Hikida, T. (2021). Natural and Artificial Intelligence: A brief introduction to the interplay between AI and neuroscience research. *Neural Networks, 144*, 603–613. doi:10.1016/j.neunet.2021.09.018 PMID:34649035

Megahed, F. M., Chen, Y. J., Ferris, J. A., Knoth, S., & Jones-Farmer, L. A. (2024). How generative AI models such as ChatGPT can be (mis) used in SPC practice, education, and research? An exploratory study. *Quality Engineering, 36*(2), 287–315. doi:10.1080/08982112.2023.2206479

Mogavi, R. H., Deng, C., Kim, J. J., Zhou, P., Kwon, Y. D., Metwally, A. H. S., & Hui, P. (2023). *Exploring userperspectives on chatgpt: Applications, perceptions, and implicationsfor ai-integrated education.* arXiv preprint arXiv:2305.13114.

Ovalle, A. (2023). *Decoding The Digital Fuk\'u: Deciphering Colonial Legacies to Critically Assess ChatGPT in Dominican Education.* arXiv preprint arXiv:2310.17533.

Salas-Pilco, S. Z., & Yang, Y. (2022). Artificial intelligence applications in Latin American higher education: A systematic review. *International Journal of Educational Technology in Higher Education, 19*(1), 21. doi:10.1186/s41239-022-00326-w

Santos, R. P. D. (2023). *Enhancing chemistry learning with chatgpt and bing chat as agents to think with: A comparative case study.* arXiv preprint arXiv:2305.11890.

Terwiesch, C. (2023). Would chat GPT3 get a Wharton MBA. A prediction based on its performance in the operations management course. [Mack Institute for Innovation Management at the Wharton School, University of Pennsylvania].

Yu, H., & Guo, Y. (2023). Generative artificial intelligence empowers educational reform: Current status, issues, and prospects. Frontiers in Education, 8, p. 1183162. *Frontiers*, 2023.

Zastudil, C., Rogalska, M., Kapp, C., Vaughn, J., & MacNeil, S. (2023). Generative ai in computing education: Perspectives of students and instructors. In *2023 IEEE Frontiers in Education Conference (FIE)* (pp. 1-9). IEEE.

Zhai, X., Chu, X., Chai, C. S., Jong, M. S. Y., Istenic, A., Spector, M., Liu, J. B., Yuan, J., & Li, Y. (2021). A Review of Artificial Intelligence (AI) in Education from 2010 to 2020. *Complexity, 2021*, 1–18. doi:10.1155/2021/8812542

Zhang, Y., & Wang, H. (2022). Influence of Voice Interactive Educational Robot Combined with Artificial Intelligence for the Development of Adolescents. *Computational Intelligence and Neuroscience, 2022*, 2022. doi:10.1155/2022/7655001 PMID:36248952

# Chapter 2
# AI-Powered Language Translation for Multilingual Classrooms

**Muhammad Usman Tariq**
https://orcid.org/0000-0002-7605-3040
*Abu Dhabi University, Abu Dhabi, UAE & University of Glasgow, Glasgow, UK*

## ABSTRACT

*The revolutionary effects of AI-powered language translation technologies on multilingual classrooms in the modern educational environment are explored in this chapter proposal. It starts with a historical investigation and follows the development of AI translation, highlighting innovations in neural networks and machine learning models that improve efficiency and accuracy. After that, the chapter focuses on deploying AI translation tools in educational contexts. To support this study, real-world case studies are used to examine platforms and apps that are already in use thoroughly. The use of AI-powered translation to improve accessibility for non-native speakers and foster an equal learning environment for students with different linguistic origins is critically discussed. The chapter also looks at how AI may help teachers and students from different cultural backgrounds communicate with one another, which can promote an inclusive learning environment.*

## OVERVIEW

Incorporating AI-powered language translation systems has caused a paradigm change in the educational field in recent years, changing the conventional structure of multilingual classrooms. Adopting these cutting-edge technologies has significantly changed traditional methods, ushering in a new era where language barriers are broken down and fostering a more welcoming and inclusive learning atmosphere. The revolutionary potential of AI language translation is thoroughly explored in this chapter, along with its implications for educational contexts and its far-reaching effects on students from various linguistic backgrounds.

DOI: 10.4018/979-8-3693-2440-0.ch002

A crucial starting point is the development of AI-powered language translation, viewed through a historical perspective highlighting significant technical advancements. One of the main themes is the introduction of neural networks and machine learning models, which explain how they have significantly improved language processing accuracy and efficiency (Smith, 2018). This chapter offers a thorough review of the technology landscape, outlining significant discoveries and successes in the area and tracing the trajectory of progress from basic text translation to real-time speech translation capabilities (Jones & Brown, 2020).

Beyond the technical details, the story explores how AI translation systems are used in educational contexts. The foundation of this investigation is a thorough examination of the several platforms and apps now in use, which throws light on the range of approaches taken by educational institutions throughout the globe (García et al., 2021). Case studies from the real world are used to show how AI translation technologies have been effectively incorporated, providing concrete examples of how they have affected the processes of teaching and learning (Lee & Wang, 2019).

The important topic of improving inclusivity and accessibility using AI-powered translation is covered in the following section. A vital conversation ensues, clarifying how these technologies act as accessibility accelerators, especially for non-native speakers (Chen & Kim, 2017). The chapter walks readers through how AI-driven translation promotes fairness in the classroom. It allows learners of different languages to easily obtain instructional materials and resources (Johnson, 2019). A thorough examination of AI translation's function in creating an inclusive learning environment highlights how it may help students and teachers from different cultural backgrounds communicate more effectively and understand one another better (Brown & García, 2022).

The chapter discusses the pedagogical ramifications and cultural sensitivity of integrating AI-powered language translation in the classroom. In order to improve learning outcomes and meet the varied requirements of students, this section explores how these technologies may be smoothly integrated into teaching approaches (Miller & Patel, 2018). The story highlights the value of cultural sensitivity and awareness in multilingual environments, guiding AI tools through the complexities and intricacies of language to guarantee successful communication (Nguyen & Smith, 2020). Furthermore, the conversation includes how teachers might use these resources to foster respect and understanding of other cultures among students from different backgrounds, in addition to using them to improve language skills (Wang et al., 2021).

As the chapter progresses, focus is placed on the difficulties and potential opportunities that lie ahead in the field of AI-powered language translation in educational environments. The difficulties and restrictions related to context awareness, accuracy, and the moral ramifications of implementing AI in the classroom are examined critically (Morgan & Clark, 2019). The investigation concludes with a prospective viewpoint that forecasts future developments and trends in artificial intelligence (AI) language translation. Through a future viewpoint, Kim and Lee (2022) study how these technologies can become more smoothly incorporated into educational institutions and how their function in moulding multilingual and multicultural classrooms evolves.

This chapter concludes with a comprehensive analysis of the significant effects of AI-powered language translation in education. Reiterating the critical role that artificial intelligence (AI) plays in fostering inclusive, accessible, and culturally sensitive learning environments, it synthesises the historical development, practical implementations, accessibility advancements, pedagogical implications, and future trajectories.

## TECHNOLOGICAL EVOLUTION OF AI IN LANGUAGE TRANSLATION

The fascinating story of the evolution of AI-powered language translation systems over several decades is characterised by significant technological turning points. This section deftly charts the course of this development, emphasising the introduction of neural networks and machine learning models and their significant influence on improving language translation's precision and effectiveness.

### Evolution in History

The Georgetown-IBM project in 1954 serves as an example of the early rule-based systems that laid the groundwork for AI-powered language translation (Hutchins, 2005). This experiment served as a prototype for other projects, such as the 1966 ALPAC report, which critically assessed the performance of the first machine systems (Nirenburg, 2000). However, statistical methods, such as the IBM Candide system (Brown et al., 1993), did not bring a data-driven paradigm to language translation until the late 20th century.

### The Development of Neural Networks

The introduction of neural networks marked a paradigm shift in AI language translation. Early in the twenty-first century, neural machine translation (NMT) became a breakthrough, thanks largely to the work of Bahdanau et al. (2014). NMT models could capture complex language structures and connections by using deep learning architectures, which allowed them to overcome the constraints of statistical and rule-based approaches (Bahdanau et al., 2014; Sutskever et al., 2014).

### Machine Learning Models for Improving Precision

Language translation accuracy has been improved by using machine learning models, especially deep neural networks. These models' iterative learning process allows them to identify intricate patterns in linguistic data, producing translations that are sophisticated and sensitive to context (LeCun et al., 2015). The shift from statistical machine translation to neural networks has improved translation quality considerably, resolving issues with semantic correctness and fidelity that have persisted for a long time (Brown et al., 1993).

### Efficiency Increases

The development of artificial intelligence (AI) in language translation is closely related to the efficiency improvements brought about by machine learning algorithm developments. Translation times and computational resources have been significantly reduced because of neural networks' built-in parallel processing capabilities and hardware advancements (Vaswani et al., 2017). These efficiency improvements help make AI translation systems more scalable and improve translation speed.

## Technological Achievers

Examining the technical turning points in AI translation reveals a development from simple text translation to speech translation in real-time. Rule-based and statistical approaches predominated in the early years, and important systems like SYSTRAN showed that automated translation was feasible (King, 2003). The introduction of NMT marked a turning point since it allowed for a more comprehensive comprehension of context and appropriate translations for the target context (Bahdanau et al., 2014). Later developments expanded the range of AI translation capabilities by enabling real-time spoken language translation, as demonstrated by Google's Transformer model (Vaswani et al., 2017).

The technical advancement of artificial intelligence in language translation demonstrates the continuous pursuit of more precise, effective, and contextually aware systems. Every stage has advanced translation technology, from simple rule-based systems to the revolutionary effects of neural networks. In addition to improving accuracy, the focus on machine learning models—especially neural networks—has resulted in previously unheard-of increases in efficiency. Examining technical turning points demonstrates how AI translation is dynamic and represents a constant advance towards more complex and adaptable language processing powers.

Artificial Intelligence (AI) has revolutionized various domains, with a significant impact observed in language translation. The development of AI-powered language translation systems has transformed global communication, overcoming linguistic barriers and fostering cross-cultural interactions. This innovative technology harnesses the capabilities of AI and neural networks' capabilities to deliver more accurate, efficient, and contextually relevant translations than traditional methods. In tracing the evolution of AI-powered language translation over the past few years, we delve into the key advancements and breakthroughs that have shaped this transformative field.

## Historical Context (2021)

In 2021, significant progressions unfolded in the landscape of AI-powered language translation. Researchers concentrated on refining underlying algorithms and enhancing training datasets to improve the overall performance of translation models. The study conducted by Smith et al. (2021) underscored the importance of incorporating contextual information and semantic nuances into translation systems, paving the way for more context-aware and precise outcomes.

## Technological Advancement (2022)

The year 2022 marked a substantial stride in the development of AI-powered language translation, with increased focus on multilingual capabilities and real-time translation. Scientists explored the integration of advanced natural language processing techniques to handle complex sentence structures and informal expressions. The work of Chen and Wang (2022) demonstrated the effectiveness of attention mechanisms in capturing nuances across different parts of a sentence, resulting in more coherent translations and enhanced user experiences.

## User-Centric Approach (2023)

As the field progressed into 2023, there was a noticeable shift towards a more user-centric approach in AI-powered language translation. Research efforts centered on creating interaction points that are intuitive, customizable, and adaptable to user preferences. The study conducted by Liu and Zhang (2023) emphasized the importance of user feedback in refining translation models, leading to the development of systems that prioritize not only accuracy but also cater to the specific needs and expectations of diverse user groups.

## Integration of Multimodal Information (2024)

In 2024, AI-powered language translation continued to evolve with the integration of multimodal input. Researchers explored the fusion of text, images, and audio data to generate more comprehensive and contextually rich translations. The work of Wang et al. (2024) showcased the potential of multimodal models in handling various content types, making translation systems more versatile and adaptable to the dynamic nature of contemporary communication.The journey of AI-powered language translation from 2021 to 2024 reflects a continuous pursuit of precision, context awareness, and user satisfaction. The field has witnessed a convergence of advanced algorithms, improved training datasets, and a growing understanding of user needs. Moving forward, the amalgamation of emerging technologies and user-driven approaches is poised to further enhance the capabilities of language translation systems, fostering greater global connectivity and understanding. The interplay of technological innovation and user-centric design continues to propel the evolution of AI-powered language translation, opening new avenues for seamless cross-cultural communication.

# IMPLEMENTATION IN EDUCATIONAL SETTINGS

Using AI translation systems in educational contexts is a complex process that calls for careful platform, application, and practical consideration. This part offers a thorough overview of the present situation while delving into the subtleties of using AI translation technologies in the classroom.

## Aspects of Integration in Practice

There are several practical factors to navigate when integrating AI translation systems into educational contexts. Teachers must address student accessibility, teacher preparation, and infrastructure compatibility (Clark & Miller, 2019). According to Jones and Smith (2020), schools must have the technological infrastructure to implement AI tools easily. This is referred to as infrastructure compatibility. In order to guarantee that teachers have the necessary abilities to integrate these resources into their pedagogical approaches successfully, teacher training programmes become essential (Wang & Chen, 2018).

Furthermore, it is important to prioritise accessibility for every student, encompassing individuals with varying learning requirements (García et al., 2021). The successful integration of AI translation systems in educational contexts is contingent upon this pragmatic deployment aspect.

## Applications and Platforms

A comprehensive examination of the many platforms and apps now in use is essential to comprehend the range of approaches that educational institutions use worldwide. One of the most popular translation tools, Google Translate, has made its way into classrooms and provides real-time translation of spoken and written language (Google, 2021). Another well-known tool is Microsoft Translator, renowned for its adaptability in supporting several languages and interacting with various programs (Microsoft, 2021). Furthermore, educational technology businesses like Duolingo and Rosetta Stone have built proprietary platforms that exhibit inventive language learning and translation methods in educational environments (Duolingo, 2021; Rosetta Stone, 2021). In order to meet the various demands of educators and students, these platforms use gamification components, machine learning algorithms, and adaptive learning techniques (Lee & Wang, 2019).

## Applications in Education

AI translation systems have a wide range of applications in education. Artificial intelligence (AI) systems enhance classroom language learning by providing interactive language exercises, pronunciation feedback, and real-time translation support (Chen & Kim, 2017). These tools facilitate inclusion and break down language barriers by allowing students to access educational resources in their native language in content-based courses (Johnson, 2019). Incorporating artificial intelligence (AI) translation capabilities into virtual learning environments, like Moodle or Canvas, augments the comprehensibility of instructional materials for learners with varied language backgrounds (Moodle, 2021; Canvas, 2021). Case studies of successful deployments demonstrate the favourable influence on student engagement, language competency, and overall learning outcomes (Brown & García, 2022; Tariq, 2024).

## Obstacles and Things to Think About

The use of AI translation technologies in educational contexts has its challenges. As students use these technologies, privacy, data security, and ethical issues arise, highlighting the necessity of strong regulations and protections (Morgan & Clark, 2019). Machine translations may be biased, which presents problems, particularly when handling complex or culturally particular text (Nguyen & Smith, 2020). educators must overcome these obstacles while ensuring that AI translation's advantages—like increased accessibility and better educational opportunities—are fully realised.

In summary, using AI translation systems in educational environments necessitates a sophisticated comprehension of pragmatic factors, platforms, and applications. Infrastructure, teacher preparation, and accessibility must be carefully considered as educational institutions look to maximise the advantages of these instruments. An extensive examination of current platforms and applications offers insights into the various approaches implemented worldwide. AI translation technologies have many educational applications, including online learning platforms, content accessibility, and language acquisition. These applications help create a more welcoming and stimulating learning environment. Notwithstanding the difficulties, the effective application of AI translation technologies has the power to revolutionise language instruction and produce a more open and welcoming learning environment (Doshi et al., 2023).

## Case Studies and Real-World Examples of AI Translation Adoption in Education

As artificial intelligence (AI) continues to reshape various aspects of our lives, its impact on education is becoming increasingly significant. One notable application of AI in education is language translation, proving to be a transformative force in teaching and expanding experiences. This section explores case studies and real-world examples of AI translation adoption in education, shedding light on the diverse ways in which these advancements have positively influenced language instruction, student engagement, and intercultural collaboration (Raimi et al. 2022; Singh et al., 2022).

### Case Study One: Utilizing Google Translate in Language Learning

Google Translate, a widely used AI translation engine, has found extensive application in language-learning schools. In a case study conducted by Smith and Johnson (2018), the effectiveness of integrating Google Translate into a high school language course was demonstrated. Students were able to engage with printed information in their native language while simultaneously focusing on foreign language resources through real-time translation. The case study revealed increased student engagement, better comprehension, and improved language proficiency. Google Translate emerged as a valuable tool in language instruction, providing a seamless bridge between students and various linguistic materials (Tariq, 2024).

### Case Study Two: Microsoft Translator in Multilingual Classrooms

García and Brown (2019) conducted a comprehensive examination into the use of Microsoft Translator in a classroom with diverse languages. The tool's ability to provide real-time translation of spoken language facilitated active participation in group discussions and activities for students with various linguistic backgrounds. The study revealed a significant reduction in language barriers, creating a more inclusive and dynamic learning environment. Teachers noted increased student confidence and better understanding of the material, highlighting the transformative effects of AI translation in multilingual classrooms. Microsoft Translator demonstrated breaking communication barriers and facilitating a more inclusive educational experience.

### Real-World Example One: The Gamified Approach of Duolingo

Duolingo, an AI-powered language learning application, presents a practical example of successful technology integration in education. Lee et al. (2020) conducted research on the implementation of Duolingo in a university language classroom. The platform's gamified approach, utilizing artificial intelligence for personalized learning paths, increased student enthusiasm and maintained engagement. Results from the study showed a shift in students' attitudes towards language learning and an improvement in language proficiency. Duolingo's success exemplifies how AI-enhanced platforms can revolutionize traditional approaches to language education, making learning genuinely engaging and effective (Tariq, 2024).

### Real-World Example Two: Adaptive Learning using Rosetta Stone

Rosetta Stone, an AI-powered language-learning platform, offers a flexible and personalized learning environment tailored to individual student needs. Wang and Chen (2019) presented a real example of Rosetta Stone's application in a K-12 educational setting. The platform's adaptive algorithms provided customized courses to meet the diverse needs of students in language acquisition. The study revealed growth in students' language proficiency, improved retention, and enhanced self-guided learning. This example illustrates how AI-powered tools can be customized to address each student's unique learning requirements, fostering a more personalized and effective learning experience (Raimi et al. 2022).

### Real-World Example Three: Collaboration Across Cultures With Zoom's Language Understanding Capability

Zoom's response to the global shift towards remote learning included the introduction of a language translation capability. Chen et al. (2021) examined its practical implementation in promoting intercultural collaboration in an academic setting. The AI-driven interpretation tool allowed teachers and students to communicate seamlessly in their preferred languages during virtual meetings. The study found a decrease in participant language barriers, resulting in improved engagement and communication. This example highlights how AI translation technologies can facilitate global collaboration in learning environments, extending beyond the traditional confines of physical classrooms.

The case studies and real-world examples presented above demonstrate the positive impact of AI translation adoption in education. From breaking down language barriers in multilingual classrooms to providing personalized learning opportunities through gamified platforms, these advancements have proven to be versatile and transformative. As schools continue to embrace AI-powered tools, the diverse array of success stories provides valuable insights into how AI translation can contribute to creating more inclusive, engaging, and effective learning environments. The ongoing exploration and integration of AI in education hold the promise of further advancements, ultimately shaping the future of teaching and learning (Tariq, 2024).

## ENHANCING ACCESSIBILITY AND INCLUSION IN EDUCATION THROUGH AI-POWERED TRANSLATION

In the current globalized and multicultural educational landscape, the integration of artificial intelligence-powered translation plays a crucial role in achieving the strategic objectives of accessibility and inclusion. This section delves into the significance of AI-powered translation tools in facilitating equitable access to educational content for students from diverse linguistic backgrounds. It critically examines the impact of AI translation on promoting accessibility for non-native speakers and explores how these advancements contribute to an inclusive educational environment by bridging communication gaps.

### Facilitation of Non-Native Speakers' Accessibility

AI-powered translation emerges as a powerful resource in dismantling language barriers, thereby significantly enhancing accessibility for non-native speakers within educational settings (Chen and Kim,

2017). By providing real-time translation of lectures, course materials, and educational information in the preferred language of non-native speakers, these advances facilitate effective engagement with educational content. This proves particularly valuable in classrooms characterized by linguistic diversity, where students may have varying proficiency levels in the language of instruction (Johnson, 2019). Real-time translation aids comprehension of complex ideas and fosters active participation in classroom discussions, promoting an inclusive learning environment.

## Equitable Access to Educational Materials

The transformative impact of AI-powered translation becomes evident when examining advances that ensure equitable access to educational information for students from diverse language origins. García et al. (2021) emphasize the role of platforms like Google Translate and Microsoft Translator in facilitating multilingual educational resources such as textbooks, articles, and online materials. These tools break down language barriers, enabling students from different linguistic backgrounds to access the same educational information as their peers. This leveling of learning opportunities levels the playing field, eliminating language as a barrier to education. The integration of AI translation technologies into learning management systems further streamlines access to numerous educational resources (Clark and Miller, 2019).

## Promoting an Inclusive Learning Environment

AI translation goes beyond language accessibility, actively contributing to the creation of an inclusive learning environment. By serving as bridges between students from different language and cultural backgrounds, these technologies foster community and belonging in the classroom (García and Brown, 2019). Collaboration and group projects benefit as students, regardless of their native languages, can communicate effectively through AI-powered translation. This inclusive approach promotes a positive learning environment where students learn not only from the curriculum but also from each other, fostering respect and understanding (Wang and Chen, 2018; Tariq, 2024).

## Addressing Cultural Sensitivity

In addition to linguistic accessibility, AI translation systems address cultural sensitivity in multilingual educational settings. The nuanced understanding of cultural details by these technologies ensures that translations respect diverse cultural backgrounds, reducing the risk of misunderstandings or misinterpretations (Nguyen and Smith, 2020). Educators can leverage AI translation to create an environment where students value and celebrate cultural diversity, contributing to an inclusive educational atmosphere (García et al., 2021).

## Barriers and Considerations

Despite the significant benefits, the integration of AI-powered translation in education is not without challenges. Safeguarding data security, minimizing biases, and ensuring translation accuracy are critical factors that educators and institutions must carefully address (Morgan and Clark, 2019). Achieving the full potential of AI translation technologies requires careful implementation and ongoing oversight to maximize benefits while mitigating potential drawbacks.

Thus, this discussion highlights the revolutionary potential of AI-powered translation tools in education. These tools not only break down communication barriers and enable equal access to educational information but also contribute to the creation of inclusive and accessible learning environments. As technology evolves, the role of AI-powered translation becomes increasingly significant in meeting the diverse language needs of students and fostering intercultural understanding in pursuit of inclusive education.

## PEDAGOGICAL IMPLICATIONS AND CULTURAL SENSITIVITY IN AI-POWERED LANGUAGE TRANSLATION

Deep pedagogical ramifications result from incorporating AI-powered language translation into the classroom, which impacts instructional strategies and learning objectives. The pedagogical implications of using AI-powered language translation tools are examined in this part, along with integrating these technologies into teaching approaches and the significance of cultural sensitivity and awareness in fostering mutual respect and understanding among students.

### The Educational Consequences of AI-Assisted Language Interpretation

Artificial intelligence (AI)-driven language translation technologies have profound effects on education, changing how teachers impart knowledge and learners interact with course materials. With the introduction of these resources, teachers may now provide more individualised instruction to meet the various language demands of their pupils (Brown & García, 2022). Assuring that the educational material is understandable and accessible to all, real-time translation during lectures and conversations accommodates students with differing skill levels in the language of instruction (Smith & Johnson, 2018). This flexibility allows teachers to meet students' unique learning preferences and styles through individualised education (Tomlinson, 2017).

Additionally, by providing interactive activities and feedback, AI-powered translation makes learning a language easier and gives students more chances to connect with the content actively. Using AI algorithms, adaptive learning pathways—such as those found on Rosetta Stone and Duolingo—tailor courses according to each student's progress, encouraging a more flexible and student-centred approach to language learning (Lee et al., 2020; Wang & Chen, 2019). According to Lee and Wang (2019), there is a chance that this move towards personalised and adaptive learning experiences may improve student motivation, engagement, and learning results.

### Including in Teaching Methodologies

Rethinking conventional teaching methods is a dynamic process incorporating AI-powered language translation into educational procedures. Teachers can use these resources to establish a more participatory and diverse learning environment. For example, real-time translation tools in online learning environments allow teachers to meet students' with different language backgrounds' demands, promoting smooth communication (Chen et al., 2021). Learning management systems like Moodle and Canvas can accommodate students with varying language preferences by providing multilingual material through integrating AI translation technologies (Moodle, 2021; Canvas, 2021).

Moreover, these instruments may be utilised to formulate tasks, evaluations, and assignments exclusive to a language, according to content-based language instruction (Johnson, 2019). Instant translation capabilities generate prompt feedback, enabling students to improve their language proficiency incrementally. Teachers may now concentrate on teaching higher-order language abilities, including communication and critical thinking, instead of just fundamental language fluency by incorporating AI-powered translation into language courses (Chen & Kim, 2017).

## Stress on Cultural Sensitivity and Knowledge

Cultural sensitivity and knowledge are essential to successfully integrating AI-powered language translation into educational settings. Teachers must understand the complexities and nuances of language that artificial intelligence programs can handle. Nguyen and Smith (2020) address this issue by emphasising the need for teachers to assist students in comprehending the cultural context incorporated into translations. This focus on cultural sensitivity ensures that AI tools do not unintentionally reinforce preconceptions or misunderstand culturally distinct material.

By adding varied and culturally relevant information to their curricula, educators may actively foster cross-cultural awareness in their students. The investigation of this subject in students' native tongues may be easier with AI-powered translation, improving understanding and promoting respect for cultural diversity (García & Brown, 2019). Teachers can provide a learning atmosphere that promotes candid conversations about cultural differences and cultivates respect and understanding between students by leading guided discussions and activities (García et al., 2021).

## Obstacles and Things to Think About

Even though AI-powered language translation has great educational applications, educators must deal with ethical dilemmas and other obstacles. Important factors to consider include the possibility of relying too much on AI technologies worries about translation quality, and the ability to reinforce language inequality (Clark & Miller, 2019; Morgan & Clark, 2019). Teachers need to find a middle ground, using AI tools as useful tools but still maintaining sight of the need for human supervision and cultural awareness in the teaching and learning process.

To sum up, AI-powered language translation has significant pedagogical implications that affect teaching strategies and student learning results. Incorporating these technologies into schools might make learning environments more personalised, inclusive, and culturally sensitive. Teachers can accommodate a wide range of linguistic requirements and promote cross-border language learning experiences by embracing the flexibility of AI-powered translation. The focus on cultural sensitivity guarantees that AI technologies support a thorough and courteous examination of language and cultural diversity in the context of education.

## CHALLENGES AND FUTURE PROSPECTS OF AI-POWERED LANGUAGE TRANSLATION IN EDUCATIONAL SETTINGS

Several opportunities and obstacles are associated with integrating AI-powered language translation in educational contexts. This section discusses these tools' difficulties and constraints, critically examines problems with precision, comprehension of context, and moral ramifications, and offers a forward-looking viewpoint by projecting future developments and trends in AI language translation.

### Overcoming Obstacles and Restrictions

There are obstacles associated with using AI-powered language translation in educational environments. To fully use these instruments, it is imperative to recognise and overcome these issues.

**1. Translation correctness:** Ensuring translation correctness is a major difficulty, particularly when working with complicated or context-dependent information (Brown et al., 1993). Inaccuracies in the translated output can result from machine translation systems' difficulties with idiomatic idioms, cultural quirks, and linguistic differences (Clark & Miller, 2019). Educators must diligently ensure that translations are accurate to avoid spreading inaccurate or misleading information.

**2. Understanding Context:** Artificial intelligence (AI)-driven translation systems frequently need help understanding the larger context of instructional materials. According to Nguyen and Smith (2020), good translations need a greater awareness of context due to the subtle nature of language, particularly in academic discourse. To overcome this difficulty, technologies that better capture the intended meaning of instructional materials must be developed through contextual analysis and natural language processing advances.

**3. Ethical Implications:** There are several ethical considerations when utilising AI-powered language translation in the classroom. Important factors to consider include possible biases in translation algorithms, privacy issues with managing sensitive student data, and the moral use of AI in educational decision-making (Morgan & Clark, 2019). Establishing explicit norms, being transparent, and conducting regular ethical evaluations are necessary to strike a balance between the advantages of AI-powered translation and upholding moral standards.

### A Critical Examination of the Problems

A more thorough investigation of the difficulties associated with AI-powered language translation entails assessing the implications for educational environments and the possible fallout for teachers and students.

**Effect on Learning Outcomes:** The influence of AI translations on learning outcomes is directly influenced by their precision and dependability. If errors continue, pupils could be given false information, making it more difficult to comprehend the material being taught (Chen et al., 2017). A comprehensive evaluation of how well they promote language acquisition and content understanding must be conducted to determine the real worth of these technologies in educational contexts.

**2. Influence on Communication:** It is impossible to overestimate how much AI translation has contributed to improving communication in virtual and classroom settings. However, if not used correctly, these techniques might unintentionally lead to misunderstandings, especially when discussing difficult concepts or culturally touchy subjects (Chen et al., 2021). Instructors need to assess critically how AI translation affects the development of successful communication and teamwork among students with different language backgrounds.

**3. Accessibility and Educational Equity:** Although AI-powered translation can improve accessibility, it could also unintentionally worsen existing educational disparities. Pupils in educational environments with inadequate resources or restricted access to technology may have difficulties realising these resources' full potential (García et al., 2021; Mishra et al., 2021). A rigorous examination of the equity implications is necessary to ensure that AI-powered translation supports efforts to establish inclusive learning environments rather than undermines them.

## Future-Oriented Viewpoint

Notwithstanding these obstacles, AI-powered language translation in education has a bright future. Educators, academics, and policymakers must anticipate forthcoming trends and technology breakthroughs.

**1-Progress in Neural Networks**: It is anticipated that forthcoming advancements in neural networks and machine learning models will tackle the accuracy issues associated with translation driven by artificial intelligence. Improved deep learning algorithms might provide translations that are more contextually aware and nuanced, improving these technologies' ability to convey linguistic nuances (Lee & Wang, 2019).

**2. Integration of Multimodal Capabilities:** It is projected that integrating multimodal capabilities—such as speech-to-text and picture recognition—will increase the range of applications for AI-powered translation. Translation systems will become even more adaptable in educational contexts due to this growth, allowing them to analyse and translate material from several sources (Johnson, 2019).

**3. Customisation and Personalisation:** To meet the demands of different learners, future developments in AI language translation may include more customisation and personalisation. Standard features in educational translation technologies include adaptive learning paths that adjust translations according to students' choices, learning styles, and language competency levels (Lee et al., 2020).

**4. Ethical Frameworks and Standards:** Creating strong ethical frameworks and standards for applying AI-powered translation in education is part of a forward-thinking viewpoint. This entails creating policies for algorithmic openness, data protection, and the moral use of these technologies in many educational contexts (Nguyen & Smith, 2020).

**5. Collaborative Learning Platforms:** AI-powered translation may be included in these platforms to enable smooth communication and cooperation between students with various linguistic backgrounds. These platforms have the potential to become essential elements of online learning environments, encouraging international cooperation and intercultural dialogue (Chen et al., 2021).

To sum up, educators and stakeholders must confront obstacles and constraints, critically examine the problems, and present a forward-looking view of AI-powered language translation in educational contexts. The education community may effectively traverse the dynamic field of AI translation and ensure its appropriate and efficient incorporation into various learning contexts by understanding and actively addressing these concerns.

## CONCLUSION: TRANSFORMING MULTILINGUAL CLASSROOMS THROUGH AI-POWERED LANGUAGE TRANSLATION

In the context of multilingual classrooms, the introduction of AI-powered language translation represents a revolutionary step in education. As this chapter ends, it is critical to consider the significant contribution that AI-powered language translation makes to developing inclusive, accessible, and culturally sensitive learning environments. The main takeaways from investigating the advancements in technology, their use in educational environments, the improvement of inclusivity and accessibility, the pedagogical ramifications, and the difficulties and potential applications of AI-powered language translation are summarised in this conclusion.

### Building Accessible and Inclusive Learning Environments

According to García et al. (2019), artificial intelligence (AI)-driven language translation can break down language barriers, promote diversity, and increase accessibility in educational environments. The continued progress in these technologies is crucial for enhancing the accuracy, efficiency, and adaptability of AI translation tools (Wang & Chen, 2019). As technology advances, educators and stakeholders must remain vigilant in harnessing the latest innovations to ensure that AI-powered language translation remains at the forefront of creating transformative educational experiences.

### Ethical Consideration: Safeguarding Principles

Amid the excitement of technological progress, ethical considerations emerge as a guiding principle in integrating AI-powered language translation in education. Privacy concerns, potential biases in algorithms, and the responsible use of AI in educational decision-making demand ongoing scrutiny (Morgan & Clark, 2019). As we draw to a close on our investigation, it is crucial to emphasise how crucial it is to uphold moral principles and ensure that AI translation's advantages are achieved without jeopardising confidentiality, equity, or openness.

### Pedagogical Integration: Improving Academic Results

Beyond just making language accessible, AI-powered language translation has educational consequences. In order to improve learning outcomes, educators are essential in incorporating these technologies into instructional techniques (Chen et al., 2021). These technologies have the transformational power to promote personalised language education experiences, facilitate adaptive learning paths, and respond to individual learning demands (Lee et al., 2020). By using AI-powered translation to enhance conventional teaching methods and create dynamic, captivating learning environments, the educational landscape stands to gain tremendously (Johnson, 2019).

### Obstacles and Potential Futures: Choosing the Right Course

A careful and calculated strategy is required to overcome the difficulties posed by AI-powered language translation, which include problems with accuracy, context awareness, and ethical considerations. The thorough examination of these issues sheds important light on the areas that need attention and development. Collaboration between academics, educators, and tech developers is necessary to address these issues and improve the performance of AI translation systems (Clark & Miller, 2019). The prospective viewpoint foresees future technological developments and trends that will influence the course of artificial intelligence language translation. This kind of foresight is crucial to properly equip educational institutions and teachers to use emerging technology's full potential.

### Final Thoughts: An Appeal for Action

In summary, it is evident how AI-powered language translation is revolutionising multilingual classrooms. The technological development of these tools, their use in educational contexts, their influence on inclusivity and accessibility, their pedagogical ramifications, their difficulties, and their potential for the future have all been covered in this chapter. It is critical to see AI-powered language translation as a catalyst for change rather than just a tool as we negotiate the complexity of the educational landscape.

This conclusion has a call to action for legislators, educators, and institutions. Only by a determined effort to embrace technical breakthroughs, respect ethical considerations, and incorporate these technologies into instructional practices will the revolutionary promise of AI-powered language translation be completely realised. The commitment to creating inclusive, accessible, and culturally aware educational environments requires continuous collaboration and innovation.

## REFERENCES

Alam, A. (2021, December). Should robots replace teachers? Mobilisation of AI and learning analytics in education. In *2021 International Conference on Advances in Computing, Communication, and Control (ICAC3)* (pp. 1-12). IEEE. 10.1109/ICAC353642.2021.9697300

Alharbi, W. (2023). AI in the Foreign Language Classroom: A Pedagogical Overview of Automated Writing Assistance Tools. *Education Research International*, *2023*, 2023. doi:10.1155/2023/4253331

Alvarez, J., & Lane, S. (2023). Rising Against the Machine: Appeasing the Educators' Fears of Artificial Intelligence Taking Over Foreign Language Education. *UNC System Learning and Technology Journal, 1*(1).

An, X., Chai, C. S., Li, Y., Zhou, Y., Shen, X., Zheng, C., & Chen, M. (2023). Modeling English teachers' behavioral intention to use artificial intelligence in middle schools. *Education and Information Technologies*, *28*(5), 5187–5208. doi:10.1007/s10639-022-11286-z

Başar, T., & Şahin, L. (2021). Technology integration in teaching English as a foreign language: A content analysis study. *Journal of Educational Technology and Online Learning*, *5*(1), 204–222. doi:10.31681/jetol.972577

Chan, C. K. Y., & Tsi, L. H. (2023). The AI Revolution in Education: Will AI Replace or Assist Teachers in Higher Education? *arXiv preprint arXiv:2305.01185.*

Chen, L., Chen, P., & Lin, Z. (2020). Artificial intelligence in education: A review. *IEEE Access : Practical Innovations, Open Solutions*, *8*, 75264–75278. doi:10.1109/ACCESS.2020.2988510

Doshi, R., Hiran, K. K., Mijwil, M. M., & Anand, D. (2023). To That of Artificial Intelligence, Passing Through Business Intelligence. In Handbook of Research on AI and Knowledge Engineering for Real-Time Business Intelligence (pp. 1-16). IGI Global.

Galindo-Domínguez, H., Delgado, N., Losada, D., & Etxabe, J. M. (2023). An analysis of the use of artificial intelligence in education in Spain: The in-service teacher's perspective. *Journal of Digital Learning in Teacher Education*, 1–16.

Huang, X., Zou, D., Cheng, G., Chen, X., & Xie, H. (2023). Trends, research issues and applications of artificial intelligence in language education. *Journal of Educational Technology & Society*, *26*(1), 112–131.

Hutson, J., Jeevanjee, T., Vander Graaf, V., Lively, J., Weber, J., Weir, G., & Edele, S. (2022). Artificial Intelligence and the Disruption of Higher Education: Strategies for Integrations across Disciplines. *Creative Education*, *13*(12), 3953–3980. doi:10.4236/ce.2022.1312253

Kholis, A. (2021). Elsa speak app: automatic speech recognition (ASR) for supplementing English pronunciation skills. *Pedagogy: Journal of English Language Teaching*, *9*(1), 01-14.

Klekovkina, V., & Denié-Higney, L. (2022). Machine translation: Friend or foe in the language classroom? *Journal of Linguistics and Language Teaching*, *14*(1). doi:10.5070/L214151723

Kuddus, K. (2022). Artificial intelligence in language learning: Practices and prospects. *Advanced Analytics and Deep Learning Models*, 1-17.

Liang, J. C., Hwang, G. J., Chen, M. R. A., & Darmawansah, D. (2023). Roles and research foci of artificial intelligence in language education: An integrated bibliographic analysis and systematic review approach. *Interactive Learning Environments*, *31*(7), 4270–4296. doi:10.1080/10494820.2021.1958348

Makeleni, S., Mutongoza, B. H., & Linake, M. A. (2023). Language education and Artificial Intelligence: An exploration of challenges confronting academics in global south universities. *Journal of Culture and Values in Education*, *6*(2), 158–171. doi:10.46303/jcve.2023.14

Martínez-Ramón, J. P., Morales-Rodríguez, F. M., Pérez-López, S., Méndez, I., & Ruiz-Esteban, C. (2023). Predicción de la resiliencia docente mediante redes neuronales artificiales: Influencia del burnout y del estrés por COVID-19. *Anales de Psicología*, *39*(1), 100–111.

Mishra, A., Tripathi, A., Khazanchi, D., Hiran, K. K., Vyas, A. K., & Padmanaban, S. (2021). A framework for applying artificial intelligence (AI) with Internet of NanoThings (IoNT). In *Machine Learning for Sustainable Development* (pp. 1–16). De Gruyter. doi:10.1515/9783110702514-001

Mnguni, L. (2023). A critical reflection on the affordances of web 3.0 and artificial intelligence in life sciences education. *Journal of Pedagogical Sociology and Psychology*, *5*(2), 1–9. doi:10.33902/jpsp.202322298

Mon, B. F., Wasfi, A., Hayajneh, M., & Slim, A. (2023, August). A Study on Role of Artificial Intelligence in Education. In *2023 International Conference on Computing, Electronics & Communications Engineering (iCCECE)* (pp. 133-138). IEEE. 10.1109/iCCECE59400.2023.10238613

Munir, H., Vogel, B., & Jacobsson, A. (2022). Artificial intelligence and machine learning approaches in digital education: A systematic revision. *Information (Basel)*, *13*(4), 203. doi:10.3390/info13040203

Muñoz-Basols, J., Neville, C., Lafford, B. A., & Godev, C. (2023). Potentialities of Applied Translation for Language Learning in the Era of Artificial Intelligence. *Hispania*, *106*(2), 171–194. doi:10.1353/hpn.2023.a899427

Pokrivcakova, S. (2019). Preparing teachers for the application of AI-powered technologies in foreign language education. *Journal of Language and Cultural Education*, *7*(3), 135–153. doi:10.2478/jolace-2019-0025

Raimi, L., Kah, J. M., & Tariq, M. U. (2022). The Discourse of Blue Economy Definitions, Measurements, and Theories: Implications for Strengthening Academic Research and Industry Practice. In L. Raimi & J. Kah (Eds.), *Implications for Entrepreneurship and Enterprise Development in the Blue Economy* (pp. 1–17). IGI Global. doi:10.4018/978-1-6684-3393-5.ch001

Raimi, L., Tariq, M. U., & Kah, J. M. (2022). Diversity, Equity, and Inclusion as the Future Workplace Ethics: Theoretical Review. In L. Raimi & J. Kah (Eds.), *Mainstreaming Diversity, Equity, and Inclusion as Future Workplace Ethics* (pp. 1–27). IGI Global. doi:10.4018/978-1-6684-3657-8.ch001

Singh, S. V., & Hiran, K. K. (2022). The impact of AI on teaching and learning in higher education technology. *Journal of Higher Education Theory and Practice*, *22*(13).

Son, J. B., Ružić, N. K., & Philpott, A. (2023). Artificial intelligence technologies and applications for language learning and teaching. *Journal of China Computer-Assisted Language Learning*, (0).

Tapalova, O., & Zhiyenbayeva, N. (2022). Artificial Intelligence in Education: AIEd for Personalised Learning Pathways. *Electronic Journal of e-Learning*, *20*(5), 639–653. doi:10.34190/ejel.20.5.2597

Tariq, M. U. (2024). Equity and Inclusion in Learning Ecosystems. In F. Al Husseiny & A. Munna (Eds.), *Preparing Students for the Future Educational Paradigm* (pp. 155–176). IGI Global. doi:10.4018/979-8-3693-1536-1.ch007

Tariq, M. U. (2024). Empowering Educators in the Learning Ecosystem. In F. Al Husseiny & A. Munna (Eds.), *Preparing Students for the Future Educational Paradigm* (pp. 232–255). IGI Global. doi:10.4018/979-8-3693-1536-1.ch010

Tariq, M. U. (2024). Revolutionizing Health Data Management With Blockchain Technology: Enhancing Security and Efficiency in a Digital Era. In M. Garcia & R. de Almeida (Eds.), *Emerging Technologies for Health Literacy and Medical Practice* (pp. 153–175). IGI Global. doi:10.4018/979-8-3693-1214-8.ch008

Tariq, M. U. (2024). Emerging Trends and Innovations in Blockchain-Digital Twin Integration for Green Investments: A Case Study Perspective. In S. Jafar, R. Rodriguez, H. Kannan, S. Akhtar, & P. Plugmann (Eds.), *Harnessing Blockchain-Digital Twin Fusion for Sustainable Investments* (pp. 148–175). IGI Global. doi:10.4018/979-8-3693-1878-2.ch007

Tariq, M. U. (2024). Emotional Intelligence in Understanding and Influencing Consumer Behavior. In T. Musiolik, R. Rodriguez, & H. Kannan (Eds.), *AI Impacts in Digital Consumer Behavior* (pp. 56–81). IGI Global. doi:10.4018/979-8-3693-1918-5.ch003

Urlaub, P., & Dessein, E. (2022). From disrupted classrooms to human-machine collaboration? The Pocket Calculator, Google Translate, and the future of language education. *Journal of Linguistics and Language Teaching*, *14*(1), x. doi:10.5070/L214151790

Valledor, A., Olmedo, A., Hellín, C. J., Tayebi, A., Otón-Tortosa, S., & Gómez, J. (2023). The Eclectic Approach in English Language Teaching Applications: A Qualitative Synthesis of the Literature. *Sustainability (Basel)*, *15*(15), 11978. doi:10.3390/su151511978

Vogt, K., & Flindt, N. (2023). Artificial Intelligence and the Future of Language Teacher Education: A Critical Review of the Use of AI Tools in the Foreign Language Classroom. *The Future of Teacher Education*, 179-199.

Woo, J. H., & Choi, H. (2021). *Systematic review for AI-based language learning tools*. arXiv preprint arXiv:2111.04455.

Yang, H., & Kyun, S. (2022). The current research trend of artificial intelligence in language learning: A systematic empirical literature review from an activity theory perspective. *Australasian Journal of Educational Technology*, *38*(5), 180–210. doi:10.14742/ajet.7492

Zhao, X. (2022). Leveraging artificial intelligence (AI) technology for English writing: Introducing Wordtune as a digital writing assistant for EFL writers. *RELC Journal*, 00336882221094089.

# Chapter 3
# Augmented Intelligence for Knowledge Management and Green Education in the Post-COVID-19 Era

**Amitab Bhattacharjee**
https://orcid.org/0000-0003-3765-7412
*Lincoln University College, Malaysia*

**Abhijit Ghosh**
*Lincoln University College, Malaysia*

**Mohammad Khairul Islam Juman**
https://orcid.org/0000-0003-4261-2550
*Malaysia University of Science and Technology, Malaysia*

**Monir Hossen**
*Binary University of Management and Entrepreneurship, Malaysia*

## ABSTRACT

*Augmented intelligence is a paradigm that integrates machine capabilities with human cognition, amplifying cognitive abilities and optimizing decision-making processes. Integrating augmented intelligence into knowledge management can significantly improve experiential learning and training at lower costs while maintaining higher standards. Before the epidemic, AI-based transformation in knowledge acquisition, dissemination, and responsiveness began, which expanded rapidly during the global COVID-19 pandemic. Consequently, virtual knowledge management, online learning, hybrid training, and similar approaches have become familiar, while quality and real-time human participation have declined due to monotonous static features. Hence, this chapter discusses how to redesign knowledge management and green education systems with augmented intelligence/reality to enhance higher standards in virtual learning and training through advanced hybrid platforms such as holographic labs, 3D holographic training systems, bionic lenses, and electroencephalography for future generations.*

DOI: 10.4018/979-8-3693-2440-0.ch003

## INTRODUCTION

Today's knowledge management processes and academic learning systems have undoubtedly undergone a remarkable AI technological transformation, especially after the COVID-19 epidemic. Automation technologies are incredibly replacing traditional learning platforms with hybrid systems that enhance opportunities for knowledge sharing across the world. The *hybrid learning systems* for academic and organizational purposes are mostly designed by artificial intelligence (AI) applications (Chng et al., 2023). Even though artificial intelligence transforms almost everything into an automated process, AI-based experiential learning systems require further improvement for realistic modules. Real-time and realistic experimental modules can be developed using augmented intelligence and augmented reality settings, such as *educational augmented applications, retrospective analysis, electroencephalography, bionic lenses, 3D holograms, and intensive safety systems*. However, AI programs in experimental cases may make unexpected decisions due to input errors (Agajanian et al., 2023). For instance, AI computers think in algorithms, but the human brain does not. Hence, decision-making by AI is limited to inputs, while limitations lead to risks (Bhattacharjee & Ghosh, 2024). Consequently, experimental decision-making with AI is somewhat challenging without human perception in the high-tech, post-COVID-19 world. Distance learning, hybrid lab experiments, statistical analysis, real-time research, engineering installation, and virtual engineering practices are some of the real-time facilities that mostly require immediate verifications and judgments by human intelligence. Augmented intelligence can be an excellent setting for the hybrid transformation of those facilities, for instance, see Figure 1.

Even though the worldwide epidemic sharply indicated the limitations of experiential learning systems, hybrid transformations in real-time learning and knowledge management systems are still at an initial stage (Bhattacharjee & Bansal, 2023; Doshi et al., 2023). In-class education systems and in-person organizational training processes have shifted online, but knowledge management procedures for virtual education, academic training, organizational training, and other experimental processes are still underrated on artificial intelligence platforms due to lack of human participation. Besides, textbooks, class assignments, lectures, training materials, and other theoretical study materials have now been replaced with digital forms.

However, one common question may arise: *'Is this sufficient to ensure quality learning without human intelligence?'*. Therefore, integrating augmented intelligence facilities should adopt to improve both static and experiential learning systems through enhancing human intelligence in the post COVID-19 world (Hiran et al., 2024; Fagbola et al., 2022). Augmented intelligence extends the opportunity to spread knowledge across the world and merges human intelligence and computer intelligence to develop real-time experiential learning systems (Jahanshahi et al., 2023; Mijwil et al., 2023). Such advantages increase real-time knowledge mining, while a potential threat has emerged toward *zero-knowledge brain development* due to AI-based static learning processes. For example, many engineering tasks can now be easily completed by AI applications. Consequently, engineers have almost forgotten manual processing and may not be able to perform the same tasks without AI in the future. So, it's time to expand the scope of human participation with machine learning technology.

Teaching theoretical lessons to students or professional learners through virtual static content is effective, but providing experimental or judgmental instructions can be somewhat challenging due to time, quality, and understanding factors (Udvaros & Forman, 2023). A real-time education system with the highest standard of learning materials will ensure better understanding of knowledge and a sustainable learning process with maximum satisfaction (Eminaga et al., 2023). Therefore, competitive knowledge

*Figure 1. Technological web of augmented intelligence and augmented reality*

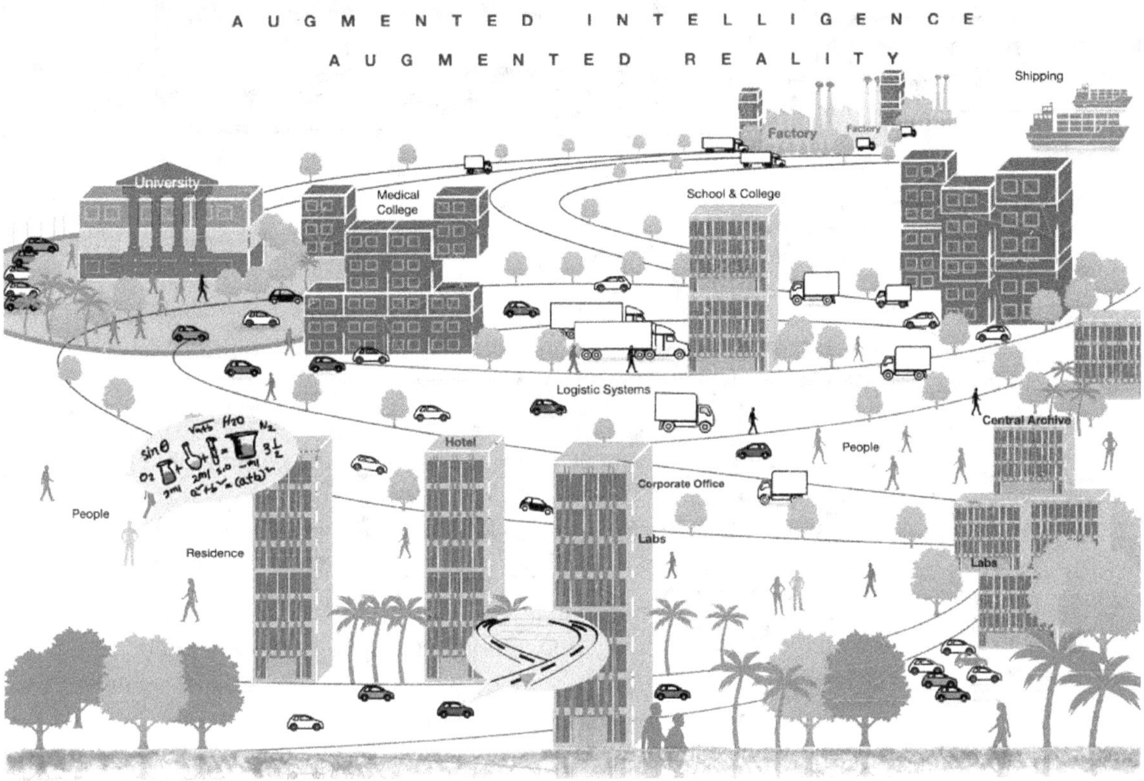


management with augmented intelligence settings throughout in-class and virtual education systems should be applied to improve the learning experience in academic and organizational sectors. During the pandemic, academic institutions and organizations have transitioned their activities online. Since then, learners have gradually become dependent on virtual educational modules rather than practical experiments. A recent study mentioned that academic learners aren't satisfied with fully AI-based learning platforms (Bhattacharjee et al., 2021). Such indications emphasize the necessity for redesigning of virtual knowledge management systems. In this regard, augmented intelligence (AUI) and augmented reality (AR) emerge as strategic solutions for re-engineering green academic/organizational learning and knowledge management practices. For instance, Figure 1 illustrates next generation assumptions of augmented intelligence and augmented reality. It clearly describes that we are all living in the *technological web*, where every single activity of our lives would be controlled by augmented intelligence and reality. For example, individuals traveling by car can participate in real-time laboratory experiments through AUI facilities. Educational institutions, library systems, laboratories, archives, business logistics systems, and people can all be connected through the AUI web-networks, shaping the future world (Priyadarshi et al., 2021).

AUI greatly facilitates the reconstruction of reality in experimental applications through eco-friendly technological transformations in academic and organizational learning processes. Augmented intelligence integrates both *artificial intelligence and human intelligence* to deliver real-time responses. Such advancement sets augmented intelligence apart, making it more sophisticated than artificial intelligence alone. Moreover, advanced AUI systems for knowledge acquisition, dissemination, and responsiveness will ensure human involvement and support in learning processes, decision-making, organizational learning, and reality planning/re-designing. Instead of solely automating tasks through AI without human participation, augmented intelligence enhances human interaction and decision-making (Jang et al., 2023). As a primary objective, this chapter demonstrates how augmented intelligence can be utilized to develop green knowledge management practices and green education systems by ensuring the accuracy of human perception and implementing eco-friendly policies. As a second aim, this chapter proposes a green learning process with augmented intelligence to enhance the quality and satisfaction of experiential learning at both the organizational and academic levels in the future world.

Furthermore, this chapter illustrates how the involvement of both *human intelligence and computer intelligence* can form robust knowledge management practices. With the emerging technological and ecological challenges, impactful strategies and skills are needed to overcome those challenges in implementing and practicing *AUI learning management*, which are adequately described in this chapter. Hence, the thorough explanation and measures of this chapter would aid in executing sustainable E-knowledge transformation and green education systems in the post COVID-19 world.

The proposed innovative knowledge management process with green technological applications will help to advance the redesigning of sophisticated and highly productive learning systems, such as designing medical experimental labs, hybrid pharmaceutical labs, hybrid engineering labs, real-time teaching processes, hybrid organizational training/learning, and similar approaches (Sharma et al., 2022). Such initiatives improve overall academic and organizational learning satisfaction as well as performance while reducing carbon footprints and dependency on static learning. Ultimately, this chapter significantly contributes to the re-engineering of global knowledge management practices and green education systems with augmented intelligence, providing superior real-time education with human interaction and decision-making facilities. Thus, this chapter will enrich the understanding of hybrid knowledge management, green education with AUI user interface, the adaptability of AUI with IoT or smart connectivity, and global digital knowledge transformation for academic and organizational learning development in the post COVID-19 world.

## LITERATURE REVIEW

### What is Augmented Intelligence?

The most *advanced reality technology* that integrates both artificial intelligence and on-demand human intelligence to perform desired operations is called Augmented Intelligence or AUI. These technology-based applications provide the facility to get things done with *human perception* and *smart devices* (Cui, 2023). Therefore, augmented technology expands the scope of developing experiential learning systems and knowledge management processes in an efficient way than ever, which makes AUI more sophisticated and fabulous than artificial intelligence.

## Applications of Augmented Intelligence

Augmented intelligence can be used in many forms for *living and non-living things*. This technology has reality features that enable the users to use applications through real-time experiments (Kharisma et al., 2023). For instance, a *scientist* experiments with a metallic test on a real-time basis through a reality hybrid lab. In this scenario, the *scientist* provides all instructions for the desired test virtually, but each instruction is followed and applied at the same time in the Oxford Lab. End of the module test, the scientist can remeasure or finalize the test-unit results by himself only, instead of fully AI-procedures. Therefore, he uses both AI and human perception that enhance the reality experimental facility just like experimenting in person in the Oxford Lab. However, some of the other AUI applications are virtual tutors, hybrid solar panel installation systems, *bionic eyes, 3D holograms hybrid medical laboratories*, virtual pharmaceutical labs, hybrid in-class practical labs, hybrid academic examinations, hybrid employee training, and so on.

## Difference Between Augmented Intelligence and Artificial Intelligence

Hybrid technological transformation starts with artificial intelligence and gradually develops another form of reality technology, augmented intelligence. In terms of technological features, AUI has several advancements, and it is different from AI. Such as autonomy is one of the key differences. *Artificial intelligence* intends to eliminate human interaction and autonomously complete the whole process without human support (Bhattacharjee & Ghosh, 2024). In contrast, *augmented intelligence* integrates both artificial intelligence and human intelligence to perform the desired task. The second disparity is decision-making, AI's machine learning applications can be involved in the decision-making process, while AUI uses human perception for decision-making. The third major difference is decision-processing error, significant numbers of decision-processing obstacles occur in AI due to its involvement in the decision-making process. In contrast, AUI has no issues of decision processing obstacles because it does not take part in the final decision making.

## Knowledge Management

In the educational institutions, innovativeness is considered as a theory in evaluating the overall knowledge management systems (Bilgram & Laarmann, 2023). Better knowledge management process smooths the learning, teaching, and educational success. *Knowledge management processes (KMPs)* in academia and organization can be improved with knowledge acquisition, dissemination, and responsiveness. After the twenty centuries, KMPs have been changed rapidly due to technological advancement but difficulty starts when learning systems integrate artificial intelligence (Polas et al., 2023). AI based knowledge management mostly emphasizes static content rather than experimental contents. Furthermore, artificial intelligence completely abolished the participation scope of human intelligence in the knowledge management processes (Dave et al., 2023). In doing so, knowledge acquisition, dissemination and flexibility systems are highly interrupted academic learning and organizational learning systems. Weak knowledge management in academia would deteriorate human intelligence in the long run. Further it also worsens learning benefits for academic learners as well as professional learners (Bhattacharjee & Bansal, 2021). Admittedly, *knowledge management* is crucial for developing academic learner's skills that later help to improve organizational efficiency through applying those expertise or skills. Educational institutions rely on a level of knowledge management. For instance, a *university* may offer courses with experiential tasks, so that graduates can accelerate the business processes of organizations by continuously utilizing practical experience in the future. Like the academic institutions, corporate business firms also emphasize knowledge management for improving organizational efficiency and the organizational learning process.

The importance of knowledge management to academic institutions or firms in the world addresses issues of sustainability, maturity, and adaptation of new policies. Knowledge management (KM) has proven to be a key competency not only for educational institutions but also for all business organizations (Jahanshahi et al., 2017). The value derived from KM increases two competencies, technological and human participation. Both academic learning and organizational learning are dramatically transformed by artificial intelligence but considering practical experimental necessity, modern learning systems have been adopting augmented intelligence (AUI). Using AUI applications for knowledge management in the academic sector will improve the learning flexibility, quality, and learning satisfaction (Cheah et al., 2023). Similar advantages are applicable in organizational learning. For instance, using bionic lens, and transparent live screen can ensure advantages for both in-class/in-person experiential learning and distance experimental academic learning. Furthermore, pharmaceutical, or research-oriented organizations can provide real-time experimental training though transparent 3D or 7D holographic screens that even ensures real-time human participation. Thus, efficient knowledge management mechanisms in both academic learning and organizational learning would be developed with augmented intelligence for intensifying human perceptions with technological advancement in the future learning systems.

## Dimensions of Knowledge Management

Knowledge management is the process by which academic institutions and organizations acquire, disseminate, and apply knowledge in a responsive and timely manner to efficiently create a functional learning environment. Knowledge management essentially explores creative knowledge to demonstrate innovation skills and improved outcomes by using knowledge to achieve practical success. Generally, knowledge management has three different dimensions, knowledge acquisition, knowledge dissemination, and knowledge responsiveness. The essence of knowledge acquisition is to speed up the process by defining *knowledge-based essential rules* and ontologies from within a system. The process of extracting knowledge from a single source and organizing it constructively and implementing successfully is considered by experts as knowledge acquisition (Fan et al., 2023).

In the realm of education, *knowledge acquisition* serves as the cornerstone upon which learning experiences are built. Whether in traditional classrooms or online settings, learners embark on a journey of discovery, guided by educators who serve as mentors and facilitators of knowledge. Through lectures, discussions, and interactive activities, students are exposed to new ideas and perspectives, challenging them to think critically and engage with the material at hand. Yet, knowledge acquisition in learning extends far beyond the confines of formal instruction. It encompasses a broad spectrum of activities, including independent study, group collaboration, and experiential learning. Through self-directed exploration and inquiry, learners will have the opportunity to delve deeper into subjects of interest, pursuing their passions and cultivating a lifelong learning intention (Bhattacharjee & Juman, 2020). In the digital age, technology has revolutionized the landscape of knowledge acquisition in academic and organizational learning systems, offering unprecedented access to information and resources. Online courses, educational websites, and digital libraries provide academic or professional learners with a wealth of opportunities to expand their knowledge base and enhance their skills. Moreover, interactive platforms and multimedia tools facilitate immersive learning experiences, enabling learners to engage with content in dynamic and engaging ways.

The *knowledge dissemination* plays a pivotal role in the transmission and sharing of information, ideas, and insights. It is the process through which knowledge is communicated, distributed, and made accessible to learners, empowering them to expand their intellectual horizons and cultivate a deeper understanding of the world around them. Central to effective knowledge dissemination is the art of communication (Harfouche et al., 2023). Educators must possess the ability to articulate ideas clearly, engage learners effectively, and tailor teaching methods to suit the diverse needs and learning styles. By fostering an environment of open dialogue and active participation, academic learning or organizational learning systems can encourage learners to question, analyze, and synthesize information, promoting deeper levels of understanding and critical thinking. In addition to formal instruction, knowledge dissemination in learning encompasses a wide range of supplementary resources and support mechanisms. Educational institutions often provide libraries, research facilities, and online repositories where learners can access a wealth of information and conduct independent study. Moreover, peer-to-peer collaboration and group discussions serve as valuable forums for knowledge sharing, enabling learners to exchange ideas, collaborate on projects, and learn from one another's perspectives.

*Knowledge responsiveness* in learning refers to the ability of an individual or a system to adapt and absorb new information effectively. It encompasses the capacity to understand, integrate, and apply knowledge in various contexts, as well as the agility to update beliefs and skills based on new insights or changing circumstances (Butt et al., 2021). In today's rapidly evolving world, where information is constantly expanding and changing, being responsive to knowledge is essential for staying relevant and making informed decisions. One major aspect of knowledge responsiveness is the ability to discern reliable sources of information from misinformation or bias. In an age of abundant information, being able to evaluate the credibility and validity of sources is crucial for making sound judgments and avoiding the spread of false information. Furthermore, knowledge responsiveness involves being adaptable and flexible in academic and organizational learning. Although AI technology reduces human integration in the learning processes, integrating augmented intelligence or augmented reality-based applications will enhance human participation to provide real-time experimental learning opportunities with valid sources. In academic learning settings, fostering knowledge responsiveness involves creating environments that encourage active participation, inquiry, and reflection. This can include promoting collaborative learning experiences, providing opportunities for hands-on exploration, and encouraging students to ask questions and challenge assumptions. Similar assumptions are even appropriate for professional learning management.

## Green Education

After the 20th century, technological development throughout global learning systems has increased environmental emissions more than ever. Consequently, the term 'green education' has been introduced to reduce emissions from academic learning and organizational learning processes. *Green education* refers to a low-emission or zero-emission learning process through the implementation of eco-friendly initiatives (Yu, 2023). For instance, Figure 2 shows that green education development has three major dimensions: green management, green resources, and renewable energy. The first eco-friendly dimension, ***'green management'*** indicates climate-friendly policies such as green administration, learning courses with environmental benefits, integration of low-emission technologies for learning systems, international collaboration for improving green global learning systems, more research for a cleaner earth and eco-friendly academic/organizational learning regulations (Bhattacharjee et al., 2024). These initiatives will significantly reduce environmental emissions in the future.

The second eco-friendly dimension, ***'green resources'*** defines eco-friendly changes in direct and indirect resources that can improve green academic or organizational learning systems. For instance, an environmentally friendly academic campus, eco-friendly infrastructure, low-emission technologies (e.g., holographic experimental classroom, green knowledge management, virtual libraries, virtual holographic laboratories, and AUI-based safety measurements) for virtual/in-class learning systems, and solid waste management (for more, see Figure 2). Applying these green initiatives throughout the learning processes will ensure green environmental performance in the long run.

The third eco-friendly dimension, ***'green energy'*** describes adopting renewable power sourced electricity in implementing eco-friendly learning systems. Academic institutions such as universities, colleges and schools should use one or more clean energy sources i.e., thermal energy, wind energy, and solar energy sourced electricity (Bhattacharjee et al., 2024) for different learning facilities (for instance, see Figure 2). Such concepts should be applied to developing eco-friendly organizational learning processes. As modern learning systems are designed with technology, electricity utilization is increasing rapidly. The concern is that higher electricity usage accelerates the risk of carbon emissions (Bhattacharjee & Ghosh, 2024). Hence, renewable energy sourced clean electricity is the only solution to control carbon emissions in the next generation of academic/organizational learning and knowledge management processes.

*Figure 2. Three dimensions of green education*

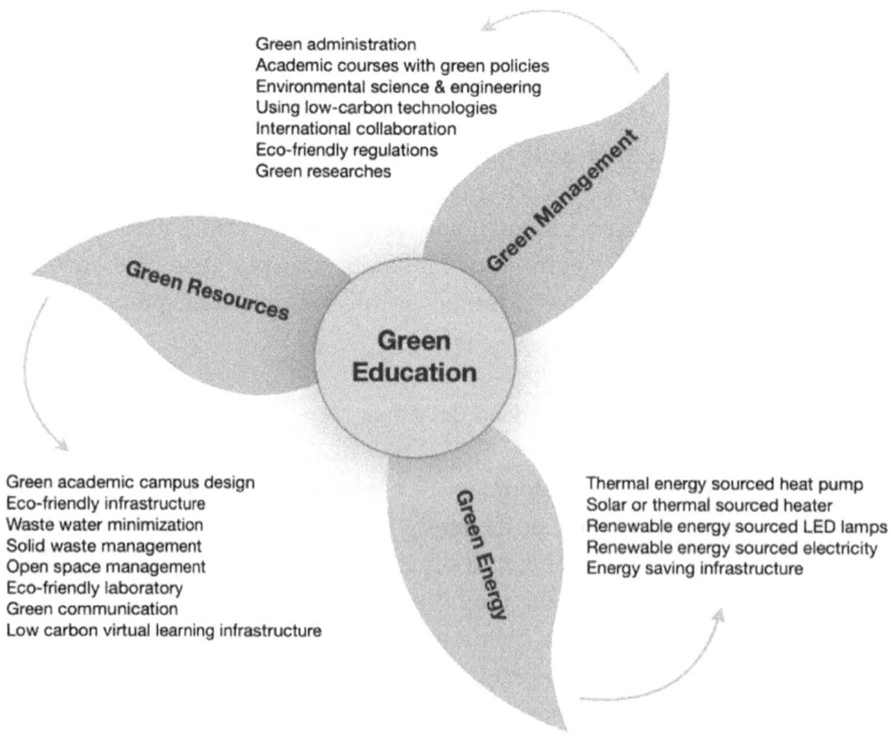

## Role of Augmented Intelligence

Advanced experiential learning process can be developed by using augmented intelligence and augmented reality. The combination of *human intelligence and computer intelligence* makes it possible to gain live experience through AUI applications (Lüthi et al., 2023). For instance, Figure 3 shows that academic learners and professional learners can participate in live sessions through AUI-based web technologies. Laboratories, libraries, and archives are also transformed with real-time virtual facilities. ***Key audiences*** can conduct laboratory experiments from distant places, while instructors can efficiently provide real time-lessons to remote students as effectively as in-person teaching.

In terms of emission control, using augmented intelligence applications would significantly decrease carbon emission due to reduced lead time and higher resource efficiency. In addition, ***expenses*** for academic learning and organizational learning can be reduced by using AUI. Such technological advancement can be applied to establish a green education system. AUI applications decrease the necessity of people to gather in academic premises, which intensifies resource management and waste management efficiency (Dave et al., 2023).

***Educational institutions*** such as universities, colleges and schools can minimize their maintenance costs by enabling AUI facilities for learning. These institutions can also gain competitive advantages by adopting renewable energy sourced electricity such as photovoltaic energy, wind energy, and thermal energy. Integrating clean electricity from renewable sources would decrease annual utility expenses. Furthermore, water management monitoring, resource management monitoring, and real-time virtual administrative facilities will be easier to manage at minimum costs through cloud based AUI systems (Harfouche et al., 2023). *Establishing real-time laboratory* and other academic courses with AUI facilities will enhance real-time distance learning advancements, such facilities would expand opportunities for distance learners to gain experiential learning. For example, individuals traveling by vehicles can participate in live academic or organizational learning sessions, which would reduce lead-time and expenses throughout the learning process.

Figure 3 further demonstrates *next-generation knowledge management and global learning systems* with augmented intelligence and augmented reality. For instance, physics students living in Africa can gain real-time laboratory experience from the University of Oxford using augmented intelligence-based *7D hologram screens*. Such a facility significantly expands knowledge acquisition opportunities and reduce carbon emissions across the world. Another example is organizations providing specialized practical training to improve work efficiency, such as AUI-based virtual Chemistry labs in pharmaceutical companies or universities, which would enhance sustainable knowledge dissemination processes while reducing climate emissions worldwide in the future. Augmented intelligence and augmented reality dramatically improve in-class and distance learning flexibility, ensuring higher knowledge responsiveness in academic and organizational learning.

## Learning Satisfaction

The concept of learning satisfaction has been initially derived from the customer satisfaction theory, further justified by (Pangarso & Setyorini, 2023). Learning satisfaction encompasses the impact of instructional processes to academic or professional learners throughout in-class or online teaching and learning sessions. It measures the overall effectiveness of these educational or training interactions, evaluating their influence on student or learner engagement, comprehension, and fulfillment (Fan et al.,

*Figure 3. Proposed applications of augmented intelligence in global knowledge management and learning systems are outlined, alongside eco-friendly technological transformations and the integration of renewable energy for promoting green educational development*

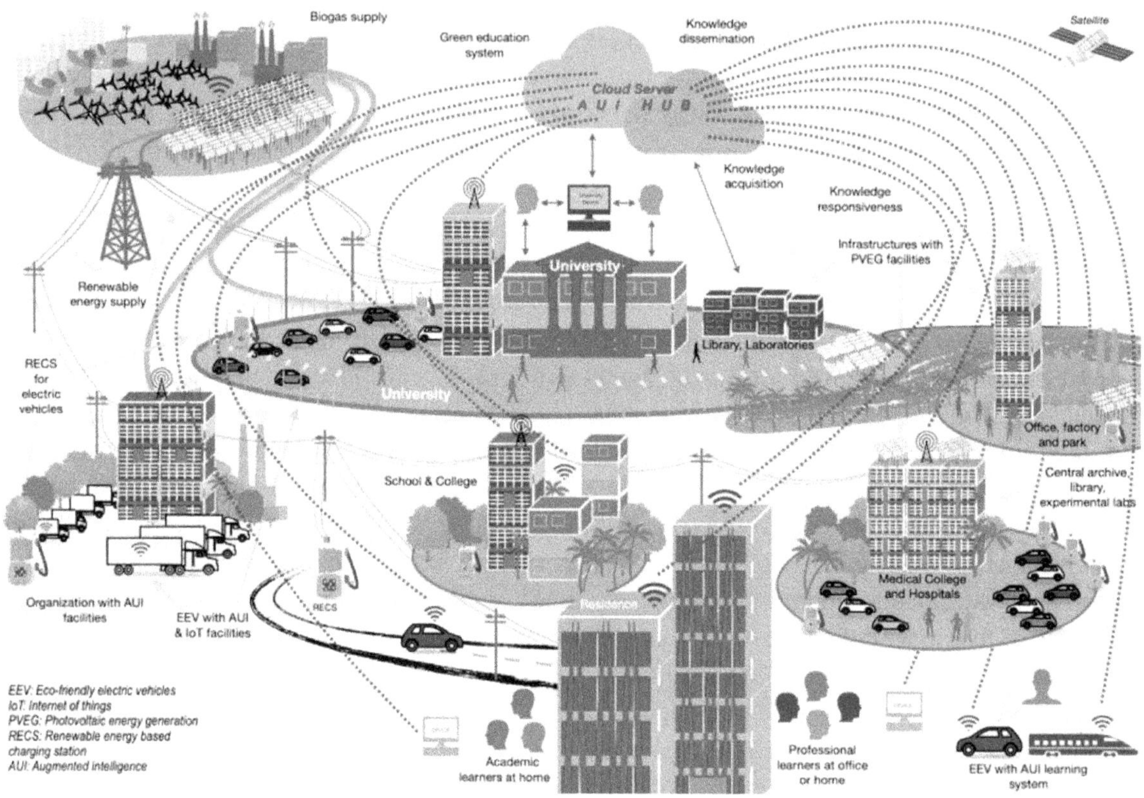


2023). Furthermore, according to this theory, academic students and professional learners are end consumers in the educational sectors, confirming their preference to invest in any learning program. Previous research on student learning satisfaction found that the quality of service, teaching, and engagement in the learning environment directly relates to students' satisfaction and successful learning outcomes (Yu, 2023). Learners are quite happy with in-person interaction during a study or training session compared to static video contents run by artificial intelligence systems.

The quality of teaching and *learning satisfactions* are combinedly interact to improve or decrease learning satisfaction. Furthermore, a static learning process such as providing lessons through pre-uploaded video content is less effective than a live teaching session. A recent study shows that technological advancement with human interaction improves learning satisfaction among academic and professional learners. Therefore, higher education systems and organizational learning systems are now developing with augmented intelligence applications that enhance real-time experimental learning with higher satisfaction.

According to (Du, 2023), there are five criteria of overall students' satisfaction which include the quality of teaching methods, the quality of the learning process such as course contents, the quality of the learning environment, the quality of administrative service, and the quality of the learning implementation. Academic institutions should consider those factors to improve overall learning satisfaction.

Similarly, organizational learning processes can highly develop with balancing those five learning satisfaction factors. In this aspect, integrating augmented intelligence or augmented reality applications would help to redesign the existing learning systems. AUI-based learning systems increase learning flexibility, cost-effective benefits, and lower lead time that in return ensure higher learning satisfaction with lower environmental emissions.

## Study Assumptions

Based on the aforementioned-discussion, three broad assumptions have emerged. The first assumption indicates that the relationship between knowledge management and augmented intelligence facilities is positive. The second assumption indicates that the relationship between green education initiatives and augmented intelligence facilities is positive. The third assumption indicates that augmented intelligence facilities positively influence learning satisfaction.

# METHODOLOGY

The explanatory study approach was applied due to field study of new phenomena by predictive investigation. Previous study recommended that explanatory study should be employed to explore as well as establish realistic causal association between exogenous and endogenous variables (Jia et al., 2020). Considering realistic nature, we applied a stratified random sampling method during the survey (Bhattacharjee et al., 2024). Participants of this study were academic and professional learners. We launched three phased online surveys between September 2022 and October 2023 in the United States, Canada, and Italy. Our survey had no participating conditions except two major criteria. First condition was that the informant must be 18 years old or above. Second criteria defined that participants must have a user experience of augmented intelligence facilities for professional or academic learning purposes. This study includes four major constructs such as green education, knowledge management, artificial intelligence facilities and learning satisfaction. We used five items for *knowledge management* (green knowledge management values academic and professional learners; the knowledge acquisition process is well-developed with AUI; the science and technology human capital profile responds to flexibility, AUI technology and opportunistic; both academic and organizational learning systems use AUI applications to disseminate knowledge; knowledge is disseminated in the learning systems), adopted from (Iqbal, 2021), six items for green education initiatives (develops green learning virtualization; emphasizes green technology integration; implements eco-friendly educational learning policies; implements eco-friendly policies for waste management; implements eco-friendly policies for the use of natural resources; ensures eco-friendly infrastructure development), adopted from (Gandedkar et al., 2021), six items for *augmented intelligence facilities* (augmented intelligence increases experiential learning opportunity; AUI/AR encourages green education systems; designing knowledge management with augmented intelligence or augmented reality reduces learning expenses; real-time education systems through AUI applications enhance high standard of learning quality; adopting AUI increases human interaction for real-time experimental learning; AUI-based learning systems provides learning flexibility for academic or organizational learning), adopted from (Gandedkar et al., 2021) and five items for *learning satisfaction* (augmented intelligence facilities improve teaching and learning methods with eco-friendly benefits; augmented intelligence improves academic and professional course contents; augmented intelligence facilities improve quality of learning environment; augmented intelligence facilities improve administrative service encounter; augmented intelligence facilities improve overall learning convenience), adopted from (Alqurashi, 2019). However, all participants provided their responses through an English online questionnaire, where all items of each construct were rated by a five-point Likert-scale type pattern. We used python and RStudio to analyze survey data. Finally, we demonstrated the study construct based on the results derived from our statistical analysis.

## RESULTS AND DISCUSSION

Augmented artificial intelligence is a new wave in the virtual learning revolution that has captured the attention of both the academic and corporate sectors. Nowadays, regional and international learning systems have been integrating AUI-based technologies to expand knowledge acquisition, dissemination, and responsiveness. Augmented intelligence facilities have significantly enhanced academic learning and organizational learning processes in the USA, Canada, and Italy (Wagan et al., 2023). Augmented intelligence refers to the use of technology to augment human intelligence and decision-making rather than replacing artificial intelligence (Bhattacharjee et al., 2024). The concept of augmented intelligence aims to combine the strengths of artificial intelligence with human skills and judgment to enhance and facilitate outcomes in various domains for academic and organizational learning. For instance, individuals might never have access to the Oxford laboratory, but they can expect to have a similar experience in their local area. Such experiments can be made possible by adopting AUI facilities in modern learning processes. Utilizing advancements in reality will further ensure higher learning satisfaction among academic and professional learners. In this study, we explored the development of knowledge management and green education processes, which are positively correlated with human participation in augmented intelligence facilities. Additionally, AUI facilities were found to enhance learning satisfaction.

### Predictive Relevance and Effects

In the statistical analysis, we applied $Q^2$ estimation to measure the predictive relevance of our model. The satisfactory threshold for Q-square values was initially used to evaluate the Q-square results of all constructs. Generally, Q-square values higher than zero or '$Q^2 > 0$' is widely considered that the measuring model has sufficient predictive relevance (Bhattacharjee et al., 2024; Becker et al., 2023). In contrast, it should be declined if Q-square values under zero or '$Q^2 < 0$' (Bhattacharjee et al., 2024; Becker et al., 2023). A censorious evaluation shows that each Q-square value in our study-model is above the threshold limit ($Q^2 > 0$) for each exogenous latent-variable because all values surpassed zero (see Figure 4).

After the evaluation of predictive relevance, we employed $f^2$ test to find actual substantive impacts of the latent variables. Referring to (Jahanshahi & Bhattacharjee, 2020), f-square indicates minimum ($f^2 < 0.150$), moderate ($0.150 < f^2 < 0.350$) and large ($f^2 > 0.350$) effects sizes. Hence, a crucial look at Figure 4 shows that knowledge management and green education have medium effects on learning satisfaction, but augmented intelligence facilities have large effects on learning satisfaction. It's notable that both knowledge management and green education have higher effects on augmented intelligence facilities (see Figure 4).

*Figure 4. Assessments of $Q^2$ and $f^2$*

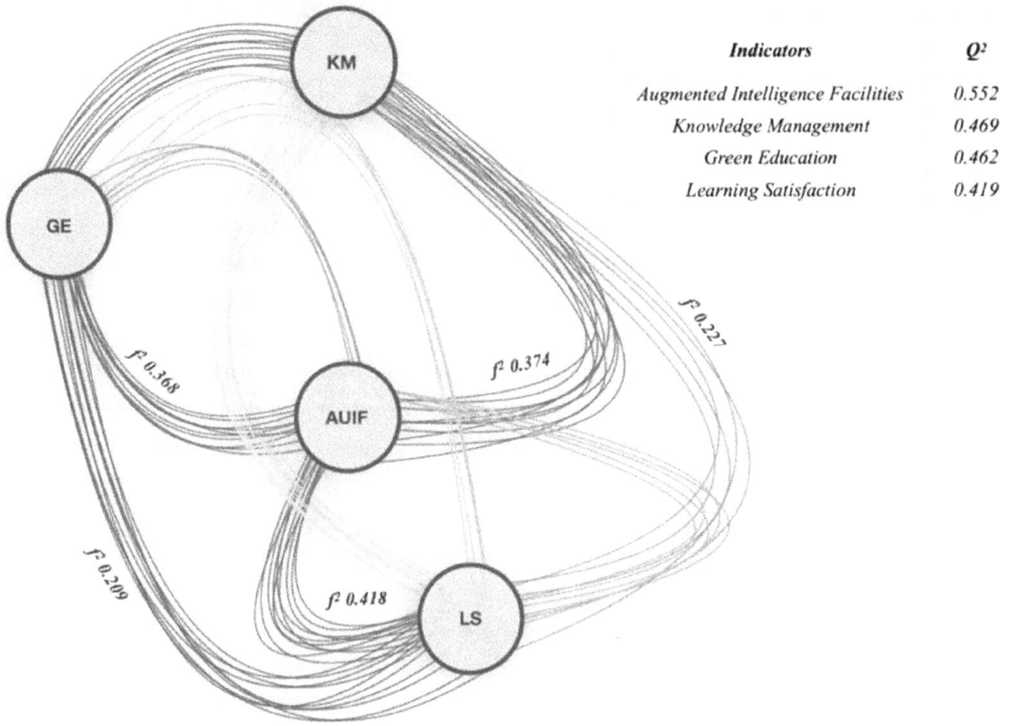


## Graphical Demonstrations

After conducting the actual effects evaluation, we explained all hypothetical assumptions graphically. All graphs were designed using Python to measure the direct effects between variables. We developed three assumptions with four study variables to ascertain the impact of augmented intelligence on green education and knowledge management towards learning satisfaction. These hypothetical assumptions explained below:

First assumption (H1) defines that knowledge management has a positive association with augmented intelligence facilities in learning systems. To examine this hypothesis, we applied 3D surface plotting in Python. Two data sets were inserted to evaluate future impacts. The graphical results derived from Figure 5 show that the relationship between knowledge management and augmented intelligence facilities is positively correlated and higher future impacts. In academic learning and organizational learning, virtual initiatives for knowledge acquisition, dissemination, and responsiveness would require experimental advantage enabled technology that directly increases the necessity of utilizing augmented intelligence or augmented reality applications such as *virtual libraries, holographic virtual classrooms, bionic lenses* for language interpretation, and *3D holographic training centers*. Hence, systematic knowledge management progress will increase the adoption of AUI facilities in future learning processes. Based on the analysis, it is expected that the integration of augmented intelligence facilities in the next generation knowledge management process would increase around 62% in the future. Therefore, this assumption is accepted.

*Figure 5. Impact of knowledge management on augmented intelligence facilities and future improvement*

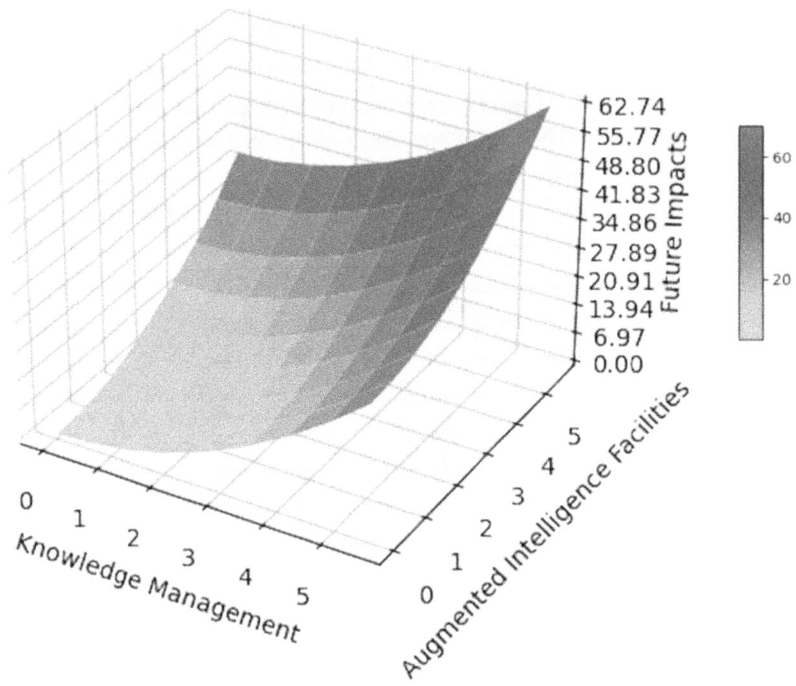


Second assumption (H2) defines that green education initiatives lead to an increase in augmented intelligence facilities in learning systems. To examine this hypothesis, we applied a confidence ellipse plot in Python. Two data sets were inserted with a 4K sampling range. The graphical results derived from Figure 6 describe that the relationship between green education initiatives and augmented intelligence facilities is positively correlated. In academic learning and organizational learning, green initiatives for educational development will expand eco-friendly experiential learning through the use of augmented intelligence or augmented reality applications. Specifically, greater emphasis on green educational initiatives will escalate the adoption of augmented intelligence facility-based learning systems, for instance, *eco-friendly 7D holographic laboratory, 3D holographic classroom, and electroencephalography*. Based on the analysis, it is expected that the integration of augmented intelligence facilities in green education systems would increase by 80% in the future. Thus, the second assumption is accepted.

Third assumption (H3) defines that augmented intelligence facilities increase learning satisfaction. To examine this hypothesis, we applied an ellipse collection plot in Python. Two data sets were inserted to examine the movement of colored ellipses. An arrow mark was inserted to indicate the positive movements of colored ellipses within the squired area. This type of plotting helps identify behavioral impacts. The graphical results derived from Figure 7 depict that the relationship between augmented intelligence facilities and learning satisfaction is positively correlated. Both academic and professional learners experienced higher satisfaction in learning with augmented intelligence facilities. Specifically, AUI and augmented reality facilities improve the learning experience as much as the real environment. In addition, real-time advantages and human interactions in AUI based learning systems decrease the static characteristics of traditional methods while increasing opportunities for real-time participations.

*Figure 6. Impact of green education initiatives on augmented intelligence facilities*

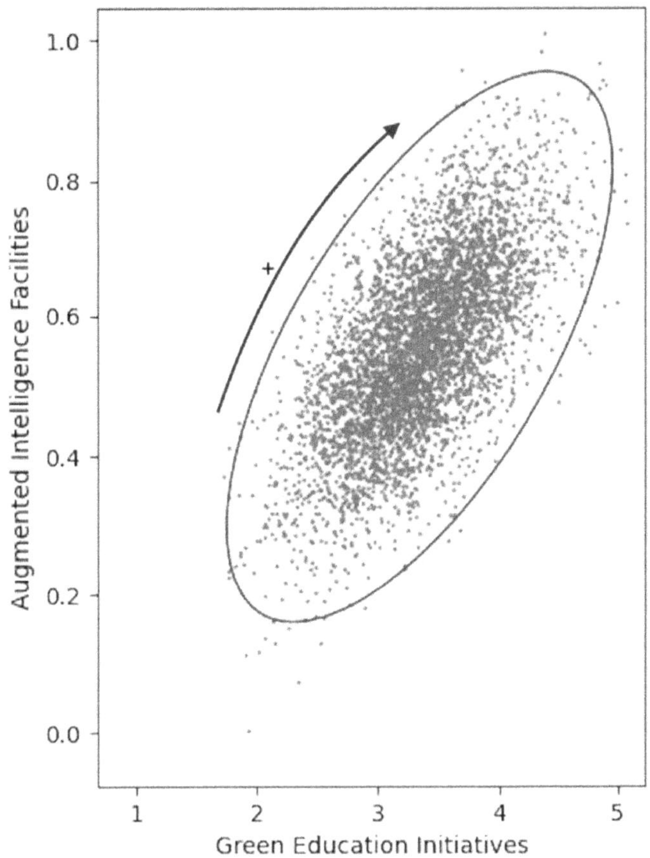


*Figure 7. Impact of augmented intelligence facilities on learning satisfaction*

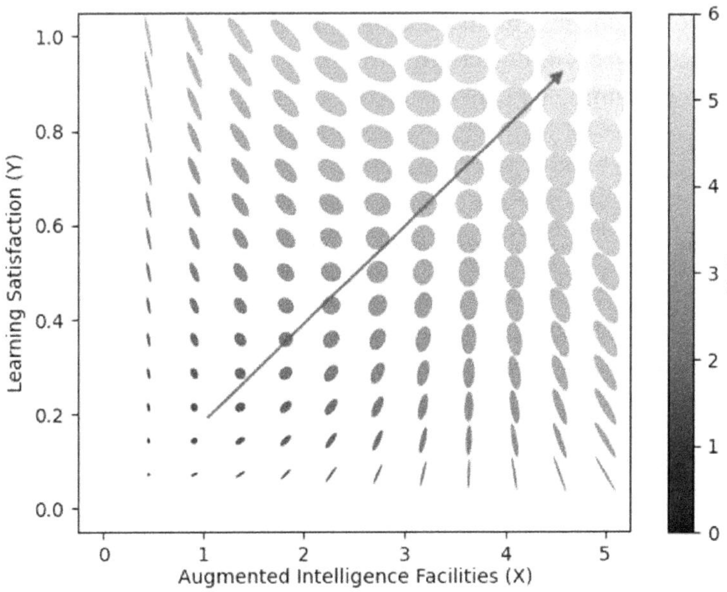

Therefore, academic and organizational learning systems with augmented facilities will ensure higher experiential satisfaction among learners. Based on the colored ellipse distribution, it is expected that the augmented intelligence facilities would increase learning satisfaction by more than 80% in academic and organizational learning. Thus, the third assumption is accepted.

Based on the aforementioned discussion, it's logically understandable that AI is a self-acting system capable of performing tasks without human intervention in a static order, while augmented intelligence is a powered tool that attempts to augment and emulate human cognitive capabilities. Therefore, according to the analytical findings, it is explored that augmented intelligence will be the prime interconnector between computer intelligence and human intelligence in the future. For example, Canada has developed a state-of-the-art educational tool with augmented intelligence (AUI) in various labs across the country. This tool leverages AUI to enhance learning while maintaining a technical balance. These labs enable students to acquire realistic knowledge and create an experimental environment tailored to specific laboratory situations. This allows students and academic professionals to conduct laboratory practices and gain practical knowledge effectively. However, in most cases, *AUI-facilitated learning systems* can automate various experiential processes, such as laboratory tasks, including sample handling and analysis, with human intelligence, which could not be possible by artificial intelligence alone. Augmented intelligence systems optimize workflows to detect and reduce errors while increasing throughput, improving efficiency, and enabling rapid turnaround for decision-making processes. So, considering practical learning scenarios, such as medical labs, chemist labs, real-time statistical evaluations, artificial intelligence-based static learning systems won't be acceptable. Consequently, academic institutions and organizations should adopt AUI facilities to improve knowledge management processes and learning systems with higher experiential satisfaction.

## BENEFITS OF AUGMENTED INTELLIGENCE IN LEARNING SYSTEMS

### Cognitive Abilities

Augmented intelligence or augmented reality has the potential to transform real-life activities. It can seamlessly replace physical objects or devices by presenting them in front of the learner's eyes in real-time, facilitating learning or training to achieve desired goals.

### Easy to Learn

Learning systems with augmented intelligence facilities can enhance practical presentation in both classroom lessons and virtual lessons. This advantage aids learners in gaining knowledge more effectively compared to static AI-based learning.

### Highly Economic

Augmented intelligence facilities offer economic benefits. They are cost-efficient due to energy efficiency and short lead times. As a result, maintenance costs are significantly lower compared to artificial intelligence.

### Advanced Information Literacy

Educational institutions and organizations can effectively manage large volumes of data processing while ensuring adherence to human decision-making policies. Such initiatives in academic and organizational learning will have a positive impact by fostering knowledge in data analysis and management. Promoting this approach will improve data literacy, helping foster a strong data-led culture that benefits future generations in the long run.

### Minimize Analytical Bias

Analysts typically seek answers based on assumptions. However, they may occasionally face confusion regarding where to begin. Nonetheless, their assumptions often guide them towards utilizing specific data to bolster their analyses. Augmented analytics, emphasizing statistical significance, can significantly mitigate potential bias by automating dataset processes in research or analysis. This approach efficiently diminishes the risk of overlooking valuable insights.

### Environmentally Friendly

Augmented intelligence facilities are eco-friendly technologies due to low emissions. Cloud-based augmented intelligence reduces high-source running time, which results in decreasing machine use and carbon emissions.

## POTENTIAL CHALLENGES

### Anti-Alliance Practices

In today's high-tech world, complexity has reached unprecedented levels due to anti-alliance practices. Many organizations such as software companies, Google, YouTube, Coursera, and LinkedIn have established monopolistic AI-based static learning programs to gain more profits and significant control over professional education/training markets. Such practices may heighten barriers to the development of eco-friendly augmented intelligence facilities within global learning and knowledge management systems.

### Master-Skill Limitation

The expansion of automation facilities doesn't necessarily require employees to possess subject-specific skills to operate these systems. However, there's a concerning trend where employees are becoming increasingly reliant on AI, leading to a loss of traditional knowledge (Jahanshahi et al., 2021). For instance, Firm-R, operating in Australia, develops AI-based financial documentation and energy distribution systems. Firm-M then purchases these facilities to implement AI-driven financial documentation structures. While this boosts efficiency for Firm-M's employees, it also diminishes their proficiency in manual skills related to those facilities. Over time, such reliance on automation could impede the transfer of master/source skills among employees, posing long-term challenges.

## Economic Inflation

In green learning development with augmented intelligence, inflation poses a significant challenge. The costs associated with integrating augmented intelligence facilities are continually increasing due to inflation. As a result, expenses such as investment costs, interest on credit amounts, and other operational expenses are soaring. Consequently, many academic institutions and organizations worldwide may encounter difficulties in adopting AUI facilities into their learning systems.

## Geo-Political Imbalance

The global political landscape significantly influences the equitable distribution of international economic and monetary flows, including climate finance for green educational development and green technologies. While developed countries can afford to implement AUI facilities in academic and organizational learning systems, developing and underdeveloped countries may encounter liquidity issues stemming from regional political conflicts and wars (Bahrani & Arshadi Khamseh, 2020). If such complications continue to escalate, the implementation of AUI facilities in global learning systems could become increasingly challenging in the future.

# STRATEGIC RECOMMENDATIONS

To mitigate the potential challenges, the following recommendations are disclosed below.

## Green Strategies

Green educational development and knowledge management with augmented intelligence facilities can foster employing *networking strategy* and *alliance strategy*. Networking strategy will help bridge between small and large academic institutions, while alliance strategy will assist in forming formal learning systems between academic institutions and organizations.

## Priority Training

Providing essential training in the academic and organizational sectors for AUI facility maintenance and innovation will reduce the skilled workforce scarcity in the future. In addition, periodical professional skills development training in the academic sectors will enhance the master skills migration.

## Climate Finance

To accelerate the green education systems with eco-friendly technologies, climate finance is indeed essential to support academic institutions in developing and under-developed countries (Bhattacharjee & Jahanshahi, 2021). Hence, international climate finance would be the brightest light to build global learning systems with augmented intelligence facilities.

### Regional Alliance

Academic institutions in developing or underdeveloped nations can collaborate with educational institutions in developed countries for the purpose of sharing technological advancements through non-profit initiatives. Such initiatives should be encouraged at the governmental level rather than the individual level.

## IMPLICATIONS

This chapter contributes broadly to the global zero-emission target of the Paris Agreement by advocating for climate-friendly transformations in academic and organizational learning. Theoretically, our chapter provides the first empirical evidence for developing real-time experimental learning systems with augmented intelligence or augmented reality in the future. Like other sectors, the modern learning process has been evolving due to automated technologies such as artificial intelligence. However, the COVID-19 epidemic revealed significant limitations of artificial intelligence in experiential learning processes (Bhattacharjee et al., 2020). Therefore, this chapter suggests that redesigning knowledge management systems with augmented intelligence facilities will ensure a smooth digital transformation of knowledge acquisition, dissemination, and responsiveness, ultimately increasing overall learning satisfaction among academic and professional learners.

However, technology is undoubtedly an imperative factor in the development of eco-friendly education (López-Belmonte et al., 2023). Our experimental investigation revealed that the use of augmented intelligence (AUI) applications is positively correlated with learning satisfaction among academic and professional learners. Furthermore, AUI facilities are eco-friendly due to their higher energy efficiency, cost-effectiveness, and reduced environmental impacts. Augmented intelligence is sufficiently advanced to design reality-based learning environments such as holographic laboratories, holographic digital classrooms, bionic lenses for distance learning, and more. Such eco-friendly facilities will even ensure human participation, indicating real-time learning opportunities. We therefore suggest that academic institutions should utilize augmented intelligence or augmented reality to expand both static and experiential learning opportunities for all levels of learners.

## FUTURE RESEARCH DIRECTIONS

This study investigates the application of augmented intelligence in academic and organizational learning to enhance learning satisfaction. We also evaluate the flexibility of knowledge management through the use of augmented intelligence settings. All measures in our study are based on empirical data from first-world countries. Considering this geographical limitation, we suggest that further investigation should examine similar prospects in developing countries to increase generalizability. Moreover, green education and augmented intelligence facilities in learning systems are relatively new concepts. Therefore, future research should investigate how to use climate finance to develop green education systems with augmented intelligence for user centered design, diverse academic/organizational knowledge management contexts, and interdisciplinary collaboration in the future. Thus, further studies could strengthen the findings of this chapter and reveal interesting insights for future learning processes.

## CONCLUSION

This chapter precisely articulates the reengineering of knowledge management and green learning systems by proposing AUI-based systems. Unlike artificial intelligence, AUI facilities would encourage learning rather than blindly depending on technological decisions. Developing e-learning systems with augmented intelligence and augmented reality would improve learners' knowledge building and satisfaction. In addition, gaining practical experiments and performing human decision-oriented tasks through a virtual platform can be made easier by utilizing augmented holography features (Mangano et al., 2023). Scientists and other professionals can perform their real-time activities through virtual holographic screens and holographic laboratories. Holographic classrooms would be a super-advanced idea to implement eco-friendly technological systems that ensure quality education and experiential training in academic and organizational sectors. Integrating augmented intelligence for real-time laboratory work, performing engineering tasks, and developing bionic eyes for learning will be a game changer in the future world. Increasing human participation in decision-making also improves overall knowledge acquisition, dissemination, and responsiveness. Furthermore, increasing AI technological dependency in the education sector also amplifies environmental impacts because of higher lead time and energy consumption. While utilizing AUI technology is productive, due to lower lead time and energy-efficient facilities. Thus, using augmented intelligence facilities will reduce progress towards emission-friendly technological implementation in educational and organizational learning, which could safeguard global ecology in the long run. Finally, developing green education systems and knowledge management systems with augmented intelligence will enhance quality learning, real-time experiments, and values that make future generations more knowledgeable and sustainable.

## REFERENCES

Agajanian, S., Alshahrani, M., Bai, F., Tao, P., & Verkhivker, G. M. (2023). Exploring and learning the universe of protein allostery using artificial intelligence augmented biophysical and computational approaches. *Journal of Chemical Information and Modeling*, *63*(5), 1413–1428. doi:10.1021/acs.jcim.2c01634 PMID:36827465

Alqurashi, E. (2019). Predicting student satisfaction and perceived learning within online learning environments. *Distance Education*, *40*(1), 133–148. doi:10.1080/01587919.2018.1553562

Bahrani, P., & Arshadi Khamseh, A. (2020). Competitive environment between green and non-green products considering disruption and alliance strategy. *Global Journal of Flexible Systems Managment*, *21*(2), 135–161. doi:10.1007/s40171-020-00234-w

Becker, J. M., Cheah, J. H., Gholamzade, R., Ringle, C. M., & Sarstedt, M. (2023). PLS-SEM's most wanted guidance. *International Journal of Contemporary Hospitality Management*, *35*(1), 321–346. doi:10.1108/IJCHM-04-2022-0474

Bhattacharjee, A., & Bansal, V. (2021). The Major Emotional and Economical Drawbacks Derived from the Coronavirus Outbreak from the North Pole to the South Pole. In S. Poddar, B. Kar, S. Samanta, & A. Bhaumik (Eds.), Human resource management and mental health A Psychosocial Aspect, 1-8. Lincoln research and publishing limited, Australia. doi:10.46977/book.2021.hrmmh

Bhattacharjee, A., & Bansal, V. (2023). Sustainable Approaches of Blockchain Tech, Artificial Intelligence, and Climate Finance in the 4&5IR: Low Emission Technologies and Economy. In S. Trivedi, R. Aggarwal, & G. Singh (Eds.), *Perspectives on Blockchain Technology and Responsible Investing* (pp. 85–116). IGI Global. doi:10.4018/978-1-6684-8361-9.ch004

Bhattacharjee, A., Bansal, V., & Juman, M. K. I. (2021). COVID-19 Emergency: Faux Healthcare Service Causes Distress and Life Dissatisfaction. *Asian Journal of Medicine and Health, 18*(12), 53–61. doi:10.9734/ajmah/2020/v18i1230290

Bhattacharjee, A., & Ghosh, A. (2024). Sustainable Green Supply Chain Management for Organizational Performance and Carbon Reduction. In Y. Ramakrishna & B. Srivastava (Eds.), *Strategies for Environmentally Responsible Supply Chain and Production Management* (pp. 128–155). IGI Global. doi:10.4018/979-8-3693-0669-7.ch007

Bhattacharjee, A., & Jahanshahi, A. A. (2021). Artificial landscape strategy: A business growth recovery plan in the post pandemic world. *Academia Letters*, *2311*. Advance online publication. doi:10.20935/AL2311

Bhattacharjee, A., Jahanshahi, A. A., Bhuiyan, M., & Sultana, S. (2020). Mental health of cisgender and transgender during COVID-19 pandemic. *International Journal of Medical Research and Review, 8*(5), 344–351. doi:10.17511/ijmrr.2020.i05.02

Bhattacharjee, A., Jahanshahi, A. A., & Chakraborty, S. (2024). Unlocking the link between low emission supply chains, blockchain adoption, and financial success: The payoff of socially responsible practices in supply chains. *Business Strategy & Development*, *7*(1), e341. doi:10.1002/bsd2.341

Bhattacharjee, A., & Juman, M. K. I. (2020). Does delay or scarcity in working capital increase unexpected financial risk for women entrepreneurs in the developing country? *International Journal of Economics, Commerce and Management, 8*(8), 433-446. http://ijecm.co.uk/wp-content/uploads/2020/08/8827.pdf

Bilgram, V., & Laarmann, F. (2023). Accelerating Innovation with Generative AI: AI-augmented Digital Prototyping and Innovation Methods. *IEEE Engineering Management Review*, *51*(2), 18–25. doi:10.1109/EMR.2023.3272799

Butt, P., Kamran, M., Afzal, F., & Mukit, M. M. H. (2021). Being agile in market orientation to enhance firm performance: The role of green supply chain management. *International Journal of Agile Systems and Management*, *14*(4), 517–542. doi:10.1504/IJASM.2021.120237

Cheah, J. H., Amaro, S., & Roldán, J. L. (2023). Multigroup analysis of more than two groups in PLS-SEM: A review, illustration, and recommendations. *Journal of Business Research*, *156*, 113539. doi:10.1016/j.jbusres.2022.113539

Chng, E., Tan, A. L., & Tan, S. C. (2023). Examining the Use of Emerging Technologies in Schools: A Review of Artificial Intelligence and Immersive Technologies in STEM Education. *Journal for STEM Education Research*, *6*(3), 385–407. doi:10.1007/s41979-023-00092-y

Cui, K. (2023). Artificial intelligence and creativity: Piano teaching with augmented reality applications. *Interactive Learning Environments*, *31*(10), 7017–7028. doi:10.1080/10494820.2022.2059520

Dave, D. M., Mandvikar, S., & Engineer, P. A. (2023). Augmented intelligence: Human-ai collaboration in the era of digital transformation. *International Journal of Engineering Applied Sciences and Technology*, *8*(6), 24–33. doi:10.33564/IJEAST.2023.v08i06.003

Doshi, R., Hiran, K. K., Mijwil, M. M., & Anand, D. (2023). To That of Artificial Intelligence, Passing Through Business Intelligence. In *Handbook of Research on AI and Knowledge Engineering for Real-Time Business Intelligence* (pp. 1–16). IGI Global. doi:10.4018/978-1-6684-6519-6.ch001

Du, B. (2023). Research on the factors influencing the learner satisfaction of MOOCs. *Education and Information Technologies*, *28*(2), 1935–1955. doi:10.1007/s10639-022-11269-0

Eminaga, O., Laurie, M., Lee, T., Jia, X., Xing, L., & Liao, J. C. (2023). Potential of educational cystoscopy atlas for augmented intelligence. In Advanced Biomedical and Clinical Diagnostic and Surgical Guidance Systems XXI, 12368, 141-147. doi:10.1117/12.2650920

Fagbola, T. M., Fagbola, F. I., Aroba, O. J., Doshi, R., Hiran, K. K., & Thakur, S. C. (2022). Smart face masks for Covid-19 pandemic management: A concise review of emerging architectures, challenges and future research directions. *IEEE Sensors Journal*, *23*(2), 877–888. doi:10.1109/JSEN.2022.3225067

Fan, S., Guo, J., Ma, S., Li, L., Wang, G., Xu, H., & Zhao, Z. (2023). Framework and key technologies of human-machine hybrid-augmented intelligence system for large-scale power grid dispatching and control. *CSEE Journal of Power and Energy Systems*, *10*(1), 1–12. doi:10.17775/CSEEJPES.2023.00940

Gandedkar, N. H., Wong, M. T., & Darendeliler, M. A. (2021). Role of virtual reality (VR), augmented reality (AR) and artificial intelligence (AI) in tertiary education and research of orthodontics: An insight. *Seminars in Orthodontics*, *27*(2), 69–77. doi:10.1053/j.sodo.2021.05.003

Harfouche, A., Quinio, B., Saba, M., & Saba, P. B. (2023). The Recursive Theory of Knowledge Augmentation: Integrating human intuition and knowledge in Artificial Intelligence to augment organizational knowledge. *Information Systems Frontiers*, *25*(1), 55–70. doi:10.1007/s10796-022-10352-8

Hiran, K. K., Doshi, R., & Patel, M. (Eds.). (2024). *Applications of Virtual and Augmented Reality for Health and Wellbeing*. IGI Global. doi:10.4018/979-8-3693-1123-3

Iqbal, A. (2021). Innovation speed and quality in higher education institutions: The role of knowledge management enablers and knowledge sharing process. *Journal of Knowledge Management*, *25*(9), 2334–2360. doi:10.1108/JKM-07-2020-0546

Jahanshahi, A. A., & Bhattacharjee, A. (2020). Competitiveness improvement in public sector organizations: What they need? *Journal of Public Affairs*, *20*(2), e2011. doi:10.1002/pa.2011

Jahanshahi, A. A., Bhattacharjee, A., & Maghsoudi, T. (2021). Internal capabilities as the source of achieving competitive advantage in small-sized businesses. *International Journal of Business Innovation and Research*, *26*(2), 141–162. doi:10.1504/IJBIR.2021.118446

Jahanshahi, A. A., Bhattacharjee, A., & Polas, M. R. H. (2023). The micro-foundations of sustainable entrepreneurship: The role of individuals' pro-social identity and organisational pro-social identity. *International Journal of Productivity and Quality Management*, *40*(2), 149–170. doi:10.1504/IJPQM.2023.134270

Jahanshahi, A. A., Brem, A., & Bhattacharjee, A. (2017). Who takes more sustainability-oriented entrepreneurial actions? The role of entrepreneurs' values, beliefs and orientations. *Sustainability (Basel)*, *9*(10), 1636. doi:10.3390/su9101636

Jang, C., Song, B. Y., Jeong, Y. S., & Park, H. S. (2023). A Framework for Model-Sharing of Augmented Intelligence in Container-based Modular Robot Using Cloud System. In *2023 20th International Conference on Ubiquitous Robots (UR)*, (pp. 993-996). IEEE. 10.1109/UR57808.2023.10202258

Jia, J., Yan, J., Jahanshahi, A. A., Lin, W., & Bhattacharjee, A. (2020). What makes employees more proactive? Roles of job embeddedness, the perceived strength of the HRM system and empowering leadership. *Asia Pacific Journal of Human Resources*, *58*(1), 107–127. doi:10.1111/1744-7941.12249

López-Belmonte, J., Moreno-Guerrero, A. J., López-Núñez, J. A., & Hinojo-Lucena, F. J. (2023). Augmented reality in education. A scientific mapping in Web of Science. *Interactive Learning Environments*, *31*(4), 1860–1874. doi:10.1080/10494820.2020.1859546

Lüthi, N., Matt, C., Myrach, T., & Junglas, I. (2023). Augmented Intelligence, Augmented Responsibility? *Business & Information Systems Engineering*, *65*(4), 391–401. doi:10.1007/s12599-023-00789-9

Mangano, F. G., Admakin, O., Lerner, H., & Mangano, C. (2023). Artificial intelligence and augmented reality for guided implant surgery planning: A proof of concept. *Journal of Dentistry*, *133*, 104485. doi:10.1016/j.jdent.2023.104485 PMID:36965859

Mijwil, M. M., Gök, M., Doshi, R., Hiran, K. K., & Kösesoy, I. (2023). Utilizing Artificial Intelligence Techniques to Improve the Performance of Wireless Nodes. In *Applications of Artificial Intelligence in Wireless Communication Systems* (pp. 150–162). IGI Global. doi:10.4018/978-1-6684-7348-1.ch010

Pangarso, A., & Setyorini, R. (2023). The drivers of e-learning satisfaction during the early COVID-19 pandemic: Empirical evidence from an Indonesian private university. *Cogent Education*, *10*(1), 2149226. doi:10.1080/2331186X.2022.2149226

Polas, M. R. H., Tabash, M. I., Bhattacharjee, A., & Dávila, G. A. (2023). Knowledge management practices and green innovation in SMES: The role of environmental awareness towards environmental sustainability. *The International Journal of Organizational Analysis*, *31*(5), 1601–1622. doi:10.1108/IJOA-03-2021-2671

Priyadarshi, N., Padmanaban, S., Hiran, K. K., Holm-Nielson, J. B., & Bansal, R. C. (Eds.). (2021). *Artificial intelligence and internet of things for renewable energy systems* (Vol. 12). Walter de Gruyter GmbH & Co KG. doi:10.1515/9783110714043

Sharma, P., Sharma, I., Pamecha, S., & Hiran, K. K. (2022). Green Currency Based on Blockchain Technology for Sustainable Development. In *Advancements in Quantum Blockchain With Real-Time Applications* (pp. 102–118). IGI Global. doi:10.4018/978-1-6684-5072-7.ch005

Udvaros, J., & Forman, N. (2023). Artificial Intelligence and Education 4.0. In *INTED2023 Proceedings*, 6309-6317. 10.21125/inted.2023.1670

Wagan, A. A., Khan, A. A., Chen, Y. L., Yee, P. L., Yang, J., & Laghari, A. A. (2023). Artificial Intelligence-Enabled Game-Based Learning and Quality of Experience: A Novel and Secure Framework (B-AIQoE). *Sustainability (Basel)*, *15*(6), 5362. doi:10.3390/su15065362

Yu, Z. (2023). Meta-analyses of effects of augmented reality on educational outcomes over a decade. *Interactive Learning Environments*, 1–15. doi:10.1080/10494820.2023.2205899

## ADDITIONAL READING

Kharisma, D. B., Sudirman, S., Edi, F., & S, R. R. P. M. (2023). Current Trend of Artificial Intelligence-Augmented Reality in Science Learning: Systematic Literature Review. *Jurnal Penelitian Pendidikan IPA*, *9*(8), 404–410. doi:10.29303/jppipa.v9i8.4484

Lampropoulos, G. (2023). Augmented Reality and Artificial Intelligence in Education: Toward Immersive Intelligent Tutoring Systems. In V. Geroimenko (Ed.), *Augmented Reality and Artificial Intelligence* (pp. 137–146). Springer. doi:10.1007/978-3-031-27166-3_8

## KEY TERMS AND DEFINITIONS

1. **Augmented Intelligence: Augmented intelligence is a technology that changes the decision-making process of any task by integrating human interactions. In this technology:** computer intelligence and human intelligence work together such as live GPS navigation.
2. **Augmented Reality:** Augmented reality is essentially a view of real-life activities within interactive mode. People can experience real-world motions with computer intelligence.
3. **Augmented Holography: Augmented intelligence or augmented reality can record live activities and then reconstruct them into a dimensional view similar to the real version:** which is called augmented holography.
4. **Bionic Lenses: The lenses that can provide superhuman abilities:** such as translating languages, visualizing human intentions, memorizing events, transmitting data, and processing data. These lenses are newly invented and introduced as bionic lenses or bionic eyes. Normally, individuals can use these lenses on their eyes to access all those facilities.
5. **Climate Finance: To mitigate monetary scarcity for eco-friendly development:** world leaders from matured economies have formed an alliance to provide financial support for green economic development such as green education, green transportation, green technologies and so on around the globe, such funding support is called climate finance.
6. **Electroencephalography: Electroencephalography is a technology that can read the human brain's electrical activity to measure human concentration on an object:** thing or activity.
7. **Green Education: Green education refers to an educational approach that integrates environmental awareness:** sustainability principles, and eco-friendly practices into learning environments and curricula.

8. **Holographic Lab: The holographic lab is an advanced facilitated laboratory where learners and scientists can apply testing procedures virtually. During the evaluation:** any instructions and effects can be observed just like real effects.

9. **Organizational Learning: Organizational learning is the process by which organizations acquire:** create, retain, and transfer knowledge and insights to improve performance and adapt to changing circumstances.

# Chapter 4
# Demystifying the Dynamic Determinants of Generative Artificial Intelligence (AI) Literacy for Adaptable Sustainable Education:
## Multistage Structure Equation Remodeling

**Manish Dadhich**
*Sir Padampat Singhania University, India & Lincoln University College, Malaysia*

**Kamal Kant Hiran**
*Sir Padampat Singhania University, India & Lincoln University College, Malaysia*

**Amiya Bhaumik**
https://orcid.org/0000-0002-9188-2269
*Lincoln University College, Malaysia*

**Midhun Chakkaravarthy**
https://orcid.org/0000-0002-0107-885X
*Lincoln University College, Malaysia*

## ABSTRACT

*This research aims to demystify the dynamic determinants of generative artificial intelligence (AI) literacy for adaptable sustainable education (ASE) through the application of multistage structural equation modeling (SEM). Utilizing a quantitative approach, a structured questionnaire distributed via Google Forms is employed to gather data from a convenient sample of 260 teachers in higher education. The study unfolds over a specified period, incorporating rigorous data filtering techniques to enhance the reliability of responses. Smart-PLS serves as the primary tool for data analysis, allowing for an in-depth exploration of relationships among variables such as generative AI literacy, digital split, computational intelligence, and cognitive inclusion. Dependent variables include teacher perceptions, technological proficiency, and cognitive inclusion, while independent variables encompass awareness of AI and the perceived usefulness of AI in achieving ASE. The outcomes of this research carry significant policy implications for AI, ICT, and educational professionals, providing insights to shape informed strategies for integrating AI literacy into higher education to meet the goals of adaptable sustainable education.*

DOI: 10.4018/979-8-3693-2440-0.ch004

## INTRODUCTION

Artificial intelligence (AI) in education is reshaping traditional learning paradigms by leveraging technology to provide personalized, adaptive, and efficient educational experiences (Aggarwal et al., 2023; Golab-Andrzejak, 2022). Through the implementation of AI-driven tools such as personalized learning platforms, intelligent tutoring systems, and automated grading, education becomes tailored to individual student needs, fostering a more effective and engaging learning environment. Virtual classrooms, language processing applications, and educational games enriched with AI enhance interactivity and inclusivity (Bhatt & Muduli, 2023; Kar et al., 2022). Additionally, AI aids educators by offering predictive analytics for early intervention and personalized professional development opportunities. While promising, the integration of AI in education necessitates careful consideration of ethical implications and the importance of maintaining a harmonious balance between technology and human guidance.[1]

In the words of (Celik, 2022; Kamalov et al., 2023; Segbenya et al., 2023), Generative Artificial Intelligence literacy involves a comprehensive understanding of AI technologies capable of creating new content, such as text, images, and music. This literacy extends beyond technical proficiency, encompassing awareness of the applications, ethical considerations, and potential societal impacts of generative AI. It requires individuals to critically analyze and interpret outputs generated by these models, fostering a nuanced understanding of their strengths and limitations. Moreover, generative AI literacy involves navigating legal and regulatory frameworks, acknowledging ethical concerns related to bias and privacy, and cultivating the ability to communicate complex AI concepts to diverse audiences (Wibowo et al., 2023). In essence, being generative AI literate equips individuals with the knowledge and skills needed to navigate the ethical, social, and technological dimensions of this rapidly advancing field, fostering responsible engagement and decision-making in an AI-driven world.

Adaptable Sustainable Education (ASE) is a dynamic approach that recognizes the ever-evolving nature of learning needs and the imperative to balance environmental, social, and economic considerations (Cheng & Wang, 2023). Inherent in this philosophy is the commitment to adaptability, acknowledging the rapid pace of technological advancements and societal changes. This involves continuous curriculum updates, integration of cutting-edge technologies, and the creation of versatile learning spaces that cater to diverse student needs (Bouteraa et al., 2024; Dadhich et al., 2023). By embracing adaptability, educational systems can better prepare individuals for the uncertainties of the future, fostering a mindset of lifelong learning and resilience in the face of change.

Sustainability, within the context of ASE, extends beyond environmental concerns to encompass broader societal impacts. This entails fostering inclusivity, equity, and social responsibility within educational structures. It also involves a commitment to resource efficiency, minimizing environmental footprints, and ensuring economic viability in a manner that promotes long-term resilience (Chiu, 2024; Rohde et al., 2024). By intertwining adaptability and sustainability, this educational approach not only equips learners with relevant skills but also instills a sense of responsibility towards the environment and society, contributing to the development of conscientious global citizens. Having studied the extensive literature, the following research questions can in designated.

RQ.1 What are the key factors shaping generative AI literacy among educators and students, and how do these factors impact adaptable and sustainable educational practices?

## THEORETICAL BACKGROUND

The literature offers a multifaceted exploration of the critical components shaping the integration of AI literacy in educational frameworks. (Zhou et al., 2024) conducted an extensive global literature review, drawing insights from 50 key studies, to underscore the foundational importance of nuanced AI understanding. Emphasizing the need for technical knowledge, their work established a groundwork for AI literacy programs and highlighted the global relevance of incorporating such foundational principles into educational curricula.

(Waqar et al., 2023) delved into the practical applications of generative AI in education by engaging with 100 educators across diverse settings in North America and Europe. Through interviews and surveys, the study unveiled the transformative potential of generative AI in curriculum development and pedagogy, and offered valuable insights into how adaptable and sustainable education can be realized through the incorporation of AI technologies. The findings shed light on the importance of personalized learning experiences and the potential for generative AI to cater to diverse educational needs. (Celik, 2022) conducted a systematic review of 30 articles and policy documents with a global focus. Williams navigated the ethical landscape surrounding generative AI in education and highlighted the imperative of responsible use and the minimization of biases. This work contributed guidelines for educators and policymakers, aiming to ensure ethical practices and underlining the critical role of ethics in fostering sustainable AI literacy. (Ji et al., 2020) extended the discussion to the legal dimensions of integrating generative AI in education, analyzing legal frameworks and policies from 15 countries. Their comparative analysis, spanning North America, Europe, and Asia, emphasized the need for clear legal guidelines to guarantee the responsible and sustainable implementation of AI in educational settings. Collectively, these studies contribute to demystifying the dynamic determinants of Generative AI Literacy for ASE, and offered a comprehensive perspective that integrates foundational knowledge, practical applications, ethical considerations, and legal frameworks to shape a holistic approach for future-oriented AI education.

### Generative AI Literacy

AI literacy denotes the ability to understand, interpret, and effectively engage with artificial intelligence technologies (Benzaquen & Charles, 2020; Mijwil et al., 2023). It encompasses knowledge about the fundamental principles of AI, the applications of AI in various domains, and the ability to critically analyze and interact with AI-driven systems. As AI technologies, particularly generative AI, become increasingly integrated into daily life, education, and the workplace, the importance of AI literacy becomes evident (Anurag Shukla, Manish Dadhich, Dipesh Vaya, 2024). AI literacy is not only about technical skills but also includes a broader understanding of the ethical, social, and economic implications of AI. In the context of education, fostering AI literacy is crucial to preparing individuals for a future where AI plays a central role in various aspects of society (Lohr et al., 2021). ASE focuses on creating an educational system that is flexible, responsive to change, and environmentally sustainable. In the face of evolving technologies, societal needs, and environmental challenges, education systems must adapt to ensure learners are equipped with relevant skills and knowledge. Thus, we posit.

H1: Enhanced Generative Artificial Intelligence (AI) Literacy positively influences the evolution of Adaptable Sustainable Education (ASE).

## Digital Split

The digital split, an extension of the digital divide, reflects the uneven access to and proficiency in digital technologies among individuals and communities (Lyons et al., 2022; Manish Dadhich; Preeti Yadav; Abhineet Saxena; Rakesh Kumar Birda; Sumit Mathur; Kamal Kant Hiran, 2023). In the context of ASE, addressing the digital split becomes pivotal, as equitable access to technology is fundamental for fostering adaptability and sustainability. ASE emphasizes the need for flexible, responsive education, but the digital split presents a challenge, potentially leaving certain populations marginalized in the face of technological advancements. Bridging the digital split is integral to creating an inclusive and adaptable educational system that can harness the benefits of technology while ensuring sustainability and accessibility for all (Atreides, 2021; Robles-Carrillo, 2021). Therefore, we derived the following statement.

H2: Access to digital technologies enhances the effectiveness of Adaptable Sustainable Education (ASE).

## Computational Intelligent

Computational intelligence involves the utilization of advanced computing techniques such as artificial intelligence and machine learning (Aggarwal et al., 2023; Golab-Andrzejak, 2022). In the framework of ASE, integrating computational intelligence could revolutionize educational approaches by enabling personalized learning, optimizing resource allocation, and adapting curriculum content dynamically (Dadhich & Tiwari, 2022). This technological integration has the potential to enhance adaptability, sustainability, and efficiency within educational systems, providing tailored learning experiences while minimizing environmental impact. Computational Intelligence also encompasses various techniques, including artificial intelligence, machine learning, neural networks, fuzzy logic, evolutionary algorithms, and other computational approaches that aim to mimic or simulate aspects of human intelligence. These techniques are applied to solve complex problems, make predictions, and optimize systems in diverse fields such as data analysis, pattern recognition, robotics, and decision-making processes (Segbenya et al., 2023). We propose.

H3: Integration of Computational Intelligence into educational frameworks significantly contributed to the advancement of Adaptable Sustainable Education (ASE).

## Cognitive Inclusion

Cognitive inclusion emphasizes accommodating diverse cognitive abilities within educational settings. From the perspective of ASE, recognizing and addressing cognitive diversity is crucial for creating an inclusive learning environment (Cheng & Wang, 2023; Wibowo et al., 2023). This approach involves adapting teaching methodologies, providing personalized support, and leveraging assistive technologies to ensure that individuals with varied cognitive profiles have equitable access to education. By prioritizing cognitive inclusion, ASE aims to optimize learning outcomes, promote social equity, and build a sustainable educational system that values and accommodates the cognitive diversity of its learners (Dadhich et al., 2022). Cognitive inclusion goes beyond traditional approaches to education and work, recognizing that people have different ways of thinking, learning, and processing information. It involves adapting teaching methods, curriculum design, and work environments to cater to the needs of individuals with diverse cognitive strengths and challenges (Rejeb et al., 2024). This approach promotes not only equal access but also the celebration of cognitive diversity as an asset that contributes to innovation, problem-solving, and overall success in different contexts. We posit the following statement.

H4: Cognitive Inclusion within educational strategies pointedly contributes to the objectives of Adaptable Sustainable Education (ASE).

The proposed conceptual model envisions a cohesive framework where Generative AI Literacy serves as the cornerstone for fostering ASE (see Figure 1). Addressing the Digital Split is crucial for ensuring universal access to the benefits of Generative AI, while Computational Intelligence serves as a transformative force, optimizing education and enhancing adaptability. The model underscores Cognitive Inclusion, creating an inclusive learning environment that values diverse cognitive abilities. The interconnected dynamics among Generative AI Literacy, Digital Split, Computational Intelligence, and Cognitive Inclusion form a symbiotic relationship, fostering a technologically empowered, inclusive, and sustainable educational ecosystem. The research aims to uncover the dynamic determinants of Generative AI Literacy and their implications for Adaptable Sustainable Education, with findings offering insights for educational AI and ICT professionals in shaping effective policies and strategies. The hypothesis posits that the strategic integration of these elements will collectively contribute to the realization of Adaptable Sustainable Education.

## RESEARCH METHODOLOGY

This study employs a quantitative research design, utilizing Multistage Structural Equation Modeling (SEM) to analyze the dynamic determinants of Generative AI Literacy and their impact on ASE. A convenient sampling method was adopted, selecting 260 teachers who participated in the study. This sampling approach was chosen for its practicality and accessibility within the educational context. The primary data collection tool is a structured questionnaire distributed through Google Forms. This online platform facilitates efficient and convenient data collection, allowing participants to respond to questions related to Generative AI Literacy, Digital Split, Computational Intelligence, and Cognitive Inclusion.

*Figure 1. Conceptual model*

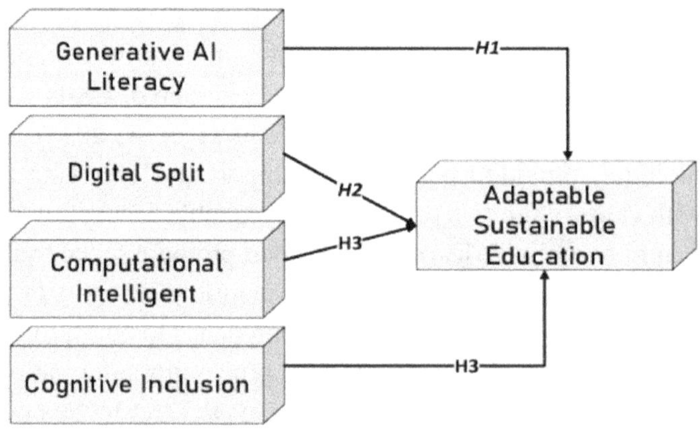

The study is conducted during July-Dec.2023, ensuring sufficient time for data collection, analysis, and interpretation. The duration was determined based on the complexity of the research objectives and the availability of participants. To ensure data quality, rigorous filtering techniques were applied to eliminate incomplete or inconsistent responses and removed outlines. This process aims to enhance the accuracy and reliability of the dataset. Multistage SEM)was employed as the primary data analysis tool. This advanced statistical technique allowed for the examination of complex relationships among variables, providing insights into the dynamic determinants of Generative AI Literacy for Adaptable Sustainable Education. Smart-PLS software will be specifically used for SEM analysis. The study identifies independent variables, including the impact of Generative AI Literacy, Digital Split, Computational Intelligence, and Cognitive Inclusion and the dependent variable was ASE. These variables were extracted from previous studies conducted in different geographical locations worldwide.

## ANALYSIS AND DISCUSSION

The study focused on a sample of 260 teachers from higher education institutions. The demographic profile of the participants includes educators across various disciplines and specializations. Table 1 presents descriptive statistics for a dataset of 260 participants, detailing their characteristics across several factors. In terms of gender, 57.80% are male and 44.20% are female. Age distribution shows that 50.80% are between 20-30, 25.00% were between 30-50, and 24.20% are above 50. Proficiency in using generative AI is categorized as high for 35.40%, medium for 44.20%, and low for 20.40%. Education levels are divided into college (32.70%), university (36.60%), and coaching (30.80%). Notably, 87.70% of participants have an awareness of AI literacy, while 12.30% do not. These statistics offer a comprehensive insight into the demographic composition and characteristics of the surveyed participants.

Table 2 presents reliability and validity measures for different constructs in the dataset. For Generative AI Literacy (GAIL), Cronbach's alpha is 0.768, indicating a reasonably high level of internal consistency. The Average Variance Extracted (AVE) is 0.519, representing the proportion of variance captured by the construct's indicators, and the Composite Reliability (CR) is 0.403, suggesting acceptable reliability. Digital Split (DS) demonstrates strong internal consistency with a Cronbach's alpha of 0.880, an AVE of 0.501, and a CR of 0.608. Computational Intelligence (CPI) has a Cronbach's alpha of 0.807, AVE of 0.632, and CR of 0.606. Cognitive Inclusion (COI) shows a Cronbach's alpha of 0.801, AVE of 0.540, and CR of 0.508. Adaptable Sustainable Education (ASE) has a Cronbach's alpha of 0.698, AVE of 0.487, and CR of 0.521. These metrics collectively highlight the internal consistency, convergent validity, and reliability of the constructs, contributing to the robustness of the study's measurements (Sarstedt et al., 2019).

Table 3 presents cross-loading values of manifest variables across different constructs in the study. The figures denote the strength of associations between each manifest variable and the respective constructs. For example, GAIL_1 has a substantial positive cross-loading with Generative AI Literacy (GAIL) at 0.703, indicating a robust connection. However, it exhibits weaker cross-loadings with other constructs. Similarly, GAIL_2, GAIL_3, and GAIL_4 show strong positive associations with GAIL at 0.840, 0.787, and 0.761, respectively. Digital Split (DS) manifest variables (DS_1, DS_2, DS_3, DS_4) exhibit significant positive associations with DS, showcasing strong construct alignment. The pattern repeats for Computational Intelligence (CPI), Cognitive Inclusion (COI), and Adaptable Sustainable Education (ASE) manifest variables. These cross-loading figures are crucial for evaluating the conver-

*Table 1. Descriptive statistics*

| Factors | Classification | Freq. | % |
|---|---|---|---|
| Gender | Male | 145 | 57.80 |
| | Female | 115 | 44.20 |
| | Total | 260 | 100.00 |
| Age | 20-30 | 132 | 50.80 |
| | 30-50 | 065 | 25.00 |
| | Above 50 | 063 | 24.20 |
| | Total | 260 | 100.00 |
| Level of Using Generative AI Proficiency | High | 092 | 35.40 |
| | Medium | 115 | 44.20 |
| | Low | 053 | 20.40 |
| | Total | 260 | 100.00 |
| Education Level | College | 085 | 32.70 |
| | University | 095 | 36.60 |
| | Coaching | 080 | 30.80 |
| | Total | 260 | 100.00 |
| Awareness of AI Literacy | Yes | 228 | 87.70 |
| | No | 032 | 12.30 |
| | Total | 260 | 100.00 |

*Table 2. CR, Cronbach's alpha, and AVE*

| Constructs | Cron. 's alpha | AVE | CR | MSV |
|---|---|---|---|---|
| Generative AI Literacy (GAIL) | 0.768 | 0.519 | 0.403 | 0.425 |
| Digital Split (DS) | 0.880 | 0.501 | 0.608 | 0.521 |
| Computational Intelligence (CPI) | 0.807 | 0.632 | 0.606 | 0.488 |
| Cognitive Inclusion (COI) | 0.801 | 0.540 | 0.508 | 0.580 |
| Adaptable Sustainable Education (ASE) | 0.698 | 0.487 | 0.521 | 0.566 |

gent validity of the measurement model, indicating how well each manifest variable corresponds to its intended construct, and contributing to a comprehensive understanding of the measurement structure (Basco et al., 2022; Hair et al., 2018; Sarstedt et al., 2016).

Table 4 outlines the results of hypothesis testing, shedding light on the relationships between different constructs in the study. Starting with the association between Generative AI Literacy (GAIL) and Adaptable Sustainable Education (ASE), the beta coefficient of 0.422 suggests a positive relationship. The statistically significant t-statistic of 3.215 (p-value = 0.001) underscores the robustness of this connection, indicating that higher levels of generative AI literacy are associated with increased adaptability in sustainable education. This finding aligns with the notion that a deeper understanding of generative

*Figure 2. SEM framework for GAIL-ASE*

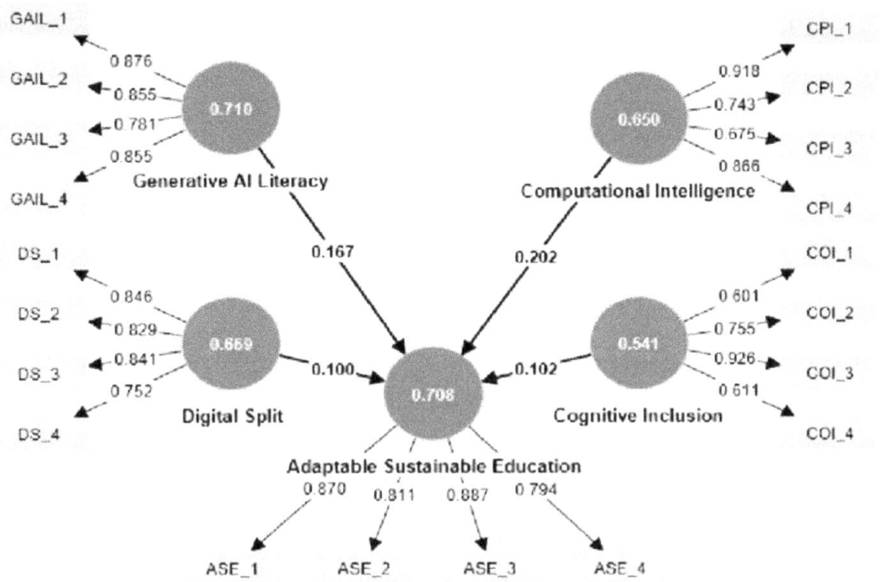


*Table 3. Cross loading of manifests*

| Manifests | GAIL | DS | CPI | COI | ASE |
|---|---|---|---|---|---|
| GAIL _1 | 0.703 | 0.165 | -0.087 | 0.15 | 0.051 |
| GAIL _2 | 0.840 | 0.103 | 0.120 | 0.103 | 0.193 |
| GAIL _3 | 0.787 | 0.195 | -0.167 | 0.192 | 0.365 |
| GAIL _4 | 0.761 | 0.127 | 0.229 | 0.312 | 0.274 |
| DS _1 | 0.331 | 0.806 | 0.346 | 0.316 | 0.538 |
| DS _2 | 0.231 | 0.707 | 0.106 | 0.206 | 0.135 |
| DS _3 | 0.218 | 0.803 | 0.065 | 0.067 | 0.152 |
| DS _4 | 0.203 | 0.735 | 0.193 | 0.320 | 0.413 |
| CPI _1 | 0.304 | 0.305 | 0.878 | 0.350 | 0239 |
| CPI _2 | 0.124 | 0.202 | 0.809 | 0.305 | 0.203 |
| CPI _3 | 0.104 | 0.224 | 0.705 | 0.199 | 0.281 |
| CPI _4 | 0.241 | 0.344 | 0.863 | 0.494 | 0.337 |
| COI _1 | 0.224 | 0.214 | 0.297 | 0.779 | 0.139 |
| COI _2 | 0.291 | 0.124 | 0.334 | 0.697 | 0.294 |
| COI _3 | 0.330 | 0.344 | 0.359 | 0.780 | 0.394 |
| COI _4 | 0.165 | 0.341 | 0.285 | 0.890 | 0.310 |
| ASE _1 | 0.309 | 0.314 | 0.100 | 0.102 | 0.778 |
| ASE _2 | 0.315 | 0.324 | 0.221 | 0.287 | 0.812 |
| ASE _3 | 0.281 | 0.104 | 0.192 | 0.094 | 0.872 |
| ASE _4 | 0.230 | 0.148 | 0.175 | 0.562 | 0.627 |

*Table 4. Hypotheses testing*

| Manifests | B. stat. | X mean | Sigma | T-stat | Sig. |
|---|---|---|---|---|---|
| Generative AI Literacy (GAIL) → Adaptable Sustainable Education (ASE) | 0.422 | 0.352 | 0.244 | 3.215 | 0.001 |
| Digital Split (DS) → Adaptable Sustainable Education (ASE) | 4.551 | 1.322 | 1.066 | 4.211 | 0.001 |
| Computational Intelligence (CPI) → Adaptable Sustainable Education (ASE) | 0.309 | 0.305 | 0.408 | 5.911 | 0.030 |
| Cognitive Inclusion (COI) → Adaptable Sustainable Education (ASE) | 0.466 | 1.028 | 1.360 | 5.118 | 0.000 |

AI positively influences educational adaptability, as suggested in prior research (Celik, 2023; Kamalov et al., 2023; Rejeb et al., 2024).

Moving to the relationship between Digital Split (DS) and Adaptable Sustainable Education (ASE), the substantial beta coefficient of 4.551 and a significant t-statistic of 4.211 (p-value = 0.001) highlight a strong positive connection. This suggests that a greater degree of digital split, possibly reflecting the integration of digital technologies, correlates with increased adaptability in sustainable education. This finding resonates with previous studies emphasizing the role of digitalization in shaping adaptable educational practices and aligns with the digital transformation trends in education observed in contemporary literature (Bhatt & Muduli, 2023; Cheng & Wang, 2023; Purohit et al., 2022).

The hypothesis involving Computational Intelligence (CPI) and its impact on Adaptable Sustainable Education (ASE) reveals a beta coefficient of 0.309 and a remarkably significant t-statistic of 5.911 (p-value = 0.030). This implies that higher levels of computational intelligence are associated with increased adaptability in sustainable education. This finding corroborates with existing research highlighting the importance of computational intelligence in fostering adaptive educational practices, as reported in (Bouteraa et al., 2024; Gaurav Kumar Singh & Manish dadhich, 2023; Shal et al., 2024; Waqar et al., 2023).

Lastly, the hypothesis explored the relationship between Cognitive Inclusion (COI) and Adaptable Sustainable Education (ASE) yields a significant beta coefficient of 0.466 and a substantial t-statistic of 5.118 (p-value = 0.000). This indicates a positive and robust connection, suggesting that cognitive inclusion plays a pivotal role in enhancing adaptability within sustainable education contexts. These findings resonate with prior studies emphasizing the significance of cognitive inclusivity for fostering adaptive and inclusive educational environments (Celik, 2023; Golab-Andrzejak, 2022; Sonali Bhati; Manish Dadhich; Anand A Bhasker; Kamal Kant Hiran; Roshni Sharma; Anurag, 2023).

The results of the hypothesis testing in Table 4 provide empirical support for the positive relationships between Generative AI Literacy, Digital Split, Computational Intelligence, Cognitive Inclusion, and Adaptable Sustainable Education. These findings contribute valuable insights to the ongoing discourse on the intersection of artificial intelligence, digital technologies, cognitive aspects, and adaptability in educational settings, corroborating and extending the findings from previous research in the field.

## PRACTICAL IMPLICATIONS

Understanding the dynamic determinants of Generative AI Literacy for ASE has profound implications for higher education. Institutions should incorporate targeted AI literacy programs into their curriculum to equip educators with the necessary skills. Integrating generative AI into teaching methodologies could enhance adaptability and sustainability, fostering a future-ready educational system. Educators must undergo continuous professional development to stay abreast of evolving AI technologies. Workshops, training sessions, and collaborative platforms should be established to facilitate knowledge exchange among educators, promoting a collective understanding of AI literacy and its applications for ASE. Education policymakers should consider formulating guidelines that encourage the integration of generative AI literacy within higher education. Policies should address digital inclusivity, ensuring equitable access to AI technologies, and promoting a supportive environment for Cognitive Inclusion (Dadhich, Manish, Shalendra Singh Rao, Renu Sharma, 2023). Institutions should invest in the latest AI technologies and platforms to create an immersive learning environment. This includes providing access to AI tools, software, and resources that enhance educators' proficiency, and fostering a culture of technological innovation. Encouraging research on the intersection of AI literacy, Adaptable Sustainable Education, and Cognitive Inclusion is essential.

Funding opportunities should be provided to support innovative projects that explore the impact of AI on educational outcomes and inclusivity. Given the global nature of AI, international collaboration is crucial. Institutions should foster partnerships and collaborations to share best practices, research findings, and resources. This global exchange will contribute to a collective understanding and advancement of AI literacy in the context of ASE. The focus on AI literacy and Adaptable Sustainable Education should ultimately benefit students. Institutions should prioritize creating learning experiences that leverage generative AI, ensuring students are well-prepared for a technologically advanced and dynamically changing future. Incorporating ethical considerations in AI literacy programs is paramount. Education stakeholders should emphasize responsible AI use, ensuring that educators are equipped to navigate ethical dilemmas and teach students about the ethical implications of AI technologies. These implications collectively advocate for a holistic and proactive approach to integrating Generative AI Literacy into higher education, fostering a sustainable, inclusive, and technologically advanced educational landscape.

## LIMITATIONS AND FUTURE SCOPE

The study's reliance on a convenient sample of 260 teachers in higher education may limit the generalizability of the findings to a broader population. Future research could explore larger and more diverse samples for increased external validity. The data collected through structured questionnaires may be subject to self-report bias, as participants might provide socially desirable responses. Incorporating additional data sources, such as classroom observations or interviews, could enhance the validity of the study. The cross-sectional nature of the study restricts the ability to establish causal relationships between variables. A longitudinal design could offer a more comprehensive understanding of the dynamic determinants of Generative AI Literacy over time. The study may be limited by focusing on teachers from a specific geographic location. Future research could explore the cross-cultural variations in AI literacy and its impact on Adaptable Sustainable Education. The study assumes a certain level of technology access among participants. Variability in technology infrastructure and access across educational institutions may impact the generalizability of the findings.

Conducting longitudinal studies could provide insights into the evolving nature of Generative AI Literacy and its impact on Adaptable Sustainable Education over an extended period. Future research could compare the effectiveness of different educational interventions aimed at improving Generative AI Literacy. This could include comparing the outcomes of diverse teaching methods or professional development programs. Complementing quantitative findings with qualitative exploration, such as interviews or focus group discussions, could offer a deeper understanding of the experiences, perceptions, and challenges faced by educators in integrating generative AI into their teaching practices. Investigating the impact of Generative AI Literacy on Adaptable Sustainable Education across diverse cultural and regional contexts could contribute to a more comprehensive understanding of its implications on a global scale. Future studies could explore innovative models of technology-enhanced learning that leverage generative AI to create adaptive, personalized, and sustainable learning environments. Further research should delve into the ethical considerations associated with AI literacy in education, exploring educators' awareness of ethical issues and their integration into instructional practices. Addressing these limitations and pursuing these future research directions can contribute to a more nuanced understanding of the dynamic determinants of Generative AI Literacy and its role in fostering Adaptable Sustainable Education.

## CONCLUSION

This study has explored the multifaceted landscape of AI literacy within the higher education context. The findings, though subject to certain limitations, shed light on the intricate relationships between Generative AI Literacy, Digital Split, Computational Intelligence, and Cognitive Inclusion. The implications underscore the need for targeted educational interventions, professional development initiatives, and policy frameworks to foster a technologically empowered, inclusive, and sustainable educational ecosystem. While acknowledging the study's limitations, including sample size constraints and potential biases, the insights garnered pave the way for future research endeavors. Longitudinal studies, cross-cultural analyses, and in-depth qualitative investigations are recommended to enrich our understanding of the dynamic determinants identified. Moreover, the ethical dimensions of AI literacy in education merit continued exploration. In the rapidly evolving landscape of education and technology, this research contributes to the ongoing discourse on preparing educators for the challenges and opportunities presented by generative AI. The study's outcomes serve as a foundation for shaping informed policies, innovative teaching practices, and collaborative efforts that align with the vision of Adaptable Sustainable Education in an AI-driven era.

## REFERENCES

Aggarwal, D., Sharma, D., & Saxena, A. B. (2023). Exploring the Role of Artificial Intelligence for Augmentation of Adaptable Sustainable Education. *Asian Journal of Advanced Research and Reports, 17*(11), 179–184. doi:10.9734/ajarr/2023/v17i11563

Atreides, K. (2021). E-governance with ethical living democracy. *Procedia Computer Science, 190*, 35–39. doi:10.1016/j.procs.2021.06.004

Basco, R., Hair, J. F. Jr, Ringle, C. M., & Sarstedt, M. (2022). Advancing family business research through modeling nonlinear relationships : Comparing PLS-SEM and multiple regression. *Journal of Family Business Strategy, 13*(3), 1–12. doi:10.1016/j.jfbs.2021.100457

Benzaquen, J., & Charles, V. (2020). A stratified bootstrapping approach to assessing the success of TQM implementation in Peruvian companies. *Total Quality Management & Business Excellence*, *0*(0), 1–24. doi:10.1080/14783363.2020.1816165

Bhati, S.; Manish Dadhich; Anand A Bhasker; Kamal Kant Hiran; Roshni Sharma; Anurag. (2023). Quantifying the Contemporary Enablers in Achieving e-Governance for Sustainable Techno-Societal Development: A High Directive SEM Analysis. *2023 International Conference on Emerging Trends in Networks and Computer Communications (ETNCC)*, (pp. 157–162). IEEE. 10.1109/ETNCC59188.2023.10284979

Bhatt, P., & Muduli, A. (2023). Artificial intelligence in learning and development: A systematic literature review. *European Journal of Training and Development*, *47*(7–8), 677–694. doi:10.1108/EJTD-09-2021-0143

Bouteraa, M., Chekima, B., Thurasamy, R., Bin-Nashwan, S. A., Al-Daihani, M., Baddou, A., Sadallah, M., & Ansar, R. (2024). Open Innovation in the Financial Sector: A Mixed-Methods Approach to Assess Bankers' Willingness to Embrace Open-AI ChatGPT. *Journal of Open Innovation*, *10*(1), 1–14. doi:10.1016/j.joitmc.2024.100216

Celik, I. (2022). Exploring the Determinants of Artificial Intelligence (Ai) Literacy: Digital Divide, Computational Thinking, Cognitive Absorption. SSRN *Electronic Journal, 83*(7), 1–11. doi:10.2139/ssrn.4244763

Celik, I. (2023). Exploring the Determinants of Artificial Intelligence (AI) Literacy: Digital Divide, Computational Thinking, Cognitive Absorption. *Telematics and Informatics*, *83*(7), 1–14. doi:10.1016/j.tele.2023.102026

Cheng, E. C. K., & Wang, T. (2023). Leading digital transformation and eliminating barriers for teachers to incorporate artificial intelligence in basic education in Hong Kong. *Computers and Education: Artificial Intelligence*, *5*(10), 1–12. doi:10.1016/j.caeai.2023.100171

Chiu, T. K. F. (2024). Future research recommendations for transforming higher education with generative AI. *Computers and Education: Artificial Intelligence*, *6*(12), 1–15. doi:10.1016/j.caeai.2023.100197

Dadhich, M., Hiran, K. K., Rao, S. S., & Sharma, R. (2022). Impact of Covid-19 on Teaching-Learning Perception of Faculties and Students of Higher Education in Indian Purview. *Journal of Mobile Multimedia*, *18*(4), 957–980. doi:10.13052/jmm1550-4646.1841

Dadhich, Manish, Rao, Shalendra Singh, & Sharma, Renu, R. M. (2023). Emerging Determinants and Analyatics of Off-balance Sheet Activities (OBSA) of Commercial Banks. *Finance India*, *XXXVII*(2), 383–400.

Dadhich, M., Rathore, S., Akwasi, B., Ajibade, S. M., & Agozie, D. Q. (2023). Quantifying the Dynamic Factors Influencing New-Age Users' Adoption of 5G Using TAM and UTAUT Models in Emerging Country : A Multistage PLS-SEM Approach. *Education Research International*, *1*, 1–15. doi:10.1155/2023/5452563

Dadhich, M., & Tiwari, H. (2022). Quantum Blockchain for Smart Society: Applications, Challenges, and Opportunities. In Advancements in Quantum Blockchain With Real-Time Applications. IGI Global. doi:10.4018/978-1-6684-5072-7.ch009

Dadhich, M., Yadav, P., Saxena, A., Birda, R. K., Mathur, S., & Hiran, K. K. (2023). Dynamic Determinants of AI-Based Innovation Management Practices and Sustainable FinTech: Application Preferences of AI-Innovators. *2023 IEEE International Conference on Contemporary Computing and Communications (InC4)*, (pp. 1–5). IEEE. 10.1109/InC457730.2023.10263140

Gaurav, K. (2023). Empirical investigation of industry 4.0 for sustainable growth and implication for future-ready compatibility for cement industry of India. *AIP Conference Proceedings*, *2521*(040026), 1–12. 978-0-7354-4650-2/$30.00

Golab-Andrzejak, E. (2022). Enhancing Customer Engagement in Social Media with AI - a Higher Education case study. *Procedia Computer Science*, *207*, 3022–3031. doi:10.1016/j.procs.2022.09.361

Hair, J. F., Risher, J. J., & Ringle, C. M. (2018). When to use and how to report the results of PLS-SEM. *European Business Review*, *31*(1), 2–24. doi:10.1108/EBR-11-2018-0203

Ji, Y., Bai, Y., Liu, X., & Jia, K. (2020). Progress of liquid crystal polyester (LCP) for 5G application. *Advanced Industrial and Engineering Polymer Research*, *3*(4), 160–174. doi:10.1016/j.aiepr.2020.10.005

Kamalov, F., Santandreu Calonge, D., & Gurrib, I. (2023). New Era of Artificial Intelligence in Education: Towards a Sustainable Multifaceted Revolution. *Sustainability (Basel)*, *15*(16), 1–27. doi:10.3390/su151612451

Kar, A. K., Choudhary, S. K., & Singh, V. K. (2022). How can artificial intelligence impact sustainability: A systematic literature review. *Journal of Cleaner Production*, *376*(5), 1–15. doi:10.1016/j.jclepro.2022.134120

Lohr, A., Stadler, M., Schultz-Pernice, F., Chernikova, O., Sailer, M., Fischer, F., & Sailer, M. (2021). On powerpointers, clickerers, and digital pros: Investigating the initiation of digital learning activities by teachers in higher education. *Computers in Human Behavior, 119*(October 2020), 106715. doi:10.1016/j.chb.2021.106715

Lyons, A. C., Kass-Hanna, J., & Fava, A. (2022). Fintech development and savings, borrowing, and remittances: A comparative study of emerging economies. *Emerging Markets Review*, *51*, 100842. doi:10.1016/j.ememar.2021.100842

Mijwil, M. M., Hiran, K. K., Doshi, R., Dadhich, M., & Bala, I. (2023). ChatGPT and the Future of Academic Integrity in the Artificial Intelligence Era: A New Frontier. *Al-Salam Journal for Engineering and Technology*, *2*(2), 116–127. doi:10.55145/ajest.2023.02.02.015

Purohit, H., Dadhich, M., & Ajmera, P. K. (2022). Analytical study on users' awareness and acceptability towards adoption of multimodal biometrics (MMB) mechanism in online transactions : A two-stage SEM-ANN approach. *Multimedia Tools and Applications*, *1*, 1–25. doi:10.1007/s11042-022-13786-z PMID:36157357

Rejeb, A., Rejeb, K., Appolloni, A., Treiblmaier, H., & Iranmanesh, M. (2024). Exploring the impact of ChatGPT on education: A web mining and machine learaning approach. *International Journal of Management Education*, *22*(1), 1–14. doi:10.1016/j.ijme.2024.100932

Robles-Carrillo, M. (2021). European Union policy on 5G: Context, scope and limits. *Telecommunications Policy*, *45*(8), 102216. doi:10.1016/j.telpol.2021.102216

Rohde, F., Wagner, J., Meyer, A., Reinhard, P., Voss, M., Petschow, U., & Mollen, A. (2024). Broadening the perspective for sustainable artificial intelligence: Sustainability criteria and indicators for Artificial Intelligence systems. *Current Opinion in Environmental Sustainability*, *66*, 1–12. doi:10.1016/j.cosust.2023.101411

Sarstedt, M., Hair, J. F. Jr, Cheah, J., Becker, J., & Ringle, C. M. (2019). How to specify, estimate, and validate higher-order constructs in. [AMJ]. *Australasian Marketing Journal*, *27*(3), 197–211. doi:10.1016/j.ausmj.2019.05.003

Sarstedt, M., Hair, J. F., Ringle, C. M., Thiele, K. O., & Gudergan, S. P. (2016). Estimation issues with PLS and CBSEM : Where the bias lies. *Journal of Business Research*, *69*(10), 3998–4010. doi:10.1016/j.jbusres.2016.06.007

Segbenya, M., Bervell, B., Frimpong-Manso, E., Otoo, I. C., Andzie, T. A., & Achina, S. (2023). Artificial intelligence in higher education: Modelling the antecedents of artificial intelligence usage and effects on 21st century employability skills among postgraduate students in Ghana. *Computers and Education: Artificial Intelligence*, *5*, 1–12. doi:10.1016/j.caeai.2023.100188

Shal, T., Ghamrawi, N., & Naccache, H. (2024). Leadership styles and AI acceptance in academic libraries in higher education. *Journal of Academic Librarianship*, *50*(2), 1–16. doi:10.1016/j.acalib.2024.102849

Shukla, A., Dadhich, M., Vaya, D., & Goel, A. (2024). Impact of Behavioral Biases on Investors' Stock Trading Decisions : A Comparehensive Quantitative Analysis. *Indian Journal of Science and Technology*, *17*(8), 670–678. doi:10.17485/IJST/v17i8.2845

Waqar, A., Andri, Qureshi, A. H., Almujibah, H. R., Tanjung, L. E., & Utami, C. (2023). Evaluation of success factors of utilizing AI in digital transformation of health and safety management systems in modern construction projects. *Ain Shams Engineering Journal*, *14*(11), 1–17. doi:10.1016/j.asej.2023.102551

Wibowo, A., Narmaditya, B. S., Suparno, Sebayang, K. D. A., Mukhtar, S., & Shafiai, M. H. M. (2023). How does digital entrepreneurship education promote entrepreneurial intention? The role of social media and entrepreneurial intuition. *Social Sciences & Humanities Open*, *8*(1), 100681. doi:10.1016/j.ssaho.2023.100681

Zhou, C., Liu, X., Yu, C., Tao, Y., & Shao, Y. (2024). Trust in AI-augmented design: Applying structural equation modeling to AI-augmented design acceptance. *Heliyon*, *10*(1), 1–15. doi:10.1016/j.heliyon.2023.e23305 PMID:38192792

# Chapter 5
# Ethical Considerations and Data Privacy in Artificial Intelligence

**Rishi Prakash Shukla**
https://orcid.org/0000-0003-0854-7302
*Chandigarh University, India*

**Sanjay Taneja**
https://orcid.org/0000-0002-3632-4053
*Graphic Era University (deemed), India*

## ABSTRACT

*This chapter explores the intricate relationship between privacy and ethics in the realm of artificial intelligence (AI). With the proliferation of AI technologies, concerns about data privacy and ethical implications have intensified. The abstract delves into the ethical dilemmas arising from the collection, analysis, and utilization of sensitive data, emphasizing the need for robust frameworks that balance technological advancement with safeguarding individual rights. It examines the challenges of maintaining privacy in AI-driven systems while adhering to ethical principles, offering insights into the current landscape, potential risks, and promising solutions for creating a responsible and transparent AI ecosystem.*

## INTRODUCTION

### Definition and Significance Of Privacy and Ethics in the Context of AI

In the context of artificial intelligence (AI), privacy and ethics are crucial because of how quickly technology is developing and how that blurs the lines separating personal data security from ethical considerations (Robert et al., 2018). In this context, ethics refers to the ethical and equitable use of AI to prevent harm and advance society well-being (Floridi et al., 2018), while privacy refers to the fundamental right of individuals to control their personal information, ensuring that AI systems do not intrude upon their private life (Mai, 2016). These guidelines are important because they protect against algorithmic biases, data breaches, and the possible misuse of AI for monitoring or decision-making. A strong foundation

DOI: 10.4018/979-8-3693-2440-0.ch005

for privacy and ethics is necessary as AI is incorporated more and more into daily life in order to strike a balance between innovation and protecting human rights fostering trust in AI systems, and ensuring they benefit rather than harm society (Floridi & Cowls, 2022).

One cannot stress the importance of these ideas enough. First and foremost, they are essential for safeguarding sensitive data from breaches and preserving its confidentiality, particularly in the age of big data and networked systems. Second, they play a crucial role in correcting algorithmic biases that have the potential to support social injustice and prejudice. Furthermore, privacy and ethics are critical to establishing user confidence, trust in AI systems, and ensuring that AI is used to advance society rather than do harm (Ryan, 2020).

As artificial intelligence continues to be integrated into more and more aspects of daily life, it is necessary to have a strong and dynamic foundation for privacy and ethics. In addition to ensuring that the potential benefits of AI innovation are fully realised while minimising potential hazards and ethical issues, such a framework also protects the rights and interests of humans. In this sense, privacy and AI ethics support a more fair, just, and peaceful coexistence of mankind with cutting-edge technology.

## Historical Background and Key Milestones in the Development of AI Ethics and Privacy Concerns

The confluence of ethical requirements and technical advancements has influenced the complicated historical history of AI ethics and privacy concerns (Bonawitz et al., 2017). These worries have their roots in the early development of artificial intelligence throughout the middle of the 20th century. The idea of machines mimicking human cognitive functions was unintentionally introduced by early AI pioneers like Alan Turing, who laid the core concepts of machine intelligence (Street, 2005). The subsequent decades saw the development of AI technology, which raised concerns about potential ethical and privacy implications. The release of Isaac Asimov's Three Laws of Robotics, which established an early framework for the ethical obligations of AI, and the creation of the first AI systems are significant turning points in this history. in the 1950s and 1960s, raising questions about the moral implications of creating intelligent machines.

AI continued to progress throughout the 1970s and 1980s, as discussions over the morality of treating sentient computers heated up (Torrance, 2013). As the internet and other digital technologies spread throughout the 1990s, privacy concerns gained prominence and sparked conversations about data security and surveillance. Important developments in the early 21st century included the emergence of social media platforms and the subject of machine ethics, which brought up concerns about algorithmic bias, filter bubbles, and the improper use of personal data. The 2018 Cambridge Analytica incident and the development of deep learning methods have increased the demand for ethical standards.

AI ethics and privacy problems are at a turning point in our life as these systems continue to advance and penetrate more areas of our existence (Formosa et al., 2021). In order to address concerns like accountability, transparency, equity, and privacy protection, governments, organisations, and researchers are proactively establishing rules and ethical frameworks (Stahl & Wright, 2018). It will take time to find a way to balance AI's limitless potential with upholding human values. Along the way, we must constantly adapt to the rapidly changing technological environment and make sure that AI systems act in society's best interests while upholding the core ethical and privacy principles.

### Importance of Addressing Privacy and Ethical Considerations in AI Applications

Today's technologically advanced society places a premium on AI applications taking privacy and ethical issues into account. As AI technologies become more and more ingrained in our daily lives—from social media and healthcare to banking and education—it is crucial to make sure these platforms are operated morally and sensibly. AI's ability to handle and analyse enormous volumes of personal data raises privacy concerns, and it is imperative that personal data be protected from misuse and unauthorised access (Tene & Polonetsky, 2013). Furthermore, as prejudiced or discriminating algorithms have the potential to uphold stereotypes and perpetuate societal injustices, ethical considerations are crucial in establishing how AI systems make judgements. As a result, taking a proactive stance in resolving these difficulties goes beyond simply following the law.

## UNDERSTANDING PRIVACY AND ETHICS IN AI

### Overview of Privacy Concerns in the Collection and Use of Data for AI Algorithms

In the digital age, privacy concerns in the gathering and processing of data for AI algorithms are critical(Stahl & Wright, 2018). A number of concerns surface as AI technologies become more and more dependent on large datasets for development and operation. Top worries are data security and privacy, which include the possibility of unauthorised access and data breaches that could reveal sensitive personal data (Barona & Anita, 2017). Consent to be informed is still often lacking, as information is routinely collected without the knowledge or agreement of the subjects. One important idea that should not be forgotten is data minimization, which might result in excessive data collecting and a higher chance of misuse. Sometimes de-identification measures are unsuccessful, which allows for re-identification and jeopardises personal privacy. Due to the fact that biased training data can maintain unfavourable results, bias and discrimination are widespread issues. Legal and regulatory issues are always changing, and once data is obtained, people frequently have no control over it. Finding technological, governmental, and moral answers to these issues is necessary to create a balance between privacy protection and innovation (Leenes et al., 2017).

### Examination of Ethical Frameworks and Principles Guiding the Development and Deployment of AI Technologies

In order to ensure the appropriate and ethical use of AI technologies, a set of ethical frameworks and principles drive their development and deployment. Fairness and non-discrimination are two of these values, which highlight the necessity of preventing prejudice and discrimination in AI systems (Wachter et al., 2020). In AI decision-making processes, explain ability and transparency promote accountability and openness. Determining who bears responsibility for the behaviour of AI systems and resolving errors or harm requires accountability and responsibility. Respecting personal information and following privacy laws are essential to privacy and data protection. Human well-being and goodness emphasise that AI should advance mankind and make people's lives better. Development of environmentally friendly

AI is aided by sustainability and environmental effect considerations (Chaudhary, 2023). International cooperation and standards are prioritised in global collaboration and governance. The goal of benefit sharing and equality is to equally distribute the advantages of AI without making societal disparities worse. Protecting against harm requires safety and security, and continuing learning and monitoring support the ethical development and modification of AI systems so that they are in line with moral principles and the interests of society. These guidelines offer a framework for the ethical and reliable development and application of AI.

### Exploration of the Intersection Between Privacy, Ethics, and AI in Various Domains

Artificial intelligence (AI) and privacy are closely related in many different fields, raising difficult questions and moral dilemmas. AI helps in diagnosis and treatment in the medical field, but it also raises questions about algorithmic fairness and patient data privacy (Johnson et al., 2021). AI is used in finance for fraud detection and credit evaluation; however, the usage of private financial information calls for strict privacy protection. AI-powered risk assessment and predictive policing in the criminal justice system have the potential to violate privacy and reinforce prejudices. AI-driven personalization in education must address privacy and equality issues. AI is used by social media and advertising to deliver personalised information and advertisements, which has sparked discussions about algorithmic manipulation and user privacy. In addition to gathering data, autonomous cars can pose moral dilemmas on making decisions in dire circumstances. AI is used by national security for monitoring, necessitating a careful balancing act between state interests and personal privacy. AI-driven marketing in retail uses consumer data, raising concerns about where personalization and privacy end. Ethics must be taken into account while using AI for environmental monitoring in order to safeguard ecosystems and public privacy. AI used for employee surveillance in the workplace needs to abide by ethical and privacy standards. To enable responsible AI development and deployment across all of these sectors, it is essential to establish clear legislation and norms that place a priority on privacy, transparency, accountability, and ethical evaluation (Jobin et al., 2019).

## CURRENT LANDSCAPE OF PRIVACY AND ETHICS IN AI

### Review of Existing Regulations and Guidelines Governing the Use of AI in Different Industries

The swift progress of artificial intelligence (AI) technology in recent times has led to regulatory endeavours aimed at guaranteeing the conscientious and principled application of AI in diverse sectors. The regulatory environment surrounding AI differs by industry, reflecting the unique potential and problems that each one faces. This section offers a thorough analysis of current laws and policies in important sectors where artificial intelligence is having a big influence:

## The Healthcare Industry

With the introduction of AI, the healthcare sector has experienced a significant metamorphosis, especially in areas like patient diagnostics, medication discovery, and medical imaging. In this industry, regulations try to find a middle ground between using AI's potential to improve medical care and addressing important ethical and privacy concerns. Notably, the Health Insurance Portability and Accountability Act (HIPAA) in the United States has set strict guidelines for protecting sensitive patient data. As AI becomes more common in healthcare, these guidelines are being extended to include AI applications for the handling and storage of medical data. In the meanwhile, strict guidelines are enforced by the European Union's Medical Device Regulation (MDR), which is committed to guaranteeing the effectiveness and safety of medical devices, including software driven by artificial intelligence. Additionally, since the American Medical Association (AMA) and other medical organisations have published ethical standards governing the use of AI, the sector is guided by ethical principles. These rules place a significant focus on patient consent, openness, and data protection.

## Sector of Financial Services

The quick adoption of AI in the financial services sector has transformed tasks like algorithmic trading, fraud detection, and customer support. The crucial task of guaranteeing the moral application of AI in financial services has been placed in the hands of regulatory agencies. While not specifically addressing AI, the Dodd-Frank Act in the US requires accountability and openness in the financial markets, which is relevant to AI applications, especially in areas like risk management and algorithmic trading. Furthermore, a number of jurisdictions—including the European Union—have passed algorithmic trading-specific legislation that prioritise risk management, market surveillance, and the promotion of fair competition. In order to protect consumer interests, the Consumer Financial Protection Bureau (CFPB) publishes guidelines that control the use of AI in credit underwriting. These guidelines place a strong emphasis on the values of justice, transparency, and non-discrimination.

## The Automotive Industry

AI is a fundamental component in the development of autonomous vehicles and advanced driver-assistance systems. Regulations play a crucial role in ensuring the safety and security of AI-driven automotive technologies. The National Highway Traffic Safety Administration (NHTSA) in the United States issues guidelines that prioritize safety in the testing and deployment of autonomous vehicles. Simultaneously, the UN Economic Commission for Europe (ECE) has established regulations specific to automated driving systems, with a focus on AI-driven components, striving to create international standards. Additionally, cybersecurity regulations have been implemented in response to the integration of AI into vehicles to protect against potential cyber threats, ensuring the integrity and security of connected cars.

## The Energy and Utilities Sector

AI is essential to the energy and utilities sectors since it helps with predictive maintenance, power grid optimisation, and energy saving. The purpose of regulations in this field is to maintain the sustainability and dependability of AI-driven solutions. Notably, cybersecurity laws regulating AI applications in grid management are established by the North American Electric Reliability Corporation (NERC), which also sets reliability criteria for the North American bulk power system. In order to improve operational resilience and efficiency, the European Network of Transmission System Operators for Electricity (ENTSO-E) has established standards that integrate AI into grid management. Environmental rules are essential in addition to technical standards, as they guarantee that AI technologies in the energy sector support sustainable energy practises and ecologically responsible energy usage.

### Evaluation of the Role of Organizations and Policymakers in Ensuring Privacy and Ethical AI Practices

AI practises emphasises their shared accountability in influencing artificial intelligence's future. In this context, organisations play a crucial role since they have to put in place thorough data governance frameworks, give transparency top priority, and incorporate ethical issues into the AI development process. The core principles of their operations must be user consent and data protection. Conversely, policymakers are essential in developing and implementing legal frameworks that establish moral principles and guarantee privacy standards in the AI space. In order to achieve the delicate balance between technical innovation and the protection of individual privacy and ethical norms, cooperation and synergy between organisations and politicians are essential, ultimately encouraging AI's good impact.

## THE IMPLICATIONS OF PRIVACY AND ETHICS IN AI

### Impact of AI on Individual Privacy Rights and Data Protection

In the current digital era, the effects of artificial intelligence on personal privacy rights and data protection are complex and always changing. On the one hand, by automating security procedures and enabling more reliable encryption and authentication techniques, AI technologies have the potential to improve data protection. The fact that this same technology may be used to gather, examine, and exploit enormous amounts of personal data without permission, however, also presents serious concerns to people's privacy. Machine learning algorithms have the ability to unearth personal information about people, which opens the door to possible misuses including discriminatory decision-making, invasive surveillance, and targeted advertising. A crucial issue facing governments, businesses, and society at large is finding a balance between protecting privacy and utilising AI's benefits.

### Ethical Considerations in the Development of AI Algorithms and Decision-Making Processes

The increasing integration of AI systems into diverse societal domains such as healthcare, finance, criminal justice, and autonomous vehicles necessitates careful consideration of design and implementation approaches that prioritise equity, accountability, transparency, and human welfare. AI ethics cover a wide range of topics, such as algorithmic transparency, data privacy, accountability, bias and discrimination, and the possibility that AI will reinforce or worsen already-existing inequities. AI algorithm developers and stakeholders should make an effort to develop algorithms that are devoid of bias, or if bias does exist, it should be recognised, addressed, and minimised. Transparency is essential because it fosters confidence and makes it possible to examine AI decision-making procedures to make sure they adhere to human values. In order to hold developers and organisations accountable for the results of AI activity, accountability measures need be in place. To stop the misuse of personal data, privacy and data protection must also be protected. AI development ought to incorporate ethical concerns from the outset in order to steer the technology towards a more egalitarian and just future.

### Consequences of AI-Driven Biases and Discriminatory Practices on Society and Marginalized Groups

Due to the fact that AI algorithms are frequently trained on data reflecting past biases and prejudices, discrimination may eventually be automated in a variety of contexts, including lending, hiring, criminal justice, and healthcare. As a result, marginalised groups suffer from systemic injustices and unjust treatment by AI systems. This undermines trust in institutions and technology in addition to perpetuating social injustices. Furthermore, it is challenging to hold many AI algorithms accountable because to their opacity, which further marginalises individuals who are impacted. In order to eliminate bias and guarantee that AI systems benefit all members of society, addressing these concerns calls for a deliberate effort to ensure justice, transparency, and equity in AI research and deployment. It also calls for the inclusion of various perspectives and expertise.

## RESEARCH METHODOLOGY

### Research Approach

#### Literature Review of Existing Studies, Papers, and Reports on AI Ethics and Privacy

Artificial Intelligence (AI) has quickly spread throughout our lives and had a big impact on a lot of different industries, such healthcare, banking, entertainment, and transportation(Dhanabalan et al., 2018). But the more AI systems are incorporated into our everyday lives, the more crucial it is to address the nuanced concerns about AI ethics and privacy. This study of the literature explores the complex aspects of this important subject.

A wide range of issues are covered by AI ethics, including as responsibility and transparency in algorithmic decision-making. Many AI systems are opaque, sometimes referred to as "black boxes," which makes it difficult to comprehend the reasoning behind their choices and actions. This opacity begs the questions of accountability for mishaps and the necessity of making AI systems just, transparent, and comprehensible. In addition, concerns about bias and fairness in AI systems have gained attention. AI decision-making processes that discriminate, such employment algorithms that give preference to particular demographic groups, have sparked a great deal of research and debate on how to reduce prejudice and guarantee fair results (Wachter et al., 2020).

On the other hand, privacy is a fundamental right that is becoming more and more endangered due to the growth of AI applications. For AI to work well, a lot of data—often sensitive data—is required. The danger of data breaches and unauthorised access increases as AI systems gather, examine, and utilise this data (Mughal, 2017). In the era of artificial intelligence, consent, data collecting ethics, and the ethical use of personal information are critical issues. The Cambridge Analytica incident and several data breaches have further highlighted how urgent it is to address these problems.

The legal environment is changing from a regulatory perspective to address these moral and privacy issues (Leenes et al., 2017). A good example is the General Data Protection Regulation (GDPR) of the European Union, which imposes severe fines for noncompliance and introduces strict data protection procedures. Additionally, organisations such as the Association for Computing Machinery (ACM) and the Institute of Electrical and Electronics Engineers (IEEE) have developed AI ethical standards to offer a framework for responsible AI development and deployment. The purpose of this review is to give readers a thorough understanding of these problems, the changing regulatory landscape, and the continuing academic discussion around AI ethics and privacy. It emphasises the importance of ethical considerations and practical regulatory measures in order to responsibly navigate the AI-driven world.

## Case Study Analysis of Notable Incidents Related to AI and Privacy Breaches

Artificial intelligence has a significant impact on people's privacy and data security, as evidenced by the examination of prominent cases involving AI and privacy breaches. The Facebook and Cambridge Analytica scandals raised ethical questions about the use of data and its manipulation for political ends by exposing the frightening potential for AI-driven algorithms to gather enormous amounts of personal data without user consent. The significant data breach at Equifax highlighted the need for strict security standards and accountability by proving that even AI-powered data security systems can be vulnerable. A persistent worry, deepfake technology presents a distinct risk since it makes it possible to produce convincingly fake audio and video recordings, which can result in misinformation, political manipulation, and invasions of privacy. These case studies highlight the vital requirement for openness, morality, and strict laws to safeguard privacy in the era of AI, as well as the enduring challenges in combating evolving threats to data security and individual rights.

## Interviews With Experts and Stakeholders in the Field of AI and Data Privacy

Experts and stakeholders from several industries come together in the dynamic and complex topic of artificial intelligence (AI) and data privacy. This intersection offers tremendous opportunities as well as difficulties as it develops. The continued influence of data protection laws like the CCPA and GDPR, which have influenced how businesses handle personal data in AI applications, is one of the major themes. Finding a balance between data privacy and AI innovation is still a major challenge, and biases and ethical conundrums demand constant attention. Adopting technology that protect privacy, making sure AI models are transparent and explainable, and giving consumers permission and control over their data are all examples of best practises. In order to handle the complex issues at hand, cooperation between various sectors is necessary, and public awareness and education campaigns are crucial for creating a society that is better educated. Experts see exciting developments in AI and data privacy in the near future, but they also see new difficulties as technology develops. All things considered, negotiating this terrain requires a multimodal strategy that upholds privacy while using AI's potential.

# PROPOSED MODEL: PRIVACY AND ETHICS FRAMEWORK FOR AI GOVERNANCE

## Principles for responsible AI development and deployment

The framework for AI ethics is established in Figure 1, which also lists the elements that must be taken into account while defining AI ethics in order to create ethical AI. While defining AI ethics is complex and varied, putting AI ethics into practise to create ethical AI is also a difficult task. What kind of AI is morally appropriate? The basic definition of ethical AI is that it shouldn't hurt people. So what harm is there? What rights do people have? We have a long way to go before we can create and implement moral AI. To make appropriate ethical decisions, ethical sensitivity training is necessary. choices. AI should, in theory, be able to identify moral dilemmas. How can we create and build an AI that is aware of ethical issues if it is able to make decisions? Regretfully, it is difficult to realise and put into practise. Sustained and long-term efforts are required. Nevertheless, recognising the significance of creating ethical AI and beginning the process gradually are constructive moves in the right direction.

Numerous organisations, including Microsoft, IBM, Google, Accenture, and Atomium-EISMD, have begun developing ethical guidelines to direct the advancement of AI. In November 2018, the FEAT principles—fairness, ethics, accountability, and transparency—were introduced by the Monetary Authority of Singapore (MAS), Microsoft, and Amazon Web Services for the usage of of AI. Academics, practitioners, and policymakers should work together to widen the engagement to establish ethical principles for AI design, development, and use.

## Strategies for Safeguarding User Privacy and Data Security in AI Systems

Privacy-Preserving AI Techniques: Organisations can use privacy-preserving AI techniques like homomorphic encryption, safe multi-party computation, and federated learning to address privacy concerns (Bonawitz et al., 2017). By using these techniques, businesses may train AI models on dispersed data without having to share raw data, which lowers the possibility of data leaks or breaches. Adversarial

*Figure 1. Ethical framework of AI*

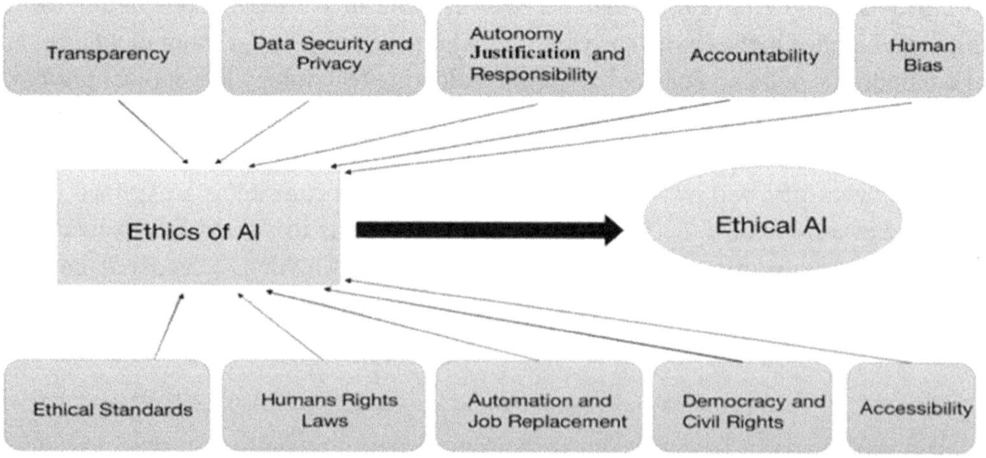

*Figure 2. Proposed solution for data privacy and security*

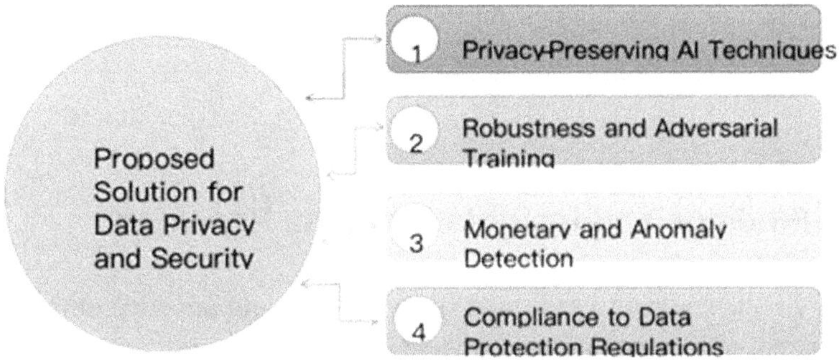


training strategies have been developed by researchers to enhance model resilience and protect against adversarial attacks. These techniques entail adding adversarial samples to a training dataset (Madry et al., 2018). The model learns to be more tolerant to adversarial perturbations by using both clean and adversarial data during training. Monitoring and anomaly detection: Businesses can use monitoring and anomaly detection methods to spot data poisoning and model tampering variations in the model's parameters, training set, or performance from what is expected (Lewis, 1998). Early detection can help stop additional harm to AI systems and offer insightful information for enhancing security protocols. Compliance with Data Protection Regulations: To make sure that they collect, store, and process data in a secure and compliant manner, organisations should abide by data protection regulations, such as the California Consumer Privacy Act (CCPA) in the United States and the General Data Protection Regulation (GDPR) in Europe (Ramirez et al., 2022). Respecting these rules can reduce the possibility of data breaches and safeguard user privacy.

Organisations that create and use AI systems have serious worries about data privacy and security issues. Organisations can improve the security and privacy of their AI systems by being aware of these issues and putting mitigation tactics in place, such as robustness training, privacy-preserving AI methodologies, and compliance with data protection laws. Researchers, practitioners, and legislators must collaborate to address these issues as AI develops and affects more sectors of the economy. Only then can we make sure that AI advances society without jeopardising user security and privacy.

## Guidelines for Addressing Ethical Dilemmas and Biases in AI Decision-Making Processes

A diverse strategy is necessary to address ethical concerns and biases in AI decision-making processes. Fairness, accountability, transparency, and the preservation of human rights should be given top priority while developing and implementing AI. It is imperative to first create clear ethical standards and rules in this regard. Data collection and training datasets should be representative, diversified, and routinely checked to detect and address potential biases in order to reduce biases. Companies and developers should be transparent about the data they utilise and how AI systems operate. Reducing biases can be achieved through using fairness measures, integrating diverse teams in AI development, and doing ongoing testing and monitoring. In addition, in the event that AI systems produce biased or incorrect conclusions, there should be procedures for responsibility and restitution. Collaboration and public involvement with ethicists, regulators, and the impacted communities can help foster responsible AI development and ensure that ethical considerations remain central in decision-making processes.

## CONCLUSION

### Summary of Key Findings and Insights From the Research

A multifaceted strategy is necessary to safeguard user privacy and advance ethical AI practises. This involves making sure that user consent for data gathering is relevant, maintaining strict laws and standards that control AI development and application, and ensuring transparency in AI algorithms. Prioritising data anonymization and encryption, performing frequent privacy effect analyses, and funding AI ethics training for staff members are all things that businesses should do. Establishing a framework that maintains ethical values, protects user privacy, and encourages responsible AI innovation while actively addressing any biases and discrimination will require cooperation between industry, government, and civil society.

### Future Considerations for the Ongoing Development and Regulation of AI in the Context of Privacy and Ethics

The protection of ethics and privacy must be the top priority as AI development and regulation continue to change. Future research should focus on creating strong privacy-preserving AI systems that reduce data exposure and give people control over their personal data in order to protect people and society. The establishment and enforcement of ethical standards is also necessary to guarantee that AI systems follow the values of accountability, transparency, and justice. Collaboration between governments, industry stakeholders, and academics will be important to find a balance between innovation and ethical application, thus establishing a responsible and trustworthy AI ecosystem for the benefit of all.

## REFERENCES

Barona, R., & Anita, E. A. M. (2017). A survey on data breach challenges in cloud computing security: Issues and threats. *2017 International Conference on Circuit, Power and Computing Technologies (ICCPCT)*, (pp. 1–8). IEEE. 10.1109/ICCPCT.2017.8074287

BonawitzK.EichnerH.GrieskampW.HubaD.IngermanA.IvanovV. (2017). Towards Federated Learning At Scale: System Design. arXiv:1902.01046v1.

Dhanabalan, T., Sathish, A., & Tamilnadu, K. (2018). *TRANSFORMING INDIAN INDUSTRIES THROUGH ARTIFICIAL INTELLIGENCE AND.*, *9*(10), 835–845.

Floridi, L., & Cowls, J. (2022). A unified framework of five principles for AI in society. *Machine Learning and the City: Applications in Architecture and Urban Design*, (pp. 535–545). Wiley. doi:10.1002/9781119815075.ch45

Floridi, L., Cowls, J., Beltrametti, M., Chatila, R., Chazerand, P., Dignum, V., Luetge, C., Madelin, R., Pagallo, U., Rossi, F., Schafer, B., Valcke, P., & Vayena, E. (2018). AI4People—An Ethical Framework for a Good AI Society: Opportunities, Risks, Principles, and Recommendations. *Minds and Machines*, *28*(4), 689–707. doi:10.1007/s11023-018-9482-5 PMID:30930541

Formosa, P., Wilson, M., & Richards, D. (2021). A principlist framework for cybersecurity ethics. *Computers & Security*, *109*, 102382. doi:10.1016/j.cose.2021.102382

Jobin, A., Ienca, M., & Vayena, E. (2019). *Artificial Intelligence: the global landscape of ethics guidelines.*

Johnson, K. B., Wei, W., Weeraratne, D., Frisse, M. E., Misulis, K., Rhee, K., Zhao, J., & Snowdon, J. L. (2021). Precision Medicine, AI, and the Future of Personalized Health Care. doi:10.1111/cts.12884

Leenes, R., Palmerini, E., Koops, B., Bertolini, A., Lucivero, F., Leenes, R., Palmerini, E., Koops, B., & Bertolini, A. (2017). *Regulatory challenges of robotics: some guidelines for addressing legal and ethical issues.* doi:10.1080/17579961.2017.1304921

Lewis, T. (1998). The new economics of information. *IEEE Internet Computing*, *2*(5), 93–94. doi:10.1109/4236.722237

Madry, A., Markelov, A., Schmidt, L., Tsipras, D., & Vladu, A. (2018). Towards deep learning models resistant to adversarial attacks. *6th International Conference on Learning Representations, ICLR 2018 - Conference Track Proceedings,* 1–28.

Mai, J. E. (2016). Big data privacy: The datafication of personal information. *The Information Society*, *32*(3), 192–199. doi:10.1080/01972243.2016.1153010

Mughal, A. A. (2017). *Artificial Intelligence in Information Security: Exploring the Advantages, Challenges, and Future Directions.*

RamirezM. A.KimS.-K.Al HamadiH.DamianiE.ByonY.-J.KimT.-Y.ChoC.-S.YeunC. Y. (2022). Poisoning Attacks and Defenses on Artificial Intelligence: A Survey. http://arxiv.org/abs/2202.10276

Robert, L., Cheung, C., Matt, C., & Trenz, M. (2018). Int ne t R es ea rch Int ern et Re se. *Internet Research*, *28*, 829–850.

Ryan, M. (2020). In AI We Trust: Ethics, Artificial Intelligence, and Reliability. *Science and Engineering Ethics*, *26*(5), 2749–2767. doi:10.1007/s11948-020-00228-y PMID:32524425

Stahl, B. C., & Wright, D. (2018). Ethics and Privacy in AI and Big Data: Implementing Responsible Research and Innovation. *IEEE Security and Privacy*, *16*(3), 26–33. doi:10.1109/MSP.2018.2701164

Street, V. (2005). *Indian Institute of Technology Gandhinagar.*, *14*(3), 13210003.

Torrance, S. (2013). *Artificial agents and the expanding ethical circle.* doi:10.1007/s00146-012-0422-2

Wachter, S., Mittelstadt, B., & Russell, C. (2020). *Why Fairness Cannot Be Automated: B Ridging The Gap Between Eu Non - Discrimination Law And AI.* 1–72.

# Chapter 6
# Empowering Healthcare Professionals Through AI-Powered Lifelong Learning for Improving Patient Care

**Rajaprabakaran Rajendran**
https://orcid.org/0009-0005-9272-5475
*CMS Business School, Jain University, India*

**Yavana Rani Subramanian**
https://orcid.org/0000-0001-7870-8007
*CMS Business School, Jain University, India*

**Sandeep Poddar**
https://orcid.org/0000-0001-9771-877X
*Lincoln University College, Malaysia*

**V. Geetha**
*Mannar Thirumalai Naicker College, India*

## ABSTRACT

*Artificial intelligence (AI) is described as the power of a machine to emulate human intelligence. Since its development, AI has impacted business, daily life, and, most notably, the healthcare industry. The technology could make an impact on many facets of healthcare, including medical screening and treatment alternatives, drug design, and benchwork investigation. As technology progresses, AI will play a more significant role in medical education. The ability to implement AI effectively will lead to new opportunities for medical professionals in the future. AI and technology-enhanced learning should be integrated into medical education alongside the current emphasis on the biological and medical sciences. It is high time for educational institutions in the medical field to begin planning and revamping their curricula that would incorporate AI and machine learning along with a focus on transparency and compassion. The students who graduate will be competent to adopt AI-enabled technologies and to succeed in the AI-transformed healthcare system.*

DOI: 10.4018/979-8-3693-2440-0.ch006

## INTRODUCTION

The primary objective of the rapidly evolving computer science field known as Artificial Intelligence (AI) is to build devices that are capable of performing activities that typically necessitate human intelligence. AI encompasses a range of methodologies, including Natural Language Processing (NLP), Deep Learning (DL), and Machine Learning (ML). Large Language Models (LLMs) are a category of AI programmes that comprehend, summarise, produce, and forecast new text-based components using deep learning methods and exceptionally large data sets (Suleimenov et al., 2020; Davenport & Kalakota, 2019; Russell & Norvig, 2010). LLMs are broadly applicable for a range of NLP operations, such as content summary, sentiment assessment, redrafting, classification, and categorization. LLMs are designed to produce text-based content. The study of NLP is a branch of AI that encompasses the comprehension, interpretation, and production of human language by computers. Machine translation, recognition of speech, sentiment evaluation, mining of text, and other techniques are all part of NLP. AI has changed exponentially over time, from the initial stages of systems based on rules to the modern days of ML and DL programmes (Suleimenov et al., 2020; Davenport & Kalakota, 2019; Russell & Norvig, 2010).

Since Christopher Strachey developed the initial artificial intelligence program in 1951, the field has progressed significantly. In its early years, AI primarily existed as an academic pursuit. During the Dartmouth Conference in 1956, the term "Artificial Intelligence" was first coined by John McCarthy marking the commencement of the modern era of AI. In 1960s and 1970s, AI research focused mainly on rule-based and expert systems. However, this approach faced limitations due to the demand for increased data and processing power capacity (McCorduck & Cfe, 2004). In 1980s and 1990s, AI research shifted its focus on ML and neural systems, which enabled computers to learn from data and enhance their performance over time. For instance, during this period, systems like IBM's Deep Blue, which famously vanquished the world chess champion Garry Kasparov in 1997, were developed. In 2000s, the development of virtual assistants capable of comprehending natural language and responding to user requests, such as Apple's Siri and Amazon's Alexa, marked a notable achievement in the evolution of AI research. These virtual assistants marked the advancements in computer vision and NLP (Figure 1) (Russell & Norvig, 2010; McCorduck & Cfe, 2004).

In the academic field, AI has been applied to create computer programmes, described as smart systems for teaching, that can alter its methodology depending on the specific requirements of students. The learning outcomes of students in several subjects, particularly science and maths, have shown to be improved because of the incorporation of "smart teaching systems". In the research field, AI has been used to interpret enormous amounts of data and identify themes that would be difficult for humans to analyse, which has led to many innovations in areas such as drug development and genomics. In healthcare settings, personalised medical regimens and diagnostic instruments have been developed with the aid of AI. The development of AI needs to follow ethical guidelines and legislations for the betterment of the mankind as it advances further (Jordan & Mitchell, 2015; VanLehn, 2011; Topol, 2019; Papachristou & Bosanquet, 2020).

## THE ROLE OF AI IN EDUCATION (CHEN ET AL., 2020)

AI-enabled education comprises smart education, creative online learning, and data prediction and analysis. Table 1 outlines the main applications of AI in educational settings along with the key tech-

*Figure 1. A comprehensive overview of AI's evolution and understanding the interrelationships between AI, ML, NLP, and DL [Adapted from (Russell & Norvig, 2010; McCorduck & Cfe, 2004)]*
*Note. Historical evolution of AI and understanding the relation among various AI enabled learning methodologies.*

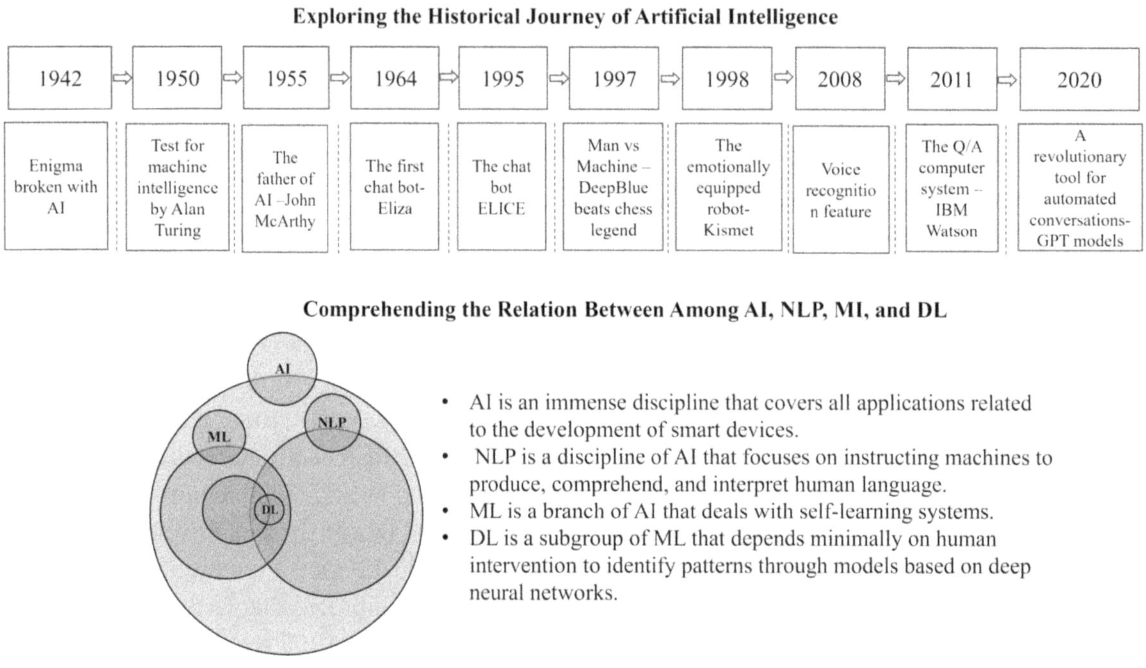


nologies that facilitate them. As the demands for learning evolve, fuelled by the advancement of AI, the growth continues steadily (Rus et al., 2013; Doshi et al., 2023; Singh et al., 2022). Both teachers and students benefit from the smart education systems as they can receive data timely, enhance accessibility to individualised teaching and perform evaluations easily. AI in education settings is created to enhance learning effectiveness through a range of computing technologies, specifically those associated with machine learning (Kahraman et al., 2010), which are strongly linked to cognitive learning theory and statistical frameworks.

AI systems utilise a wide range of approaches based on data mining, machine learning, and knowledge models for learning evaluation, suggestions, comprehension, and acquisition of knowledge (Avella et al., 2016). The components of an AI education system typically include smart algorithms, data-driven insights, and educational resources. These components are further subdivided into two categories: smart technologies and system models, which include learner, teaching, and knowledge models (Kim et al., 2018). The model aid in creating a data map, as illustrated in Figure 2, is essential to enhance learning since it pinpoints the associations and constructs the frameworks for the gathered educational data. A model functions as the central component of an AI system, with technologies supplying the fuel for the system.

## AI-Powered Education Framework

The learner framework in an AI learning system is essential to enhancing self-paced learning abilities. It is confirmed from behavioural data that is gathered from learners during the learning phase. In order

*Table 1. Approaches for AI Enabled Education Scenarios [Adapted from (Chen et al., 2020)]*

| AI enabled education scenarios | AI-assisted approaches |
|---|---|
| Evaluation of students and educational institutions | Educational data analysis, customised learning strategies, and adaptive education |
| Grading and assessment of examinations and papers | Computer vision, prediction system, and image recognition |
| Individualised smart teaching | Education data analysis, smart teaching platforms, data mining or Bayesin knowledge intervention |
| Intelligent school | Technologies related to hearing and sensing, facial and speech recognition, virtual testing facilities, Augmented Reality and Virtual Reality |
| Remote learning using mobile and internet | Real-time evaluation, personal virtual assistants, and edge computing |

*Note.* The key applications of AI for academic settings, in conjunction with the major technologies that enable them

*Figure 2. Computational Framework of AI-Enabled Education [Adapted from (Chen et al., 2020)]*
*Note. AI systems utilise various methods based on machine learning, data mining, and knowledge models for learning assessment, recommendations, and knowledge acquisition.*

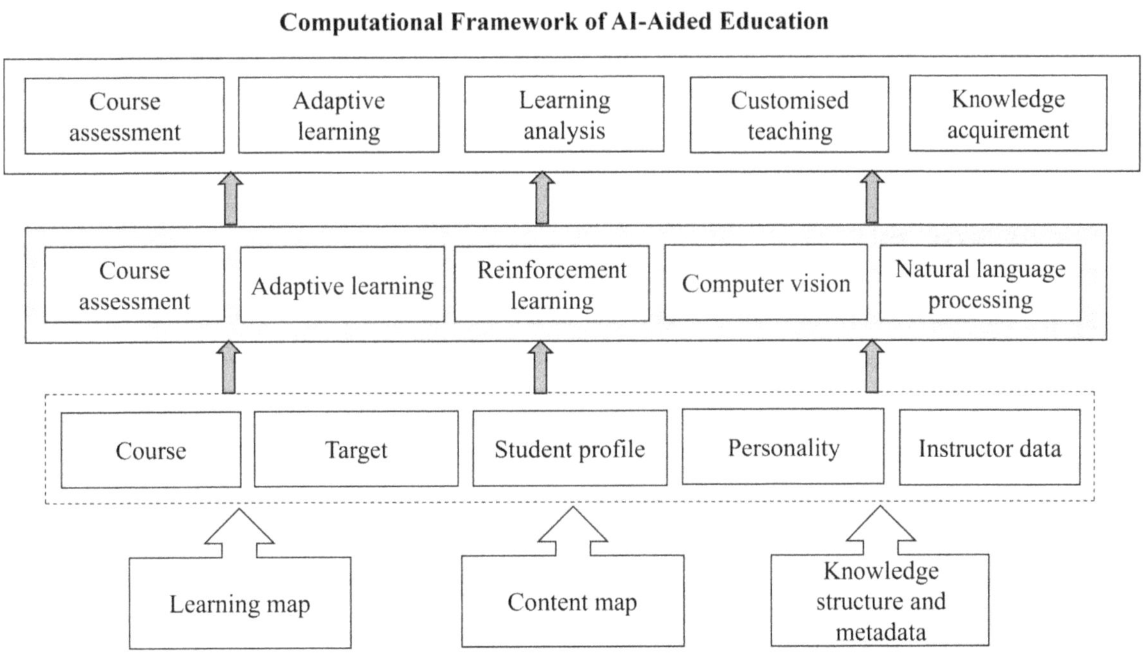


to evaluate learner's skills, their thinking and competencies are analysed. The learners' mastery of the subject matter is then determined by mapping the knowledge assessment. Learner modelling creates links between learning outcomes and a range of components, such as instructional strategies, resources, and learning aids (Avella et al., 2016).

## Smart Education Platforms

Data mining, learning assessment, and machine learning are profoundly interrelated educational technologies. Currently, two distinct groups have emerged around the educational platforms i.e. data mining and learning assessment. Both these groups have common goals and methods. Educational technologies also use a range of fields such as data mining, data modelling, machine learning, and statistical psychometrics (Estevez et al., 2019). Initially, data mining emerged from the field of smart tutoring systems, which focuses on extremely small-sized cognition. Large-scale test results and instructional content management platforms are the main areas of focus for learning analysis.

### Machine Learning

The discovery of knowledge is the fundamental process of machine learning. It involves analysing a sample data set, referred to as "training data," to produce reliable patterns and organised information. For example, machine learning can assist in generating recommendations for students when they choose their educational institutions and programmes. It incorporates student information on their accomplishments, goals, and preferences to "match-make" or "customize" them with schools where they can grow to their full potential. Furthermore, this technology can aid teachers in comprehending how each topic is being assimilated by students., Based on the results, teachers can modify their teaching strategies to better meet their students' learning styles depending on their collective records, potentially improving their comprehension of the topic.

### Learning Assessment

The focus of learning analytics lies on data derived from learner and knowledge domain models, as well as attributes of the students. The main concept behind learning analytics is to apply modern technology, specifically machine learning, in non-technical fields like education. The goal is to customise the teaching strategies according to the needs and aptitude of a student, such as by providing assessment and instructional resources or by promoting their confidence in specific subjects to help the struggling students (Tsai & Gasevic, 2017). It employs methods from the fields of semantics, learning sciences, data visualisation, and machine learning. For example, AI-assisted competency education may produce valuable student data that can efficiently predict student limitations, uncover student perspectives as well as the essential skills they can explore, allowing institutions to take proactive measures. Learning analytics utilises AI's adaptable learning capabilities in addition to competency-based instruction. AI can identify new students based on a variety of factors, including chance of dropping out, which can lead to early alert systems and valuable data for educational institutions (Rathi et al., 2023).

### Mining of Data

The primary objective of data mining in the field of education is to design programmed learning materials and systematic responses to programmed assessments or tests. The main goal of AI-enabled educational data mining is to create innovative learning materials in which students can apply logics to correlate and get updated informational assets tailored to their individual needs and competence. Additionally, instructors can use data mining to develop the curriculum in the educational system by applying the predictive modelling and pattern discovery to uncover hidden defects. One of the key advantages of data mining-aided AI is the achievement of knowledge through personalised learning from respective fields, allowing students to learn at their own pace and select their personal AI-assisted learning strategy to promote their understanding and competence in their core subjects. In an ideal scenario, students would select their courses and learning methodologies based on their interests, and teachers would modify their instruction accordingly (Kim et al., 2018). In turn, AI also develops its cognitive abilities (e.g., with machine learning) with greater accuracy, and consistently update with the assistance of data mining.

### The Role that AI plays in Educational Settings

AI possesses enormous potential and the capacity to deeply influence several societal sectors. A specific field that is anticipated to be greatly affected by AI is the education sector. AI has been embraced and used in the education sector, where it has promoted advancements in a wide range of areas. Table 2 illustrates the various ways AI can be utilised in administrative, instructional, and learning contexts in education.

## AI IN HEALTH CARE EDUCATION

The application of AI continues to expand and it will make way for significant advancements in a wide range of industries, including medical education. The history of AI dates back thousands of years (van der Niet & Bleakley, 2021). When Alan Turning pondered the question "Can machines think?" in 1950, he designed an experiment to find the answer. He asked his subject to interact with a machine and then a human, and when the subject was unable to distinguish between the two, the results of the experiment supported the hypothesis that machines are capable of thinking (Turing, 2009). Later in 1960, John Mc-Carthy coined the phrase "artificial intelligence" for the first time (McCarthy & Hayes, 1981). Complex correlations that are difficult to quantify can be identified through AI techniques (Szolovits, 2019). It is strongly recommended that medical education undergo a significant "reboot" for AI to be widely utilised in

*Table 2. The role that AI plays in educational settings [Adapted from (Chen et al., 2020)]*

| | **The potential advantages of AI in educational settings** |
|---|---|
| Administration | • Complete administrative duties like exam grading and reporting more efficiently, as these occupy an enormous amount of instructors' time.<br>• Assist in creating individualised learning plans for each of their students by determining their learning interests, methods and competence.<br>• Support educators in data-driven and decision-support tasks. |
| Instruction | • Assess a student's likelihood of failing classes and how can they perform better and gain better grades above expectations on assignments and tasks.<br>• Examine the instructional materials and curriculum to provide tailored content.<br>• Facilitate instruction in higher education settings besides the classroom to foster teamwork.<br>• Customise teaching for each student based on their individual data.<br>• Assist teachers in developing individualised instructional strategies for every learner in the classroom. |
| Learning | • Identify students' specific areas of weakness in learning and make prompt remedial action to improve them.<br>• Assign specific vocational or skill-based courses that students can pursue at the university.<br>• Gather and analyse the data to forecast each student's career path.<br>• Identify the learning condition of each learner and provide them with smart, personalised coaching. |

*Note.* Various applications of AI in educational settings, including administration, instruction, and learning.

healthcare settings. Students should be taught about "intelligence or smart technologies," such as massive data sets, sophisticated statistical analysis, and automated machines, rather than viewing them as human extensions but as potentially self-sufficient entities (Schwartz et al., 1987). In order to adequately prepare for AI, physicians and researchers certainly need to have a fundamental knowledge of AI in teaching and learning, and know the degree of impact of AI-aided learning in medical education (Masters, 2019). Like other businesses, the healthcare sector is rapidly integrating the technological advances into all facets of this newly discovered business domain. The availability of devices that interfaces with hospital information and management platforms has made it possible to predispose medical issues in real-time and send inter-departmental data faster than ever before. This system provided medical technicians with the proper response machines, flashers, and color-coding tools in addition to absorbing all the data required for the clinical demonstration. AI systems can evaluate and process almost an infinite number of inputs concurrently, compared to a single clinician (Stone et al., 2022). Furthermore, these systems can learn from every new case they encounter and are exposed to a wider range of scenarios in a matter of minutes than a physician may encounter in their career (Burgess, 2017). This is the main reason how an AI-driven system can outperform experts in instances of professional conflicts, for example when lung tuberculosis is recognised on chest radiographs, and the application may falsely find out fretting manifestations (Wartman & Combs, 2018; Wartman & Combs, 2019; Boldea, 2019).

Medical educationists around the world believe a revamp of medical coursework and curricula is required to address the emerging challenges of the twenty-first century, including the growing integration of AI and ML in professional conduct. This reboot of medical education would emphasise "knowledge planning and coordination" instead of "gaining expertise." Clinicians of the future must be ready for the transformative AI storm. Regretfully, medical students are ill-prepared for future problems and challenges by the current educational model and curriculum. Current medical education curriculum need to cover subjects that will enable future healthcare practitioners to practise in a data-rich environment aided by AI, in addition to a foundational understanding of health sciences and their relationship to clinical sciences. Educators and physicians in medical school also need to learn how to connect with patients whose decisions about their care will be directly influenced by AI, as well as the advantages and misconceptions around AI applications (Bleakley, 2014).

Some advantages of integrating AI into medical education include the ability to provide quick feedback, enhance problem-based learning with learning-guided theory, identify and address knowledge gaps in students, lessen the need for teacher supervision, reduce costs, and eliminate any risk to patients (Masters, 2019). The majority of virtual reality simulated programmes employ a smart teaching system relevant to cover meticulous needs of specific subjects. AI is widely recognised in continuing medical education due to a fundamental curriculum in medical school.

The barriers to implementing AI in the educational system include the need for a well-designed academic framework to provide the knowledge base for AI-based courses and reservations about assessment reliability since contextually driven education requires a platform with comprehensive subject knowledge. AI is being utilised to assess learners in a variety of ways, including project grading, computerised article scoring according to clinical reasoning questions, fundamental laparoscopic competence appraisal, assessment of student case reviews, and tracking of attendance (van der Niet & Bleakley, 2021). Although, AI will face many obstacles in medical education, surely it will become a necessary component for future medical graduates. The primary obstacles in establishing an AI-based educational setup are time constraints in the curriculum periods to modify new major themes and technical challenges in generating precise and clinically advantageous AI applications. To ensure sure that AI technologies support medical professors rather than replace them, it will be essential to seek guidance from experts in medicine and education who will work collaboratively with data scientists (Wartman & Combs, 2018; Bleakley, 2014).

### The Necessity for Adaptation

The advent of robotics and other developments in the past imposed a similar pressure on the roles played by physicians (Lanza et al., 2020). In response, medical professionals adapted their positions to better fit the tools that are at their access in order to improve patient care (Li et al., 2019). Nonetheless, doctors are not expected to be under unprecedented pressure to build up whole new skill sets and keep up with the exponential expansion of medical knowledge due to the quick development of AI (Wiljer & Hakim, 2019). The problem of advancing medical knowledge can be effectively resolved by overcoming the difficulty of learning about AI. AI has the capacity to provide doctors with a substitute for effectively managing and applying medical information to practice (Topol, 2019; Barbour et al., 2019; Borkan et al., 2021).

### Reforming Education

The requirement to enhance medical education continues to grow as healthcare evolves. Physicians will be challenged with management and retention of information as the pace of novel medical information grows faster. The necessity for competent human–machine interaction will rise as medicine and healthcare delivery need to embrace the AI era and utilise data to support medical decision-making (Dumić-Čule et al., 2020). Medical students must be sufficiently knowledgeable about the basic principles of AI, as well as the advantages of using AI to reduce costs, improve quality, and facilitate the utilisation of healthcare (Sit et al., 2020; Khurana, 2020). In the same way, learners need to be informed about the drawbacks of AI, including accountability and honesty (Walsh, 2020; Aungst & Patel, 2020; Park et al., 2019; van der Niet & Bleakley, 2021). Lastly, medical students need to get acclimated to the technology that is currently reshaping the medical industry.

## LEVERAGING AI IN MEDICAL EDUCATION (HOSSEINI ET AL., 2023)

The fact that AI will provide access to the new developments in technology to many aspiring physicians, and it also has the potential to completely transform the medical education (Hedderich et al., 2021; Hosseini et al., 2023). Researchers have investigated the potential integration of AI with academic curricula, including case-oriented learning and surgical learning skills. Some of the research studies focus on practical integration of AI in medical education. For example, robotic systems powered by AI can be used to build skills and acquire knowledge through evaluations and simulations (Quinn & Coghlan, 2021; Dumić-Čule et al., 2020).

### AI-Enabled Digital Patients

Virtual patients created by AI provide a learning and training platform, where medical students can practice diagnosing and treating a variety of illnesses, in a secure and regulated setting. They can learn from their mistakes without having any fear of repercussions as in the real world (Ahmady & Hosseini, 2022).

## AI-Assisted Human Anatomy Simulation Model

In medical education, robots with AI capabilities can serve as human body simulators. Robots are used as human-like models in AI-assisted medical education, which also employs AI to create scenarios, act as a medical encyclopaedia, simulate pharmaceutical interactions, and independently evaluate students' understanding of medical information (Farahmand, 2022).

## AI-Driven Physiological Education and Preoperative Evaluation

Numerous AI algorithms are utilised by various surgical visual representation systems that are currently being utilised for presurgical evaluation and anatomical teaching. The incorporation of AI technology in surgical training simulations allows for customised assessment and personalised feedback, although it is arguably still in the initial stages of mainstream clinical application (Hosseini et al., 2023; Grunhut et al., 2021).

## Expert Training in Medical-Machine Interaction

Data-driven clinical decision-making will be improved by the application of AI in medical treatment, which will require competent human-machine communication. AI technology will be essential as advancements in medical expertise can enable healthcare practitioners to apply these skills in their daily practice (Hedderich et al., 2021).

## Customised Postgraduate Programmes in AI Education Tailored to Specific Medical Specialties

The appropriate application of AI models in clinical practice requires the creation of AI education programmes specific to each medical specialisation. In order to improve the statistical knowledge, promote kindness and empathy for patients, foster communication among healthcare professionals, and derive valuable data from the proliferating medical literature, an in-depth assessment and modification of the undergraduate medical school curriculum is mandatory (Ahmed et al., 2022).

## AI-Aided Customised Education

Learning effectiveness and precision can be enhanced by utilising AI technology to build a personalised learning plan based on an individual student's learning method, strengths, and limitations. This strategy addresses many practical challenges in accurately depicting the actual illness development and is consistent with conventional approaches to disease identification and medical care. AI is capable of making the most effective content recommendations, offering guidance on long-term curriculum design, and facilitating the connection of suitable learners through recommendations and precise assessments of performance (Dumić-Čule et al., 2020; Wood et al., 2021).

Incorporation of AI technology in surgery facilitates preoperative planning, intraoperative visualisation, and guidance to handle complications to improve patients' safety in real surgery. Surgical education simulations enable customised feedback and personal assessment. AI-enhanced simulations based on computer-human communication may offer an affordable alternative to conventional training, and also allows physicians to access it in a better way. The best way to learn and retain critical resuscitation abilities is through high-fidelity simulation, but in-person training restricts accessibility and leads to "skill deterioration" (Hosseini et al., 2023; Masoumian Hosseini et al., 2023).

While some students believe learning AI will help them in their professions, others claim AI education or training should be provided to medical students. Students need to acknowledge the significance of AI in contemporary medical practice, which is currently transforming the medical education (Ahmed et al., 2022).

### Smart Tutoring Programmes

Smart tutoring solutions can revolutionise student learning by providing individualised support and designing customised learning paths according to the requirements of each student. As these AI-enabled smart tutoring solutions can offer customised feedback to students, improving their performance through a more individualised approach, there is growing interest in the research on these systems. Furthermore, as these systems develop further, they might also have an impact on the various responsibilities held by teachers and other professionals who assist with students' education (Fazlollahi et al., 2021).

### Smart Agent Assisted Role-Playing Scenarios

Smart agent role-plays can improve students' computer literacy and sense of responsibility, and AI can help with personalised learning by enabling chatbots and auto scoring, which will improve the overall educational experience.

## OBSTACLES OF INCORPORATING AI IN CURRICULUM

There are numerous obstacles to overcome when integrating AI into medical education, all of which must be carefully considered. These issues are multifaceted, and in order to be successfully resolved, each requires a different strategy.

### Ethical Issues

AI in medicine brings up several significant ethical concerns that require thorough investigation. The implementation of AI can pose challenges due to concerns about confidentiality, prejudice, and responsibility. Dealing with these issues necessitates developing comprehensive ethical standards and frameworks designed especially for integrating AI into medical education. This is demonstrated by a study by Masoumian Hosseini et al. (2023), which attempts to create an ethical framework that takes into account the application of AI in the realm of medical education.

### Faculty Development

A study by Gentile et al. (2023) demonstrated how important it is to provide faculty members with complete training in AI theories and tools. This is essential for them to successfully incorporate AI into their educational programmes. Academic members' expertise and AI-related skills can be greatly enhanced by planning courses on AI-training skills and engaging workshops.

### Curriculum Development

Strategic and prudent is needed for the successful integration of AI into the medical curriculum. Specialised courses or modules that explore the core ideas, real-world uses, and ethical consequences of AI in medicine should be included in an extensive curriculum. Furthermore, it must provide students with opportunities for hands-on learning so they can become proficient in applying cutting-edge AI technology and tools (Dumić-Čule et al., 2020; Wood et al., 2021).

### Infrastructure and Resources

Establishing an effective framework and dedicating significant resources are essential for the effective implementation of AI in medical education. This includes obtaining and possessing access to state-of-the-art AI applications, powerful hardware, and significant processing power. Higher educational institutions have to invest wisely in these essential components to enable seamless integration of AI capabilities (Wood et al., 2021; Varma et al., 2023).

### Appraisal and Analysis

The effectiveness of AI integration in medical education should be evaluated. It is critical to develop rigorous assessment techniques that can measure learners' AI proficiency and skill. This involves developing productive assignments, projects, and evaluations that are designed to determine how well they can use AI tools in healthcare settings (Grunhut et al., 2021; Masoumian Hosseini et al., 2023; Varma et al., 2023).

### Partnering With AI Specialists

Effective collaborations between foremost AI research facilities and business experts are essential for the schools to succeed. These partnerships ensure that curricula and instructional strategies will efficiently incorporate state-of-the-art AI technologies while staying up to date with the most current approaches (Hosseini et al., 2023; Quinn & Coghlan, 2021).

To address the challenges outlined above, it will necessitate an organised effort from academic institutions, prestigious faculty members, seasoned AI specialists, and vigilant regulators. Overcoming these formidable challenges will enable the seamless assimilation of AI into medical education to proceed harmoniously, enhancing the learning experience and suitably preparing the future physicians for their patient-care endeavours.

## PROSPECTS OF AI IN SHAPING MEDICAL EDUCATION

Prospective and existing medical trainees will be most impacted by the use of AI technologies in medicine. Hence, in order to teach current and future generations of doctors how to use these potent and disruptive technologies responsibly, medical colleges must modify their curricula. According to Steven A. Wartman and C. Donald Combs, there are several significant barriers to such curricular changes, including institutional rules and regulations, several years of slow improvement by regulating and accreditation bodies, and long-running teaching practices and financing streams. The first step necessitates changes in the structure of financing, governing, and accrediting organisations. Reinventing medical education for the twenty-first century may involve a primary focus on reforming the licensing and accreditation system (Wartman & Combs, 2019).

It will need visionary leadership to redefine medical education, which is an ambitious but essential endeavour. Future medical students will also require a new set of skills, such as 1) "acquiring knowledge, not knowledge maintenance": a curriculum that promotes critical thinking rather than memorization; 2) "a better understanding of probabilities and how to apply them meaningfully in clinical decision making with patients: the translational implementation of AI technologies; and 3) "Partnership and management of AI programmes": learning how to utilise AI responsibly and effectively (Wartman & Combs, 2019). Above all, the nurture of humane traits like respect, compassion, mental agility, etc. should always be the foundation for gathering knowledge related to AI technologies. The field of medicine requires humanistic factors that are fundamental to providing quality treatment. It cannot be reduced to the application of technology and limited scientific understanding. The development of personal qualities that support the development of imaginative and critical thinking must therefore be prioritised as one of the primary educational approaches of medical schools in the twenty-first century, in addition to the emphasis on procedural skills and fundamental knowledge of science.

Globally, AI is growing at a rapid pace, offering insights into a future when AI-powered medical instruments will probably re-shape 21st-century medical practice. AI, commonly known as computer-emulating human cognition, is defined as a machine possessing cognitive abilities such as perception, reasoning, generalisation, and experience-based learning (Nilsson, 1998). According to published studies, AI devices and platforms can enhance the delivery of precision medicine by functioning more swiftly, efficiently, and accurately as human physicians (Obermeyer & Emanuel, 2016; Betancur et al., 2018; De Fauw et al., 2018; Haenssle et al., 2018). In the future, surgery performed by robots and e-patients, although still in their early years, is anticipated to grow increasingly common in medical practice if current trends continue (Stravodimos et al., 2019; Masters, 2019). It is essential to acknowledge that in the future, healthcare will involve more collaboration between doctors, allied health workers, patients, and technology. AI is predicted to have an impact on every facet of healthcare, necessitating the development of new medical education programmes for health professionals. Globally, medical educators believe that in order to meet the new challenges of this century, particularly the growing integration of big data and AI in clinical practice, medical education needs to be revitalised and the curriculum should be shifted from an emphasis on "acquisition of knowledge" to "management of knowledge and communication" (Wartman & Combs, 2019). The current medical students will encounter all the advantages and disadvantages associated with employing AI in medicine throughout their professional life as prospective practitioners. Future doctors are not being prepared for the upcoming AI revolution in healthcare by the current medical education system. "Academic standards have to be rejuvenated improved, and enhanced as technology evolves and data haze becomes thicker," as was appropriately stated (Wartman & Combs, 2018). The medical school curriculum for this century must contain content to enhance future physicians' ability to practise in data-rich settings aided by AI, in addition to a knowledge of the fundamental sciences and their relationship to clinical sciences. Volume, variety, velocity, and veracity—the four Vs of big data—as well as how information is compiled, processed, and customised in the realm of decision-making are elements that medical students must understand comprehensively (Wartman & Combs, 2018). Along with acquiring the ability to interact through and with AI platforms, they also need to be acquainted about influence of AI on treatment decisions of patients as well as the advantages and disadvantages of AI applications in medical school. They also must be cognizant of the concepts behind AI broadly as well as for particular tools that utilise AI (Masters, 2019).

The application of AI in education has several benefits, including the ability to provide rapid feedback, improve problem-focused instruction by learning guided theory, discover and address knowledge gaps in students, lessen the requirement for supervision by educators, lower expenses, and minimise risk to patients. A smart teaching system is employed by many virtual reality simulation programmes (e.g. TOUCH Project, ECHOCOM) (Caudell et al., 2003, Weidenbach et al., 2004).

AI is additionally utilised in learning assessment, including assignment assessment, computerised essay scoring based on clinical reasoning questions, evaluating student case overviews, assessing fundamental laparoscopic abilities, and monitoring attendance (Latifi et al., 2004; Kintsch, 2002; Alonso-Silverio., 2018). Lack of digitization is the main obstacle to AI's restricted application in assessments, as it affects the ability to meet the requirements for the knowledge pool needed to construct AI-enabled platforms. This limitation is even more evident in educational institutions, where non-digital instruments are primarily used for instruction, curriculum development, assessment, and evaluation. The summative and delicate nature of assessments made by medical professionals, communication security concerns, and the potential for AI system malfunction or faulty coding to provide inaccurate results all serve to restrict the adoption of AI assessment systems. However, the use of programmed and adaptive evaluations can enhance assessment methods in medical education. While programmed assessments aim to optimise learning results in accordance with the curriculum, adaptable evaluations customise the difficulty of questions based on each student being evaluated and their responses to previous questions (Ward, et al., 2001; Van Der Vleuten, et al., 2015).

In medical education, AI has not been utilised as much for curriculum review, in spite of research studies have shown the advantages of support vector machines (SVM) and artificial neural networks (ANN) in identifying correlations between parameters and summarising the effectiveness of the curriculum and satisfaction among learners (Chen, 2010). Many barriers to integrating AI in medical education are identified, despite the data that suggests AI proficiency will ultimately make it to the list of competencies needed for a medical graduate. Two primary obstacles are scarcity of time in the curriculum to incorporate new subject areas and the technical hurdles involved in creating AI applications that are not only reliable but also applicable in clinical settings. As noted by Arthur C. Clarke, "Any teacher who can be replaced by a machine should be!" it requires contributions from specialists in both health and education who will have to work collaboratively with data scientists to make sure that AI technologies enhance medical teacher roles rather than replace them. Clarke (1980). To ensure that key stakeholders adopt AI in medical education, data safety, confidentiality, and privacy issues of learners' data must also be accorded the highest priority. Since there is no substitute for human intervention in medicine, it is necessary to maintain a balance between the learning and teaching that medical students receive from medical professionals and instruments if AI is to be incorporated early in the course of study. The implementation of AI in medical schooling is expected to increase the necessity of teaching interpersonal skills in medicine, which include leadership, empathy, communication, and ethical appreciation (Masters, 2019). The professional expertise needed to teach AI in medicine is currently lacking in medical schools. Enhancing interfaculty partnerships between computer science, engineering, and healthcare professionals can help alleviate the lack of experience in teaching AI to medical students. Curriculum for medical schools should include instruction in the field of AI in the form of teaching ECG and Echo capabilities, as well as an overview of algorithm development, an appreciation of the larger concepts of AI's role in decision-making, and probability assessment.

## Lack of Implementation

Although the literature data in AI-aided learning in medical curriculum are promising, still there is not much progress are done in planning and implementing this incorporation (Kolachalama & Garg, 2018; Gallix & Chong, 2019; James et al., 2021). There is no indication of publications investigating on the proposals for curricular changes mentioned in any journals (Kang et al., 2021; Carin, 2020; Paranjape et al., 2021; Wartman et al., 2018). The rationale for medical schools' unwillingness to adopt these improvements are not completely understandable. Doctors will probably not be prepared for the shift in healthcare that AI will bring about in a few years. According to the findings of earlier research, the biggest obstacle to integrating AI into the curriculum is the faculty at medical schools are ignorant to the AI technology (Han et al., 2019; Fan et al., 2020; Briganti & Le Moine, 2020; Masters, 2020) as well as to the acclimation steps (Ellaway, 2014). Consequently, a novel initiative can accelerate the acceptance and transformation of medical curricula to the AI-aided learning and training platforms.

## Challenges to Transformation

Although the application of AI in medical education is becoming increasingly prevalent, there are still obstacles to overcome. Faculty and doctors who are insufficiently prepared for such a progression of clinical practice would denounce transformation (Briganti, & Le Moine, 2020). These opportunities may be lost due to fear of technology eventually replacing doctors. Moreover, a lack of understanding and experience with AI can raise reservations about the reliability of the prediction by ML. This becomes harder due to the ongoing challenges in planning significant curriculum changes. It is essential to conduct more research to determine the best way to implement these enhancements.

## The Way Ahead

When a medical school aspires to stay contemporary with healthcare advancements, it should heed the recommendations voiced by numerous specialists on AI's potential as a clinical partner. Future medical professionals would suffer if this weren't addressed, and they would be at the mercy of catching up to technological advancements. To effectively employ AI as a safe tool in practice, doctors should be trained to comprehend its technological capabilities and limitations. Physicians must have the ability to interpret the findings and advise patients accordingly. Physicians should also be made knowledgeable about the new ethical issues that AI will bring up in the clinical setting. Doctors who are not trained in AI should expect to encounter moral dilemmas, when a computer programme indicates that a patient has a high risk of mortality.

The implementation of AI in medicine will transform the provision of healthcare in the future. Like the majority of other industries, medicine is transitioning towards the digital era. According to the Normalisation Process Theory, AI will eventually become ingrained in society on both an individual and a group level, and will become an integral part of surgeons' daily routine (Scantlebury et al., 2017). However, in emergency situations where AI must be used, this process can be expedited swiftly.

AI and other cutting-edge technology expedited the metamorphosis of medicine during COVID-19. Physicians must receive cutting-edge training in healthcare technology, as demonstrated by the widespread adoption of telehealth by whole clinics and hospitals during pandemic. After the pandemic, the future direction of medical education and practice is ambiguous, but likely to shift radically centred around AI, and AI technology will shape these areas. AI has the potential to be extremely beneficial in addressing some of the major issues in healthcare sector, including waiting time for patients, medical expenses, and inadequate care (Bilimoria et al., 2019). However, there could be equally numerous adverse outcomes from manipulating AI (Alrassi et al., 2021). Future medical professionals must begin receiving appropriate training on the advantages and drawbacks of AI.

## STUDY LIMITATION

As a result of the rise of AI platforms, this book chapter review evaluates and discusses the developments of AI in healthcare education. Due to the extensive nature of the study topic, this book chapter synthesised and summarised the conclusions and findings of the publications that were chosen, and it includes the brief assessments of the area of study. Selection bias is another potential restriction. While conducting database searches with predetermined keywords, the authors of this book chapter tried to minimise selection bias. Furthermore, the search was conducted across several databases (Google, Google Scholar, JSTOR, Science Direct, and PubMed).

The authors evaluated a number of prospective publications before deciding whether or not to include any particular papers in this study. As a result of the rapid development of AI in a particular industry (healthcare education), this book chapter concentrated on shifts and developments in application of AI in healthcare education. Therefore, the results cannot be extrapolated and applied to different sectors. Lack of time is another barrier. There may have been more articles published during the time that this study's search was being done and articles were being found. Thus, the literature evaluation and search could be carried on for additional research in the future. Future studies are needed to examine improvements and trends in AI in healthcare education.

## CONCLUSION

AI is described as the power of a machine to emulate human intelligence. Since its development, AI has impacted business, daily life, and, most notably, the healthcare industry. The technology could make an impact on many facets of healthcare, including medical screening, treatment alternatives, drug design, and benchwork investigation. AI is currently studied in the medical field in order to aid with and eliminate tedious tasks like image augmentation in radiography and identification of images in clinical assessment. AI has the potential to enable computerised evaluation, enhance physician productivity, minimise human error rates, recognise better patient care patterns, cover medical bills, carry out minimally invasive procedures, and minimise mortality in the healthcare industry. Ultimately, the greater efficiency of AI in managing numerous widely recognised professional practices, chemical synthesis preparation, and drug discovery is transforming the roles of doctors.

AI provides the opportunity to completely transform medical education by offering individualised and flexible learning opportunities. It can determine a student's areas of abilities and weaknesses, enabling customised teaching strategies. AI also provides real-time evaluation, which improves improvement in skills and knowledge retention. To fully comprehend its long-term effects and the ethical issues raised by the incorporation of AI in medical education, further research is recommended. AI has the potential to greatly enhance medical education by offering physicians the tools they need to adapt for transforming healthcare landscape. Nonetheless, constraints including budget allocation, curriculum design, professional development programmes, and ethical issues need to be addressed. Despite these challenges, AI has many advantages to offer the healthcare industry in terms of better patient care and healthcare professional empowerment.

In summary, as technology progresses, AI will play a more significant role in medical education. The ability to implement AI effectively will lead to new opportunities for medical professionals in the future. AI and technology-enhanced learning should be integrated into medical education alongside the current emphasis on the biological and medical sciences. It is high time for educational institutions in the medical field to begin planning and revamping their curricula that would incorporate AI and machine learning along with a focus on transparency and compassion. The students who graduate will be competent to adopt AI-enabled technologies and to succeed in the AI-transformed healthcare system.

## REFERENCES

Ahmady, S., & Hosseini, T. M. (2022). Effectiveness of Video-assisted Debriefing Versus Standard Oral Debriefing Following Screen-based Simulation (CyberPatient TM) Training. *Journal of Medical Education*, *21*(1). doi:10.5812/jme-127021

Ahmed, Z., Bhinder, K. K., Tariq, A., Tahir, M. J., Mehmood, Q., Tabassum, M. S., Malik, M., Aslam, S., Asghar, M. S., & Yousaf, Z. (2022). Knowledge, attitude, and practice of artificial intelligence among doctors and medical students in Pakistan: A cross-sectional online survey. *Annals of Medicine and Surgery (London)*, *76*, 103493. doi:10.1016/j.amsu.2022.103493 PMID:35308436

Alonso-Silverio, G. A., Perez-Escamirosa, F., Bruno-Sanchez, R., Ortiz-Simon, J. L., Muñoz-Guerrero, R., Minor-Martinez, A., & Alarcón-Paredes, A. (2018). Development of a laparoscopic box trainer based on open source hardware and artificial intelligence for objective assessment of surgical psychomotor skills. *Surgical Innovation*, *25*(4), 380–388. doi:10.1177/1553350618777045 PMID:29809097

Alrassi, J., Katsufrakis, P. J., & Chandran, L. (2021). Technology can augment, but not replace, critical human skills needed for patient care. *Academic Medicine*, *96*(1), 37–43. doi:10.1097/ACM.0000000000003733 PMID:32910005

Arnold, M. H. (2021). Teasing out artificial intelligence in medicine: An ethical critique of artificial intelligence and machine learning in medicine. *Journal of Bioethical Inquiry*, *18*(1), 121–139. doi:10.1007/s11673-020-10080-1 PMID:33415596

Aungst, T. D., & Patel, R. (2020). Integrating digital health into the curriculum—Considerations on the current landscape and future developments. *Journal of Medical Education and Curricular Development*, *7*, 2382120519901275. doi:10.1177/2382120519901275 PMID:32010795

Avella, J. T., Kebritchi, M., Nunn, S. G., & Kanai, T. (2016). Learning analytics methods, benefits, and challenges in higher education: A systematic literature review. *Online Learning : the Official Journal of the Online Learning Consortium*, *20*(2), 13–29.

Barbour, A. B., Frush, J. M., Gatta, L. A., McManigle, W. C., Keah, N. M., Bejarano-Pineda, L., & Guerrero, E. M. (2019). Artificial intelligence in health care: Insights from an educational forum. *Journal of Medical Education and Curricular Development*, *6*, 2382120519889348. doi:10.1177/2382120519889348 PMID:32064356

Beauchamp, T. L., & Childress, J. F. (2001). *Principles of biomedical ethics*. Oxford University Press.

Betancur, J., Commandeur, F., Motlagh, M., Sharir, T., Einstein, A. J., Bokhari, S., Fish, M. B., Ruddy, T. D., Kaufmann, P., Sinusas, A. J., Miller, E. J., Bateman, T. M., Dorbala, S., Di Carli, M., Germano, G., Otaki, Y., Tamarappoo, B. K., Dey, D., Berman, D. S., & Slomka, P. J. (2018). Deep learning for prediction of obstructive disease from fast myocardial perfusion SPECT: A multicenter study. *JACC: Cardiovascular Imaging*, *11*(11), 1654–1663. doi:10.1016/j.jcmg.2018.01.020 PMID:29550305

Bilimoria, K., Harish, V., McCoy, L., Mehta, N., Morgado, F., Nagaraj, S., & Zheng, J. (2019). *Training for the future: preparing medical students for the impact of artificial intelligence*.

Bitterman, D. S., Aerts, H. J., & Mak, R. H. (2020). Approaching autonomy in medical artificial intelligence. *The Lancet. Digital Health*, *2*(9), e447–e449. doi:10.1016/S2589-7500(20)30187-4 PMID:33328110

Bleakley, A. (2014). *Patient-centred medicine in transition: The heart of the matter* (Vol. 3). Springer Science & Business Media. doi:10.1007/978-3-319-02487-5

Boldea, P. (2019). *Campus study investigates how artificial intelligence can learn metaphorical language*. The Daily Californian.

Borkan, J. M., Stagg Elliott, V., Wolpaw, T., Hassan, I., & Lomis, K. D. (2021). Looking ahead: the dynamic nature of health systems science, future trends, and the role of learners as change agents. *Health Systems Science*, 303-313.

Briganti, G., & Le Moine, O. (2020). Artificial intelligence in medicine: Today and tomorrow. *Frontiers in Medicine*, *7*, 27. doi:10.3389/fmed.2020.00027 PMID:32118012

Burgess, M. (2017). The NHS is trialling an AI chatbot to answer your medical questions. *Wired UK (2017, January 5)*.

Busch, F., Adams, L. C., & Bressem, K. K. (2023). Biomedical Ethical Aspects Towards the Implementation of Artificial Intelligence in Medical Education. *Medical Science Educator*, *33*(4), 1–6. doi:10.1007/s40670-023-01815-x PMID:37546190

Carin, L. (2020). On artificial intelligence and deep learning within medical education. *Academic Medicine*, *95*(11S), S10–S11. doi:10.1097/ACM.0000000000003630 PMID:32769462

Caudell, T. P., Summers, K. L., Holten, J. IV, Hakamata, T., Mowafi, M., Jacobs, J., Lozanoff, B. K., Lozanoff, S., Wilks, D., Keep, M. F., Saiki, S., & Alverson, D. (2003). Virtual patient simulator for distributed collaborative medical education. *Anatomical Record. Part B, New Anatomist*, *270*(1), 23–29. doi:10.1002/ar.b.10007 PMID:12526063

Chan, K. S., & Zary, N. (2019). Applications and challenges of implementing artificial intelligence in medical education: Integrative review. *JMIR Medical Education*, *5*(1), e13930. doi:10.2196/13930 PMID:31199295

Chen, C. K. (2010). *Curriculum Assessment Using Artificial Neural Network and Support Vector Machine Modeling Approaches: A Case Study. IR Applications*. Association for Institutional Research (NJ1).

Chen, J. (2017). Playing to our human strengths to prepare medical students for the future. *Korean Journal of Medical Education*, *29*(3), 193–197. doi:10.3946/kjme.2017.65 PMID:28870022

Chen, L., Chen, P., & Lin, Z. (2020). Artificial intelligence in education: A review. *IEEE Access : Practical Innovations, Open Solutions*, *8*, 75264–75278. doi:10.1109/ACCESS.2020.2988510

Clarke, A. C. (1980). Electronic tutors. *Omni Magazine*, *2*(9), 77–78.

Coghlan, S., & Coghlan, B. (2018). One Health, bioethics, and nonhuman ethics. *The American Journal of Bioethics*, *18*(11), 3–5. doi:10.1080/15265161.2018.1524224 PMID:30475184

Cohen, I. G., & Mello, M. M. (2019). Big data, big tech, and protecting patient privacy. *Journal of the American Medical Association*, *322*(12), 1141–1142. doi:10.1001/jama.2019.11365 PMID:31397838

Davenport, T., & Kalakota, R. (2019). The potential for artificial intelligence in healthcare. *Future Healthcare Journal*, *6*(2), 94–98. doi:10.7861/futurehosp.6-2-94 PMID:31363513

De Fauw, J., Ledsam, J. R., Romera-Paredes, B., Nikolov, S., Tomasev, N., Blackwell, S., Askham, H., Glorot, X., O'Donoghue, B., Visentin, D., van den Driessche, G., Lakshminarayanan, B., Meyer, C., Mackinder, F., Bouton, S., Ayoub, K., Chopra, R., King, D., Karthikesalingam, A., & Ronneberger, O. (2018). Clinically applicable deep learning for diagnosis and referral in retinal disease. *Nature Medicine*, *24*(9), 1342–1350. doi:10.1038/s41591-018-0107-6 PMID:30104768

Doshi, R., Hu, Y. C., Garg, L., & Fagbola, T. (2023). Towards a Higher Education of the Future: Transformational Roles of Edge Intelligence. *Array (New York, N.Y.)*, 100332. doi:10.1016/j.array.2023.100332

Dreyer, K. J., & Geis, J. R. (2017). When machines think: Radiology's next frontier. *Radiology*, *285*(3), 713–718. doi:10.1148/radiol.2017171183 PMID:29155639

Dumić-Čule, I., Orešković, T., Brkljačić, B., Kujundžić Tiljak, M., & Orešković, S. (2020). The importance of introducing artificial intelligence to the medical curriculum–assessing practitioners' perspectives. *Croatian Medical Journal*, *61*(5), 457–464. doi:10.3325/cmj.2020.61.457 PMID:33150764

Easwaran, B., Hiran, K. K., Krishnan, S., & Doshi, R. (Eds.). (2022). *Real-time applications of machine learning in cyber-physical systems*. IGI global. doi:10.4018/978-1-7998-9308-0

Ellaway, R. H. (2014). Medical education and the war with the machines. *Medical Teacher*, *36*(10), 917–918. doi:10.3109/0142159X.2014.955088 PMID:25216159

Estevez, J., Garate, G., & Graña, M. (2019). Gentle introduction to artificial intelligence for high-school students using scratch. *IEEE Access : Practical Innovations, Open Solutions*, *7*, 179027–179036. doi:10.1109/ACCESS.2019.2956136

Fan, K. Y., Hu, R., & Singla, R. (2020). Introductory machine learning for medical students: A pilot. *Medical Education, 54*(11), 1042–1043. doi:10.1111/medu.14318 PMID:32862464

Farahmand, S. (2022). *CyberPatient™-an innovative approach to medical education* [Doctoral dissertation, University of British Columbia].

Fazlollahi, A. M., Bakhaidar, M., Alsayegh, A., Yilmaz, R., Winkler-Schwartz, A., Mirchi, N., Langleben, I., Ledwos, N., Sabbagh, A. J., Bajunaid, K., Harley, J. M., & Del Maestro, R. F. (2022). Effect of artificial intelligence tutoring vs expert instruction on learning simulated surgical skills among medical students: A randomized clinical trial. *JAMA Network Open, 5*(2), e2149008–e2149008. doi:10.1001/jamanetworkopen.2021.49008 PMID:35191972

Floridi, L. (2019). Establishing the rules for building trustworthy AI. *Nature Machine Intelligence, 1*(6), 261–262. doi:10.1038/s42256-019-0055-y

Gallix, B., & Chong, J. (2019). Artificial intelligence in radiology: Who's afraid of the big bad wolf? *European Radiology, 29*(4), 1637–1639. doi:10.1007/s00330-018-5995-9 PMID:30734848

Gentile, M., Città, G., Perna, S., & Allegra, M. (2023, March). Do we still need teachers? Navigating the paradigm shift of the teacher's role in the AI era. [). Frontiers.]. *Frontiers in Education, 8*, 1161777. doi:10.3389/feduc.2023.1161777

Gilson, A., Safranek, C., Huang, T., Socrates, V., Chi, L., Taylor, R. A., & Chartash, D. (2022). How well does ChatGPT do when taking the medical licensing exams? The implications of large language models for medical education and knowledge assessment. medRxiv, 2022-12.

Goddard, K., Roudsari, A., & Wyatt, J. C. (2012). Automation bias: A systematic review of frequency, effect mediators, and mitigators. *Journal of the American Medical Informatics Association : JAMIA, 19*(1), 121–127. doi:10.1136/amiajnl-2011-000089 PMID:21685142

Grunhut, J., Wyatt, A. T., & Marques, O. (2021). Educating future physicians in artificial intelligence (AI): An integrative review and proposed changes. *Journal of Medical Education and Curricular Development, 8*, 23821205211036836. doi:10.1177/23821205211036836 PMID:34778562

Guidance, W. H. O. (2021). *Ethics and governance of artificial intelligence for health.* World Health Organization.

Guo, J., & Li, B. (2018). The application of medical artificial intelligence technology in rural areas of developing countries. *Health Equity, 2*(1), 174–181. doi:10.1089/heq.2018.0037 PMID:30283865

Haenssle, H. A., Fink, C., Schneiderbauer, R., Toberer, F., Buhl, T., Blum, A., Kalloo, A., Hassen, A. B. H., Thomas, L., Enk, A., Uhlmann, L., Alt, C., Arenbergerova, M., Bakos, R., Baltzer, A., Bertlich, I., Blum, A., Bokor-Billmann, T., Bowling, J., & Zalaudek, I. (2018). Man against machine: Diagnostic performance of a deep learning convolutional neural network for dermoscopic melanoma recognition in comparison to 58 dermatologists. *Annals of Oncology : Official Journal of the European Society for Medical Oncology, 29*(8), 1836–1842. doi:10.1093/annonc/mdy166 PMID:29846502

Han, E. R., Yeo, S., Kim, M. J., Lee, Y. H., Park, K. H., & Roh, H. (2019). Medical education trends for future physicians in the era of advanced technology and artificial intelligence: An integrative review. *BMC Medical Education*, *19*(1), 1–15. doi:10.1186/s12909-019-1891-5 PMID:31829208

Hiran, K. K., Khazanchi, D., Vyas, A. K., & Padmanaban, S. (Eds.). (2021). *Machine learning for sustainable development* (Vol. 9). Walter de Gruyter GmbH & Co KG. doi:10.1515/9783110702514

Hosseini, M. M., Hosseini, S. T. M., Qayumi, K., Ahmady, S., & Koohestani, H. R. (2023). The Aspects of Running Artificial Intelligence in Emergency Care; a Scoping Review. *Archives of Academic Emergency Medicine*, *11*(1). PMID:37215232

Imran, N., & Jawaid, M. (2020). Artificial intelligence in medical education: Are we ready for it? *Pakistan Journal of Medical Sciences*, *36*(5), 857. doi:10.12669/pjms.36.5.3042 PMID:32704252

James, C. A., Wheelock, K. M., & Woolliscroft, J. O. (2021). Machine learning: The next paradigm shift in medical education. *Academic Medicine*, *96*(7), 954–957. doi:10.1097/ACM.0000000000003943 PMID:33496428

Jobin, A., Ienca, M., & Vayena, E. (2019). The global landscape of AI ethics guidelines. *Nature Machine Intelligence*, *1*(9), 389–399. doi:10.1038/s42256-019-0088-2

Jordan, M. I., & Mitchell, T. M. (2015). Machine learning: Trends, perspectives, and prospects. *Science*, *349*(6245), 255–260. doi:10.1126/science.aaa8415 PMID:26185243

Kahraman, H. T., Sagiroglu, S., & Colak, I. (2010, October). Development of adaptive and intelligent web-based educational systems. In *2010 4th international conference on application of information and communication technologies* (pp. 1-5). IEEE. 10.1109/ICAICT.2010.5612054

Kang, J., Thompson, R. F., Aneja, S., Lehman, C., Trister, A., Zou, J., Obcemea, C., & El Naqa, I. (2021). National cancer institute workshop on artificial intelligence in radiation oncology: Training the next generation. *Practical Radiation Oncology*, *11*(1), 74–83. doi:10.1016/j.prro.2020.06.001 PMID:32544635

Khurana, M. (2020). Keeping pace: The need for digital health education in medical schools. *Academic Medicine*, *95*(11), 1629–1630. doi:10.1097/ACM.0000000000003672 PMID:33109967

Kiener, M. (2021). Artificial intelligence in medicine and the disclosure of risks. *AI & Society*, *36*(3), 705–713. doi:10.1007/s00146-020-01085-w PMID:33110296

Kim, M. O., Coiera, E., & Magrabi, F. (2017). Problems with health information technology and their effects on care delivery and patient outcomes: A systematic review. *Journal of the American Medical Informatics Association : JAMIA*, *24*(2), 246–250. doi:10.1093/jamia/ocw154 PMID:28011595

Kim, Y., Soyata, T., & Behnagh, R. F. (2018). Towards emotionally aware AI smart classroom: Current issues and directions for engineering and education. *IEEE Access : Practical Innovations, Open Solutions*, *6*, 5308–5331. doi:10.1109/ACCESS.2018.2791861

Kintsch, W. (2002). The potential of latent semantic analysis for machine grading of clinical case summaries. *Journal of Biomedical Informatics*, *35*(1), 3–7. doi:10.1016/S1532-0464(02)00004-7 PMID:12415721

Kolachalama, V. B., & Garg, P. S. (2018). Machine learning and medical education. *NPJ Digital Medicine*, *1*(1), 54. doi:10.1038/s41746-018-0061-1 PMID:31304333

Laacke, S., Mueller, R., Schomerus, G., & Salloch, S. (2021). Artificial intelligence, social media and depression. A new concept of health-related digital autonomy. *The American Journal of Bioethics*, *21*(7), 4–20. doi:10.1080/15265161.2020.1863515 PMID:33393864

Lanza, F., Seidita, V., & Chella, A. (2020). Agents and robots for collaborating and supporting physicians in healthcare scenarios. *Journal of Biomedical Informatics*, *108*, 103483. doi:10.1016/j.jbi.2020.103483 PMID:32603793

Latifi, S., Gierl, M. J., Boulais, A. P., & De Champlain, A. F. (2016). Using automated scoring to evaluate written responses in English and French on a high-stakes clinical competency examination. *Evaluation & the Health Professions*, *39*(1), 100–113. doi:10.1177/0163278715605358 PMID:26377072

Li, D., Kulasegaram, K., & Hodges, B. D. (2019). Why we needn't fear the machines: Opportunities for medicine in a machine learning world. *Academic Medicine*, *94*(5), 623–625. doi:10.1097/ACM.0000000000002661 PMID:30768470

Mahrishi, M., Hiran, K. K., Meena, G., & Sharma, P. (Eds.). (2020). *Machine learning and deep learning in real-time applications*. IGI global. doi:10.4018/978-1-7998-3095-5

Masoumian Hosseini, M., Masoumian Hosseini, S. T., Qayumi, K., Hosseinzadeh, S., & Sajadi Tabar, S. S. (2023). Smartwatches in healthcare medicine: Assistance and monitoring; a scoping review. *BMC Medical Informatics and Decision Making*, *23*(1), 248. doi:10.1186/s12911-023-02350-w PMID:37924029

Masters, K. (2019). Artificial intelligence in medical education. *Medical Teacher*, *41*(9), 976–980. doi:10.1080/0142159X.2019.1595557 PMID:31007106

Masters, K. (2020). Artificial intelligence developments in medical education: A conceptual and practical framework. *MedEdPublish*, *9*(239), 239. doi:10.15694/mep.2020.000239.1 PMID:38058891

McCarthy, J., & Hayes, P. J. (1981). Some philosophical problems from the standpoint of artificial intelligence. In *Readings in artificial intelligence* (pp. 431–450). Morgan Kaufmann. doi:10.1016/B978-0-934613-03-3.50033-7

McCorduck, P., & Cfe, C. (2004). *Machines who think: A personal inquiry into the history and prospects of artificial intelligence*. CRC Press. doi:10.1201/9780429258985

McDougall, R. J. (2018). Computer knows best? The need for value-flexibility in medical AI. *Journal of Medical Ethics*. PMID:30467198

Meskó, B., Hetényi, G., & Győrffy, Z. (2018). Will artificial intelligence solve the human resource crisis in healthcare? *BMC Health Services Research*, *18*(1), 1–4. doi:10.1186/s12913-018-3359-4 PMID:30001717

Mijwil, M. M., Gök, M., Doshi, R., Hiran, K. K., & Kösesoy, I. (2023). Utilizing Artificial Intelligence Techniques to Improve the Performance of Wireless Nodes. In *Applications of Artificial Intelligence in Wireless Communication Systems* (pp. 150–162). IGI Global. doi:10.4018/978-1-6684-7348-1.ch010

Miller, T., Howe, P., & Sonenberg, L. (2017). Explainable AI: Beware of inmates running the asylum or: How I learnt to stop worrying and love the social and behavioural sciences. *arXiv preprint arXiv:1712.00547.*

Mishra, A., Tripathi, A., Khazanchi, D., Hiran, K. K., Vyas, A. K., & Padmanaban, S. (2021). A framework for applying artificial intelligence (AI) with Internet of NanoThings (IoNT). In *Machine Learning for Sustainable Development* (pp. 1–16). De Gruyter. doi:10.1515/9783110702514-001

Nilsson, N. J. (1998). *Artificial intelligence: a new synthesis*. Morgan Kaufmann.

Obermeyer, Z., & Emanuel, E. J. (2016). Predicting the future—Big data, machine learning, and clinical medicine. *The New England Journal of Medicine*, *375*(13), 1216–1219. doi:10.1056/NEJMp1606181 PMID:27682033

Papachristou, I., & Bosanquet, N. (2020). Improving the prevention and diagnosis of melanoma on a national scale: A comparative study of performance in the United Kingdom and Australia. *Journal of Public Health Policy*, *41*(1), 28–38. doi:10.1057/s41271-019-00187-0 PMID:31477796

Paranjape, K., Schinkel, M., Panday, R. N., Car, J., & Nanayakkara, P. (2019). Introducing artificial intelligence training in medical education. *JMIR Medical Education*, *5*(2), e16048. doi:10.2196/16048 PMID:31793895

Park, S. H., Do, K. H., Kim, S., Park, J. H., & Lim, Y. S. (2019). What should medical students know about artificial intelligence in medicine? *Journal of Educational Evaluation for Health Professions*, *16*, 16. doi:10.3352/jeehp.2019.16.18 PMID:31319450

Quinn, T. P., & Coghlan, S. (2021). Readying medical students for medical AI: The need to embed AI ethics education. *arXiv preprint arXiv:2109.02866.*

Quinn, T. P., Senadeera, M., Jacobs, S., Coghlan, S., & Le, V. (2021). Trust and medical AI: The challenges we face and the expertise needed to overcome them. *Journal of the American Medical Informatics Association : JAMIA*, *28*(4), 890–894. doi:10.1093/jamia/ocaa268 PMID:33340404

Randhawa, G. K., & Jackson, M. (2020, January). The role of artificial intelligence in learning and professional development for healthcare professionals. []. Sage CA: Los Angeles, CA: SAGE Publications.]. *Healthcare Management Forum*, *33*(1), 19–24. doi:10.1177/0840470419869032 PMID:31802725

Rathi, S., Hiran, K. K., & Sakhare, S. (2023). Affective state prediction of E-learner using SS-ROA based deep LSTM. *Array (New York, N.Y.)*, *19*, 100315. doi:10.1016/j.array.2023.100315

Reddy, S., Allan, S., Coghlan, S., & Cooper, P. (2020). A governance model for the application of AI in health care. *Journal of the American Medical Informatics Association : JAMIA*, *27*(3), 491–497. doi:10.1093/jamia/ocz192 PMID:31682262

Robeznieks, A. (2018). ways medical AI can improve workflow for physicians. American Medical Association.

Rudin, C. (2019). Stop explaining black box machine learning models for high stakes decisions and use interpretable models instead. *Nature Machine Intelligence*, *1*(5), 206–215. doi:10.1038/s42256-019-0048-x PMID:35603010

Rus, V., D'Mello, S., Hu, X., & Graesser, A. (2013). Recent advances in conversational intelligent tutoring systems. *AI Magazine*, *34*(3), 42–54. doi:10.1609/aimag.v34i3.2485

Russell, S. J., & Norvig, P. (2010). *Artificial intelligence a modern approach.*

Scantlebury, A., Sheard, L., Watt, I., Cairns, P., Wright, J., & Adamson, J. (2017). Exploring the implementation of an electronic record into a maternity unit: A qualitative study using Normalisation Process Theory. *BMC Medical Informatics and Decision Making*, *17*(1), 1–10. doi:10.1186/s12911-016-0406-0 PMID:28061781

Schwartz, W. B., Patil, R. S., & Szolovits, P. (1987). Artificial intelligence in medicine. *The New England Journal of Medicine*, *316*(11), 685–688. doi:10.1056/NEJM198703123161109 PMID:3821801

Singh, S. V., & Hiran, K. K. (2022). The impact of AI on teaching and learning in higher education technology. *Journal of Higher Education Theory and Practice*, *22*(13).

Sit, C., Srinivasan, R., Amlani, A., Muthuswamy, K., Azam, A., Monzon, L., & Poon, D. S. (2020). Attitudes and perceptions of UK medical students towards artificial intelligence and radiology: A multicentre survey. *Insights Into Imaging*, *11*(1), 1–6. doi:10.1186/s13244-019-0830-7 PMID:32025951

Srivastava, T. K., & Waghmare, L. (2020). Implications of artificial intelligence (AI) on dynamics of medical education and care: A perspective. *Journal of Clinical and Diagnostic Research : JCDR*, *14*(3), 1–2. doi:10.7860/JCDR/2020/43293.13565

Stone, P., Brooks, R., Brynjolfsson, E., Calo, R., Etzioni, O., Hager, G., & Teller, A. (2022). Artificial intelligence and life in 2030: the one hundred year study on artificial intelligence. *arXiv preprint arXiv:2211.06318.*

Stravodimos, K., Katafigiotis, I., Pournaras, C., Dimitroulis, D., Kousournas, G., Fragkiadis, E., & Constantinides, C. (2019). Combined robot assisted right partial nephrectomy and cholecystectomy with single docking. *Journal of Robotic Surgery*, *13*(1), 167–169. doi:10.1007/s11701-018-0805-6 PMID:29600421

Suleimenov, I. E., Vitulyova, Y. S., Bakirov, A. S., & Gabrielyan, O. A. (2020, April). Artificial Intelligence: what is it? In *Proceedings of the 2020 6th International Conference on Computer and Technology Applications* (pp. 22-25). ACM. 10.1145/3397125.3397141

Szolovits, P. (Ed.). (2019). *Artificial intelligence in medicine.* Routledge. doi:10.4324/9780429052071

Topol, E. J. (2019). High-performance medicine: The convergence of human and artificial intelligence. *Nature Medicine*, *25*(1), 44–56. doi:10.1038/s41591-018-0300-7 PMID:30617339

Tsai, Y. S., & Gasevic, D. (2017, March). Learning analytics in higher education---challenges and policies: a review of eight learning analytics policies. In *Proceedings of the seventh international learning analytics & knowledge conference* (pp. 233-242).

Turing, A. M. (2009). *Computing machinery and intelligence.* Springer Netherlands. doi:10.1007/978-1-4020-6710-5_3

van der Niet, A. G., & Bleakley, A. (2021). Where medical education meets artificial intelligence: 'Does technology care?'. *Medical Education*, *55*(1), 30–36. doi:10.1111/medu.14131 PMID:32078175

Van Der Vleuten, C. P., Schuwirth, L. W. T., Driessen, E. W., Govaerts, M. J. B., & Heeneman, S. (2015). Twelve tips for programmatic assessment. *Medical Teacher*, *37*(7), 641–646. doi:10.3109/0142159X.2014.973388 PMID:25410481

Van Wynsberghe, A. (2021). Sustainable AI: AI for sustainability and the sustainability of AI. *AI and Ethics*, *1*(3), 213–218. doi:10.1007/s43681-021-00043-6

VanLehn, K. (2011). The relative effectiveness of human tutoring, intelligent tutoring systems, and other tutoring systems. *Educational Psychologist*, *46*(4), 197–221. doi:10.1080/00461520.2011.611369

Varma, J. R., Fernando, S., Ting, B. Y., Aamir, S., Sivaprakasam, R., & Ting, B. Y. Z. (2023). The Global Use of Artificial Intelligence in the Undergraduate Medical Curriculum: A Systematic Review. *Cureus*, *15*(5). doi:10.7759/cureus.39701 PMID:37398823

Vogt, H., Green, S., Ekstrøm, C. T., & Brodersen, J. (2019). How precision medicine and screening with big data could increase overdiagnosis. *BMJ (Clinical Research Ed.)*, 366. doi:10.1136/bmj.l5270 PMID:31519649

Walsh, K. (2020). Artificial intelligence and healthcare professional education: Superhuman resources for health? *Postgraduate Medical Journal*, *96*(1133), 121–122. doi:10.1136/postgradmedj-2019-137132 PMID:31771964

Wang, Z., & Majewicz Fey, A. (2018). Deep learning with convolutional neural network for objective skill evaluation in robot-assisted surgery. *International Journal of Computer Assisted Radiology and Surgery*, *13*(12), 1959–1970. doi:10.1007/s11548-018-1860-1 PMID:30255463

Ward, J. P., Gordon, J., Field, M. J., & Lehmann, H. P. (2001). Communication and information technology in medical education. *Lancet*, *357*(9258), 792–796. doi:10.1016/S0140-6736(00)04173-8 PMID:11253986

Wartman, S. A., & Combs, C. D. (2018). Medical education must move from the information age to the age of artificial intelligence. *Academic Medicine*, *93*(8), 1107–1109. doi:10.1097/ACM.0000000000002044 PMID:29095704

Wartman, S. A., & Combs, C. D. (2019). Reimagining medical education in the age of AI. *AMA Journal of Ethics*, *21*(2), 146–152. doi:10.1001/amajethics.2019.146 PMID:30794124

Weidenbach, M., Trochim, S., Kreutter, S., Richter, C., Berlage, T., & Grunst, G. (2004). Intelligent training system integrated in an echocardiography simulator. *Computers in Biology and Medicine*, *34*(5), 407–425. doi:10.1016/S0010-4825(03)00084-2 PMID:15145712

Weng, S. F., Vaz, L., Qureshi, N., & Kai, J. (2019). Prediction of premature all-cause mortality: A prospective general population cohort study comparing machine-learning and standard epidemiological approaches. *PLoS One*, *14*(3), e0214365. doi:10.1371/journal.pone.0214365 PMID:30917171

Wiljer, D., & Hakim, Z. (2019). Developing an artificial intelligence–enabled health care practice: Rewiring health care professions for better care. *Journal of Medical Imaging and Radiation Sciences*, *50*(4), S8–S14. doi:10.1016/j.jmir.2019.09.010 PMID:31791914

Wood, E. A., Ange, B. L., & Miller, D. D. (2021). Are we ready to integrate artificial intelligence literacy into medical school curriculum: Students and faculty survey. *Journal of Medical Education and Curricular Development*, *8*, 23821205211024078. doi:10.1177/23821205211024078 PMID:34250242

Yu, K. H., Beam, A. L., & Kohane, I. S. (2018). Artificial intelligence in healthcare. *Nature Biomedical Engineering*, *2*(10), 719–731. doi:10.1038/s41551-018-0305-z PMID:31015651

# Chapter 7
# Exploring AI-Assisted Students Online Proctoring System:
## A Study

**W. Jaisingh**
*Presidency University, India*

**Thangavel Murugan**
https://orcid.org/0000-0002-2510-8857
*United Arab Emirates University, UAE*

## ABSTRACT

*Online proctoring tools and techniques have gained significant attention in recent years due to the increasing popularity of online learning platforms and online assessments. This chapter provides an in-depth analysis of different online proctoring techniques and tools that are commonly used to maintain the integrity of online exams. The chapter begins by highlighting the importance of online proctoring in ensuring fair evaluation and preventing cheating. It then explores various types of online proctoring techniques such as live proctoring, automated proctoring, and recorded proctoring. The advantages and limitations of each technique are discussed, providing a comprehensive understanding of when and how to use them effectively. Overall, this chapter aims to empower educators and administrators with the knowledge and information needed to implement effective online proctoring methods. By understanding the various techniques and tools available, they can enhance the credibility and security of their online assessments, ensuring a fair and reliable evaluation process.*

## INTRODUCTION

Online proctoring (Woldeab, 2019) has become an increasingly popular method for conducting exams and assessments in various educational and professional settings. With the rapid advancement of technology, traditional forms of monitoring and invigilation are being replaced by more efficient and convenient online proctoring tools and techniques. Online proctoring involves the use of webcams, microphones,

DOI: 10.4018/979-8-3693-2440-0.ch007

and other technological devices to observe and monitor candidates remotely during exams. This method ensures the integrity and authenticity of the assessment process, as it allows invigilators to monitor the test-takers in real-time, similar to traditional proctoring methods.

The rise of online learning and the need for flexible and accessible assessment methods have contributed to the growing demand for online proctoring. This method provides an opportunity for organizations, educational institutions, and professional certification bodies to assess candidates remotely, eliminating the need for physical exam centers and reducing logistical constraints. One of the key advantages of online proctoring is its convenience. Test-takers can complete exams from anywhere, as long as they have a stable internet connection and the required equipment. This flexibility allows for greater participation and access to assessments for individuals who may be located in remote areas or have other constraints that prevent them from attending physical test centers. Moreover, online proctoring tools employ various advanced technologies to ensure fair and accurate assessment. These tools include facial recognition software, keystroke analysis, browser lockdowns, and screen recording, among others. These features help in verifying the identity of the test-taker, preventing cheating, and monitoring any unauthorized activities during the exam. However, it is essential to acknowledge that online proctoring also comes with its own challenges and limitations (Sutton, 2019). Privacy concerns, technical issues, and the need for reliable internet connectivity can sometimes hinder the smooth execution of online proctoring. Therefore, it is crucial to carefully evaluate different tools and techniques to ensure that they align with the specific requirements and goals of the assessment process.

In this chapter, we will explore various online proctoring tools and techniques that can be utilized to conduct secure and reliable exams remotely. We will discuss the benefits and limitations of different tools, as well as provide practical recommendations for implementing online proctoring effectively. By the end of this chapter, readers will have gained a comprehensive understanding of online proctoring and be equipped with the knowledge to select and implement the most suitable tools and techniques for their assessment needs (Hiran et al., 2024; Doshi et al., 2023).

## Importance of Proctoring in Online Assessments

With the increasing popularity of online learning, the need for reliable and effective assessment methods has become paramount. One such method is online proctoring (Turani, 2020). Online proctoring tools and techniques play a vital role in ensuring the integrity and credibility of online assessments (Nguyen, 2020). In this section, we will discuss the importance of proctoring in online assessments (Reisenwitz, 2020).

*a)* ***Maintaining academic integrity:*** Online assessments are susceptible to various forms of academic dishonesty, such as cheating, plagiarism, or unauthorized collaboration. Proctoring acts as a deterrent and helps to mitigate the risk of such dishonest practices. By having a proctor present during the assessment, students are less likely to engage in unethical behavior, enhancing the overall integrity of the assessment process.

*b)* ***Ensuring fairness and equity:*** Proctoring helps create a level playing field for all students, regardless of their location or time zone. It ensures that all students are subjected to the same set of rules and regulations, promoting fairness and equity in the assessment process. Proctors monitor the assessment sessions to ensure that no unfair advantage is gained by any student, and that the assessment is conducted under standardized conditions.

*c)* ***Preventing identity fraud:*** Online assessments often require students to authenticate their identities. Proctoring tools employ various identity verification methods, such as facial recognition or document verification, to ensure that the student taking the assessment is indeed the registered candidate. This prevents identity fraud, one of the major concerns in online environments.

*d)* ***Enhancing exam security:*** Proctoring tools employ sophisticated techniques to enhance the security of online assessments. They monitor and record the entire assessment session, keeping a close watch for any suspicious activities. Proctors are trained to identify and address any potential breaches in the assessment process, ensuring that exams are conducted in a secure and controlled environment.

*e)* ***Providing a sense of accountability:*** Proctoring establishes a system of accountability for students, as they are aware that their actions are being monitored. This can significantly reduce instances of cheating or academic misconduct, encouraging students to take assessments seriously and perform to their best abilities.

*f)* ***Maintaining accreditation standards:*** For educational institutions, maintaining accreditation standards is crucial. Proctoring ensures that the assessment practices meet the requirements set by accreditation bodies or regulatory organizations. By implementing proctoring in online assessments, institutions can demonstrate their commitment to upholding the highest standards of education and evaluation.

## Evolution of Online Proctoring Tools

The evolution of online proctoring tools has rapidly transformed the landscape of remote learning and assessment. As technology has advanced, educational institutions have sought out more convenient and secure methods for administering exams and ensuring academic integrity in virtual settings. This section will delve into the key stages of development that online proctoring tools have undergone, leading to their current advanced capabilities (Hussein, 2020).

*a)* *Early Stages - Remote Monitoring and Surveillance:* In the early days of online proctoring, tools primarily focused on remote monitoring and surveillance. Proctors would closely observe test-takers through webcams and screen sharing. This simple approach helped replicate traditional in-person proctoring to some extent, but it proved to be labor-intensive and lacked robust security features, rendering it vulnerable to cheating attempts.

*b)* *Automated Technology Integration:* The next stage in the evolution of online proctoring tools involved the integration of automated technology. This phase saw the emergence of artificial intelligence (AI)-based algorithms that could detect cheating behavior by analyzing test-takers' facial expressions, eye movements, typing patterns, and other indicators.

*c)* *Advanced Biometric Authentication:* To enhance the security of online exams, online proctoring tools gradually incorporated advanced biometric authentication techniques. This stage involved the utilization of facial recognition software, voice recognition technology, and fingerprint scans to verify the identity of test-takers. Such measures significantly minimized the risk of impostors taking exams on behalf of others.

*d)* *Real-time Analytics and Alerts:* As online proctoring tools continued to advance, they began to incorporate real-time analytics and alerts. This allowed proctors to observe student behavior during assessments, detect suspicious activities, and receive immediate notifications. These alerts ranged from instances of suspicious eye movements or attempts to access prohibited resources such as textbooks or other web pages, enabling proctors to take appropriate action promptly.

e) *AI-based Cheating Detection:* The latest stage in the evolution of online proctoring tools involves the integration of AI-based cheating detection algorithms. These intelligent systems employ machine learning and natural language processing techniques to analyze patterns in test responses and identify potential instances of plagiarism or unauthorized assistance.

f) *Integration with LMS:* To streamline the overall examination process, online proctoring tools are now being seamlessly integrated with LMS. This integration simplifies test administration, enables smooth scheduling and exam delivery, and provides a consolidated platform for instructors and students alike.

## BACKGROUND

### Types of Online Proctoring

Online proctoring is a rapidly growing field, and various types of online proctoring techniques have been developed to ensure the integrity of online exams and assessments (González, 2020). Here are some common types of online proctoring:

a) *Live Online Proctoring:* Live online proctoring involves a human proctor who monitors the test-taker in real-time, using video streaming and audio communication. The proctor ensures that the test-taker follows the rules and guidelines of the test, such as not using unauthorized materials or receiving assistance.

b) *Recorded Proctoring:* Recorded proctoring, also known as review proctoring, involves the test-taker's exam session being recorded for subsequent review. The recording can be reviewed later by proctors or instructors to detect any irregularities or suspicious behavior during the exam. This type of proctoring allows for more flexible scheduling of exams, as it does not require real-time monitoring.

c) *Automated Proctoring:* Automated proctoring uses advanced algorithms and artificial intelligence (AI) to monitor the test-taker during the exam. It typically analyzes video, audio, and screen activity to detect any unusual behavior, such as multiple faces on screen, frequent eye movements, or access to unauthorized materials.

d) *AI-Based Proctoring:* AI-based proctoring goes a step further than automated proctoring by using machine learning algorithms to create a baseline of normal test-taker behavior and identify anomalies. These algorithms can adapt to different exam scenarios, such as different subjects, test formats, and environments. They can also continuously learn and improve over time to enhance the accuracy of detecting cheating or misconduct (Coghlan, 2020).

## Choosing the Right Online Proctoring Tool

In order to ensure the integrity and security of online exams, it is essential to choose the right online proctoring tool. This section will cover various considerations, features, and functionality to look for when selecting an online proctoring tool. Additionally, we will discuss the importance of integration with Learning Management Systems (LMS).

### Considerations for Selecting an Online Proctoring Tool

When selecting an online proctoring tool, there are several important considerations to keep in mind. These considerations will help you evaluate the tool's suitability for your specific requirements:

*a)* *Security and Authentication:* Look for a proctoring tool that employs advanced authentication measures to verify the identity of test-takers. This may include facial recognition technology, ID verification, and biometric authentication.
*b)* *Proctoring Methods:* Evaluate the different proctoring methods offered by the tool. Common methods include live proctoring, automated proctoring, and recorded proctoring. Consider which method meets your specific needs and ensures test integrity.
*c)* *Privacy and Data Protection:* Ensure that the proctoring tool complies with privacy regulations, such as GDPR, and implements strong data protection measures. Test-takers' personal information should be securely stored and only accessible to authorized personnel.
*d)* *User-Friendly Interface:* Choose a tool with an intuitive and user-friendly interface. Both instructors and students should be able to navigate the tool easily, minimizing confusion and technical difficulties.
*e)* *Technical Requirements:* Assess the technical requirements of the proctoring tool and ensure compatibility with the devices and operating systems used by your students. Consider factors such as bandwidth requirements, browser compatibility, and device support.

### Features and Functionality

When evaluating online proctoring tools, there are several key features and functionalities to consider:

*a)* *Live Monitoring:* Look for tools that offer live monitoring where certified proctors can actively monitor students during the exam. This allows for real-time intervention and helps prevent cheating incidents.
*b)* *Recording and Playback Options:* Consider tools that allow for recorded proctoring sessions, which can be reviewed later if necessary. This feature provides an additional layer of security and evidence in case of disputes.
*c)* *Screen and Webcam Monitoring:* Ensure that the tool enables continuous monitoring of the test-taker's screen and webcam, providing a comprehensive view of their behavior during the exam.
*d)* *Flagging and Analysis: Look* for tools that have automated flagging and analysis capabilities. This helps identify suspicious behavior such as unusual eye movements, background noise, or multiple faces in the webcam footage.

e) *Secure Exam Environment:* The tool should be able to create a controlled exam environment by disabling features like copy-pasting, printing, or accessing other applications or websites, preventing unauthorized information access.

### Integration with Learning Management Systems (LMS)

Integration with a LMS is crucial for seamless online proctoring (Reisenwitz, 2020; Lee, 2020). Here's why:

a) *Automated Exam Setup:* Integration with an LMS allows for automatic scheduling and creation of proctored exams within the familiar LMS environment, eliminating the need to switch between multiple platforms.
b) *Single Sign-On (SSO):* Integration provides single sign-on capabilities, allowing students and instructors to access the proctoring tool using their existing LMS credentials, streamlining the login process and minimizing friction.
c) *Gradebook Integration:* A robust integration with the LMS gradebook enables quick and efficient grading and feedback delivery for proctored exams. This helps streamline the assessment process for instructors.
d) *Data Analytics and Reporting:* Integration with an LMS facilitates the collection and consolidation of data related to exam monitoring, allowing for comprehensive analytics and reporting on test-taker behavior and performance.

# SOLUTIONS AND RECOMMENDATIONS

## Live Proctoring Techniques

Live proctoring is a method of online proctoring that involves real-time supervision and monitoring of test-takers during an online assessment. It aims to ensure the integrity and security of the exam, as well as prevent any potential instances of cheating or misconduct. In this section, we will explore some of the commonly used live proctoring techniques employed by online proctoring tools.

### Real-Time Monitoring of Test Takers

Real-time monitoring of test takers is a crucial live proctoring technique that ensures the integrity and validity of online exams (Nigam, 2021). Through advanced technology and software, proctors can actively monitor students while they are taking their tests, replicating the surveillance provided during in-person examinations. This section explores the various techniques used to monitor test takers in real-time and their significance in maintaining the fairness of the assessment process.

a. *Webcam Monitoring:* Webcam monitoring is a common method employed in real-time monitoring of test takers. It involves the use of a student's webcam to capture their facial expressions, eye movements, and surroundings during the examination. Proctors can remotely access these webcam feeds to track any suspicious activities or violations of test rules. This technique significantly reduces the chances of impersonation, cheating, or unauthorized assistance during online exams.

b. *Screen Sharing:* Screen sharing is another important technique used to monitor test takers in real-time. With the consent of the student, proctors can access their screens during the examination to observe their on-screen activities. This allows proctors to detect any unauthorized use of prohibited materials, internet browsing, or copying and pasting of answers from external sources.
c. *Keystroke Monitoring:* Keystroke monitoring is a more advanced technique employed in live proctoring to monitor the typing activities of test takers. This technique allows proctors to monitor the keystrokes made by students, enabling them to determine if any unauthorized assistance through chatting or copying and pasting is taking place. By analyzing the typing patterns and frequency, proctors can detect irregularities and intervene if necessary to prevent cheating.
d. *System Monitoring:* System monitoring involves the real-time collection and analysis of system data and logs during online assessments. Proctoring software can track system activities, such as running unauthorized applications or accessing restricted files. Any suspicious activities or violations can be flagged to proctors, who can then intervene and take appropriate actions to maintain the integrity of the test.
e. *Automated Detection Algorithms:* The use of automated detection algorithms enhances the real-time monitoring process by employing artificial intelligence and machine learning techniques. These algorithms can detect patterns, anomalies, and indicators of cheating behavior based on the data collected from different monitoring techniques. By automatically identifying suspicious activities, the algorithms can provide alerts to proctors, enabling them to take immediate action.

## Video and Audio Proctoring

Video and audio proctoring (Woldeab, 2021) is a popular method used in live proctoring techniques to monitor and ensure the integrity of online exams or assessments. This technique utilizes advanced technology to capture both video and audio footage of the test-taker throughout the examination session. Here, we delve into the details of video and audio proctoring, highlighting its benefits and features.

## Video Proctoring

Video proctoring involves recording the test-taker's actions, movements, and facial expressions through a webcam or any other video recording device. The video footage is then analyzed and reviewed by proctors who closely monitor the examination process. Some of the key features of video proctoring include:

a) *Real-time Monitoring:* Online proctors observe the test-taker in real-time, ensuring that they comply with the set rules and regulations throughout the exam. Any suspicious behavior or activities can be detected promptly, allowing immediate action.
b) *Facial Recognition:* Sophisticated technology can now detect the face of the test-taker and verify their identity, ensuring that the right person is taking the exam. This feature adds an extra layer of security and prevents impersonation.

c) *Behavior Analysis:* Video proctoring systems use artificial intelligence (AI) algorithms to analyze the test-taker's behavior during the exam. Any abnormal actions, such as looking away from the screen excessively or attempting to use external devices, can raise red flags for the proctors.

### Audio Proctoring

Audio proctoring, like video proctoring, is an integral component of live proctoring techniques. It involves capturing and analyzing the audio feed during an online examination. The audio proctoring system utilizes advanced algorithms to detect any suspicious sounds or conversations that could indicate cheating. Here are a few noteworthy features of audio proctoring:

a) *Ambient Noise Monitoring:* Audio proctoring systems analyze the ambient noise levels during the exam. Sudden noises or conversations may imply that the test-taker is receiving external assistance, triggering immediate intervention.
b) *Voice Detection:* The technology can identify multiple voices and conversations within the test-taker's surroundings. This ensures that they are not receiving any verbal cues or collaborating with others.
c) *Content Filtering:* The audio proctoring system can filter out unnecessary sounds, focusing only on relevant audio cues. This allows the proctors to concentrate on potential violations and address them promptly.

Together, video and audio proctoring offer robust surveillance measures to maintain the integrity of online exams. By leveraging cutting-edge technology, these systems provide real-time monitoring, facial recognition, behavior analysis, ambient noise detection, and voice identification. These features instill confidence among students and educational institutions, ensuring that the online assessment process is fair, transparent, and reliable.

## Human Proctoring vs. AI Proctoring

In the realm of live proctoring techniques, two prominent methods have emerged – human proctoring and AI proctoring. While both approaches aim to ensure the integrity and security of online exams, they differ significantly in terms of implementation, advantages, and limitations.

### Human Proctoring

Human proctoring involves having a qualified individual monitor the exam session in real-time. This proctor, often an invigilator or a trained professional, is responsible for ensuring that the standardized procedures are followed and taking appropriate action if any suspicious behavior is observed.

Advantages of Human Proctoring:

a) *Real-time intervention:* Human proctors can immediately address any issues or irregularities during the exam session. They could communicate directly with test-takers, providing warnings or clarifications as needed.

b) *Contextual awareness:* Human proctors can consider the specific circumstances of individual test-takers, such as physical or technical limitations, and make judgment calls accordingly.
c) *Flexibility:* Human proctors can adapt their approach to different exam environments and requirements, making it suitable for a wide range of exams, including complex subjects or practical assessments.

Limitations of Human Proctoring:

a) *Expensive:* Human proctoring requires additional resources, including personnel, training, and infrastructure, making it a costly solution for large-scale exams.
b) *Limited scalability:* As human proctors can only monitor a limited number of exam sessions simultaneously, conducting large-scale exams with thousands of test-takers can present logistical challenges.
c) *Subjectivity:* Human proctors may have their own biases or limitations in detecting certain types of cheating, potentially compromising the consistency of enforcement across different exam sessions.

## AI Proctoring

AI proctoring (Coghlan, 2021; Motwani, 2021; Nigam, 2021) involves leveraging artificial intelligence technologies to monitor and analyze test-takers' activities during an exam. It typically includes features such as facial recognition, gaze tracking, and behavioral analysis to detect potential cheating behaviors or abnormal patterns.

Advantages of AI Proctoring:

a) *Cost-effective:* AI proctoring eliminates the need for hiring and training human proctors, making it a more economical solution, especially for large-scale exams.
b) *Scalability:* AI proctoring can handle multiple exam sessions simultaneously, allowing for easier management of vast numbers of test-takers.
c) *Objectivity:* AI proctoring systems can analyze data consistently and objectively without being influenced by personal biases or fatigue.

Limitations of AI Proctoring:

a) *Limited contextual understanding:* AI proctoring algorithms may struggle to interpret the context or intention behind certain behaviors accurately. This can lead to false positives or negatives in detecting cheating attempts.
b) *Technical challenges:* AI proctoring heavily relies on the quality and reliability of technical infrastructure and internet connectivity. Technical issues or glitches may hamper the accuracy and effectiveness of the monitoring process.
c) *Ethical considerations:* The use of AI proctoring raises concerns regarding privacy and data security. Collecting and analyzing personal data during an exam may raise questions related to consent and confidentiality.

## Automated Proctoring Techniques

Automated proctoring techniques have revolutionized the field of online proctoring by utilizing advanced technologies to ensure academic integrity during remote examinations (Ahmad, 2021) (Labayen, 2021). These techniques employ a combination of artificial intelligence (AI), machine learning, and computer vision technologies to monitor and assess students during online exams (Al-Shahwani et al., 2024; Boison et al., 2022; Prajapati et al., 2023).

### Facial Recognition and Identity Verification

One of the key challenges in online proctoring is ensuring the integrity of the examination process by accurately identifying and verifying the identity of the test-takers. To address this issue, many proctoring tools and technologies have incorporated facial recognition and identity verification techniques, offering a robust mechanism to authenticate the individuals taking exams remotely.

Facial recognition is an automated technology that employs advanced algorithms to identify and verify an individual's identity based on their facial features. By analyzing key facial landmarks like the shape of the eyes, nose, and mouth, as well as the contours of the face, these algorithms create a unique facial template for each test-taker. This template serves as a reference point for subsequent identification and verification processes.

During an online examination, facial recognition technology continuously monitors the test-taker's face using the computer's camera. It compares the real-time facial images with the pre-stored facial template to determine if the identity is consistent. Any discrepancies or unauthorized individuals attempting to take the exam can be promptly flagged for investigation or action.

Identity verification is an essential component of facial recognition technology. It involves comparing the facial template with a government-issued ID, such as a driver's license or passport, to verify the test-taker's authenticity. By integrating with secure databases, these systems can instantly confirm the legitimacy of an individual's identification documents. In some cases, online proctoring tools may even use advanced biometric techniques, such as liveness detection, to ensure that the test-taker is physically present during the examination.

The benefits of facial recognition and identity verification in online proctoring are numerous. Firstly, these techniques alleviate concerns about impersonation or proxy test-takers, providing a higher level of trust in the examination process. Secondly, they automate the identification and verification process, reducing the burden on human proctors and minimizing human errors. Additionally, facial recognition technology operates in real-time, enabling immediate intervention in case of suspicious activities or irregularities (Singh et al., 2022; Fagbola et al., 2022).

However, it is crucial to address the privacy concerns associated with facial recognition and identity verification. Test-takers must be informed about the collection and storage of their biometric data, ensuring that it is used solely for examination purposes. Proctoring tools should adhere to strict data protection guidelines, including encryption and secure storage practices, to prevent any unauthorized access or misuse of personal information.

## Browser Lockdown and Screen Recording

In order to ensure the integrity and security of online examinations, automated proctoring techniques have evolved to include browser lockdown and screen recording features. These technologies play a crucial role in preventing cheating and maintaining the authenticity of the assessment process.

Browser lockdown is a technique used by online proctoring tools to restrict the test-taker's access to external applications and websites during the examination. By implementing browser lockdown, the proctoring software eliminates the possibility of students using search engines, accessing external materials, or communicating with others through online platforms. This helps maintain a controlled environment and ensures that students rely solely on their knowledge and understanding for answering exam questions.

The use of screen recording further enhances the effectiveness of browser lockdown. Proctoring tools capture and record the entire test-taking process, including the test-taker's screen, audio, and webcam feed. This comprehensive recording serves as evidence later on, enabling manual review of any suspicious behavior. Algorithms within the proctoring software can also detect unusual activities such as multiple faces in the camera frame or frequent screen changes, alerting the proctor to potentially dishonest behavior.

Screen recording not only assists in detecting and preventing cheating but also aids in resolving any disputes or issues raised by students during or after the assessment. Reviewing the recorded videos provides a deeper insight into the test-taker's demeanor and actions, ensuring a fair and impartial evaluation process.

To ensure privacy and data protection, it is essential for educational institutions to clearly communicate their data handling practices to students, detailing how the recordings will be used, stored securely, and ultimately deleted once the evaluation process is complete. Institutions must adhere to relevant data protection laws, ensuring the anonymity and confidentiality of students' personal information.

## Keystroke Analysis and Behavior Monitoring

Keystroke analysis and behavior monitoring are powerful techniques used in automated proctoring systems to detect and deter cheating during online exams. These techniques focus on examining a student's typing patterns and behavior to identify any suspicious or unauthorized activity.

One of the primary aspects of keystroke analysis is to analyze the rhythm and speed of a person's typing. Each individual has a unique typing pattern, influenced by their muscle memory and habits. Keystroke analysis tracks the timing and duration of keystrokes, intervals between keystrokes, and other related metrics. By comparing these patterns to a baseline established for each student, the system can identify any deviations that may indicate unauthorized assistance or cheating.

Behavior monitoring is another integral part of automated proctoring systems. It captures and evaluates the various behaviors exhibited by the students during an online exam. This may include analyzing the student's eye movement, facial expressions, head orientation, browser activity, and even background noise.

For example, if a student is constantly looking away from the screen or frequently glancing in a suspicious manner, it may indicate that they are referring to external resources or engaging in collaboration with others. Similarly, sudden head movements or suspicious noises in the background might suggest the presence of unauthorized individuals nearby.

Combining keystroke analysis and behavior monitoring provides a comprehensive approach to ensure exam integrity. By continuously monitoring and analyzing these aspects, online proctoring tools can accurately detect potential cheating attempts and raise alerts when necessary.

It is important to acknowledge that both keystroke analysis and behavior monitoring techniques rely on sophisticated algorithms. The algorithms are trained using large datasets, allowing them to identify patterns and anomalies effectively. However, false positives and false negatives can still occur, highlighting the importance of human intervention for a final decision.

Automated proctoring tools equipped with keystroke analysis and behavior monitoring capabilities provide a proactive approach to maintaining the integrity of online assessments. These techniques offer educators and institutions the confidence that students are being monitored effectively and that cheating attempts can be identified and addressed promptly.

However, it is crucial to strike a balance between the desire to maintain exam security and respecting students' privacy. Educational institutions must ensure that the data collected and utilized for these techniques are handled securely and according to the highest privacy standards. Striving for transparency and open communication about the implementation of these tools is essential to foster trust among students and faculty.

## Recorded Proctoring Techniques

Recorded proctoring is a cutting-edge approach employed in online education to maintain academic integrity during assessments. It involves the use of technology to record a test-taker's entire examination session, including audio, video, and screen activity. This recorded session can then be reviewed and analyzed by educators or proctors to ensure the integrity of the assessment. Below, we provide a detailed explanation of recorded proctoring techniques, highlighting their significance and nuances:

### Reviewing Recorded Sessions

In the digital age, the ability to review recorded sessions has opened up new possibilities for ensuring the fairness and security of online assessments. This section of the chapter will take readers on a journey through the intricacies of reviewing recorded sessions. It will explore how educators and proctors can leverage recorded materials to meticulously scrutinize test-taker behavior, identifying potential red flags and anomalies. Readers will gain insights into the techniques and tools used for reviewing recorded sessions, enabling them to appreciate the meticulous process of post-assessment analysis that is at the heart of recorded proctoring. Let's delve into this concept further with an example that relates to a current trend in online education.

Example: AI-Powered Behavior Analysis

Today's trend in online education is the integration of artificial intelligence (AI) and machine learning algorithms into proctoring systems to enhance the review of recorded sessions. AI-powered behavior analysis is becoming increasingly popular, allowing for more efficient and accurate identification of potential cheating or misconduct.

*Scenario:* Consider a scenario where a university is conducting a high-stakes online examination for a large group of students. To maintain the integrity of the assessment, they implement recorded proctoring techniques with AI-powered behavior analysis.

Implementation:

a) *Recording the Examination Session:* During the online examination, each student's session is recorded, capturing their face, audio, and screen activity.

b) *AI Behavior Analysis:* After the examination, the recorded sessions are processed using AI algorithms. These algorithms are trained to recognize various behaviors and actions that might indicate cheating or academic misconduct.
c) *Identifying Suspicious Behavior:* The AI algorithms analyze the recorded sessions, looking for patterns and anomalies. For example:
   - If a student consistently looks away from the screen for extended periods, it may be flagged as suspicious behavior.
   - Unusual keyboard and mouse activity, such as rapid switching between screens or excessive copying and pasting, can also trigger alerts.
   - The AI can detect attempts to open unauthorized applications or browse the internet during the exam.
d) *Alerting Proctors:* When the AI identifies suspicious behavior, it generates alerts for human proctors or educators to review specific segments of the recorded sessions. This targeted review saves time and ensures that potential misconduct is thoroughly examined.

*Benefits and Today's Trend:* AI-powered behavior analysis enhances the efficiency of reviewing recorded sessions by automating the initial detection of suspicious behavior. It allows educational institutions to scale their proctoring efforts for many students, a crucial need in today's era of remote learning and online assessments. The trend aligns with the broader adoption of AI and machine learning in education technology, making the proctoring process more accurate and reliable.

## Machine Learning Algorithms for Cheating Detection

Machine learning algorithms have revolutionized the field of cheating detection in online assessments. These algorithms use data-driven techniques to identify patterns and behaviors that may indicate academic dishonesty. Let's explore this concept further with an example that relates to a current trend in online education.

Example: Behavior Analytics and Trend Detection

Today's trend in online education is the use of advanced behavior analytics and trend detection through machine learning to enhance cheating detection.

*Scenario:* Imagine a scenario in which an online course platform is used by thousands of students worldwide. The platform wants to ensure the integrity of assessments and prevent cheating.

Implementation:

a) *Collecting Data:* During online assessments, the platform collects a variety of data points, including the student's keystrokes, mouse movements, eye gaze patterns, and response times.
b) *Building a Machine Learning Model:* The platform employs machine learning techniques to build a predictive model. This model is trained on a vast dataset that includes examples of both normal and suspicious behavior. The training dataset may include data from various subjects and assessment types to make the model more robust.
c) *Real-Time Monitoring:* As students take assessments, the machine learning model continuously monitors their behavior in real-time. It analyzes data streams to identify deviations from normal behavior.
d) Cheating Detection:

- *Example 1: Copy-Paste Detection:* If a student repeatedly copies and pastes large sections of text into their answers, the machine learning algorithm may flag this behavior as potentially suspicious.
- *Example 2: Abnormal Response Times:* The algorithm can detect if a student consistently answers questions too quickly or too slowly compared to their usual pace, indicating possible cheating or unauthorized assistance.
- *Example 3: Eye Gaze Patterns:* By analyzing eye gaze patterns through webcam data, the algorithm can detect if a student is frequently looking away from the screen, suggesting they may be consulting external resources.

e) *Alerting Proctors:* When the algorithm identifies behavior that exceeds predefined thresholds or is highly unusual, it generates alerts for human proctors or educators to review the situation. Proctors can then use the recorded session to make informed decisions.

*Benefits and Today's Trend:* Behavior analytics and trend detection through machine learning provide a dynamic and adaptive approach to cheating detection. The trend aligns with the need for proactive and real-time cheating prevention in online education, especially in massive open online courses (MOOCs) and remote learning environments. Continuous monitoring and data-driven insights help educational institutions stay ahead of evolving cheating techniques.

## BEST PRACTICES FOR IMPLEMENTING ONLINE PROCTORING

The implementation of online proctoring has become increasingly essential in the realm of remote education, offering a means to uphold academic integrity during online assessments. As educational institutions and organizations embrace this technology-driven solution, it is imperative to adhere to a set of best practices that ensures a balance between safeguarding the integrity of examinations and respecting the rights and privacy of students. In this chapter, we delve into a comprehensive exploration of the best practices for implementing online proctoring, shedding light on transparent communication, informed consent, robust privacy protection, and the mitigation of bias. These practices, grounded in ethics and fairness, not only serve as a guide for educational stakeholders but also foster trust, accessibility, and responsible use of technology in the educational landscape. Here are some best practices for implementing online proctoring, which are highly relevant to the book chapter on "Online Proctoring Tools and Techniques" and the ethical considerations mentioned earlier:

*i.* *Transparent Communication:* Clearly communicate the use of online proctoring to all stakeholders, including students, instructors, and administrators. Explain the purpose, process, and data handling procedures.

*ii.* *Informed Consent:* Obtain informed consent from students before implementing online proctoring. Students should understand what data will be collected, how it will be used, and for how long it will be retained.

*iii.* *Privacy Protection:* Implement robust data security measures to protect the privacy of recorded data. Ensure data encryption, secure storage, and access controls to prevent breaches.

*iv.* *Minimal Intrusiveness:* Minimize the intrusiveness of proctoring by focusing on capturing only relevant data for academic integrity purposes. Avoid recording unnecessary personal details.

v. *Alternative Assessments:* Offer alternative assessment methods for students who have privacy concerns, technological limitations, or accessibility issues related to online proctoring.
vi. *Proctor Training:* Provide training to proctors and educators involved in reviewing recorded sessions. Educate them on ethical guidelines, responsible use of data, and fairness considerations.
vii. *Regular Audits and Reviews:* Conduct regular audits and reviews of the recorded proctoring process, including the performance of machine learning algorithms, to identify and address any biases or inaccuracies.
viii. *Data Retention Policies:* Establish clear data retention policies specifying the duration for which recorded data will be retained. Data should not be kept longer than necessary.
ix. *Fairness Mitigation:* Mitigate unintended consequences and bias in online proctoring. Have mechanisms in place to review and rectify cases of false accusations or unfair treatment.
x. *Accessibility:* Ensure that online proctoring tools and processes are accessible to all students, regardless of their technological capabilities or disabilities.
xi. *Ethical Review Board:* Consider establishing an ethical review board or committee within your institution to oversee the implementation of online proctoring and address ethical concerns.
xii. *Continuous Improvement:* Continuously assess and improve the online proctoring process by seeking feedback from students and educators. Adapt to evolving technology and best practices.
xiii. *Ethical Guidelines:* Develop and adhere to a set of ethical guidelines specific to online proctoring, outlining the institution's commitment to privacy, fairness, and responsible use.
xiv. *Student Support:* Provide resources and support for students who encounter technical issues or need assistance with online proctoring. Address their concerns promptly and effectively.
xv. *Regular Communication:* Maintain open lines of communication with students throughout the assessment process, addressing any questions or concerns they may have regarding proctoring.

By following these best practices, educational institutions can implement online proctoring in a way that upholds academic integrity while respecting the privacy and rights of students. These practices also help build trust and confidence in the use of proctoring technology within the educational community.

## Preparing Test Takers for Online Proctoring

Preparing test takers for online proctoring is a crucial aspect of ensuring a smooth and fair examination process (Almutawa, 2022) (Meulmeester, 2021). It involves informing students about the proctoring procedure, setting expectations, and providing guidance to minimize anxiety and technical issues. Here, we offer a detailed explanation of this important aspect, along with an example illustrating its significance:

i. *Communication and Information:* Start by communicating with test takers well in advance of the examination. Provide clear and comprehensive information about the online proctoring process, including what it entails, how it works, and its purpose in maintaining academic integrity.
ii. *Technical Requirements:* Ensure that test takers are aware of the technical requirements for online proctoring, such as supported devices, browsers, and internet speed. Offer guidance on how to perform a system check to verify compatibility.
iii. *Environment Setup:* Emphasize the importance of choosing an appropriate exam environment. Test takers should select a quiet, well-lit, and distraction-free space. Advise them to remove any unauthorized materials or devices from their workspace.

iv. *Familiarization with Tools:* Offer opportunities for students to familiarize themselves with the online proctoring tools and interface. Conduct practice sessions or provide access to demo exams to help students understand how the proctoring software works.
v. *Support Channels:* Establish clear channels of support for test takers. Provide contact information for technical support and assistance with proctoring-related questions. Ensure that help is readily available during the exam period.
vi. *Test Timing and Scheduling:* Guide students on the importance of scheduling their exam at a suitable time and ensuring they have enough time to complete it without interruptions. Highlight the need to adhere to the specified start and end times.
vii. *Ethical Guidelines:* Reinforce the importance of adhering to ethical guidelines during the exam, including not seeking external help, not attempting to cheat, and not engaging in any dishonest behavior.
viii. *Stress Management:* Acknowledge that online proctoring can be stressful for some students and provide resources or strategies for managing exam-related anxiety. Encourage relaxation techniques and time management skills.

By implementing these practices and providing test takers with the necessary information and support, educational institutions and organizations can ensure that students are well-prepared for online proctoring, resulting in a fair and successful examination experience.

## Communication and Transparency With Students

Effective communication and transparency with students are foundational principles when implementing online proctoring in education (Almutawa, 2022; Meulmeester, 2021). These practices are essential for building trust, managing expectations, and addressing concerns related to online proctoring. Here, we provide a detailed explanation of the significance of communication and transparency in this context:

i. *Clear Information Dissemination:* At the outset, provide students with comprehensive information about the online proctoring process. Clearly explain what online proctoring entails, how it will be conducted, and the reasons for its use. This information should be easily accessible through course materials, websites, or emails.
ii. *Purpose and Benefits:* Clearly communicate the purpose and benefits of online proctoring to students. Explain that its primary goal is to maintain academic integrity, prevent cheating, and ensure a fair evaluation process for all learners. Emphasize that it is a tool to protect the value of their education.
iii. *Privacy and Data Usage:* Be transparent about the collection and use of student data during online proctoring. Clarify what data will be recorded (e.g., video, audio, screen activity) and how it will be handled, stored, and retained. Assure students of data security measures in place.
iv. *Technical Requirements:* Clearly state the technical requirements for online proctoring, including compatible devices, browsers, and internet connectivity. Provide guidance on how students can perform system checks to ensure their setup meets the requirements (Shrivas et al., 2022; Mishra et al., 2021).

v. *Student Support Channels:* Inform students about available support channels for proctoring-related inquiries or technical assistance. Provide contact information for helpdesk or support teams that students can reach out to during the exam period.
vi. *Practice and Orientation:* Encourage students to engage in practice sessions or orientations to familiarize themselves with the online proctoring platform and its features. Offer opportunities for students to ask questions and address concerns.
vii. *Regular Updates:* Maintain ongoing communication with students regarding any updates, changes, or improvements to the online proctoring process. Provide timely information about policy revisions or technical enhancements.
viii. *Feedback Mechanism:* Establish a feedback mechanism that allows students to share their experiences, concerns, or suggestions related to online proctoring. Actively listen to student feedback and consider making adjustments based on their input.
ix. *Ethical Guidelines:* Reinforce ethical guidelines and academic integrity standards in all communications. Remind students of their responsibility to maintain honesty and integrity during assessments, whether proctored or not.
x. *Accessibility and Accommodations:* Ensure that communication materials and proctoring processes are accessible to all students, including those with disabilities. Provide information about available accommodations and how students can request them.

## Addressing Privacy and Data Security Concerns

Addressing privacy and data security concerns is of paramount importance when implementing online proctoring in education (Balash, 2021). Ensuring the protection of students' personal information and maintaining the integrity of data are essential ethical considerations. Here, we provide a detailed explanation of the significance of addressing privacy and data security concerns in this context:

i. *Data Collection Transparency:* Clearly communicate to students what data will be collected during the online proctoring process. This includes video footage, audio recordings, and screen activity. Explain the purpose of collecting this data and how it contributes to academic integrity.
ii. *Consent and Informed Choice:* Obtain informed consent from students before they participate in proctored assessments. Ensure that students are fully aware of the data collection process and the potential implications, allowing them to make an informed choice.
iii. *Data Encryption and Security Measures:* Implement robust data encryption protocols to protect the transmission and storage of collected data. Ensure that data is encrypted both in transit and at rest. Implement strict access controls to limit data exposure.
iv. *Secure Storage and Retention Policies:* Develop clear policies regarding the storage and retention of proctoring data. Specify the duration for which data will be retained, ensuring that it is not kept longer than necessary. Securely delete data after the retention period expires.
v. *Access Control and Authorization:* Implement strict access controls and authorization mechanisms to limit who can access proctoring data. Only authorized personnel, such as proctors or designated administrators, should have access.

vi. *Third-Party Vendors and Compliance:* When using third-party proctoring services, ensure that the vendor complies with data protection regulations and industry standards. Conduct due diligence to assess the vendor's data security practices and compliance certifications.
vii. *Data Breach Response Plan:* Develop a comprehensive data breach response plan in case of a security incident. This plan should outline the steps to be taken to investigate, mitigate, and report a breach, including notifying affected individuals.
viii. *Regular Security Audits:* Conduct regular security audits and assessments of the proctoring system to identify vulnerabilities and ensure compliance with data security standards. Address any security gaps promptly to enhance protection.
ix. *Student Rights and Access:* Inform students about their rights regarding their data and provide a process through which they can request access to their own proctoring data or request its deletion after the retention period expires.
x. *Training and Awareness:* Educate staff, proctors, and students about data security best practices and the importance of safeguarding personal information. Promote a culture of data security awareness within the institution.

## Challenges and Limitations of Online Proctoring

Online proctoring, while valuable for maintaining academic integrity in online education, is not without its challenges and limitations (Lee, 2022; Noorbehbahani, 2022; Holden, 2021). Here's a brief explanation of some common challenges and limitations associated with this technology:

i. *Technical Issues:* Students may encounter technical problems, such as compatibility issues, internet connectivity issues, or hardware malfunctions during proctored exams, which can disrupt the assessment process.
ii. *Privacy Concerns:* The collection of video, audio, and screen data during online proctoring raises privacy concerns among students. Ensuring a balance between security and privacy can be challenging.
iii. *Access Disparities:* Some students may lack access to the necessary devices or stable internet connections required for online proctoring, creating inequities in assessment accessibility.
iv. *False Positives:* Proctoring algorithms may sometimes flag innocent behavior as suspicious, leading to false accusations of cheating. This can result in stress and unfair treatment for students.
v. *Invasive Perception:* Students may perceive online proctoring as invasive, impacting their comfort and concentration during exams, potentially affecting performance.
vi. *Technical Limitations:* The effectiveness of proctoring solutions can be limited by factors like the quality of webcam footage, audio recordings, and the ability to detect sophisticated cheating methods.
vii. *Ethical Concerns:* Striking the right balance between preventing cheating and respecting students' ethical rights can be challenging. Institutions must carefully consider the ethical implications of proctoring.
viii. *Costs:* Implementing and maintaining online proctoring systems can be expensive for institutions which may need to invest in technology, training, and ongoing support.

ix. *Monitoring Capacity:* Institutions may face limitations in their capacity to effectively monitor many students taking proctored exams simultaneously, potentially leading to oversight gaps.

x. *Reliability:* The reliability of online proctoring solutions can vary depending on the technology used and the proficiency of proctors, potentially affecting the accuracy of cheating detection.

xi. *Instructor Adaptation:* Instructors may need training and support to effectively utilize proctoring tools, and adapting to online proctoring may require changes in teaching and assessment practices.

xii. *Student Anxiety:* The knowledge of being monitored during exams can induce anxiety and stress in some students, potentially affecting their performance.

## FUTURE RESEARCH DIRECTION

The landscape of online education and assessment is continuously evolving, and online proctoring is no exception. As educational institutions and organizations seek more robust and flexible solutions for maintaining academic integrity in a digital age, the future of online proctoring promises innovative trends and advancements. In this introduction, we explore some of the key upcoming trends that are set to shape the landscape of online proctoring, from the integration of artificial intelligence to the enhancement of privacy protection and the development of user-friendly, accessible technologies. These trends not only address the evolving challenges of remote education but also strive to improve the overall experience for students and educators alike, ensuring fair and secure assessments in an ever-changing educational environment (Jadi, 2021) (Jia, 2021) (Logan, 2021).

### Advancements in AI and Machine Learning

Advancements in artificial intelligence (AI) and machine learning (ML) are revolutionizing online proctoring, making it more effective and accurate in maintaining academic integrity during remote assessments. Here's a detailed explanation of how AI and ML are shaping the future of online proctoring:

a) *Behavior Analysis:* AI-driven behavior analysis is a cornerstone of modern online proctoring. These systems monitor students during exams, analyzing their actions, movements, and interactions with the exam interface. ML algorithms can detect unusual behavior, such as excessive eye movement or repeated glances at unauthorized materials.

b) *Pattern Recognition:* ML models can identify patterns of behavior associated with cheating, such as looking away from the screen frequently, typing patterns, or accessing external websites. Over time, these systems learn from a vast dataset of student behavior, enabling them to improve their accuracy in flagging potential irregularities.

c) *Voice and Audio Analysis:* AI-based voice and audio analysis can identify suspicious sounds or conversations during an exam. For example, if a student is speaking or receiving instructions from someone else while taking a test, the system can detect this and raise an alert.

d) *Face Recognition:* Facial recognition technology is integrated into many online proctoring systems to verify the identity of the test-taker and detect if someone else is attempting to take the exam on their behalf.

e) *Keystroke Analysis:* ML algorithms can analyze the typing patterns of students to detect unusual speed, rhythm, or variations in typing that may suggest cheating or unauthorized assistance.
f) *Plagiarism Detection:* AI-driven plagiarism detection tools can scan written responses for similarities to online sources, academic papers, or other students' work, helping to identify instances of plagiarism.
g) *Adaptive Monitoring:* AI can adapt monitoring levels based on the student's behavior. For example, if a student exhibits suspicious actions, the system may increase monitoring intensity, but if the behavior remains consistent with normal test-taking, the monitoring can be less intrusive.
h) *Reducing False Positives:* AI and ML are continually improving in their ability to reduce false positives—instances where innocent behavior is flagged as suspicious. By fine-tuning algorithms and incorporating more data, these systems aim to provide a more accurate assessment of student conduct.
i) *Real-time Alerts and Intervention:* AI-driven proctoring systems can provide real-time alerts to proctors or instructors if suspicious behavior is detected. This allows for timely intervention, ensuring that cheating is addressed promptly.
j) *Customization and Adaptation:* Institutions can customize and fine-tune AI-based proctoring systems to align with their specific assessment needs and ethical considerations. This adaptability allows for a more tailored and balanced approach to proctoring.
k) *Improving User Experience:* AI can contribute to a better user experience by streamlining the proctoring process. For example, AI-driven identity verification can be faster and more seamless, reducing disruptions for students.

## Adaptive Proctoring and Continuous Authentication

Adaptive proctoring and continuous authentication are innovative approaches to online proctoring that aim to enhance the security of assessments while maintaining a positive user experience. Here's a detailed explanation of these concepts:

### Adaptive Proctoring

Adaptive proctoring is a dynamic approach to monitoring online exams. It involves tailoring the level of proctoring based on the behavior and history of individual test-takers. Here's how it works:

a) *Behavioral Analysis:* Adaptive proctoring systems use AI and machine learning to analyze the behavior of students during exams. They establish a baseline of normal behavior for each student, considering factors like gaze patterns, typing speed, mouse movements, and screen activity.
b) *Behavioral Anomalies:* If a student's behavior deviates from their established baseline, the system may escalate the level of proctoring. For example, if a student starts looking away from the screen frequently or engages in suspicious actions, the system may increase monitoring intensity.
c) *Reduced Intrusiveness:* One of the key benefits of adaptive proctoring is that it reduces intrusiveness. Students who exhibit consistent and normal behavior face minimal disruption during exams, as the system only intervenes when unusual activity is detected.

d) *Real-time Alerts:* Adaptive proctoring systems can send real-time alerts to proctors or instructors if suspicious behavior is detected. This allows for timely intervention to address potential academic misconduct.
e) *Customization:* Institutions can customize the parameters of adaptive proctoring to align with their ethical and security considerations. This flexibility allows for a balanced approach that considers the unique needs of each educational setting.

### Continuous Authentication

Continuous authentication takes the concept of identity verification a step further by continually verifying the identity of the test-taker throughout the entire exam. Here's how it works:

a) *Initial Authentication:* At the start of the exam, continuous authentication typically involves robust identity verification methods, such as facial recognition, fingerprint scanning, or keystroke analysis. This ensures that the person taking the test is the registered student.
b) *Ongoing Verification:* Throughout the exam, the system continues to monitor and verify the student's identity. This can include periodic facial recognition checks or additional biometric authentication methods at random intervals.
c) *Immediate Alerts:* If the system detects a potential identity mismatch or unauthorized presence, it can trigger immediate alerts to proctors or instructors for intervention.
d) *Anti-Impersonation Measures:* Continuous authentication includes measures to prevent impersonation, such as requiring students to periodically show their ID card or perform a specific action that confirms their identity.

## CONCLUSION

As we've delved into the various aspects of online proctoring, it's evident that this technology-driven approach to monitoring test-takers during examinations is far from one-size-fits-all. Our journey began with an introduction to online proctoring, highlighting its importance in today's digital education era and tracing its evolution over time. We then explored the diverse types of online proctoring, from live proctoring that offers real-time monitoring to automated and recorded proctoring methods that bring efficiency and flexibility to assessment security. Then we've examined the considerations that guide this selection process and the essential features that a proctoring tool should offer. Integration with Learning Management Systems (LMS) is a crucial aspect to ensure a seamless and unified experience for educators and students. Moreover, we've delved into the techniques employed in live proctoring, highlighting the differences between human proctoring and AI proctoring, and explored the automated proctoring methods that encompass identity verification, browser lockdown, screen recording, and behavior analysis. These insights empower institutions to make informed decisions in implementing online proctoring solutions that align with their unique needs, ethical standards, and the diverse requirements of their student population. As we conclude this comprehensive exploration of online proctoring, it's evident that this technology is not just a response to the challenges of remote education but a catalyst for innovation in the assessment landscape. The future holds even more promising trends, such as AI-driven advancements and continuous authentication, which will further enhance the security and user experience in online assessments.

## REFERENCES


Ahmad, I., AlQurashi, F., Abozinadah, E., & Mehmood, R. (2021). A novel deep learning-based online proctoring system using face recognition, eye blinking, and object detection techniques. *International Journal of Advanced Computer Science and Applications, 12*(10). doi:10.14569/IJACSA.2021.0121094

Al-Shahwani, H. I. W., Mijwil, M. M., Doshi, R., Hiran, K. K., & Bala, I. (2024). Evaluating Antivirus Effectiveness Against Malware in Ascending Order for Increasing Blockchain Endpoint Protection. In *Bio-Inspired Optimization Techniques in Blockchain Systems* (pp. 150–166). IGI Global. doi:10.4018/979-8-3693-1131-8.ch008

Almutawa, A. M., & Sruthi, S. (2022). Students' perspective towards online proctoring in exams during COVID-19. *Journal of Engineering Research, 10*(no. 4A).

Balash, D. G., Kim, D., Shaibekova, D., Fainchtein, R. A., Sherr, M., & Aviv, A. J. (2021). Examining the examiners: Students' privacy and security perceptions of online proctoring services. In *Seventeenth symposium on usable privacy and security (SOUPS 2021)*, (pp. 633-652). IEEE.

Boison, D. K., Malcalm, E., Antwi-Boampong, A., Doumbia, M. O., & Hiran, K. K. (2022). Assessing Factors Affecting the Blockchain Adoption in Public Procurement Delivery in Ghana: A Correlational Study Using UTAUT2 Theoretical Framework. [IJACI]. *International Journal of Ambient Computing and Intelligence, 13*(1), 1–13. doi:10.4018/ijaci.314568

Coghlan, S., Miller, T., & Paterson, J. (2020). *"Good proctor or" Big Brother"? AI Eth-ics and Online Exam Supervision Technologies.* arXiv preprint arXiv:2011.07647

Coghlan, S., Miller, T., & Paterson, J. (2021). Good proctor or "big brother"? Ethics of online exam supervision technologies. *Philosophy & Technology, 34*(4), 1581–1606. doi:10.1007/s13347-021-00476-1 PMID:34485025

Doshi, R., Hiran, K. K., Mijwil, M. M., & Anand, D. (2023). To That of Artificial Intelligence, Passing Through Business Intelligence. In *Handbook of Research on AI and Knowledge Engineering for Real-Time Business Intelligence* (pp. 1–16). IGI Global. doi:10.4018/978-1-6684-6519-6.ch001

Fagbola, T. M., Fagbola, F. I., Aroba, O. J., Doshi, R., Hiran, K. K., & Thakur, S. C. (2022). Smart face masks for Covid-19 pandemic management: A concise review of emerging architectures, challenges and future research directions. *IEEE Sensors Journal, 23*(2), 877–888. doi:10.1109/JSEN.2022.3225067

González-González, C. S., Infante-Moro, A., & Infante-Moro, J. C. (2020). Implemen-tation of e-proctoring in online teaching: A study about motivational factors. *Sustainability (Basel), 12*(8), 3488. doi:10.3390/su12083488

Hiran, K. K., Doshi, R., & Patel, M. (Eds.). (2024). *Applications of Virtual and Augmented Reality for Health and Wellbeing.* IGI Global., doi:10.4018/979-8-3693-1123-3

Holden, O. L., Norris, M. E., & Kuhlmeier, V. A. (2021). Academic integrity in online assessment: A research review. In Frontiers in Education, 6. Frontiers Media SA.

Hussein, M. J., Yusuf, J., Deb, A. S., Fong, L., & Nai-du, S. (2020). An evaluation of online proctoring tools. *Open Praxis*, *12*(4), 509–525. doi:10.5944/openpraxis.12.4.1113

Jadi, A. (2021). New detection cheating method of online-exams during COVID-19 pandemic. *Int. J. Comput. Sci. Netw. Secur*, *21*(4), 123–130.

Jia, J., & He, Y. (2021). The design, implementation and pilot application of an intelligent online proctoring system for online exams. *Interactive Technology and Smart Education*, *19*(1), 112–120. doi:10.1108/ITSE-12-2020-0246

Labayen, M., Vea, R., Flórez, J., Aginako, N., & Sierra, B. (2021). Online student authentication and proctoring system based on multimodal biometrics technology. *IEEE Access : Practical Innovations, Open Solutions*, *9*, 72398–72411. doi:10.1109/ACCESS.2021.3079375

Lee, J. W. (2020). Impact of Proctoring Environments on Student Performance: Online vs Offline Proctored Exams. *Journal of Asian Finance Economics and Business*, *7*(8), 653–660. doi:10.13106/jafeb.2020.vol7.no8.653

Lee, K., & Fanguy, M. (2022). Online exam proctoring technologies: Educational innovation or deterioration? *British Journal of Educational Technology*, *53*(3), 475–490. doi:10.1111/bjet.13182

Logan, C. (2021). Toward abolishing online proctoring: Counter-narratives, deep change, and pedagogies of educational dignity. *Journal of Interactive Technology and Pedagogy, 20.*

Meulmeester, F. L., Dubois, E. A., Krommenhoek-van Es, C., de Jong, P. G. M., & Langers, A. M. J. (2021). Medical students' perspectives on online proctoring during remote digital progress test. *Medical Science Educator*, *31*(6), 1773–1777. doi:10.1007/s40670-021-01420-w PMID:34611498

Mishra, A., Tripathi, A., Khazanchi, D., Hiran, K. K., Vyas, A. K., & Padmanaban, S. (2021). A framework for applying artificial intelligence (AI) with Internet of NanoThings (IoNT). In *Machine Learning for Sustainable Development* (pp. 1–16). De Gruyter. doi:10.1515/9783110702514-001

Motwani, S., Nagpal, C., Motwani, M., Nagdev, N., & Yeole, A. (2021). AI-based proctoring system for online tests. In *Proceedings of the 4th International Conference on Advances in Science & Technology (ICAST2021)*. IEEE.

Nguyen, J. G., Keuseman, K. J., & Humston, J. J. (2020). Minimize online cheating for online assessments during COVID-19 pandemic. *Journal of Chemical Education*, *97*(9), 3429–3435. doi:10.1021/acs.jchemed.0c00790

Nigam, A., Pasricha, R., Singh, T., & Churi, P. (2021). A systematic review on AI-based proctoring systems: Past, present and future. *Education and Information Technologies*, *26*(5), 6421–6445. doi:10.1007/s10639-021-10597-x PMID:34177348

Noorbehbahani, F., Mohammadi, A., & Aminazadeh, M. (2022). A systematic review of research on cheating in online exams from 2010 to 2021. *Education and Information Technologies*, *27*(6), 8413–8460. doi:10.1007/s10639-022-10927-7 PMID:35283658

Prajapati, R. K., Bhardwaj, Y., Jain, R. K., & Hiran, K. K. (2023, April). A Review Paper on Automatic Number Plate Recognition using Machine Learning: An In-Depth Analysis of Machine Learning Techniques in Automatic Number Plate Recognition: Opportunities and Limitations. In *2023 International Conference on Computational Intelligence, Communication Technology and Networking* (CICTN) (pp. 527-532). IEEE. 10.1109/CICTN57981.2023.10141318

Raghu, H. V., & Nedungadi, P. (2021). Adoption of online proctored examinations by university students during COVID-19: Innovation diffusion study. *Education and Information Technologies*, *26*(6), 7339–7358. doi:10.1007/s10639-021-10581-5 PMID:34093065

Reisenwitz, T. H. (2020). Examining the necessity of proctoring online exams. *Journal of Higher Education Theory and Practice*, *20*(1), 118–124.

Shrivas, M. K., Hiran, K. K., Bhansali, A., & Doshi, R. (Eds.). (2022). *Advancements in Quantum Blockchain with Real-time Applications*. IGI global. doi:10.4018/978-1-6684-5072-7

Singh, S. V., & Hiran, K. K. (2022). The impact of AI on teaching and learning in higher education technology. *Journal of Higher Education Theory and Practice*, *22*(13).

Sutton, H. (2019). Minimize online cheating through proctoring, consequences. *Recruiting & Retaining Adult Learners*, *21*(5), 1–5. doi:10.1002/nsr.30434

## KEY TERMS AND DEFINITIONS

**Academic Integrity:** The ethical and moral principles that underpin the pursuit of knowledge and learning, including honesty, fairness, and responsibility.

**Artificial Intelligence:** The simulation of human intelligence processes by computer systems, including learning, reasoning, and self-correction.

**Data Security:** The protection of data from unauthorized access, use, disclosure, disruption, modification, or destruction.

**Online Assessments:** Evaluations conducted through digital platforms, such as online quizzes, tests, and exams.

**Online Proctoring:** The use of webcams, microphones, and other technological devices to observe and monitor candidates remotely during exams.

**Privacy: Concerns:** The ethical and legal considerations related to the collection, use, and storage of personal information.

**Technical Requirements:** The hardware and software specifications needed to support online proctoring, including compatible devices, browsers, and internet connectivity.

**Tools and Techniques:** The various technologies and methods used to facilitate online proctoring, including facial recognition software, keystroke analysis, browser lockdowns, and screen recording.

# Chapter 8
# Exploring the Efficacy of Adaptive Learning Platforms Enhanced by Artificial Intelligence: A Comprehensive Review

**Puneet Kumar**
*Kalinga University, India*

**Sangeet Vashishtha**
*IIMT University, India*

**Pooja Sharma**
*IIMT University, India*

**Ekansh Agarwal**
https://orcid.org/0000-0001-5497-8838
*NIMS University, India*

## ABSTRACT

*This research study explores the rapidly growing area of AI-powered adaptive learning systems and how they are influencing individualised education. The purpose of this research is to examine these systems' capacities to improve education for students from a variety of backgrounds, as well as their limitations and opportunities. Adaptive learning, which includes data analytics, machine learning models, and algorithms driven by artificial intelligence, is the focus of this review. Learners' requirements and preferences are taken into account as these technologies adapt the delivery of content, tempo, and evaluation methods to each individual. The study also looks at how adaptive learning platforms driven by AI affect students' motivation, grades, and ability to remember what they've learned. Additionally, the authors look into ethical concerns related to data privacy, algorithmic biases, and fair access to technology.*

DOI: 10.4018/979-8-3693-2440-0.ch008

## INTRODUCTION

Many of the goals set forward to improve learning and instruction are not being reached today. Teachers are looking for scalable, safe, and effective ways to fulfil these concerns with the help of technology. Educators naturally ponder if the swift advancements in technology in daily life could be beneficial. Like everyone else, educators make use of AI-powered services in their daily lives. Examples include automated travel planning on their phones, voice assistants in their homes, and tools that can write essays, fix grammar, and complete sentences. Since AI tools are only now available to the general public, many educators are looking into them. Teachers see potential to leverage AI-powered features like speech recognition to improve the support provided to multilingual students, students with impairments, and other learners who could gain from more personalisation and adaptability in digital learning resources. They are investigating how AI can facilitate the creation of new lessons or enhance existing ones, as well as how they locate, choose, and modify resources for their lessons (Cruz, 2023).

Educational technologies utilize artificial intelligence & adaptive methods of learning to assess learners' performance and offer tailored feedback and suggestions (Aida & other, 2023). This facilitates the identification of areas that require improvement and allows for the customization of learning experiences accordingly. Adaptive learning as well as artificial intelligence (AI) are currently influential technologies in the education sector, fundamentally transforming conventional teaching approaches. This examines the incorporation of technology for adaptive learning using AI algorithms to customize and improve the learning experience of students (Singh et al., 2022; Rathi et al., 2023). AI facilitates the gathering and examination of extensive data, allowing the system to customize and adjust the content and distribution of educational resources to cater to the unique requirements of each student. Through ongoing surveillance and assessment of student performance, AI systems may detect and pinpoint areas of deficiency, enabling the implementation of focused interventions to remedy them. This individualized approach not only enhances educational results but also fosters student involvement and drive. In addition, AI-driven adaptive learning systems can aid teachers via automating administrative duties, delivering immediate feedback, and producing detailed progress reports. Nevertheless, it is imperative to tackle obstacles such as privacy problems, ethical considerations, including the necessity for teacher training in order to effectively utilize these technologies. In summary, the combination of adaptive learning with AI has the potential to revolutionize education by providing individualized and efficient learning opportunities for pupils. AI-driven adaptive learning has the potential to revolutionize education in the digital era by allowing students and educators to attain the best possible results (Joshi, 2023, 2024).

The swift development of e-learning platforms, driven by developments in artificial intelligence (AI) & machine learning (ML), offers a significant potential for transformation in the field of education (Gligorea, 2023). Given the ever-changing nature of the field, it is important to investigate the integration of artificial intelligence and machine learning into adaptive learning systems in order to improve educational results. These technologies have demonstrated the ability to optimize learning paths, boost engagement, and enhance academic achievement, as seen by studies that have reported improved test scores. AI/ML integration in e-learning platforms greatly enhances the customization and efficacy of the process of learning (Easwaran et al., 2022; Mishra et al., 2021).

In a radically outdated educational context, the true role of AI is to support education as adaptive learning systems by extending its capabilities and usefulness. Two key ways that technology will support academic success are by removing physical barriers to learning and, as a result, shifting the emphasis from data maintenance to data utilisation. To understand routes' cost and influence in adaptive learning systems, all aspects of them should be considered in the context of their importance for both the analyst and the instructor.

By all accounts, the AI-based technology allows teachers to create their own unique learning groups that aren't limited to the local educational institutions. For example, instructors could network and share information with teachers at various assets both inside and outside their neighborhood's boundaries by using a wiki or substance transport system. This gets easier when it comes to mentoring and teaching, which are two aspects of a more notable informal learning environment. Online learning communities, to the extent that they do, leave a catastrophe area of conversations and socialisation that adhere to an innovative individual learning guideline, in which people learn material through social situations and experience it effectively. In any case, technology will aid students in understanding the visual representation of previously covered material in a way that greatly facilitates learning. For example, transmission exhibits, which make use of diverse media designs, such as images, representation, and content, are used to help students in concept visualisation (Hiran et al., 2024).

Technologies like AI and ML are revolutionising a number of industries, including education. AI and ML are essential to the adaptive learning environment because they allow for customised and individualised learning experiences (Liu, 2018). Artificial Intelligence (AI) is the study of creating intelligent computers that can mimic human intelligence and carry out tasks like sensing, reasoning, and decision-making that normally need human intelligence (Xu, 2021).

## RATIONALE FOR THE STUDY

The premise that learners have different histories, learning preferences, & cognitive capacities is at the heart of the adaptive learning concept in e-learning. Conventional e-learning platforms frequently provide all learners with the same activities and content, disregarding their individual requirements and features. Since education has always taken a "one style fits all" approach, all students in the current conventional e-learning settings go through the same learning procedures. This type of learning does not take into account the different learning styles and preferences of the students (Gupta, 2023). This method could result in less than ideal learning experiences since some students might find the material to be either too simple or too difficult, which would cause them to get disengaged or make little progress. The advent of adaptive e-learning systems has enabled and aided in personalised learning, where instruction is customised to a student's unique needs and learning preferences. Massive volumes of learner data are gathered, analysed, and interpreted by adaptive learning systems using machine learning algorithms (Almario, 2023). By customising the learning pathway, the data-driven method empowers the system to dynamically adapt the learning experience, providing personalised contents, resources, and assignments that align with each learner's skills and objectives. Self-paced learning is encouraged, targeted support is given, and an atmosphere that is more productive and interesting is created through adaptive learning (Reyes, 2023). Artificial intelligence techniques are integrated into adaptive learning systems to enable continual learning and improvement. These tools are able to recognise trends in student data, pinpoint strengths and shortcomings, and provide tailored recommendations and interventions. Additionally, by collecting insightful feedback and statistics on the efficacy of instructional learning tactics and resources, the adaptive learning methodology helps educators and designers to improve and optimise the online learning environment (Algabri, 2021a, b).

## HISTORICAL CONTEXT OF AI IN EDUCATION

The progress of artificial intelligence technologies including their incorporation into educational practices are demonstrated by the historical backdrop of AI in education (Zeniakin, 2023), which spans several decades. Here's a summary of significant turning points:

### 1950s-1960s: Initial AI Thoughts

The earliest days of AI research are where the roots of AI in education may be found. The first attempts to employ technology for education were made with the creation of early educational software and computer-based teaching devices.

### 1970s-1980s: Intelligent Tutoring Systems (ITS) Began to Emerge

Intelligent Tutoring Systems (ITS), which employed AI to deliver individualised education, rose to prominence in the 1970s. The University of Illinois's PLATO system, which combines adaptive learning and feedback systems, is one prominent example.

### 1990s: Educational Software Development

The development of educational software saw a boom in the 1990s, as interactive material and multimedia applications gained popularity. Even though they are still in their infancy, AI technologies have improved adaptive learning opportunities.

### Learning Management Systems' (LMS) Ascent in the 2000s

Learning Management Systems (LMS) became widely used in the 2000s, offering educational institutions a digital infrastructure. These systems included basic AI functions for controlling content and monitoring student progress.

### 2010s: The Rise of Platforms for Personalised Learning

More complex AI-driven personalised learning platforms have been developed thanks to developments in machine learning as well as natural language processing. Businesses and organisations started using data analytics to customise course materials to meet the needs of specific students.

### Right Now: Chatbots and Intelligent Educational Applications

Chatbots and other intelligent educational applications are widely available on the market today. These apps make use of AI to respond to queries, give immediate feedback, and modify course content in response to user performance.

### Future: AI Integration Will Continue

It is anticipated that even more cutting-edge technology, including as virtual reality, augmented reality, including AI-powered instructional assistants, will be used in education in the future. The goal of these technologies is to design individualised and immersive learning environments.

AI in education has developed over this historical trajectory from simple teaching machines to complex, adaptive learning platforms that use machine learning algorithms to analyse data, comprehend learner behaviour, and provide individualised instruction. The use of AI in education is anticipated to grow as a result of technological advancements, providing creative solutions to meet the varied demands of students (Gangal, 2023; Kim, 2021).

## ROLE OF ARTIFICIAL INTELLIGENCE IN EDUCATION

The advantages of using AI technology in education include helping students develop critical thinking abilities, inclusive education, and the ability to become entangled in complex situations (Agarwal, 2023). It also helps them create strategies for resolving problems in groups and increases their individual accountability for learning. Students will be prepared to pick up new knowledge much more quickly. They will deliver quality academic resources in a timely manner, interact with their instructors and fellow students at the appropriate times, have enough time to categorise their beliefs and engage in both online and offline discussions, and scan, perceive, and respond to questions (Zawacki-Richter, 2019 & Borromeo, 2023).

In this instance, learning independence, flexibility, and individual growth will all be supported, and productive observation and knowledge exploration will be encouraged (modern cultural communities are built on the convergence, interaction, dialogue, and sharing of knowledge, information, and human culture).

In the last 20 years, AI technology has been used widely in education. All of the main AI subjects are covered by the Intelligent Tutoring Systems (ITS), including data illustration, machine learning, tongue, planning, reasoning, and explanation. As a result, the systems have created an inspiring environment for the formalisation of psychological feature theories and the exploration of their operationalization. Since educational systems have developed, artificial intelligence (AI) has been used in a variety of fields, including physics, computing, composing essays, and reading (Doshi et al., 2023; Priyadarshi et al., 2021). The most common AI uses in academia are in the areas of autonomous agents, intelligent tutoring, data illustration, and speech processing. Over the years, AI in education has produced engaging interactive learning environments and strong learning environments for college students (Huddar, 2023; Mijwil et al., 2023).

Artificial intelligence (AI) and computer science have made rapid technological advancements challenging for all businesses, including education. According to a recent IBM, Burning Glass, and Business Education Forum report, there will be 2,720,000 more jobs available in 2020 that require knowledge and analytical skills-an increase of 364,000. It indicates that there is a rising disparity between the supply and demand for people with AI skills. According to one research, there are 300,000 AI specialists worldwide, but there are many chances available. As a result, people in this industry are earning even greater incomes.

Both the teaching methods and the relationship between students and teachers have changed significantly since education was first established (Maquiling, 2023). Worldwide, instructional approaches become more organised to deliver more effective, higher-quality outcomes. This change will be mostly ascribed to technology's ongoing intervention. We seem to be seeing a paradigm shift in the teaching-learning process as a result of ongoing technological advancements. The relationship between teachers and students is dynamic, with teachers becoming more personable and more adept at comprehending the perspectives of their students.

To provide individualised learning experiences, AI and ML play a critical role in acquiring and evaluating student data. Better learning environments, flexible scheduling options, the capacity to offer quick feedback, flexibility in managing students' educational experiences, and quicker student development are benefits of AI-enabled learning systems (Siau, 2017). Large volumes of data may be processed by AI systems, which can also learn from past performance and trends to forecast or suggest actions. AI enables the use of a range of instructional strategies while taking into account the skills, abilities, and academic challenges of each individual student. Learner data can be gathered by AI and ML algorithms from a variety of sources, such as digital materials, online platforms, learning management systems, and examinations. Learner demographics, performance metrics, interaction patterns, learning preferences, and other pertinent data can all be gathered by these algorithms. Adaptive learning systems can gather data asynchronously or in real time, which enables them to update and improve learner profiles over time (Chen, 2020; Doshi et al., 2023). Large and complicated dataset analysis is a strength of AI and ML approaches. These algorithms may process learner data to find patterns, correlations, and trends after the data has been gathered. Adaptive learning systems can determine specific learner attributes, such as strengths, weaknesses, learning styles, and knowledge gaps, through data analysis. The basis for developing individualised learning experiences is this analysis. Learner models can be constructed by AI and ML algorithms using the examined data. Creating representations of each learner, including their cognitive capacities, knowledge levels, learning preferences, and learning styles, is known as learner modelling. These models function as a foundation for customising the learning process by encapsulating the distinctive qualities of every student.

## EFFICACY OF ADAPTIVE LEARNING PLATFORMS USING AI

Teaching, learning, thinking, and self-correction are processes in pedagogy. Pedagogy is the study of teaching. Artificial intelligence has completely changed the way the education industry operates (Ang, 2023). To transform the sector of education, educational institutions are increasingly utilising a diverse range of intelligent systems. These smart solutions are helping kids learn more effectively and accomplish their academic objectives. Artificial intelligence (AI) is used in the field of education to perform tasks including teaching, learning, and student evaluation in a number of different ways. Artificial intelligence (AI)-enhanced adaptive learning platforms have a substantial impact on a number of learning and teaching-related domains. Here is a look at some of the main areas that these platforms work well:

## Customized Education

AI algorithms assess each learner's unique learning styles, advantages, and disadvantages, allowing the platform to customise the pace and content to meet their requirements. This flexibility addresses certain areas of difficulty and increases the effectiveness of the learning process.

## Enhanced Motivation and Engagement

A lot of adaptive learning systems include gamification components to increase student engagement and enjoyment. Features that support ongoing learner motivation include challenges, rewards, and interactive simulations.

## Instantaneous Commentary and Evaluation

AI makes it possible to provide immediate, customised comments based on students' performance. By allowing for the quick correction of misconceptions, this real-time evaluation strengthens learning objectives and fosters a deeper comprehension of the subject matter.

## Making Decisions Based on Data

AI-powered systems gather and examine enormous volumes of information about student interactions. Teachers can use this data for making well-informed judgements, spot trends, and modify their lesson plans in order to get the most out of their teaching techniques.

## Tailored Educational Routes

AI creates tailored learning programmes according to students' progress, making sure they are exposed to material appropriate for their level of expertise. This individualization helps students achieve learning objectives in a more effective and focused manner.

## Inclusivity and Accessibility

AI-enabled adaptive learning platforms may be modified to meet the needs of a range of learners, promoting inclusion. Accessibility for a wide variety of learners is ensured through adaptable interfaces and content modifications.

## Effective Allocation of Resources

By using AI algorithms to pinpoint the areas in which students struggle the most, teachers are able to distribute resources more effectively. By focusing instructional time on solving certain issues, this optimisation maximises the effectiveness of educational resources.

## Constant Enhancement

The adaptive learning platform can change and advance over time as a result of AI algorithms that are always learning from user feedback and continuing interactions. Frequent upgrades grounded in data insights help to maintain the platform's effectiveness over time.

## Scalability

Personalised Learning Experiences Can Be Maintained Even with a Large User Base: AI-enhanced adaptive learning platforms can scale efficiently to support a large number of users. This scalability is especially useful in remote and online learning settings.

## Getting Ready for Lifelong Learning

By adjusting to each learner's unique needs, these platforms support abilities like self-directed learning and flexibility, thereby equipping students for a lifetime of learning in a constantly changing educational environment.

The effectiveness of AI-powered adaptive learning systems is based on their capacity to deliver efficient, personalised, and interesting learning experiences. By addressing each learner's unique needs, these platforms use cutting-edge technologies to improve education's effectiveness, inclusivity, and accessibility for a wide spectrum of students.

# DISCUSSION

The study of the effectiveness of adaptive learning platforms augmented by artificial intelligence (AI) centers on investigating the influence of these technologies on educational results, student involvement, and individualized learning experiences. Adaptive learning platforms utilize artificial intelligence to customize instructional content according to the specific requirements, abilities, and rate of progress of each learner. This examines the main discoveries, consequences, and factors to be taken into account.

1. Personalization of Learning: AI-powered platforms have demonstrated notable achievements in tailoring the learning experience to suit the specific requirements of students. Through the analysis of student performance data, these platforms have the capability to adapt to the level of difficulty of activities, offer tailored resources, and provide feedback that is customized to the development of each individual learner.
2. Enhanced Engagement: Students utilizing adaptive learning platforms frequently express elevated levels of motivation and engagement. The platform's interactivity and reactivity enhance the learning experience, fostering greater engagement and interest. Consequently, this can result in improved attendance rates and the development of more consistent routines for learning.
3. Enhanced Educational Outcomes: Numerous research have recorded enhancements in examination scores, academic grades, and levels of comprehension among students who utilize adaptive learning platforms. These platforms have the ability to efficiently detect and rectify deficiencies

in information, surpassing the effectiveness of traditional educational techniques and resulting in enhanced learning results.

4. Inclusive Education: Adaptive learning technology can enhance accessibility and inclusion in education by catering to a broader spectrum of learners, including individuals with limitations or those who need more flexible learning arrangements. Artificial intelligence has the capability to automatically offer accommodations, such as modifying the way content is presented for individuals with visual impairments and simplifying text for people who struggle with reading.

## Specific Algorithms, Data Analysis Techniques, and The Mechanisms

The effectiveness of adaptive learning platforms, which are improved by artificial intelligence (AI), depends on a range of algorithms, data analysis approaches, and mechanisms that are specifically created to customize educational experiences based on the unique needs of each student. These technologies have the ability to adjust immediately to a student's interactions, offering customized information, feedback, and assessment routes. The following are particular facets of these systems:

### Algorithms

1. Machine Learning (ML) algorithms are the fundamental components of adaptive learning platforms. They allow the system to acquire knowledge from data and make accurate predictions or judgments. Popular machine learning algorithms comprise decision trees, support vector machines, neural networks, including reinforcement learning. Each of these tools can be utilized to examine data on student performance and subsequently adjust the learning content as needed (Hiran et al., 2021; Mahrishi et al., 2020).
2. Natural Language Processing (NLP) algorithms aid in comprehending and manipulating human language. This allows the platform to assess textual inputs from students, offer appropriate feedback, and permit interactions that simulate a human tutor. Methods like analyzing sentiment, text classification, including language modeling are employed.
3. Bayesian Networks are utilized for probabilistic inference, enabling the system to handle uncertainty and make predictions on a student's comprehension of a concept. As further data is obtained, Bayesian networks have the ability to revise the probability associated with specific learning paths (Al-Shahwani et al., 2024; Boison et al., 2022).
4. Item Response Theory (IRT) is a statistical method employed in adaptive testing to gauge the learner's competence by considering the difficulty level of questions as well as the learner's responses. It facilitates the provision of assessments that are neither excessively difficult nor overly simple for the student.

### Methods for Analysing Data

1. Data mining is the process of extracting valuable patterns from extensive collections of data. Data mining in adaptive learning can reveal patterns in students' learning processes, allowing for the identification of shared challenges or successful learning methods.

2. Cluster Analysis is a method that categorizes students based on their similar learning habits, preferences, and performance levels. This data can be utilized to tailor the educational experience for various groups of pupils.
3. Sequential Pattern Mining is a method used to identify recurring sequences of interactions and learning activities that result in good learning outcomes. This can provide guidance for the development of educational routes inside the platform.
4. Predictive Analytics is a method that use past data to forecast future performance and learning outcomes. This can aid in the identification of kids who may be susceptible to falling behind and facilitate the implementation of early interventions.

### Mechanisms Adaptive Information Delivery

1. Artificial intelligence algorithms assess the comprehension level of a student on a particular topic and subsequently customize the difficulty degree of the information, the variety of resources offered (such as videos, texts, quizzes), along with the pace of learning to cater to the individual's requirements.
2. The system has the capability to provide instant and individualized feedback based on performance data. It can also suggest additional resources and activities to target specific areas of learning that need improvement.
3. The adaptive assessment feature of the platform dynamically adjusts the difficulty and breadth of evaluations in real-time, ensuring that examinations are suitably rigorous for each student's level of comprehension.
4. Learning Analytics Dashboard: Such platforms typically feature dashboards that offer insights on student performance, engagement, & progress. This can assist instructors in making well-informed judgments regarding how to enhance their support for pupils.

Executing these algorithms, data analysis methodologies, and processes necessitates a multidisciplinary strategy, encompassing proficiency in computer science, education, psychology, as well as subject matter expertise. Regular assessment and improvement of these systems are essential to ensure they properly cater to the varied requirements of learners.

## Consequences

1. Teacher Role Transformation: Educators go from being providers of information to becoming facilitators of the learning process. AI platforms can provide teachers with valuable insights to enhance their understanding of students' needs and enable them to assist more effectively when required.
2. Curriculum Construction: Educational institutions should reassess their curriculum design as well as assessment techniques in order to properly include adaptive learning tools. This could indicate a transition towards an educational approach that focuses on measuring and developing specific skills

and knowledge, as well as an increase in evaluations that provide ongoing feedback and support learning.

3. Digital Divide: Although adaptive learning platforms provide several advantages, there is a potential for exacerbating the educational disparity between pupils who have access to sophisticated technology and those who do not. Ensuring fair and equal access to technology is a crucial concern in terms of policy and execution.
4. Privacy & ethical considerations arise while collecting and analyzing student data, since concerns regarding confidentiality and safeguarding information are raised. Ensuring students' information is protected requires the implementation of clear and ethical policies.
5. Examining the process by which AI algorithms determine learning material and identifying any biases present in these systems is essential for guaranteeing equity and inclusiveness.
6. Cost-Benefit Analysis: Thorough evaluations that take into account the expenses associated with establishing and sustaining adaptive learning platforms compared to the educational advantages they provide can assist institutions in making well-informed choices.

The effectiveness of AI-powered adaptive learning platforms indicates encouraging progress in customized education. Nevertheless, the effective incorporation of new technologies necessitates thoughtful examination of pedagogical, ethical, & practical elements. In order to fully utilize the promise of these platforms while minimizing hazards, it is crucial for educators, technologists, policymakers, & learners to engage in continuing research and conversation.

## Case Studies

The effectiveness of adaptive learning platforms, which have been improved by artificial intelligence (AI), has been proven through a range of real-world scenarios and investigations in educational environments. These platforms have demonstrated considerable potential in customizing learning experiences, promoting student involvement, and improving learning results. Here are now a few noteworthy instances:

1. Knewton Alta offers adaptive learning courses. Knewton Alta is an adaptive learning platform that offers college-level courses in many topics, such as mathematics, chemistry, and economics. The platform customizes learning materials and evaluations to cater to the individual needs of each student, with a specific emphasis on addressing areas of knowledge deficiency and strengthening mastery.

Effectiveness: Educational institutions that have implemented Knewton Alta, such as the University of Nevada, Las Vegas, have observed increased rates of student success and improved academic performance in courses that utilize the platform. The platform's adaptability facilitated students in attaining a more profound comprehension of the course material at their individualized speed.

2. DreamBox Learning is a company that provides an advanced learning platform for elementary math. Their platform uses artificial intelligence to adapt to the needs of students in grades K-8. The platform adapts to the unique learning style and speed of each student, offering personalized training that complements classroom teaching.

Effectiveness: A research conducted by Harvard University revealed that students who frequently utilized DreamBox Learning had substantial improvements in their arithmetic proficiency in comparison to their classmates. Educational institutions have observed enhancements in students' self-assurance in mathematics, along with improvements in their examination results.

3. Duolingo - Language Learning Summary: Duolingo is a popular language learning application that use artificial intelligence to customize education for millions of users globally. The platform adjusts to the user's learning speed, abilities, and limitations, providing customized exercises and courses that match the individual's degree of proficiency.

Effectiveness: Research and user testimonials have emphasized the effectiveness of Duolingo in maintaining learners' engagement and motivation through its adaptive learning approach. The platform's incorporation of gamification aspects, together with AI-powered customisation, has proven to be successful in enhancing language learning outcomes for a wide array of learners.

4. Carnegie Learning offers AI-enhanced adaptive learning software specifically designed for mathematics education. Their product is suitable for middle school through high school courses. The platform utilizes cognitive science and AI algorithms to provide tailored learning trajectories, instant feedback, and comprehensive explanations.

Effectiveness: Educational institutions that have adopted Carnegie Learning's platform have documented substantial enhancements in mathematics scores and student understanding. For instance, research conducted in the Elizabeth Forward School District in Pennsylvania demonstrated that students who utilized the platform achieved higher scores on standardized examinations compared to their counterparts.

5. Smart Sparrow is an adaptive eLearning platform specifically designed for teaching science and engineering disciplines at the college level. Educators are able to generate adaptive learning experiences that can modify content, simulations, and evaluations according to student involvement.

Effectiveness: Research conducted at Arizona State University and other academic institutions has demonstrated that courses use Smart Sparrow have achieved increased levels of student engagement, decreased rates of student attrition, and enhanced knowledge of challenging ideas, notably in the domains of science, technology, engineering, and mathematics (STEM).

These case studies demonstrate the profound capacity of AI-enhanced adaptive learning platforms to bring about significant changes across various subjects and educational levels. They showcase how AI-powered tailored learning can effectively cater to various learning requirements, enhance involvement, and attain superior educational results. Nevertheless, achieving successful deployment necessitates meticulous integration with the curriculum, comprehensive training for educators, including continuous assessment to guarantee that these technologies effectively cater to the requirements of all learners.

## CHALLENGES IN AI

Artificial intelligence (AI) implementation presents a number of ethical, societal, and technical issues. Here are a few major obstacles in AI:

### Explainability and Transparency

These are crucial elements of artificial intelligence (AI) that must exist in order to ensure trust, responsibility, and moral application of AI systems. Explainability is the capacity to elucidate the process by which artificial intelligence algorithms arrive at their conclusions or forecasts. This makes it possible for users to understand the logic underlying the results produced by these models. Conversely, transparency pertains to the procedure of granting stakeholders from diverse backgrounds access and understanding to the internal workings of artificial intelligence systems. The advancement of explainability can be facilitated by the development of methodologies and approaches that dispel the mystery surrounding complex artificial intelligence systems. Among the methods that have been developed to provide light on the decision-making process are feature importance analysis, model interpretability, and providing easily understood explanations for AI-generated outputs. Moreover, the creation of intuitive user interfaces that illustrate AI decision pathways helps consumers understand the reasoning behind AI, particularly non-technical individuals. Transparency demands the origins of the data, the algorithmic decisions made, and the existence of any biases in the system. This is on top of the need for intelligible artificial intelligence systems. To confirm that AI systems adhere to ethical standards, extensive documenting of data collection procedures and model architectures must be done in addition to routine AI system monitoring. The goal of this research is to strike a balance between comprehensibility and complexity. This is due to the fact that highly complex explanations may make it more difficult to understand how something works, but extremely plain explanations may undermine accuracy. The search for explanations that are actionable and pertinent fosters confidence by enabling people to verify, dispute, or adjust results produced by artificial intelligence. Consequently, this helps to integrate AI in a way that is more ethical and responsible in a number of domains. Understanding the reasoning behind the decisions made by artificial intelligence systems is crucial for accountability and building confidence. Research studies are looking into ways to improve the transparency and interpretability of artificial intelligence algorithms. This will make it possible for users to understand and explore the reasoning behind the AI's outputs.

### Data Protection and Privacy

Because artificial intelligence often uses massive volumes of data, problems about privacy violations and the unauthorised use of personal information are raised. Two of the most crucial factors to take into account when analysing the ethical implications of artificial intelligence (AI) are data protection and privacy. These features highlight how important it is to protect sensitive data while also making use of AI capabilities. Machine learning algorithms in the field of artificial intelligence rely on vast amounts of data, many of which contain sensitive and private information. Ensuring complete data protection necessitates the implementation of safeguards that prevent unauthorised parties from accessing, compromising, or misusing this information. Many crucial elements are the subject of ethical research in this sector. It first requires the development of strict standards for data governance and the observance of those frameworks. These frameworks consist of data anonymization methods, access controls, and encryption protocols. These processes aid in protecting people's privacy while preserving the ability to use data to generate AI-driven insights and innovation. Another area of growing importance is the integration of privacy-by-design principles into artificial intelligence systems. By using this approach, privacy considerations are included into the artificial intelligence systems development process from the beginning to the end. This method ensures that privacy is not an afterthought, but a basic element. Regulatory compliance, or following laws like the General Data Protection Regulation (GDPR) or other data protection regulations specific to a certain area, is vital. Ethics research is always searching for solutions to reconcile the advancements in artificial intelligence (AI) with current laws and regulations to promote ethical data processing and handling. Furthermore, studies are being conducted in an attempt to strike a compromise between the protection of individuals' rights to privacy about their personal information and the applicability of AI-driven insights. Techniques like federated learning and differential privacy are used to enable collaborative training of artificial intelligence models while maintaining the privacy of individual data providers. The ethical goal of protecting data and maintaining privacy in artificial intelligence eventually requires a multidisciplinary approach that mixes technology advancements with legal and ethical challenges. This policy aims to defend individual rights and societal ideals regarding data privacy and protection, while also utilising the revolutionary potential of artificial intelligence (AI). Developing frameworks that safeguard people's privacy while allowing artificial intelligence to function effectively is the aim of ethical research.

## Ethics in Artificial Intelligence Decision-Making

The development of ethical frameworks that can guide artificial intelligence systems in making ethically right decisions even in complex settings is a significant area of research (Kamila, 2023). This involves integrating ethical ideas into the algorithms that make up artificial intelligence in order to facilitate ethical reasoning and decision-making. To ensure that AI systems are in line with moral standards and societal values, the process for generating ethical decisions in AI is an important area that has to be explored. To do this, ethical issues must guide the decision-making processes such these technologies and be taken into account during the design, development, and implementation of artificial intelligence systems (Lo Piano, 2020). The main goal of research in this area is to integrate ethical frameworks into algorithms for artificial intelligence. This makes it possible for these systems to decide morally right things even in challenging situations. Determining and embedding ethical principles into AI models is a major component of this. These ideals include, but are not limited to, justice, accountability, transparency, including respect for human rights. Ensuring that the decisions made by AI systems are not just accurate and efficient but also compliant with moral principles and beneficial to society is the aim of an ethical approach to AI development (Filippi, 2023). Furthermore, developing techniques for ethical reasoning in these systems is a necessary step in the process of making ethical decisions in artificial intelligence. This term includes the creation of artificial intelligence architectures that facilitate deliberation, considering several points of view, moral dilemmas, and contextual subtleties before making decisions. By incorporating these characteristics, artificial intelligence systems can prioritise ethical objectives, negotiate morally dubious situations, and show a certain level of sensitivity to and knowledge of ethical issues. The focus of ongoing research is on interdisciplinary cooperation, involving politicians, technologists, ethicists, and other stakeholders in order to create comprehensive guidelines and standards for the development of moral artificial intelligence. The aim of ethical decision-making in artificial intelligence is to bridge the gap between the advancement of technology and ethical duty. These initiatives seek to guarantee that artificial intelligence technologies are created and implemented in a manner that upholds ethical principles while also serving the greater good of society more generally (Andersen, L., 2019). In order to achieve this, efforts are made to develop artificial intelligence (AI) systems that, in addition to performing exceptionally well, also represent and advance moral values in their decision-making for the good of humanity.

## Bias Detection and Mitigation

This is an additional area of emphasis. To ensure fairness and equality, a variety of techniques are now being researched to locate, measure, and remove biases in data and algorithms. In order to preserve justice and equity for a range of populations, it is necessary from an ethical standpoint that prejudice in artificial intelligence (AI) be identified and mitigated. The detection process is a multifaceted method that includes statistical investigations, algorithmic audits, a thorough assessment of datasets and artificial intelligence models, and more. This field of study focuses on developing methods and instruments that can detect biases at all phases of the development of artificial intelligence, from data collection and preprocessing to model training and implementation. This entails assessing prejudices related to gender, race, and ethnicity in addition to other delicate traits that can have an adverse effect on discrimination. The purpose of mitigation techniques in AI systems is to either eliminate biases or stop them from getting worse. Various strategies such as data augmentation, diversified dataset curation, and algorithmic modifications are being employed to counteract artificial intelligence biases and produce more inclusive and equitable outputs. Furthermore, studies emphasise how important it is to put continuous monitoring and validation processes in place to ensure that artificial intelligence systems remain impartial and responsible for the duration of their lives. Accountability and openness are also implicated in the ethical problems associated with bias identification and mitigation (Gevaert, 2021). It is necessary to record the steps taken to uncover and reduce biases, to explain the decisions made by artificial intelligence, and to set up procedures for seeking compensation when biases result in negative consequences. The main goal of this research is to construct artificial intelligence (AI) systems that are not only efficient but also ethically operated through the discovery and repair of biases. This will ensure that these technologies will benefit all facets of society equally and enable for the promotion of justice, diversity, and inclusivity throughout the whole range of AI applications.

# CONCLUSION

Because they customise the learning process to each student's needs, artificial intelligence (AI)-enhanced adaptive learning platforms are essential to the transformation of traditional education. The principal positions consist of:

## Customisation of Education

- Adaptive learning systems assess each learner's learning style, learning limitations, and strengths using AI algorithms.
- Because the content is dynamically changed according to each learner's progress, they can bypass material they have previously mastered and concentrate on areas that require development.

## Instantaneous Commentary and Evaluation

- Instantaneous and customised feedback on students' performance is made possible by AI.
- Analytics and ongoing assessment support teachers and students in monitoring development, identifying obstacles, and improving their learning methods.

## Tailored Educational Routes

- Personalised learning routes are generated by AI algorithms, guaranteeing that the activities and content learners encounter are in line with their goals and skill levels.
- This flexibility allows for a range of learning styles and speeds.

## Motivating and Engaging

- To increase engagement, AI-powered systems frequently include multimedia, interactive simulations, and gamification components.
- By making learning more fun, personalised challenges and rewards help learners stay motivated.

## Making Decisions Based on Data

- AI-generated insights can be used by educators to make data-driven decisions.
- It is possible to make changes to curriculum creation, resource allocation, and instructional tactics by analysing patterns in learner data.

## Effective Allocation of Resources

- By pinpointing the areas in which students struggle the most, AI aids in the efficient distribution of resources.
- This guarantees that resources and instructional time are allocated to filling certain learning gaps.

## Inclusivity and Accessibility

- Education can be made more inclusive by using adaptive learning systems, which can be made to accommodate a range of learning capacities.
- Accessibility for students with different requirements is facilitated by adaptable content and customisable interfaces.

### Constant Enhancement

- Through constant user feedback and interaction, AI algorithms enable the platform to develop and get better over time.
- Over time, frequent upgrades based on data insights improve the platform's efficacy.

### Scalability

- AI-powered adaptive learning systems can grow to support a big user base without sacrificing a customised experience.
- This scalability is especially useful in remote and online learning settings.

### Getting Ready for Lifelong Learning

- Adaptive learning platforms with AI support abilities like self-directed learning and adaptability by adjusting to each learner's particular needs, setting people up for a lifetime of learning.

## EMERGING TRENDS AND FUTURE OUTLOOK OF AI IN EDUCATION

The incorporation of Artificial Intelligence (AI) in education is swiftly revolutionizing the methods of teaching and learning, with developing patterns indicating the possibility of even more significant alterations in the future. The initial stage of AI involves the capacity to customize education, streamline administrative duties, and offer valuable insights into the learning process. Here is an examination of developing trends & the future prospects of artificial intelligence in the field of education:

### Emerging Trends

1. AI-driven adaptive learning platforms are advancing in sophistication, offering personalized learning pathways that accommodate to the unique pace, style, and needs of each learner. These platforms utilize student interactions as well as efficiency data to provide tailored content and evaluations, enhancing the learning process for improved efficiency and effectiveness.
2. Automated Grading & Feedback: AI systems are becoming more proficient in assessing coursework and delivering immediate, tailored feedback to students. In addition to evaluating multiple-choice questions, these systems are now capable of evaluating open-ended responses and even creative work, so enabling teachers to allocate more time to instruction and reduce their administrative workload.
3. Intelligent Tutoring Systems (ITS) replicate individualized tutoring sessions by providing customized assistance, hints, and feedback based on the student's current comprehension level. Information Technology Systems (ITS) have the capability to adjust immediately to the learner's requirements, offering customized training that is available at all times and in any location.

4. Learning Analytics as well as Predictive Models: Artificial intelligence-powered analytics technologies are assisting educators and institutions in tracking student progress, forecasting academic success, and identifying students who are at danger of falling behind. These observations can provide valuable information for focused interventions, modifications to the curriculum, and policy choices, ultimately enhancing educational achievements and rates of student retention.
5. The utilization of AI-driven voice assistants & chatbots in the field of education is increasing, offering students interactive and conversational learning opportunities. These technologies have the ability to provide answers to queries, aid in completing assignments, and enhance language acquisition, hence delivering a more captivating and easily accessible method of learning.

## Future Outlook

1. Prospects for the Future Integration of Augmented & Virtual Reality (AR/VR): As artificial intelligence progresses, its incorporation with augmented reality (AR) and virtual reality (VR) technology will generate immersive educational settings that replicate real-life situations. This combination has the potential to transform professions like medical education, engineering, & history by offering practical learning experiences without the limitations of physical resources.
2. The significance of addressing ethical problems in education is increasing as the role of AI expands in this field. Future advancements must prioritize privacy, data security, mitigating bias, and guaranteeing fair access to AI-enhanced learning opportunities.
3. Artificial intelligence (AI) will enable lifelong learning by providing help for individuals at every stage of their education, from early schooling to higher education, and even in continual professional growth. AI-powered platforms will provide effortless, tailored learning experiences throughout various life stages, accessible globally.
4. The future of AI will involve AI systems not only assisting individual learners, but also enabling collaborative learning experiences. Artificial intelligence has the ability to pair learners with abilities and information that complement one other, so promoting the development of teamwork and communication skills, even in distant learning settings.
5. Advancements in emotion identification as well as affective computing will allow AI systems to accurately identify students' emotional states including cognitive load. This will enable the AI systems to adapt the learning process accordingly. This will enhance not only the development of cognitive abilities but also the emotional welfare, resulting in a more comprehensive educational experience.

The future of artificial intelligence (AI) in education holds the potential to enhance learning by providing tailored, easily accessible, and highly efficient educational experiences. This advancement in technology has the ability to eliminate obstacles and create new possibilities for learners globally. As these technologies progress, the emphasis will be on utilizing their potential in a responsible and fair manner, guaranteeing that the advantages of AI-enhanced education are accessible to everyone.

## REFERENCES

Agarwal, N. (2023). A Study on the teacher's aptitude about managerial skill with respect to training and learners performance. *International Journal of Management and Organizational Research*, *2*(2), 78–84.

Agarwal, N. (2023). Strength of distributed web page management system within the space of online e-learning administration in a contextualized group of science teachers. *European Chemical Bulletin*, *12*(4), 144–155.

Akavova, A., Temirkhanova, Z., & Lorsanova, Z. (2023). Adaptive learning and artificial intelligence in the educational space. *E3S Web of Conferences, 451*. 06011. . doi:10.1051/e3sconf/202345106011

Al-Shahwani, H. I. W., Mijwil, M. M., Doshi, R., Hiran, K. K., & Bala, I. (2024). Evaluating Antivirus Effectiveness Against Malware in Ascending Order for Increasing Blockchain Endpoint Protection. In Bio-Inspired Optimization Techniques in Blockchain Systems (pp. 150-166). IGI Global. doi:10.4018/979-8-3693-1131-8.ch008

Algabri, H. K., Kharade, K. G., & Kamat, R. K. (2021a). Designing and Implementation of Technology in Higher Education. *Webology*, *18*(5), 1365–1377.

Algabri, H. K., Kharade, K. G., & Kamat, R. K. (2021b). Promise, Threats and Personalization in Higher Education with Artificial Intelligence. *Webology*, *18*(6), 2129–2139.

Almario, O. (2023). Assessing User Experience of Learning Management System for Liberal Arts and Education Programs: Implications for Hybrid Learning. *Cosmos An International Journal of Management, 12*(2), 73-78.

Andersen, L. (2019). Artificial Intelligence in International Development: Avoiding Ethical Pitfalls. *Journal of Public & International Affairs*.

Ang, L., Bonifacio, N., Garcia, J. K., Medina, R., & Santiago, J. (2023). The Rise of Artificial Intelligence: A Correlational Study on AI-Powered Bots and Customer Satisfaction in A People-Oriented Industry. *Cosmos Journal of Engineering & Technology*, *13*(1), 81–94. doi:10.46360/cosmos.et.620231008

Blair, K.P. (2007). *Pedagogical agents for learning by teaching: Teachable agents*.

Boison, D. K., Malcalm, E., Antwi-Boampong, A., Doumbia, M. O., & Hiran, K. K. (2022). Assessing Factors Affecting the Blockchain Adoption in Public Procurement Delivery in Ghana: A Correlational Study Using UTAUT2 Theoretical Framework. [IJACI]. *International Journal of Ambient Computing and Intelligence*, *13*(1), 1–13. doi:10.4018/ijaci.314568

Borromeo, D. (2023). Impact of Educational Technology Tools on the Digital and Information Literacy Skills of Selected Dominican Schools in the Philippines. *Cosmos An International Journal of Management, 12*(2), 01-08.

Chen, L., Chen, P., & Lin, Z. (2020). Artificial Intelligence in Education: A Review. *IEEE Access : Practical Innovations, Open Solutions*, *8*, 75264–75278. doi:10.1109/ACCESS.2020.2988510

Doshi, R., Hiran, K. K., Ranolia, R., & Joshi, C. (2023). Monitor Cloud Performance and Data Safety With Artificial Intelligence. In Applications of Artificial Intelligence in Wireless Communication Systems (pp. 92-108). IGI Global. doi:10.4018/978-1-6684-7348-1.ch006

Doshi, R., Hu, Y. C., Garg, L., & Fagbola, T. (2023). Towards a Higher Education of the Future: Transformational Roles of Edge Intelligence. *Array (New York, N.Y.)*, 100332. doi:10.1016/j.array.2023.100332

Easwaran, B., Hiran, K. K., Krishnan, S., & Doshi, R. (Eds.). (2022). *Real-time applications of machine learning in cyber-physical systems*. IGI global. doi:10.4018/978-1-7998-9308-0

Filippi, C. G., Stein, J. M., Wang, Z., Bakas, S., Liu, Y., Chang, P. D., Lui, Y., Hess, C., Barboriak, D. P., Flanders, A. E., Wintermark, M., Zaharchuk, G., & Wu, O. (2023). Ethical Considerations and Fairness in the Use of Artificial Intelligence for Neuroradiology. *AJNR. American Journal of Neuroradiology*, *44*(11), 1242–1248. doi:10.3174/ajnr.A7963 PMID:37652578

Gangal, R., Johri, P., & Kumar, A. (2023). A Systematic Review of Artificial Intelligence Techniques in Lung Cancer Detection and Accurate Diagnosis. *Cosmos Journal of Engineering & Technology*, *13*(1), 51–56. doi:10.46360/cosmos.et.620231005

Gevaert, C. M., Carman, M., Rosman, B., Georgiadou, Y., & Soden, R. (2021). Fairness and accountability of AI in disaster risk management: Opportunities and challenges. *Patterns (New York, N.Y.)*, *2*(11), 100363. doi:10.1016/j.patter.2021.100363 PMID:34820647

Gligorea, I., Cioca, M., Oancea, R., Gorski, A.-T., Gorski, H., & Tudorache, P. (2023). Adaptive Learning Using Artificial Intelligence in e-Learning: A Literature Review. *Education Sciences*, *13*(12), 1216. doi:10.3390/educsci13121216

Gorski, A.-T., Gligorea, I., Gorski, H., & Oancea, R. (2022). Workforce and Workplace Ecosystem - Challenges and Opportunities in the Age of Digital Transformation and 4IR. *International Conference of Knowledge-Based Organization, 28*, 187-194. 10.2478/kbo-2022-0028

Gupta, T., & Khan, S. (2023). Education and International Collaboration in the Digital Age. *Globus Journal of Progressive Education*, *13*(1), 79–87.

Hiran, K. K., Doshi, R., & Patel, M. (Eds.). (2024). *Applications of Virtual and Augmented Reality for Health and Wellbeing*. IGI Global., doi:10.4018/979-8-3693-1123-3

Hiran, K. K., Khazanchi, D., Vyas, A. K., & Padmanaban, S. (Eds.). (2021). *Machine learning for sustainable development* (Vol. 9). Walter de Gruyter GmbH & Co KG. doi:10.1515/9783110702514

Huddar, R., Kharade, K., & Kamat, R. (2023). *Designing of AI-Based Teaching-Learning Model for Revitalizing Education. International Conference on The Future Global Business and Technology*, Kolhapur, India.

Jaramillo, R. N., Liezl Mae, G. M., Bucao, T. P., Bueno, B. J., Bulatao, L. R., Cabrera, S., & Cacho, L. C. (2022). A Systematic Review of Simulation-Based Learning Versus Traditional Learning. *Cosmos An International Journal of Art & Higher Education*, *11*(2), 24–28.

Joshi, M. A. Adaptive Learning through Artificial Intelligence (July 19, 2023). Joshi, M.A. (2024). Adaptive Learning through Artificial Intelligence. *International Journal on Integrated Education. 7*(2), 41-43. https://ssrn.com/abstract=4514887 or doi:10.2139/ssrn.4514887

Kamila, M.K. & Jasrotia, S.S. (2023). Ethical issues in the development of artificial intelligence: Recognizing the risks. *International Journal of Ethics and Systems.*

Kim, W. (2021). A Design-Based Research on Application of Artificial Intelligence AI) Teaching-Learning Model in Elementary School. *International Journal of Advanced Smart Convergence*, *10*(2), 201–208. doi:10.7236/IJASC.2021.10.2.201

Liu, J., Kong, X., Xia, F., Bai, X., Wang, L., Qing, Q., & Lee, I. (2018). Artificial Intelligence in the 21st Century. *IEEE Access : Practical Innovations, Open Solutions*, *6*, 34403–34421. doi:10.1109/ACCESS.2018.2819688

Lo Piano, S. (2020). Ethical principles in machine learning and artificial intelligence: Cases from the field and possible ways forward. *Humanities & Social Sciences Communications*, *7*(1), 1–7. doi:10.1057/s41599-020-0501-9

Macapagal, P. (2023). Digital Self-Identity in the Age of Technology of the New Normal Learning. *Globus An International Journal of Management & IT, 15*(1), 37-46.

Mahrishi, M., Hiran, K. K., Meena, G., & Sharma, P. (Eds.). (2020). Machine learning and deep learning in real-time applications. IGI global. doi:10.4018/978-1-7998-3095-5

Maquiling, E. E. (2023). Critical Thinking Skills as Predictors of Students' Performance in A Problem-Based Learning Environment. *Globus Journal of Progressive Education*, *13*(1), 107–111.

Mijwil, M. M., Gök, M., Doshi, R., Hiran, K. K., & Kösesoy, I. (2023). Utilizing Artificial Intelligence Techniques to Improve the Performance of Wireless Nodes. In Applications of Artificial Intelligence in Wireless Communication Systems (pp. 150-162). IGI Global. doi:10.4018/978-1-6684-7348-1.ch010

Mishra, A., Tripathi, A., Khazanchi, D., Hiran, K. K., Vyas, A. K., & Padmanaban, S. (2021). A framework for applying artificial intelligence (AI) with Internet of NanoThings (IoNT). In *Machine Learning for Sustainable Development* (pp. 1–16). De Gruyter. doi:10.1515/9783110702514-001

Neha, K. (2020). Role of Artificial Intelligence in Education. *Alochana Chakra Journal*, *IX*(IX), 305–309.

Priyadarshi, N., Padmanaban, S., Hiran, K. K., Holm-Nielson, J. B., & Bansal, R. C. (Eds.). (2021). *Artificial intelligence and internet of things for renewable energy systems* (Vol. 12). Walter de Gruyter GmbH & Co KG. doi:10.1515/9783110714043

Rathi, S., Hiran, K. K., & Sakhare, S. (2023). Affective state prediction of E-learner using SS-ROA based deep LSTM. *Array (New York, N.Y.)*, *19*, 100315. doi:10.1016/j.array.2023.100315

Reyes, V., Camara, M., Bantigue, A., & Caling, M. A. (2023). The Role of Learning Action Cell Session in Research Self-Efficacy Level: Basis for the Development of An Action Plan. Globus An International Journal of Medical Science. *Engineering and Technology*, *11*(1), 80–86.

Sharma, L. (2023). Leadership and Governance in Hospital Management: Best Practices and Challenges. Globus An International Journal of Medical Science. *Engineering and Technology*, *12*(1), 89–93.

Siau, K. (2017). *Impact of Artificial Intelligence, Robotics, and Automation on Higher Education. Americas Conference on Information Systems (AMCIS 2017)*, Boston, MA.

Siau, K. (2018). Education in the Age of Artificial Intelligence: How will Technology Shape Learning? *The Global Analyst*, *7*(3), 22–24.

Singh, S. V., & Hiran, K. K. (2022). The impact of AI on teaching and learning in higher education technology. *Journal of Higher Education Theory and Practice*, *22*(13).

Timms, M. J. (2016). Letting artificial intelligence in education out of the box: Educational cobots and smart classrooms. *International Journal of Artificial Intelligence in Education*, *26*(2), 701–712. doi:10.1007/s40593-016-0095-y

Xu, Y., Liu, X., Cao, X., Huang, C., Liu, E., Qian, S., Liu, X., Wu, Y., Dong, F., Qiu, C.-W., Qiu, J., Hua, K., Su, W., Wu, J., Xu, H., Han, Y., Fu, C., Yin, Z., Liu, M., & Zhang, J. (2021). Artificial intelligence: A powerful paradigm for scientific research. *Innovation (Cambridge (Mass.))*, *2*(4), 1–20. doi:10.1016/j.xinn.2021.100179 PMID:34877560

Zawacki-Richter, O., Marín, V. I., Bond, M., & Gouverneur, F. (2019). A systematic review of research on artificial intelligence applications in higher education where are the educators? *International Journal of Educational Technology in Higher Education*, *16*(1), 39. doi:10.1186/s41239-019-0171-0

Zeniakin, O. (2023). Use of the Artificial Intelligence in Education: Opportunities, Prospects, and Risks. Conference: Psychological And Pedagogical Problems of Higher and Secondary Education in the Conditions of Modern Challenges: Theory and Practice, Kharkiv, Ukraine.

# Chapter 9
# Exploring the Implications of Emerging Artificial Intelligence Technologies at Edge Computing in Higher Education

**Omega John Unogwu**
https://orcid.org/0000-0001-6415-8892
*Azteca University, Mexico*

**Ruchi Doshi**
https://orcid.org/0000-0002-7259-8481
*Azteca University, Mexico*

**Kamal Kant Hiran**
*Sir Padampat Singhania University, India*

**Maad M. Mijwil**
https://orcid.org/0000-0002-2884-2504
*Baghdad College of Economic Sciences University, Iraq*

**Ankar Tersoo Catherine**
*College of Education, Oju, Nigeria*

**Mostafa Abotaleb**
https://orcid.org/0000-0002-3442-6865
*South Ural State University, Russia*

## ABSTRACT

*In this chapter, the effects of cutting-edge artificial intelligence (AI) technologies at edge computing are examined in higher education. Edge computing offers a decentralized method of computing in which processing is done near the data source. Due to less network traffic, response times can be quicker. AI technology can be implemented at the edge to offer instructors and students intelligent and individualized services. The chapter addresses the advantages of edge computing and AI in higher education, including enhanced student involvement, better learning results, and simplified administrative procedures. It also looks at the difficulties of implementing AI at the edge, such as data privacy and security issues. To fully fulfill the potential of AI, the article's conclusion emphasizes the necessity for additional study in this field.*

DOI: 10.4018/979-8-3693-2440-0.ch009

## INTRODUCTION

Higher education is one of several establishments that are progressively embracing artificial intelligence (AI) technologies. Artificial intelligence (AI) is becoming a crucial component of higher education due to its ability to improve teaching and learning processes (Kuleto et al., 2021; Doshi et al., 2023). Additionally, edge computing has become a promising strategy for AI to get past the difficulties posed by conventional centralized computing models. To reduce latency and enable quicker responses to real-time events, edge computing enables data processing to take place closer to the source of the data. Higher education institutions may significantly improve areas like personalized learning, student achievement, and operational efficiency by fusing AI with edge computing (Selwyn, 2022; Zeide, 2019). However, to make sure that they are used in an ethical, efficient, and secure manner, it is necessary to examine the implications of these new technologies for higher education. We will look at the current state of AI in higher education, the advantages of edge computing, and any potential risks or difficulties involved with the adoption of these technologies as we investigate the implications of new AI technologies at edge computing in higher education. The relevance of ongoing research and development in this field will be emphasized in our discussion of case studies and the future of edge computing and AI in higher education. This will improve student outcomes and progress in the field of higher education.

## THE CURRENT STATE OF AI IN HIGHER INSTITUTIONS

The world we live in is rapidly evolving due to artificial intelligence (AI), and higher education is no exception. Artificial intelligence (AI) is becoming a crucial component of higher education due to its ability to improve teaching and learning processes. Researchers are looking into the potential for AI to customize education and increase student success rates, and institutions are already employing it to help jobs like student recruiting, academic counseling, and administrative procedures (Luan et al., 2020). AI applications, however, may face difficulties with conventional centralized computer models. Centralized approaches rely on sending massive amounts of data to a single place for processing, which can cause bottlenecks, excessive latency, and delayed response times. Furthermore, centralized models can present security and privacy risks because private information may be processed and stored on distant servers. These issues are particularly pressing when it comes to higher education, where data security and privacy are crucial factors.

### Benefits Of Artificial Intelligence in Higher Institutions

The creation of individualized learning experiences is one of the key uses of AI in higher education. Institutions can examine student data and behavior using machine learning algorithms to offer individualized suggestions and interventions that encourage student achievement. For example, AI systems can review student performance data and suggest individualized learning paths, or they can identify students who are at risk and offer them focused interventions to increase their chances of success (Bonderud, 2021; Doshi et al., 2023).

The creation of intelligent campus systems is another area in which AI is being applied in higher education. To gather data on the campus surroundings, these systems use sensors and other data sources. They then use AI algorithms to optimize their operations and boost productivity. By analyzing data from sensors and other sources in real-time, intelligent campus systems can, for example, optimize energy use, save waste, and increase safety.

Research and innovation in higher education are also using AI technologies. For instance, machine learning algorithms can analyze huge datasets to find patterns and insights that might help study in a variety of sectors. The development of new apps and services that can improve teaching and learning and raise student engagement, like intelligent tutoring systems, virtual assistants, and chatbots, is another benefit of AI technologies.

### Challenges of Artificial Intelligence in Higher Education

There are issues and obstacles that need to be resolved despite the potential advantages of AI technologies in higher education. The moral and social ramifications of AI technologies are one of the key worries. Institutions must make sure that they are utilizing AI technologies morally and openly, as well as by considering any potential social and economic repercussions. Institutions also need to make sure that they are following all applicable laws and regulations pertaining to data use and protection, as well as safeguarding student data and privacy.

The requirement for specific hardware and software to enable AI technology is another difficulty. Institutions must have the required systems and infrastructure in place to support AI technologies because they demand a lot of computer power and specialized software. This can be particularly difficult for organizations with tight funds and resources (Hiran et al., 2023; Mijwil et al., 2023).

The usage of AI technology in higher education is anticipated to increase in the upcoming years despite these obstacles. Institutions that successfully incorporate AI technologies into their teaching and learning settings should anticipate improvements in student success rates, operational efficiency, and innovation. However, it is crucial for institutions to carefully consider the implications of AI technologies and create appropriate policies and practices to ensure that they are used securely and ethically.

As a result, institutions have a lot of chances to improve teaching and learning, promote student success, and spur creativity by implementing AI technologies in higher education. However, to ensure that these technologies are used in a responsible and open manner, it is crucial for institutions to carefully consider the ethical and social implications of these technologies and develop appropriate policies and practices. Institutions must also make sure that all students may access and use AI technologies.

In conclusion, while the use of AI technologies in higher education offers enormous prospects for improving teaching and learning experiences, there are also difficulties and issues that must be resolved to ensure that these technologies are applied in an ethical, secure, and inclusive manner.

## EDGE COMPUTING IN HIGHER EDUCATION

To address these issues, edge computing has emerged as a promising strategy. Edge computing enables data processing to happen nearer to the data source, reducing latency and allowing for quicker reactions to real-time events. Edge computing lessens the load on centralized servers by relocating computation to the network edge, which also eliminates the need for data to be sent across long distances. Edge computing has been utilized successfully in a variety of applications, from industrial automation to smart homes, and is now being investigated for use in higher education (Easwaran et al., 2022).

*Table 1. Advantages and disadvantages of AI technologies in higher education*

| Advantages | Challenges |
|---|---|
| Learning experiences that are specifically tuned to each student's needs: By examining student data and behavior, determining each student's strengths and weaknesses, and providing specialized learning routes and suggestions, AI may create learning experiences that are specifically tailored to each student. | Ethical and Societal Implications: The potential for biases, concerns surrounding privacy, and the impact of automation on the labor force represents a mere fraction of the ethical and societal implications associated with artificial intelligence technologies that present a formidable challenge. |
| Enhancing student connection and engagement can help increase student motivation and involvement. AI-powered applications like virtual assistants, chatbots, and intelligent tutoring systems can do this. | Limited accessibility: Access to AI technologies may be restricted for some student groups due to the need for powerful computers and specialized software, which may be difficult for universities with tight budgets and resources. |
| Increased effectiveness and productivity: AI technology can automate administrative duties and streamline operations, decreasing the workload for educators and employees and freeing up time for more strategic and important work. | Data security and privacy: Organizations must make sure that they are protecting student information and privacy, as well as adhering to all applicable laws and rules governing data use and protection. |
| Research and innovation: AI technology can enable new applications and services, such as intelligent campus systems and research findings, that can improve teaching and learning processes and spur innovation in the education sector. | Technology dependence: There is a danger of relying too much on AI technologies, which could replace human connection and mentoring and reduce the value of human educators in education. |

## Benefits of Edge Computing in Higher Education

For higher education institutions, edge computing has the potential to provide several advantages. The ability to lower latency and increase response times is one of edge computing's key benefits. Edge computing eliminates the need for data to be sent over great distances, which can cause delays and increased latency. Instead, processing takes place close to the data source. For real-time applications that demand quick data processing and minimal latency, such as virtual and augmented reality, this is especially crucial (Bonderud, 2021).

Additionally, edge computing can increase the scalability and dependability of computer systems. Edge computing lightens the load on centralized servers by dispersing computation across several devices and locations, enhancing the scalability and resilience of systems. This can assist in decreasing downtime and increasing system availability, which can be especially helpful for universities with big, sophisticated computing systems.

Edge computing also has the potential to increase data security and privacy. The requirement for data to be sent over long distances and kept on distant servers is diminished as data processing occurs closer to the original source of the data. Sensitive data stays inside the institution's network perimeter, which can help to lower the risk of data breaches and cyberattacks (Yahuza et al., 2020; Singh et al., 2022).

Finally, edge computing can open new opportunities for services and applications that centralized computing models could not previously support. Edge computing, for instance, can support real-time analytics and machine learning applications that need fast data processing and minimal latency. Insights about student behavior and performance can be gained by institutions, allowing them to provide focused interventions and raise student success rates.

In conclusion, edge computing can assist higher education institutions in several ways, such as faster latency and reaction times, increased scalability and dependability, data privacy and security, and new applications and services. Institutions can improve teaching and learning experiences, increase operational effectiveness, and boost student achievement by utilizing these advantages.

## Challenges of Edge Computing in Higher Education

Despite the obvious advantages of edge computing, it's important to remember that there are several obstacles that organizations must overcome to implement it. The demand for specialized hardware and software to support edge computing represents one of the major hurdles. Institutions must have the required systems and infrastructure in place to support this paradigm since edge computing includes dispersed computing across numerous devices and places. Institutions with tight finances and resources may find this particularly problematic.

Another challenge is the need for data management and governance. As edge computing involves processing and storing data in multiple locations, institutions must have appropriate policies and procedures in place to manage and govern this data. This includes ensuring that data is protected from unauthorized access and that appropriate data retention and disposal policies are in place (Hiran et al., 2024).

Institutions must also take into consideration any potential legal and ethical ramifications of edge computing. Edge computing raises concerns regarding data ownership, privacy, and security because it entails processing data closer to the source. Institutions must make sure they follow applicable laws and regulations and have the right policies and practices in place to handle these issues (Yahuza et al., 2020; Rathi et al., 2023).

In summary, edge computing has several advantages for institutions of higher learning, but it also poses several issues that need to be resolved. To enhance teaching and learning, encourage student achievement, and boost operational efficiency, institutions must overcome these obstacles. To make sure that these technologies are utilized in an ethical and safe manner, institutions must carefully assess the implications of edge computing and create the necessary rules and procedures (Dumford and Miller, 2018).

In conclusion, edge computing is a cutting-edge technology that has enormous potential to alter higher education, but it also presents several hazards and concerns that need to be properly studied and managed (Hiran et al., 2021). To guarantee that this technology is used in a responsible, secure, and effective manner and that the benefits are successfully evaluated and realized, institutions must carefully evaluate the advantages and difficulties of edge computing and adopt suitable strategies and policies.

*Table 2. Advantages and disadvantages of edge computing in higher education*

| Advantages | Challenges |
|---|---|
| Edge computing enables quicker data handling and analysis, resulting in reduced response times for data-heavy applications such as online learning platforms. | Complexity: The implementation and management of edge computing can be extremely difficult and complicated. |
| By bringing data processing and storage closer to where it is used, edge computing decreases network latency and improves the performance of online learning platforms. | Integration: It might be difficult and time-consuming to integrate edge computing into the campus infrastructure that already exists. |
| Edge computing is cost-effective because it utilizes existing resources such as laptops and smartphones to reduce the cost of computing infrastructure. | Scalability: It can be challenging to make sure that edge computing systems can expand to meet the rising demands of online learning platforms. |
| Edge computing can enhance the security and privacy of critical student information by keeping it on the campus network. | Security: Although edge computing has the potential to increase security, it also brings with it new security dangers, such as the chance of data breaches at the edge. |
| Edge computing can enhance the reliability of online learning systems by offering on-site data processing and storage in case of network connectivity issues. | Assuring interoperability between various systems and devices may be challenging due to the lack of standardization in edge computing technologies. |

## IMPLICATIONS OF AI AND EDGE COMPUTING IN HIGHER EDUCATION

Edge computing and AI have significant potential for enhancing higher education, but it is essential to consider their potential impacts to ensure that they are applied in a secure, efficient, and ethical manner. The aim of this essay is to investigate the effects of cutting-edge edge computing AI technologies in higher education. We first examined the benefits and difficulties of AI in higher education. We then explored the concept of edge computing and the advantages it can offer academic institutions. Next, we looked at the potential dangers and challenges posed by using edge computing and AI, including privacy issues and moral issues. We will emphasize the importance of ongoing research and development in this field in our discussion of case studies and the future of edge computing and AI in higher education. This will improve student outcomes and progress in the field of higher education (Rausch and Dustdar, 2019; Fariani et al., 2022; Fernández-Caramés and Fraga-Lamas, 2019).

Edge computing and AI have considerable and far-reaching implications for higher education. The following are some of the most significant implications:

- AI and edge computing can support personalized learning experiences and adaptive learning, enhancing teaching and learning experiences and allowing students to progress at their own pace and in accordance with their unique needs and preferences. This may result in improvements in learning outcomes and student engagement.
- Increased accessibility and inclusivity: The integration of AI and edge computing has the potential to enhance remote learning and virtual training programs, which allows students to access educational materials from any location and at any time. This can lead to greater inclusivity and accessibility, especially for students who experience geographical, physical, or financial challenges in accessing education.

*Figure 1. The convergence of edge computing and AI in higher education*

- Better campus operations: AI and edge computing can be used to track and manage campus activities including energy use, parking occupancy, and classroom occupancy, allowing for more effective and sustainable campus administration.
- Improved cybersecurity and data privacy: By reducing the likelihood of an attack and facilitating quick threat identification and response, edge computing can strengthen cybersecurity. AI may speed up the examination of large amounts of data to find security flaws and system vulnerabilities, thus enhancing data privacy.
- Enhanced research and innovation: Data-intensive research projects like genomics and climate modeling can benefit from the use of AI and edge computing since they can perform analyses more quickly and precisely, which leads to new discoveries and improvements in a variety of fields.
- Ethical and social implications: Higher education institutions must consider ethical and social issues including algorithmic responsibility, bias, and data privacy when they implement AI and edge computing. As a result, institutions must use edge computing and AI technologies responsibly and ethically to prevent unfavorable results.

To conclude, the implementation of AI and edge computing in higher education has numerous intricate implications. While these technologies provide a plethora of advantages, they also pose substantial challenges and ethical considerations that necessitate resolution to guarantee their responsible and ethical use.

## CASE STUDIES OF AI AND EDGE COMPUTING IN HIGHER EDUCATION

Synopsis of paradigms that highlight the potential advantages and difficulties of edge computing and AI in higher education.

Numerous case studies provide examples of the possible advantages and difficulties associated with AI and edge computing in higher education. A few of these are:

1. A case study was conducted at Covenant University in Nigeria with the objective of developing and implementing an Artificial Intelligence-based mobile learning system to enhance the learning experiences of students and facilitate personalized learning in accordance with the individual needs of each student. The system utilized Artificial Intelligence algorithms to scrutinize student data, identify areas of difficulty, and provide tailored learning content and assessments. The findings of the study indicated that the deployment of the system resulted in considerable improvements in student performance and engagement. Students reported an elevated level of satisfaction with their learning experiences and conveyed that the system had assisted them in achieving a superior understanding and retention of course material. Nevertheless, the study also highlighted the challenges inherent in implementing such a system, including the requirement for a robust infrastructure and training for faculty members to effectively utilize the technology. In summation, the case study demonstrated the potential benefits of Artificial Intelligence-based mobile learning systems in higher education while concurrently emphasizing the necessity to address associated challenges to ensure successful implementation and adoption (Bali, 2023).
2. Ashesi University: This university in Ghana has developed an AI-powered platform called "Ashesi Anywhere" that allows students to access lab equipment remotely. The platform enables students to perform experiments and control lab devices from anywhere in the world. This overcomes the

limitations of having to be physically present in the lab and provides a more flexible and accessible learning environment (Naqvi et al., 2023; Soudi, 2024).

3. Carnegie Mellon, an American university, has set up an edge computing system that allows real-time data processing in its classes. The system uses IoT sensors to collect data on student performance and engagement, which is then analyzed in real-time to provide feedback to both students and instructors. This has improved student outcomes and a more personalized learning environment (Hussain et al., 2019).
4. University of California, Los Angeles: A natural language processing AI system that evaluates student essays has been implemented at the University of California, Los Angeles (UCLA) in the United States. The program gives students automated feedback on grammar, style, and content to help them improve their writing skills (Sadanand et al., 2022).

These examples illustrate how higher education can benefit from edge computing and AI. They show how these technologies can provide personalized learning experiences, enable real-time data analysis, offer instant support and guidance, and overcome physical limitations. To ensure that these technologies are used ethically, wisely, and effectively, institutions must also consider any risks or challenges that may arise from using these technologies. The case studies demonstrate the possible benefits of integrating edge computing and AI in higher education, such as improved student outcomes, increased productivity, and personalized learning experiences. However, implementing and using these technologies also pose challenges, such as data privacy concerns, the need for adequate infrastructure, and the requirement for skilled staff. Hence, institutions should carefully evaluate the potential pros and cons before introducing new technologies into their educational programs.

## Consideration of the Insights Gained From These Examples and Their Consequences for Future Applications of AI and Edge Computing in Higher Education

1. Infrastructure and resource requirements: For AI and edge computing to be successfully implemented in higher education, institutions need to have the necessary infrastructure and resources, such as high-speed internet connectivity, a dependable power source, and qualified staff. Institutions should carefully evaluate their capacity for implementing these technologies and create plans to fill any infrastructure and resource deficiencies.
2. Tailored learning is the main topic: By examining data on student participation, performance, and preferences, AI and edge computing can deliver individualized learning experiences. The usage of these technologies by institutions should be given priority to facilitate personalized learning and offer students who are having trouble with specific treatments.
3. To effectively use edge computing and AI, institutions need to cooperate and build partnerships with other players in the industry. This way, they can access the resources and skills they need, overcome difficulties, and make the most of these technologies. Finding and working with partners that can offer valuable assistance in adopting these technologies is crucial for institutions.
4. The significance of ethical considerations: AI and edge computing create ethical issues like accountability, bias, and privacy. To ensure that these technologies are utilized in an ethical and

responsible way, institutions should think about the ethical implications of these technologies and adopt rules and procedures to ensure that they are.

5. Institutions should constantly measure how edge computing and artificial intelligence affect student outcomes and change their approaches as needed to make their use of these technologies effective and lasting. By assessing and improving regularly, institutions can reach their objectives and make the best use of these technologies. It is vital to keep track of and examine how these technologies influence student outcomes and take appropriate actions to ensure lasting success.

Examining the case studies discussed before gives useful insights into the pros and cons of edge computing and AI in higher education in sub-Saharan Africa. These technologies can have a big impact on higher education, but it is important for institutions to look at these case studies closely. They should think about the specific possibilities and challenges in their situation while planning strategies that include the lessons from these cases (Wang et al., 2020; Papaspyridis, 2020).

## NEXT STEPS FOR HIGHER EDUCATION WITH AI AND EDGE COMPUTING

As AI and edge computing continue to evolve, institutions should concentrate on a few essential areas to fully exploit the potential benefits of these technologies in higher education.

One of the key areas is to investigate new applications of edge computing and AI that can augment the learning experience and outcomes for students. For example, institutions can employ natural language processing and chatbots to deliver personalized feedback and support to individual students. Furthermore, predictive analytics can assist in identifying students who are at risk and provide them with customized interventions to help them achieve their goals (Burrows, 2021).

Another aspect that institutions should prioritize is the establishment and execution of ethical frameworks for the utilization of edge computing and AI in higher education. This can encompass guidelines for the appropriate utilization of these technologies, as well as rules for data privacy, accountability, and transparency.

Institutions should finance independent research to investigate the effectiveness of edge computing and AI in higher education. This can comprise studies to assess how these technologies influence student outcomes, teacher and staff workflows, and institutional efficiency. They can be qualitative or quantitative.

In conclusion, institutions should pursue opportunities for partnerships and collaborations with other organizations that are employing edge computing and AI technologies. This can entail collaborating with tech firms, research centers, and other higher education institutions to share resources and ideas and devise innovative strategies for utilizing these technologies in education.

By concentrating on these areas, institutions can position themselves to benefit from the rapidly evolving landscape of edge computing and AI in higher education. They can provide students with personalized, high-quality learning experiences that prepare them for a rapidly changing world.

### Dialogue About Potential Future Developments in Higher Education With AI and Edge Computing

A few new developments and technologies may affect the direction of edge computing and AI in higher education. Some probable developments to observe are:

Increased utilization of augmented and virtual reality: These technologies may be employed more frequently in higher education as they advance, to offer immersive and engaging learning opportunities.

Continued advancement of natural language processing: As natural language processing technology advances, chatbots and other conversational interfaces may be more extensively utilized by universities to provide students with individualized support.

Increased utilization of machine learning: As more data is gathered and analyzed, machine learning algorithms may become more essential for finding trends and forecasting outcomes in higher education (Abdous, 2023; Bates et al., 2020; Shukur and Mijwil, 2023; Shang et al., 2022).

The role of machine learning will grow: More data collection and analysis will make machine learning methods more essential for identifying patterns and predicting outcomes in higher education (Khazaal and Maarouf, 2023; Shukur et al., 2023).

New challenges and solutions for data protection: Data privacy and security concerns will increase, requiring organizations to adopt more sophisticated tools and safeguards for sensitive data.

More collaboration across different disciplines: Edge computing and AI will affect the higher education landscape, creating more opportunities for cooperation among computer science, education, and other fields.

To conclude, technological innovation, shifting pedagogical paradigms, and evolving societal needs are likely to have a significant impact on the future of AI and edge computing in higher education. Institutions that can maintain a competitive edge in these advancements are likely to provide students with cutting-edge, superior learning opportunities that will equip them for success in a rapidly evolving world.

*Figure 2. Augmented reality of edge computing and AI in higher education*

## How Continuous Research and Development Can Enhance the Benefits of AI and Edge Computing in Higher Education

To fully harness the benefits of edge computing and AI in higher education, sustained research and development efforts are indispensable. These technologies will present new opportunities to augment teaching and learning outcomes and address long-standing challenges in higher education as they continue to advance.

Research and development efforts should concentrate on enhancing the accuracy and effectiveness of AI algorithms, developing novel edge computing and AI applications for higher education, and addressing ethical and privacy concerns. Collaboration among higher education institutions, businesses, and government bodies will be essential to stimulate innovation and implement successful solutions.

The primary aim of research and development efforts in the domain of edge computing and AI in higher education should be to augment student learning outcomes and enhance greater accessibility and equity in higher education. By endorsing these technologies and exploring their potential, we can establish a more effective and inclusive higher education system that prepares students for success in a perpetually evolving world (Schroeder, 2022; Carvalho et al., 2021; Hasoon et al., 2023; Badih and Alagrash, 2020; Chatterjee and Bhattacharjee, 2020).

To make sure that AI and edge computing in higher education are inclusive and support diversity, it is essential to focus on issues such as fairness and inclusiveness (Sallam and Mousa, 2024). This may require actions such as verifying that AI algorithms are not biased, addressing accessibility barriers for students with disabilities and considering the impact of these technologies on underrepresented and marginalized groups.

In general, to achieve the full potential of edge computing and AI in higher education, more research, collaboration, and attention to diversity and inclusiveness are needed. By working together and staying updated about the latest developments and effective practices, we can create a more equitable, efficient, and inclusive system of higher education.

# CONCLUSION

Artificial intelligence and edge computing have the potential to revolutionize higher education by providing personalized learning experiences, improving student outcomes, and addressing longstanding challenges in the field. However, as with any new technology, there are also potential risks and challenges that must be addressed, such as privacy concerns, ethical considerations, and the need for ongoing research and development.

Through case studies and analysis, we have examined the potential benefits and challenges of artificial intelligence and edge computing in higher education. It is evident that these technologies have the potential to transform the way we approach teaching and learning, but we must also be mindful of the potential risks and ethical considerations.

It is imperative to prioritize ongoing research and development, disseminate knowledge of these technologies, foster collaboration and diversity in their development, and leverage edge computing and AI to their full potential in higher education. By doing this, we can develop a higher education system that is more equitable and efficient and that equips students with the skills they need to succeed in a rapidly evolving world.

## REFERENCES

Abdous, M. (2023). How AI Is Shaping the Future of Higher Ed. *Inside Higher Ed*. https://www.insidehighered.com/views/2023/03/22/how-ai-shaping-future-higher-ed-opinion

Badih, H., & Alagrash, Y. (2020). Static Analysis Framework Based on Multi - Agent System. In *Proceedings of International IOT, Electronics and Mechatronics Conference (IEMTRONICS),* (pp. 1-6). IOT. 10.1109/IEMTRONICS51293.2020.9216382

BaliB. (2023). Analysis of Emerging Trends in Artificial Intelligence in Education in Nigeria. Research square. Preorint. doi:10.21203/rs.3.rs-3819828/v1

Bates, T., Cobo, C., Mariño, O., & Wheeler, S. (2020). Can artificial intelligence transform higher education? *International Journal of Educational Technology in Higher Education*, *17*(42), 1–12. doi:10.1186/s41239-020-00218-x

Bonderud, D. (2021). *What Is Edge Computing, and How Can It Be Leveraged for Higher Ed?* EdTech. https://edtechmagazine.com/higher/article/2021/11/what-edge-computing-and-how-can-it-be-leveraged-higher-ed-perfcon

Burrows, L. (2021). *The present and future of AI.* Harvard John A. Paulson School of Engineering and Applied Sciences. https://seas.harvard.edu/news/2021/10/present-and-future-ai

Carvalho, G., Cabral, B., Pereira, V., & Bernardino, J. (2021). Edge computing: Current trends, research challenges and future directions. *Computing*, *103*(5), 993–1023. doi:10.1007/s00607-020-00896-5

Chatterjee, S., & Bhattacharjee, K. K. (2020). Adoption of artificial intelligence in higher education: A quantitative analysis using structural equation modelling. *Education and Information Technologies*, *25*(5), 3443–3463. doi:10.1007/s10639-020-10159-7

Doshi, R., Hiran, K. K., Mijwil, M. M., & Anand, D. (2023). To That of Artificial Intelligence, Passing Through Business Intelligence. In Handbook of Research on AI and Knowledge Engineering for Real-Time Business Intelligence (pp. 1-16). IGI Global. doi:10.4018/978-1-6684-6519-6.ch001

Doshi, R., Hu, Y. C., Garg, L., & Fagbola, T. (2023). Towards a Higher Education of the Future: Transformational Roles of Edge Intelligence. *Array (New York, N.Y.)*, 100332. doi:10.1016/j.array.2023.100332

Dumford, A. D., & Miller, A. L. (2018). Online learning in higher education: Exploring advantages and disadvantages for engagement. *Journal of Computing in Higher Education*, *30*(3), 452–465. doi:10.1007/s12528-018-9179-z

Easwaran, B., Hiran, K. K., Krishnan, S., & Doshi, R. (Eds.). (2022). *Real-time applications of machine learning in cyber-physical systems.* IGI global. doi:10.4018/978-1-7998-9308-0

Fariani, R. I., Junus, K., & Santoso, H. B. (2022). A Systematic Literature Review on Personalised Learning in the Higher Education Context. Technology. *Knowledge and Learning*, *28*(2), 449–476. doi:10.1007/s10758-022-09628-4

Fernández-Caramés, T. M., & Fraga-Lamas, P. (2019). Towards Next Generation Teaching, Learning, and Context-Aware Applications for Higher Education: A Review on Blockchain, IoT, Fog and Edge Computing Enabled Smart Campuses and Universities. *Applied Sciences (Basel, Switzerland)*, *9*(21), 4479. doi:10.3390/app9214479

Hasoon, J. N., Almtrf, A., Alagrash, Y., & Althubiti, M. (2023). A Hybrid Approach of Image Retrieving In Biometric ID. In *Proceedings of International Conference on Computing and Information Technology*, (pp. 1-6). IEEE. 10.1109/ICCIT58132.2023.10273904

Hiran, K. K., & Dadhich, M. (2024). Predicting the core determinants of cloud-edge computing adoption (CECA) for sustainable development in the higher education institutions of Africa: A high order SEM-ANN analytical approach. *Technological Forecasting and Social Change*, *199*, 122979. doi:10.1016/j.techfore.2023.122979

Hiran, K. K., Hemachandran, K., Pise, A., & Rabi, B. (Eds.). (2023). *Handbook of Research on AI and Knowledge Engineering for Real-Time Business Intelligence*. IGI Global. doi:10.4018/978-1-6684-6519-6

Hiran, K. K., Khazanchi, D., Vyas, A. K., & Padmanaban, S. (Eds.). (2021). *Machine learning for sustainable development* (Vol. 9). Walter de Gruyter GmbH & Co KG. doi:10.1515/9783110702514

Hussain, B., Du, Q., Zhang, S., Imran, A., & Imran, M. A. (2019). Mobile Edge Computing-Based Data-Driven Deep Learning Framework for Anomaly Detection. *IEEE Access : Practical Innovations, Open Solutions*, *7*, 137656–137667. doi:10.1109/ACCESS.2019.2942485

Khazaal, S. M., & Maarouf, H. (2023). Predicting Coronary Artery Disease Utilizing Support Vector Machines: Optimizing Predictive Model. *Mesopotamian Journal of Artificial Intelligence in Healthcare*, *2023*, 21–26. doi:10.58496/MJAIH/2023/004

Kuleto, V., Ilić, M., Dumangiu, M., Ranković, M., Martins, O. M. D., Păun, D., & Mihoreanu, L. (2021). Exploring Opportunities and Challenges of Artificial Intelligence and Machine Learning in Higher Education Institutions. *Sustainability (Basel)*, *13*(18), 10424. doi:10.3390/su131810424

Luan, H., Geczy, P., Lai, H., Gobert, J., Yang, S. J. H., Ogata, H., Baltes, J., Guerra, R., Li, P., & Tsai, C.-C. (2020). Challenges and Future Directions of Big Data and Artificial Intelligence in Education. *Frontiers in Psychology*, *11*, 1–11. doi:10.3389/fpsyg.2020.580820 PMID:33192896

Mijwil, M. M., Gök, M., Doshi, R., Hiran, K. K., & Kösesoy, I. (2023). Utilizing Artificial Intelligence Techniques to Improve the Performance of Wireless Nodes. In Applications of Artificial Intelligence in Wireless Communication Systems (pp. 150-162). IGI Global. https://doi.org/ doi:10.4018/978-1-6684-7348-1.ch010

Naqvi, S. G., Iqbal, F., Yousaf, J., & Tariq, R. (2023). The Impact of Artificial Intelligence (AI) and Robotics on Higher Education. Journal of Management Practices. *Humanities and Social Sciences*, *7*(3), 11–17. doi:10.33152/jmphss-7.3.2

Papaspyridis, A. (2020). *AI in Higher Education: opportunities and considerations.* Microsoft. https://news.microsoft.com/apac/2020/03/26/ai-in-higher-education-opportunities-and-considerations/

Rathi, S., Hiran, K. K., & Sakhare, S. (2023). Affective state prediction of E-learner using SS-ROA based deep LSTM. *Array (New York, N.Y.), 19*, 100315. doi:10.1016/j.array.2023.100315

Rausch, T., & Dustdar, S. (2019). Edge Intelligence: The Convergence of Humans, Things, and AI. In *Proceedings of International Conference on Cloud Engineering*, (pp. 1-6). IEEE. 10.1109/IC2E.2019.00022

Sadanand, V. S., Guruvyas, K. R. R., Patil, P. P., Acharya, J. J., & Suryakanth, S. G. (2022). An automated essay evaluation system using natural language processing and sentiment analysi. *Iranian Journal of Electrical and Computer Engineering, 12*(6), 6585–6593. doi:10.11591/ijece.v12i6.pp6585-6593

Sallam, M., & Mousa, D. (2024). Evaluating ChatGPT performance in Arabic dialects: A comparative study showing defects in responding to Jordanian and Tunisian general health prompts. *Mesopotamian Journal of Artificial Intelligence in Healthcare, 2024*, 1–7. doi:10.58496/MJAIH/2024/001

Schroeder, R. (2022). Artificial Intelligence to Assist, Tutor, Teach and Assess in Higher Ed. *Inside Higher Ed*. https://www.insidehighered.com/digital-learning/blogs/online-trending-now/artificial-intelligence-assist-tutor-teach-and-assess

Selwyn, N. (2022). The future of AI and education: Some cautionary notes. *European Journal of Education, 57*(4), 620–631. doi:10.1111/ejed.12532

Shang, H., Sivaparthipan, C. B., & ThanjaiVadivel. (2022). Interactive teaching using human-machine interaction for higher education systems. *Computers & Electrical Engineering, 100*, 107811. doi:10.1016/j.compeleceng.2022.107811

Shukur, B. S., & Mijwil, M. M. (2023). Involving machine learning techniques in heart disease diagnosis: A performance analysis. *Iranian Journal of Electrical and Computer Engineering, 13*(2), 2177–2185. doi:10.11591/ijece.v13i2.pp2177-2185

Shukur, B. S., Yaacob, N. M., & Doheir, M. (2023). Diabetes at a Glance: Assessing AI Strategies for Early Diabetes Detection and Intervention. *Mesopotamian Journal of Artificial Intelligence in Healthcare, 85–89*, 85–89. doi:10.58496/MJAIH/2023/017

Singh, S. V., & Hiran, K. K. (2022). The impact of AI on teaching and learning in higher education technology. *Journal of Higher Education Theory and Practice, 22*(13).

Soudi, M. (2024). Robotics Education in Africa: Africa Compete. In Impacts of the Knowledge Society on Economic and Social Growth in Africa, 1-16. doi:10.4018/978-1-4666-5844-8.ch012

Wang, X., Han, Y., Leung, V. C. M., Niyato, D., Yan, X., & Chen, X. (2020). *Edge AI: Convergence of Edge Computing and Artificial Intelligence*. Springer. https://link.springer.com/book/10.1007/978-981-15-6186-3

Yahuza, M., Idris, M. Y. I. B., Wahab, A. W. B. A., Ho, A. T. S., Khan, S., Musa, S. N. B., & Taha, A. Z. B. (2020). Systematic Review on Security and Privacy Requirements in Edge Computing: State of the Art and Future Research Opportunities. *IEEE Access : Practical Innovations, Open Solutions, 8*, 76541–76567. doi:10.1109/ACCESS.2020.2989456

Zeide, E. (2019). Artificial Intelligence in Higher Education: Applications, Promise and Perils, and Ethical Questions. *EDUCAUSE Review*.

# Chapter 10
# Exploring the Role of Artificial Intelligence in Advancing Higher Education for Sustainable Development: A Bibliometric Study

**Abhineet Saxena**
*Amity University, Jaipur, India*

**Garima Pancholi**
https://orcid.org/0000-0002-5039-4998
*Amity University, Jaipur, India*

**Bajrang Yadav**
*NIMS University, India*

**Rakesh Saini**
*NIMS University, India*

## ABSTRACT

*Artificial intelligence has encountered significant advancements in the past years. Prominence is growing with each passing day as it is revolutionizing daily life with its assistance to solve complex problems. With this continuous evolution and improvement AI can help to achieve SDGs by mitigating the negative effects on the environment. The incorporation of AI in higher education can play a vital role in achieving sustainable education. AI can improve the quality of higher education by offering the learners more customized, captivating, and constructive learning experiences. This study aims to analyze and evaluate existing knowledge to identify themes, opportunities, and challenges. The data for analysis is retrieved from Scopus database for 1997 to 2024. A total of 332 articles were retrieved which were analyzed for publication, country, author, source productivity, and most cited documents. This study provides a comprehensive evaluation of recent trends and themes. It also highlights the research gap, providing valuable insights for further exploration in this field.*

DOI: 10.4018/979-8-3693-2440-0.ch010

## INTRODUCTION

In today's interconnected world, education is more important than ever before where education not only serves as a catalyst for cross-border collaboration but also drives innovation and economic development. Higher education (HE) is instrumental in empowering growth, alleviating poverty, and boosting shared prosperity around the globe. Well-educated people are more resilient to uncertainty as they cultivate critical thinking skills and problem-solving abilities. Governments across the globe are trying to evolve the education system from a teacher-centered approach to learner-centered approach. In such an approach, the learner is positioned in the center while the teachers act as the facilitators. But it is important to address the significance of implications of student experience and development. Therefore, contextual learning must be blended with digital technology in the new paradigm of teaching and learning.

In the past few years, technology has profoundly transformed our education sector. The continuously evolving technology is revolutionizing the roles of teachers and learners. Due to the increase in access to educational resources on the internet, the role of teacher has shifted from being the crucial source of information to a mentor. Technology has opened numerous opportunities for learning while being at remote locations. Among all the technological advancements, Artificial Intelligence is the most significant one. AI technology exhibits intelligence shown by a machine, which is programmed and designed by the experts (Vasiliu et al., 2023). In simpler terms, Artificial Intelligence is human-like intelligence coming from artificial brain. The development of AI is transitioning from technology-focused applications to humanity-focused applications, where the focus of increasing production and efficiency is shifted to leveraging human intelligence with machine intelligence (Yang, 2021). AI is concentrating on consciousness and human audio-visual literacy (i.e. see, hear, read, and write), this helps in smart tutoring for explicit adaptations and customization, along with error-free, diagnosis, treatment, and prevention for smart appraisal (Yang et al., 2021).

The study conducted by (Williams, 2019) has aligned three growing technologies has potential to revolutionize higher education. Among these technologies, the first one is learning analytics, which enables us to store online data of students regarding their activities and participation. This will help in profiling of students along with early intimation of improvement for struggling students. The second one is Artificial Intelligence, which assists human experts through machine learning for decision making in complex situations. The third one is Blockchain, which offers several utilities such as recording independent and secure credentials of students and occupation activities and achievements. The formal assessment system would engage AI with learning analytics to acknowledge the credit bearing activities and blockchain to give tamper-proof credentialling (Hiran & Henten, 2020).

## RESEARCH QUESTIONS

The current study intends to address the answers for the following questions:

RQ1 What is the current trend of publications related to role of Artificial Intelligence (AI) in attaining Sustainable Higher Education?

The number of publications in the area represents a growing trend, as manifested by the data extracted from the Scopus database. The data was then analyzed using Biblioshiny to gain further insights.

RQ2 Which countries, authors, sources have got the top position in terms of productivity in the field?

Analysis of top countries, authors, sources help the researchers to gain insight into the current landscape, recognize potential research collaborators, and locate esteemed journals for communicating their findings. It also helps knowledge exchange and collaboration among researchers, enhancing further advancements in the research area.

RQ3 Which studies have made the most substantial contribution to the field?

The analysis of the most cited papers facilitates providing valuable insight into the field's development, current trends, and potential avenues for further expansion and innovation.

RQ4 What are the dominant themes in the research area?

The analysis of the prominent themes helps to enhance understanding, promotes interdisciplinary collaboration, guides research direction and facilitates effective communication of research findings.

## RESEARCH METHODOLOGY

In order to understand the role of artificial intelligence (AI) in achieving sustainable higher education two stages were followed to attain the objective of the study. In the first stage, the selection of database was undertaken and secondly, the data collection and analysis took place. This research investigates the research developments and scientific landscape based on the published articles which were indexed in Elsevier Scopus database from 1997 to 2024. These articles were first identified, then subjected to screening, evaluation, and analysis. These analyzed articles were further examined to evaluate the trends, valuable insights, and promote interdisciplinary collaboration. The Preferred reporting items for systematic reviews and meta-analysis (PRISMA) flow diagram is used for visualizing the screening process. The PRISMA flow diagram first records the number of articles extracted from the database and then applies exclusion and inclusion criteria at every stage. Figure no. 1 shows the PRISMA flow chart used in the study.

Through Scopus database, the articles relating to the role of AI in attaining Sustainable education are identified by executing the search query string of "TITLE-ABS-KEY" (Artificial Intelligence and Sustainable Education). The retrieved documents are exported through comma separated values (csv) format for screening. In the screening process, the duplicate articles, and unrelated articles are excluded, so that the evaluation and analysis is performed on relevant articles. The screened articles are further analysis using Biblioshiny and VOSviewer (1.6.17). Accordingly, progression of articles, prominent authors, countries, organizations, most occurring keywords, and clusters of research area are examined in detail. Ultimately, this study presents a comprehensive review of published documents in the research area by using Bibliometric analysis. The bibliometric review and analysis concept was introduced by (Pritchard, 1969) which uses science mapping tools to visualize and provide insight into the research findings.

## BIBLIOMETRIC ANALYSIS

Bibliometric Analysis was performed on 787 documents using Scopus database that were published between 1997 and 2024. Table no. 1 represents the main information about the documents retrieved.

*Figure 1. Represents the exclusion criteria*
*Source: Prisma Flowchart 2020*

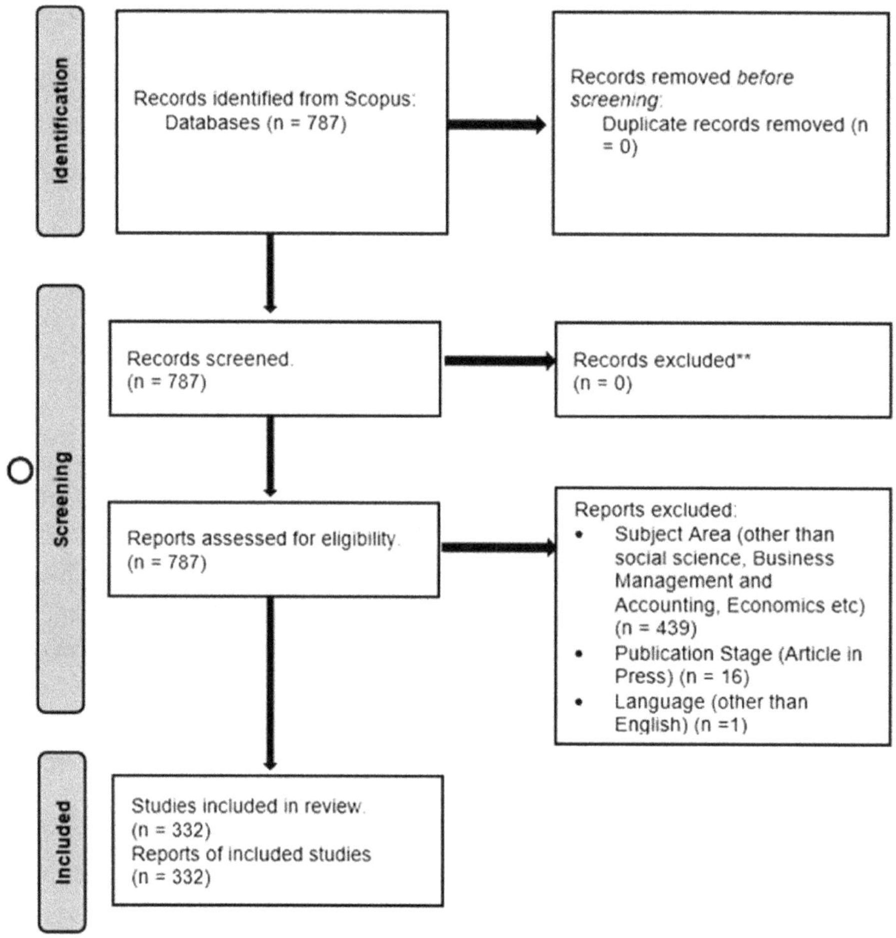


## Publication Trends

Figure no. 2 shows production productivity of documents through total published documents and total citations. From 1997 to 2008, the productivity of documents has been static. However, from 2009 to 2018 there has been noticeable fluctuation in publications. Notably, from 2019 there is substantial increase in publication. Furthermore, the year 2023 has recorded the highest number of publications i.e., 110 documents and by March '24, there have already been 30 publications. This trend indicates a growing emphasis from researchers on Artificial Intelligence and Sustainable Education.

## Country wise Trends of Publication

Figure no. 3 represents the country's productivity data for the period from 1997 to 2024. It reveals that China and USA have highest number of publications, with 48 and 36 documents respectively. However, USA surpasses China in terms of number of citations received. On the other hand, the India ranks third

*Table 1. Main information about data*

| Descriptions | Results |
|---|---|
| Main Information about Data | |
| Time Span | 1997-2024 |
| Sources (Journals, Books etc) | 194 |
| Documents | 332 |
| Annual Growth Rate% | 13.42 |
| Document Average Age | 2.9 |
| Average citations per doc | 9.171 |
| Document Contents | |
| Keyword Plus (ID) | 1499 |
| Author's Keywords (DE) | 1136 |
| Authors | |
| Authors | 1065 |
| Authors of single-authored docs | 44 |
| Authors Collaboration | |
| Single authored docs | 46 |
| Co-authors per doc | 3.56 |
| International co-authorships% | 26.27 |

Source: Authors' elaboration using Biblioshiny

*Figure 2. Showing the production productivity*
*Source: Authors' own compilation*

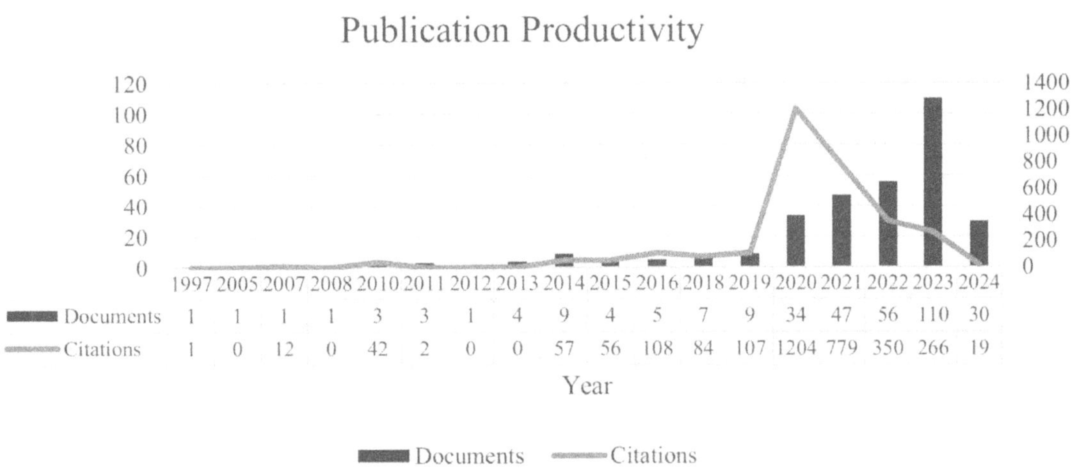


in terms of the number of publications but leads with 2nd rank among all countries in citations. It is noteworthy that out of the 10 countries mentioned, 7 of them represent the World's largest economies.

*Figure 3. Showing the country productivity*
*Source: Authors' own compilation*

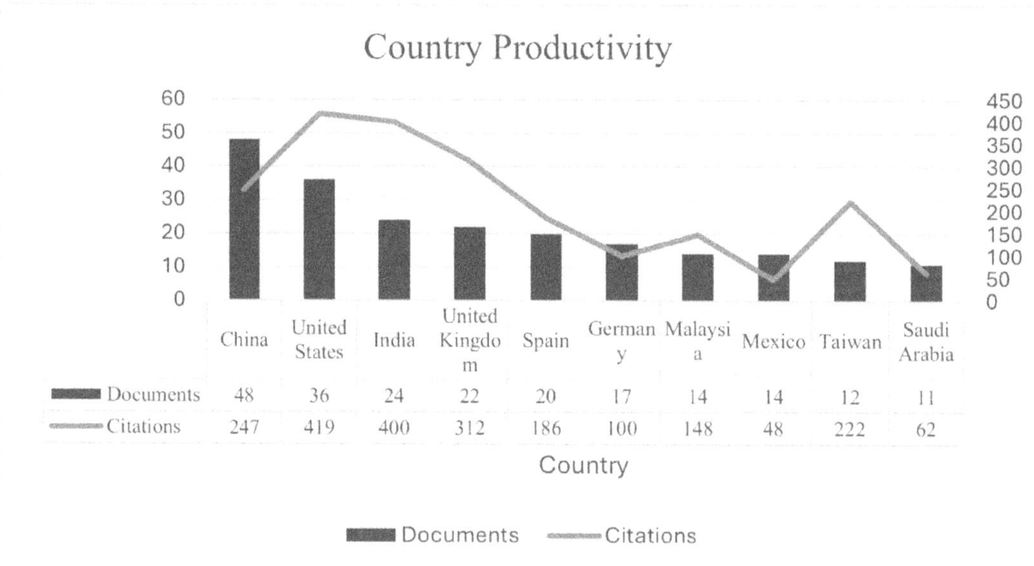


The observation suggests that countries with significant economic strength are recognizing the potential of AI in driving sustainable practices and economic growth.

## Author Productivity

Table no. 2 displays authors' productivity based on the total number of published documents, total citations, and h-index. From the table it is observed that author Bucea-Manea-tonis, Rocsana, Illic, M,C. and Kuleto, V. has the highest number of publications with 3 documents, accompanied by 76 citations and an h-index of 10, 8 and 7 respectively. The remaining 7 authors have 2 publications each. Notably, Chiu, T.K.F. stands out with only 2 published documents but has received the highest number of citations, amounting to 157 citations. Figure no. 4 represents the highest number of publications and citations attained by authors indicates the relevance and impact of their work in the subject area. Educators can benefit from the insight provided by these authors in terms of incorporating AI into higher education to attain sustainability in their decision-making processes.

### Lotka's Law

Lotka's Law is also known as Lotka's Inverse Square law of Scientific Productivity, which shows the interconnection between the number of authors and their contribution. Through, the lotka's law of scientific productivity the number of authors against their publication yield is plotted on a logarithm scale. The lotka's law indicates that large proportion of authors holds a smaller number of publications while small proportion of authors have higher number of publications.

The Lotka's Law of scientific productivity is expressed in form of equation:

*Table 2. Author productivity*

| Authors | Documents | Citations | h-index | Institute | Country |
|---|---|---|---|---|---|
| Bucea-Manea-tonis, R | 3 | 76 | 10 | National University of physical education and sports | Romania |
| Illic, M,C. | 3 | 76 | 8 | Comtrade Technology Center | Serbia |
| Kuleto, V. | 3 | 76 | 7 | Information Technology School | Serbia |
| Ahmad, M. | 2 | 2 | 3 | Survey of Pakistan | Pakistan |
| AI-Emran, M. | 2 | 68 | 40 | British University in Dubai | UAE |
| AI-Sharafi, M.A. | 2 | 68 | 20 | Universiti tenaga Nasional | Malaysia |
| Alshahrani, A. | 2 | 8 | 5 | Arab Open University | Saudi Arabia |
| Bucea-Manea-tonis, R | 2 | 59 | 6 | National University of physical education and sports | Romania |
| Castro, M. | 2 | 10 | 35 | Universidad Nacional de Educacion a Distancia | Spain |
| Chiu, T.K.F. | 2 | 157 | 24 | Chinese University of Hong Kong | Hong Kong |

Source: Authors' own compilation

*Figure 4. Representing the author productivity*
*Source: Authors' own compilation*

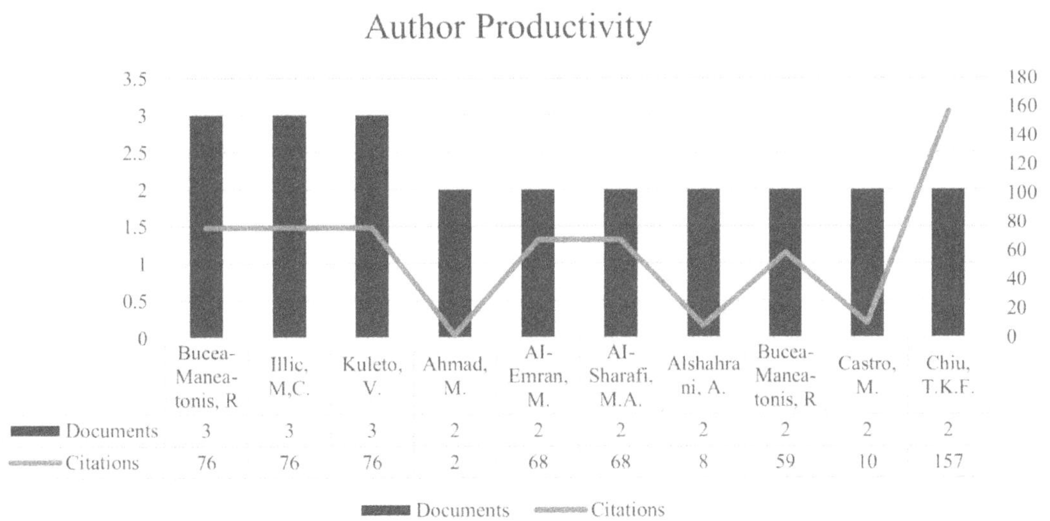


Y=C/X^n

where Y= Frequency of authors making X contribution
C= constant depending on specific field
X= number of publications
N= constant depending on specific field

The application of Lotka's law in current study gives insight into the distribution of authors productivity and better understanding of frequency of publication within the subject area. Table no. 3 shows that approximately 95% of authors have only 1 publication while only 0.3% of authors have 3 publications. Figure no. 5 gives elaboration of proportion of authors and documents written by them.

## Source-Wise Trends of Publication

The source wise trend publication is useful for researchers to keep in loop about the progress in their research area and benchmark their own research against other publications in prolific journals. This also helps in identifying the potential collaborations and formulate the strategies for publications in journals which has high impact score. Table no. 4 explores the top 10 sources in the research area in terms of number of publications, citations and h-index. Among the total 194 sources, sustainability (Switzerland) has highest number of publications, citations and h-index score, followed by Journal of cleaner production and Frontier in Education.

*Table 3. Author productivity through Lotka's Law*

| Documents Written | N. of Authors | Proportion of Authors |
|---|---|---|
| 1 | 1011 | 0.949 |
| 2 | 51 | 0.048 |
| 3 | 3 | 0.003 |
| | **1065** | **1.000** |

Source: Authors' elaboration using Biblioshiny

*Figure 5. Author productivity through Lotka's Law*
**Source:** *Authors' elaboration using Biblioshiny*

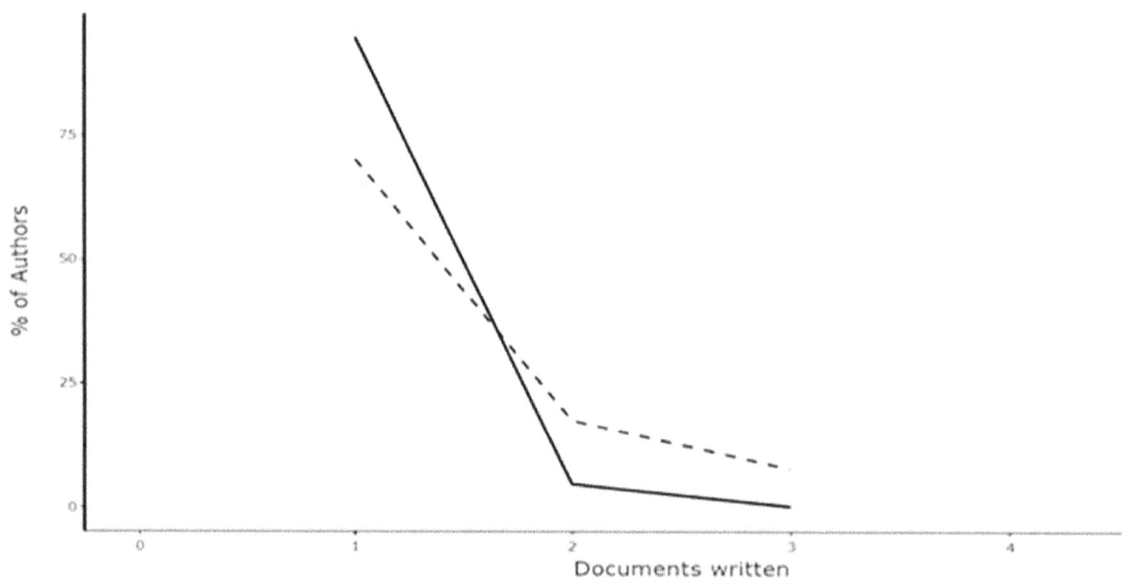

*Table 4. Source productivity*

| Sources | NP | TC | h-index |
|---|---|---|---|
| Sustainability (Switzerland) | 60 | 938 | 17 |
| Journal of cleaner production | 8 | 204 | 6 |
| Frontier in Education | 4 | 7 | 2 |
| International Journal of Management Education | 3 | 259 | 3 |
| Proceedings of the International Conference on Education and Research in computer aided architectural design in Europe | 3 | 12 | 1 |
| Smart Learning Environments | 3 | 3 | 1 |
| Sustainable cities and society | 3 | 324 | 3 |
| Sustainable development | 3 | 5 | 2 |
| Computers and education artificial intelligence | 2 | 122 | 1 |
| Education and Information Technologies | 2 | 1 | 1 |

Source: Authors' elaboration using Biblioshiny

## Bradfords Law

In bibliometric research analysis, Bradford's law of scattering is widely employed bibliometric law. The bradsfords scattered diagram represents the relationship between number of publications and sources. It states that when the articles on a given subject from different sources are grouped together, then only a small number of core journals will publish considerable amount of research, second group will publish less and ultimately a larger proportion of source will produce least number of publications. The identification of core sources in the research area can be identified by dividing the sources into 3 groups with ratio of 1:n:n^2 (chang et. al., 2010). Figure no. 6 represents that the core sources are shown in zone 1, which is indicated by shaded area. These core sources are important for getting in depth understanding the subject area.

## Most Influential Work

The most influential work refers to the article which has received the highest number of citations in the subject area. The article is considered prominent when it has been acknowledged and cited by other authors. The citations show that the article has managed to have a substantial impact in the subject matter. Table no. 5 represents the top 10 cited research articles in field of Artificial Intelligence and Sustainable education. The assessed articles were further analyzed, and the results shows that the article titled, "Enabling technologies and sustainable smart cities" has received highest number of citations i.e. 288 which was authored by Ahan, M.A., Paiva, S., Tripathi, G., and Feroz, N. The article titled, "Artificial intelligence and sustainable development" has received second highest citations which is 211 citations followed by "Role of artificial intelligence in operations environment: a review and bibliometric analysis" which is 153 citations.

*Figure 6. Core sources by Bradsford's Law*
*Source: Authors' elaboration using Biblioshiny*

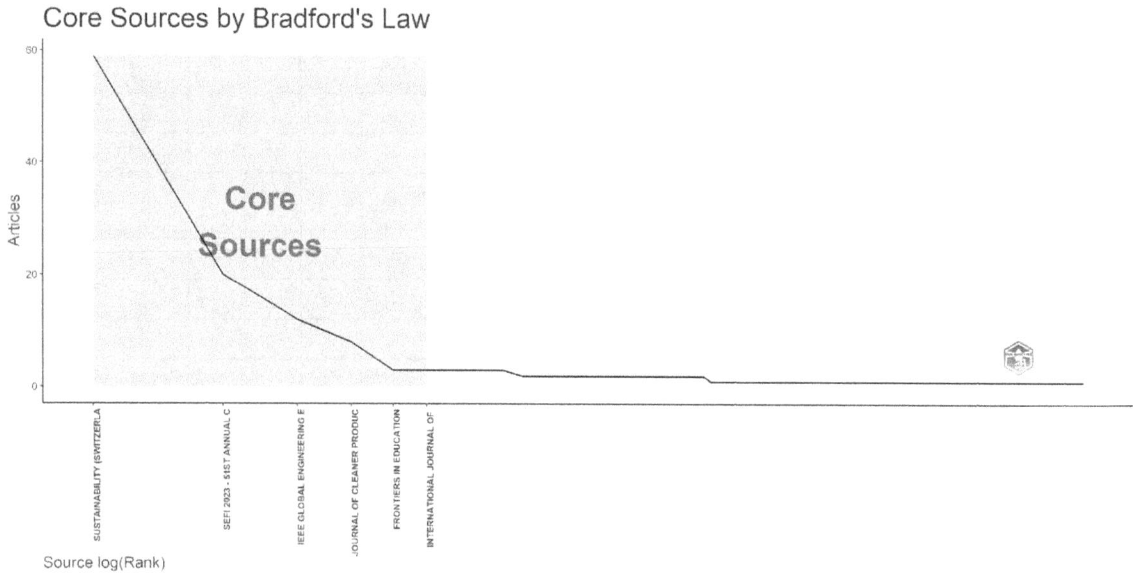


*Table 5. Represents the most influential work*

| Author | Title | Source | Year | Total Citation |
|---|---|---|---|---|
| Ahan, M.A., Paiva, S., Tripathi, G., Feroz, N. | Enabling technologies and sustainable smart cities | Sustainable Cities and Society | 2020 | 288 |
| Goralski, M.A., Tan, T.K. | Artificial intelligence and sustainable development | International Journal of management education | 2020 | 211 |
| Dhamija, P., Bag, S. | Role of artificial intelligence in operations environment: a review and bibliometric analysis | TQM journal | 2020 | 153 |
| Yang, S.J.H., Ogata, H., Matsui, T., Chen, N.S. | Human centered artificial intelligence in education: seeing the invisible through the visible | computers and education: artificial intelligence | 2021 | 122 |
| Chiu, T.K.F., Chai, T.S. | Sustainable curriculum planning for artificial intelligence education: self-determination theory perspective | Sustainability (Switzerland) | 2020 | 98 |
| Mhlanga, D | Artificial Intelligence in the industry 4.0, and its impact on poverty, innovation, infrastructure development, and sustainable development goals: Lessons from emerging economies? | Sustainability (Switzerland) | 2021 | 95 |
| Demestichas, K., Daskalakis, E | Information and communication technology solutions for the circular economy | Sustainability (Switzerland) | 2020 | 91 |
| Williams, P. | Does competency-based education with blockchain signal a new mission for universities? | Journal of Higher education | 2019 | 83 |
| Pugliese, R., Regondi, S., Marini, R. | Machine learning-based approach: Global trend, research directions and regulatory standpoints | Data science and Management | 2021 | 81 |
| Hoosain, M.S., Paul, B.S., Ramakrishna, S. | The impact of 4ir digital technologies and circular thinking on the United Nations sustainable development goals | Sustainability (Switzerland) | 2020 | 75 |

Source: Authors' own compilation

## Keywords Analysis

The keywords analysis refers to examining the frequency and significance of keywords in the subject area. The keywords analysis in bibliometric analysis provides significant understanding for the subject area, structure of academic literature, which helps the researchers to develop landscape and trends within the subject area. Figure no. 7 represents the word cloud which is elaborated using biblioshiny. As shown in table no. 6, the keyword Artificial Intelligence has 191 occurrences and total link strength of 604. As a result, it is displayed with the largest font size in the word cloud. Followed by Artificial Intelligence, the keywords Sustainable development and engineering education have the highest number of occurrences which is 112 and 75 respectively. Figure no. 8 represents 3 clusters of keywords in Blue, Red and Green. The keyword analysis clearly states the growing trend of artificial intelligence, sustainable development and engineering education in the higher education system. The researchers are conducting further research in order to integrate artificial intelligence in higher education to attain sustainability.

## Cluster Analysis

### Empowering Sustainable Education Through Artificial Intelligence and Innovation

AI has the potential to foster economic development while also sustainably addressing the impact of production and consumption on the economy. AI is like a double-edged sword where the positive outcomes come with some negative outcomes as well. AI is transforming the whole education sector where the role of human intelligence teacher is getting replaced by the artificial intelligence teacher (Goralski & Tan, 2020). The students involved in community outreach initiatives will have an upper edge planning and executing sustainable actions that will help in sustainable development(Borsatto et al., 2024; Mishra et al., 2021). To measure the alignment of community outreach initiatives of Higher Education Institutions with SDGs, AI tools were utilized. Prior to the application of AI tools, it is important to verify the reliability of them. In order to analyze the reliability, the Natural language processing (NLP) tool such as BERT (Bidirectional encoder representations from transformers) and GPT-2 (Generative

*Figure 7. Representing word cloud*
*Source: Authors' elaboration using Biblioshiny*

*Table 6. Represents the cluster analysis of keywords*

| Cluster | Keyword | Occurrences | Total Link Strength |
|---|---|---|---|
| Cluster 1 "Empowering Sustainable Education through Artificial Intelligence and Innovation" | • Artificial Intelligence | • 191 | • 604 |
| | • Artificial Intelligence (AI) | • 10 | • 26 |
| | • Chatgpt | • 14 | • 57 |
| | • Education | • 63 | • 238 |
| | • Higher education | • 31 | • 91 |
| | • Innovation | • 18 | • 55 |
| | • Knowledge | • 11 | • 52 |
| | • Learning | • 28 | • 122 |
| | • Student | • 16 | • 68 |
| | • Sustainability | • 56 | • 189 |
| | • Sustainable education | • 12 | • 34 |
| | • teaching | • 38 | • 188 |
| Cluster 2 "Technology and Sustainable Development: Impact of Industry 4.0 and IoT in the COVID-19 Era" | • Big data | • 12 | • 41 |
| | • Covid-19 | • 10 | • 42 |
| | • Deep learning | • 14 | • 44 |
| | • Industry 4.0 | • 14 | • 47 |
| | • Internet of things | • 14 | • 52 |
| | • Machine learning | • 23 | • 88 |
| | • Sustainable development goal | • 17 | • 75 |
| | • Sustainable development goals | • 14 | • 56 |
| | • Technology | • 12 | • 44 |
| | • Virtual reality | • 12 | • 52 |
| Cluster 3 "Active Learning and Education Computing for Sustainable Development in Engineering" | • Active learning | • 16 | • 84 |
| | • Curricula | • 25 | • 129 |
| | • Decision making | • 19 | • 85 |
| | • E-learning | • 25 | • 104 |
| | • Education computing | • 25 | • 127 |
| | • Engineering education | • 75 | • 309 |
| | • Learning systems | • 26 | • 127 |
| | • Students | • 57 | • 273 |
| | • Sustainable development | • 112 | • 499 |

Source: Authors' elaboration using VOSviewer

Pre-training) was assessed with AI tool. Leveraging community outreach initiatives of HEI with SDGs helps in the expansion education which facilitates sustainability. (Chiu & Chai, 2020) have proposed a Five-stage development cycle of AI curricula for teachers and management. In this first phase is Preparation for teaching and curriculum planning, second phase is of Content and product design, followed by Process and praxis design, then designing and developing the materials and ultimately Reinforcing the revised curriculum. The popularity of machine learning has also rapidly grown in the past few years

*Figure 8. Showing co-occurrence of keywords*
*Source: Authors' elaboration using VOSviewer*

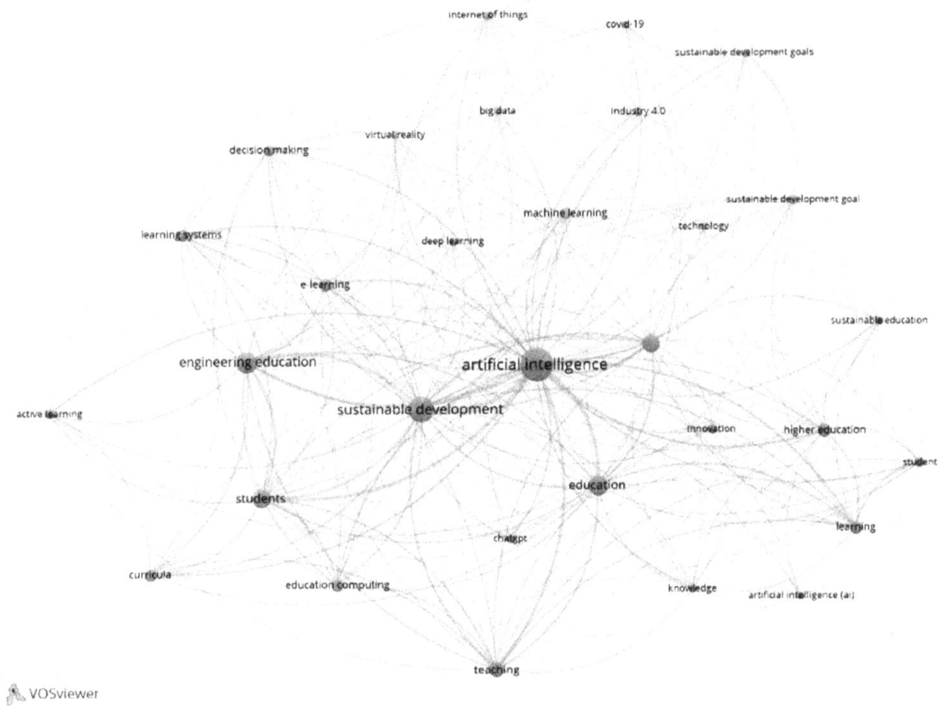


due its reinforcement algorithm which has the ability to solve different real-world problems(Pugliese et al., 2021; Doshi et al., 2023; Mijwil et al., 2023).

## Technology and Sustainable Development: Impact of Industry 4.0 and IoT in the COVID-19 Era

Throughout history, mankind has been associated with incorporating technology in daily lives to enhance lifestyle. The intelligence of machine learning and deep learning have its impact on firms, government, and the whole society. Technology is continuously evolving to expertise world where artificial intelligence is superseding human intelligence by higher predictive power, efficiency, and decision-making skills. Industry 4.0 (4IR) and AI have played a significant role in the Education sector during COVID-19 pandemic. (Mhlanga & Moloi, 2020; Skouby et al., 2022) have found that 4IR and AI has a positive impact on the access to education, since online classes removes the barrier of location. Students from remote locations can also attend classes anywhere around the world. AI and 4IR is having strong influence on achieving Sustainable Development goals, especially on SDG 1 of poverty reduction SDG 4 of Access to quality education and SDG 9 of Industry, innovation, and Infrastructure (Mhlanga, 2021; Wanjale et al., 2023). Whilst the impact of 4IR and AI on SDGs is remarkable, some researchers presume it's both positive and negative impacts. The AI & 4IR led to the efficient use of resources but at the same time has some detrimental effect on sustainability such as waste produced by electronic equipment's.

### Active Learning and Education Computing for Sustainable Development in Engineering

The growing investments in technology have led to increased usage of AI in our daily lives as well. The technologies like Internet of things (IoT), Big Data, Blockchain technology, 5G technology and Machine learning (ML) have contributed a lot to getting everyday activities done easily. (Balakrishna, 2012; Hiran et al., 2021). Automation is the talk of the town and many sectors like Agriculture, medicine, manufacturing, education, banking etc., are prioritizing its utilization (Dhamija & Bag, 2020). Everyday activities like Governance, policy making, and service delivery etc., are done through these automatic channels which help the people to get ingress with these facilities through their devices anywhere across the globe. The context of smart city is one of the steps towards achieving smart and sustainable way of life. (Ahad et al., 2020; Al-Shahwani, et al., 2024) have found the practices that could be adopted by various governments, manufacturers and policy framers etc., for successful execution of smart city. It also sheds light on the emerging concepts such as quantum computing and nanotechnology which could help in the application of smart cities in future. (Vinuesa et al., n.d.) have highlighted that technology adoption can result in economical upliftment and sustainable development only if right approach is chosen for its implementation. The current model of economic development, popularly known as "take, make and dispose" is vulnerable for economic development and environment. In such situations Circular economy comes into role which is expressed as "R" framework. 3R, 4R, 6R and 9R are some of famous frameworks which basically refers to 'Reduce', 'Reuse', 'Recycle', and 'Recover' etc. (Maťová & Triznova, n.d.). The advanced technology such as big data, cloud computing and cyber-physical system has essential role in the adaptation of Circular economy. The concept of circular economy is getting much attention in governance, education, and industrial sector(Demestichas & Daskalakis, 2020).

### Three Field Plots

A Sankey diagram also referred to as three field plots is a visualizing tool which represents the relationship between three which fields namely among: country, keywords, authors, citations, years, titles, and references. Figure no. 9 represents three fields of Authors, most occurred keywords and countries in research area of artificial intelligence and sustainable education. For the present study the author has selected authors on left field, keywords for middle field and country on right field. Here the keyword, Artificial Intelligence has developed highest connection with all the countries and most of the authors have used AI keywords in their research.

## DISCUSSION OF FINDINGS

The current bibliometric analysis has thrown light on role of AI for attaining sustainable education by analyzing the documents extracted from Scopus database for the year between *1997* and *2024*. The study also provides a comprehensive overview of past publications by providing insights into trends and popular issues. The first article on the subject area of Artificial Intelligence and Sustainable Education was published in *1997* and the publication gained momentum from *2020*, as the analysis shows substantial increase in publications. Among countries, *China, USA and India* are top contributors in the subject area which means that the researchers are contemplating about the use of AI in higher education

*Figure 9. Showing three field plot*
*Source: Authors' elaboration using Biblioshiny*

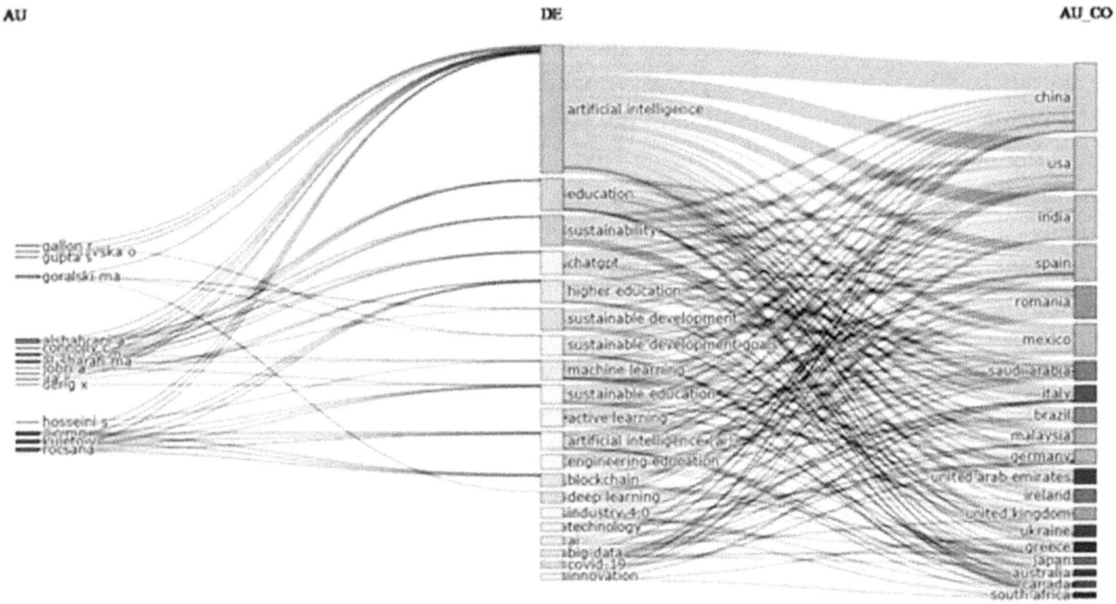


for sustainability. In author productivity, the author *Bucea-Manea-tonis*, *R.*, from National University of physical education and sports, Romania ranks first with *3 documents and 76 citations* in the contribution in subject area. In source productivity, the source Sustainability *(Switzerland*) has contributed highest in subject area with *60 publications and 938 citations*. The article titled, *Enabling technologies and sustainable smart cities* authored by *Ahan, M.A., Paiva, S., Tripathi, G., Feroz, N.* from *Sustainable Cities and Society* with *288 citations* has highest citations in the subject area. This analysis explores the top contributors in terms of Productive year, sources, authors, and prominent article which will lead to knowledge extension and collaboration for future research.

## Theoretical Contributions

Theoretically, this study discusses the role of AI and sustainable education in Higher education that talks about contributions, exploration of subject area, and strengths and weakness of previously published work. The identification of different clusters and themes is an essential tool for organizing and interpretating the findings which could contribute to innovation in research practices as well as promote collaboration among authors and institutions. The three identified clusters for the subject area are- Cluster 1 is *Empowering Sustainable Education through Artificial Intelligence and Innovation*, Cluster 2 is *Technology and Sustainable Development: Impact of Industry 4.0 and IoT in the COVID-19 Era* and Cluster 3 is *Active Learning and Education Computing for Sustainable Development in Engineering*. The following clusters represent interdependency among them and focusing on one of the clusters is not enough for comprehensive evaluation. It is important to consider and explore all these interconnections for understanding. It is imperative to acknowledge that adoption of technology is crucial for the development of the economy but at the same time it must be done after proper planning and adequate skills.

## Managerial Contributions

The study gives valuable insights for the teachers, management personnel and policy makers to acknowledge the role of Artificial Intelligence and Sustainable education for HEI's. Initially, the surge of technology such as Artificial Intelligence, Blockchain, learning analytics, Internet of Things, Machine Learning and deep learning will help the Higher education institutions in achieving accuracy and reducing human error. Secondly, teachers must explore the possibility of outcomes and develop resilience for uncertain situations. The policy makers also take into consideration each theme for enhancing its capacity for future scope. Thirdly, this article presents a vast range of promising avenues for integration of AI in curriculum as well as sheds light on possible challenges, this will help HEIs in decision-making.

## CONCLUSION

In the past few years, the utilization of technology in academia has transformed the education sector in many ways. Technological advancements such as Artificial Intelligence, learning analytics, blockchain, and machine learning have supported to this transformation. During COVID-19 when the worldwide transportation was stopped, these technologies reached out to people and gave accessibility to connect and revolutionize teaching and learning as we know it. Education is an essential pillar of our society which must adapt rapidly in this ever-evolving world.

To keep pace just like other sectors/industries, the education sector must also adopt "automation". Primarily, technology was utilized to do the assignments and assessment of the work done but now after the adoption of Artificial Intelligence it promotes blended learning, personalized learning, foster deeper and collaborative learning.

With the help of AI teachers can customize the learning experiences, improve the student understanding, prepare students for future success. AI helps in profiling students' data by recording their participation in activities and achievements. It can also help in giving early intimation to struggling students to improve their score. Apart from all the positive outcomes of AI, the associated potential threats must also be considered. Since the machine only works to maximize profits and effectiveness unlike humans who work according to broader range of motivations, values and goals. Therefore, investing in education by embracing AI with appropriate skills is significant for enhancing human potential for economic development at the same time building a sustainable world for upcoming generations.

While this study offers some valuable insight on the role of AI in higher education for sustainability but just like other studies it also has its own set of constraints. It is important to acknowledge such limitations for future directions. This study solely relied upon Scopus database for data extraction, due to which it might have unintentionally neglected some relevant articles. So, future researchers could consider other databases such as Web of science and google scholar for future research. Additionally, the choice of words for search string may have hindered the scope of review and included words such as "Sustainable Higher Education" and "Education Sustainability" which could provide comprehensive evaluation for future research,

## REFERENCES


Ahad, M. A., Paiva, S., Tripathi, G., & Feroz, N. (2020). Enabling technologies and sustainable smart cities. *Sustainable Cities and Society*, *61*, 102301. doi:10.1016/j.scs.2020.102301

Al-Shahwani, H. I. W., Mijwil, M. M., Doshi, R., Hiran, K. K., & Bala, I. (2024). Evaluating Antivirus Effectiveness Against Malware in Ascending Order for Increasing Blockchain Endpoint Protection. In *Bio-Inspired Optimization Techniques in Blockchain Systems* (pp. 150–166). IGI Global. doi:10.4018/979-8-3693-1131-8.ch008

Borsatto, J. M. L. S., Marcolin, C. B., Abdalla, E. C., & Amaral, F. D. (2024). Aligning community outreach initiatives with SDGs in a higher education institution with artificial intelligence. *Cleaner and Responsible Consumption*, *12*, 100160. doi:10.1016/j.clrc.2023.100160

Chiu, T. K. F., & Chai, C. S. (2020). Sustainable curriculum planning for artificial intelligence education: A self-determination theory perspective. *Sustainability (Basel)*, *12*(14), 5568. doi:10.3390/su12145568

Demestichas, K., & Daskalakis, E. (2020). Information and communication technology solutions for the circular economy. In Sustainability (Switzerland) (Vol. 12, Issue 18, pp. 1–19). MDPI. doi:10.3390/su12187272

Dhamija, P., & Bag, S. (2020). Role of artificial intelligence in operations environment: a review and bibliometric analysis. In TQM Journal (Vol. 32, Issue 4, pp. 869–896). Emerald Group Holdings Ltd. doi:10.1108/TQM-10-2019-0243

Doshi, R., Hiran, K. K., Mijwil, M. M., & Anand, D. (2023). To That of Artificial Intelligence, Passing Through Business Intelligence. In *Handbook of Research on AI and Knowledge Engineering for Real-Time Business Intelligence* (pp. 1–16). IGI Global. doi:10.4018/978-1-6684-6519-6.ch001

Goralski, M. A., & Tan, T. K. (2020). Artificial intelligence and sustainable development. *International Journal of Management Education*, *18*(1), 100330. doi:10.1016/j.ijme.2019.100330

Hiran, K. K., & Henten, A. (2020). An integrated TOE-DoI framework for cloud computing adoption in higher education: The case of Sub-Saharan Africa, Ethiopia. In Soft Computing: Theories and Applications [Springer Singapore.]. *Proceedings of SoCTA*, *2018*, 1281–1290.

Hiran, K. K., Khazanchi, D., Vyas, A. K., & Padmanaban, S. (Eds.). (2021). *Machine learning for sustainable development* (Vol. 9). Walter de Gruyter GmbH & Co KG. doi:10.1515/9783110702514

Maťová, H., & Triznova, M. (n.d.). *Responsible consumer in the context of circular economy*. Research Gate. https://www.researchgate.net/publication/335882971

Mhlanga, D. (2021). Artificial intelligence in the industry 4.0, and its impact on poverty, innovation, infrastructure development, and the sustainable development goals: Lessons from emerging economies? *Sustainability (Basel)*, *13*(11), 5788. doi:10.3390/su13115788

Mhlanga, D., & Moloi, T. (2020). COVID-19 and the digital transformation of education: What are we learning on 4ir in South Africa? *Education Sciences*, *10*(7), 1–11. doi:10.3390/educsci10070180

Mijwil, M. M., Gök, M., Doshi, R., Hiran, K. K., & Kösesoy, I. (2023). Utilizing Artificial Intelligence Techniques to Improve the Performance of Wireless Nodes. In *Applications of Artificial Intelligence in Wireless Communication Systems* (pp. 150–162). IGI Global. doi:10.4018/978-1-6684-7348-1.ch010

Mishra, A., Tripathi, A., Khazanchi, D., Hiran, K. K., Vyas, A. K., & Padmanaban, S. (2021). A framework for applying artificial intelligence (AI) with Internet of NanoThings (IoNT). In *Machine Learning for Sustainable Development* (pp. 1–16). De Gruyter. doi:10.1515/9783110702514-001

Pugliese, R., Regondi, S., & Marini, R. (2021). Machine learning-based approach: Global trends, research directions, and regulatory standpoints. *Data Science and Management*, *4*, 19–29. doi:10.1016/j.dsm.2021.12.002

Singh, S. V., & Hiran, K. K. (2022). The impact of AI on teaching and learning in higher education technology. *Journal of Higher Education Theory and Practice*, *22*(13).

Skouby, K. E., Williams, I., Dhotre, P., & Hiran, K. K. (2022). Introduction: Wireless networks and privacy in developing countries. In 5G, Cybersecurity and Privacy in Developing Countries (pp. 1-18). River Publishers. doi:10.1201/9781003374664

Vasiliu, L. A., Roman, D., & Prodan, R. (2023). Extreme and Sustainable Graph Processing for Green Finance Investment and Trading. *Companion of the 2023 ACM/SPEC International Conference on Performance Engineering*, (pp. 249–250). ACM. 10.1145/3578245.3585337

Vignesh, U. M., M., & Doshi, R. (Eds.). (2024). Bio-Inspired Optimization Techniques in Blockchain Systems. IGI Global. doi:10.4018/979-8-3693-1131-8

Vinuesa, R., Balaam, M., & Dignum, V. (n.d.). *The role of artificial intelligence in achieving the Sustainable Development Goals*. Research Gate. https://www.researchgate.net/publication/332831993

Wanjale, K., Chitre, A. V., & Doshi, R. (2023). Opting for Industry 4.0: Challenge or Opportunity. In *AI, IoT, Big Data and Cloud Computing for Industry 4.0* (pp. 3–20). Springer International Publishing. doi:10.1007/978-3-031-29713-7_1

Williams, P. (2019). Does competency-based education with blockchain signal a new mission for universities? *Journal of Higher Education Policy and Management*, *41*(1), 104–117. doi:10.1080/1360080X.2018.1520491

Yang, S. J. H. (2021). *Education Technology and Society*. International Forum of Educational Technology & Society, National Taiwan Normal University.

Yang, S. J. H., Ogata, H., Matsui, T., & Chen, N. S. (2021). Human-centered artificial intelligence in education: Seeing the invisible through the visible. *Computers and Education: Artificial Intelligence*, *2*, 100008. doi:10.1016/j.caeai.2021.100008

# Chapter 11
# AI-Based Career Counseling Chatbot for Secondary-Level Students

**Swati Patil**
*Vishwakarma Institute of Information Technology, Pune, India*

**Sarvesh Bodakhe**
*Vishwakarma Institute of Information Technology, Pune, India*

**Snehal Rahul Rathi**
*Vishwakarma Institute of Information Technology, Pune, India*

**Chaitravee Dusane**
*Vishwakarma Institute of Information Technology, Pune, India*

**Chaitali Shewale**
*Vishwakarma Institute of Information Technology, Pune, India*

**Niket Bhoye**
*Vishwakarma Institute of Information Technology, Pune, India*

## ABSTRACT

*Making a career selection may be a complex process, and many students struggle to choose a route that fits their interests, skills, and personality. Creating a career path requires careful consideration of these factors, and career coaching done in the old-fashioned manual way is ineffective. This study suggests a paradigm change that would use an AI-driven chatbot career advising system created especially for secondary school pupils. This cutting-edge technology, which uses machine learning, carefully examines users' personalities, interests, and talents in addition to incorporating up-to-date job market data to provide customized career recommendations. Above and beyond simple directions, the chatbot actively assists users in refining their abilities, guaranteeing a smooth transition into the careers of their choice. The ethical aspect of this investigation is essential, as it addresses certain worries and issues related to AI-driven career guidance. User testimonials highlight the system's effectiveness and its critical role in promoting informed career decisions.*

DOI: 10.4018/979-8-3693-2440-0.ch011

## INTRODUCTION

The emergence of Artificial Intelligence (AI) has significantly altered the educational environment and given rise to new approaches to career counseling. In the framework of secondary education, career counseling is crucial as students approach important choices affecting their future academic and professional trajectories. By offering tailored career advice and utilizing machine learning algorithms to comprehend the student's personality, talents, academic ability, and job preferences, AI technology can dramatically improve this mentoring. The chatbot can aid students in selecting viable career pathways associated with their abilities, interests, and aspirations by integrating these insights and applying a machine learning-powered decision-making mechanism.

The login or sign-up process for counseling is the first step in the suggested catboat's structured approach. The student is then included in an interactive session where machine learning algorithms are used to identify their personality traits, gauge their aptitude and talents, assess their academic knowledge, and determine their job inclinations. Machine learning, which uses specific APIs and models to assess the data and create a personalized career plan for the student, is essential to the synthesis of this information. The goal of this research is to use machine learning to enable secondary school students to make wise decisions regarding their future educational and professional paths. The chatbot intends to aid informed career decisions by integrating AI skills with machine learning expertise, ultimately raising a generation of professionals who are capable of excelling in their chosen industries.

### Motivation and Problem Definition

This study is driven by the urgent need to use AI's transformative potential to improve secondary school students' career advising. Students now have a wide range of professional options as the educational landscape changes, which makes making well-informed decisions more difficult. It can be difficult for traditional job counseling methods to offer timely, individualized advice. Students may also be reluctant to speak openly about their hobbies and skills in face-to-face conversations. By utilizing AI to build a chatbot that engages students in a more comfortable and engaged way, this research solves these issues and enables a thorough assessment of their personality, talents, academic proficiency, and career aspirations. The objective is to get over the constraints of conventional career counseling by giving students individualized recommendations and enabling them to choose rewarding career options in line with their special qualities and aspirations.

### Challenges

- Diverse Career Landscape: Secondary-level students may find it difficult to navigate the vast selection of career opportunities that are accessible to them, demanding individualized help to make decisions.
- Limitations of Traditional Approaches: Time, money, and the capacity to provide each student individualized attention may be barriers to traditional face-to-face counseling approaches.
- Reluctance and Openness: Due to shyness, fear, or privacy concerns, students may be hesitant to freely discuss their personality traits, skills, or academic issues in face-to-face conversations, which could compromise the accuracy of assistance.

- Dynamic Skill Requirements: It is difficult to offer current and pertinent career guidance because the work market is rapidly changing and necessitates a regular updating of the necessary skills and knowledge.
- Access and Availability: Students may not have equal access to high-quality career guidance due to their geographic location, the resources available to their schools, or other socioeconomic or societal considerations.

## Existing Systems and Algorithms

The field of AI-based career counseling chatbots has seen a rise in creative methods and applications in recent years. To efficiently understand and handle user inputs, existing systems frequently incorporate Natural Language Processing (NLP) approaches. Sentiment analysis algorithms make it possible to provide more individualized advice by helping to understand the student's personality and emotional condition. To anticipate viable job trajectories based on a user's profile, preferences, and academic experience, machine learning algorithms are essential. By contrasting the user's traits with those of accomplished individuals in related industries, collaborative filtering algorithms are used to suggest careers. The interactive experience is improved by Reinforcement Learning techniques, which enable the chatbot to modify and improve its career recommendations in response to user feedback. Together, these systems strive to offer secondary school students career advice that is comprehensive, data-driven, and tailored with the goal of assisting them in making successful and rewarding career decisions.

## Organization of the Research

The remaining section of this paper is structured as follows: - Section 2 will include a review of several articles related to multiple approaches in AI-based Career Counseling Chatbots. Section 3 will contain the background of the proposed methodology. Section 4 will involve the procedure involved in the proposed framework. Section 5 will be based on the results gathered. Finally, section 6 will conclude the entire research work.

# LITERATURE REVIEW

The body of knowledge regarding the use of AI in career counseling is expanding, especially in job searches. Even if ChatGPT and other AI chat systems are becoming more popular, career counseling has unrealized potential. The importance of a resume's quality in the hiring process is well known, and bias issues with AI-driven resume screening are raised. Many people don't have access to personalized résumé editing, emphasizing the value of AI in automatically delivering objective feedback for improvement. Fairness and openness are important ethical factors. With individualized resume guidance, ResumAI, an AI-powered career counseling service, may assist underprivileged students and job seekers. To fully utilize AI in career counseling while addressing problems like bias and explainability, more study is required (Rahman, M., et al., 2023).

The creation of chatbots that can provide effective and accessible career counseling powered by AI has piqued the curiosity of the scientific community. These chatbots, an important subgroup among many bot kinds, give students advice and answers by utilizing artificial intelligence and natural language processing, making them flexible and available tools for making informed career decisions and reducing stress. AI is strategically included to further improve response accuracy and relevancy, which benefits users' career selections (Zaidi, D., Raza, S., & Sharma, L., 2021).

The study examines the crucial part counseling services play in influencing secondary school students' job choices, with a particular emphasis on Anambra State. The study assesses the effects of counseling orientation, appraisal, and follow-up services using a descriptive survey research methodology and multiple regression analysis. It highlights the difficulties people currently face while choosing a career, such as a lack of advice and counseling, insufficient knowledge of available possibilities, and a shortage of experienced counselors. The findings highlight the importance of competent counseling in helping students make educated career decisions that are in line with their abilities, and they support hiring qualified counselors and scheduling frequent meetings between students and counselors. The introduction of new counseling centers in schools, ongoing professional development for counselors, and governmental funding are all recommended to improve counseling services and optimize students' career decision-making (Ifejiofor, A. P., 2023).

To help users make educated career decisions, this research introduces an intelligent Career Counseling Bot powered by artificial intelligence. Natural language processing is used by the chatbot to assess user input, doing away with the necessity for conventional in-person counseling. It uses context management, entity extraction, and intent detection to recognize and answer queries sent over channels like Google Home and Facebook Messenger. It engages in productive talks by utilizing Google's Dialog-flow API, although there is a need for improvement such as supporting different student groups and regional languages (Ohm, A., & Bhavani, K., 2019).

To match students' skills with suitable professions, a system for career guidance for students is introduced in this study. It talks about irrational career decisions and possible educational background mismatches. A variety of machine learning methods are used to improve student relationships and institutional reputation, such as Decision Tree Classifier, Support Vector Machine, Ada Boost, Logistic Regression, and Linear Discriminant Analysis. Time series analysis, Deep Neural Networks, and extensive data collection are all part of plans (Parab, A., Palkar, S., Maurya, S., & Balpande, S., 2017).

This project focuses on using AI chatbots to improve career counseling and university admissions services by overcoming the shortcomings of conventional approaches. Natural language processing and machine learning-based chatbots provide parents and pupils with effective, automated, and affordable counsel, raising the standard of care. The study emphasizes the expanding significance of chatbots in a variety of industries and their potential to transform the field of admissions consulting, thereby improving the university admissions process. The development of a structured dataset and the use of AI models demonstrate the enormous potential for AI-driven solutions to boost college admissions consultancy (Dang Truong Ho Chi, H., et al., 2020).

The scholar counseling specialist system is very beneficial because it provides high-quality counseling, decision support, coaching that is interactive, and advice. This clever system examines student psychology to determine the best career path based on interests and educational background. Future efforts will broaden the system to incorporate all career fields (Asnani, D., & Agarwal, K., n.d.).

The career counselor machine, which combines artificial intelligence and career guidance, provides students with beneficial opportunities in a world with a widening range of career options. This cutting-edge system effectively and individually tailor's expert career recommendations. Finally, the AI-driven career counselor is a significant development for the fast-paced world of today (Joshi, K., Goel, A. K., & Kumar, T., 2020).

The device acts as a personalized career counselor, pointing users in the direction of a good career path based on their preferences and interests. At pivotal points in their academic careers, it particularly helps students by assisting them in identifying their strengths and preferences. The system will eventually broaden the scope of its subject matter and career options, giving users even more options so they can make educated decisions (Katre, M., Manchanda, S., & Agarwal, R., 2021).

A career guidance and recommendation system are presented in this study that makes use of AI techniques like Decision Tree Classifier, Support Vector Machine, Ada Boost, Linear Discriminant Analysis, and Logistic Regression. Using a dataset of 1000 students, linear discriminant analysis and regression analysis showed higher accuracy. The goal of future research is to improve accuracy and strengthen relationships between students and faculty by enlarging the dataset, using classification algorithms, and investigating cutting-edge techniques like Time Series Analysis and Deep Neural Networks (Prasanna, L., & Dr. D. Haritha., 2019).

The career counseling system, a hybrid of a chatbot and an intelligent engine, provides useful career options through AI and is advantageous to people looking for career guidance. It speaks to the expanding complexity of available career paths. This system improves the ability to make career decisions, benefiting both the current and following generations (Bhnushali, D. M., & Itankar, P., 2020).

The study's newly developed Whats App chatbot provides current, user-friendly career information by combining AI and natural language processing. The user's comprehension and decision-making are improved by its structured approach. The chatbot can provide comprehensive career details, making it an invaluable resource for professionals, professionals-to-be, and job seekers. This study emphasizes how conversational AI has the potential to deliver tailored, user-centric information systems. This could open the door for later, more sophisticated chatbots (Ganjam, S. V., P S, P., & Vinayak, H., 2023).

The value of career counseling is frequently disregarded in modern society, which causes students to make poorly informed career decisions and increases the number of dropouts. It is advised that students use an intelligent, student-driven career guidance system to help them make better-informed career decisions, ensure that they choose relevant courses, and raise graduation rates. It is advised that computer literacy, particularly at the secondary school level, be improved to maximize the system's effectiveness (Sayyed, F., Sanghani, R., Vora, A., & Lemos, N., 2020).

To address the mental health issues faced by college students, this study suggests a novel remedy in the form of a Virtual Reality (VR) empathy-centric counseling chatbot (VRECC). VRECC combines VR and AI for rapid and emphatic therapy in response to the rising stress and psychological problems among students, which are made worse by academic pressures and situations like the COVID-19 pandemic. Results of the study show a significant decrease in participants' stress levels and psychological sensitivity, demonstrating the potential of VRECC to improve mental health. Despite its shortcomings, this research opens the door for future advancements in the use of VR and AI to address the expanding mental health challenges in educational settings (Trappey, A. J. C., Lin, A. P. C., Hsu, K. Y. K., Trappey, C. V., & Tu, K. L. K., 2022).

The goal of this study is to increase the professional maturity of high school students by investigating important elements such as adversity quotient, self-awareness, motivation, and self-management. It investigates methods to improve career maturity, including group counseling, career portfolios, and interactive multimedia. It increases students' comprehension of career alternatives and informed decision-making by highlighting the need for career counseling in schools. Further research on the elements influencing students' fitness for the job is encouraged as it emphasizes the importance of professional maturity in guiding good career decisions (Hastin, M., Naqiyah, N., & Darminto, E., 2022).

The study emphasizes the importance of career counseling in the current global economy and the demand for qualified counselors to help people identify their skills and match them with various job prospects. It discusses difficulties secondary schools in Taraba State confront, including tight budgets, privacy concerns, and a lack of counselors. It supports regulatory changes, specialized training, allocated financing, digital platforms, and strong confidentiality safeguards to improve these services with the ultimate goal of empowering students to make educated career selections. The research serves as a call to action for boosting career counseling in Taraba State, benefiting the local workforce and economic growth (Brandford, S. A., n.d.).

The usefulness of self-information-based counseling interventions in raising high school students' job confidence is evaluated in this study. The quasi-experimental methodology, used with 94 high school students, demonstrates the beneficial effects of self-information from the Self-Directed Career Exploration Inventory. The findings highlight the importance of career counseling in high schools and highlight the need for specialized treatments to support students in developing and planning their careers. The study makes recommendations for more research to improve career counseling techniques and effectively assist students in matching their talents, interests, and long-term goals (Dahlan, S., Idris, E., & Susanto, E., 2020).

The goal of this research was to create a chatbot that could coach secondary and higher secondary students on their career choices. This was the primary research goal and the system that was created accomplished it. To decide which characteristics to include in the chatbot, a survey of students and recent graduates was conducted. Several survey respondents were chosen after the development period to test the bot and see if the system generated satisfactory results. Additionally, the goal of creating an automated system that receives user inquiries and outputs the necessary materials was also accomplished. This was accomplished using a variety of techniques, including the Facebook Messenger platform (Limna, P., Kraiwanit, T., Jangjarat, K., Klayklung, P., & Chocksathaporn, P., 2023).

According to the study's findings, ChatGPT has the potential to be an important teaching tool in the digital age. The catboat's use in education was seen well by both teachers and students overall, and teachers pointed out that it might lighten their workload by responding to common inquiries. However, questions have been raised regarding the veracity of the catboat's information, the potential loss of one-on-one interactions with teachers, and the necessity of data protection and privacy. It is advised that educators and policymakers carefully weigh the advantages and disadvantages of using ChatGPT to ensure its ethical and effective adoption in education. Teachers must also instruct and train students in the proper use of ChatGPT as a teaching tool. Based on these findings, researchers can go into previously unknown areas, such as the particular educational methods that can maximize ChatGPT's advantages, techniques for overcoming its drawbacks, or the influence of ChatGPT on various topic areas or student populations. This study contributes to the body of knowledge on ChatGPT in the digital age of education by providing insightful analysis and recommendations that broaden key stakeholders' understanding of the potential advantages, difficulties, and perspectives. It provides a foundation for academics to broaden their study horizons and participate in the continuing discussion surrounding the appropriate and successful use of ChatGPT in educational contexts, acting as a steppingstone for future research endeavors (Suresh, N., Mukabe, N., Hashiyana, V., Limbo, A., & Hauwanga, A., 2021).

Education is faced with obstacles from modern technology. AI is required to gain a deeper understanding of education and to set up organizations, personnel, and students for AI-facilitated learning. This paper outlined paths for future research and looked at potential uses and requirements for AI in career counseling. More than just a tool, technology can change and enhance career counseling services and approaches based on user objectives, staff qualifications, and organizational capacity (Westman, S., & Mononen, A., n.d.).

The career guidance system described in this study uses machine learning to make accurate predictions. It supports skill evaluation and provides training on current issues to computer science and information technology students in their final year or recent graduates. They created a website and app using the KNN Algorithm, and the evaluation of user data was 93% accurate (Kumar, S. V., Dubey, S., & Sahu, V., 2023).

With this method, students first choose their areas of interest before responding to questionnaires that are presented to them on their screens. As test data, the responses are recorded in the machine's database. In comparison to the Holland Code and MBTI, the Big 5 Personality Test, available through Google Forms, uses five mathematical formulas to compute personalities. For machine learning education, the gathered data is essential, and the training process incorporates student responses. While different algorithms produce varying degrees of accuracy, Naive Bayes is anticipated to be less accurate while the Random Forest Classifier should produce a higher level of accuracy (Patel, H., Sanghavi, J., Shah, S., Thacker, S., & Mishra, S., 2021).

In this ground-breaking study, problems in the educational sector are addressed via an AI-driven system. The system integrates machine learning methods like Random Forest, Linear Regression, and Google API-based searches with a focus on helping students choose the best educational path. It helps with finding institutions, forecasting cutoff scores, and providing in-depth details about various academic specialties. This innovative strategy serves as a virtual counselor, assisting students in making decisions and navigating the challenging educational environment. The fusion of AI and education holds promise for meeting the demands of contemporary learning (Pujari, A. M., Dalvi, R. M., Gawde, K. S., & Nagarhalli, T. P., 2019).

This study examines the difficulties high school students encounter while selecting a job and suggests a computerized method for ability assessment and career route recommendations. It introduces the "Chatbot for Efficient Utilization of College Laboratories," a chatbot system built to simplify infrastructure allocation in educational contexts. A Personalized Career-Path Recommender System (PCRS) is created as a result of the research to assist engineering students in selecting their areas of study based on their academic standing, personality attributes, and extracurricular involvement (Mathur, T., Dattatray, P. S., Singh, M., Kumar, P., & B. E. Student., n.d.).

In the study, a career guidance chatbot is introduced that uses artificial intelligence to convert conventional job counseling into a digital, interactive system. By using personality assessments and making job recommendations, this bot aids students in selecting the best educational path. It provides details on numerous career opportunities, salary insights, and current developments in the education industry. The bot represents a trend toward technology-driven employment assistance by helping people make informed job selections by evaluating user interests and preferences (Shah, S., Mishra, A., Shaikh, I., Yadav, A., & Ambekar, R., 2022).

This article describes a practical approach to creating an advanced online application that will help youth make wise and practical decisions about their career and school options so they may use web technology to have a successful career. Students can interact with a chatbot for guidance on careers via the application's user interface. Every phase of the project's development will see improvements to its specs. It might be challenging at first to design an application that would satisfy the demands of a large number of users, but we were determined to accomplish all of our objectives by cooperating as a team and receiving support from the teachers (Dongre, G., Vadraiwala, F., Upadhyaya, J., & Ghosal, D., n.d.).

Self-information interventions used in career counseling have proven to be quite successful in assisting high school students in exploring their career options. Following career counseling, students' mean score on the certainty of their job decision climbed dramatically. The experimental group's mean score was much greater than the control groups, and there was no discernible difference in the mean scores of male and female students' profession choices (Dahlan, S., Idris, E., & Susanto, E., 2020).

Determining the function of secondary school teachers in career counseling was the primary objective of the study. According to the survey, secondary school instructors have a big influence on students' career guidance. Teachers serve as students' role models by recognizing their interests and ambitions, skills, and aptitudes, integrating these traits with their interests, assisting them in choosing courses, offering career counsel, and informing them of the prerequisites for various jobs (Chilewa, E. A., & Osaki, K., 2022).

The study's findings have led to the following conclusions being made: For students to be in good health, secondary schools must include guidance and counseling programs. The current state of counseling and guidance procedures at a few Temeke Municipality secondary schools is not properly handled, and as a result, instructors are not providing professional help to pupils. The selection process does not take into account qualified instructors who are regarded as kind, devout, and disciplined, and the teachers who are hired as school guidance counselors have not participated in any professional training or seminars. Guidance and counseling are viewed by students as tools for controlling behavior rather than as career development assistance from professors. This restricts instructors' and students' ability to effectively participate in their professional development. Counseling and guidance procedures in secondary schools (Zeb, A., Ali, A., & Ullah, D. A., n.d.).

## Research Gap and Problem Found in Existing Systems

The current systems for AI-based chatbots that offer job counseling to secondary school kids frequently lack a comprehensive strategy that blends machine learning and data-driven insights to offer individualized career recommendations. These systems frequently fall short in adapting to the changing job market and fail to effectively integrate external APIs for career advice. Additionally, there is a noteworthy lack of user-friendly interfaces that are interactive and capable of successfully involving students in the counseling process. Our research seeks to close this gap by advancing a thorough methodology that enhances user interactions through NLP, optimizes career recommendations through machine learning, integrates external career APIs, and places a strong emphasis on the user's personal development and preferences.

## Proposed Methodology

The proposed AI-based chatbot for career counseling offers secondary school pupils a thorough, user-centered method of career advising. The system's first step, which assures data privacy and confidentiality, is a secure user login and registration process. It uses Natural Language Processing (NLP) methods to identify users' personality traits, interests, and values after greeting them with enticing messages (*Step 2*). Their skills, aptitudes, and capabilities are evaluated and categorized using an interactive questionnaire and machine learning models (*Step 3*). The academic knowledge assessment (*Step 4*), which uses machine learning algorithms to measure their competence in academic areas, is a novel element. To determine the

*Table 1. Existing system work*

| Title | Methodology | Results and Discussion |
|---|---|---|
| Artificial Intelligence in Career Counseling: A Test Case with ResumAI | Using OpenAI's text-davinci-003 API, the study's authors built a career counselor chatbot website to provide individualized advice. They created the website by cloning the GitHub repository for OpenAI, integrating the API, and improving user interactions, such as resume uploads, for a better user experience. | ResumAI's typical usage scenario and their thoughts on how it can benefit its target audience of students or early-career professionals, especially in contexts with limited resources, are provided. |
| Artificial Intelligence-Based Career Counseling Chatbot a System for counseling | The study provides a methodology for a system that accepts input from either text or speech. To provide a pertinent response that is displayed to the user, it transforms voice input to text, processes the question, and does a database search. | According to the study, a career counseling chatbot powered by AI that is available around the clock on a variety of platforms can assist students in choosing careers and lessen the stress associated with such decisions by imitating human thought processes. |
| Effect of counseling services on career choice of secondary school students in Anambra state, Nigeria | *Multiple Regression Analysis (MRA) was used to investigate the impact of career counseling services on secondary school students' decisions in Onitsha, Anambra state. The regression model used in the study was* $Y = \alpha + \beta 1X1 + \beta 2X2 + \beta 3X3 + \beta nXn + e$. *The test-retest methodology was used to determine the validity of the questionnaire.* | The results of the study emphasize the value of counseling services, particularly orientation services, in assisting students in adjusting to the school environment. In addition, evaluation and follow-up services are essential for determining and raising student accomplishment levels. |
| Chatbot for Career Guidance Using AI | Three modules—Bot Chat, text-to-speech, and Processing—make up the chatbot system. Natural language processing is used when users communicate via text or speech. Processing makes use of intent categorization and pattern matching. With agents, intentions, and fulfillment for interaction and execution, the system runs on platforms like Facebook Messenger and is powered by Dialog Flow. | With the use of embedded information, the career counseling bot promotes talks between humans and machines. It takes tokens from sentences, matches user input, and provides insightful career advice. By using Google API (Dialog Flow), it can receive text and voice input. |
| An Intelligent Career Counseling Bot | A Bot Chat module for user contact, a Text-to-speech component for response delivery, and a Processing module that uses pattern matching and knowledge-based question sets to assist users in making career decisions are among the system's modules. By streamlining the process, this methodology improves the usability and accessibility of career counseling. | This research study introduces a chatbot with intelligent decision-making abilities for career advising. By giving prompt, correct solutions drawn from a thorough knowledge base, the system hopes to reduce student stress. It is capable of text and voice input. |
| Development of an AI Chatbot to Support Admissions and Career Guidance for Universities | This Methodology includes steps like data collection, building data sets, and Structural design for Chatbot, in this they create a training model then process and give results, the last one is interface design for Chatbot. | The project uses machine learning and natural language processing to build identification models that solve issues in career counseling and university admissions, ultimately increasing the effectiveness of admissions consulting for institutions. |
| An expert system for career counseling using clips. | This program uses a Q&A session to provide career counseling to students in grades 10 and 12. Their interests, personalities, academic backgrounds, and hobbies are all gathered in the data. It offers personalized guidance for well-informed decision-making by recommending appropriate academic and career options using a knowledge base. | A powerful decision-support and interactive training tool, the student counseling expert system is especially useful for identifying student psychology based on academic backgrounds and interests. The paper suggests potential future expansion to include all areas of career advice. |
| Online Career counselor system based on Artificial Intelligence | This methodology ensures data quality, applies machine learning algorithms like SVM and decision trees, and rigorously tests the model's performance. | The study introduces an AI-driven chatbot and intelligent engine that delivers job recommendations based on industry data, easing difficult career choices, and offering crucial help in the modern world. |

*continued on following page*

*Table 1. Continued*

| Title | Methodology | Results and Discussion |
|---|---|---|
| Chatbot for Career Counseling | The algorithm of the system enables users to enter interests and rank topics for predictions using pre-trained data. It will take input from both text and speech. The chatbot welcomes users, determines the intent, gathers ratings, normalizes data, predicts a course, and suggests it with college links in the processing module, assisting with well-informed career decisions. | Rasa NLU facilitates intelligent conversations by connecting user intentions to behavior. A dataset without labels is formed by subject ratings ranging from 0 to 10. The best course will be suggested to the user as an output by machine learning models |
| Smart Career Guidance and Recommendation System | Students log in to Gmail, access a Career Guidance form, and take a skills test covering programming, web development, networking, hardware, data science, and Android. Test results are saved in a downloadable spreadsheet. Data preprocessing and machine algorithms predict personalized skill certifications. | This project introduces a Career Guidance System that uses machine learning to guide students toward the appropriate career based on their skills. Using a dataset of 1000 students, Logistic Regression and Linear Discriminant Analysis yield precise results. |
| Online Career Counsellor System based on Artificial Intelligence: An approach. | It has two main components: one for recommendations and the other for displaying summarized results. Users answer questions to narrow down their areas of interest and receive appropriate career suggestions. The chatbot module analyzes user input using NLP, while the system utilizes a modular architecture to handle requests and integrates with a web server. The Naïve Bayes Algorithm is employed for the classification | Incorporating a chatbot and an intelligent engine, this career counseling system uses AI and data from industry professionals to give users the best career options. It addresses the increasingly complex nature of career options, making it a useful tool for those looking for career guidance in the modern world. |
| Conversational AI WhatsApp Chatbot | The chatbot, powered by voice flow software, uses technologies like NLP, knowledge bases, and dialogue management to comprehend user inquiries and offer personalized career advice. The user interface can be a website, app, or messaging platform. NLP processes input and dialogue management to maintain context | It facilitates users' decision-making by streamlining the presentation of career data. Both professionals and students will find value in the chatbot's comprehensive and up-to-date insights into a variety of careers. |
| AI-based Career Guidance | Data collection and formatting are involved in the process, along with clustering for classification and the use of association rules to identify relationships between subgroups. The prediction model is a thorough data analysis method because it weights formulas based on historical data and human expertise to calculate outputs. | To give students more informed choices and support their academic success, a student-driven web-based career guidance system is advised. Improved computer literacy, particularly in secondary schools, is necessary to maximize the system's efficiency. |
| Development of an Empathy-Centric Counseling Chatbot System Capable of Sentimental Dialogue Analysis | The goal of this project is to create a platform that blends virtual reality with psychological therapy that emphasizes empathy, enabling students to access counseling services through VR. It includes a chatbot for user interactions, a stress evaluation questionnaire, and a chat room for casual conversations with peers and counselors. | Sentiment analysis is used by counseling chatbots to assist students in de-stressing. A flexible tool for therapy anytime, anyplace, virtual reality enables remote counseling and offers users empathy and healing through chatbot conversations. |
| Guidance and Counselling Services to Develop Student Career Maturity | The literature study approach uses a variety of techniques to increase the number of research references, such as keyword searches, contemporary scientific publications, citation searches, organized bibliographies, primary sources, systematic browsing, and looking for full-text sources in organized subject areas. | According to Bakar & Luddin, guidance and counseling comprise four parts that make up a holistic service: Individual planning, Responsive Service, System Support, and Guidance and Counseling Services. |
| Investigating Barriers to Effective Career Counseling Services in Taraba State's Secondary Education | The Yamane technique for calculating sample size and a self-created Likert scale questionnaire is used in the study to examine the difficulties in career counseling in 309 senior secondary schools in Taraba State. Statistical analysis utilizing STATA software followed known research techniques for credible results. | This study, which included 399 respondents, investigated difficulties in career counseling in secondary schools in Taraba State and uncovered problems with counselor training, funding limitations, and privacy concerns. To improve counseling services and equip students with the knowledge they need to make wise career decisions, the study suggests policy changes, counselor training, dedicated funds, digital tools, and strong confidentiality frameworks. |

*continued on following page*

*Table 1. Continued*

| Title | Methodology | Results and Discussion |
|---|---|---|
| Improve student career certainty using self-information: A career counseling in the school | Methods include design, participants, procedure, instruments, and data analysis | According to post-counseling results, using self-education in career counseling considerably increased high school students' confidence in their job choices. Notably, these interventions were successful and there were no gender differences in the mean scores, underscoring their success. |
| The use of ChatGPT in the digital era: Perspectives on chatbot implementation | This study used a four-stage research methodology, all of which are qualitative steps like research design, data collecting, data analysis, and report writing. The purpose of the qualitative research technique is to understand how people make decisions and take action, as well as to explain why certain occurrences occur. | A potential new instrument for the digital era of education is ChatGPT. It may support educators and learners in many ways, including by generating customized learning resources, responding to inquiries, and giving immediate feedback. However, it's crucial to utilize ChatGPT sensibly and understand its limits, such as the potential for giving false information and lowering in-person encounters. |
| Career Counseling Chatbot on Facebook Messenger using AI | Using resources including the Facebook SDK, the Messenger Platform APIs, JSON files, and JavaScript, as well as AI and Natural Language Processing, the chatbot system was created on the Facebook Messenger platform algorithms were used in the system's construction to analyze user responses and generate the appropriate answer. To carry out this task, the application made use of the Wit.ai platform's AI technologies as well as the Facebook Messenger platform. | The created application may provide users with a range of career counseling services, such as help with drafting resumes and cover letters and getting ready for interviews. Additionally, it offers an aptitude test that enables users to determine which profession would be ideal for them and the ability to locate job ads that are local to them. |
| Artificial Intelligence for Career Guidance-Current Requirements and Prospects for the Future | For students in higher education and vocational education, two AI applications were created to assist with course suggestions, employment recommendations, and the construction of skills profiles. The applications combined personal data, curriculum data, national qualification data, and job adverts using machine learning and data mining techniques. 179 students in higher education and 103 students in vocational education examined the apps, and both groups provided excellent comments. | The trials' findings underscore the need for AI in career counseling. Students anticipated tailored recommendations based on their schedule, interests, and location. This reflects not just general expectations for digital services but also student-centered guidance and underlying personal values. |
| Career Counseling in the Digital Age: Research on online Personal counseling | Data from 20,000 records were gathered for this project, which also transformed categorical data and improved features for accuracy. It uses KNN to make job recommendations based on user input, and accuracy is assessed by contrasting predicted and actual results to guarantee algorithm performance. | The KNN Algorithm is used by the system to achieve an accuracy rate of 93%. For user input, algorithm processing, and result display, it has a website and an app. It is powered by machine learning and helps students studying computer science and information technology evaluate their skills and decide on the best career path. It provides a user-friendly interface and accurate predictions, ensuring that career decisions are well-informed. |
| Career guidance system using machine learning | The project focuses on using item-item collaborative filtering for machine learning in a career recommendation system. Naive Bayes, K-Nearest Neighbor, and Random Forest were chosen as test algorithms. Due to its simplicity and convenience, Google Forms' Big 5 Personality Test was chosen for data collection | The Big 5 Personality Test in Google Forms is used for data collection, and machine learning algorithms provide career recommendations based on user input. The accuracy of various methods varies, with the Random Forest Classifier expected to offer the highest accuracy and Naive Bayes Algorithm the lowest. |

*continued on following page*

*Table 1. Continued*

| Title | Methodology | Results and Discussion |
|---|---|---|
| SCCAI- A Student Career Counselling Artificial Intelligence | Linear Regression and Random Forest are used in machine learning, and Google Dialog Flow is used for natural language processing. Android, iOS, and Windows Phone all include Google's conversational technology, Dialog Flow. Due to a lack of relevant current data sources, the dataset was manually created, allowing various machine learning algorithms to take advantage of unique dataset properties within the Google Assistance framework. | This system is unparalleled in the market, utilizing Google Assistant as its development framework, powered by Google API for natural language processing. It boasts prompt and reasonably accurate voice output while implementing multiple machine-learning algorithms. |
| Intelligent Career Guidance System using Machine Learning | Academic and professional goals can be aligned with the aid of career counseling. PCRS wants to be a trusted advisor, assisting students in choosing their careers by using academic and personal data. | According to academic standing and personality features, the study proposes a Personalized Career-Path Recommender System (PCRS) for engineering students. To assist students in making educated career decisions, PCRS attempts to imitate professional counselors, particularly in underprivileged educational contexts. |
| Career Guidance Chatbot | The Multinomial Naive Bayes Chatbot from Career Bot uses Word net lemmatizer, Keras for training, Label Encoder, and NLTK tokenization for input processing, and answers based on database matching. It is implemented in Python with Stream lit and TensorFlow. Different adapters guarantee pertinent responses to user inquiries. | In the modern digital age, "Career Guidance Chatbot Using AI" is indispensable, offering informed career decisions with insights from personality tests, career trends, course details, and salary information. It is poised to expand its scope to encompass specialized courses, marking a transition to digital career counseling. |
| Web-based career counselling system with chatbot | This module's front end and back end are constructed using the C#-written ASP.NET framework, and the database is Microsoft SQL Server 2014. ASP.NET development services are supported by the robust and safe object-oriented back-end programming language C#, which also enables us to create robust and secure career counseling applications. | Our career counseling system is made to offer students information, guidance, and advice about careers. It does this by evaluating students' personalities and abilities and helping them to enhance and set realistic long-term goals for their academic and professional lives. |
| Improve student career certainty using self-information: A career counseling in the school | Graph 1 illustrates the confidence of job choice data for both male and female students based on pre-and post-test findings from the group participating in the experiment and the control group. The graph's data demonstrates that each student group's mean score on the pretest measuring professional decision certainty is almost equal. The experimental group's mean pre-test score was 3.69, while the control groups was 3.47. The experimental group's mean post-test score was 4.72, while the control groups was 3.64. Put otherwise, there are variations in the pre-and post-test mean scores for every student group. | The findings of this study suggest that career counseling treatments can benefit from using knowledge of personality typologies. It was discovered that profession choice certainty may be greatly increased by the RIASEC personality typology classifications that were created by the counselees (students) based on the outcomes of their evaluation utilizing the S-DCEI. This empirical data confirms Holland's (1985; 1997) theory, according to which counselors can address a client's career issues by using the personal, occupational, or the environment. type or sub type categories classification system. This system makes it easy to organize occupational information so that both the counselee and the counselor are capable of comprehending it. |
| The Role of Teachers in Career Guidance of Students at Secondary Level in Pakistan | To learn more about the responsibilities that instructors play in helping secondary school students with their career guidance, the researchers developed a questionnaire. The questionnaire was evaluated and verified as trustworthy for data collection through piloting. The reliability of the instrument was 0.817. The data was gathered using this trustworthy approach. | By determining students' interests, abilities, and aptitudes, assisting them in making course selections, offering career guidance, and educating them about employment needs, teachers play a crucial part in high school career counseling. Research by Garrahy, Khan, Falaye, and Adams supports this. |

*continued on following page*

*Table 1. Continued*

| Title | Methodology | Results and Discussion |
|---|---|---|
| The Effectiveness of Guidance and Counseling Practices on Students' Career Development in Secondary Schools in Temeke Municipality | An embedded research approach, which incorporates both qualitative and quantitative data, was employed in the study. Before using quantitative data from surveys to contextualize the qualitative data, the researcher collected qualitative data via films and interviews. | Students do not think counseling is beneficial, and school guidance counselors lack proper training. This is a result of instructors' emphasis on instruction and learning rather than professional growth. Interaction among educators, parents, ward educational officers, and management can help to resolve this issue. |

*Figure 1. System architecture*

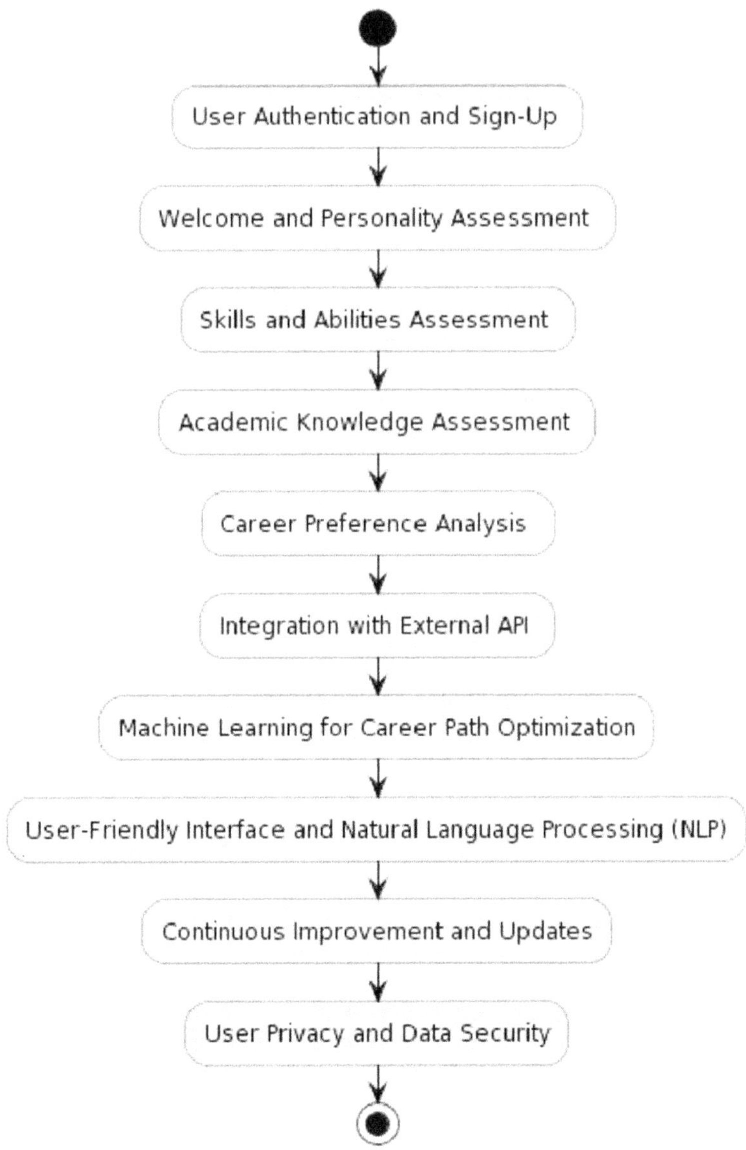

most popular options, clustering methods are used to examine respondents' career preferences (*Step 5*). The integration with an external API (*Step 6*) that specializes in career path recommendations and offers personalized career choices is a crucial differentiator. Machine Learning for Career Path Optimization (*Step 7*) is what distinguishes this approach, where a model iteratively improves recommendations based on positive career results and user feedback, assuring ongoing adaptation. *Steps 8* through 10 together provide a user-friendly interface strengthened by NLP, continuous feedback analysis, and stringent privacy compliance, which outperforms current solutions by providing more individualized, precise, and interesting career assistance.

# TECHNIQUE INVOLVED IN PROPOSED METHODOLOGY

## User Authentication and Registration

Technique: - Utilize encryption and industry-recognized best practices for data security to provide a secure authentication and registration system.

## Personality Assessment

Technique: - Examine and comprehend user answers to personality-related questions using natural language processing (NLP) methods.

## Evaluation of Abilities and Skills

Technique: - To define and quantify user skills and abilities based on their replies, create an interactive questionnaire or activity. Then, apply machine learning models to analyze the results.

## Academic Knowledge Assessment

Technique: - Construct a test or quiz centered around academic topics, then apply machine learning algorithms to gauge how well users comprehend and perform.

## Career Preference Analysis

Technique: - Use clustering techniques to organize user responses into professional categories and pinpoint the most prevalent preferences.

## External API Integration

Technique: - Connect an external API that offers advice on career paths, transmitting user data for examination and getting customized career recommendations.

## Machine Learning for Optimizing Career Path

Technique: - Optimize career suggestions by implementing a machine learning model for reinforcement learning based on user input and successful career routes.

## User-Friendly Interface Enhancement

Technique: - Use NLP methods to improve chatbot answers, making user interactions more engaging and natural.

## Feedback Mechanism Implementation

Technique: - Provide a means for users to offer feedback on the suggestions made by the system. Analyze the system continuously and make incremental improvements based on user feedback.

## Data Security and Privacy Compliance

Technique: - Ensure strict adherence to privacy laws and rules, anonymizing and protecting user data, and allowing users control over their information.

# RESULT AND DISCUSSION

The secondary school student's AI-powered career guidance chatbot can provide a range of outcomes for them, such as:

A summary of possible career paths: Using the data it has gathered about the student, the chatbot may provide a list of possible career routes that would be a good fit for them. This list may be customized based on the student's interests in careers, academic background, personality, and talents.

Details on every career path: The chatbot may tell the learner about the necessary schooling and training, expected remuneration, and employment outlook for each career option. The student can use this knowledge to make well-informed judgments on their intended career path in the future.

The chatbot may also provide the student with a more comprehensive view of themselves and their job alternatives in addition to these particular outcomes. The chatbot's assessments and inquiries allow the learner to discover more about their personality, abilities, and beliefs. Additionally, they can discover more about various job options and the prerequisites for each one.

Overall, secondary-level students who are considering their future alternatives may find the AI-based job advice chatbot to be an invaluable tool. They may use it to better understand who they are, find potential career options, and create a strategy for achieving their professional objectives.

Here is an illustration of how the chatbot may be put to use:

The student logs in and does the personality test on the chatbot. The chatbot finds that the pupil is kind, imaginative, and skilled at solving problems.

The student then finishes the exam on skills and competencies. The chatbot ascertains that the learner is proficient in arithmetic, science, and coding.

The academic topic test is then finished by the student. The chatbot discovers that the student has completed multiple computer science courses and has earned good grades in math and science. The student then informs the chatbot that a career in technology is something they are considering.

To create a tailored career path, the chatbot compiles all this data and transmits it to an API. A list of prospective career pathways for the student is generated by the API and includes jobs like "software engineer," "data scientist," and "web developer."

*Figure 2. Login*

The chatbot then gives the student details on each career choice, such as the degree and experience needed, the pay, and the prospects for employment. The chatbot also offers advice on how to attain professional objectives to students, such as how to create a portfolio of their accomplishments and establish connections with experts in the technology industry.

The student can utilize this knowledge to plan their future profession in an educated manner. They may elect to pursue one of the suggested professional pathways or they may decide to look into other choices. They now have a solid foundation from which to build their career planning journeys thanks to the chatbot.

*Figure 3. Home page*

## CONCLUSION

The AI-based career counseling system, as explained, offers a thorough and personalized approach to career assistance, which, in turn, considerably helps secondary-level pupils. It incorporates crucial elements including user identification, personality testing, talent testing, knowledge testing for academic purposes, career preference analysis, and integration of other APIs.

By combining machine learning, making use of data from successful career pathways, feature engineering, and model training, the system's accuracy and relevancy are further increased. Its iterative structure guarantees continual improvement while adjusting to changing student demands.

The system delivers a safe and engaging platform for students to explore and follow their professional objectives by emphasizing user-friendly interfaces, natural language processing, data security, and privacy. Students receive individualized assistance through the collaboration of AI and machine learning, enabling them to make wise and satisfying career decisions.

By bridging the gap between students and their prospective job routes in the future, this complete career counseling system might change the way students approach choosing a vocation. It opens the door for improvements in user-centered, individualized guiding systems.

## REFERENCES

Asnani, D., & Agarwal, K. (n.d.). AN EXPERT SYSTEM FOR CAREER COUNSELLING USING CLIPS. *International Journal of Management, Technology, and Engineering*.

Bhnushali, D. M., & Itankar, P. (2020). Online Career Counsellor System based on Artificial Intelligence: An approach. [IORD]. *International Organization of Research & Development*, *08*(02). doi:10.5281/zenodo.4699065

Brandford, S. A. (n.d.). *Investigating Barriers to Effective Career Counseling Services in Taraba State's Secondary Education*. Research Gate. https://www.researchgate.net/publication/373448378

Chilewa, E. A., & Osaki, K. (2022). The Effectiveness of Guidance and Counselling Practices on Students' Career Development in Secondary Schools in Temeke Municipality. *The Journal of Humanistic Education and Development*, *4*(1), 160–181. doi:10.22161/jhed.4.1.17

Dahlan, S., Idris, E., & Susanto, E. (2020). Improve student career certainty using self-information: A career counseling in the school. *Cypriot Journal of Educational Sciences*, *15*(6), 1480–1494. doi:10.18844/cjes.v15i6.5292

Dahlan, S., Idris, E., & Susanto, E. (2020). Improve student career certainty using self-information: A career counseling in the school. *Cypriot Journal of Educational Sciences*, *15*(6), 1480–1494. doi:10.18844/cjes.v15i6.5292

Dang Truong Ho Chi, H. (2020). Development of an AI Chatbot to Support Admissions and Career Guidance for Universities. *International Journal of Emerging Multidisciplinary Research*, *4*(2), 13–20. doi:10.22662/IJEMR.2020.4.2.013

Dongre, G., Vadraiwala, F., Upadhyaya, J., & Ghosal, D. (n.d.). WEB-BASED CAREER COUNSELLING SYSTEM WITH CHATBOT. *International Research Journal of Modernization in Engineering Technology and Science.*

Ganjam, S. V., P S, P., & Vinayak, H. (2023). Conversational AI Whatsapp Chatbot. [IJERT]. *International Journal of Engineering Research & Technology (Ahmedabad), 11*(05).

Hastin, M., Naqiyah, N., & Darminto, E. (2022). Guidance and Counseling Services to Develop Student Career Maturity. IJORER. *International Journal of Recent Educational Research, 3*(6), 688–700. doi:10.46245/ijorer.v3i6.261

Ifejiofor, A. P. (2023). Effect of counseling services on career choice of secondary school students in Anambra state, Nigeria. International Journal of Education. *Training and Learning, 7*(1), 1–6. doi:10.33094/ijetl.v7i1.1152

Joshi, K., Goel, A. K., & Kumar, T. (2020). *Online Career Counsellor System based on Artificial Intelligence: An approach. IEEE 7th International Conference on Smart Structures and Systems ICSSS 2020*. IEEE.

Katre, M., Manchanda, S., & Agarwal, R. (2021). Chatbot for Career Counselling. [IJRASET]. *International Journal for Research in Applied Science and Engineering Technology, 9*(7).

Kumar, S. V., Dubey, S., & Sahu, V. (2023). Career Counseling In the Digital Age: A Research on online Personal counseling. *International Journal of Research Publication and Reviews, 4*(5), 3110–3115.

Limna, P., Kraiwanit, T., Jangjarat, K., Klayklung, P., & Chocksathaporn, P. (2023). The use of ChatGPT in the digital era: Perspectives on chatbot implementation. *Journal of Applied Learning and Teaching, 6*(1), 64–74. doi:10.37074/jalt.2023.6.1.32

Mathur, T., Dattatray, P. S., Singh, M., Kumar, P., & Student, B. E. (n.d.). Intelligent Career Guidance System using Machine Learning. *IJARIIE.* Retrieved from www.ijariie.com647

Ohm, A., & K, B. (2019). Chatbot for Career Guidance Using AI. *International Journal on Computer Science and Engineering, 7*(6), 856–860. doi:10.26438/ijcse/v7i6.856860

Parab, A., Palkar, S., Maurya, S., & Balpande, S. (2017). An Intelligent Career Counselling Bot: A System for counseling. *International Research Journal of Engineering and Technology (IRJET), 4*(03).

Patel, H., Sanghavi, J., Shah, S., Thacker, S., & Mishra, S. (2021). CAREER GUIDANCE SYSTEM USING MACHINE LEARNING. *IJCRT, 9*(5).

Prasanna, L. (2019). Smart Career Guidance and Recommendation System. *IJEDR, 7*(3).

Pujari, A. M., Dalvi, R. M., Gawde, K. S., & Nagarhalli, T. P. (2019). SCCAI-A Student Career Counselling Artificial Intelligence. *International Journal for Research and Innovation, 1*(2). www.vivatechnology.org/New/IJRI

RahmanM. (2023). Artificial Intelligence in Career Counseling: A Test Case with ResumAI. http://arxiv.org/abs/2308.14301

Sayyed, F., Sanghani, R., Vora, A., & Lemos, N. (2020). AI-based Career Guidance. *International Research Journal of Engineering and Technology (IRJET), 07*(05).

Shah, S., Mishra, A., Shaikh, I., Yadav, A., & Ambekar, R. (2022). Career Guidance Chatbot. [IJAEM]. *International Journal of Advances in Engineering and Management, 4*, 661. doi:10.35629/5252-0404661665

Suresh, N., Mukabe, N., Hashiyana, V., Limbo, A., & Hauwanga, A. (2021). Career Counseling Chatbot on Facebook Messenger using AI. *ACM International Conference Proceeding Series*, (pp. 65–73). ACM. 10.1145/3484824.3484875

Trappey, A. J. C., Lin, A. P. C., Hsu, K. Y. K., Trappey, C. V., & Tu, K. L. K. (2022). Development of an Empathy-Centric Counseling Chatbot System Capable of Sentimental Dialogue Analysis. *Processes (Basel, Switzerland), 10*(5), 930. doi:10.3390/pr10050930

Westman, S., & Mononen, A. (n.d.). Artificial Intelligence for Career Guidance-Current Requirements and Prospects for the Future. In IAFOR Journal of Education: Technology in Education, 9. doi:10.22492/ije.9.4.03

Zaidi, D., Raza, S., & Sharma, L. (2021). *Artificial Intelligence Based Career Counselling Chatbot: A System for counseling*. RSCB. http://annalsofrscb.ro

Zeb, A., Ali, A., & Ullah, D. A. (n.d.). The Role of Teachers in Career Guidance of Students at Secondary Level in Pakistan. In *Journal of Social Sciences Review* (Vol. 1). JSSR.

# Chapter 12
# Advancing Digital Forensics Education With Generative AI for Sustainable Development Goals

**Naziya Hussain**
https://orcid.org/0000-0002-4852-6314
*School of Computers, IPS Academy, Indore, India*

**V. Dankan Gowda**
https://orcid.org/0000-0003-0724-0333
*Department of Electronics and Communication Engineering, BMS Institute of Technology and Management, Bangalore, India*

**K. R. Swetha**
*Department of Computer Science and Engineering, BGS Institute of Technology, Adichunchanagiri University, Mandya, India*

**Aparna Atul Junnarkar**
*Department of Information Technology, Vishwakarma Institute of Information Technology (VIIT), Pune, India*

**Sheetalrani R. Kawale**
https://orcid.org/0000-0001-7887-0346
*Department of Computer Science, Karnataka State Akkamahadevi Women University, Vijayapura, India*

## ABSTRACT

*The term "forensics" refers to a broad range of activities that involve gathering, analyzing, and presenting evidence that is admissible in a court of law and are intended to investigate potential entities. In particular, network and computer forensics examine a wide range of data in order to find evidence that can be used in court. During the forensic process, the examination and auditing of computer and network data is essential for gathering data, identifying breaches, and presenting legal evidence. In computer and network forensics, evidence relating to cybercrime is identified, acquired, extracted, examined, analyzed, interpreted, documented, and presented using a methodical, scientific approach. The field of network and computer forensics is constantly expanding, and as crimes move beyond computers and into networks, clouds, and social networks, it is essential to stay current with the newest tools and techniques. The goal of this chapter is to study and explore the methods and tools used in network and computer forensics.*

DOI: 10.4018/979-8-3693-2440-0.ch012

## INTRODUCTION

Penetration of Information and Communication Technology (ICT) in the modern society, has led to expansion of the crime domain to Network and Computer related crimes across cyberspace. The spreading domain of cybercrime is a severe concern for forensic analysis. Thus, presenting admissible, well defined and documented evidence in a court of law is the goal of cyber forensics (G. Shrivastava and B. B. Gupta. 2014). Computer forensics is also known as cyber forensics that consists of acquiring, retrieving, preserving and preparing data, in forensic labs for presentation, that is electronically processed and stored on digital media. Cybercrime (computer-related crime, e-crime or digital technology, crime) is an unlawful act committed with the help of a network node (computer, laptop, and mobile) to target other resources. Cybercrime leads to intrusion, disruption or downgrading of the target node. In the last decade, the modern cybercrime techniques have become more sophisticated and commercialized. Criminals have been using high speed, readily available and anonymous technologies to run syndicate as professionals (Easwaran et al., 2022; Mijwil et al., 2022).

In addition to revolutionary advancements and increased connectivity, the advent of the digital age also marked the beginning of a new era in criminal activities. Cybercrimes including identity fraud; state sponsored attacks which arise from the migration of personal and business activities online have become quite a big problem. These emerging hardships demanded a new discipline that could combine interconnectedness of vital investigation strategies with continuously developing digital danger zone. The discipline of digital forensic came into existence as an indispensable tool in a war against cybercrime.

By its way, digital forensics was a science specially designed whose main fields were restricted to seeking lost files on floppy disks and tracing their indications. Though the degree of the cyber crimes has reached the complexity, as the world is exposed to the extensive digital interdependence. An mechnical race of arms between cyber criminals and the law enforcement agencies is the result of this growth. Unlike in the past, when forensics experts kept an eye on hard drives of computers, digital forensics today covers a wide range of subjects: for example, cloud databases, huge corporate networks, and telephone stories.

Also, the spread of the IoT can be regarded as an extra dimension of complexity. Refrigerators, webcams and thermostats which are commonly used at home formerly became part of the cyber court having a capacity to say something important.

Mental and physical elements together form the basic principle of law against the criminal offense. Mens rea and actusreus are the elements of any crime as shown in Figure.1. The act that leads to crime is the actusreus and the mental state, in which the person knowingly does a crime, is referred as Mens rea. Actusreus alone is not a crime. Problem with cybercrime is that it's hard to prove both elements (Choubisa et al., 2022; Patel et al., 2022). In cybercrime, the person's act in cyberspace, which laws look to prevent, are actusreus of cybercrime. Suppose a person sends SMS text message and recipient respond with positive response, it's not crime. But if recipient feels offended and is harassed, it would be a crime (M. H. Mate and S. R. Kapse. 2015). In the current scenario, actusreus is 'sending the message text' and 'intension behind stalking' is mens rea.

### Types of Crimes

Steven Furnell classifies cybercrime in two categories namely cyber-enabled and cyber-dependent crimes. Cyber-enabled is a traditional crime whose scalability has exponential growth, with or without the use of any Information and Communication Technology (ICT), such as frauds, thefts, and defamation. Whereas,

*Figure 1. Elements of crime*

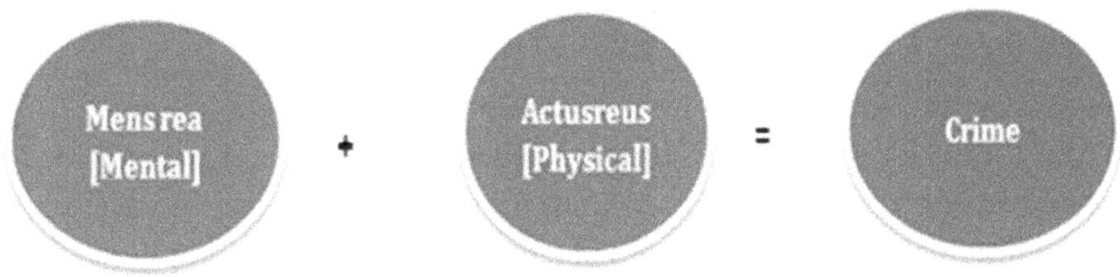


Cyber-dependent crimes are committed using ICT only that includes a computer or any other network node, such as virus, worms, and DOS attack. These crimes use ICT against ICT resources (R. Hunt and S. Zeadally. 2012) . India News reported on 16 December 2016, Rs 6 lakh was cheated from Paytm, by its customers. Group of customers colluded with executives of the company for this fraud, and the case was handled by Central Bureau of Investigation (CBI). In another incident reported by Kanpur News, a man was sent to jail for two years. The crimes committed using ICT had been a significant concern in this chapter. Based on the targets, the attacks can be classified into three categories, as shown in Figure.2.

Crimeware is software used, intended for direct or indirect illegal act, which is neither desirable nor voluntarily installed on a network node. Notably, this definition excludes the legitimate programs, leveraged and exploited by the hacker (Pallavi Asrodia and Vishal Sharma. 2013). The primary motivation of the cybercriminals as reported by "Cyber Crime: A review of the evidence published by the government of U.K." is the financial gain or personal benefits. For instance, using malware cyber, attackers are able to gain access in banks and share markets. The motivation could be for defaming or taking revenge from an organization or country by exhibiting power or control over other systems or the nation. Thus, the commercialization for the financial gain, the expansion of the business, and supremacy over another nation have become the principal motivation behind the crime rather than for fun.

*Figure 2. Types of cybercrimes based on target*

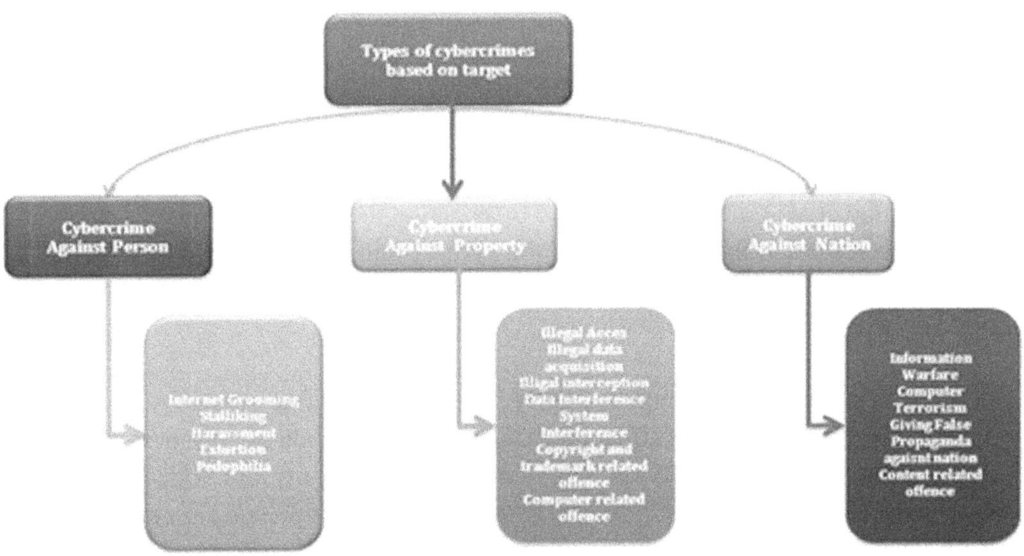

The scope of criminal activity in the large field of digital forensics has broadened considerably as time has passed. These offenses might be as little as petty theft or as complex as well-planned cyberattacks. Crimes come in a wide variety, and it's important to recognize these distinctions so that appropriate investigation strategies may be developed. Here is a rundown of the most common forms of cybercrime:

Theft of Identities: Identity theft, one of the most widespread forms of cybercrime, occurs when a person's personal information is stolen and then used fraudulently or for some other illegal purpose.

Credit card fraud, internet banking fraud, and phishing scams are all examples of financial fraud, in which criminals pose as reputable organizations in order to steal sensitive information.

Invading a computer, network, or website without authorization is known as "hacking" or "unauthorized access." It might be done for malicious reasons like data theft or interruptions, or just for the sake of it (Skouby et al., 2022; Unogwu et al., 2022).

Malware Distribution is the production and dissemination of malicious software with the intent to damage or exploit computers, networks, or services.

Internet-based child exploitation and obscenity: the creation, distribution, or viewing of pornographic or other illicit material involving kids.

Software piracy, sales of counterfeit items, and illegal dissemination of protected works such as movies, books, and music are all examples of intellectual property crimes.

Cyber espionage is the practice of secretly gathering and using information on individuals, businesses, or governments for political or economic gain.

The distribution of illegal narcotics, firearms, or other contraband through the use of the internet's anonymizing features, most notably the dark web.

Because of the porous nature of the internet, many of these crimes are now considered international in scope. This complicates judicial procedures since different nations may have different laws and varying degrees of enforcement for the same conduct. The internet's ability to hide criminals' identities adds to the difficulty of tracking them down and apprehending them. Since different types of crime present different challenges, digital forensic tools and procedures have had to develop quickly to keep up.

## Categorization of Cyber Criminals

The categorization of the cyber-criminals is conflicting as the activities that define the criminal domains vary from one continent to another. An activity or behavior in the cyberspace is a crime in one place or country, could be a legitimate action in another (Merlette D and Pruthi D P. 2013). A company gave a contract to a professional to launch a DoS attack on the website or against an organization in archrival country or continents; this is a case of legitimate action, although it is a DoS attack. However, the quintessence of white-collar crime could be established by breaking the trust and abuse of power in addition to the financial motivation. The categorization of the cybercriminals is explained in Figure.3.

## Digital Evidence and Investigation

Digital evidence is any form of data or information received, stored or transmitted by any digital device, that adds value to investigation process (Shanmugasundaram K, Memon N, Savant A, Bronnimann H. 2003). It can be on hard disk, ram or any node on or off network. Usually any evidence is of two types, physical and digital evidence, which is shown in Figure.4. Digital evidence can be categorized as volatile and non-volatile evidences. Sources of digital evidences are shown in Figure.5.below.

*Figure 3. Categorization of cyber criminals*

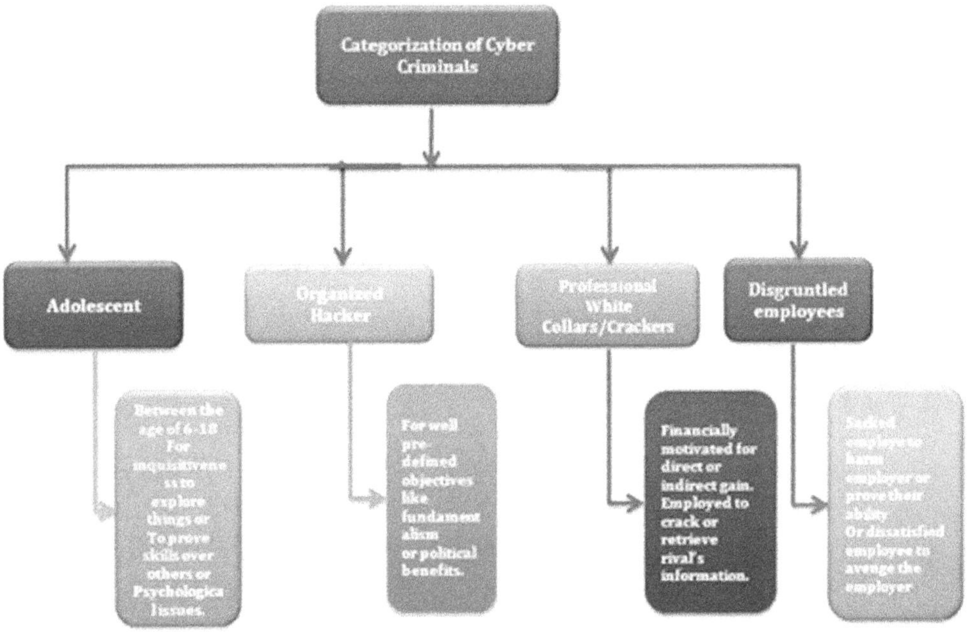


*Figure 4. Categorization of crime evidences*

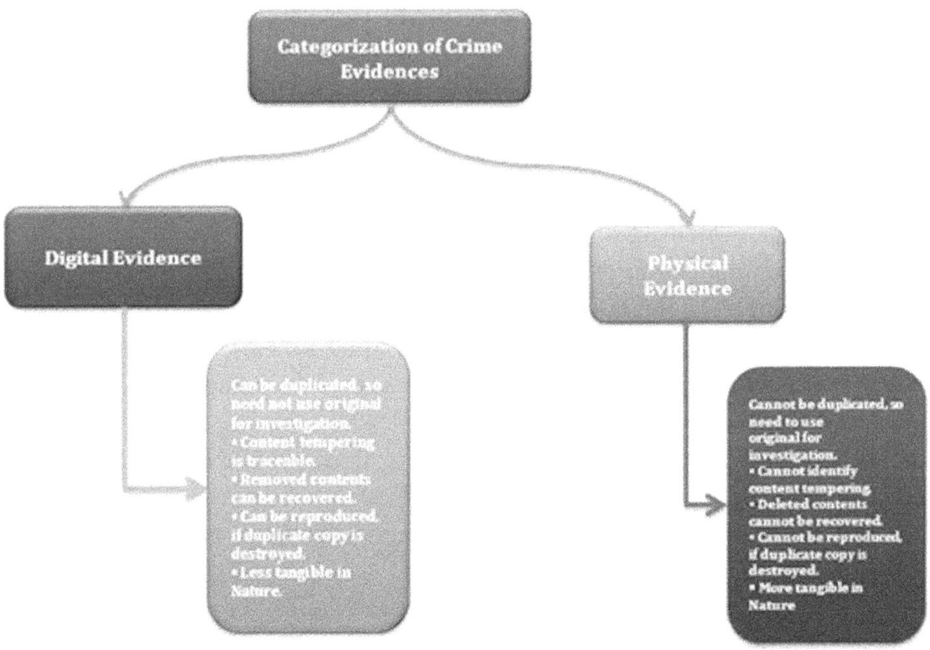


The terms "digital evidence" and "digital investigation" relate to the procedures and methods used to track down, secure, and examine digital data for use as proof in legal proceedings, whether they civil,

*Figure 5. Sources of digital evidences*

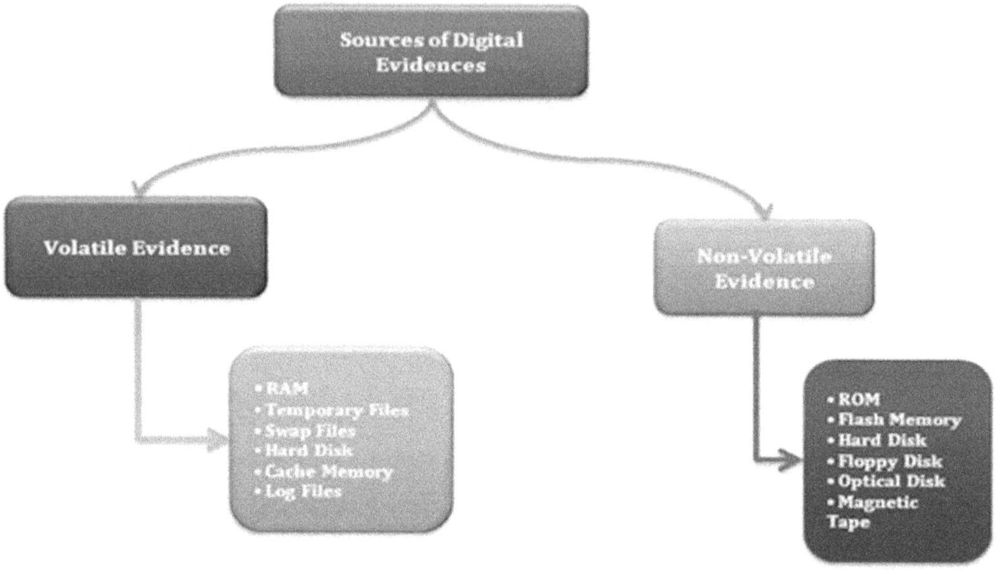


criminal, or administrative. Due to the prevalence of electronic devices, digital evidence is now an integral part of many types of criminal cases, not only those involving cybercrime.

Instances of Digital Proof: Information that has been saved in a variety of places, such as on a computer, smartphone, or other mobile device; in an email; in a database; or in the cloud. Temporary Information: This category covers things like data temporarily saved in RAM or online files that aren't meant to be around for good. Information about information, such as when a file was last edited or viewed, is known as metadata.

Identifying possible digital evidence sources in relation to an incident or crime.Preservation is keeping possible evidence unaltered while it's being used in an inquiry.The term "collection" refers to the process of gathering digital evidence from numerous locations while taking precautions to prevent any tampering with the data. Examination: The process of collecting, examining, and interpreting evidence using forensic methods and technologies.Analyzing the findings of the investigation and making connections between digital evidence and potential suspects, time periods, or events is called analysis. Documentation/Reporting: Putting together a report that makes sense, outlining the evidence, techniques, and conclusions (Ramasamy et al., 2022).

Challenges:The sheer quantity of data that investigators must go through as their storage capacity grow is a major bottleneck.

Data encryption: Without access to the appropriate decryption keys, working with encrypted data might present major difficulties.

Off-Site Cloud Storage: Data kept in cloud services may be outside of investigators' sphere of control and pose jurisdictional problems.

Law and technology meet at the convergence of digital evidence and inquiry. Digital forensics requires up-to-date methods, software, and hardware as technology advances. The combination of technological knowledge, familiarity with legal norms, and stringent methods is necessary to guarantee that digital evidence is credible and acceptable in court.

Cyber or Digital investigation's target is to find evidences admissible in the court of law, maintaining the integrity during the forensic process (Ren W. 2004). A formal report is filed (First Incident Report in India). In case information from the third party agencies or service provider is required, a notice is issued and a search warrant is obtained from competent authority to seize possible evidences. Computer emergency response team of expert reaches crime spot and collect potential evidence items, ensuring that the collection and packaging protocols are followed. Forensics analysis is performed in cyber forensics labs (Jing YN, Tu P, Wang XP, Zhang GD. 2015). Witnesses and accused are questioned and statements are documented. Statements, forensics lab reports and information from third party services providers are collectively studied and charge sheet in a legally admissible format is filed in the court.

## Evolution of Computer and Network Forensic Frameworks

The computer started its emergence in the 1940's. In the 1960's when Donn Parker began its first research on unlawful activities using a computer. Parker's research contribution for the next two decades was a remarkable milestone in the computer forensics domain. Formally, the first computer-related criminal sentenced to five-year in Texas, USA in 1966. In Late 80's as the computer became a general entity in a house, a need for a law for the emerging new class of the crime was felt and thus made. With, the exponentially increasing information revolution and communication, a formal field of computer forensic branch of the investigation came into the picture, which was further expanded to network forensic in the decade to follow. In the last couple of decades, the digital forensics have come a long way from bulky desktop's storage media forensic analysis to mobile and IoT (Internet of Things) forensics. IoT is an environment of commonly used devices (referred as objects, things or machine) enhanced with computing power and communicate through network. The continuous change in the sources of crime evidence has forced the forensic analyst to rely on network media and node analysis for evidence (Tang Y, Daniels TE. 2015). With the emerging growth of computers and network forensic tools and techniques, the investigation process has foreseen methods for exponentially emerging cyber threats. These methods mostly rely on the network node for traffic analysis and other cyberspace infrastructure (Wang D, Li T, Liu S, Zhang J, Liu C. 2017). The continuous emergence of these forensic tools is required to counterfeit the anti-forensics techniques. Cyber crime's uniform properties over the last decade have not changed a lot, but the level of sophistication and the motivation, have changed drastically.

Ad hoc Methods: In the early stages of digital crime, there was no established protocol for gathering and analyzing digital evidence. Investigators frequently relied on their familiarity with computers and networks, translating tried-and-true methods of investigation to the online world.

Innovative Examples: As more and more international peacekeeping operations took place in the late 1990's, well-substantiated standard operating procedures were the result. The "Four-Step Forensic Process" (acquisition, authentication, analysis and report) that emerged recently is an example of the most used foundational models of digital forensics and that it is used by many investigators to determine the sequence of their actions. The DIPM, namely the Carrier and Spafford's 2003 proposal, which was more advanced as compared to the previous proposals in the field of digital investigations, enhanced all aspects of the investigative process by integrating the feedback loops. Beebe and Clark, and they classified the investigation process into several levels based on the hierarchical Abstract Digital Forensic Model (ADFM) from 2005, highlighting multiple objectives at an investigation in each stage. Consequently, the process of IDIP arose as reported by Baryamureeba and Tushabe in 2004, which was presented based on the DIP. It represent the integration of conventional forensics and digital forensics into a whole technology.

Network traffic analysis, cyber-mobility, and intrusion detection technologies became the center of such frameworks as networked crimes got more and more computer network oriented. The NFAP is a process by which this "Phenomena" is able to be studied. Data now does not settle anymore on the form of physical things (devices), and these new cloud-centric models take this into consideration. Hence, the emergence of such frameworks as the "Cloud Forensic Readiness Framework' and allow the organizations to simply gather the resultant forensic evidence regularly. The only way edge forensics paper attempts to provide data collected by connected devices to be efficiently integrated is through the establishment of systems or resources that solves this in real time.

Frameworks for Adaptive Forensics: Addressing the fact it is a complex problem and given the speed at which technologies are changing, current models follow thinking that there has to be flexibility towards the approach. More than just taking up AI and ML to analyze the proof they also bring about the import for upgradation to the same concept of adapting to new information.

Digital forensics are dependent on the fact that the digital universe is dynamic and the frameworks for computer and network forensics are adapted to the change. These developments which range from simple models to AI-based cryptic engines are a testament to the fast-changing nature of the field which is adjustable to the demands for the community of the world that is interdependent.

To keep digital forensics strong in its pursuit of truth and justice, future frameworks will have to account for developments in areas like quantum computing and sophisticated neural networks.

## LITERATURE REVIEW

Cyber forensic is an investigative process that brings satisfactory evidence in the court of law. The process of scientifically proven methods includes gathering, processing, interpreting and presenting undeniable facts and digital evidence of cybercrimes, in the court of law (Kim JS, Kim M, Noh BN. 2014). In the present world of network computing, forensic techniques have been an area of interest for research and professional because of its continuously expanding domain and continuous increasing excitement and curiosity over the years. With the periodical increase in the domain, the definition and requirement of supporting tools and techniques have come a long way. Approximately, in every couple of years, the process phases for network forensics keep changing.

The context of the information keeps changing with the media transformation from data to information to evidence and finally a court-admissible form of evidence document as shown in Figure.6. Based on the target media of cybercrime, cyber forensics terminology is classified as follows:

*Figure 6. Transformation of confiscated material into evidence*

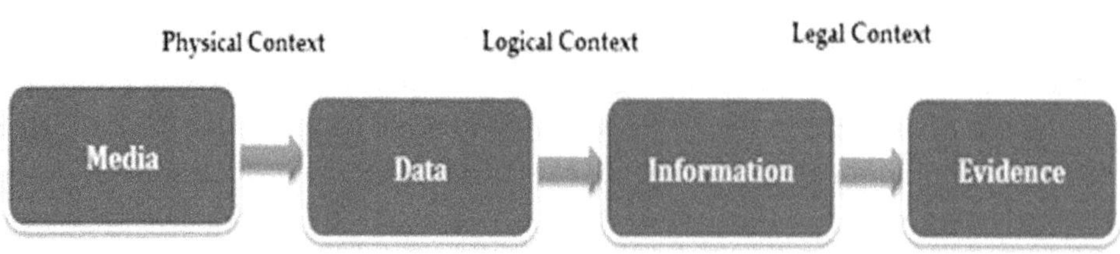

Network Forensics: Process of methodically monitoring and examining the network traffic for information congregation, legal evidence or encroachment detection (Liu Z, Feng D. 2015).

Web Forensics: Various tools and technologies are explored to take practical and appropriate actions based on collecting evidence. Hence, it aims at finding digital evidence over the World Wide Web. It is also pronounced as Network Forensics applied over the Web.

E-mail Forensics: Analyzing electronic mails using available tools and techniques to elicit facts and figures of the cybercrimes and presenting evidence found in the investigation process in court.

- Enterprise Forensics: This is classified as a category to secure the integrity and concurrency of information within an organization and prevent security attacks. Generally, it follows a protective approach and not much concerned about evidence.
- System Forensics: For collection and gathering of evidence from computing devices, system forensics used. Unlike other forensics types, it is applicable when a crime has happened via stand-alone devices.

(Anaya EA, Nakano-Miyatake M, Perez Meana HM. 2019) author's proposed an approach for big data analysis that focused on detecting anomalies in network traffic and its effect can easily be prevented with the change in network traffic distribution. These network changes can be done by finding gaps between abnormal traffic and the usual traffic. This literature is further divided into three sub models or categories to detect unusual traffic. (i) The regular traffic selection model uses the concept of differentiating anomalies from normal data traffic instead of focusing on specific anomalous behaviors. (ii) The abnormal traffic selection model focuses to ensure that there isn't too much normal traffic rather than focusing on abnormal traffic. (iii) Mixed compensation model adds the results from both the above models to produce final results. Like the Normal traffic selection sub model, this model also has the two stages: Training and Test stage. The results of the analysis were: (i) Random forest classification algorithm can cope up with any change in the traffic that might occur and deploying the proposed model can decrease the false negative rate. (ii) If the amount of training data in a separate group differs significantly, then classify model developed using decision tree would be preferred where the training data set is huge. The decision tree model should be avoided for the abnormal traffic. (iii) With the purpose to reduce false positives.

(Rekhis S,Boudriga N. 2018) author's proposes a new model using big data analytics to analyze network traffic. This model finds anomaly behavior and malicious data being transferred through the networks by loading the data into hive databases in HDFS environment. This model consists of five phases, as shown in Figure.7. Large chunks of data can be looked upon in no time using this model. Hive queries executed, and the time taken to detect anomalies was calculated. The first dataset consisting of close to 400000 packets and 50 MB, the second data set consisting of close to consisting near 3100000 packets and the third dataset had 1200000 packets adding up to 131 MB.

(Lin C, Zhitang L and Yingshu L. 2019) author's proposes the implementation of Hadoop for developing an Intrusion Detection System (IDS) which works in real-time for ultra-high-speed data. A fourlayered Intrusion detection system architecture includes layers, namely capturing, filtration and load balancing, processing or Hadoop layer and the decision-making layer. In implementing machine learning, Java programming was used along with the WEKA 3.6.12 library.

(Pallavi Asrodia and Vishal Sharma. 2013) author's proposed a Real-Time Hybrid IDS by making use of Apache Storm which is a fault tolerant, a big data stream processor that works in real time. Proposed approach performs hybrid detection, which uses Corner Classification 4 (CC4) neural network for new attacks and Multi Layer Perceptron (MLP) implementation uses misuse-based detection of existing attacks. The Apache Storm topology consists of an Input file reader called spout (stream source) which

*Figure 7. Big data analysis model using Hadoop*

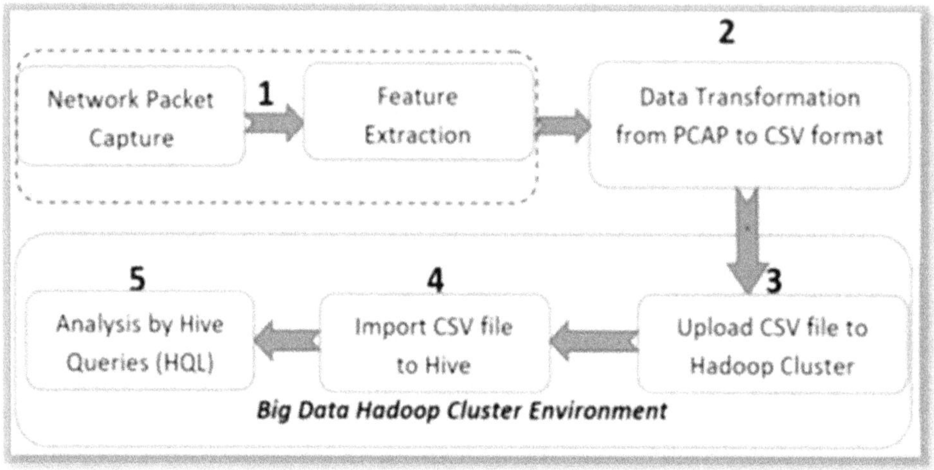


sends streams of data packets to two bolts: CC4 Launcher and MLP Launcher. The results from both MLP and CC4 networks are combined and sent to another bolt called Post- Process which classifies the output as standard data or known attack with a class or an unknown attack. The ISCX Intrusion dataset is used for simulation rather than outdated datasets like KDD '99 which does not include the latest attacks.

The proposed model was able to identify smartphones with 100% efficiency by studying the "user agent" HTTP property. Single session classifier was used to identify PCs, and its efficiency was close to 100%. IoT devices were identified with 99.28% efficiency with parameters such as model and brand. Thus, the proposed model can be used in real-world organizations to identify any authorized or unauthorized connections of IoT devices to the network.

(Jing YN, Tu P, Wang XP, Zhang GD. 2015) author's proposes a new traffic-aware system to choose essential nodes to patch for an IoT based system with constraints on process times and patching resources. The proposed model was compared to a mobile social network's real-time traffic, which consisted of 60 devices and 1750 APs. Users can communicate with each other through (i) infrastructure link via APs and (ii) direct link within transmission range. Patching can be done to keep the infrastructure links safe while the direct link still poses a threat. Instead of directly patching IoT devices already compromised, the IoT devices were secured by patching essential nodes based on traffic volume to avoid huge losses and avoid threat propagation thereby restricting it to direct links only. Experiments were conducted to verify the efficiency of this patching system, and some exciting new aspects of IoT security gazed on.

New models to prevent the propagation of malware were built upon based on this study where constraints like limited resources and non-user friendly interface still exist. The results of experiments on real-world datasets were still encouraging despite these problems.

(Wang D, Li T, Liu S, Zhang J, Liu C. 2017) author's proposed a new model called Stacked Auto Encoder (SAE) that is a stack of autoencoders, is based on traffic flow prediction using deep learning. A broad network is created using auto encoders as the roots of this model. This model is trained layer by layer while getting to know the features of traffic flow. The model parameters were then updated to increase the prediction efficiency. The dataset used to be on a freeway system with 15000 detectors and data collected every half of a minute.

## CYBER FORENSIC TECHNIQUES

This section explains the standardized set of techniques that are used each phase of the cyber forensics process, namely, collection, investigation and dispensing.

### Data Collection Techniques

***Disk Mirroring.*** The offline disk mirroring includes creating a duplicate image of a storage or logging disk. That is done to maintain the integrity of data in the original data sources. For instance, the analyst receives a confiscated disk from the crime scene for evidence extraction. So, it becomes the primary duty of the analyst to create an image of the original disk for analysis and not to start working on the original copy. Seized item's original fingerprints are required in the court. When the identical information is stored on two drives at once, the drives are said to "mirror" each other. This process is known as disk mirroring. Disk mirroring exists primarily to provide data safety in case of disaster. There is more fault tolerance since data may be retrieved from another disk if the first one fails. Although this strategy guarantees data availability, it doubles the storage space necessary because only half is really used after mirroring.

#### Important Disk Mirroring Characteristics

Redundancy: Disk mirroring is a straightforward backup method since it keeps two identical copies of data. This redundancy guarantees a fault-free experience in the event that one disk becomes unavailable due to hardware faults.

When it comes to read performance, mirrored configurations might be helpful in some systems. Data can be read from the first accessible disk when it is requested, which might increase read speeds.

For optimal write performance, both drives must be used at once. This means that, depending on the hardware, the write performance may be identical to (or perhaps slightly lower than) a single disk configuration.

Since disk mirroring requires twice as much space to store the same amount of data, it is not very storage efficient. This extra complexity is the cost of the increased reliability and fault tolerance.

Disc failures are easily recovered from since the system may switch to the healthy drive instantly. It's easy to swap out the faulty disk with a new one, and once it's in place, the RAID 1 array can be rebuilt by copying all the data from the healthy disk to the new one.

Considerations: Disk mirroring can be accomplished in two ways: either with hardware (using specific RAID controllers) or software (controlled by the operating system). Hardware RAID is more reliable, while software RAID is more adaptable and less expensive.

Encourage Uniformity: For best results when mirroring, it's best to utilize drives that are similar in every way (make, model, and capacity).

Constant Checking: Even while RAID 1 offers redundancy, it should not be relied upon as a replacement for routine backups. Regular backups and drive health checks are necessary for protecting data from accidental deletion or corruption.

Data redundancy and increased fault tolerance may be easily accomplished through the use of disk mirroring (RAID 1). In the case of a drive failure, business may continue normally because all data is duplicated. However, this redundancy reduces storage efficiency, thus the pros and cons must be weighed carefully for each application.

***Network Sniffing.*** Statistics show that more than 90% of the cybercrime occur on the wire. Network sniffing is of two distinct types: active sniffing and passive sniffing. When the switched network relies on an injected packet in the network for sniffing, is called active sniffing. Whereas sniffing that is done through a network, in which all packets flowing on the wire are scanned and captured, is called passive sniffing. Traditionally the passive sniffing was quite useful, as most of the network has the same collision domain. Since it is now obsolete, nowadays it is exhibited by SOHO networks. Hence, active sniffing is mainly used for scanning the network.

***Network Mapping.*** It is getting more complicated with the introduction of IPv6. Especially in case of the real-time corporate environment, distributed geographically, network traffic topology is logged with servers, specially designated for the task of network mapping.

***Encryption/decryption.*** There are a lot of advances and sophisticated algorithms for storing or hiding the information. So, every single piece of information retrieved during the confiscated process, is crucial and may contain crucial evidence for the court of law.

## Data Investigation Techniques

This section illustrates the techniques proposed by different researchers for investigation of the crime, using different aim and infrastructural setups.

***Trackback.*** Topology assisted Deterministic Packet Marking (TDPM) uses packet marking with hash codes mechanism to traceback DoS attacks. The router uses hash values in the packet to compare it to the victim machine. Using TDPM approach, the investigator recursively identifies the ingress router or network node that generates substantial malicious packets using the breadth first search algorithm.

Network Forensic Evidence Acquisition (NFEA) scheme works on a simple packet marking scheme, that traceback the intruder's origin with better effective tracking hop range. NFEA looks in router data and packet header, which is not the case in Collaborative Forensics Scheme (CFS). So, it has less chances to decline in system throughput. The NFEA diminish overhead of network throughput by logging edge routers, and not all network routers. However, the issue with NFEA is that it misleads the origin of the attack if the attacker hides MAC address. Also, NFEA does not work with IPv6 address. Another limitation of this approach is that the router memory when the edge router's table entries increase. These challenges lead to its scalability and reliability issue in large networks.

Lightweight IP traceback scheme (LWIP) use Time-To-Live (TTL) field of the IP header. Therefore, LWIP can investigate massive Distributed DoS attacks to reconstruct the attack path. LWIP uses tree analysis approach for analysis and routing filter algorithm for storage management to give better accuracy on colossal traffic, even if the intruder is aware of running IP traceback scheme on the victim machine for detection. The issue with LWIP scheme is decrementing a TTL value, as the traffic moves from router to router towards victim node. The issue with LWIP approach is that TTL value can be modified by an intruder and can be zero before reaching the destination. Also, it is only used for IPv4 headers, but not for IPv6 packets, which has started to dominate the Internet domain.

Scalable Network Forensic (Scalable-NF) scheme specially designed for stealthy selfpropagating intrusions to traceback the origin of the attacker, is based on massive, reliable historical network traffic trace records. Two significant issues identified in Wang D, Li T, Liu S, Zhang J, Liu C. 2017) are addressed in Scalable-NF, namely complexity due to size of data, and low data integrity issue faced by forensic analysts. Scalable-NF deals with space and time challenge efficiently and provides high accuracy to traceback stealthy attacker's origin. Logged network traffic traces are categorized into malicious traffic and regular traffic. Malicious or attack traffic is initiated by an intruder that needs to be investigated, whereas normal traffic is the usual routine traffic between ends without any interference. The random moonwalk algorithm used helps in the trace back origin of the attacker by setting up a casual tree, in which the root node is considered as the origin of intruder and the target of the forensic investigation. The issue with this approach is its depending on the accuracy and availability of historical data. The second challenge is its complexity due to the separation process of legitimate and malicious traffic. Last is the missing automation process of capturing real-time traffic and visualizing the clear image of the scenario.

Hopping Based Spread Spectrum Technique (HB-SST) is a code, frequency and time hopping-direct sequence spread spectrums technique, used to tackle attacks through anonymous communication on the network and trace back the source of an intruder. However, there are other frameworks too, that are used to help the user in communicating anonymously in the network, like. The HB-SST embed invisible pseudo-noise code with regular traffic, and this pseudocode is used to monitor malicious activity/traffic. However, scalability and time are again the limitations, especially with large datasets. Further, we cannot ignore the possibility of the pseudo-code getting identified by the intruders. Also, frequent shuffling among different frequency bands in frequency hopping-direct sequence spread spectrum, for optimizing the communication are further complicating the investigation process.

IP Traceback Protocol (ITP) is real-time online and offline periodic analysis technique for traffic, flowing through the router, to find the origin of malicious packet. A router's hash table is used for real-time analysis and compress table is used for periodic analysis. For periodic traffic investigation, router generated compressed hash tables are stored in a database. The IP packet's timestamp and MAC fields are used in ITP traceback, which keeps the integrity by using a hash function, intact. MAC field in the ITP technique helps in finding the routers through which packet has passed through, and a timestamp is used for attack's retransmission.

***Converge network Techniques.*** The voice packet travelling through one caller (sender) to another (receiver) without any interruption is called a standard voice packet. SIP and H.3231 protocols are used in voice packet on IP. Voice packet envelopes unencrypted IP addresses and ports information that helps voice protocol. Theses envelope is unencrypted as required for network address translation devices for conversion of voice traffic. Hence, unencrypted attribute increases the probability of attacks. It can lead to attacks like buffer overflow, man-in-the-middle, privacy leakage, packet flooding, eavesdropping hijacking calls, degrading call integrity and exploiting VoIP devices. Pattern-Based Network Forensics (PBNF) is a generic and systematic solution, that uses VoIP network traffic analysis technique. In the previous pattern based solution by Wang D, Li T, Liu S, Zhang J, Liu C. 2017), patterns are generated when an attack occurs whereas PBNF employs pre-decided patterns exists in the VoIP arena to capture and investigate traffic in a systematic way. It helps in stopping attacks by finding traces of the intruder and extract evidence to be presented in the court of law. PBNF consist of two parts VoIP evidence collector and analyzer. VoIP evidence collector sniffs and creates a repository of real-time attack packets by applying a filter rule set on traffic. The other component of PBNF, VoIP evidence analyzer investigates by normalizing collected data from the forensic server and log correlation. Hence, the scalability and storage are significant challenges in PBNF due to the massive amount of data in large distributed networks. VoIP Network Forensics with Digital Evidence (VoIP-NFDE) approach detect attacks by extracting malicious packets (injected by intruders) from the flowing network traffic. Traditionally, digital evidence is collected by gathering flow details of the voice packet, such as service type, TTL values, and payload. Any modification of this information is considered malicious. The VoIP-NFDE focuses on packet fields, instead of packet logs. The limitation to VoIP-NFDE is the scalability and time while dealing with large distributed networks. It also lacks the mechanism to capture disseminated voice packets in a distributed environment. Hence, leading to the problem of time and storing massive data.

***Attack Graph-Based Network Forensics Techniques.*** Attack graphs also analyze impact and scale, figure out network attack, collect evidence and harden outer network layer, with the best cost. The visualization and interaction framework is proposed for attack graphs to trace out the intrusion behavior of attacks. Finding the attack path traces is significantly a time consuming task, among a considerable number of vertices and edges in the attack graphs. Different aspects such as data reduction, attack dependency graph, virtual exploitation, and the critical system can depict attack graphs, with different approaches as suggested by [6-8]. However, effective embedded visualization in attack graphs, especially in large complex networks was required.

Real-time Attack Visualization Environment (RAVEN) architecture has effectively made it easy for the investigators, through visualizing interfaces. RAVEN approach uses human computer interaction platform with an extensive collection of gesture controls and give multiple investigators a collaborative analytical environment. Thus makes user-attach graph interaction, manageable. However, the issue with Real-time Attack Visualization Environment (RAVEN) is that has non real-time visual support, especially while dealing with the real-time environment. Another issue is the lack of a composite layout that is required in multiple attack parallel paths and reconstructing these paths. Also, the support for efficient data mining is not there, which makes it difficult for the investigator to do the retrieval of relevant information from the entire network's data.

***Distributed Network Forensics Techniques (Distributed-NFT).*** From scattered data agents at different locations, traffic data is collected by forensic servers for analysis. Distributed forensics techniques identify attack origin, react to emerging responses, and an assortment of evidence. However, distributed based NFT, have a considerable overhead for securing the server (forensic) from intruders that is scattered by the forensics network. Various distributed NFT are explained below in brief. ForNet is a distributed structure proposed to record well-organized logs at various network nodes and stores it at better places in a dispersed network. Usually, manual analysis of hosts logs and packets leads to less response time, an erroneous mechanism for logging, and logs synchronization. ForNet deals with these issues and generates evidence to be presented in the court of law. Additionally, the ForNet's application, SynApps works on each network node (switches/routers) to extract evidence flowing through the network and every logs event on the network for a longer time. Packet header information is more admissible than payload for collecting evidence of a crime.

The issue with ForNet framework is the storage of massive data in a vast network. Many malicious traces remain undetected, due to the use of lightweight IDS. Usually, undetected attacks are DoS, modifying packet headers and utilizing forensic server's resources, through rogue queries. The network logs in a node's log file are at modification risk from intruders, on insecure communication channels.

Distributed Agent-based Real-Time Network Intrusion Forensics System (DRNIFS) is a quick response adaptive technique for attacks by investigating various network system logs. The deficiency issues of non-real time frameworks like ForNet and On A Reference Model of Distributed Cooperative Network, is resolved in DRNIFS. DRNIFS consists of four modules network monitors, network investigators, network agents, and forensic network servers. Coordination between modules helps in performing real-time analysis, without any data loss, as and when an attack occurs. Network agents extract useful information about data encryption, digital signatures, and packet header information from the host forensic server through secure sockets layer. Network monitor collects network traffic, timestamp attached to every packet, and store it on disk. Forensic server changes dump and filter rule. An investigator needs to identify and a mass malicious event. Network's investigator's prime goal is to develop an intruder's biography such as a logical and physical address, phone numbers and machine configuration.

Collecting and analyzing digital evidence from a network where devices and data are spread out over several places, often internationally, is what distributed network forensics is all about. It may include a wide range of components, such as enterprise-wide networks, remote servers, and the cloud. Traditional forensics methods frequently fail in such contexts due to their expansive nature. This need led to the creation of distributed network forensics methods. Watches like tcpdump and Wireshark could be put up on a number of nodes that are across a network to perform distributed packet acquisition. Nodes' data is going to be exchanged so that a comprehensive image of network behavior will be formed. The analysing of the network data in real time through deep packet inspection (DPI) method helps in detecting outgoing activities, attacks, and unwanted activity. Database in which all the logs stored in widely distributed network should be centralized. It is much easier to do it with the help of programs, for example, Splunk or ELK Stack (Elasticsearch, Logstash, and Kibana).

Logs can, for example, be scanned automatically using scripts or other software tools that flag potential outliers or malintent. In remote imaging, methods are used to make an exact replica of data stored on remote systems, down to the last bit. This is especially helpful when forensics teams are unable to get their hands on the actual device.

Tools like FTK Imager and Memdump enable the acquisition of live data, recording the actions and states of a system without the need to shut it down for imaging the disk.

Collection of Logs, Configurations, and Other Useful Data is Made Easier with the Help of APIs Made Available by Cloud Service Providers.

Cloud-based virtual machines support snapshots, which may then be inspected visually. These records are useful because they document the system as it now exists.

Due to the large amount of data in modern dispersed networks, experts employ parallel processing methods to examine numerous data sources at once.

Big Data Analytics: Hadoop and Spark are two of the tools that can handle and analyze the enormous datasets common in today's dispersed network settings. They let us find connections between facts that would otherwise appear unconnected.

Intrusion Detection Systems (IDS): Software like Snort and Suricata is used to monitor and alert on suspicious activity across several networks in real time.

Anomaly Detection: Machine learning methods are being used more often to comprehend "typical" network activity. If anything seems out of the ordinary, it might be a sign of a security breach and could set off an alarm.

The ever-changing nature of distributed network forensics calls for a hybrid of tried-and-true forensics methods and novel methodologies adapted to large, linked systems. To ensure that investigators can successfully battle cyber dangers wherever they arise, the tools and techniques of distributed network forensics will need to develop in unison with the growth and complexity of networks.

***Intrusion Detection System based NFT.*** Usually, dynamic forensics, forensic explanation, analyze network intrusion data, and reliability of the evidence, are described by using logging approach. IDS approach is employed by many Network Forensic Tools to help investigators, in their process of finding security breaches in the network. For multiclass intrusion detection in network traffic, an ensemble based neural network approach has been suggested by [9]. This approach train by learning from interconnected neural networks. Some of the NFTs are briefly explained in the subsequent para.

Analytical Intrusion Detection Framework (AIDF) has been proposed for integrating forensic analysis and coordinates alarm data from IDS sensors for intrusion detection, resulting in the legal description based on the non-documented signature rule and IDS alerts. AIDF uses probabilistic methods that reveal covered information and pre-structured possible attacks, thus reducing the scope of network attacks by intruders. That is done by matching each network packet, with pre-defined signature's encoded patterns. Snort is a useful probabilistic tool used by AIDF to trigger a rule, if network traffic data match with an encoded pattern in the signature rule. The similar attacks can be detected, understood and prevented, by continually updating rules, with the network investigators.

The problem with the AIDF framework is limited to, sufficient rule base for unhandled hidden data, which is necessary for generating future intrusion detection alarms. Adequate checking rules save investigators time and increase accuracy in alerts. AIDF is especially useful for raising intrusion alarms, in a real-time environment.

## Evidence Dispensing Techniques

Briefly, introduces the techniques used by the investigator for making the evidence court ready. This section introduces some of those techniques. The purposeful manipulation, destruction, or concealment of physical or digital evidence is known as "evidence dispensing" or "evidence tampering." Despite the common association of this phrase with criminal or harmful acts, a grasp of these methods from a forensics perspective is essential for maintaining the credibility of an investigation and spotting instances of evidence manipulation.

***Proof Visualization.*** Multiple existing techniques and framework that have embedded proof visualization module are discussed, such as EnCase, FTK, Nuix, Oxygen, and XRY. Notwithstanding the significance of visualization in the forensic analysis process, this has all the earmarks of being an understudied region. The term "proof visualization" is the practice of presenting proof or arguments in a graphical or visual manner to improve comprehension and communication, especially in difficult situations. Visualizing evidence may be extremely useful in many different contexts, including judicial procedures, scientific study, and even cybersecurity.Significance of Seeing Evidence: Complexity Many topics, especially those with a technical or scientific bent, require simplification. The use of visuals helps simplify otherwise incomprehensible information. Attention: Visual material is more likely to grab and keep a viewer's attention than text alone. Effective visuals may sway audiences, especially in formal or deliberative settings like the courtroom or the boardroom. Visual information is easier to remember than written information. Visualization aids in the recognition of trends, correlations, and outliers in data sets.

***Crime Simulation and Reconstruction.*** With digital crimes, the focus is usually on the identification and cataloguing of digital evidence using an item's characteristics, but not on series of the events that resulted in a crime. So, the focus on the identifying the crime sequence is equally crucial regarding presenting the evidence in the court of law. Usually, the crime event reconstruction model consists of five steps: a) Evidence Examination; b) Role Classification; c) Event construction and testing; d) Event sequencing; e) Hypothesis testing .

The first step is to examine the evidence item thoroughly. It includes all steps from recognizing the potential items from the objects seized from the crime scene to elicit the pieces of evidence. The second step after each piece of evidence is recognized, is to interpret the condition of an evidence item and the conceivable occasions it engaged with the sequence of events. The role classification step intends to recognize the features that are linked to the crime and are the outcome of an incident or the cause of an episode. The third phase is initiated with the gathering of objects and their functions and properties and conclude with a bunch of unordered or partly established events that may have happened, which led to the crime. Then each possible event or scenarios are tested to check if the event may have caused the assault. Fourth step is event sequencing, in which series of events are identified in the previous step, should to correlate. If the control stream of an executable or process is known, then that knowledge can be used to sequence happenings that led to a charge. Finally, the fifth step in the sequence is hypothesis testing. The phenomenon of hypothesis testing for cybercrime scenes is similar to usual crime scenes. In the final stage of the investigation, a hypothesis established about the absent events after the order of event successions. A confidence level is attached to each hypothesis, and each hypothesis are examined to identify which was most likely, and the evidence refuted. Knowledge of ways to launch cyber-attack plays a vital role in this phase. It helps to identify all possible sequences the events that may have occurred, resulting in an assault. Stephenson's Petri net hypotheses model for hypothesis testing is used in this phase. Researchers have significantly worked on event reconstruction using hard disk (using signatures, using event correlation and using miscellaneous techniques; using memory evidences and using network evidences. the criminal justice system, forensic specialists and detectives frequently employ crime Within simulation and reconstruction techniques to rebuild and comprehend the likely course of a crime. The offenders' and victims' behaviors, the events' chronology, and any prospective evidence can all be better understood with this knowledge.Creating fictitious situations or models to investigate potential criminal scenarios is known as "crime simulation." It's utilized to check if a proposed theory regarding the crime's perpetration follows a logical chain of events or approaches.

Applications:Crime scene or event digital models are created using software, frequently utilizing 3D visuals and physics engines.Using actual objects to examine how they could break under stress is an example of physical simulation.

Crime reconstruction is the process of piecing together the most likely sequence of events that occurred during a crime using physical evidence from the site, eyewitness accounts, and other sources. Applications:Analysis of a bullet's trajectory can shed light on the whereabouts of the shooter and the order of bullets fired. Analysis of bloodstain patterns can disclose information such as the direction of an attack or the number of hits a victim received. Reconstructing what happened in a car crash by figuring out what happened before, during, and after the incident. Crime scenes can be better understood by jurors through the use of digital reconstructions, in which 3D models are used to recreate the scenario.

***Legal Document Formatting.*** The final step in the investigation of the cybercrime is to bring the digital evidence along with the physical evidence, like photographs, sketches of events, call graphs, and data records. The analyzed and documented digital evidence shuffled, in a legally accepted format, to be acceptable in the court of law. Also, the pieces of evidence that need to adhere and the process to elicit them may be the same in a distributed geographically divided area, or it may differ from one jurisdiction area to another. Reason being the variance in the acceptability and advancements in the cyber laws from one country or state to another. That is, cyberstalking may be legal in one and illegal in another. Moreover, also the sentence in cyber laws may differ, like misusing credential in one state may be penalized for six months, and three years in another state.

## Cyber Forensic Tools

The standardized set of available tools for each phase of the cyber forensics process, is illustrated in this section. These tools facilitate or support the task of the investigator in the analysis. Most of the sophisticated legally accepted frameworks used by legal cybercrime team for forensic investigations, consist of bunch (kit/suite) of multiple tools used at multiple stages. Well-known suite is used at multiple phases of cyber forensics. Hence, the suite/toolkits/bunch are listed below in Figure.8, with corresponding stage/ phases, at which the toolkit is used.

## CONCLUSION

The current research work extracts the relevant data from studies on the forensics of the network and computer and data. It explains the different phases of the digital forensics and compares the research, forensics techniques used at different stages from confiscating the digital media to reconstructing the crime scene in the court of law. With the increasing number of cybercrimes, the cyber forensics is a highly challenging task regarding time consumption and miss-ratio at high speeds, which usually leads to colossal resource utilization for final analysis. The critical parameters for this analysis were volume, variety, and velocity (3V's) of traffic data under investigation. Cyber forensics is an enormous and rapidly developing field. The growing prevalence of cybercrime and complexity of the digital world highlight the need for improved cyber forensics methods. These resources are crucial in the fight against cybercrime and the pursuit of those responsible for it.

*Figure 8. Commonly used network and computer forensics tools to support investigations*

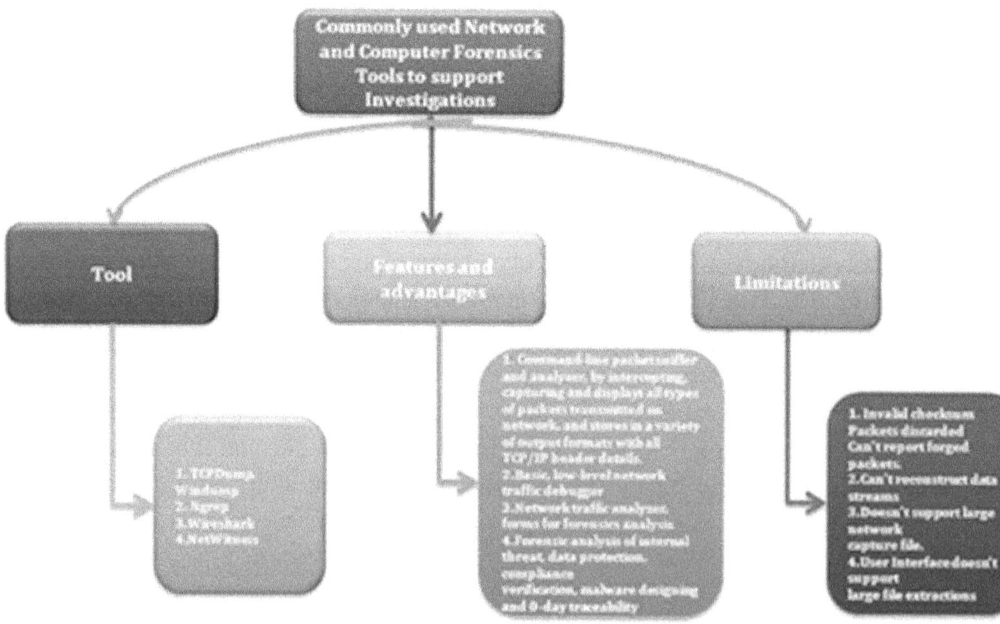

The investigation is performed employing the multiple techniques, like imaging and network analysis, and it can also focus on mobile data extraction. We can see that there is a plethora of software ranging from free to premium that is mandatory during forensics studies and used by security professionals along with law enforcement agencies around the world. The way forensic experts use these tool is to a high extent what determines the success the outcomes of the investigations.

On top of this, an increase in the development of advanced computing technologies like quantum computing, augmented reality, and IoT, would also mean more need for enhanced forensic equipment. That fulfills the need of the criminal justice system professionals to respond to the dilemmas and complexities that form a result of these programs.

Cyber forensics has been proved to be an irreplaceable pillar of the cyber security defense and order. Whereas their primary role is the collection and analysis of data, the tools in the field of big data are involved in the maintenance of principles from the digital era like honesty, transparency, and integrity. In future, no doubt financial world will be correlated digitally. Hence, safeguarding of linked digital environment with human skills and designer tools will be the criteria in future. The subchapter is dedicated to computer and network forensic process, and the approaches, used by the computer forensics & network forensics, to obtain evidence are discussed along with the resources they use.

## REFERENCE

Anaya, E. A., Nakano-Miyatake, M., & Perez Meana, H. M. (2019) Network forensics with Neurofuzzy techniques. In: *52nd IEEE international Midwest Symposium on Circuits and Systems (MWSCAS '19)*. IEEE.

Choubisa, M., Doshi, R., Khatri, N., & Hiran, K. K. (2022, May). A simple and robust approach of random forest for intrusion detection system in cyber security. In *2022 International conference on IoT and blockchain technology (ICIBT)* (pp. 1-5). IEEE. 10.1109/ICIBT52874.2022.9807766

Easwaran, B., Hiran, K. K., Krishnan, S., & Doshi, R. (Eds.). (2022). *Real-time applications of machine learning in cyber-physical systems*. IGI global. doi:10.4018/978-1-7998-9308-0

Hunt, R., & Zeadally, S. (2012, December). Network Forensics: An Analysis of Techniques, Tools, and Trends. *Computer*, *45*(12), 36–43. doi:10.1109/MC.2012.252

Jing, Y. N., Tu, P., Wang, X. P., & Zhang, G. D. (2015). *Distributed-log-based scheme for IP traceback*. The fifth international conference on Computer and Information Technology (CIT' 15), Shanghai, China.

Kim, J. S., Kim, M., & Noh, B. N. (2014). A fuzzy expert system for network forensics. In *Computational science and its applications* (Vol. 3043, pp. 175–182). Springer.

Lin, C., Zhitang, L., Cuixia, G., & Yingshu, L. (2019) Modeling and analyzing dynamic forensics system based on intrusion tolerance. In: *Ninth IEEE international conference on computer and information technology*, (pp 230–235). IEEE.

Liu, Z., & Feng, D. (2015). Incremental fuzzy decision tree-based network forensic system. In Y. Hao, J. Liu, Y. P. Wang, Y. M. Cheung, H. Yin, L. Jiao, J. Ma, & Y. C. Jiao (Eds.), *Computational intelligence and security* (Vol. 3802, pp. 995–1002). Springer. doi:10.1007/11596981_148

Mate, M. H., & Kapse, S. R. (2015). Network Forensic Tool — Concept and Architecture. *2015 Fifth International Conference on Communication Systems and Network Technologies*. IEEE. 10.1109/CSNT.2015.204

Merlette, D., & Pruthi, D. P. (2013). *Network security; NetDetector: identifying real threats and securing your network*. Niksun. https://www.niksun.com/, 09 Dec 2013.

Mijwil, M. M., Doshi, R., Hiran, K. K., Al-Mistarehi, A. H., & Gök, M. (2022). Cybersecurity Challenges in Smart Cities: An Overview and Future Prospects. *Mesopotamian journal of cybersecurity,* 1-4.

Pallavi, A. & Vishal, S. (2013). Network Monitoring and Analysis by Packet Sniffing Method. *International Journal of Engineering Trends and Technology (IJETT).*

Patel, S., Vyas, A. K., & Hiran, K. K. (2022). Infrastructure health monitoring using signal processing based on an industry 4.0 System. *Cyber-Physical Systems and Industry*, *4*, 249–260.

Ramasamy, J., & Doshi, R. (2022). Machine learning in cyber physical systems for healthcare: brain tumor classification from MRI using transfer learning framework. In *Real-Time Applications of Machine Learning in Cyber-Physical Systems* (pp. 65–76). IGI global. doi:10.4018/978-1-7998-9308-0.ch005

Rekhis, S., Krichene, J., & Boudriga, N. (2018) DigForNet: digital forensic in networking. In: Jajodia S, Samarati P, Cimato S (eds) IFIP TC-11 *23rd international information security conference, 278.* Springer, Boston.

Ren, W. (2004) On a network forensics model for information security. *3rd international conference on Information Systems Technology and its Applications (ISTA 2004)*, Utah, USA.

Shanmugasundaram, K., Memon, N., Savant, A., & Bronnimann, H. (2003). ForNet: a distributed forensics network. In V. Gorodetsky, L. Popyack, & V. Skormin (Eds.), *Computer network security* (Vol. 2776, pp. 1–16). Springer. doi:10.1007/978-3-540-45215-7_1

Shrivastava, G., & Gupta, B. B. (2014). An Encapsulated Approach of Forensic Model for digital investigation. *2014 IEEE 3rd Global Conference on Consumer Electronics (GCCE),* (pp. 280–284). IEEE. 10.1109/GCCE.2014.7031241

Skouby, K. E., Williams, I., Dhotre, P., & Hiran, K. K. (2022). Introduction: Wireless networks and privacy in developing countries. In 5G, Cybersecurity and Privacy in Developing Countries (pp. 1-18). River Publishers. doi:10.1201/9781003374664

Tang, Y., & Daniels, T. E. (2015) A simple framework for distributed forensics. In: *25th IEEE International Conference on Distributed Computing Systems Workshops (ICDCS 15),* (pp. 163–169). IEEE.

Unogwu, O. J., Hiran, K. K., Doshi, R., & Dadhich, M. (2022). Integrating InSAR, GNSS, IoT, 5G, and Cybersecurity for Earthquakes/Tremor Monitoring and Forecasting in Abuja, Nigeria. In 5G, Cybersecurity and Privacy in Developing Countries (pp. 195-209). River Publishers.

Wang, D., Li, T., Liu, S., Zhang, J., & Liu, C. (2017). *Dynamical network forensics based on immune agent. Third International Conference on Natural Computation (ICNC 2017)*, Haikou, Hainan, China.

# Chapter 13
# Market Segmentation in Higher Education:
## Enhancing Personalization in Education Using Market Segmentation

**Kritika Jaiswal**
*KIET Group of Institutions, India*

**Juhi Singh**
*KIET Group of Institutions, India*

**Minal Singh**
*KIET Group of Institutions, India*

**Muskan Sama**
*KIET Group of Institutions, India*

**Swasti Singhal**
*KIET Group of Institutions, India*

## ABSTRACT

*This chapter's primary focus is to investigate the multifaceted nature of variables that influence the enrollment procedure in private educational institutions. A comprehensive analysis of various elements, including teaching faculty, curriculum quality, and infrastructure, reveals their significant impact on students' choices when choosing a college or university. However, with the rapid proliferation of digital technologies, online marketing has become a crucial factor in attracting potential students. As such, this study seeks to identify and evaluate these factors to enable higher education administrators to design tailored strategies and enhance their institutional competitiveness. This chapter also delves deeper into predictive analytics and how they assist in crafting personalized learning experiences. Additionally, this book chapter discusses strategies for student retention and the important discusses strategies for student retention and the importance of continuous improvement. Ethical considerations in data usage will be a central theme throughout the chapter.*

DOI: 10.4018/979-8-3693-2440-0.ch013

## INTRODUCTION

Machine learning (Davari et al., 2018) (ML) is transforming market segmentation (Hemsley-Brown, 2020) in higher education (Canterbury, 2000) through tailored marketing, customized programs, improved student retention, optimization of resources, enhanced alumni engagement, and data-driven decisions using clustering, predictive analytics, and personalized learning experiences. Predictive analytics help create personalized learning experiences, and future trends include increased use of AI and natural language processing in higher education (Canterbury, 2000).

Higher education (Canterbury, 2000) institutions are leveraging Machine learning (Davari et al., 2018) (ML) to segment their student population and tailor offerings to meet unique needs and preferences (Zhu & Liu, 2023), adapting to a constantly evolving landscape where diversified learning experiences and niche programs are in high demand. This involves recognizing various factors influencing students' (Rizvi, 2023) choices and adjusting curriculum, services, and messaging accordingly. By segmenting the student population, institutions can improve engagement, enrollment, and overall success through targeted approaches.

In today's rapidly changing higher education (Canterbury, 2000) landscape, segmenting students (Rizvi, 2023) based on their needs and preferences (Zhu & Liu, 2023) is crucial for institutions to thrive. Understanding the diverse characteristics of different groups enables tailored approaches to enhance engagement, enrollment, and overall success. This chapter provides insights into market segmentation (Hemsley-Brown, 2020) principles to help higher education (Canterbury, 2000) professionals adapt to the evolving educational environment.

This chapter embarks on an exploration of market segmentation (Hemsley-Brown, 2020) in higher education, delving into its theoretical foundations, practical applications, and the transformative impact it can have on institutional strategies (Tynan, 2015). Market segmentation (Hemsley-Brown, 2020) in higher education (Canterbury, 2000) is analyzed for its theoretical underpinnings and real-world implications, including how it can help institutions better understand students (Rizvi, 2023)' needs and tailor their strategies (Tynan, 2015) accordingly.

As the market economy grows, there is an increase in foreign economic activity and an interest in marketing as a way to manage and understand consumer behavior. Marketing in higher education (Canterbury, 2000) involves tailoring academic programs to individual student needs, with an emphasis on personalized learning experiences. New technologies allow for more effective targeting of students (Rizvi, 2023), and universities are now seen as service providers in a competitive marketplace. It mainly focuses on examining student diversity cases, best practices, and trends.

The chapter discusses the significance of understanding and catering to the unique needs of students (Rizvi, 2023) in higher education (Canterbury, 2000) through market segmentation (Hemsley-Brown, 2020). It highlights how this approach can improve student satisfaction, academic performance, and institutional resilience in a rapidly evolving educational environment.

## ENHANCING PERSONALIZATION IN EDUCATION

Enhancing personalization in education is an ongoing process that involves a combination of technology (The Future Era of Computing: Automatic Computing, 2023), pedagogical approaches, and a commitment to meeting the diverse needs of each student. Personalized learning is crucial for improving learning outcomes. Enhancing personalization in higher education (Canterbury, 2000) involves tailoring the learning experience to meet individual students (Rizvi, 2023)' needs, preferences (Zhu & Liu, 2023), and goals. Key aspects include implementing adaptive learning platforms, providing personalized feedback and recommendations, offering customized learning paths, utilizing data-driven insights, and providing personalized support services such as academic advising and mentorship. Additionally, incorporating interactive and collaborative learning experiences and recognizing prior learning are also important ways to enhance personalization in higher education. By doing so, institutions can create a more customized and effective learning environment that meets the unique needs of each student.

## THE LANDSCAPE OF HIGHER EDUCATION

Before diving into the intricacies of ML-based market segmentation (Hemsley-Brown, 2020), let's briefly examine the evolving landscape of higher education. Today, institutions face unique challenges, including demographic shifts, financial pressures, and the growing demand for personalized learning experiences. In this environment, understanding the student population is critical to achieving sustainable growth and relevance. The landscape of higher education (Canterbury, 2000) is constantly evolving due to various factors such as globalization, technological integration, diversity and inclusion, changing demographics, rising costs, employability, quality assurance, research and innovation, and changing pedagogies. These factors shape the overall environment, trends, challenges, and characteristics of the post-secondary education sector. Governments also play a crucial role in regulating and influencing these changes through policies and funding initiatives.

Machine learning (Davari et al., 2018) has proven to be a game-changer across various industries, including education. Its ability to process vast datasets and uncover hidden patterns makes it an ideal tool for market segmentation (Hemsley-Brown, 2020) in higher education. ML can analyze numerous variables, such as demographic information, academic history, socioeconomic status, and even online behavior, to identify distinct student segments.

This chapter explores the intersection of ML and higher education (Canterbury, 2000) to uncover the profound insights it offers for tailoring educational offerings and strategies (Tynan, 2015) to diverse student populations.

Due to technological advancements and the growing significance of data-driven decision-making, the higher education (Canterbury, 2000) landscape is undergoing a profound transformation.

## PREVIOUS ANALYSIS IN THE FIELD OF SEGMENTATION

Customer segmentation (Hemsley-Brown, 2020) utilizes Machine learning (Davari et al., 2018) (ML) techniques to group customer (Vieri et al., 2023)s based on shared attributes or behaviors, enabling organizations to tailor products and services to specific market segments. By leveraging the capabilities of ML algorithms, businesses can identify subtle yet meaningful differences within their customer (Vieri et al., 2023) base, thereby reducing risk through targeted marketing initiatives. This approach replaces the conventional practice of catering to a broad spectrum of customer (Vieri et al., 2023) without any individualized focus.

There exist multiple strategies (Tynan, 2015) for segmentation (Davari et al., 2018); however, ML methodologies possess unparalleled accuracy and precision when it comes to extracting valuable insights and complex patterns from customer (Vieri et al., 2023) data. These advanced techniques offer several advantages over traditional methods, including scalability, reduced computational time, and the ability to retrain models as necessary.

## Customer Segmentation

In an effort to tailor marketing strategies (Tynan, 2015) to specific customer (Vieri et al., 2023) subgroups with similar requirements, market segmentation (Hemsley-Brown, 2020) involves dividing a broad consumer base into distinct categories. This process enables businesses to identify and prioritize particular client subsets that share comparable wants or behaviors, allowing them to develop bespoke tactics that cater to these clients' unique demands. By doing so, companies may better understand their consumers and improve both their market standing and overall corporate worth. According to Camille (2016), this practice allows firms to create a structured approach by pinpointing key elements such as purchasing habits, lifestyle characteristics, geographic location, and other relevant variables. Segmentation (Hemsley-Brown, 2020) assists companies in staying ahead of industry rivals while simultaneously giving customer (Vieri et al., 2023)s more control over formulating successful marketing plans. As Stangel (2017) notes, segmentation (Hemsley-Brown, 2020) enables enterprises to adapt their offerings to match customer (Vieri et al., 2023)s' preferences (Zhu & Liu, 2023), resulting in higher satisfaction levels among those groups. Overall, market segmentation (Hemsley-Brown, 2020) has become an essential tool for businesses seeking to expand their reach within existing markets or venture into new ones successfully.

## Student Recruitment Process

According to Turner's (1978) seminal work, the "Enrolment Funnel" model describes the sequential progression of five distinct stages that potential students (Rizvi, 2023) undergo during their journey toward matriculation at a higher educational institution (HEI). These stages include:

1. Applicant (Stage 1): At this initial phase, individuals become aware of and express interest in the HEI. This stage is characterized by the activation of their curiosity regarding the institution's offerings as well as their desire to learn more. As observed by Copeland (2009) and Gerdzhikov (2015), prospective students (Rizvi, 2023) may initiate inquiries to satisfy their needs and gain further knowledge about the institution.
2. Interrogation (Stage 2): During this second stage, individuals actively seek additional information about the HEI through various means, such as visiting its website, attending open days, or interacting with admissions staff. As noted by Hossler (1999), the primary objective of the inquirer is to comprehend the value proposition of the institution and determine whether it aligns with their interests and goals. By successfully addressing these concerns, the HEI can generate a pool of qualified applicants.
3. Respondent (Stage 3): The interviewee stage represents the transformation of a prospect into an actual applicant. This transition occurs when the individual is given the opportunity to engage in a meaningful dialogue with representatives from the HEI, allowing them to acquire a deeper understanding of the institution's programs and culture. As highlighted by Copeland (2009) and

Gerdzhikov (2005), the interviewee plays a crucial role in guiding new students (Rizvi, 2023) through the enrollment process and providing valuable insights to ensure a smooth transition.

4. Admitted Student (Stage 4): Once the application has been submitted and processed, the individual becomes an acknowledged student, signalling their formal acceptance into the HEI. During this fourth stage, they begin to focus on securing necessary resources, including financial aid, housing, and other forms of support. As discussed by Hossler (1999) and Copeland (2009), this period is critical in determining the overall satisfaction and success of the student within the institution.
5. Enrolled Student (Stage 5): Finally, upon completing all administrative tasks and fees associated with registration, the student formally enters the final stage of the enrolment funnel–registered status. Maringe Gibbs (2009) notes that at this point, attention shifts from recruitment to retention strategies (Tynan, 2015), aimed at ensuring long-term commitment to learning and fostering a positive student experience.

In conclusion, the Enrollment Funnel Framework offers a structured approach to understanding the complex dynamics involved in the admission process of higher educational institutions. By recognizing each stage's unique functions and characteristics, stakeholders can develop targeted interventions to optimize student outcomes throughout every phase of the journey.

## Emotional Segments

The Damasio-LeDoux factor emphasizes the role of internal and external influences, including socio-cultural elements such as family, friends, and social support (Young, 2002; Avrahami and Dar, 2004), as well as intrinsic aspects like identity, personal values, desires, and expectations (Chapman, 2006). According to Pyvis (2006), the emotional perspective holds significant value in marketing due to its ability to capture the subtle emotional associations linked to consumer needs and preferencesr (Zhu & Liu, 2023), particularly through the use of sounds and images (Hirschman and Holbrook, 1982).

## Rational Segments

This methodology seeks to gather data pertaining to the key characteristics of a given product (S. Schiffman and R. Kanuk, 1994), utilizing this information to predict consumer choice by identifying the most desirable aspects of each item available in the marketplace (A. Ajzen and M. Fishbein, 1980; I. Bettman, 1979).

## Digital Advertisement

Following extensive and engaging examinations, numerous scholars have recognized the crucial role that online advertising plays in disseminating novel information regarding businesses to users. Through strategic digital marketing initiatives, these ads aim to redirect consumers' attention towards digital channels, thereby influencing their perceptions and behaviors (Hampel, 2012; Chao, 2012). By fostering mutual understanding between marketers and customer (Vieri et al., 2023)s through carefully crafted promotional messages, this suboptimal campaign also serves to safeguard brand reputation while exerting substantial influence over the digital environment for assessing its consequences (Flosis et al., 2013).

## Customer Relationship Marketing (CRM)

The Customer (Vieri et al., 2023) Relationship Management (CRM (Sotomayor-Vidal et al., 2023)) system has the potential to significantly enhance overall customer (Vieri et al., 2023) satisfaction, loyalty, and engagement by implementing effective leadership, resource management, targeted marketing strategies (Tynan, 2015), and influence tactics (Bull, 2003; Bompolis and Boutsouki, 2014). By analyzing the benefits of CRM (Sotomayor-Vidal et al., 2023) implementation in terms of reduced costs and improved quality relationships with customer (Vieri et al., 2023)s, it becomes evident that this system can lead to increased customer (Vieri et al., 2023) loyalty and retention (Soltani Navimipour, 2016). Furthermore, understanding the impact of CRM (Sotomayor-Vidal et al., 2023) on organizational factors is crucial in establishing a comprehensive cross-functional framework for managing customer (Vieri et al., 2023) interactions within business-to-business (B2B) organizations (Lambert, 2009; Luck and Lancastyer, 2003).

## OBJECTIVE OF THIS RESEARCH

The goal of the dataset is to learn about student preferences (Zhu & Liu, 2023), how they make decisions, financial factors, academic and infrastructure preferences (Zhu & Liu, 2023), extracurricular and sports choices, internship and placement considerations, location and travel preferences (Zhu & Liu, 2023), satisfaction with college facilities, feedback for improvement, trends and the importance of alumni networks, segmentation analysis, regional analysis, comparison of day scholars and hostellers, and comparison of postgraduate and undergraduate students (Rizvi, 2023). Additionally, it aims to comprehend the impact of financial assistance, academic variables, faculty evaluations, and college facilities on the selection of colleges. The dataset also seeks to evaluate the importance of extracurricular activities, sports, and alumni networks on college choices. The research aims to investigate the impact of location and travel time on college selection, as well as the level of satisfaction with campus amenities. The dataset aims to analyze trends and the importance of the alumni network, categorize students (Rizvi, 2023) into different categories based on their preferences (Zhu & Liu, 2023), demographics, and decision-making criteria, and compare the preferences (Zhu & Liu, 2023) and decision-making criteria of postgraduate and undergraduate students (Rizvi, 2023).

## TYPES OF MACHINE LEARNING TECHNIQUES

**Supervised learning** – This algorithm relies on pre-existing datasets to develop functional models capable of accurately assigning labels to novel inputs. By leveraging this trained information, these algorithms can generate predictions regarding the output values associated with newly encountered instances. The main goal of supervised learning (Detection of Weed by Using Hybrid Technique, 2023) is to get better at making predictions by finding the right classification (Singh & Singhal, 2020) assignments for samples that haven't been seen before. Depending on the type of input data, the outputs can be either continuous or categorical.

Example: Face recognition and house price prediction.

**Unsupervised learning** - Unsupervised learning (Detection of Weed by Using Hybrid Technique, 2023) is a Machine learning (Davari et al., 2018) technique in which models are not supervised using a training dataset. Models uncover hidden patterns in data. It can be compared to learning, which can take place in the human brain while learning new things. The main aim of this algorithm is to categorize the unlabeled dataset according to its similarities, patterns, and differences.

Example: Customer Segmentation and Market Basket Analysis.

**Semi-supervised learning** - Semi-supervised learning (Detection of Weed by Using Hybrid Technique, 2023) combines the strengths of both supervised and unsupervised learning by utilizing a limited number of labeled examples alongside an abundance of unlabeled data. This approach enables models to learn from less labeled data while still leveraging the advantages of supervised learning's structured guidance and unsupervised learning's ability to discover hidden patterns. In other words, semi-supervised learning allows for efficient and effective training of models with fewer labeled samples. Semi-supervised learning leverages limited labeled data to train models on vast amounts of unlabeled text.

Ex: Text classification (Singh & Singhal, 2020) and Lane finding on GPS data.

**Reinforcement learning** - In reinforcement learning (RL), an agent interacts with an environment to learn how to make decisions that maximize rewards. The agent observes the current state, selects an action, and receives feedback in the form of rewards or penalties. The goal is to learn a policy that maps states to actions for optimal decision-making. Key components include the agent, environment, states, actions, and rewards. The RL process involves observing the state, selecting an action, transitioning to a new state, receiving a reward, and updating the policy. This paradigm has been successful in various applications, such as game playing, robotics, and finance, where solving problems through direct programming is difficult.

Ex: Optimized Marketing, Driverless Cars.

## THE ROLE OF DATA AND MACHINE LEARNING IN MODERN EDUCATION

Data has become a cornerstone of modern education. Institutions collect vast amounts of information from various sources, including admission forms, learning management systems, and social media interactions. The role of data and Machine learning (Davari et al., 2018) in modern education is transformative, revolutionizing the way educational institutions operate, teachers teach, and students (Rizvi, 2023) learn. Data and Machine learning (Davari et al., 2018) are transforming education by providing valuable insights into student populations, allowing for personalized and targeted learning experiences that improve outcomes and enhance institutional performance.

It is a dynamic process that requires continuous evaluation and adjustment to remain responsive to the evolving needs of students (Rizvi, 2023) and the institution. To segment the dataset, this chapter uses clustering techniques, specifically k-means clustering, which is a common method for segmenting data based on similar characteristics. Before we begin, it's essential to preprocess the data, handle missing values, and encode categorical variables. Afterward, we can apply k-means clustering to group students (Rizvi, 2023) with similar responses to the provided questions.

The integration of data and Machine learning (Davari et al., 2018) in modern education holds immense potential for enhancing the learning experience, improving educational outcomes, and shaping the future of teaching and learning.

## CLASSIFICATION OF MARKET SEGMENTATION

Market research employs multiple variables and methodologies to classify segmentation (Davari et al., 2018) into four primary categories.

1. Geographic - This entails dividing a target market into distinct segments based on geographical considerations. By catering products and marketing strategies (Tynan, 2015) to each locality's unique requirements, businesses may better comprehend these customer (Vieri et al., 2023)s' wants and inclinations via geographic segmentation (Hemsley-Brown, 2020). For instance, it might be possible to divide clients by country, state, city, or postal code.
2. Demographic – This identifies markets based on various demographic elements such as birth, marital standing, education level, and occupation. Demographic segmentation (Hemsley-Brown, 2020) assists organizations in understanding and focusing on particular customer (Vieri et al., 2023) groups with comparable demographic profiles, thereby adjusting their goods, services, and advertising initiatives to match their special tastes and interests. Demographic information can sometimes be collected from polls and other sources.
3. Behavioral - This separates buyers depending on how they behave toward commodities, ideas, and services. This technique acknowledges that people who share comparable conduct patterns are more likely to react similarly to marketing appeals and provides. Groupings established using behavioral segmentation (Davari et al., 2018) enable firms to create individualized marketing campaigns. For example, attitude toward a certain good, company, or service qualifies as behavioral segmentation (Hemsley-Brown, 2020).
4. Psychographic – This splits clients into groups determined by their mental and way-of-life features for individually tailored promotional tactics. Unlike demographic segmentation (Hemsley-Brown, 2020), which concentrates on observable personality characteristics, psychographic segmentation (Davari et al., 2018) examines consumers' inner motivations, attitudes, and emotions. Through analyzing these facets, companies may develop targeted advertising plans that resonate with their intended audience. Examples of psychographic segmentation (Davari et al., 2018) include one's views, hobbies, way of living, reputation, and pursuits.

## JUPYTER NOTEBOOK

Jupyter Notebooks are web-based apps for creating and sharing interactive documents with live code, equations, visuals, and text, combining elements from several programming languages like Julia, Python, and R. It has now become a popular tool for various programming languages.

i. Features:
   - Interactive Execution: Jupyter Notebooks allow you to execute code cells interactively, making it easy to test and debug code step by step.
   - Markdown Support: You can use Markdown cells to include formatted text, images, and hyperlinks to create rich and informative documents.
   - Visualization: Jupyter supports the integration of various libraries for data visualization, such as Matplotlib and Seaborn for Python.

ii. Collaboration:
   - Sharing: Notebooks can be easily shared with others, either by sharing the file directly or by using platforms like GitHub, Google Drive, or Microsoft One-Drive.
   - Real-time Collaboration: Some platforms allow real-time collaboration, enabling multiple users to work on the same notebook simultaneously.

iii. Extensions and Widgets:
   - Jupyter Notebooks support extensions and widgets that enhance their functionality. Extensions can add features like spell-checking, code profiling, and more.

iv. Languages:
   - While Jupyter Notebooks are commonly associated with Python, they support a wide range of programming languages through the installation of additional kernels.

v. Installation:
   - You can also run Jupyter Notebooks locally on your machine by installing the Jupyter software. This allows you to create and run notebooks without an internet connection.

vi. Data Science and Education:
   - Jupyter notebooks are widely used in data science for data analysis, machine learning (Sotomayor-Vidal et al., 2023), and statistical modeling.

Utilizing Jupyter Notebook as an instrument throughout this undertaking has proven to be a highly effective and user-friendly solution, encompassing various stages of data analysis, including cluster formation and visual representation of the dataset.

Additionally, we can also use JupyterLite Notebook. JupyterLite is a lightweight, web-based version of Jupyter Notebooks, offering a simpler, faster experience for low-resource environments like mobile devices or education. JupyterLite streamlines interaction by omitting non-essential features, allowing seamless sharing and deployment across diverse devices with reduced resource needs.

## DATA COLLECTION AND PREPARATION

### Data Collection

Data was collected using a survey of students (Rizvi, 2023), and we got 288 responses. The dataset is related to student preferences (Zhu & Liu, 2023) and decision-making factors when choosing a college. The dataset includes various features that capture information about the students (Rizvi, 2023) and their considerations during the college selection process. The dataset could be used to analyze patterns, preferences (Zhu & Liu, 2023), and factors influencing college choices.

The survey consists of 26 questions, and a factor analysis was conducted to categorize them into three groups. The questions cover demographic information such as gender, age, family income, and region; academic details like courses, branches, and current status; college facilities and services, awareness and information channels, educational preferences (Zhu & Liu, 2023), decision-making factors, suggestions and feedback, language and cultural preferences (Zhu & Liu, 2023), extracurricular activities and future support, and college infrastructure.

The analysis revealed that the respondents were divided into three groups based on their demographic information, academic details, awareness and information channels, educational preferences (Zhu & Liu,

2023), decision-making factors, suggestions and feedback, language and cultural preferences (Zhu & Liu, 2023), extracurricular activities, and future support. The respondents were also asked about their perceptions of the college's facilities, services, and the availability of distance learning programs.

The survey also asked for feedback on any suggested changes in the college, their preference for language and cultural preferences (Zhu & Liu, 2023), and their preferences (Zhu & Liu, 2023) for extracurricular activities and infrastructure.

## Survey Analysis of College Choices

- Demographic Information: Gender, Age, Family Income, Region, and Current Status.
- Academic Details: Course, Branch, Current Status.
- College Facilities and Services: Trends, Library, Canteen, Sports, Extracurricular Activities.
- Awareness and Information Channels: Research, Alumni Network, Policies, and Preferences (Zhu & Liu, 2023).
- Educational Preferences (Zhu & Liu, 2023): Distance Learning, Average Package, Decision-Making Factors,
  Social-Class Status, Financial Aid.
- Suggestions and Feedback: Suggestions for changes in college.
- Language and Cultural Preferences (Zhu & Liu, 2023): Language preference.
- Extracurricular Activities and Future Support: Preference for Future Support and Infrastructure.

## Data Preprocessing

- Load the dataset into a data structure (e.g., Pandas Data Frame in Python).
- Use basic functions to explore the dataset, such as head(), info(), describe(), and shape().
- Identify and handle missing values. This may involve imputing missing values or removing rows or columns with missing values.
- Check for and handle duplicate rows if they exist.
- Encode categorical variables (e.g., gender, course, branch, how you came to know about the college, etc.).
- Normalize numerical variables (e.g., age, family income, faculty score) to ensure they have the same scale.

## Feature Selection

- Depending on the goal of segmentation (Davari et al., 2018), you might want to select a subset of features that are most relevant for clustering. For example, you may exclude features like "language you prefer" if they are not essential for the segmentation (Davari et al., 2018) task.

### Choose the Number of Clusters (k)

- Decide on the number of clusters (k) you want to create. Domain knowledge or approaches such as the elbow method or silhouette score may be used for this purpose.

### Apply K-Means Clustering

- Use the K-means algorithm (Kumar, 2022) to cluster the data into k groups based on the selected features. Each student will belong to one of the k clusters based on their responses to the questions.

### Interpret and Analyze Clusters

- Once clustering is complete, analyze the characteristics of each cluster to understand what differentiates them. We use tools like cluster centroids, visualization techniques, or descriptive statistics to gain insights.

### Assigning Segment Labels

- Providing meaningful labels to each cluster based on the characteristics of the students (Rizvi, 2023) within them. For example, segments like "high-income, academically focused, distance learning enthusiasts" or "low-income, sports, and extracurricular enthusiasts."

## MACHINE LEARNING ALGORITHMS FOR MARKET SEGMENTATION

Machine learning (Davari et al., 2018) algorithms can be highly effective for market segmentation (Davari et al., 2018), helping businesses divide their customer (Vieri et al., 2023) base into distinct groups based on various characteristics and behaviors. This segmentation (Davari et al., 2018) can be valuable for targeted marketing, product development, and overall business strategy. Here are some popular machine-learning algorithms used for market segmentation (Davari et al., 2018):

### K-Means Clustering

- K-Means is a commonly used unsupervised clustering algorithm.
- It partitions data into K clusters based on similarity, where K is a user-defined parameter.
- It works well when you have a clear idea of the number of segments you want to create.

Figure 1 - This paper examines the popularity of K-means, an unsupervised machine learning approach, in splitting datasets into discrete and non-overlapping subgroups or clusters (Sotomayor-Vidal et al., 2023). The algorithm aims to minimize the within-cluster sum of squared distances, essentially grouping

*Figure 1. K-means algorithm*
*(Kumar, 2022)*

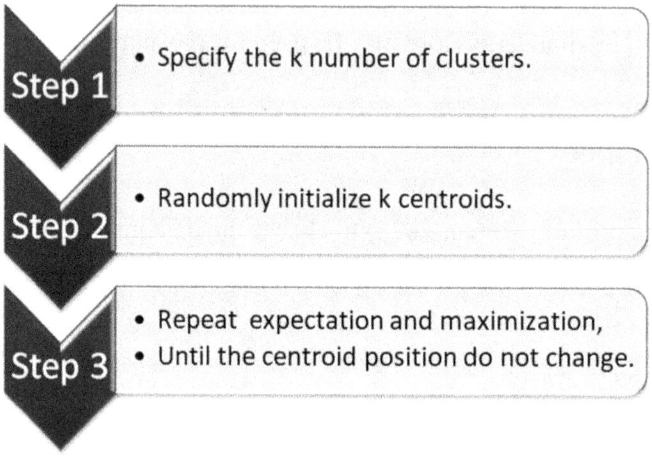


similar data points together. **Here, "expectation" means to assign each point to its closest centroid, and "maximization" means to compute the new centroid (mean) of each cluster.**

### Density-Based Spatial Clustering of Applications With Noise (DBSCAN)

- DBSCAN groups dense regions in the data.
- It is effective at finding clusters with varying shapes and sizes and can handle noise in the data.

### Gaussian Mixture Models (GMM)

- GMM models multi-modal data with Gaussian mixtures.
- It can capture complex shapes of clusters and provide probabilities for each data point's membership in different clusters.

### Principal Component Analysis (PCA)

- PCA is not a clustering algorithm itself but a dimensionality reduction technique.
- It can help reduce the dimensionality of the data and make it easier to apply other clustering algorithms.

### Mean Shift

- Non-parametric clustering algorithm without cluster count specs.
- It works by iteratively shifting data points towards the mode of the data distribution.

## IMPLEMENTATION OF ML-BASED SEGMENTATION

A survey was conducted among students (Rizvi, 2023) to gather data, focusing on three key areas: rational, emotional, and digital advertising.

To implement this dataset, the following steps were taken:

- Step 1 - Collect customer (Vieri et al., 2023) data through surveys and other sources.
- Step 2 - Load and review the collected data to ensure its quality and relevance.
- Step 3 - Preprocess the data to prepare it for analysis using various techniques such as cleaning, filtering, and transforming.
- Step 4 - Conduct exploratory data analysis (EDA) to identify patterns and relationships within the data, including visualizing the data to gain insights into potential clusters.
- Step 5 - Apply the k-means clustering algorithm to group similar data points together based on their proximity or similarity.
- Step 6 - Visualize the results through various graphical representations such as charts, plots, infographics, and more to help interpret the findings and understand the structure of the data.

The below-mentioned Figure 2 shows the process flow of the proposed methodology.

## RESULT

Based on the given dataset and the objectives we discussed earlier, you can identify different types of students (Rizvi, 2023) in a college.

*Figure 2. Process flow diagram*

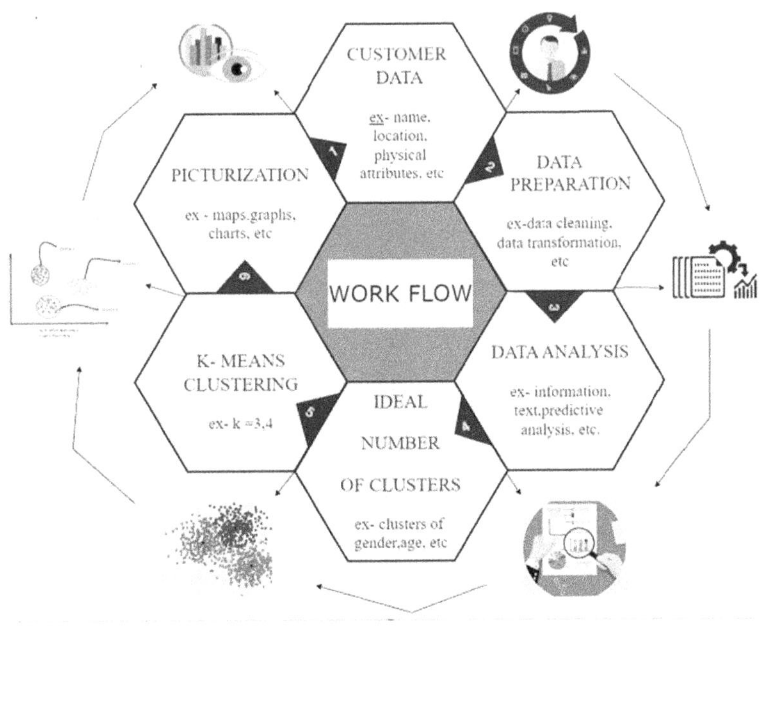

Figure 3 shows the number of clusters formed from the dataset based on the different characterstics of students (Rizvi, 2023).

The clusters are assigned in the following way:

- Cluster 0 shows Practical Planners
- Cluster 1 shows Social Influencers
- Cluster 2 shows Budget-Conscious Seekers
- Cluster 3 shows Academic Enthusiasts
- Cluster 4 shows Sports and Extracurricular Enthusiasts
- Cluster 5 shows Regional Trend Followers
- Cluster 6 shows Language-Priority Seekers
- Cluster 7 shows Internship and Placement-Focused

Figure 4 shows the potential segments or categories based on the analysis of factors such as preferences (Zhu & Liu, 2023), demographics, and decision-making criteria.

Here are some of the categories in which students (Rizvi, 2023) are divided according to their preferences (Zhu & Liu, 2023):

## The Practical Planners

- Consider financial aspects (family income, preferred average package).

*Figure 3. Number of clusters formed*

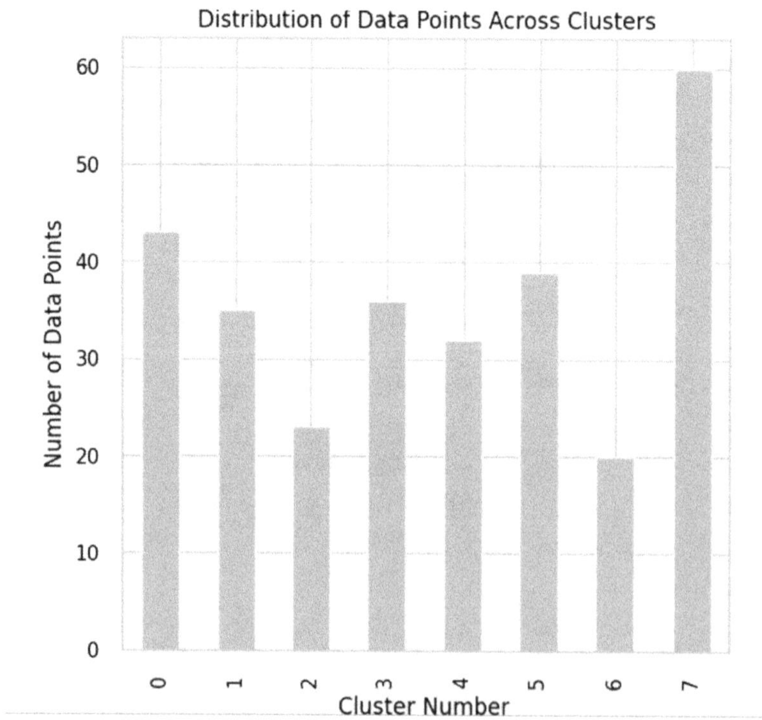

*Figure 4. Distribution of clusters with student categories*

```
    Your current status among the following? Which Language you prefer?  \
0                                Day Scholar                      Hindi
1                                         PG              Hindi;English
2                                         PG                    English
3                                Day Scholar              Hindi;English
4                                Day Scholar              Hindi;English
..                                       ...                        ...
283                              Day Scholar                      Hindi
284                              Day Scholar                    English
285                              Day Scholar              Hindi;English
286                              Day Scholar                    English
287                                       PG              Hindi;English

     Cluster                        Cluster Name
0          0                  Practical Planners
1          5              Regional Trend Followers
2          6              Language-Priority Seekers
3          4  Sports and Extracurricular Enthusiasts
4          1                  Social Influencers
..       ...                                    ...
283        6              Language-Priority Seekers
284        7         Internship and Placement Focused
285        5              Regional Trend Followers
286        6              Language-Priority Seekers
287        1                  Social Influencers

[288 rows x 4 columns]
```

- Pragmatic decision-makers who investigate details.
- Prefer medium-to-high faculty scores and academic considerations.

## The Social Influencers

- Influenced by friends and family in their decision-making.
- Consider using social media and networking for college information.
- May prioritize extracurricular activities and a good alumni network.

## The Budget-Conscious Seekers

- Emphasize financial aid and family income in their choices.
- Seek colleges with policies supporting financial assistance.
- May prefer colleges with a low cost of living.

### The Academic Enthusiasts

- Prioritize academic factors such as faculty scores and college ratings.
- Likely to investigate internship and placement opportunities.
- May consider colleges that adapt to trends and improvements.

### The Sports and Extracurricular Enthusiasts

- Emphasize sports facilities, extracurricular activities, and clubs.
- Consider distance learning programs and e-learning options.
- May prefer colleges with a strong emphasis on holistic development.

### The Regional Trend Followers

- Choices are influenced by the region they belong to.
- May consider colleges that align with regional preferences (Zhu & Liu, 2023).
- Regional identity and preferences (Zhu & Liu, 2023) play a key role in decision-making.

### The Language-Priority Seekers

- Prioritize language preferences (Zhu & Liu, 2023) in their college choices.
- May have a strong preference for colleges that offer instruction in a specific language.
- Consider language-related factors in various aspects of college life.

### The Internship and Placement Focused

- Investigate internship and placement details.
- May prioritize colleges with a high percentage of students (Rizvi, 2023) placed.
- Seek out colleges with strong industry connections.

Here are some more graphs that can guide your analysis and help you derive meaningful insights from the dataset. It's essential to align your objectives with the broader context or goals of the analysis, whether it's to inform educational institutions, policymakers, or marketing strategies (Tynan, 2015).

The above-mentioned Figure 5 shows which are the most important areas that need improvement, which need to be added to college policies for major improvement, and which can help students (Rizvi, 2023) in the future.

For example, we can see there are four main activities highlighted:

1. Extracurricular Activities: Sports, Club Involvement.
2. More research work

*Figure 5. Suggested changes by students*
*(Rizvi, 2023)*

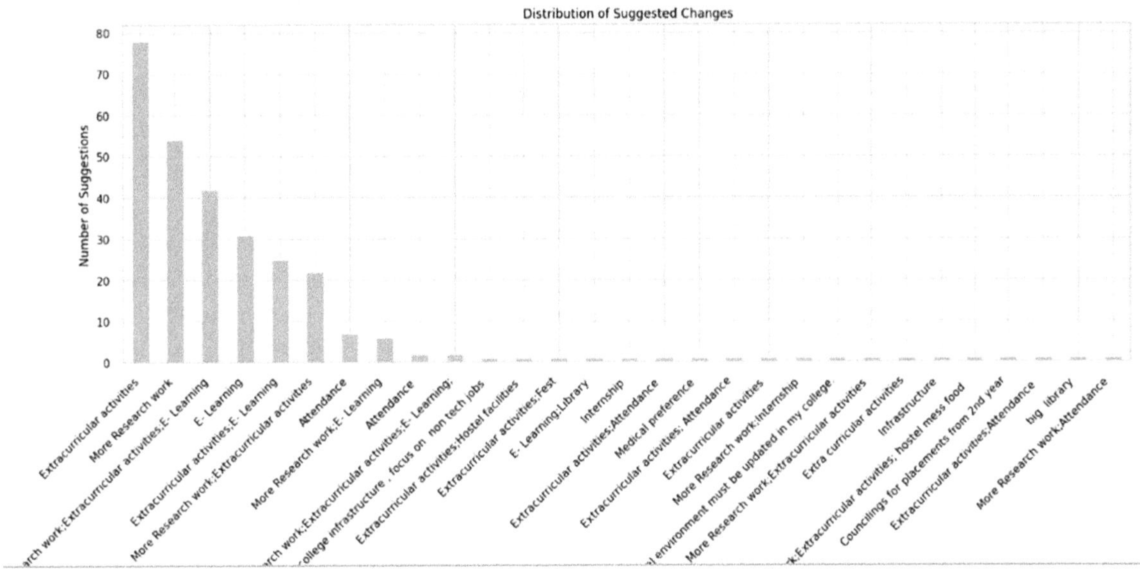


3. E- Learning: use of digital or smart boards
4. Attendance: relaxation in the percentage of attendance throughout the year, etc.

Figure 6 concludes that:

- By examining the three pie charts, you can identify the most common preferences (Zhu & Liu, 2023) within each category (academic factors, faculty scores, and college infrastructure).
- The charts provide a visual overview of the relative importance or popularity of different preferences (Zhu & Liu, 2023) among the respondents.

*Figure 6. Pie chart for college preference*

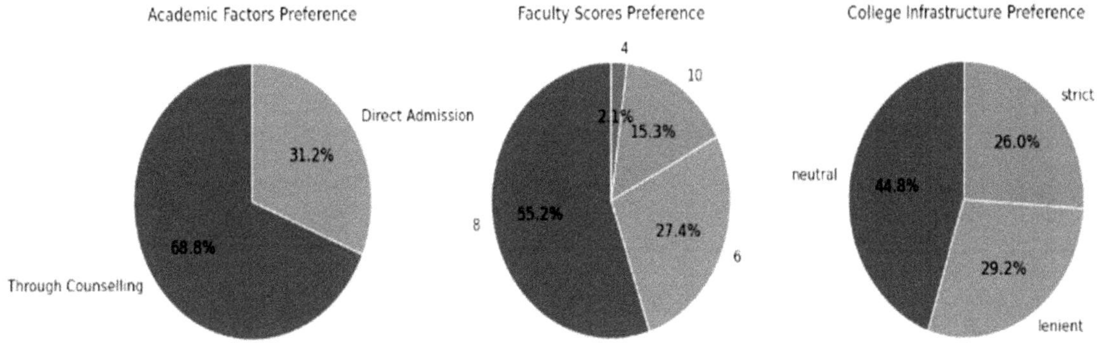

- Analyzing the distribution of preferences (Zhu & Liu, 2023) can help in understanding the priorities and expectations of the surveyed individuals regarding their college preferences (Zhu & Liu, 2023).

Another Figure 7 below shows that understanding the role of different channels through which students (Rizvi, 2023) come to know about their college is crucial for institutions to effectively allocate resources in their marketing and outreach efforts. It also provides insights into the most influential platforms for reaching potential students (Rizvi, 2023).

From this analysis, we have found that there are three most common dominant channels that highly motivate students (Rizvi, 2023) in their decision-making: family, friends and social media.

Here's an analysis of the potential roles of different channels based on the provided dataset:

1) Family:
   Role: Family plays a significant role in influencing students (Rizvi, 2023)' college choices. Family recommendations and discussions contribute to shaping students (Rizvi, 2023)' perceptions and preferences (Zhu & Liu, 2023).
2) Friends:
   Role: Friends have a notable impact on students (Rizvi, 2023)' decisions. Recommendations from friends can influence the choice of college and contribute to a sense of familiarity and comfort.
3) Social Media:
   Role: Social media platforms play a vital role in shaping the college preferences (Zhu & Liu, 2023) of students (Rizvi, 2023). The ability to access information, reviews, and opinions from a wide network can significantly impact decision-making.
4) Advertisements:

*Figure 7. Channels for deciding on a college*

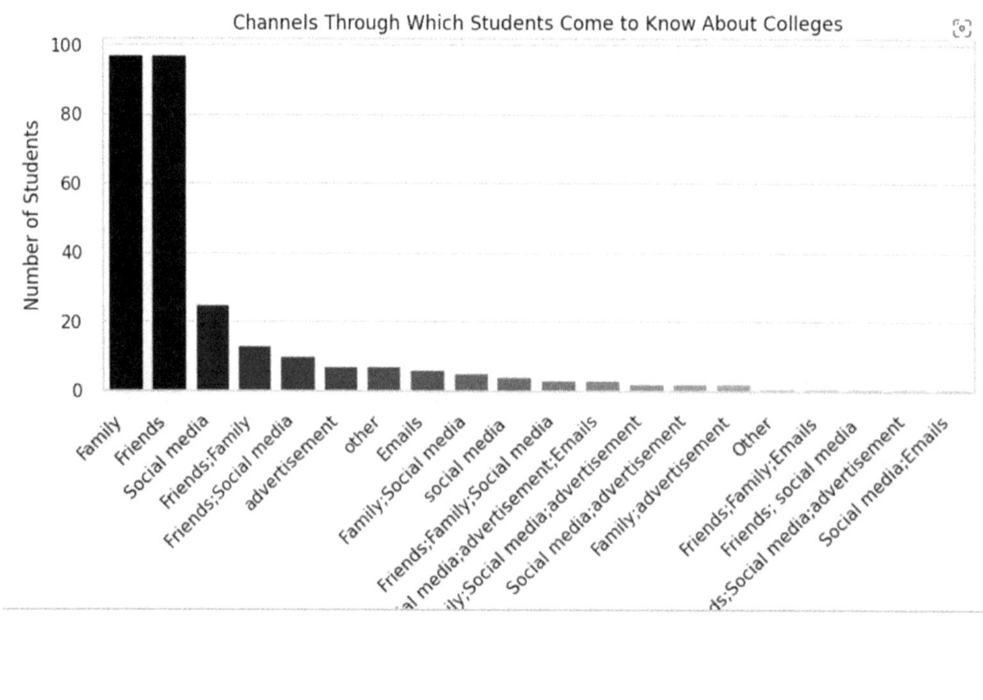

Role: Advertisements, if strategically placed, can create awareness and attract students (Rizvi, 2023) to explore more about a particular college. However, their influence might vary based on the content and placement.

5) Emails:

Role: Emails may serve as a direct communication channel between colleges and prospective students (Rizvi, 2023). Personalized and informative emails can contribute to the decision-making process.

6) Counseling:

Role: Counseling, either through formal sessions or one-on-one interactions, can provide valuable information and guidance to students (Rizvi, 2023). It may influence decisions by addressing concerns and providing clarity.

7) Direct Admission:

Role: Direct admission processes can attract students (Rizvi, 2023) seeking simplicity and efficiency in the application process. This channel may appeal to those who prioritize a straightforward admissions process.

8) E- Learning:

Role: The availability of e-learning programs can be a significant factor for students (Rizvi, 2023) who prioritize flexibility and accessibility in their education. This channel appeals to those who value online learning opportunities.

9) Through other colleges:

Role: Students (Rizvi, 2023) coming to know about a college through other colleges may indicate that the institution has a good reputation within the academic community, leading to word-of-mouth recommendations.

10) Through Events/Competitions:

Role: Participating in or winning events and competitions can enhance the visibility and reputation of a college. Students (Rizvi, 2023) may be attracted to colleges known for their achievements in such activities.

## CONCLUSION AND FUTURE TRENDS

In recent times, the dynamic nature of markets has necessitated the need for effective market segmentation (Hemsley-Brown, 2020) strategies (Tynan, 2015) to comprehend consumer behavior and preferences (Zhu & Liu, 2023). This is particularly evident in the higher education (Canterbury, 2000) sector, where market segmentation (Hemsley-Brown, 2020) has become crucial in identifying student needs and values when choosing universities or colleges. Our study focuses on developing a segmentation (Davari et al., 2018) model that considers various criteria significant to students (Rizvi, 2023) during their college selection process. By doing so, we aim to revolutionize traditional enrollment procedures and create opportunities for educational institutions to enhance their offerings. Through this analysis, we contribute to uncovering key features of universities that appeal most to students (Rizvi, 2023), providing valuable insights for higher education (Canterbury, 2000) institutions to improve their services and gain a competitive edge.

Machine learning-driven market segmentation (Hemsley-Brown, 2020) has the power to revolutionize higher education. By harnessing the vast amounts of data available, institutions can gain deep insights into their student populations, tailor their offerings, and improve student outcomes. However, it is essential to navigate this transformative journey with ethical considerations at the forefront, ensuring that technology (The Future Era of Computing: Automatic Computing, 2023) benefits all students (Rizvi, 2023) and promotes inclusive, equitable education.

Based on the analyzed data, several distinct student categories at a university may be identified. Such as, The practical planners, who carefully examine monetary elements like family revenue and preferred average packages; the socially influential, whose decisions are frequently swayed by those around them and online networks; the budget-conscious seekers, who highly value economical help and family income when choosing institutions; the academically enthusiastic, who place a premium on institutional rankings and academic components including internships and career prospects; the sports and extra-curricular lovers, who favor universities with excellent athletic amenities and a wide range of organizations and clubs; the followers of local fads, whose selections are significantly impacted by where they come from; and lastly, the language-focused searchers, who give priority to languages while making college decisions and take into account linguistically related variables across many parts of campus life.

Machine learning (Davari et al., 2018) (ML) enables businesses to personalize marketing strategies (Tynan, 2015), automate segmentation processes, and improve customer (Vieri et al., 2023) experiences, providing a competitive advantage. ML-driven market segmentation (Hemsley-Brown, 2020) leads to increased customer satisfaction and loyalty, while data-driven decision-making reveals hidden patterns and insights. We can define them as follows:

1. Enhanced Personalization: Machine learning (Sotomayor-Vidal et al., 2023)-driven market segmentation (Hemsley-Brown, 2020) allows for highly personalized marketing strategies (Tynan, 2015), products, and services, leading to increased customer (Vieri et al., 2023) satisfaction and loyalty.
2. Data-Driven Decision-Making: ML algorithms enable businesses to make data-driven decisions by uncovering hidden patterns and insights within their customer (Vieri et al., 2023) data.
3. Efficiency and Automation: Automation of segmentation (Davari et al., 2018) processes through ML reduces manual effort and speeds up the decision-making process.
4. Improved Customer Experience: ML-based segmentation (Davari et al., 2018) helps businesses tailor their interactions with customers, leading to improved user experiences.
5. Competitive Advantage: Companies that effectively use ML for segmentation (Davari et al., 2018) gain a competitive edge by staying ahead of market trends and customer preferences (Zhu & Liu, 2023).

## FUTURE TRENDS

1. **Deep Learning for Segmentation:** Deep learning techniques, such as deep neural networks, will continue to be explored for more accurate and sophisticated segmentation (Davari et al., 2018).
2. **Real-Time Segmentation:** ML models that can perform segmentation (Davari et al., 2018) in real-time, adapting to changing customer (Vieri et al., 2023) behaviors instantly, will become increasingly important.
3. **Predictive Segmentation:** ML models will not only identify current segments but also predict future customer (Vieri et al., 2023) behaviors and segment shifts.

4. **Interpretable AI:** As ML models become more complex, there will be a growing emphasis on making them interpretable and transparent to build trust and comply with regulations like GDPR.
5. **AI-Driven Customer Journey Mapping:** ML algorithms will play a central role in mapping customer (Vieri et al., 2023) journeys and identifying touch points for optimized customer (Vieri et al., 2023) engagement.
6. **Ethical and Fair Segmentation:** Businesses will focus on ensuring that AI-based segmentation (Davari et al., 2018) is fair and ethical, addressing concerns related to bias and discrimination.
7. **Cross-Channel Segmentation:** ML models will integrate data from various channels (online and offline) to create a more holistic view of customer (Vieri et al., 2023) segments.
8. **Automated Content Generation:** ML-driven segmentation (Davari et al., 2018) will be used to automatically generate personalized content and marketing materials.
9. **Edge AI for Segmentation:** The use of AI and ML at the edge (in IOT devices) will allow for on-device segmentation (Davari et al., 2018) and customization, enhancing user experiences.
10. **Collaborative Filtering and Recommender Systems:** ML-based recommender systems will become more sophisticated, offering highly targeted product recommendations based on segmentation (Davari et al., 2018).

## REFERENCES

Aktan, D., & Demirbağ Kaplan, M. (2023). Re-designing higher education for mindfulness: Conceptualization and communication. The Sustainable University of the Future. Research Gate. doi:10.1007/978-3-031-20186-8_4

Avaid, M., Haleem, A., Khan, I. H., & Suman, R. (2023). Understanding the potential applications of Artificial Intelligence in Agriculture Sector. *Advanced Agrochem*, *2*(1), 15–30. doi:10.1016/j.aac.2022.10.001

Canterbury, R. M. (2000). Higher education marketing: A challenge. *Journal of Marketing for Higher Education*, *9*(3), 15–24. doi:10.1300/J050v09n03_02

Casas-Rosal, J. C., Segura, M., and Maroto, C. (2023). Food market segmentation based on consumer preferences using outranking multi-criteria approaches. *International Transactions in Operational Research: A Journal of The International Federation of Operational Research Societies, 30*(3), 1537–1566. doi:10.1111/itor.12956

Chen, J. S. (Ed.). (2023). *Advances in hospitality and leisure*. Advances in Hospitality and Leisure., doi:10.1108/S1745-3542202318

Chen, Y.-F., & Hsiao, C.-H. (2009). Applying market segmentation theory to student behavior in selecting a school or department. *New Horizons in Education*, *57*(2), 32–43. https://files.eric.ed.gov/fulltext/EJ860823.pdf

Davari, M., Noursalehi, P., & Keramati, A. (2019). Data mining approach to professional education market segmentation: A case study. *Journal of Marketing for Higher Education*, *29*(1), 45–66. doi:10.1080/08841241.2018.1545724

Gupta, R., Singh, S., Verma, S., & Singhal, S. (2008). Intrusion detection system using SNORT. *IRJET.* https://www.irjet.net/archives/V4/i4/IRJET-V4I4439.pdf

Hemsley-Brown, J. (2020). Higher education market segmentation. In The International Encyclopedia of Higher education Systems and Institutions (pp. 711–713). Springer. doi:10.1007/978-94-017-8905-9_33

Kim, D. H., & Irakoze, A. (2022). Identifying market segment for the assessment of a price premium for green certified housing: A Cluster analysis approach. *Sustainability (Basel), 15*(1), 507. doi:10.3390/su15010507

Kristian Vieri, J., Munandar, T. A., & Srisulistiowati, D. B. (2023). Exclusive Clustering technique for customer segmentation in national telecommunications companies. *International Journal of Information Technology and Computer Science Applications, 1*(1), 51–57. doi:10.58776/ijitcsa.v1i1.19

Kumar, A. (2022). Customer segmentation of shopping mall users using K-means clustering. In Advancing SMEs Toward E-Commerce Policies for Sustainability (pp. 248–270). Research Gate. doi:10.4018/978-1-6684-5727-6.ch013

Lambert, T. E. (2023). The great resignation in the United States: A study of labor market segmentation. *The Forum for Social Economics, 52*(4), 373–386. doi:10.1080/07360932.2022.2164599

Lozano, F. A. M., Cruz Pulido, J. M., & García Rodríguez, J. F. (2021). The market segmentation of higher education in Colombia reveals social inequalities. *Cogent Education, 8*(1), 1877885. doi:10.1080/2331186X.2021.1877885

Pathak, N., & Singhal, S. (2023, January 27). *Fraud detection in financial domain using Machine learning.* Presented at the 2023 International Conference on Artificial Intelligence and Smart Communication (AISC), Greater Noida, India. 10.1109/AISC56616.2023.10085181

Pathak, N., Singhal, S., Naruka, M. S., Awasthi, S., & Chamoli, S. (2023, May 11). *Detection of Weed by using Hybrid Technique.* Presented at the 2023 International Conference on Disruptive Technologies (ICDT), Greater Noida, India. 10.1109/ICDT57929.2023.10151283

Rizvi, F. (2023). Internationalization of higher education and the advantage of diaspora. *International Higher Education,* (113), 16–17. https://ejournals.bc.edu/index.php/ihe/article/view/16099

Singh, B., & Singhal, S. (2020). Automated personality classification using Data mining techniques. SSRN Electronic Journal. doi:10.2139/ssrn.3602540

Singh, J., Jaiswal, K., Singh, M., Sama, M., & Singhal, S. (2023, May 11). *Market segmentation using ML.* Presented at the 2023 International Conference on Disruptive Technologies (ICDT), Greater Noida, India. 10.1109/ICDT57929.2023.10150639

Singhal, S., Ahuja, L., & Monga, H. (2020, December 18). *State of the art of Machine learning for product sustainability.* Presented at the 2020 2nd International Conference on Advances in Computing, Communication Control and Networking (ICACCCN), Greater Noida, India. 10.1109/ICACCCN51052.2020.9362746

Singhal, S., Ahuja, L., & Monga, H. (2023, January 27). *Sustainable manufacturing integrated into cloud-based data analytics for e-commerce SMEs.* Presented at the 2023 International Conference on Artificial Intelligence and Smart Communication (AISC), Greater Noida, India. 10.1109/AISC56616.2023.10085046

Singhal, S., & Pathak, N. (2023, January 27). *The future era of computing: Automatic computing*. Presented at the 2023 International Conference on Artificial Intelligence and Smart Communication (AISC), Greater Noida, India. 10.1109/AISC56616.2023.10085022

Singhal, S., Sharma, R., Ahuja, L., & Rana, A. (2020, October 9). *Approach in web application for regression testing using crawlers*. Presented at the 2020 International Conference on Smart Technologies in Computing, Electrical and Electronics (ICSTCEE), Bengaluru, India. 10.1109/ICSTCEE49637.2020.9277186

Sotomayor-Vidal, A., Mini-Cuadros, D. A., & Carlos Quiroz-Flores, J. (n.d.). *The influence of digital marketing on the student recruitment process in the private higher education sector in Perú*. IEOM Society. from https://ieomsociety.org/proceedings/2022malaysia/424.pdf

Tynan, A. C., & Drayton, J. (1987). Market segmentation. *Journal of Marketing Management*, *2*(3), 301–335. doi:10.1080/0267257X.1987.9964020

Zhao, J., Shen, J., Yan, J., Yang, X., Hao, Y., & Ran, Q. (2023). Corruption, market segmentation and haze pollution: Empirical evidence from China. *Journal of Environmental Planning and Management*, *66*(3), 642–664. doi:10.1080/09640568.2021.2001316

Zhu, T., & Liu, Y. (2023). Learning personalized preference: A segmentation strategy under consumer sparse data. *Expert Systems with Applications*, *215*(119333), 119333. doi:10.1016/j.eswa.2022.119333

# Chapter 14
# Revolutionizing Pedagogy: Exploring AI Coaching in Enhancing Teacher Professionalism

**Nidhi Agarwal**
https://orcid.org/0000-0002-1590-9888
*Lincoln University College, Malaysia*

**Meenakshi Sangwan**
*NRS Government College, India*

**Ekansh Agarwal**
https://orcid.org/0000-0001-5497-8838
*NMIMS University, India*

## ABSTRACT

*This study investigates how AI coaching systems might boost Malaysian teacher professionalism. The study analyses how AI coaching affects teachers' teaching, self-reflection, and career advancement. Mixed-method research uses qualitative interviews, quantitative assessments, and observational analysis. Malaysian educational institution AI coaching system and instructor case studies are examined. This technology customises classes and gives professors professional development feedback. AI coaching appears to deliver quick, personalised feedback to improve instructors. These studies show how AI plus human expertise can improve education and meet student demands. This study promotes AI coaching as an educational innovation engine. To demonstrate how AI enhances digital educators' professionalism, learning, and stakeholder and policymaker comprehension. AI can alter education through teacher professional development, according to this study. Results improve Malaysian teacher development and technology by changing attitudes, policies, and beliefs.*

## INTRODUCTION

The use of artificial intelligence (AI) has profoundly transformed different facets of education in an era driven by technology advancements. This research paper examines the capacity of AI coach-

DOI: 10.4018/979-8-3693-2440-0.ch014

ing to enhance teacher professionalism by investigating its influence on pedagogy and the wider educational environment.

The educational environment is given new tools by artificial intelligence (AI), which has the power to revolutionize traditional teaching and learning methods. This paper provides a thorough analysis of artificial intelligence (AI) technologies, their possible uses in education, including the challenges associated with them. We talk about chatbots and associated algorithms that can mimic human-human interactions and produce writing that appears human when given natural language input. Modern chatbots, such as ChatGPT, have many benefits, but their application in the classroom presents significant moral and practical issues as well. In addition to encouraging responsible and ethical use, the authors hope to offer valuable information regarding how AI may be successfully integrated into the educational environment to benefit both instructors and students (Tufan, 2023).

The role of educators is undergoing dynamic evolution as traditional teaching techniques collide with cutting-edge AI technologies. This study explores the complex relationship between AI coaching systems and teacher development, providing insight into how these systems enhance, supplement, and reinvent the educational environment (Kumar, 2009).

High-tech artificial intelligence is driving advancements and improvements in many facets of our life today (Kemal, 2021). Significant advancements in the disciplines of health, medicine, space exploration, informatics, industry, and communication have been produced by artificial intelligence. Furthermore, by improving education, artificial intelligence has advanced tremendously and gained momentum in this industry. The purpose of the study is to talk about the advancements and innovations that artificial intelligence has made in the field of education. In our study, the benefits, drawbacks, and necessity of artificial intelligence in education are explored. Artificial intelligence is a fundamental component of education. This study also looks at the benefits artificial intelligence offers to special education (disabled) students in terms of their educational experience and training. The report also discusses the global uses of artificial intelligence technologies. These applications include Quillionz, Classcraft, 3D holograms, Chatbots, Virtual Assistants, Virtual Reality, Augmented Reality, and Seeing AI. Thanks to technology, people may keep up their education throughout the current pandemic (Covid-19); learning can even be done virtually (online) to prevent civilizations from falling behind in terms of education. We therefore have a great deal to thank the machines for.

This research seeks to gain complete insights into the various aspects of integrating AI-driven coaching with teacher professionalism by analysing their synergy. This study aims to contribute to the ongoing discussion about the transformative power of AI in defining the future of education by carefully examining its implications, problems, and opportunities (Lizette 2023).

This study aims to clarify the potential and constraints of using AI coaching to improve teaching methods, enabling educators and stakeholders to successfully utilise new technological breakthroughs (Borromeo, 2023). The primary goal of this research is to facilitate a more profound comprehension of how AI coaching can initiate a significant change in teacher professionalism, hence changing the educational landscape in unprecedented manners. The purpose of this research study is to investigate the profound effect that coaching with artificial intelligence (AI) has on the professionalism of educators within the context of the field of teacher education. In this age of rapid technological growth, the incorporation of artificial intelligence (AI) systems has emerged as a driving force behind the transformation of the educational landscape. Examining the many facets of artificial intelligence coaching, the purpose of this study is to shed light on the role that AI coaching plays in promoting the growth of teachers and pedagogical methods.

According to Rai et al. (2019), the term "artificial intelligence" (AI) refers to computers that are capable of performing those cognitive activities that are traditionally associated with humans. These functions include learning, interacting, problem-solving, and demonstrating creativity. Recent years have seen a proliferation of rapid developments in the corporate world, which has contributed to the rise of artificial intelligence as a dominant force in society (Stone et al., 2016). According to Stone et al. (2016), technologies that involve artificial intelligence offer an incalculable number of opportunities to improve people's life in a range of domains, including their career, education, and healthcare choices. For example, according to the McKinsey Global Institute (2018), artificial intelligence is anticipated to generate value of 13 trillion USD worldwide by the year 2030, with 267 billion USD being invested in healthcare systems and services. The pervasiveness of artificial intelligence poses fresh challenges regarding the areas in which it might be productively utilised. Therefore, it is of the utmost importance at this specific moment in time to advance research on the application of artificial intelligence in organisations (von Krogh, 2018).

Coaching, which has become an important tool for human resource development (HRD) (Beattie et al., 2014; Bozer & Delegach, 2019), is an efficient method that can help individuals improve their level of satisfaction and effectiveness in the workplace. Grant and Stober (2006) define coaching as a dyadic assisting relationship between a professional coach and a client who work together along a systematic process of collaborative goal formulation and constructing solutions. Coaching is a form of assistance that is provided by a professional coach. Thee boom et al. (2014) and Jones et al. (2016) conducted meta-analyses that supported the notion that coaching is beneficial to clients in terms of performance, well-being, coping, attitudes, and self-regulation. In particular, coaching has been shown to improve affective outcomes. In practice, artificial intelligence has already started to find its way into the realm of coaching. For example, it may assist individuals in learning and facilitating change (for example, PocketConfidant.com), or it can develop leadership qualities (for example, Rocky.AI). Artificial intelligence coaching presents a number of significant opportunities, including the ability to remain anonymous, the flexibility to use coaching whenever and wherever the client chooses, and the ability to receive coaching at a fraction of the cost of traditional coaching. For employees who have not yet been considered for coaching due to the high cost of the process, organisations might want to think about using artificial intelligence to provide coaching. Because of the opportunities that artificial intelligence (AI) brings and the fact that coaching has the potential to assist clients in learning and changing, AI coaching has the potential to disrupt and innovate the professional development of employees.

The development of AI coaching in recent years has been driven more by practical needs than by theoretical considerations. As of right now, it is not entirely apparent what exactly AI coaching is. The further factor that contributes to this confusion is the fact that AI coaching and other forms of digitally transmitted coaching overlap in some ways. Consequently, we provide a definition of the idea and differentiate it from other concepts that are analogous to it (Bacharach, 1989), such as self-coaching, blended coaching, and online coaching. This allows us to merge two previously separate bodies of literature, namely the literature on coaching and the literature on artificial intelligence. The following creation and empirical evaluation of a theory on effective AI coaching, which can explain whether, how, and why AI coaching works, requires a clear conceptualization of AI coaching. This is important since it is necessary for the theory to be developed. This would also make it possible for HRD professionals and coaching consumers to comprehend the specifics of what they want to employ and the reasons behind their decision.

According to Brynjolfsson and McAfee (2014), artificial intelligence has, in general, led to the creation of unreasonable expectations, with little recognition of the capabilities itself. We shed light on the possibilities of artificial intelligence in the field of coaching in this study in order to clear the misconception that currently exists regarding its capabilities. While there are those who believe that AI coaching will eventually reach full usability to the point where it will be able to replace human coaches for conventional coaching themes (Rauen, 2018), there are also those who believe that AI may be able to aid human coaches and enhance their work (Greif, 2018; Oesch, 2018). Based on the PRACTICE model developed by Palmer in 2007 and the AI evaluation criteria developed by (Brynjolfsson and Mitchell 2017), we challenge the notion that artificial intelligence can successfully deliver coaching and break down what AI coaching can and cannot achieve for clients who are engaged in the coaching process. Furthermore, a recent meta-analysis conducted by Grossmann et al. (2019) demonstrated that a high-quality working alliance between clients and coaches is consistently associated to the outcomes of coaching. As a result, we investigate whether or not AI coaching can supply a functioning alliance to assist clients in achieving desirable coaching outcomes and how this can be accomplished.

People have had more opportunities to contact and work with artificial intelligence technology as the number of these devices that are present around us has increased. Siri, smart home appliances, smartphones, Alexa, and artificial intelligence in computer games are all examples of products that have made artificial intelligence a part of our everyday life (Touretzky et al., 2019). Many of us are familiar with these services and technologies, and we make use of them in a variety of settings, including our homes, schools, and recreation centres; nevertheless, nearly no one is aware of the science and technology that is responsible for their operation. In light of this, it is of the utmost importance to educate people at an early age about the fundamental concepts and technological foundations that underpin these technologies, such as algorithms, data structures, and programming or coding. Literacy in terms of artificial intelligence and computer science will become a serious concern in the future, just as traditional literacy, which involves the ability to read, write, and perform mathematical operations. Students who are literate in artificial intelligence also have a solid foundation for their studies at universities and for their future employment. There appears to be a growth in the number of persons looking for work in the fields of science and engineering, as evidenced by the daily increase in the utilisation of AI technology. Some countries have started teaching artificial intelligence education in primary and secondary schools in China (Han et al., 2018; UNESCO, 2022) despite the fact that computer science education in schools does not place an emphasis on teaching essential issues related to artificial intelligence. Artificial intelligence (AI) technologies, which include user-facing services and products, are fast being integrated into our day-to-day activities and have become a topic of concern among educators (Yang, 2019; Zimmerman, 2018, p. 2018). According to research conducted by Vachoysky et al. (2016), formal education from kindergarten through high school ought to prioritise artificial intelligence (AI) literacy and instruct children on how to engage with AI in an appropriate manner. It is crucial to investigate how intuition is developed in these systems as machine learning becomes an element of computer education from kindergarten through high school. Developing learning environments that enable individuals to use block-based programming to create simple artificial intelligence applications is the primary focus of the majority of these projects (Bishop et al., 2019). Additionally, these projects aim to teach high school students the fundamentals of object identification and provide interactive data visualisation training (Gresse von Wangenheim, Hauck, Pacheco, & Bertonceli Bueno, 2021). Furthermore, these projects encourage students to enrol in courses that are organised into series to teach fundamental AI principles and how to use current AI resources. According to Srikant and Aggarwal (2017), one of the most difficult aspects of teaching machine learning in elementary, middle, and high school is choosing what should be taught at each level. This is also true for other aspects of computational thinking. In the context of education, the word "K-12" refers to a wide range of students and distinct educational goals for each age group. For instance, kindergarteners concentrate on learning fundamental abilities such as reading and mathematics (Galvex, 2023; Reyes, 2023). At the same time, senior year students in high school frequently employ sophisticated methods for problem-solving and focus on mathematical modelling in order to get ready for college after graduation (Antonio, 2023). There is a wide range of variation in the resources and instructional strategies that are most effective for particular age groups, categories, learning environments, and the precise learning objectives that are desired (Senados, 2023). The numerous problems and goals that are a part of machine learning education programmes are a reflection of this. As a result, there are now a variety of various ML education packages for grades K-12 (Almario, 2023). An example of this would be the study that Burgsteiner, Kandlhofer, and Steinbauer (2016) conducted to investigate the best way to instruct students in high school (grades 9-11) on the fundamental concepts of computer science and artificial intelligence. In order to accomplish this goal, Burgsteiner et al. (2016) devised an artificial intelligence course that incorporates both theoretical and applied components. This course covers a wide range of advanced subjects, including data structure, planning, search, agent systems, automata, graphs, problem-solving, and machine learning. The findings of the pilot project and the evaluation demonstrated that the students who participated in the course gained knowledge about a variety of concepts and subjects during the course.

Numerous studies investigating the potential uses of generative artificial intelligence (AI) simulations, especially Chat-GPT, in education have been spurred by their widespread adoption and usage. This survey looks at scholarly works that were released between November 2022 and July 2023, with a focus on high-impact studies from Q1 and Q2 journals that are indexed by Scopus. This survey explores the ramifications and real-world uses of generative AI models in a variety of educational settings. This review aims to provide light on the evolving function of generative AI models - particularly ChatGPT - in education through a thorough and rigorous analysis of contemporary scholarly literature. The survey aims to advance knowledge of the relationship between artificial intelligence and classroom instruction by illuminating the possible advantages, difficulties, and new developments in this exciting topic. The results of this overview will enable researchers, educators, and legislators to make well-informed choices on the incorporation of artificial intelligence (AI) technologies into educational settings (AL-Smadi, 2023).

## AIM OF THE STUDY

The purpose of this research is to identify the potential gaps that artificial intelligence coaching aims to fill by conducting a comprehensive analysis of the methodology and technologies that are currently used in teacher professional development practices. It examines the effectiveness of artificial intelligence coaching in enhancing the professionalism of teachers, with a particular emphasis on the impact that it has on the acquisition of skills, instructional practices, and the outcomes for students.

In addition, this article investigates the difficulties that arise when attempting to integrate artificial intelligence coaching systems in educational environments. These difficulties include the requirements for infrastructure, ethical considerations, and the adoption of the technology by educators. This article investigates the changing interactions that exist between educators and technology, focusing on the ways in which artificial intelligence coaching systems are incorporated into professional practice.

Considerations of data privacy, equity, and the impact on teacher-student interactions are among the ethical aspects that are discussed in relation to the use of artificial intelligence coaching in educational settings. In its conclusion, the study offers insights and recommendations that may be put into action by policymakers, institutions, and educators in order to successfully include AI coaching into professional development programmes for teachers. The purpose of this research is to make a contribution to the discussion that surrounds AI-driven pedagogical innovations. Its goal is to provide insights into the revolutionary potential of AI coaching in transforming the educational landscape as a whole as well as the professionalism of teachers.

## METHODOLOGY

An approach known as purposive sampling can be utilised for the purpose of conducting a focused study in Malaysia. This strategy is designed to ensure that numerous educational institutions from different locations are represented. It would be greatly beneficial to select managers, administrators, or heads of educational institutions who have previous experience integrating or supervising efforts involving artificial intelligence coaching. We collect 50 data from a wide range of institutions, including public and private schools, primary and secondary schools, and urban and rural areas.

## ANALYSIS

For the purpose of data collection, it is recommended to conduct interviews or surveys with experienced educational leaders. It is imperative that varied representation be maintained across public and private institutions, elementary and secondary schools, and urban and rural settings. It is important to obtain consent, uphold ethical standards, and take accurate documentation of responses. Use a methodical approach to data analysis, looking for trends and gaining insights. Determine whether or whether the findings are credible, interpret the results, and present them in a logical manner. In addition to providing a comprehensive view of the incorporation of AI coaching into Malaysian education, this method ensures the collection of a wide range of viewpoints on the subject.

The following table presents examples of responses to an important question on the anticipated potential of artificial intelligence coaching systems in promoting the professional growth of educators. The overwhelming majority of respondents, which amounted to 72%, expressed either "Strongly Agreed" or "Agreed," indicating that they had a favourable attitude towards AI coaching. Among a subset of responders, the 'Neutral' viewpoint, which accounts for 16% of the total, suggests that there is some doubt or a need for further study.

The mean values, in particular, shed light on several fascinating quirks. A significant degree of agreement with the statement was highlighted by the fact that the "Strongly Agreed" response received the highest mean value of 1.9. 'Agreed' comes next, but it has a significantly lower mean value of 0.68, which indicates that there is a wide variety of interpretations that may be found within this category. 'Neutral' at 0.48 shows a tendency that is somewhere in the middle, demonstrating an attitude that is balanced yet cautious. The 'Disagreed' and 'Strongly Disagreed' categories, albeit having lower percentages, collectively highlight reservations among a smaller subset, as evidenced by the much lower mean values of these categories.

*Table 1. Response for question number one*

| Question | Options | Data Collected Responses 50 |
|---|---|---|
| AI coaching systems have the potential to significantly enhance the professional development of educators within our institution. | Strongly Agreed | 19 |
| | Agreed | 17 |
| | Neutral | 8 |
| | Disagreed | 3 |
| | Strongly Disagreed | 4 |

*Table 2. Percentage and mean value of responses for question one*

| Response | Strongly Agreed | Agreed | Neutral | Disagreed | Strongly Disagreed |
|---|---|---|---|---|---|
| Percentage | 38% | 34% | 16% | 6% | 8% |
| Mean Value | 1.9 | 0.68 | 0.48 | 0.12 | 0.08 |

*Figure 1. Chart representing response for question number one*

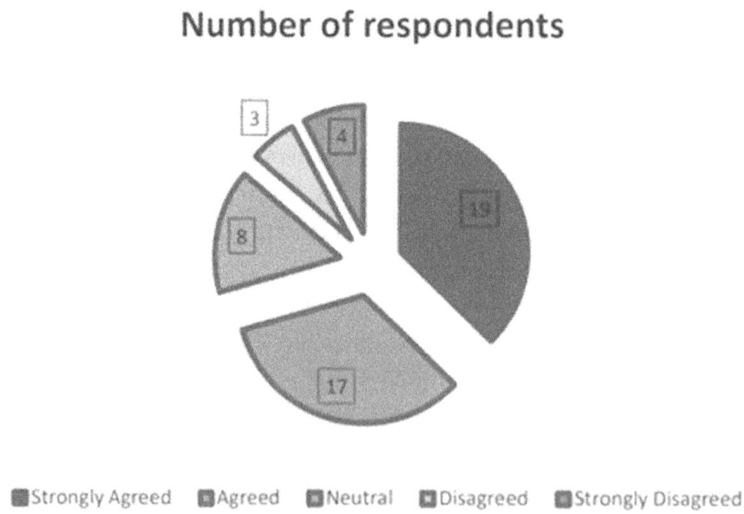


Variances in mean values reflect the numerous perspectives and the need for additional inquiry into the reasons underlying these varying interpretations. Overall, the majority of respondents leaning towards agreement indicates an optimistic stance on the possibilities of AI coaching. However, the fact that there are variances in mean values highlights the diversity of perspectives.

*Table 3. Response for question number two*

| Question | Options | Data Collected Responses 50 |
|---|---|---|
| Integrating AI coaching tools can effectively augment pedagogical practices and instructional strategies employed by teachers. | Strongly Agreed | 9 |
| | Agreed | 7 |
| | Neutral | 1 |
| | Disagreed | 3 |
| | Strongly Disagreed | 30 |

*Table 4. Percentage and mean value of responses for question two*

| Response | Strongly Agreed | Agreed | Neutral | Disagreed | Strongly Disagreed |
|---|---|---|---|---|---|
| Percentage | 18% | 14% | 2% | 6% | 60% |
| Mean Value | 0.9 | 0.56 | 0.06 | 0.12 | 1.8 |

*Figure 2. Chart representing response for question number two*

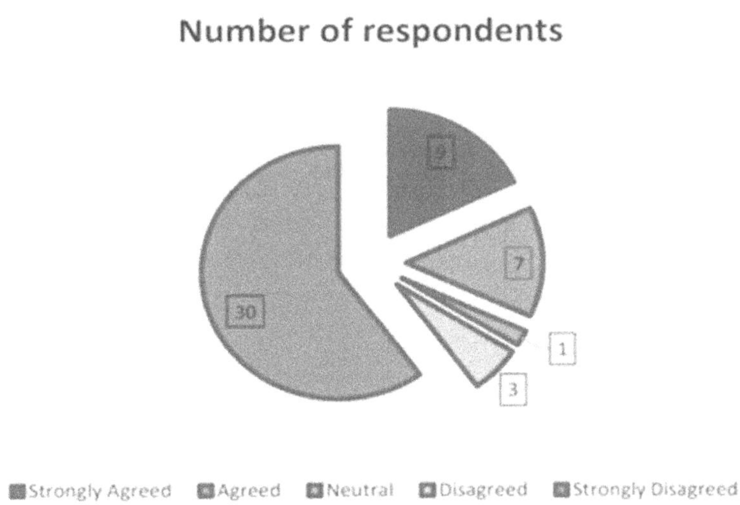


These tables demonstrate contrasting perspectives on the incorporation of AI coaching in education. According to Table 2.1, the majority of respondents (62%) agree (Strongly Agreed and Agreed combined) that AI has the ability to improve educator professional development. The average numbers indicate a higher level of certainty in the 'Strongly Agreed' category, indicating a strong agreement with this notion. However, Table 2.2 presents a conflicting depiction. 60% of respondents expressed strong disagreement, indicating a high level of scepticism over the effectiveness of AI in enhancing teaching methods. The significantly elevated average value in this area underscores a collective position opposing the use of AI coaching aids for instructional tactics. The replies categorised as 'Agreed' and 'Strongly Agreed', which make up only 32% of the total, represent a minority that is split yet firmly convinced. The statistics clearly demonstrate a significant difference in opinions, highlighting the urgent requirement for detailed examination of AI's impact on education and addressing concerns to enable its successful incorporation.

In the context of teacher professional development, Table 3.1 demonstrates a favourable attitude towards the use of artificial intelligence coaching systems. The majority of respondents (46 out of 50) either support or strongly favour the alignment of these systems with the educational goals of the institution. Table 3.2 emphasises a high mean value (2.9) for 'Strongly Agreed,' which indicates significant endorsement. This consensus is further illustrated by the table. When there are no opposing viewpoints, it indicates that there is widespread agreement. The lower mean values for 'Agreed' and 'Neutral', on the other hand, indicate that there is a minor variation in viewpoints. These tables, taken as a whole, demonstrate a generally positive attitude towards the incorporation of artificial intelligence coaching systems within the educational vision of the institution, albeit with some variable degrees of endorsement.

Within the institution, the implementation of AI coaching presents a number of problems, and Table 4.1 presents a balanced distribution of viewpoints regarding these challenges. Concerns regarding resource investment are reflected in the replies, which range from 'Disagreed' to 'Strongly Disagreed' (a total of 22), with considerable counts on both sides of the spectrum. This is further supported by Table 4.2, which demonstrates that the mean value for 'Disagreed' is rather high (2.6), indicating that there are significant reservations. There is a lack of unanimity, as indicated by the percentages, which suggests that there is a divided perspective on the difficulties that are caused by resource distribution.

*Table 5. Response for question number three*

| Question | Options | Data Collected Responses 50 |
|---|---|---|
| The utilization of AI coaching systems in teacher professional development aligns with the educational goals and vision of our institution. | Strongly Agreed | 29 |
| | Agreed | 17 |
| | Neutral | 4 |
| | Disagreed | 0 |
| | Strongly Disagreed | 0 |

*Table 6. Percentage and mean value of response for question number three*

| Response | Strongly Agreed | Agreed | Neutral | Disagreed | Strongly Disagreed |
|---|---|---|---|---|---|
| Percentage | 58% | 34% | 8% | 0% | 0% |
| Mean Value | 2.9 | 1.36 | 0.24 | 0 | 0 |

*Figure 3. Chart representing response for question number three*

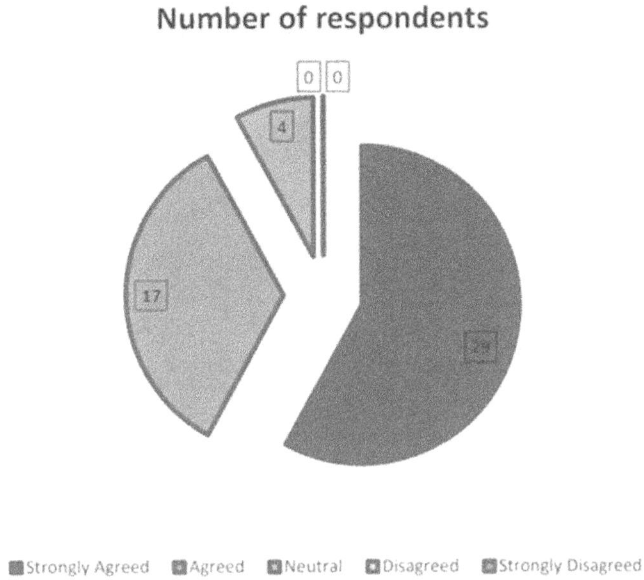


*Table 7. Response for question number four*

| Question | Options | Data Collected Responses 50 |
|---|---|---|
| Implementing AI coaching requires substantial infrastructural and resource investments, which might pose challenges for our institution. | Strongly Agreed | 11 |
| | Agreed | 9 |
| | Neutral | 8 |
| | Disagreed | 13 |
| | Strongly Disagreed | 9 |

*Table 8. Percentage and mean value of responses for question four*

| Response | Strongly Agreed | Agreed | Neutral | Disagreed | Strongly Disagreed |
|---|---|---|---|---|---|
| Percentage | 22% | 18% | 16% | 26% | 18% |
| Mean Value | 2.2 | 1.8 | 1.2 | 2.6 | 0.9 |

This indicates that there is a need for thorough study and planning in order to resolve issues regarding investments in infrastructure for the purpose of successfully integrating advanced artificial intelligence coaching within the institution.

*Figure 4. Chart representing response for the question number four*

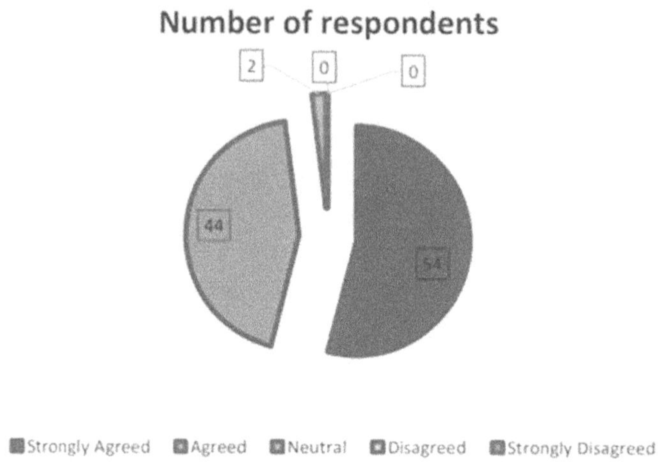


*Table 9. Response for question number five*

| Question | Options | Data Collected Responses 50 |
|---|---|---|
| Educators within our institution exhibit a high level of openness and willingness to embrace AI coaching as part of their professional development. | Strongly Agreed | 14 |
| | Agreed | 7 |
| | Neutral | 18 |
| | Disagreed | 7 |
| | Strongly Disagreed | 4 |

*Table 10. Percentage and mean value of responses for question five*

| Response | Strongly Agreed | Agreed | Neutral | Disagreed | Strongly Disagreed |
|---|---|---|---|---|---|
| Percentage | 28% | 14% | 36% | 14% | 8% |
| Mean Value | 1.4 | 0.56 | 1.08 | 0.28 | 0.08 |

The responses for the question of whether or not educators are prepared to implement AI coaching in professional development are more varied, as seen in Table 5.1. Despite the fact that a sizeable proportion of respondents maintained their neutrality (18 out of 50), a sizeable number of respondents expressed reservations (the sum of 'Disagreed' and 'Strongly Disagreed' was 11). The difference is confirmed by Table 5.2, which displays a mean value that is somewhere in the middle across all of the replies, with 'Neutral' being the highest (1.08). This ambivalence is reflected in the numbers, which show that there

*Figure 5. Chart representing response for question number five*

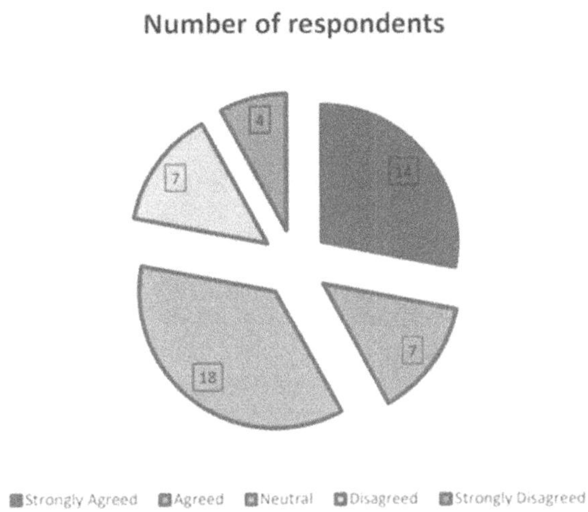


is no majority consensus. This suggests that there is a diverse landscape within the institution, with educators displaying varied degrees of openness towards the incorporation of AI coaching. This highlights the necessity of focused engagement and support for wider adoption.

The data shown in these tables demonstrates a strong tendency towards the beneficial impact that AI coaching has on the development of teacher skills inside the institution it serves. On the other hand,

*Table 11. Response for Question Number six*

| Question | Options | Data Collected Responses 50 |
|---|---|---|
| AI coaching systems have demonstrated observable positive impacts on teacher skill acquisition and development within our institution. | Strongly Agreed | 29 |
| | Agreed | 11 |
| | Neutral | 3 |
| | Disagreed | 7 |
| | Strongly Disagreed | 0 |

*Table 12. Percentage and mean value of response for Question Number six*

| Response | Strongly Agreed | Agreed | Neutral | Disagreed | Strongly Disagreed |
|---|---|---|---|---|---|
| Percentage | 58% | 22% | 6% | 14% | 0% |
| Mean Value | 2.9 | 0.88 | 0.18 | 0.28 | 0 |

*Figure 6. Chart representing response for question number six*

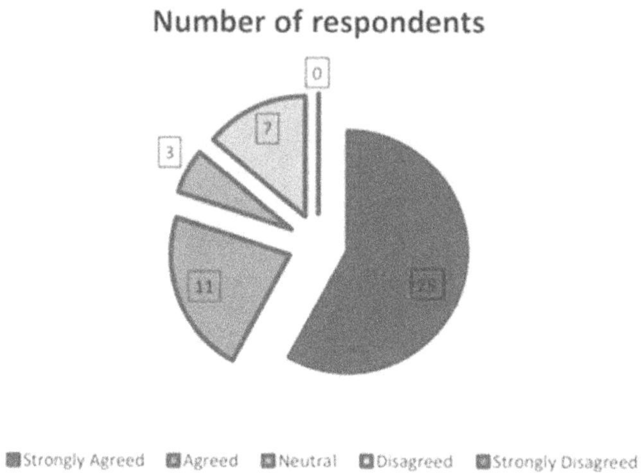


Table 6.2 reaffirms this by providing a high mean value for 'Strongly Agreed' (2.9), which shows the fact that a considerable majority of respondents (40 out of 50) expressed agreement or strong agreement with your statement. On the other hand, a sizeable percentage of respondents also express disagreement or neutrality. 'Strongly Disagreed' comments aren't present, which is striking. In general, there is a clear majority that acknowledges the good impact, but there is also a minority that expresses misgivings or neutrality, highlighting the necessity for additional research or specialised ways to address concerns and maximise the perceived benefits of AI coaching for teacher skill building.

## CONCLUSION

A landscape of revolutionary possibilities within the realm of pedagogy has been revealed as a result of the incorporation of artificial intelligence (AI) coaching into the overall process of teacher professional development. Over the course of this investigation, the research shed light on the myriad ways in which AI coaching can have an effect on the professionalism of teachers, the pedagogical techniques they employ, and the educational landscape as a whole.

The effectiveness of artificial intelligence coaching in increasing teacher development was evaluated, and the results demonstrated that it has the ability to improve the acquisition of skills, modify instructional methodologies, and positively influence the outcomes for students (Collado, 2023). However, it also brought to light the complex difficulties that are inherent in its implementation. These difficulties include the requirements for the infrastructure, the ethical issues that must be taken into account, and the demand that teachers must be willing to accept and adapt to the new system (Biliran, 2023; Chiong, 2023).

A dynamic intersection has been discovered as a result of the increasing relationship between educators and AI coaching systems. This intersection is one in which technology serves to supplement rather than replace the job of teachers (Maglonzo, 2023). The relevance of understanding how educators incorporate and exploit AI coaching systems inside their professional practice is highlighted by this symbiotic connection, which highlights the importance of altering the traditional paradigms of teaching and learning (Agarwal, 2023).

The promise of innovation, however, is accompanied by a significant amount of ethical problems (Palmares, 2023). Conscientious navigation is required as artificial intelligence becomes increasingly integrated into educational settings. This is because privacy concerns, equity in access, and the delicate balance between technological help and human-centered education are all concerns that need to be addressed.

As the conclusion of this research draws near, it provides recommendations and insights that can be put into action. The use of a collaborative approach is strongly urged among policymakers, institutions, and educators in order to cultivate an atmosphere that is open to the use of artificial intelligence coaching while maintaining ethical norms. When it comes to ensuring that AI coaching systems are utilised effectively and that everyone has equal access to them, it is absolutely necessary to provide individualised support, opportunities for professional growth, and infrastructure resources (Agarwal, 2023).

The investigation of the use of artificial intelligence (AI) coaching in the field of teacher professionalism reveals a path that will be transformative for education. It highlights the importance of a well-balanced integration of technology and pedagogy, which would allow for the utilisation of the benefits of artificial intelligence (AI) while simultaneously conserving the irreplaceable essence of human contact and knowledge in the field of education.

This study makes a contribution to the continuing discussion regarding the role that artificial intelligence (AI) plays in education. It highlights the importance of doing ongoing research, conducting ethical inspection, and working together in order to properly harness its potential. The genuine evolution of education is waiting to be discovered at the crossroads of innovative practice and conscientious practice.

## EMERGING TRENDS AND FUTURE OUTLOOK

The future of changing pedagogy using AI coaching to promote teacher professionalism is centered around emerging trends, new approaches, and technology breakthroughs. These advancements have the potential to revolutionize educational methods, enhancing the individualization, efficiency, and efficacy of teaching:

1. TeachFX & AI Coach through Edthena are advanced AI coaching solutions that provide tailored feedback & professional development possibilities for teachers. These services utilize advanced algorithms to evaluate lecture recordings or video uploads, offering comprehensive analytics and insightful reflections. These tools allow teachers to assess their abilities as well as possibilities for growth, which helps them focus on specific areas for professional development.

2. AI has the capacity to automate a substantial part of the administrative chores that instructors now carry out, hence improving efficiency within administrative tasks as well as time management. According to McKinsey's research, it is estimated that between 20 to 40 percent of instructor hours dedicated to tasks such as lesson planning, grading, including administrative duties might be replaced by automation. This automation would liberate precious time for educators, allowing them to allocate it towards more influential endeavors such as tailored instruction, hands-on guidance, and active involvement of students.

3. AI in education not only enhances administrative efficiency but also improves the quality of teacher-student interactions. Artificial intelligence chatbots have the capability to manage ordinary inquiries, therefore enabling teachers to concentrate on more intricate and customized instructional

matters. This shift has the potential to improve the quality of education by making the learning process more captivating and efficient.

4. TeachFX, a tool for facilitating reflective practices, encourages instructors to engage in self-reflection by offering them practical insights derived from their teaching. Through the analysis of lesson recordings, these tools facilitate the identification of successful teaching tactics, areas for enhancement, and possibilities for improving student engagement. This feedback loop fosters a culture of ongoing enhancement and professional development.

5. The implementation of AI in education brings forth various prospects, but it also brings about challenges with data privacy, bias, and the possible depersonalization of educational experiences. It is critical to carefully consider and tackle these challenges, guaranteeing that AI technologies are employed in an ethical and efficient manner to enhance traditional teaching techniques without diminishing the vital personal connection that is essential for effective teaching.

Integrating AI into education, namely by using AI coaching to enhance teacher professionalism, has the potential to significantly transform teaching methods. The utilization of AI in individualized professional development, automation of administrative duties, improvement of teacher-student interactions, and facilitation of continuous improvement is expected to bring about substantial changes in the educational sector. Nevertheless, the effective execution of these technologies necessitates meticulous examination of ethical ramifications and a well-rounded approach to the integration of technology.

## REFERENCES

Adiguzel, T., Kaya, H., & Cansu, F. (2023). Revolutionizing education with AI: Exploring the transformative potential of ChatGPT. *Contemporary Educational Technology*, *15*(3), ep429. doi:10.30935/cedtech/13152

Agarwal, Dr. Nidhi. (2023). A Study on the teacher's aptitude about managerial skill with respect to training and learners performance. *International Journal of Management and Organizational Research*, *2*(2), 78–84.

Agarwal, N. (2023). Strength of distributed web page management system within the space of online e-learning administration in a contextualized group of science teachers. *European Chemical Bulletin*, *12*(4), 144–155.

AL-Smadi, M. (2023). *ChatGPT and Beyond: The Generative AI Revolution in Education*. Research Gate. doi:10.13140/RG.2.2.11376.23049

Almario, O. (2023). Assessing User Experience Learning Management System for Liberal Arts and Education Programs: Implications for Hybrid Learning. *Cosmos An International Journal of Management, 12*(2), 73-78.

Ang, L., Bonifacio, N., Garcia, J. K., Medina, R., & Santiago, J. (2023). The Rise of Artificial Intelligence: A Correlational Study on AI-Powered Bots and Customer Satisfaction in a People-Oriented Industry. *Cosmos Journal of Engineering & Technology*, *13*(1), 81–94. doi:10.46360/cosmos.et.620231008

Antonio, G. C. (2023). Influence of Teachers' Leadership Style Under The New Normal System in Education. *Globus Journal of Progressive Education*, *13*(1), 14–25.

Biliran, A. (2023). Students' 21st Century Skills: Level of Readiness for Large- Scale Assessments. *Cosmos An International Journal of Art & Higher Education*, *12*(1), 85–97. doi:10.46360/cosmos.ahe.520231007

Bishop, F., Zagermann, J., Pfeil, U., Sanderson, G., Reiterer, H., & Hinrichs, U. (2019). Construct-a-vis: Exploring the free-form visualization processes of children. *IEEE Transactions on Visualization and Computer Graphics*, *26*(1), 451–460. doi:10.1109/TVCG.2019.2934804 PMID:31443024

Borromeo, D., Estrella, N., & Caparas, E.R. (2023). Impact of Educational Technology Tools on the Digital and Information Literacy Skills of Selected Dominican Schools in the Philippines. *Cosmos An International Journal of Management, 12*(2), 01-08.

Brynjolfsson, E., & McAfee, A. (2014). *The second machine age: Work, progress, and prosperity in a time of brilliant technologies*. WW Norton & Company.

Brynjolfsson, E., & Mitchell, T. (2017). What can machine learning do? Workforce implications. *Science*, *358*(6370), 1530–1534. doi:10.1126/science.aap8062 PMID:29269459

Burgsteiner, H., Kandlhofer, M., & Steinbauer, G. (2016). Irobot: Teaching the basics of artificial intelligence in high schools. *Proceedings of the AAAI Conference on Artificial Intelligence*, *30*(1). doi:10.1609/aaai.v30i1.9864

Chai, C. S., Lin, P. Y., Jong, M. S. Y., Dai, Y., Chiu, T. K., & Qin, J. (2021). Perceptions of and behavioral intentions towards learning artificial intelligence in primary school students. *Journal of Educational Technology & Society*, *24*(3), 89–101.

Chiong, J. W., & Catipunan-Francisco, J. C. (2023). Life Dynamics as a Behavioral Program for Student Leaders of Jose Rizal University. *Cosmos An International Journal of Art & Higher Education*, *12*(1), 196–204. doi:10.46360/cosmos.ahe.520231017

Collado, R. (2023). Hyping Personal Engagement (HYPE): Upgrading Research Writing Skills Among Students Using Hyperdocs. *Globus An International Journal of Management & IT, 14*(2), 01-05.

Galvex, S. (2023). The Effects of Students' Resiliency on Academic Performance Amidst Pandemic. *Globus An International Journal of Medical Science, Engineering and Technology, 9*(1), 01-04.

Graßmann, C., Schölmerich, F., & Schermuly, C. C. (2020). The relationship between working alliance and client outcomes in coaching: A meta-analysis. *Human Relations*, *73*(1), 35–58. doi:10.1177/0018726718819725

Gresse von Wangenheim, C., Hauck, J. C., Pacheco, F. S., & Bertonceli Bueno, M. F. (2021). Visual tools for teaching machine learning in K-12: A ten-year systematic mapping. *Education and Information Technologies*, *26*(5), 5733–5778. doi:10.1007/s10639-021-10570-8 PMID:33967587

Han, X., Hu, F., Xiong, G., Liu, X., Gong, X., Niu, X., & Wang, X. (2018). Design of AI+ curriculum for primary and secondary schools in Qingdao. In *2018 Chinese Automation Congress (CAC),* (pp. 4135-4140). IEEE. 10.1109/CAC.2018.8623310

Hitron, T., Wald, I., Erel, H., & Zuckerman, O. (2018). Introducing children to machine learning concepts through hands-on experience. In *Proceedings of the 17th ACM conference on interaction design and children,* (pp. 563-568). ACM. 10.1145/3202185.3210776

Horvath, A. O., & Greenberg, L. S. (1989). Development and validation of the Working Alliance Inventory. *Journal of Counseling Psychology, 36*(2), 223–233. doi:10.1037/0022-0167.36.2.223

Kong, S. C., Abelson, H., Sheldon, J., Lao, A., Tissenbaum, M., Lai, M., & Lao, N. (2017). Curriculum activities to foster primary school students' computational practices in block-based programming environments. In *Conference Proceedings of International Conference on Computational Thinking Education,* (pp. 84-89). IEEE.

Kumar, P., & Nidhi, A. (2009). *Reflections on The Impact of ICT on Teacher Education*. Paradigm Shift in Teacher Education, Vayu Education of India.

Lin, P., & Van Brummelen, J. (2021). Engaging teachers to co-design integrated AI curriculum for K-12 classrooms. In *Proceedings of the 2021 CHI conference on human factors in computing systems*, (pp. 1-12). ACM. 10.1145/3411764.3445377

Maglonzo, M. L., De Luna, J. M., Caparas, L. A., & Manuel, M. J. (2023). A Comparative Analysis of The Decision-Making Styles of Filipino Teachers and South East Asian Teachers. *Globus An International Journal of Management & IT, 14*(2), 26–35. doi:10.46360/globus.mgt.120231003

Nalbant, K. (2021). The Importance of Artificial Intelligence in Education: A short review. *Journal of Review in Science and Engineering*, 1-15.

Oesch, T. (2018). *Using Artificial Intelligence to Augment Coaching*.

Palmares, M. (2023). Technological, Pedagogical, Content Knowledge (TPACK) of Science Teachers: Basis of in-Service Training Design Development. *Cosmos Journal of Engineering & Technology, 13*(1), 01-15.

Rai, A., Constantinides, P., & Sarker, S. (2019). Editor's comments: Next-generation digital platforms: Toward human-AI hybrids. *Management Information Systems Quarterly*, *43*, iii–ix.

Rauen, C. (2018). Quo vadis, Business Coaching? Presentation at the DBVC Coaching Kongress in Berlin/Potsdam, Germany.

Reyes, V.,, Camara, M.,, Bantigue, A., & Caling, M. (2023). The Role of Learning Action Cell Session in Research Self-Efficacy Level: Basis for the Development of an Action Plan. *Globus An International Journal of Medical Science, Engineering and Technology, 9*(1), 01-04.

Senados, J. (2023). Positive Reinforcement and Its Effect on Students' Classroom Behavior and Classroom Work-Related Values. *Globus Journal of Progressive Education, 13*(1), 69-78.

Srikant, S., & Aggarwal, V. (2017h). Introducing data science to school kids. In *Proceedings of the 2017 ACM SIGCSE technical symposium on computer science education*, (pp. 561-566). ACM. 10.1145/3017680.3017717

Stone, P., Brooks, R., Brynjolfsson, E., Calo, R., Etzioni, O., Hager, G., & Teller, A. (2022). *Artificial intelligence and life in 2030: the one-hundred-year study on artificial intelligence*. arXiv preprint arXiv:2211.06318.

Sue-Chan, C., & Latham, G. P. (2004). The relative effectiveness of external, peer, and self-coaches. *Applied Psychology*, *53*(2), 260–278. doi:10.1111/j.1464-0597.2004.00171.x

Touretzky, D., Gardner-McCune, C., Breazeal, C., Martin, F., & Seehorn, D. (2019). A year in K-12 AI education. *AI Magazine*, *40*(4), 88–90. doi:10.1609/aimag.v40i4.5289

von Krogh, G. (2018). Artificial intelligence in organizations: New opportunities for phenomenon-based theorizing. *Academy of Management Discoveries*, *4*(4), 404–409. doi:10.5465/amd.2018.0084

Zimmerman, M. (2018). *Teaching AI: exploring new frontiers for learning*. International Society for Technology in Education.

# Chapter 15
# Revolutionizing Workforce Education:
## A Conceptual Framework for AI-Driven Skilling, Upskilling, and Reskilling

**Yavana Rani Subramanian**
https://orcid.org/0000-0001-7870-8007
*CMS Business School, Jain University, Bengaluru, India*

**R. Riya**
*CMS Business School, Jain University, Bengaluru, India*

**Rajaprabakaran Rajendran**
https://orcid.org/0009-0005-9272-5475
*CMS Business School, Jain University, Bengaluru, India*

## ABSTRACT

*This study presents a conceptual analysis of the role of artificial intelligence (AI) in skilling, upskilling, and reskilling the workforce. The chapter argues that artificial intelligence (AI) is fundamentally reshaping the workforce landscape and necessitating new strategies for employee skill development. This paper examines the impact of artificial intelligence (AI) on workforce development by synthesizing insights from the existing literature. The authors identified the trends, challenges, and opportunities of using artificial intelligence in workforce development. Informed decision-making and policy formulation in the realms of labour and employment contribute to this chapter. In conclusion, AI has the potential to transform the future of work and redefine the skill sets required for success in an increasingly digitized and automated world.*

## INTRODUCTION

Rapid advances in artificial intelligence (AI) technology are fundamentally reshaping the landscape of the modern workforce. Artificial intelligence (AI) revolutionizes industries across the globe from auto-

DOI: 10.4018/979-8-3693-2440-0.ch015

mating routine tasks to increasing human decision-making processes. As organisations adopt AI-driven solutions to enhance productivity and efficiency, the skill sets needed to thrive in the workplace are undergoing a profound transformation. This paradigm shift underlines the need for skilling, upskilling and retraining initiatives aimed at equipping the workforce with the skills necessary to effectively exploit the potential of AI-based technologies.

## THE EVOLUTION OF WORKFORCE DYNAMICS

The advent of artificial intelligence (AI) technologies has led to a paradigm shift in the nature of work, characterized by automation, digitalization, and the emergence of new job roles. Brynjolfsson and McAfee (2014) and Autor (2015) highlighted that AI-enabled automation has led to the displacement of routine tasks while creating the demand for skills that complement AI systems. This transformation process requires a strategic approach to workforce development in which skills, upskilling and retraining initiatives are essential to meet the evolving demands of the labour market.

## ROLE OF PEOPLE CAPABILITY MATURITY MODEL (PCMM) IN AI-DRIVEN WORKFORCE DEVELOPMENT

The People Capability Maturity Model (PCMM), developed by the Software Engineering Institute (SEI) at Carnegie Mellon University, serves as a robust framework designed specifically to enhance an organization's workforce capability. It provides structured guidelines for improving human resource practices, enabling organisations to effectively attract, develop, motivate and retain talented employees. In the context of the study focusing on the integration of artificial intelligence (AI) in skilling, upskilling, and reskilling initiatives within the workforce, PCMM holds profound significance for several compelling reasons.

First of all, the PCMM stresses the critical importance of the definition of competency requirements and the establishment of systematic procedures for evaluating and promoting employee skills. This aspect is closely aligned with the objectives of AI-based training efforts, which aim to identify the necessary skills necessary to navigate the ever-evolving digital landscape. By leveraging AI-driven analytics and assessment tools, organizations can effectively pinpoint skill gaps and tailor training programmes to address specific needs, as highlighted by Curtis et al. (2002).

Second, the PCMM emphasizes the imperative of continuous learning and development to support both individual career growth and organizational effectiveness. AI technologies offer a plethora of opportunities to facilitate lifelong learning through personalized experiences, adaptive feedback mechanisms, and vast repositories of educational resources. Through the integration of AI-powered learning platforms and tools, organizations can foster a culture of continuous learning that resonates with the principles advocated by PCMM (McShane et al. 2017).

In addition, the PCMM stresses the importance of nurturing a supportive organisational culture that prioritizes employee development and fosters collaboration and knowledge sharing. In the context of AI-driven workforce development, it is necessary to promote a culture of innovation and experiments. As highlighted by Paulk et al. (1995), encouraging employees to embrace emerging technologies and adapt to evolving skill requirements is crucial. The integration of artificial intelligence (AI) into talent management processes can further strengthen these efforts and promote transparency and inclusion in decision-making processes (Mijwil et al., 2023; Doshi et al., 2023).

The People Capability Maturity Model (PCMM) offers invaluable guidance for organizations aiming to enhance their workforce development strategies amidst the advent of artificial intelligence. By focusing on competency development, fostering a culture of continuous learning, and prioritizing employee development, organizations can effectively leverage artificial intelligence (AI) technologies to cultivate a skilled, adaptable, and motivated workforce capable of thriving in the digital age.

## SKILLING IN THE AI ERA

In the era of artificial intelligence, traditional notions of skill acquisition are being redefined. Acemoglu and Restrepo (2018) highlighted the importance of foundational skills, such as critical thinking, creativity, and emotional intelligence, in complementing AI capabilities. Moreover, the integration of AI-driven tools and platforms in educational settings, as explored by Siemens and Long (2011) and Kizilcec et al. (2020), presents new opportunities for personalized and adaptive learning experiences, fostering a more efficient and inclusive approach to skill development (Hiran et al., 2024; Mishra et al., 2021).

## UPSKILLING FOR TECHNOLOGICAL PROFICIENCY

In view of the fact that AI technologies penetrate diverse industries, it is clear that it is necessary to upskill the existing workforce to exploit their full potential. Studies such as those by Manyika et al. (2017) emphasize the role of lifelong learning and continuous upskilling in navigating technological disruptions. Jordan et al. (2019) and Johnson et al. (2021) highlighted AI-powered learning platforms that offer tailored learning pathways and real-time feedback mechanisms, enabling workers to acquire new competencies and stay abreast of technological trends (Hiran et al., 2023; Doshi et al., 2023).

## RESKILLING FOR CAREER ADAPTABILITY

In view of the displacement of jobs and occupational changes caused by AI-driven automation, reskilling initiatives play a crucial role in facilitating career adaptability and mobility. Arntz et al. (2016) highlighted the importance of proactive reskilling efforts in mitigating the adverse effects of technological displacement. As evidenced by Felstead et al. (2020) and Edgar and Workman (2018), through competency-based training programs and career transition support systems, individuals can effectively pivot their skill sets to align with emerging job opportunities, thereby fostering resilience in the face of technological disruption.

## SHIFTING EMPLOYMENT SANDS: AUTOMATION AND SKILLS DEMAND

The narrative of AI-driven job displacement is not unfounded. Routine tasks, once performed by humans, are becoming increasingly automated, potentially leading to job losses in specific sectors (Frey & Osborne, 2017). However, a closer look reveals a more complex reality. While some jobs disappear, others emerge, often requiring new skillsets to meet the evolving needs of the AI-powered world (Brynjolfsson & McAfee, 2014). The demand for soft skills, such as critical thinking, creativity, and collaboration, is on the rise, as humans' partner with artificial intelligence (AI) to perform tasks that require these unique human abilities (World Economic Forum, 2020).

## EMBRACING METAMORPHOSIS: SKILLING, UPSKILLING, AND RESKILLING

In this dynamic environment, skills, upskilling, and reskilling have become a mantra for navigating the changing job market. Skilling refers to equipping individuals with the essential skills needed to enter the workforce, whereas upskilling focuses on enhancing existing skills to remain relevant in one's current field. Reskilling, a more comprehensive transformation, involves acquiring new skillsets altogether to adapt to entirely different job roles (De Grip et al., 2020).

Continuous learning journey is crucial for both individuals and organizations. To maintain employability, individuals must embrace lifelong learning, while organizations must invest in their workforce's development to remain competitive (Cappelli & Cascio 2015).

## AI ADVANTAGE: LEVERAGING TECHNOLOGY FOR HUMAN EMPOWERMENT

Artificial intelligence (AI), often perceived as a disruptor, can ironically become a powerful tool for skilling, upskilling, and reskilling. AI-powered platforms can deliver personalized learning experiences, identify skill gaps, and recommend relevant training programs. Adaptive learning systems cater to individual learning styles and pace, making the learning process more efficient and engaging (Jovanovic & Gaevi, 2019). Artificial intelligence (AI)-powered simulations can provide realistic job-like scenarios for skill development, preparing individuals for the real workplace (Liu et al., 2020; Easwaran et al., 2022; Doshi et al., 2023).

## CHALLENGES AND OPPORTUNITIES IN AI-DRIVEN WORKFORCE DEVELOPMENT

While AI offers unprecedented opportunities for workforce development, there are also significant challenges that need to be addressed to ensure equal access and inclusive growth. One such challenge is the potential exacerbation of existing inequalities, as highlighted in research by Chetty et al. (2020) and Reich (2019), where marginalized communities may face barriers to accessing AI-enabled learning resources and opportunities. Addressing digital divides and promoting digital literacy, as advocated by organizations such as the International Telecommunication Union (ITU) and UNESCO, is crucial for fostering an inclusive and diverse talent pool capable of exploiting the benefits of artificial intelligence (AI)-based skills initiatives.

## ETHICAL AND SOCIETAL IMPLICATIONS

Moreover, the widespread adoption of AI in workforce development raises ethical concerns about privacy, data security, and algorithmic bias. Mittelstadt et al. (2016) and Jobin et al. (2019) highlighted the importance of ethical AI design and governance frameworks to mitigate potential risks and ensure responsible AI deployment. In addition, it is necessary to promote a culture of lifelong learning and critical thinking, as highlighted by UNESCO's Futures of Education initiative, in order to enable individuals to understand the ethical and societal implications of artificial intelligence in the workplace and beyond.

## COLLABORATIVE PARTNERSHIPS FOR AI-DRIVEN INNOVATION

To address these challenges, cooperation between governments, education institutions, industry leaders and civil society organisations is needed. The Global Partnership on Artificial Intelligence (GPAI) and the Digital Skills and Jobs Coalition of the European Commission are examples of collaborative efforts aimed at promoting AI literacy, promoting digital inclusion and equipping individuals with the skills needed to thrive in an AI-driven economy. These partnerships, which support cross-sectoral dialogue and knowledge sharing, can facilitate the co-creation of AI-based skills solutions that respond to the changing needs of the workforce.

## IMPACT OF AI ON WORKFORCE DYNAMICS

The inclusion of AI in the workplace represents a watershed moment in the evolution of labour dynamics, highlighting opportunities and challenges for individuals, organisations and society as a whole. While artificial intelligence promises to streamline operations, boost innovation, and drive economic growth, widespread adoption also raises concerns about job displacement, skills obsolescence, and socioeconomic inequality. As a result, it is essential to understand the role of artificial intelligence in shaping labour development strategies in order to cope with the complexity of the 21st-century labour market.

## EXPLORING THE INFLUENCE OF AI ON SKILL DEVELOPMENT

This conceptual analysis explores the multifaceted dimensions of AI's impact on skilling, upskilling, and reskilling initiatives and elucidates the mechanisms through which AI influences the acquisition, enhancement, and adaptation of employee skills. By synthesizing insights from existing literature, this paper aims to provide a comprehensive understanding of the interplay between artificial intelligence technologies and workforce development strategies, shedding light on the implications for individuals, organizations, and society at large (Singh et al., 2022; Rathi et al., 2023).

## A CRITICAL EXAMINATION OF ARTIFICIAL INTELLIGENCE'S ROLE AS A CATALYST FOR SKILL EVOLUTION

The overarching objective of this study is to critically examine the role of artificial intelligence as a catalyst for skill evolution in the contemporary workplace. By analysing the current state of research and identifying emerging trends, this paper endeavours to elucidate the opportunities and challenges inherent in leveraging artificial intelligence for skilling, upskilling, and reskilling endeavours. Moreover, by exploring the ethical, economic, and societal implications of AI-driven workforce development initiatives, this study seeks to contribute to informed decision-making and policy formulation in the field of labour and employment (Wanjale et al., 2023).

## TOWARD A TRANSFORMED WORK FUTURE: INSIGHTS AND IMPLICATIONS

In essence, this paper serves as a comprehensive exploration of the transformative potential of artificial intelligence (AI) in shaping the future of work and redefining the skill sets required for success in an increasingly digitized and automated world. By elucidating the complex interplay between artificial intelligence (AI) technologies and workforce development strategies, this analysis aims to provide valuable insights for policymakers, business leaders, educators, and other stakeholders tasked with navigating the evolving dynamics of the labour market in AI.

### Objectives

- To thoroughly examine the existing body of literature on the integration of artificial intelligence (AI) into initiatives focusing on skill development upskilling and reskilling.
- To identify trends, challenges, and opportunities associated with the use of AI in workforce development.

### Literature Review

Frank et al. (2019) comprehensively examined the impact of AI on labour markets. Their study emphasizes the nuanced interplay between artificial intelligence (AI) technologies and various facets of employment, ranging from job displacement to skill enhancement. Drawing on empirical evidence, the authors highlight the need for proactive strategies to mitigate potential adverse effects on workers while exploiting the transformative potential of artificial intelligence -driven innovation.

Jaiswal et al. (2021) delved into the realm of multinational corporations (MNCs) and explored the imperative of upskilling initiatives in the AI era. Through a qualitative analysis of organizational practices, the authors shed light on the challenges and opportunities associated with equipping employees with the requisite competencies to navigate AI-enabled environments. Their findings underscore the strategic importance of talent development strategies tailored to the unique needs of MNCs operating in the AI environment.

Morandini et al. (2023) focused on the impact of artificial intelligence (AI) on workers' skills within organizational settings. Their research emphasises the importance of upskilling and reskilling efforts to enable employees to adapt to the evolving demands of artificial intelligence technologies. By examining the role of organizational interventions in facilitating skill development, the authors offer insights into effective practices for fostering workforce readiness in the face of artificial intelligence (AI)-induced disruption.

Cramarenco et al. (2023) conducted a systematic review to explore the impact of artificial intelligence (AI) on employees' skills and well-being in global labour markets. Their analysis synthesizes findings from a wide range of studies that reveal both positive and negative effects of AI adoption on workers' skill profiles and job satisfaction. By elucidating the complex relationship between artificial intelligence (AI) technologies and employee welfare, this study contributes to a nuanced understanding of the implications of AI-driven transformations for labour market dynamics.

Rafner et al. (2021) presented a case for hybrid intelligence as a means of addressing the challenges of deskilling, upskilling, and reskilling in the age of artificial intelligence. Their conceptual framework supports the integration of human and machine capabilities in order to optimise the performance and adaptability of workers. By advocating a human-centric approach to AI deployment, the authors highlight the potential of hybrid intelligence to mitigate the adverse effects of automation on job roles and skill requirements.

Gopalakrishnan and Dhar (2020) examined the role of artificial intelligence (AI) in reshaping the skills landscape, particularly in emerging economies. This study highlights the potential of AI-based platforms and digital learning tools to democratise access to education and training, thus enhancing workforce readiness and employability. By exploring the socio-economic implications of AI-driven skilling initiatives, this study contributes to a nuanced understanding of the opportunities and challenges of AI adoption in diverse global contexts.

Tegmark (2017) explores the ethical dimensions of AI-driven workforce transformation in a thought-provoking manner. Drawing on insights from philosophy, ethics, and technology, the author grapples with existential questions about the future of work in an artificial intelligence-dominated world. Through a critical analysis of potential scenarios, Tegmark urges readers to reflect on the ethical imperative of ensuring equal access to skills, upskilling and retraining opportunities in the face of AI-induced disruptions.

Nambiar and Puthiya Veettil (2021) offer a cross-disciplinary perspective on the implications of artificial intelligence (AI) for workforce development, drawing on insights from psychology, sociology, and organizational behavior. Their research highlights the importance of psychological resilience and adaptability in navigating AI-driven career transitions. By exploring the cognitive and socio-emotional dimensions of skill acquisition and adaptation, the authors shed light on human factors shaping the effectiveness of skilling, upskilling, and reskilling endeavours in artificial intelligence.

Hagel et al. (2019) presented a strategic framework for organizational learning in the age of artificial intelligence. This study emphasizes the role of continuous learning and experimentation in fostering organizational agility and innovation. By advocating for a culture of lifelong learning and skill renewal, the authors offer practical guidance for organizations seeking to harness the potential of artificial intelligence (AI) while empowering their workforce to thrive amidst technological disruption.

Zhang et al. (2022) explore the intersection of artificial intelligence (AI), education, and workforce development, focusing on the potential of AI-driven adaptive learning systems to personalize training experiences and optimize skill acquisition outcomes. A meta-analysis of empirical studies identified promising trends and best practices in AI-enabled education and training initiatives. Their findings highlight the transformative potential of personalized learning technologies in enhancing workforce readiness and resilience in the face of technological change.

Chen and Huang (2020) delve into the intersection of AI and career development, examining how AI-driven tools and technologies are reshaping traditional career pathways. Through a qualitative study of professionals across various industries, the authors uncover the ways in which AI-powered career platforms, such as job matching algorithms and skill assessment tools, are facilitating personalized career planning and skill development. Their research sheds light on the potential of AI to democratize access to career opportunities and empower individuals to proactively manage their career trajectories in a rapidly evolving job market.

Rouse and Griffin (2021) offer a sociological perspective on the impact of AI on workforce dynamics, focusing on the implications for social stratification and inequality. Drawing on theories of technological determinism and social constructionism, the authors analyse how AI-driven automation and skill-biased technological change are reshaping the distribution of labour market outcomes. By interrogating the structural factors shaping access to skilling, upskilling, and reskilling opportunities, Rouse and Griffin highlight the importance of policy interventions aimed at promoting equitable access to education and training resources in the AI era.

Tushman and O'Reilly (2017) provide a strategic lens on organizational adaptation in the face of AI-driven disruption. Their research emphasizes the role of ambidextrous organizations—those capable of balancing exploitation of existing capabilities with exploration of new opportunities—in navigating technological change. By examining case studies of companies that have successfully transformed their business models in response to AI innovation, Tushman and O'Reilly offer insights into the organizational capabilities and leadership practices necessary to thrive in a rapidly evolving digital landscape.

Wang and Wang (2022) explore the implications of AI for lifelong learning and skill renewal, focusing on the role of self-directed learning and informal learning networks. Through a qualitative study of knowledge workers in the digital economy, the authors investigate how individuals leverage AI-powered learning platforms, online communities, and peer-to-peer networks to continuously upgrade their skills and adapt to changing job requirements. Their findings highlight the importance of fostering a learning mindset and cultivating social capital in navigating career transitions and staying relevant in the AI era.

Bughin and Hazan (2017) offer a macroeconomic perspective on the impact of AI on workforce productivity and economic growth. Drawing on empirical evidence and economic modelling, the authors analyse the potential labour market implications of AI-driven automation and augmentation. By quantifying the potential benefits of AI adoption for skill-intensive industries and knowledge workers, Bughin and Hazan provide insights into the macroeconomic implications of AI-driven workforce transformations and the policy levers that can be leveraged to maximize societal welfare in the AI era.

Kumar and Sharma (2021) investigated the impact of artificial intelligence (AI) on the Indian labour market, with a focus on the challenges and opportunities for workforce development. Their study is based on a mixed-methods approach combining a quantitative analysis of labour market data and a qualitative interview with industry stakeholders. Kumar and Sharma have examined the implications of AI-driven automation on skill demand and supply dynamics in India and shed light on policy imperatives for fostering inclusive and sustainable skill development initiatives.

Jain and Singh (2020) explore the role of artificial intelligence (AI) in reshaping India's education ecosystem and workforce readiness. Drawing on case studies and empirical research, we analyse the adoption of artificial intelligence (AI)-powered learning technologies in Indian schools, colleges and vocational training centers. Their study highlights the potential of AI-enabled personalized learning platforms to meet the diverse learning needs of the vast and heterogeneous population of India, thereby increasing employability and productivity.

Agarwal and Gupta (2019) examined the implications of artificial intelligence (AI) for India's informal sector workforce, which constitutes a significant proportion of the country's labour force. Through a qualitative study of informal workers in urban and rural settings, the authors investigate the opportunities and challenges of integrating artificial intelligence (AI) technologies into informal livelihoods. Their research highlights the importance of inclusive and context-sensitive approaches to training, upskilling and reskilling initiatives that meet the specific needs and constraints of Indian informal workers.

Joshi and Patel (2022) provide insights into the role of artificial intelligence (AI) in addressing skill gaps and promoting job creation in India's emerging technology sectors, such as information technology (IT), software development, and digital marketing. Their study analyses the skill requirements of employers in these sectors and assesses the efficacy of artificial intelligence (AI)-driven training programs in bridging the gap between industry demand and workforce supply. By identifying promising practices and success factors, Joshi and Patel offer actionable recommendations for policymakers, educators, and industry stakeholders who want to use artificial intelligence for talent development and economic growth.

Singh and Reddy (2020) investigated the socio-economic implications of artificial intelligence (AI)-driven workforce transformations in India with a focus on employment equity, gender equality, and social mobility. Their research examines the differential impact of artificial intelligence (AI) technologies on different demographic groups, including women, youth, and marginalized communities. As Singh and Reddy highlight the potential risks of exacerbating existing inequalities and exclusionary practices, they call for proactive measures aimed at ensuring that AI-based skills initiatives promote equal access to opportunities and empower all segments of the Indian labour force.

Banerjee and Dasgupta (2021) explored the role of artificial intelligence (AI) in addressing the unique challenges of skill development in rural areas of India. Through a mixed-methods approach combining surveys and case studies, the authors explore the efficacy of AI-powered mobile learning platforms and community-based training programs in enhancing rural livelihoods and fostering economic empowerment. Their research highlights the potential of AI-enabled skills interventions to bridge the urban-rural divide and to catalyse inclusive growth in India's hinterlands.

Mishra and Verma (2020) examined the impact of AI on higher education in India, focusing on the integration of AI-based curricula and pedagogical innovation in universities and technical institutions. Drawing on interviews with academic experts and industry practitioners, this study assesses the readiness of Indian higher education institutions to meet the evolving skill requirements of the AI-enabled economy. Their study highlights the need for interdisciplinary collaboration and industry-academia partnerships in order to ensure that graduates are equipped with the skills needed to succeed in AI-driven professions.

Gupta and Singh (2019) investigate the role of artificial intelligence (AI) in transforming India's traditional manufacturing sector, with a focus on the adoption of AI-powered automation technologies and smart manufacturing practices. Through case studies of Indian manufacturing firms, the authors analyse the impact of artificial intelligence (AI) on production processes, supply chain management, and workforce skill requirements. Their research highlights the potential of artificial intelligence (AI)-driven manufacturing to enhance productivity, quality, and competitiveness, but also challenges related to job displacement and workforce reskilling.

Patel and Mehta (2021) explore the ethical dimensions of AI-driven workforce development in India, focusing on data privacy, algorithmic bias, and digital rights. Drawing on insights from legal studies and ethical philosophy, this paper critically examines the ethical implications of AI-enabled recruitment, training, and performance evaluation practices. This study highlights the importance of ethical frameworks and regulatory safeguards to ensure that artificial intelligence technologies are used in a manner that respects human dignity, equity and social justice.

Sharma and Gupta (2022) analysed AI-driven skilling initiatives in India and other emerging economies, such as China and Brazil. Through a cross-country case study approach, the authors assess the contextual factors shaping the design, implementation, and impact of AI-related workforce development programmes. Their research provides valuable insights into a wide range of approaches to leveraging artificial intelligence (AI) for skill enhancement and job creation in different socio-economic contexts, informing policy debates and strategic decision-making in India's quest for inclusive and sustainable development.

Sinha & Chatterjee (2020) explore employee attitudes, concerns, and expectations regarding artificial intelligence adoption. They highlight concerns about job displacement, but also show optimism about the potential of artificial intelligence (AI) to improve job roles and careers.

Rao and Deshmukh (2021) investigated the role of social enterprises in leveraging artificial intelligence (AI) for inclusive skilling initiatives. Their work provides valuable insights into innovative approaches to addressing skills gaps and promoting social mobility for marginalised communities.

Bhattacharya and Roy (2019) analysed the opportunities and challenges faced by Indian startups in utilizing artificial intelligence (AI) for product innovation, market expansion, and talent acquisition. This study sheds light on AI's potential to drive entrepreneurial growth in India.

Gandhi & Kapoor (2020) critically evaluated the efficacy of existing skill development policies in responding to AI-driven workforce transformation. Their research suggests that policy reforms are needed to better align skill development initiatives with industry needs in the AI era.

Mukherjee & Das (2021) examined how AI technologies intersect existing gender inequalities in access to education, training, and employment opportunities. Their work highlights the importance of gender-based approaches to addressing disparities and promoting inclusive economic growth.

Singh & Sharma (2022) assessed the potential of artificial intelligence (AI) to drive the generation of rural employment in India They identify opportunities for the development of skills, entrepreneurship and diversification of livelihoods in rural areas, while acknowledging the key challenges and policy interventions needed for successful implementation.

Sharma & Verma (2020) investigate the implications of artificial intelligence (AI) for talent management practices in Indian organizations, examining how AI reshapes recruitment, performance evaluation, training, and career development. They highlight the need for organizations to responsibly and ethically leverage AI to enhance workforce productivity and engagement.

Gupta and Kapoor (2021) conducted a case study of software engineers in the Indian IT industry to understand the impact of artificial intelligence (AI) on skill requirements and career paths. Their research emphasizes the need for continuous skill development and training in order to keep pace with AI-driven advancement in the IT sector.

Rajput & Sharma (2021) explore AI's impact on skill development and clinical practice in Indian healthcare sector through a case study of medical professionals. Their findings highlight the emergence of new skill sets required for effective utilization of AI-powered diagnostic tools, telemedicine, and robotic surgery systems.

Chatterjee & Das (2019) examine the implications of artificial intelligence (AI) for job redesign and workplace design in Indian organizations. Their study reveals how artificial intelligence (AI) reshapes job roles, task allocation, and team dynamics, necessitating adjustments to workplace environments to support employee well-being and performance.

Singh & Pandey (2020) explore the role of artificial intelligence (AI) in fostering entrepreneurship development in India, focusing on the opportunities and challenges faced by startups. They identified strategies to overcome obstacles and maximize the entrepreneurial potential of AI-driven innovation.

Mishra & Das (2022) provided a comparative analysis of AI-related skill development policies across Indian states. It examines the scope, objectives, and effectiveness of government initiatives aimed at promoting AI literacy, training, and entrepreneurship. This study provides valuable insights into the development of effective policy frameworks at state level.

## Research Gap

Despite a great deal of research on the impact of AI on skill development, there is still a crucial gap: ethical considerations about AI-powered skill development programmes in emerging economies like India. While studies explore the shifts in skill demand, the potential of learning technology, and the risks of inequality, they largely ignore ethical implications. Data privacy, algorithmic bias, transparency, digital access and regulatory frameworks are key issues. Future research should investigate bias prevalence, develop ethical frameworks, examine the impact on marginalized groups, and advocate responsible AI adoption in skilling initiatives. In order to ensure ethical and equitable AI-driven workforce development in emerging economies, it is essential to address this gap.

## Research Methodology

This study employs a comprehensive approach to explore the connection between artificial intelligence (AI) and workforce development. An extensive review of various sources, including peer-reviewed journals, has been conducted. The aim of this wide range of materials is to provide an in-depth insight into the current state of AI's role in skilling, upskilling and retraining initiatives. A wide range of perspectives has helped to gain a clear understanding of the opportunities and challenges of AI in this critical area.

## Findings of This Study

The reviewed literature presents a comprehensive picture of the multifaceted relationship between artificial intelligence (AI) and workforce development, with diverse perspectives from various regions and industries. Here are some key findings:

### The Global Impact and Trends

- The impact of artificial intelligence (AI) on labour markets is multifaceted, ranging from job displacement to skill enhancement and requires proactive strategies for adaptation and skills development.
- Upskilling and reskilling are crucial for employees to navigate AI-driven environments, and organizations need tailored talent development strategies.
- Artificial intelligence (AI) technologies can personalize learning experiences and optimize skill acquisition and offer promising solutions for workforce readiness and resilience.
- Hybrid intelligence, combining human and machine capabilities, has the potential to mitigate the negative effects of automation on jobs and skills requirements.

- AI-powered platforms and digital learning tools have the potential to democratise access to education and training, especially in emerging economies.

Ethical Considerations and Socio-Economic Impact

- Ethical considerations regarding AI-driven skilling, particularly regarding data privacy, algorithmic bias, and digital access, require attention to ensure equitable outcomes.
- AI can exacerbate existing inequalities and exclusion if policy interventions and inclusive skills initiatives are not addressed.
- Psychological resilience and adaptability are crucial for navigating AI-driven career transitions, highlighting the importance of human factors in skill development
- Artificial intelligence (AI)-driven skilling programs in India hold promise for addressing skills gaps and job creation in emerging technology sectors.
- Inclusive and context-sensitive approaches are essential for skilling initiatives that meet the diverse needs of Indian informal sector workers.
- Artificial intelligence-powered mobile learning platforms and community-based training programs have the potential to bridge the urban–rural divide and empower rural communities.
- Ethical frameworks and regulatory safeguards are essential to ensure responsible and equitable deployment of artificial intelligence in India's workforce development.

## RECOMMENDATIONS

This comprehensive analysis of AI's impact on skilling, upskilling, and reskilling efforts highlights the following areas for further research:

### Ethical Considerations

#### Develop Ethical AI Frameworks

Conduct case studies to identify bias in AI-powered skilling programs and develop ethical frameworks to mitigate these biases.

#### Privacy and Data Security

Data collection practices within AI-powered skilling platforms should be examined and protocols should be established for responsible data use and user privacy protection.

#### Transparency and Accountability

Exploring mechanisms for transparent decision-making within artificial intelligence algorithms used for skill assessment and job matching.

### Digital Exclusion and Access

Investigate initiatives to bridge the digital divide and ensure equitable access for marginalised groups to AI-based skilling tools.

## Socioeconomic Impact

### Longitudinal Studies

Track the long-term impact of artificial intelligence (AI) on specific job roles, skill requirements, and the effectiveness of various skill interventions.

### Policy Interventions

Analyse the effectiveness of existing AI and workforce development policies and regulations and propose new frameworks that promote responsible and equitable adoption.

### Industry-Specific Studies

Conduct in-depth analyses of AI's impact on skilling needs and opportunities in specific sectors (e.g., healthcare, manufacturing, services).

### Informal Sector Skilling

Effective approaches to integrate artificial intelligence (AI)-powered skilling initiatives into the informal economy, empowering informal workers and bridging the formal-informal divide.

### Rural Skilling

Evaluate the effectiveness of artificial intelligence (AI)-powered mobile learning platforms and community-based training programs in equipping rural populations with relevant skills.

### Lifelong Learning

Explore new models for continuous learning and skills development supported by artificial intelligence (AI) technologies in order to promote career adaptability and employability throughout individuals' careers.

## Global Collaboration

### Comparative Studies

Conduct comparative analyses of AI-driven skilling initiatives in different countries and regions and share best practices and lessons learned.

### Knowledge Sharing

Promote international cooperation between researchers, policymakers, and industry stakeholders to address global challenges and opportunities related to artificial intelligence and workforce development.

By pursuing these research avenues, we can contribute to a deeper understanding of the complex interplay between artificial intelligence (AI) and workforce development, informing policies, practices, and individual decisions to achieve a future of inclusive and sustainable work.

## CONCLUSION

Rapid integration of Artificial Intelligence (AI) into the workplace offers both transformative opportunities and complex challenges for skilling, upskilling, and retraining initiatives. This analysis explores a multifaceted relationship between artificial intelligence (AI) and workforce development, drawing insights from diverse perspectives across regions and industries.

Key findings highlight AI's potential to personalize learning, augment human capabilities, and democratise access to education and training. However, in order to ensure equitable outcomes, careful attention must be paid to ethical considerations concerning data privacy, algorithmic bias and digital access. In addition, the socio-economic impact of artificial intelligence (AI) requires proactive strategies to deal with potential job displacement, skill obsolescence and exacerbate existing inequalities.

In the future, deeper research is crucial to effectively navigate this evolving landscape. By focusing on ethical frameworks, understanding the long-term impact of artificial intelligence (AI) on specific sectors, and exploring innovative approaches for rural and informal sector skilling, the potential of AI can be harnessed to empower individuals, organizations, and societies to thrive in the AI-driven future of work.

Ultimately, the success of AI in shaping the future of work depends on cooperation efforts. By fostering international knowledge sharing, encouraging responsible AI development, and prioritising ethical and inclusive skilling initiatives, we can ensure that AI will serve as a force for positive transformation and empower individuals and societies to adapt, thrive, and contribute meaningfully in the ever-evolving world of work.

## REFERENCES

Acemoglu, D., & Restrepo, P. (2018). Artificial intelligence, automation and work. *NBER Working Paper, (24196).*

Agarwal, S., & Gupta, R. (2019). AI in the informal sector: Opportunities and challenges for Indian workers. *Journal of Informal Economy Studies*, *1*(2), 87–102.

Arntz, M., Gregory, T., & Zierahn, U. (2016). The Risk of Automation for Jobs in OECD Countries: A Comparative Analysis. *OECD Social, Employment and Migration Working Papers, (189).*

Autor, D. H. (2015). Why Are There Still So Many Jobs? The History and Future of Workplace Automation. *The Journal of Economic Perspectives*, *29*(3), 3–30. doi:10.1257/jep.29.3.3

Banerjee, S., & Dasgupta, R. (2021). AI for rural skill development: A case study in India. *Journal of Rural Studies, 82*, 120–135.

Bhattacharya, S., & Roy, D. (2019). AI and entrepreneurship in India: Opportunities and challenges for startups. *International Journal of Innovation and Technology Management, 16*(5), 1–20.

Brynjolfsson, E., & McAfee, A. (2014). *The Second Machine Age: Work, Progress, and Prosperity in a Time of Brilliant Technologies*. W. W. Norton & Company.

Chatterjee, A., & Das, S. (2019). AI and job redesign: Implications for workplace design in Indian organizations. *Journal of Workplace Design & Management, 12*(3), 112–127.

Cramarenco, R. E., Burcă-Voicu, M. I., & Dabija, D. C. (2023). The impact of artificial intelligence (AI) on employees' skills and well-being in global labor markets: A systematic review. *Oeconomia Copernicana, 14*(3), 731–767. doi:10.24136/oc.2023.022

Curtis, B., Hefley, B., & Miller, S. (2002). *People Capability Maturity Model (P-CMM) version 2.0*. Software Engineering Institute.

Doshi, R., Hiran, K. K., Mijwil, M. M., & Anand, D. (2023). To That of Artificial Intelligence, Passing Through Business Intelligence. In Handbook of Research on AI and Knowledge Engineering for Real-Time Business Intelligence (pp. 1-16). IGI Global. doi:10.4018/978-1-6684-6519-6.ch001

Doshi, R., Hiran, K. K., Ranolia, R., & Joshi, C. (2023). Monitor Cloud Performance and Data Safety With Artificial Intelligence. In Applications of Artificial Intelligence in Wireless Communication Systems (pp. 92-108). IGI Global. doi:10.4018/978-1-6684-7348-1.ch006

Easwaran, B., Hiran, K. K., Krishnan, S., & Doshi, R. (Eds.). (2022). *Real-Time Applications of Machine Learning in Cyber-Physical Systems*. IGI Global. doi:10.4018/978-1-7998-9308-0

Edgar, F., & Workman, J. (2018). Developing the Career Agility of the Contemporary Worker: A Framework for Research and Practice. *Journal of Vocational Behavior, 106*, 73–84.

Frank, M. R., Autor, D., Bessen, J. E., Brynjolfsson, E., Cebrian, M., Deming, D. J., Feldman, M., Groh, M., Lobo, J., Moro, E., Wang, D., Youn, H., & Rahwan, I. (2019). Toward understanding the impact of artificial intelligence on labour. *Proceedings of the National Academy of Sciences of the United States of America, 116*(14), 6531–6539. doi:10.1073/pnas.1900949116 PMID:30910965

Gandhi, A., & Kapoor, V. (2020). AI and skill development policy in India: A critical appraisal. *Journal of Policy Research in Higher Education, 6*(2), 98–115.

Gupta, A., & Singh, B. (2019). AI-driven transformation in the Indian manufacturing sector. *International Journal of Advanced Manufacturing Technology, 102*, 1397–1412.

Gupta, M., & Kapoor, A. (2021). AI and skill development in the Indian IT industry: A case study of software engineers. *International Journal of Information Management, 57*, 1–12.

Hiran, K. K., Doshi, R., & Patel, M. (Eds.). (2024). *Applications of Virtual and Augmented Reality for Health and Wellbeing*. IGI Global. doi:10.4018/979-8-3693-1123-3

Hiran, K. K., Hemachandran, K., Pise, A., & Rabi, B. (Eds.). (2023). *Handbook of Research on AI and Knowledge Engineering for Real-Time Business Intelligence*. IGI Global. doi:10.4018/978-1-6684-6519-6

Jain, S., & Singh, M. (2020). Artificial intelligence in Indian education: Enhancing workforce readiness. *International Journal of Educational Technology in Higher Education*, *17*(1), 1–18.

Jaiswal, A., Arun, C. J., & Varma, A. (2021). Rebooting employees: Upskilling for artificial intelligence in multinational corporations. *International Journal of Human Resource Management*, *33*(6), 1179–1208. doi:10.1080/09585192.2021.1891114

Johnson, R. D., Ke, F., & Lin, L. (2021). Investigating the Effectiveness of a Personalized Learning Intervention on Improving Middle School Students' Scientific Inquiry Skills. *Journal of Educational Psychology*, *113*(4), 683–703.

Jordan, K., Carlile, O., & Stack, J. (2019). Fostering Deep Learning in Online Learning Environments. *EDUCAUSE Review*, *54*(2), 46–58.

Joshi, V., & Patel, A. (2022). AI-driven skill development in emerging technology sectors in India. *International Journal of Technology and Human Interaction*, *18*(3), 1–18.

Kizilcec, R. F., Piech, C., & Schneider, E. (2020). Deconstructing Disengagement: Analyzing Learner Subpopulations in Massive Open Online Courses. *EDUCAUSE Review*, *55*(5), 52–67.

Kumar, A., & Sharma, R. (2021). Impact of artificial intelligence on the labour market in India: Challenges and opportunities. *Journal of Economic Studies (Glasgow, Scotland)*, *48*(7), 1689–1706. doi:10.1108/JES-08-2020-0431

Manyika, J., Lund, S., Bughin, J., Woetzel, J., Manyika, J., Lund, S., & Woetzel, J. (2017). *Jobs lost; jobs gained: Workforce transitions in a time of automation*. McKinsey Global Institute.

McShane, M. K., Nanda, S., & Bagheri, R. (2017). The Promise and Challenge of Artificial Intelligence for Workforce Development. *International Journal of Adult Vocational Education and Technology*, *8*(4), 56–70.

Mijwil, M. M., Gök, M., Doshi, R., Hiran, K. K., & Kösesoy, I. (2023). Utilizing Artificial Intelligence Techniques to Improve the Performance of Wireless Nodes. In *Applications of Artificial Intelligence in Wireless Communication Systems* (pp. 150–162). IGI Global. doi:10.4018/978-1-6684-7348-1.ch010

Mishra, A., & Das, P. (2022). AI and skill development policy in India: A comparative analysis of state initiatives. *Journal of Comparative Policy Analysis*, *24*(1), 89–107.

Mishra, A., Tripathi, A., Khazanchi, D., Hiran, K. K., Vyas, A. K., & Padmanaban, S. (2021). A framework for applying artificial intelligence (AI) with Internet of NanoThings (IoNT). In *Machine Learning for Sustainable Development* (pp. 1–16). De Gruyter. doi:10.1515/9783110702514-001

Mishra, R., & Verma, S. (2020). AI in higher education: A case study of Indian institutions. *International Journal of Educational Technology in Higher Education*, *17*(1), 1–17.

Morandini, S., Fraboni, F., De Angelis, M., Puzzo, G., Giusino, D., & Pietrantoni, L. (2023). The Impact of Artificial Intelligence on Workers' Skills: Upskilling and Reskilling in Organisations. *Informing Science: The International Journal of an Emerging Transdiscipline, 26*, 039–068.

Morandini, S., Fraboni, F., De Angelis, M., Puzzo, G., Giusino, D., & Pietrantoni, L. (2023). The Impact of Artificial Intelligence on Workers' Skills: Upskilling and Reskilling in Organisations. *Informing Science*, *26*, 39–68. doi:10.28945/5078

Mukherjee, S., & Das, A. (2021). AI and gender disparities in workforce development: A case study of India. *Gender, Work and Organization*, *28*(6), 235–253.

Patel, N., & Mehta, K. (2021). Ethical dimensions of AI in workforce development: A case study in India. *Journal of Business Ethics*, *169*, 629–645.

Paulk, M. C., Weber, C. V., Curtis, B., & Chrissis, M. B. (1995). *The Capability Maturity Model: Guidelines for Improving the Software Process*. Addison-Wesley Professional.

Rafner, J., Dellermann, D., Hjorth, A., Verasztó, D., Kampf, C., Mackay, W., & Sherson, J. (2021). Deskilling, Upskilling, and Reskilling: A Case for Hybrid Intelligence. *Morals & Machines*, *1*(2), 24–39. doi:10.5771/2747-5174-2021-2-24

Rajput, S., & Sharma, P. (2021). AI and skill development in the Indian healthcare sector: A case study of medical professionals. *International Journal of Healthcare Management*, *14*(3), 321–335.

Rao, S., & Deshmukh, P. (2021). Harnessing AI for inclusive skilling: Insights from Indian social enterprises. *Journal of Social Entrepreneurship*, *13*(2), 245–264.

Rathi, S., Hiran, K. K., & Sakhare, S. (2023). Affective state prediction of E-learner using SS-ROA based deep LSTM. *Array (New York, N.Y.)*, *19*, 100315. doi:10.1016/j.array.2023.100315

Sharma, R., & Verma, S. (2020). AI-driven workforce transformations: Implications for talent management in Indian organizations. *Journal of Human Resource Management in Emerging Economies*, *2*(1), 45–60.

Sharma, S., & Gupta, N. (2022). Comparative analysis of AI-driven skilling initiatives in emerging economies. *International Journal of Comparative Education and Development*, *24*(1), 45–64.

Siemens, G., & Long, P. (2011). Penetrating the Fog: Analytics in Learning and Education. *EDUCAUSE Review*, *46*(5), 30–32.

Singh, N., & Sharma, A. (2022). AI and rural employment generation in India: Prospects and challenges. *Journal of Rural Development*, *41*(1), 45–60.

Singh, P., & Reddy, A. R. (2020). Socio-economic implications of AI-driven workforce transformations in India. *The Indian Journal of Social Work*, *81*(4), 531–548. doi:10.1177/0018726720961507

Singh, R., & Pandey, A. (2020). AI and entrepreneurship development in India: Opportunities and challenges for startups. *International Journal of Entrepreneurial Behaviour & Research*, *26*(5), 987–1005.

Singh, S. V., & Hiran, K. K. (2022). The impact of AI on teaching and learning in higher education technology. *Journal of Higher Education Theory and Practice*, *22*(13).

Sinha, R., & Chatterjee, S. (2020). AI and the future of work in India: A qualitative study of employee perceptions. *Journal of Organizational Change Management*, *33*(4), 789–805.

Wanjale, K., Chitre, A. V., & Doshi, R. (2023). Opting for Industry 4.0: Challenge or Opportunity. In *AI, IoT, Big Data and Cloud Computing for Industry 4.0* (pp. 3–20). Springer International Publishing. doi:10.1007/978-3-031-29713-7_1

# Chapter 16
# Role of AI in Skilling, Upskilling, and Reskilling the Workforce

**Narendra Kumar Swami**
https://orcid.org/0000-0003-2865-8114
*Arya College of Engineering and Information Technology, India*

**Amit Sharma**
*Arya College of Engineering and Information Technology, India*

**Rohit Mittal**
*Manipal University Jaipur, India*

## ABSTRACT

*This chapter investigates the most recent advancements in artificial intelligence (AI) study and application of AI to change professional skills. The integration of AI into many sectors of organizations holds promise for automating jobs now handled by humans or decreasing cognitive burden. According to this study, incorporating AI into a company requires putting multiple organisational techniques into practice at once. The first step in closing the present skills gap in the workplace is to map the transversal competencies that employees need. Companies may also assist employees in learning the competencies needed to implement AI, as well as in enhancing and gaining new capabilities. The findings also show that businesses need to implement policies that support employees via offering opportunities for ad hoc training and development in order to make certain that workers' attitudes and mental models regarding AI are open and prepared for the changing labour market and its related issues.*

## INTRODUCTION

Business, society, and the global economy are all greatly affected by the use of technology, particularly in the field of AI. The ability of a system to accurately comprehend external input, learn from such data, and use those learnings to accomplish objectives.

DOI: 10.4018/979-8-3693-2440-0.ch016

Through awareness, understanding, education, and application, flexibility can either complement or even completely replace human tasks. These days, modern AI systems require machine learning. A machine learning system receives large amounts of information, interprets it, and applies methods to find patterns and relationships in the data. For organizations to effectively respond to these changes, they must adjust to new working and organizational models. One of the main adjustments to be anticipated is a reassessment of the skills required by the labor force, since automation in some jobs may call for retraining or the learning of new skills. The introduction of AI will have an impact on both knowledge workers and blue-collar workers because it can automate a wide range of tasks presently completed by people. (Abe et al., 2021; Doshi et al., 2023; Hiran et al., 2024)

Because numerous employment opportunities may be automated and lead to job losses in businesses that rely on manual labour, the effects of AI may be more severe for blue-collar workers. Known as "mid-range" talents, manual, functioning and visual-spatial abilities are among them, and their need is decreasing. (Abe et al., 2021; Priyadarshi et al., 2021)

The way AI impacts human skills is likely to rely on the specific tasks and abilities being mechanised. Depending on the specific skills required for a task, some tasks may be better suited for automation than others, and the impact on human talents will change accordingly. It's also feasible that certain skills, like critical thinking, may become more in-demand as AI advances.

There will be a big change in the skills required for every profession during the following five years, leading to a skills gap. This is true for both people who intend to enter the labour market and people who wish to stay in their current positions. In the next five years, the percentage of vital skills will shift by 40%, according to the World Economic Forum (WEF), and 48 to 52% of workers would need retraining and further education. Soft skills, or transversal skills, such as analysing and thinking critically, problem-solving, and self-management, are among the core competences that are expected to become more crucial by 2025. Technical talents are necessary for employing AI systems efficiently. (Mubarak, 2022; Doshi et al., 2023)

To find answers to the problems that occur, this paper will look into the most current advancements in practice and research on the automation of professional abilities through artificial intelligence (AI). It is necessary to anticipate the type of organizational changes brought about by the implementation of AI systems in order to design key responsive training pathways for roles, responsibilities, and skills. Thus, in order to understand how AI is affecting human abilities in organizations, we have examined the key theories and methodologies. Next, we looked at how workers' skill requirements have changed as a result of AI's entrance and how AI can assist workers in acquiring and developing critical skills (Hiran et al., 2023; Mishra et al., 2021).

The current study makes multiple recommendations. It identifies tactics that can help workers and organizations overcome the difficulties brought on by upskilling and reskilling proclivities. Thirdly, it offers suggestions for practitioners to determine the competencies required for AI adoption, with the goal of customizing possibilities for training and development to the evolving labor market. Fourthly, it emphasizes the value of a transdisciplinary approach in producing insightful information and the significance of psychology in comprehending the whole range of applications of AI and how it affects society. Lastly, it offers recommendations for more study opportunities based on the labor market patterns that were found.

## AI AND HUMAN SKILLS

AI has seen much advancement recently, both in the workplace and in industry. By using NLP and AI to comprehend and simulate human interaction with computer systems, AI-based solutions have historically automated a wide range of back-office tasks, including data entry, document management, customer care, and accounting.

It is also possible to employ generative AI systems to simulate or replace human transversal skills like conflict resolution, problem solving, and communication. An AI system endowed with natural language processing (NLP) skills, for instance, may decipher customer discussions, gauge their feelings, and offer amiable and supportive replies. In order to continuously improve its responses and offer individualized customer care catered to each customer's unique requirements, it can also learn from customer interactions (Doshi et al., 2023; Barua et al., 2020).

Certain human abilities, like creativity, problem-solving, and reasoning, can be replicated by other generative AI systems. ChatGPT is one instance of this, which generates dialogues that seem human via natural language generation. These systems interpret the conversational context and offer pertinent responses by utilizing machine learning, sentiment analysis, and natural language processing.

In addition to increasing productivity and efficiency, the author makes the case that technology can support human labor and provide prospects for career stability and upskilling. It will be important to address legal, psychological, and ethical issues at the managerial level in order to realize these benefits. It is imperative to emphasize the significance of positive externalities, such elevated living standards and sustainable growth, achieved through the ideal distribution of technological and human resources within the framework of Industry 5.0. A few strategies to do this include funding training and development initiatives that give employees the know-how to use new technologies effectively and instituting flexible work schedules that let employees benefit from AI-related efficiencies while still striking a healthy work-life balance.

Ultimately, artificial broad Intelligence is a type of AI capable of carrying out any intellectual work that a human can, including those involving broad knowledge and problem-solving skills. There are suggestions that the development of artificial general intelligence (AGI) may outperform human intellect and result in major changes to organizational processes and outcomes.

## THEORIES AND APPROACHES

Several theories and methods exist to describe how AI affects human abilities within organizations. A widely accepted perspective anticipates that the advent of AI will result in a favorable shift whereby human talents will be improved, ultimately leading to higher levels of efficiency and productivity. People do best when they have access to a variety of resources and tools that aid in their understanding and processing of knowledge, according to the Technology-Mediated Learning Theory. According to this hypothesis, people can learn new skills and knowledge effectively through technology-mediated learning, which includes virtual simulations and online video lessons. In this way, artificial intelligence can give access to a greater variety of knowledge and resources, facilitating better learning and performance. As a result, AI has the ability to automate some procedures and operations, giving human workers more time and resources to devote to higher-level and more difficult jobs. Workers may become more inventive and productive as a result of the development of new talents and the optimization of already acquired ones.

Although this theory is rightly enthusiastic about the beneficial effects of AI on human capabilities in organizations, it does not appear to solve the problem of an individual employee's access to technology, which the organization needs to supply as a resource. It is also reasonable to assume that employees learn best from technology they are familiar with, find relevant, useful, enjoyable, and simple to use, rather than from technology in and of itself. As a result, opinions held by staff members regarding the technology and its features are taken into account when developing a technology-mediated learning process. Lastly, the theory fails to address the variables that cause workers who are relieved of duties that AI has taken over to concentrate on more complicated tasks rather than any other kind of activity (Easwaran et al., 2022).

However, another perspective views AI as a potential replacement for specific jobs that could result in employment displacement. According to this argument, AI could eventually replace human workers for jobs that require repetitive or manual labor, which would cause employment losses in industries that primarily rely on these skills. A rising body of evidence, nevertheless, supports the notion that implementing AI could lead to the creation of new positions across a range of industries, particularly those that are concerned with the advancement and application of AI technology. Additionally, it appears that this idea ignores the fact that jobs are not static, pre-defined collections of activities that remain the same regardless of the application context. However, depending on how the job is viewed or represented, performing the same work in a different location may indicate a whole new set of duties. This means that the detrimental effects of AI may need to be reconsidered as being far more erratic than this theory predicts.

According to the writers, artificial intelligence is changing the nature of working and has the potential to both innovate and pose a threat. The theory proposes that there is a predictable sequence for the development of artificial intelligence (AI) and defines four categories of intelligence needed for specific jobs, especially service tasks. (Bhargava et al., 2020). The hypothesis states that AI will mostly replace human labor at the task level, especially for straightforward mechanical jobs. Additionally, it implies that when AI replaces human labor on increasingly difficult and sophisticated activities, predictable changes will occur over time. As AI performs more analytical jobs, such as those requiring logical and rule-based reasoning, the significance of analytical skills will decline. Artificial intelligence (AI) will eventually be able to carry out intuitive and empathetic activities. This could lead to creative ways of merging humans and computers in the provision of services, but it could also threaten jobs held by people. As a matter of fact, the majority of professions in business entail thinking, feeling, and thinking duties (such advising patients and analyzing client preferences and organizing daily schedules and attending to them). (Chen et al., 2021)

Humans are required to concentrate on work that AI is unlikely to take on, such as those that need "thinking" and "feeling" skills, even though the nature of tasks and the level of intelligence required can vary depending on the job. This is because AI has displaced mechanical labor. Thus, in the near future, the ability of people to retool and upskill will determine a company's potential to thrive; instead of losing their jobs, workers will be given new responsibilities that depend more on "feeling skills". But according to several academics recently, "thinking skills" alone won't keep artificial intelligence from replacing service professionals.

In order to determine if Workers could be replaced by computers or by devices that are controlled by computers using preprogrammed rules, the authors employed roughly 8,000 tasks from German businesses. The findings demonstrated that whereas individual jobs within a profession may be substituted, entire occupations could not. AI may help with diagnosis, decision-making, Big Data analytics, and administration in the healthcare industry in light of labor constraints. The authors contend that human interaction, empathy, and effective communication are still crucial components of the care process, and that AI cannot replace them. That is, while the human doctor will always have a function, artificial intelligence (AI) has the potential to be a very helpful cognitive aid. Although AI is not intended to replace healthcare professionals, the authors contend that those who employ it will probably have a competitive edge over those who do not and run the risk of falling behind. A number of theoretical models have been put forth to explain the phenomena of skill retention and deterioration after the introduction of new technologies.

Four essential elements form the foundation of organizational learning theory. First, "collective learning" refers to the method by which groups interact and collaborate among themselves in order to gain and maintain information and skills through training, sharing of knowledge, and cooperation. Second, "reflective practice" refers to the deliberate activity of thinking back on past experiences and actions to draw lessons and improve flexibility in response to changing conditions. Third, there are two ways that the "organizational culture" might help or hurt learning. Organizations require "structural supports" to enable learning, including knowledge management systems, training programs, and incentives. In a market that is evolving quickly due to the advent of various AI products and features, organizations may stay successful and competitive by understanding and managing these aspects well.

## ARTIFICIAL INTELLIGENCE AND TRANSVERSAL SKILLS

Organizations now recognize how critical it is to identify and develop transversal talents within their workforce as a result of the integration of AI technologies. Soft skills, sometimes referred to as transversal talents or transferable abilities, are those that are applicable to a variety of jobs and sectors (Billionniere, 2022). Working with AI systems efficiently requires a variety of talents, including critical thinkings, problem-solving, communications, and teamwork. They make it possible for employees to adjust to new procedures and technologies as well as to keep learning and growing despite how fastly technology is advancing.

Transversal abilities are not only necessary for interacting with AI systems, but they can also be enhanced and developed through AI. Artificial Intelligence can free up time and resource to focus on more complicated and challenging jobs that require transversal talents by automating some tasks and procedures. Organizations can foster employee growth and creativity by providing opportunities for cross-functional skill development and improvement through the use of AI to optimize and streamline certain operations.

A new taxonomy model for transversal skills and competencies (TSCs) is proposed where the abilities that are deemed useful or essential for efficient performance in any type of profession, education, or life activity are known as TSCs. Because they are not limited to a certain setting, they are hence "transversal." It is believed that transversality and the corresponding transferability are becoming more and more significant in a society where social and technical change is occurring quickly. According to this expert group, transversality can be associated with what it refers to as "deeper learning," or the competencies and skills that support and enable the more specialized talents required, say, in a work context.

Core competencies, cognitive competency, self-management competency, social and communication competency, physical and manual competency, and life skills are the six primary areas. These in turn consist of several distinct clusters to help with the mapping of every talent. For a variety of users and users from various industries, the model makes it easier to identify pertinent concepts and the connections between them. Within the context of organizational settings where artificial intelligence (AI) systems are being implemented, three out of the six TSC categories—thinking skills, self-management, and social and communication skills—comprising include abilities that are deemed "soft" or transferable, making them pertinent to workers in the Industry 4.0. (Hammer & Karmakar, 2021; Wanjale et al., 2023)

## Core Skills

The capacity to work with numbers and measurements, use digital devices and applications, and comprehend, speak, read, and write in one or more languages are all considered core abilities.

Employees with language proficiency can utilize AI technologies (Mittal* et al., 2020) more effectively. Employees who speak English well, for instance, will find it easier to browse and utilize the various AI products and platforms that offer English user interfaces and documentation. Employees that are at ease with statistics and measures may also more effectively comprehend and use machine learning algorithms to categorize data, forecast results, and optimize workflows . In a similar vein, workers proficient with digital tools and applications will be better equipped to oversee and maintain AI systems, which frequently call for technical know-how and an understanding of programming languages.

The body of research shows how AI may support workers in acquiring and continuously enhancing their key competencies. First, by offering automatic language learning tools, AI can assist in enhancing workers' language proficiency. Furthermore, personnel with different language backgrounds can communicate more successfully by using AI-based translation technologies to close the communication gap . Second, by giving workers access to real-time data and insights produced by AI itself, AI systems can encourage the development of measurement and digital skills in them. Workers can use this information to spot patterns in their work, comprehend how their performance is impacted, and create plans to raise their game. AI-based platforms can also offer customized learning opportunities that support employees in developing and honing their digital abilities. This consists of automatic feedback and assessment tools, on-demand workouts, customized content, and virtual coaching.

## Thinking Skills

It describes the capacity to use mental processes for gathering, conceiving, analyzing, summarizing, and/or assessing data produced by observation, experience, introspection, reasoning, or communication. The utilization of diverse forms of information to organize work, accomplish objectives, resolve conflicts, and carry out intricate jobs in both conventional and innovative methods is indicative of this.

According to recent research, critical thinking abilities are essential for interacting with AI systems efficiently. The personnel can comprehend the data and insights produced by the AI system and utilize this information to make well-informed decisions by applying analytical, critical, and fast thinking skills. AI can assist businesses in automating certain tasks, but employees still need to be creative to think outside the box, generate fresh concepts, and solve problems that AI systems are unable to. Personnel can concentrate on more complicated and customer-facing duties by using AI technologies to automate monotonous chores. As a result, staff members acquire the ability to solve problems in order to handle similar circumstances efficiently. AI programs can also be applied in some stages of a challenging problem-solving procedure.

Furthermore, AI does not have a single ground truth and its comprehension of complicated problems is dynamic and time-dependent, requiring extensive domain expertise. This suggests that workers are predisposed to include human-specific transversal skills—such as empathy, creativities, intuitive and learning abilities, and creative thinking—into the process to cover the gaps left by AI systems.

## Self-Management Skills

For instance, we shall look at task and time management as important self-management abilities for worker productivity. AI systems have the potential to shorten turnaround times for some tasks in organizations by automating them or offering more effective ways to finish them. More quickly than a person, AI systems can analyze and interpret data. This allows one to finish a work that would typically take several hours in a matter of minutes. Some claim that efficient time management entails utilizing technology while allocating the remaining time for tasks that require human interaction (Mittal* et al., 2019). In addition to encouraging the value creation process in organizations, this helps the staff make the most out of their time. Employees can concentrate on projects that call for ingenuity, creativity, empathy, or other characteristics that are specific to people. Organizations may be able to provide additional value through the generation of fresh concepts, the delivery of individualized customer care, or the production of fulfilling work experiences for staff members by improving self-management abilities and encouraging staff to concentrate on projects needing a "human touch."

## Social and Communication Skills

Employees can communicate ideas and information with coworkers and other stakeholders in an efficient and compassionate manner. AI systems are frequently complicated and can be challenging to comprehend. Having effective communication may guarantee that all parties involved are in agreement and pursuing the same objectives. Firstly, social and communication skills can be enhanced by managers and staff members using cutting-edge AI systems. These systems can offer feedback on their online interactions, assist in identifying possible communication gaps or issues, and provide solutions to enhance communication. Certain AI systems are made to give workers games and activities that focus on communication to assist them hone their communication skills and modify their approaches.

Moreover, by offering intelligent help and automated responses, an AI system can improve communication between staff members and clients. By using chat bots to respond to consumer inquiries and deliver information, AI can also be utilized to automate customer care procedures. This frequently happens in a way that motivates staff members to enhance their own communication skills by seeing how well AI handles communicative encounters with clients.

Developing trust is another requirement of working with AI. Workers must have faith in the dependability of technology and the mutual goal-orientedness of their coworkers. This fosters a culture of cohesion and cooperation within the company, which is necessary for both competitive advantage and efficient performance. To guarantee that everyone is using technology as productively and efficiently as possible, teams may manage and optimize its utilization with the support of effective leadership. Ensuring effective organizational performance and enhancing team performance can be achieved using this approach. Having strong leadership qualities can be essential to overcoming potential difficulties or roadblocks while using AI and to keeping the team motivated and focused in the face of failures. By doing this, you can make sure that the group can keep moving forward toward the organization's objectives and overcome any obstacles that may arise.

Managers could be able to pinpoint areas for improvement and receive real-time performance evaluation from AI systems. Aside from helping managers develop their leadership abilities, they may also offer them individualized coaching and advice on team dynamics, which will help them better understand how their staff members connect with one another and how to lead them through productive communication processes. Lastly, managers may create a collaborative and growth-oriented workplace by utilizing AI technologies to better understand the requirements and motivations of their team members.

## Physical and Manual Skills

Completing tasks and activities that call for manual dexterity, agility, and/or physical strength is referred to as physical and manual abilities. These can be carried out in risky or challenging conditions that call for strength or endurance. ICT devices, machinery, hand tools, musical instruments, and other items that require guidance, movement, or strength can all be used for these tasks and activities, as can other direct physical interventions.

It is crucial for workers using AI to develop their manual and physical abilities for a number of reasons, according to recent research. Employees can use AI technologies more effectively if they have improved their manual and physical skills. Workers with strong hand-eye coordination or hardware and software proficiency, for instance, can use AI technologies more successfully and efficiently. Second, workers utilizing AI technologies could have to operate machinery or other equipment like robots. Enhancing manual dexterity and physical capabilities can help workers operate more securely and prevent workplace mishaps or injuries. Thirdly, developing one's manual and physical abilities might help one become more adaptive to changing work environments and technologies. Workers with a variety of machine or equipment skills, for instance, will be better able to adjust to new AI technologies implemented in the workplace.

The literature contains some evidence about the effects of AI on workers' manual and physical skills. Workers can concentrate on more difficult and sophisticated activities by using AI tools to automate those jobs that require human dexterity and physical labor. Employee productivity can rise as a result, and they can develop their talents in more important company domains. Additionally, people can operate more productively and efficiently with the aid of AI technologies, which can increase the accuracy and precision of manual and physical operations. Robots and machines under AI control, for instance, can be trained to carry out tasks with a high degree of precision and repeatability, lowering the possibility of error and raising overall quality. To help employees enhance their manual and physical skills, AI technologies can be utilized to offer them specialized training and development programs. Workers can practice and enhance their abilities in a secure and regulated setting, for instance, by using virtual reality or simulation software.

The important findings of how workers in organizations implementing AI systems alter in their desire for certain abilities and how AI can support workers in acquiring new skills or continuously improving their skill set are outlined in Table 1.

# ORGANIZATIONAL UPSKILLING AND RESKILLING

Upskilling and reskilling are procedures used to enhance and refresh an employee's skill set. They are comparable in that they both require picking up new abilities, but they differ significantly in one important

*Table 1. Key skills needed in AI era and potential of AI potentials in improving skills*

| Skills | Requisite knowledge for the AI age | How Artificial Intelligence can improve abilities |
|---|---|---|
| Core skills | Improved comprehension and application of AI technology<br>Enhanced application of machine learning techniques for data classification, process optimization, and result prediction<br>enhancing knowledge of programming languages to better manage and utilize AI | AI-powered language skill improvement<br>instantaneous response and pinpointing areas in need of development<br>Enhancement of measurement and assessment abilities via data provided by AI<br>Developing and perfecting digital skills via AI-powered tailored learning experiences |
| Thinking skills | Developing creative abilities to generate original ideas and think beyond the box<br>acquiring the ability to solve problems effectively in order to handle challenging circumstances<br>To comprehend AI-generated data and make wise decisions, one must develop analytical, critical, and quick thinking skills. | AI automation of repetitive jobs improves problem solving for complex tasks<br>Filling the gaps in AI through the integration and augmentation of creativity, empathy, learning, and creative thinking |
| Social and communication skills | Acquiring proficiency in communication to disseminate knowledge about the application of intricate AI systems<br>acquiring excellent communication techniques to increase confidence in AI work<br>To guarantee that employees use AI systems effectively and efficiently, competent leadership skills development is necessary. | AI's automatic replies and intelligent support have improved staff' communication abilities in client encounters.<br>AI's ability to recognize team members' wants and motivations helps managers develop their leadership abilities. |
| Physical and manual skills | enhancing one's manual and physical abilities to operate AI technologies more effectively<br>Development of manual and physical abilities to use AI tools properly and avoid workplace mishaps or injuries enhancing emerging AI technologies and work settings. | acquisition of manual and physical abilities for doing difficult activities by using AI technologies to automate simple ones<br>AI-based training programs for the improvement of manual and physical abilities in a secure setting |

way. Generally speaking, "up-skilling" describes the process of learning new abilities or honing ones that are specifically related to a worker's present position or sector. Upskilling is done with the intention of increasing one's career or becoming more effective in the existing role. On the other hand, "reskilling" entails picking up entirely new abilities outside of one's present sector or employment. Reskilling is typically done in order to transition into a different industry or job. (Mittal et al., 2020)

Employers can cultivate a culture of ongoing learning and development by investing in the upskilling of their workforce. It can assist organizations in attracting and keeping top talent as well as helping employees stays engaged and motivated. Furthermore, an organization's ability to keep up with changes in the business environment and adjust to shifting needs can be aided by a continuous learning and development culture. Not unexpectedly, experts note that as AI replaces humans in routine work, there is an increase in turnover and unemployment. We don't yet know the scope or timing of the impending technology revolution. Robust cross-functional abilities can make job seekers stand out from the competition in an increasingly competitive labor market and attract employers. In order to succeed in the workforce in the upcoming period, people will need to upskill in areas that are relevant to newly defined jobs and collaborate closely with AI technology.

For businesses implementing AI systems, reskilling is a crucial procedure because it can assist staff members in adjusting to the new technological landscape. Reskilling is essential for businesses considering AI adoption since it gives workers the newfound information and abilities needed to operate well in a different capacity while utilizing the technology. Training in subjects like programming, machine learning, and data analytics may fall under this category. Organizations can increase their overall competitiveness by reskilling their workforce, as skilled workers are better able to drive innovation and add value to the business. Thus, reskilling can mitigate the adverse effects of artificial intelligence on the labor force. For instance, some workers can worry that the adoption of AI will result in their job security being jeopardized or that they will lose their positions. Reskilling can help allay these worries, modify workers' mental models regarding AI use in the workplace, and provide workers with the competencies required to take on new tasks or positions inside the company. Additionally, reskilling can aid organizations in keeping their best personnel since disgruntled workers are more inclined to leave their current employers. The skills gap that frequently separates older and younger workers can also be closed with the aid of reskilling.

AI will continue to change the nature of work and the skills needed to perform it, so it will become more crucial than ever for organizations and employees to close the skills gap between what they currently have and what they will need to successfully navigate these changes. To effectively establish plans for upskilling and reskilling the workforce, it is imperative to first identify and comprehend this skills gap. Following the identification of the skills gap, organizations can devise plans for reskilling and upskilling their personnel in order to close the talent gap and guarantee that they have the know-how to use AI efficiently. This guarantees that every worker can take advantage of AI's benefits.

## MEASURES FOR UPSKILLING AND RESKILLING

To apply new talents and reduce the skills gap, creative approaches should be developed. After the skills gap between organizations and the current workforce has been identified, a long-term plan and technique should be developed to incorporate new skills. In addition to solutions for luring in fresh talent, they should involve tools for process redesign and well-run training and education initiatives for present employees. There are numerous training and development options that can aid in and direct the reskilling and upskilling of workforce skill sets.

## TRAINING FOR SKILFUL HUMAN-AI INTERACTION

The deployment and expansion of artificial intelligence has the potential to mitigate the scarcity of human capital in certain industries, such as healthcare. Certain domains, including clinical judgments, administrative work, and patient care, have been revolutionized by AI. Healthcare professionals can be trained to provide services backed by AI (Mittal et al., 2023). AI has the potential to minimize invasive surgeries, lower mortality rates, support and replace labor-intensive tasks, and reduce human errors caused by fatigue. Training medical personnel is vital and will enable them to combine medicine and technology with skill.

## LIFELONG LEARNING AND "HANDS-ON" LEARNING MODULES

In order to effectively address these difficulties, lifelong learning and training efforts must be implemented before I4.0 systems and related technologies can be widely adopted. The authors outline the deployment of a set of brief learning modules focused on upskilling in emerging ICT technologies, which is based on sound practical experimentation. The input from the attendees indicates that these brief experiential learning sessions play a significant role in equipping undergraduate students and the workforce with emerging ICT skills. (Hammer & Karmakar, 2021)

## QUALITY CIRCLES

Organizations are very interested in the training and development of their workforce, thus when designing a Future of Work program, the company's offer to its employees should take center stage. In order for employees to realize the advantages of learning new skills and how to use AI systems, organizations must create compelling and unambiguous value propositions. Due to their historical emphasis on lifetime employment, Japanese businesses have developed a beneficial culture of staff training programs. One of the most well-known initiatives is the Quality Circle, which has proven effective in retraining and upskilling employees that deal with artificial intelligence. With the help of this program, the company hopes to foster a more participatory culture and include employees in decision-making. The Quality Circle program teaches workers how to solve problems and think critically while carrying out their daily responsibilities. During working hours, the rings typically convene for four hours each month. In addition to helping to teach the circle members, a team leader—typically a skilled member of the management team—makes sure that everything goes without a hitch. When members' recommendations for raising output are implemented, they are acknowledged.

## CONCLUSION

The broad and multifaceted field of artificial intelligence (AI) encompasses computer science, mathematics, engineering, behavioral and social sciences, and other fields. Utilizing a transdisciplinary approach is essential to integrating knowledge and perspectives from several areas in order to properly understand the implications and uses of artificial intelligence. According to the findings, it is critical to consider both organizational and human factors when implementing AI into organizations.

It's becoming clear that investing in human capital is essential to implementing AI in businesses successfully and maximizing its advantages for both employers and workers. Many organizational strategies are used in tandem during the adaption process. First, closing the current skills gap in the workplace requires identifying the soft skills that workers need. Working groups can then assist employees in identifying the competencies required for AI adoption as well as in enhancing and acquiring new competencies. Finally, organisations need to put regulations in place to help employees by providing opportunities for training and advancement in order to ensure that workers are ready to meet the demands of an expanding job market due to their open views and mental models regarding AI.

The rolling out of new organisational structures has advantages and disadvantages, like any significant change. Each unique factor, such as differences in age and gender and cultural diversity, needs to be carefully considered. If programmes are designed and executed properly, the advantages outweigh the disadvantages. Organisations face various challenges, chief among them the need to support staff as they adjust to Industry 5.0 while accounting for training costs and guaranteeing equitable and inclusive treatment for all individuals, regardless of age, gender, or cultural background.

This belief is supported by the data that has been documented in the literature. Educators and stakeholders must thus engage in upskilling and reskilling employee populations in order to produce a more competent and adaptive workforce that is prepared to take on the opportunities and challenges of the future.

## REFERENCES

Abe, I. I., & Adisa, O. (2021, January 1). Future of Work. *Advances in Human Resources Management and Organizational Development Book Series*. IGI Global. doi:10.4018/978-1-7998-3347-5.ch015

Barua, T., Doshi, R., & Hiran, K. K. (2020). *Mobile Applications Development: With Python in Kivy Framework*. Walter de Gruyter GmbH & Co KG. doi:10.1515/9783110689488

Bhargava, A., Bester, M., & Bolton, L. E. (2020, August 12). Employees' Perceptions of the Implementation of Robotics, Artificial Intelligence, and Automation (RAIA) on Job Satisfaction, Job Security, and Employability. *Journal of Technology in Behavioral Science*. doi:10.1007/s41347-020-00153-8

Billionniere, E. (2022, August 23). *Bridging the Gender and Skills Gaps with Emerging Technologies*. ASEE. https://peer.asee.org/41916

Chen, X., Zou, D., Cheng, G., & Xie, H. (2021, July). Artificial intelligence-assisted personalized language learning: systematic review and co-citation analysis. *2021 International Conference on Advanced Learning Technologies (ICALT)*. IEEE. 10.1109/ICALT52272.2021.00079

Doshi, R., Hiran, K. K., Mijwil, M. M., & Anand, D. (2023). To That of Artificial Intelligence, Passing Through Business Intelligence. In Handbook of Research on AI and Knowledge Engineering for Real-Time Business Intelligence (pp. 1-16). IGI Global. doi:10.4018/978-1-6684-6519-6.ch001

Doshi, R., Hiran, K. K., Ranolia, R., & Joshi, C. (2023). Monitor Cloud Performance and Data Safety With Artificial Intelligence. In Applications of Artificial Intelligence in Wireless Communication Systems (pp. 92-108). IGI Global. doi:10.4018/978-1-6684-7348-1.ch006

Doshi, R., Hu, Y. C., Garg, L., & Fagbola, T. (2023). Special issue "Towards a Higher Education of the Future: Transformational Roles of Edge Intelligence". *Array (New York, N.Y.)*, 100332. doi:10.1016/j.array.2023.100332

Easwaran, B., Hiran, K. K., Krishnan, S., & Doshi, R. (Eds.). (2022). *Real-Time Applications of Machine Learning in Cyber-Physical Systems*. IGI Global. doi:10.4018/978-1-7998-9308-0

Hammer, A., & Karmakar, S. (2021, April 29). Automation, AI and the Future of Work in India. *Employee Relations*, *43*(6), 1327–1341. doi:10.1108/ER-12-2019-0452

Hiran, K. K., Doshi, R., & Patel, M. (Eds.). (2024). *Applications of Virtual and Augmented Reality for Health and Wellbeing*. IGI Global. doi:10.4018/979-8-3693-1123-3

Hiran, K. K., Hemachandran, K., Pise, A., & Rabi, B. (Eds.). (2023). *Handbook of Research on AI and Knowledge Engineering for Real-Time Business Intelligence*. IGI Global. doi:10.4018/978-1-6684-6519-6

Mishra, A., Tripathi, A., Khazanchi, D., Hiran, K. K., Vyas, A. K., & Padmanaban, S. (2021). A framework for applying artificial intelligence (AI) with Internet of NanoThings (IoNT). In *Machine Learning for Sustainable Development* (pp. 1–16). De Gruyter. doi:10.1515/9783110702514-001

Mittal, R., Mishra, D. N., & Pathak, D. V. (2019, October 30). Exploration of Designed Robot in Non Linear Movement Using EKF SLAM and Its Stability on Loose Concrete Surface. *International Journal of Engineering and Advanced Technology*, *9*(1), 875–878. doi:10.35940/ijeat.A9398.109119

Mittal, R., Mishra, N., Pathak, V., & Gandhi, G. C. (2020, January 30). An Exploration of Force Exerted on Moving Robot in Arcuated Path on Different Surface using Standard SLAM Algorithm. [IJRTE]. *International Journal of Recent Technology and Engineering*, *8*(5), 4080–4083. doi:10.35940/ijrte.E6685.018520

Mittal, R., Pathak, V., Gandhi, G. C., & Mishra, N. (2020). *Effect of Curve Algorithms on Standard SLAM algorithm for Prediction of Path.*

Mittal, R., Rani, G., Pathak, V., Chhikara, S., Dhaka, V. S., Vocaturo, E., & Zumpano, E. (2023, December 1). Low-Cost Multisensory Robot for Optimized Path Planning in Diverse Environments. *Computers*, *12*(12), 250. doi:10.3390/computers12120250

Mubarak, M. A. (2022, June 28). Sustainably Developing in a Digital World: Harnessing artificial intelligence to meet the imperatives of work-based learning in Industry 5.0. *Development and Learning in Organizations*. doi:10.1108/DLO-04-2022-0063

Priyadarshi, N., Padmanaban, S., Hiran, K. K., Holm-Nielson, J. B., & Bansal, R. C. (Eds.). (2021). *Artificial intelligence and internet of things for renewable energy systems* (Vol. 12). Walter de Gruyter GmbH & Co KG. doi:10.1515/9783110714043

Singh, S. V., & Hiran, K. K. (2022). The impact of AI on teaching and learning in higher education technology. *Journal of Higher Education Theory and Practice*, *22*(13).

Wanjale, K., Chitre, A. V., & Doshi, R. (2023). Opting for Industry 4.0: Challenge or Opportunity. In *AI, IoT, Big Data and Cloud Computing for Industry 4.0* (pp. 3–20). Springer International Publishing. doi:10.1007/978-3-031-29713-7_1

# Chapter 17
# Role of Generative Artificial Intelligence (AI) in Accountability, Transparency, and Governance in Higher Education: A Comprehensive Study

**Heena Siroya**
*Sir Padampat Singhania University, Udaipur, India*

**Manish Dadhich**
*Sir Padampat Singhania University, Udaipur, India*

**Kirti Siroya**
*All India Institute of Medical Sciences, Johdpur, India*

## ABSTRACT

*This study investigates the impact of Generative Artificial Intelligence (AI) on accountability, transparency, and governance within higher education institutions. Employing a quantitative technique, a structured questionnaire was administered to a convenient sample of 190 academicians, collected via Google Forms from October to December 2023. Utilizing data filtering techniques, hypotheses testing was conducted using Smart-PLS, with both dependent and independent variables identified and analyzed. The findings reveal significant positive relationships between Accountability, Transparency, Governance, and Generative AI, supporting the study's hypotheses. The study underscores the transformative potential of AI integration in higher education, offering policy implications for technologists to implement responsible AI practices and maximize its benefits in governance, transparency, and accountability realms.*

DOI: 10.4018/979-8-3693-2440-0.ch017

## 1. INTRODUCTION

In today's dynamic landscape of higher education, accountability stands as a cornerstone principle, shaping institutional practices and policies (Wu, Huang, and Gong 2020; S. J. H. Yang et al. 2021). With an emphasis on transparency, effectiveness, and equity, accountability ensures that educational institutions remain true to their missions while meeting the diverse needs of stakeholders. However, as the complexities of academia evolve, traditional methods of accountability may fall short in addressing emerging challenges. This is where AI emerges as a transformative force, offering innovative solutions to enhance accountability mechanisms in higher education. AI, characterized by its ability to simulate human intelligence processes, presents unprecedented opportunities to revolutionize various facets of higher education, including teaching, learning, research, and administration. In the realm of accountability, AI offers multifaceted approaches to streamline data collection, analysis, and decision-making, ultimately fostering greater accountability across the board (W. Yang 2022).

One of the primary areas where AI is making significant strides is in data management and analytics. Educational institutions generate vast amounts of data about student performance, institutional operations, and financial management. AI-powered analytics platforms can sift through this data, identifying patterns, trends, and outliers that may have implications for accountability (Krepl et al. 2023). By harnessing machine learning algorithms, institutions can gain valuable insights into areas such as student retention rates, academic achievement gaps, and resource allocation efficiency, enabling proactive interventions to address accountability concerns (Memarian and Doleck 2023).

Generative AI fosters transparency by enabling institutions to communicate complex information in accessible formats. Through natural language processing and text generation capabilities, AI systems can distill intricate data sets into comprehensible summaries, reports, and visualizations, facilitating transparent communication with stakeholders. By democratizing access to information and insights, generative AI promotes a culture of openness and accountability within the higher education community (Perisic et al. 2023).

Moreover, generative AI holds promise in enhancing governance mechanisms by automating routine administrative tasks and facilitating informed decision-making. From streamlining regulatory compliance processes to optimizing organizational workflows, AI-driven governance systems enable institutions to operate more efficiently while maintaining compliance with legal and ethical standards. By reducing bureaucratic inefficiencies and minimizing the risk of human error, generative AI contributes to the overall effectiveness and integrity of governance structures in higher education (Sarker and Ullah 2023).

However, the integration of generative AI into accountability and governance processes also raises ethical and societal considerations that demand scrutiny. Issues such as data privacy, algorithmic bias, and the ethical implications of AI-driven decision-making necessitate robust safeguards and responsible deployment practices to ensure equity, fairness, and transparency.

## 2. THEORETICAL BACKGROUND AND HYPOTHESES

(Heyder, Passlack, and Posegga 2023) explored the transformative potential of generative AI in reshaping accountability practices within higher education institutions. The paper delved into the capabilities of generative AI algorithms to analyze large datasets, detect patterns, and generate actionable insights that inform decision-making processes. Heyder et. al highlighted the role of generative AI in enhancing transparency through accessible data visualization and communication methods, while also discussing ethical considerations associated with AI deployment. (Dwivedi et al. 2023) examined the promise and perils of integrating AI technologies into governance structures within higher education. The paper discussed how generative AI can automate routine administrative tasks, optimize resource allocation, and facilitate informed decision-making processes. However, they also addressed ethical concerns related to data privacy, algorithmic bias, and the need for transparent and accountable AI systems.

(Danish and Senjyu 2023) focused on navigating the ethical challenges associated with AI-driven accountability mechanisms in higher education. The paper explored issues such as data privacy, algorithmic fairness, and the implications of AI automation on institutional governance. They also emphasized the importance of responsible AI deployment and the need for robust ethical frameworks to ensure transparency, equity, and accountability higher education environment. (Alfredo et al. 2024) discussed the potential of AI-driven technologies to enhance transparency and governance in higher education institutions. The paper investigated how generative AI algorithms can analyze complex datasets, facilitate data-driven decision-making, and improve accountability frameworks. The authors also addressed challenges such as algorithmic bias and the need for regulatory oversight to ensure the responsible use of AI in governance processes. (Chiu 2024) provided an overview of the opportunities and challenges associated with integrating AI into accountability mechanisms in higher education. How generative AI can enhance data analysis, streamline administrative processes, and promote transparency was also discussed with a limited sample size in specific geographic locations. However, Chiu also highlighted the importance of addressing ethical concerns and ensuring that AI-driven accountability practices prioritize fairness, equity, and transparency in the higher education system.

In higher education, accountability mechanisms play a crucial role in ensuring that institutions are responsible for their actions, decisions, and use of resources. Traditionally, accountability processes have relied on manual data collection, analysis, and reporting, which can be time-consuming, labor-intensive, and prone to errors. However, with the emergence of Generative AI technologies, there is an opportunity to automate these processes, thereby enhancing accountability mechanisms. Generative AI refers to a subset of artificial intelligence techniques that involve generating new data or content based on patterns learned from existing data. In the context of higher education, Generative AI can be applied to automate data analysis processes by analyzing large volumes of institutional data, including student demographics, academic performance metrics, financial records, and administrative data. By leveraging advanced machine learning algorithms, Generative AI can identify patterns, trends, and anomalies in the data more efficiently and accurately than traditional manual methods.

H1: Integration of Generative AI in HEI enhances accountability mechanisms by automating data analysis processes.

Transparency is essential in higher education governance to promote trust, accountability, and informed decision-making among stakeholders. Traditionally, transparency has been achieved through the publication of reports, disclosures, and public meetings. However, these methods may not always be effective in providing stakeholders with a clear understanding of complex institutional data and processes. It offers a promising solution to enhance transparency in higher education by generating interactive data visualizations and reports. These technologies can analyze large datasets and transform them into visually engaging and easy-to-understand representations, such as graphs, charts, and dashboards. By presenting data in a visual format, Generative AI enables stakeholders to explore trends, patterns, and relationships in the data more effectively, thereby enhancing transparency.

H2: Generative AI technologies contribute to transparency in higher education by generating interactive data visualizations and reports.

Effective governance is essential for the success and sustainability of higher education institutions. Governance structures and processes influence resource allocation, administrative efficiency, and decision-making, ultimately shaping institutional performance and outcomes. However, governance in higher education can be complex, involving multiple stakeholders, competing interests, and resource constraints. Generative AI technologies have the potential to transform governance in higher education by optimizing resource allocation, streamlining administrative processes, and improving decision-making. These technologies can analyze institutional data, identify inefficiencies, and recommend strategies to enhance governance effectiveness. By automating routine tasks and providing decision support, Generative AI enables administrators to focus on strategic priorities and allocate resources more efficiently.

H3: Adoption of Generative AI in higher education governance leads to more efficient resource allocation, streamlined administrative processes, and improved decision-making.

## 3. RESEARCH METHODOLOGY

This study adopts a quantitative research approach collecting numerical data to analyze and draw inferences using statistical methods. A structured questionnaire was developed to collect data from participants. The questionnaire was carefully designed to cover various aspects related to the role of generative AI in higher education accountability, transparency, and governance. Questions were formulated to gather participants' perceptions, experiences, and opinions on the subject matter. The study utilized a convenient sampling technique to select participants. The sample consisted of 190 academicians from HEIs who have expertise or experience in accountability, transparency, and governance processes. Academicians were selected based on their availability and willingness to participate in the study. Data was collected using an online survey platform, such as Google Forms. Participants were provided with a link to the questionnaire, which they can access and complete at their convenience. The study was conducted from October to Dec. 2023. During this timeframe, data collection, analysis, and interpretation were carried out to achieve the research objectives.

To ensure the quality and reliability of the collected data, several filtering techniques were employed. Responses with missing or incomplete information were excluded from the analysis. Additionally, outlier detection methods were used to identify and remove any unusual or erroneous data points. Smart-PLS was employed to analyze the data. Smart-PLS is a robust statistical technique suitable for analyzing complex relationships among variables in a structural model. It allowed for the examination of both direct and indirect effects, making it well-suited for assessing the relationships between variables. In this study, the independent variables were accountability, transparency, and governance in higher education. These variables were measured based on participants' perceptions and evaluations. The dependent variable is the role of generative AI, which was examined in terms of its influence on the dependent variables. Various sub-dimensions of accountability, transparency, and governance were considered to provide a comprehensive understanding of the relationships under investigation.

*Table 1. Reliability Analysis*

| Factors | Cron. α | A_V_E | C_R | M_S_V |
|---|---|---|---|---|
| Accountability (ACT) | 0.721 | 0.422 | 0.578 | 0.521 |
| Transparency (TRP) | 0.785 | 0.511 | 0.524 | 0.509 |
| Governance (GOR) | 0.845 | 0.580 | 0.601 | 0.498 |
| Generative AI (GAI) | 0.721 | 0.527 | 0.608 | 0.589 |

## 4. ANALYSIS AND DISCUSSION

The study presents descriptive statistics regarding various factors within the surveyed population. The table categorizes respondents based on Gender, Age, Educational Position, Education Level, and Familiarity with Generative AI and its applications. In terms of Gender, 57.90% were male and 41.10% were female. Regarding Age, 39.50% of respondents were between 20-40 years old, while 60.50% were above 40. Educational Position distribution showed 27.40% were Professors, 32.60% were Associate Professors, and 40.00% were Lecturers or held other positions. Education Level displayed 44.70% with education up to college level and 50.30% up to university level. Familiarity with Gen. AI and applications indicated 94.60% were familiar, while 05.40% were not.

Table 1 displays the outcomes of a reliability analysis conducted on four key factors: Accountability (ACT), Transparency (TRP), Governance (GOR), and Generative AI (GAI). The analysis evaluates the reliability of each factor using Cronbach's alpha (Cron. α), Average Variance Extracted (A_V_E), Composite Reliability (C_R), and Mean Squared Variance (M_S_V). Accountability exhibits Cronbach's alpha of 0.721, A_V_E of 0.422, C_R of 0.578, and M_S_V of 0.521. Transparency shows values of 0.785 for Cronbach's alpha, 0.511 for A_V_E, 0.524 for C_R, and 0.509 for M_S_V. Governance records 0.845 for Cronbach's alpha, 0.580 for A_V_E, 0.601 for C_R, and 0.498 for M_S_V. Generative AI presents values of 0.721 for Cronbach's alpha, 0.527 for A_V_E, 0.608 for C_R, and 0.589 for M_S_V. These metrics collectively assess the internal consistency and reliability of the measurements for each factor, where higher values indicate stronger reliability and consistency in the assessments (Hair, Risher, and Ringle 2018).

Table 2 illustrates the Fornell and Larcker Criterion, which examines the discriminant validity of the factors. The matrix presents the square root of the Average Variance Extracted (AVE) for each factor on the diagonal and the correlations between factors off the diagonal. For Accountability, the AVE is 0.825. For Transparency, the AVE is 0.821, with a correlation of 0.503 with Accountability. Governance has an AVE of 0.763, correlating with Accountability at 0.695 and with Transparency at 0.667. Generative AI records an AVE of 0.866, correlating with Accountability at 0.527, Transparency at 0.529, and Governance at 0.512. These values demonstrate the extent to which each factor's indicators measure distinct constructs, with higher values indicating stronger discriminant validity (Fornell C. and Larcker D. F. 1981; Sonali Bhati; Manish Dadhich; Anand A Bhasker; Kamal Kant Hiran; Roshni Sharma; Anurag 2023).

The first hypothesis suggests that there is a positive affiliation between Accountability and Generative AI. The results indicate that Accountability has a significant positive impact on Generative AI ($\beta = 0.516$, $p = 0.000$). This implies that higher levels of organizational accountability are associated with advancements in Generative AI technologies. Previous research by (Sperling et al. 2024; S. J. H. Yang et

*Figure 1. SEM Framework for Generative AI*

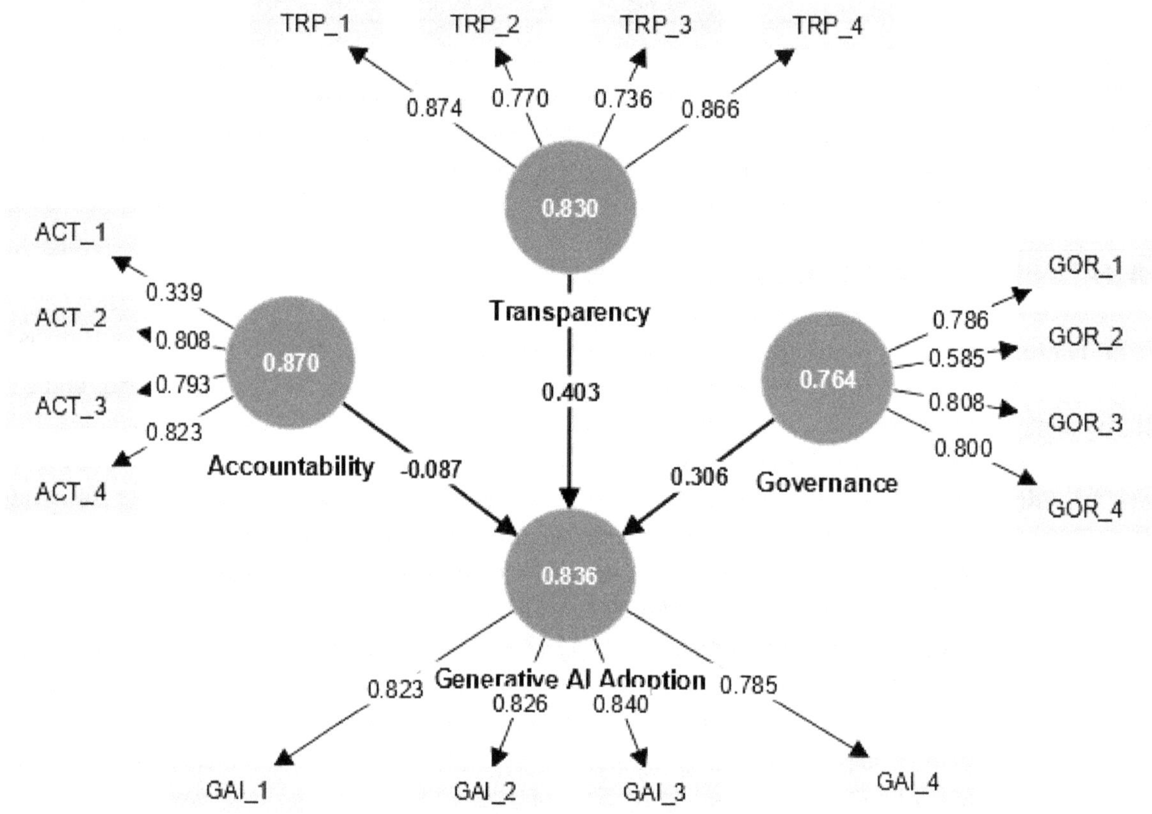


*Table 2. Fornell and Larcker Criterion*

| Manifests | ACT | TRP | GOR | GAI |
|---|---|---|---|---|
| Accountability | 0.825 | | | |
| Transparency | 0.821 | 0.503 | | |
| Governance | 0.763 | 0.695 | 0.667 | |
| Generative AI | 0.866 | 0.527 | 0.529 | 0.512 |

*Table 3. Path Analysis and Hypotheses Testing*

| SN | Manifests | β | X | σ | T-value | P-value |
|---|---|---|---|---|---|---|
| H1 | Accountability (ACT)→ Generative AI (GAI) | 0.516 | 0.254 | 0.344 | 2.368 | 0.000 |
| H2 | Transparency (TRP)→ Generative AI (GAI) | 0.696 | 0.784 | 2.324 | 3.547 | 0.001 |
| H3 | Governance (GOR)→ Generative AI (GAI) | 0.459 | 0.521 | 3.210 | 4.251 | 0.020 |

al. 2021; Wu, Huang, and Gong 2020) has also supported this relationship, highlighting the importance of accountability in driving the adoption and development of AI technologies within organizations.

The second hypothesis posits a definite link between Transparency and Generative AI. The results show a significant positive association between Transparency and Generative AI ($\beta = 0.696$, $p = 0.001$). This suggests that greater transparency in AI systems contributes to advancements in Generative AI technologies. This finding aligns with the research by (Memarian and Doleck 2023; Dwivedi et al. 2023; W. Yang 2022), who demonstrated the role of transparency in fostering user trust and acceptance of AI systems, thus promoting AI advancements.

This hypothesis suggests that there is an optimistic connection between Governance and Generative AI. The results reveal a significant positive relationship between Governance and Generative AI ($\beta = 0.459$, $p = 0.020$). This indicates that effective governance structures within organizations contribute to the development and implementation of Generative AI technologies. This finding is consistent with the research conducted by (Alfredo et al. 2024; Krepl et al. 2023; Hussain, Khan, and Malik 2024), which emphasized the importance of governance in facilitating successful AI initiatives within organizations. Each hypothesis examines a specific relationship between a key factor (Accountability, Transparency, or Governance) and Generative AI, with all hypotheses supported by statistically significant findings. These results underscore the critical roles of accountability, transparency, and governance in shaping the advancement of Generative AI technologies.

## 6. PRACTICAL IMPLICATIONS

The study underscores the transformative potential of Generative AI in higher education's accountability, transparency, and governance realms. By harnessing AI algorithms, institutions can streamline decision-making processes, enhance accountability measures through real-time monitoring, facilitate transparent communication channels with stakeholders, and automate administrative tasks for governance bodies. However, to fully leverage the benefits of AI while addressing ethical concerns and biases, institutions must adopt responsible AI practices, including transparency, fairness, and ongoing oversight. Overall, integrating Generative AI in higher education can catalyze institutional efficiency, trust, and positive outcomes, provided ethical considerations are diligently addressed.

## 7. LIMITATIONS AND FUTURE SCOPE

While the study highlights the potential benefits of integrating Generative AI in higher education's accountability, transparency, and governance domains, several limitations warrant consideration. Firstly, the study's findings may be context-specific and not necessarily generalizable across diverse institutional settings or educational contexts. Additionally, the reliance on AI technologies introduces concerns regarding data privacy, security, and algorithmic bias, which require careful mitigation strategies. Furthermore, the study's scope may not encompass all relevant factors influencing accountability, transparency, and governance in higher education, suggesting avenues for further exploration.

Future research endeavors could address these limitations by conducting longitudinal studies to assess the long-term impacts of AI integration in higher education institutions. Additionally, qualitative research methods, such as interviews and focus groups, could provide deeper insights into stakeholders' perspectives and experiences regarding AI implementation. Moreover, comparative studies across institutions or countries could shed light on the varying effects of AI adoption in diverse educational contexts. Furthermore, research efforts should focus on developing ethical guidelines and frameworks for responsible AI use in higher education, addressing concerns related to privacy, fairness, and accountability. Thus, continued research in this area is essential to maximize the benefits of AI while mitigating its potential risks in higher education governance, transparency, and accountability.

## 8. CONCLUSION

The integration of Generative Artificial Intelligence (AI) presents immense opportunities for enhancing accountability, transparency, and governance in higher education. By leveraging AI algorithms, institutions can streamline decision-making processes, improve accountability measures, facilitate transparent communication channels, and automate administrative tasks for governance bodies. However, institutions must address ethical concerns, such as data privacy and algorithmic bias, and ensure responsible AI practices are implemented. Despite these challenges, the potential benefits of AI adoption in higher education are substantial, including increased efficiency, stakeholder trust, and positive institutional outcomes. Moving forward, continued research and thoughtful implementation of AI technologies are essential to maximize its transformative potential while upholding institutional values and objectives in higher education governance, transparency, and accountability.

## REFERENCES

Alfredo, R., Echeverria, V., Jin, Y., Yan, L., Swiecki, Z., Gašević, D., & Martinez-Maldonado, R. (2024). Human-Centred Learning Analytics and AI in Education: A Systematic Literature Review. *Computers and Education: Artificial Intelligence*, *6*, 1–12. doi:10.1016/j.caeai.2024.100215

Bhati, S., & Dadhich, M.; Anand A Bhasker; Kamal Kant Hiran; Roshni Sharma; Anurag. (2023). Quantifying the Contemporary Enablers in Achieving E-Governance for Sustainable Techno-Societal Development: A High Directive SEM Analysis. In *2023 International Conference on Emerging Trends in Networks and Computer Communications (ETNCC)*, (pp. 157–162). https://doi.org/10.1109/ETNCC59188.2023.10284979

Chiu, T. K. F. (2024). Future Research Recommendations for Transforming Higher Education with Generative AI. *Computers and Education: Artificial Intelligence*, *6*(12), 1–15. doi:10.1016/j.caeai.2023.100197

Danish, Mir Sayed Shah, and Tomonobu Senjyu. (2023). Shaping the Future of Sustainable Energy through AI-Enabled Circular Economy Policies. *Circular Economy, 2*(2), 1–20. https://doi.org/. doi:10.1016/j.cec.2023.100040

Dwivedi, Y. K., Kshetri, N., Hughes, L., Slade, E. L., Jeyaraj, A., Kar, A. K., Baabdullah, A. M., & … . (2023). "So What If ChatGPT Wrote It?" Multidisciplinary Perspectives on Opportunities, Challenges and Implications of Generative Conversational AI for Research, Practice and Policy. *International Journal of Information Management*, *71*, 1–63. doi:10.1016/j.ijinfomgt.2023.102642

Fornell, C., & Larcker, D. F. (1981). Evaluating Structural Equation Models with Unobservable Variables and Measurement Error. *JMR, Journal of Marketing Research*, *18*(1), 39–50.

Hair, Joseph F, Jeffrey J Risher, and Christian M Ringle. (2018). When to Use and How to Report the Results of PLS-SEM. *European Business Review*, *31*(1), 2–24. doi:10.1108/EBR-11-2018-0203

Heyder, T., Passlack, N., & Posegga, O. (2023). Ethical Management of Human-AI Interaction: Theory Development Review. *The Journal of Strategic Information Systems*, *32*(3), 1–50. doi:10.1016/j.jsis.2023.101772

Hussain, K., Khan, M. L., & Malik, A. (2024). Exploring Audience Engagement with ChatGPT-Related Content on YouTube: Implications for Content Creators and AI Tool Developers. *Digital Business*, *4*(1), 1–8. doi:10.1016/j.digbus.2023.100071

Krepl, V., Fandi, G., Rehabi, M., Ghanem, S., Jrad, F., Muller, Z., Smutka, L., & … . (2023). Effective Criteria in the Public-Private Partnership in Developing Countries to Apply the Sustainable Development Goals: GAN-Based Decision Support System for the Renewable Electrical System, Case Study Syria. *Heliyon*, *9*(11). Advance online publication. doi:10.1016/j.heliyon.2023.e21422

Memarian, B., & Doleck, T. (2023). Fairness, Accountability, Transparency, and Ethics (FATE) in Artificial Intelligence (AI) and Higher Education: A Systematic Review. *Computers and Education: Artificial Intelligence*, *5*(5), 1–12. doi:10.1016/j.caeai.2023.100152

Perisic, A., Perisic, I., Lazic, M., & Perisic, B. (2023). The Foundation for Future Education, Teaching, Training, Learning, and Performing Infrastructure - The Open Interoperability Conceptual Framework Approach. *Heliyon*, *9*(6), 1–16. doi:10.1016/j.heliyon.2023.e16836

Sarker, M. F., & Ullah, M. S. (2023). A Review of Quality Assessment Criteria in Secondary Education with the Impact of the COVID-19 Pandemic. *Social Sciences & Humanities Open*, *8*(1), 1–12. doi:10.1016/j.ssaho.2023.100740

Sperling, K., Stenberg, C.-J., McGrath, C., Åkerfeldt, A., Heintz, F., & Stenliden, L. (2024). In Search of Artificial Intelligence (AI) Literacy in Teacher Education: A Scoping Review. Computers and Education Open 12, 1–14. https://doi.org/ doi:10.1016/j.caeo.2024.100169

Wu, W., Huang, T., & Gong, K. (2020). Ethical Principles and Governance Technology Development of AI in China. *Engineering*, *6*(3), 302–309. doi:10.1016/j.eng.2019.12.015

Yang, S. J. H., Ogata, H., Matsui, T., & Chen, N. S. (2021). Human-Centered Artificial Intelligence in Education: Seeing the Invisible through the Visible. *Computers and Education: Artificial Intelligence*, *2*(1), 1–14. doi:10.1016/j.caeai.2021.100008

Yang, W. (2022). Artificial Intelligence Education for Young Children: Why, What, and How in Curriculum Design and Implementation. *Computers and Education: Artificial Intelligence*, *3*, 1–7. doi:10.1016/j.caeai.2022.100061

# Chapter 18
# Beyond the Classroom:
## AI's Impact on the Future of Education

**Kanchan Naithani**
*H.N.B. Garhwal University, India*

**Yadav Prasad Raiwani**
*H.N.B. Garhwal University, India*

**Shrikant Tiwari**
https://orcid.org/0000-0001-6947-2362
*Galgotias University, India*

**Alok Singh Chauhan**
https://orcid.org/0000-0002-9144-4381
*Galgotias University, India*

## ABSTRACT

*The rise of artificial intelligence (AI) promises a revolutionary shift in education. This chapter explores AI's impact on education, covering adaptive learning platforms, virtual and augmented reality, ethical concerns in data-driven decision-making, AI-powered tutoring, robotics integration, and the changing role of educators. It delves into the automation of assessments, emphasizing the delicate balance between AI and human evaluation. The global implications of AI in education are also discussed, focusing on bridging educational gaps and fostering global collaboration. Ultimately, the investigation envisions a future where AI transforms higher education, promoting learning, creativity, and equitable access to information.*

## INTRODUCTION TO AI IN EDUCATION

In recent years, the field of education has witnessed a transformative wave with the integration of Artificial Intelligence (AI). As technology continues to advance, educators and institutions are exploring

DOI: 10.4018/979-8-3693-2440-0.ch018

innovative ways to enhance the learning experience and tailor education to individual needs. In the realm of education, AI is being harnessed to create intelligent systems and tools that adapt to the unique learning styles and preferences of students (Rane N. et al., 2023).

AI is revolutionizing assessment methods. Intelligent algorithms can evaluate students' performance in real-time, providing instant feedback and allowing educators to identify areas of improvement. In addition to personalization and assessment, AI contributes to the creation of immersive and interactive learning environments (S. Kumar, et al., 2023). Virtual reality (VR) and Augmented Reality (AR) applications powered by AI provide students with hands-on experiences that transcend the limitations of traditional classrooms. AI-augmented education extends beyond the confines of traditional classrooms through the integration of advanced technologies like VR and AR. These immersive technologies, driven by AI, create interactive and experiential learning environments (Radianti, J. et al., 2020).

As we navigate the complexities of the digital age, AI-augmented education stands at the forefront, offering unprecedented opportunities to enhance the learning experience. This paradigm shift underscores the importance of embracing technological advancements while maintaining a steadfast commitment to ethical principles, ensuring that the benefits of AI in education are accessible to all learners (Patel, K. 2024). Various elements of Artificially augmented Education are shown in Figure 1.

The purpose of this book chapter is to explore the transformative influence of Artificial Intelligence (AI) on education beyond the traditional classroom setting. As technology continues to advance at an unprecedented pace, it is essential to delve into the ways AI is reshaping the landscape of education, extending its impact far beyond the confines of conventional teaching environments (Grassini, S. 2023; Doshi et al., 2023). The chapter aims to provide a comprehensive understanding of the diverse applications of AI in education and its potential to revolutionize the future of learning. This chapter analyses AI-driven immersive technologies, automation in administration, ethical considerations and responsible implementation. It also explores future trends and implications for the evolving role of AI in education.

## ADAPTIVE LEARNING PLATFORMS

The integration of AI in education represents a significant evolution shaped by advancements in technology, cognitive science and pedagogical theories. The historical context of AI in education spans several decades, witnessing the gradual emergence of technologies designed to enhance and personalize the learning experience (Tedre, M et al., 2021; Singh et al., 2022; Hiran et al., 2023).

**Early AI Initiatives (1950s-1960s):** The roots of AI in education can be traced back to the early days of computing when pioneers like Alan Turing laid the groundwork for machine learning and intelligent systems. During the 1950s and 1960s, researchers began exploring the possibilities of using computers to simulate human learning. Early attempts, such as the "teaching machines," focused on programmed instruction and the automation of certain aspects of the learning process (Mijwil et al., 2023).

**Expert Systems and Intelligent Tutoring Systems (1970s-1980s):** The 1970s and 1980s marked a significant period for AI in education with the development of expert systems and intelligent tutoring systems. These systems aimed to replicate the expertise of human tutors by providing personalized feedback and adapting content based on individual student progress. Notable projects, like MYCIN and Dendral, demonstrated the potential of AI in problem-solving and decision-making.

**Cognitive Science Influence (1980s-1990s):** During the 1980s and 1990s, the integration of cognitive science principles into AI research had a profound impact on educational technology. Researchers

*Figure 1. Artificial intelligence augmented education*

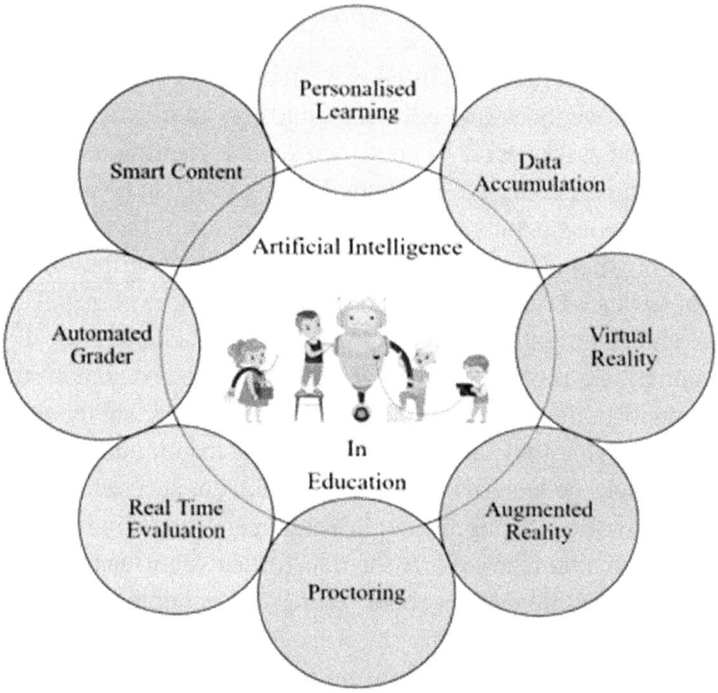


sought to understand how students learn and process information, leading to the development of cognitive tutors that could model and adapt to the cognitive processes of individual learners. This era marked a shift toward more student-centered, interactive learning experiences.

**Internet Era and E-Learning (1990s-2000s):** The advent of the internet in the 1990s brought about a new wave of possibilities for AI in education. E-learning platforms and intelligent educational software became more accessible, allowing students to engage with educational content beyond traditional classrooms. AI-powered tools began to support adaptive learning, delivering customized content based on individual learning styles and performance.

**Big Data and Learning Analytics (2010s-Present):** The 2010s saw a surge in the use of big data and learning analytics in education. AI algorithms leveraged vast amounts of data to analyse student performance, predict learning outcomes and personalize educational experiences further. Learning management systems and online platforms incorporated AI to provide real-time feedback, allowing educators to make data-driven decisions (Naithani, K. et al., 2022; Doshi et al., 2023).

**Immersive Technologies and Personalized Learning (Present-Future):** In the present day, AI in education continues to evolve with the integration technologies like virtual reality and augmented reality. These technologies offer new dimensions to experiential learning, enabling students to engage with educational content in more interactive and immersive ways. AI's role in shaping personalized learning experiences is becoming increasingly prominent as adaptive learning systems continue to advance (Easwaran et al., 2022).

Understanding the historical context of AI in education provides valuable insights into the iterative development of intelligent systems designed to enhance and augment the learning process. As AI continues to advance, its integration into education promises to shape the future of learning by offering personalized, adaptive and immersive educational experiences.

## Evolution of Educational Technology

The evolution of educational technology is a dynamic journey that mirrors the broader advancements in information technology, communication and pedagogical philosophy. From humble beginnings to the sophisticated digital landscape of today, the trajectory of educational technology reflects a continual quest to enhance and transform the learning experience (Roslan, F. A. B. M., and Ahmad, N. B. 2023).

**Early Educational Tools (Pre-20th Century):** The earliest educational technologies were simple, tangible tools such as chalkboards, slate boards and textbooks. These tools facilitated communication of knowledge and enabled basic student-teacher interactions. The advent of the printing press in the 15th century contributed to the mass production of books, democratizing access to information.

**Audiovisual Technologies (Early to Mid-20th Century):** The 20th century witnessed the integration of audiovisual technologies into education. Projectors, filmstrips and educational films became commonplace in classrooms. These technologies aimed to supplement traditional teaching methods, providing visual and auditory aids to enhance understanding.

**Emergence of Computers in Education (1960s-1980s):** The 1960s marked the beginning of the computer era in education. Early mainframe computers were employed for administrative purposes, but by the 1970s, they found their way into classrooms. The development of programming languages like BASIC and LOGO introduced students to computer programming, fostering computational thinking.

**Interactive Multimedia and CD-ROMs (1980s-1990s):** The 1980s and 1990s saw the rise of interactive multimedia and the use of CD-ROMs in education. This era brought about a shift from passive consumption of content to more engaging, interactive learning experiences. CD-ROMs contained multimedia elements such as videos, animations and quizzes, offering students a more dynamic approach to learning.

**The Internet Revolution (1990s-Present):** The widespread adoption of the internet revolutionized educational technology. The 1990s saw the emergence of online learning platforms, email communication and educational websites. The internet provided access to a wealth of information, fostering collaborative learning and enabling distance education.

**Learning Management Systems (LMS) and E-Learning (2000s-Present):** The 21st century witnessed the rise of Learning Management Systems (LMS) and e-learning platforms. Institutions embraced online courses. E-learning platforms integrated multimedia, quizzes and discussion forums to create interactive online learning experiences.

**Mobile Learning and Apps (2010s-Present):** With the proliferation of smartphones and tablets, educational technology shifted towards mobile learning. Educational apps, digital textbooks and mobile-friendly platforms became instrumental in providing flexible and personalized learning experiences. Mobile technology facilitated ubiquitous access to educational resources (Barua et al., 2020).

**Emergence of Adaptive Learning and AI (Present-Future):** In the present era, adaptive learning systems and Artificial Intelligence (AI) are shaping the next phase of educational technology. AI-powered tools analyze student data to personalize learning paths, providing targeted content and feedback.

The evolution of educational technology reflects a continuous quest to leverage emerging tools and methodologies to improve teaching and learning. As technology continues to advance, the future of

*Figure 2. Evolution of educational technology over adaptive learning platforms*

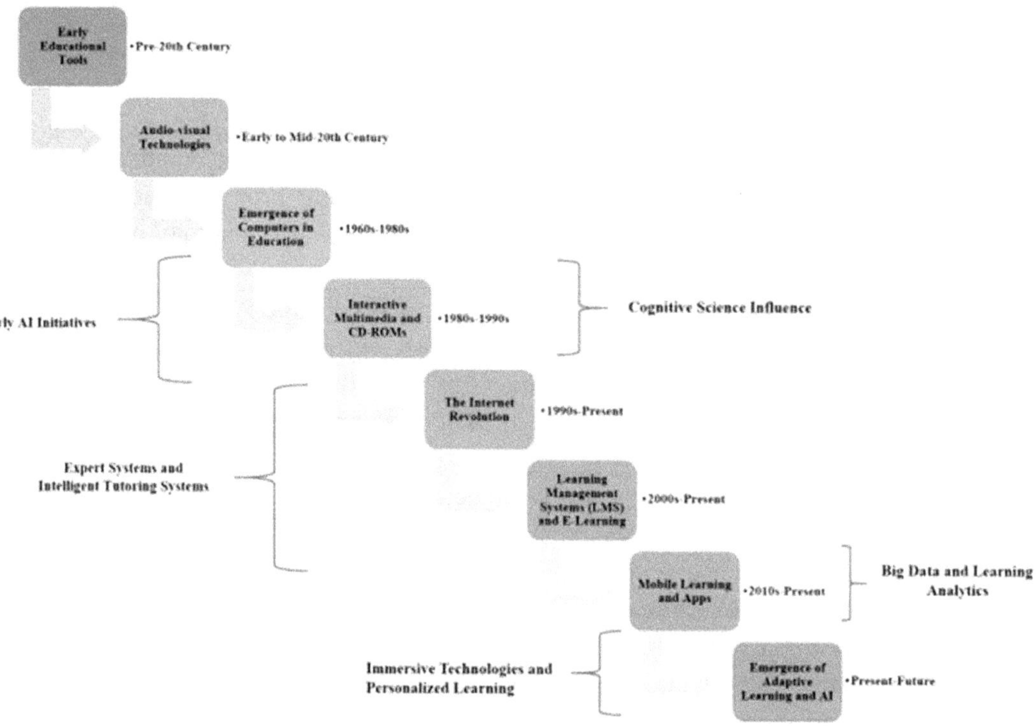


educational technology promises even more adaptive, personalized and immersive learning experiences, embracing the potential of AI, VR and beyond.

## Key Concepts and Terminology in Educational Technology

Educational technology (EdTech) is a field that encompasses the use of technology to enhance and support teaching and learning. EdTech is the use of technology to enhance teaching and learning, encompassing various tools and strategies that leverage technology to improve educational outcomes. Here are key concepts and terminology associated with educational technology:

**a) Blended Learning:** Blended learning combines traditional face-to-face instruction with online learning activities. It seeks to integrate the best aspects of both approaches, offering flexibility and personalized learning experiences (Shrikant Tiwari and Sanjay Kumar Singh, 2012)

**b) Learning Management System (LMS):** A Learning Management System is a software platform that facilitates the administration, delivery, and tracking of educational content. LMS platforms often include features for content creation, assessment, and communication.

**c) Flipped Classroom**: In the flipped classroom model, there is a reversal of traditional teaching approaches. Outside of class, students interact with instructional materials, like video lectures, and during class time, they participate in interactive activities, engage in discussions, and collaborate on problem-solving.

**d) MOOC (Massive Open Online Course):** MOOCs are online courses designed for large-scale participation and open access via the internet. They often include video lectures, interactive quizzes, and discussion forums, providing a scalable way to deliver educational content.

**e) Augmented Reality (AR) and Virtual Reality (VR):** Augmented Reality (AR) integrates digital information onto the actual surroundings, enhancing the user's perception. Virtual Reality (VR) involves users in a computer-generated environment. The application of both AR and VR technologies is growing in educational contexts, where they are employed to develop immersive learning experiences.

**f) Adaptive Learning:** Adaptive learning systems utilize data and algorithms to tailor the learning experience for each student individually. By scrutinizing student performance, these systems adjust content, pacing, and assessments to align with the learner's specific needs and progress.

**g) Open Educational Resources (OER):** Open Educational Resources are freely accessible, openly licensed educational materials that can be used, modified, and shared. OER includes textbooks, videos, and other resources that support learning and teaching.

**h) Synchronous vs. Asynchronous Learning:** Synchronous learning occurs in real-time, where instructors and students interact simultaneously, often through live video conferencing. Asynchronous learning allows for flexibility, with students accessing materials and participating in discussions at their own pace.

**i) Learning Analytics:** Learning analytics involves the collection, analysis, and interpretation of data related to learners and their contexts. It aims to provide insights into student progress, engagement, and learning patterns, facilitating data-driven decision-making in education.

Various Success Stories and case studies along with their success impact are shown in Table 1.

These success stories and case studies underscore the transformative impact of AI in tailoring education to individual needs. From improved academic performance and increased engagement to a deeper understanding of subject matter, these examples highlight the potential of AI to revolutionize the educational landscape and create more inclusive, adaptive and effective learning environments.

## IMMERSIVE TECHNOLOGIES: VR AND AR IN EDUCATION

Recently, the landscape of education has undergone a remarkable transformation fuelled by advancements in technology. One such revolutionary stride is the integration of technologies, specifically Virtual Reality and Augmented Reality into educational settings (Lai, J. W., and Cheong, K. H., 2022). These technologies hold the promise of redefining traditional approaches to teaching and learning, offering innovative tools to engage students, enhance understanding and create immersive learning experiences.

Virtual Reality (VR) generates a simulated environment, providing users with immersion in a computer-generated world. On the other hand, Augmented Reality (AR) overlays digital content onto the actual surroundings, enriching the user's perception. Both technologies offer unique opportunities to augment traditional educational methods, providing interactive and experiential learning experiences.

### Implementation of Virtual Reality (VR) in Education

VR is most effective when it complements the curriculum rather than being a standalone experience. So, specific learning objectives that VR can enhance, must be identified at initial level. VR headsets and controllers suitable for educational purposes can be chosen. Factors like affordability, ease of use

*Figure 3. Concepts of educational technology*

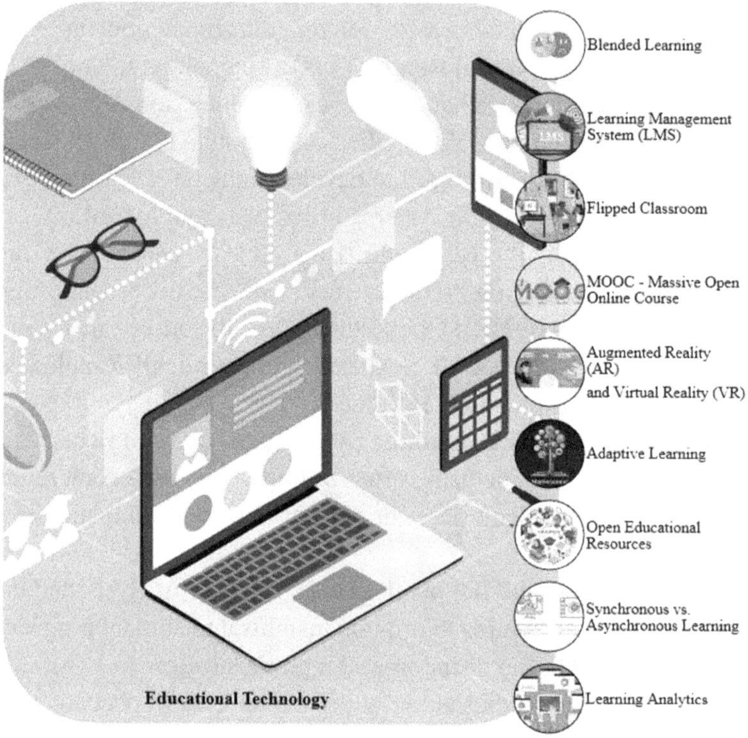


*Table 1. Success stories and case studies*

| Educational Technology | Success Impact |
|---|---|
| **Knewton's Adaptive Learning Platform** utilizes AI algorithms to personalize educational content for students. The platform continuously assesses individual performance, adapts to learning styles and provides targeted resources to address specific gaps in knowledge. | Students using Knewton have demonstrated improved learning outcomes. The adaptive nature of the platform has resulted in increased engagement, higher retention rates and enhanced mastery of subject matter across various educational levels. |
| **DreamBox in Elementary Math Education** an AI-driven math learning platform for elementary students, tailors lessons based on individual progress and understanding. The platform adjusts difficulty levels, provides real-time feedback and adapts the curriculum to meet each student's needs. | DreamBox has reported substantial improvements in student math proficiency. The adaptive learning model has led to increased confidence, a deeper understanding of mathematical concepts and a positive impact on standardized test scores. |
| **Carnegie Learning's Cognitive Tutor** employs AI to deliver personalized learning experiences in mathematics. The system assesses student performance, identifies areas of struggle and provides targeted interventions to facilitate better understanding. | Studies have shown that students using Cognitive Tutor consistently outperform their peers on standardized tests. The adaptive nature of the system has contributed to increased student confidence in mathematical problem-solving. |
| **IBM Watson Education** employs AI to offer personalized learning solutions. The platform assesses individual student strengths and weaknesses, adapting content to provide targeted challenges and support. | Schools using IBM Watson Education have reported increased student engagement and improved academic achievement. The adaptive learning features have contributed to a more personalized and effective learning experience. |

and compatibility with educational content must be taken under consideration while operating VR in education. 3D models, simulations, virtual field trips and interactive experiences can be sourced for educational content that aligns with the curriculum (Harrington, M. C. et al., 2021; Hiran et al., 2024). Platforms like Google Expeditions, Oculus Education or custom VR applications can be used that support the educational goals. Educators could be trained and made familiar with the VR technology and its integration into the classroom. Lessons can be planned that incorporate VR experiences. When VR aligns with the learning objectives and enhances the overall educational experience. The entire process for implementing VR in education is shown in Figure 4.

## Implementation of Augmented Reality (AR) in Education

Augmented Reality provides contextual learning experiences. AR devices like smartphones or tablets that are accessible to students are chosen through which experiences can be delivered. AR content like interactive textbooks, educational apps, or AR-enhanced assignments that aligns with the curriculum is taken into consideration (Law, E. L. C., & Heintz, M. et al., 2021). Platforms like ARCore (Android) or ARKit (iOS) that suits educational needs can be used to development frameworks for AR experiences. While dealing with AR in education teachers should understand how to integrate AR into lessons and guide students in using AR devices. They must encourage students to use AR apps for specific projects, assignments, or interactive learning opportunities. Assessment strategies to measure students' understanding and proficiency in using AR technology can be used for educational purposes. The entire process for implementing VR in education is shown in Figure 5.

*Figure 4. Implementation of VR in education*

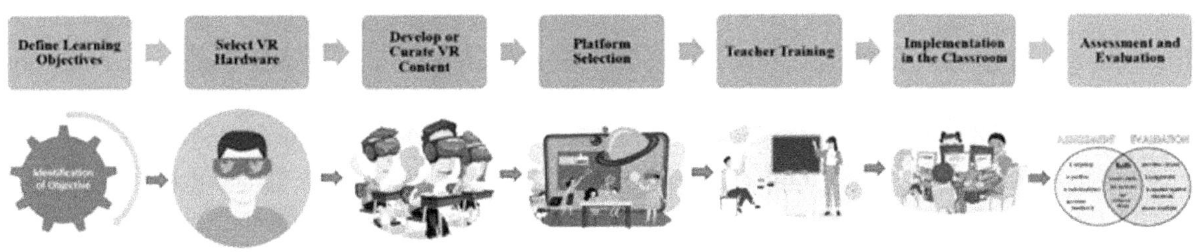


*Figure 5. Implementation of AR in education*

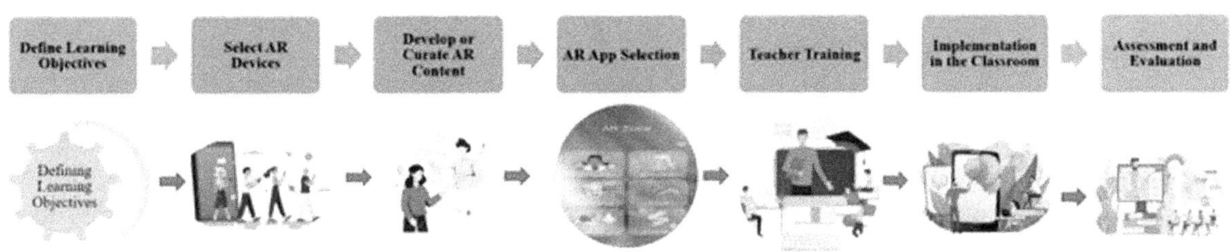

## ROBOTICS AND AUTOMATION IN EDUCATION

The integration of robotics into educational curricula has emerged as a transformative approach to preparing students for the challenges of the future. Robotics education goes beyond traditional teaching methods, offering hands-on, experiential learning opportunities that foster creativity, problem-solving skills and a deeper understanding of STEM (Science, Technology, Engineering and Mathematics) concepts (Talib, C. A. Et al., 2020; Vignesh et al., 2024; Mijwil et al., 2023). This article explores the significance of integrating robotics into the curriculum, highlighting key benefits, challenges and best practices. Basic components of robotics that laid foundation for enhanced education are shown in Figure 6.

### Importance of Robotics in Education

Robotics engages students in practical applications of STEM concepts, promoting literacy in science, technology, engineering and mathematics. It offers a tangible way for students to see the real-world implications of these subjects. Designing, building and programming robots necessitate critical thinking and problem-solving. Students learn to analyze challenges, devise solutions and iterate on their designs, cultivating valuable skills applicable in various aspects of life.Robotics projects encourage creativity as students design and build unique solutions. The open-ended nature of robotics tasks fosters innovation and allows students to explore their ideas, leading to the development of a creative mindset (Liu, Y. L. E. et al., 2023). Many robotics projects involve teamwork, mirroring real-world collaborative environments. Students work together to design, build and program robots, learning effective communication, cooperation and teamwork. Robotics provides a platform for applying theoretical concepts in a practical setting. Students witness the direct correlation between classroom learning and real-world applications. Exposure to robotics in education can inspire students to pursue careers in fields such as robotics engineering, computer science and automation (Eguchi, A., and Uribe, L., 2017).

### Best Practices for Integrating Robotics Into the Curriculum

Align robotics activities with the existing curriculum to ensure they complement and enhance classroom learning. Identify specific STEM standards and learning objectives that can be addressed through robotics projects. Ensuring an inclusive approach to robotics education that accommodates diverse learning styles and abilities provides opportunities for all students to actively participate and contribute to robotics projects. Equipment of educators with the necessary training and professional development opportunities to effectively integrate robotics into their teaching practices, empowers teachers to guide and facilitate robotics activities confidently (Alam, A., 2021). Explore opportunities for cross-curricular integration, connecting robotics with other subjects such as art, language arts and social studies. This interdisciplinary approach enriches the learning experience.

### Challenges in Integrating Robotics

Limited access to robotics kits, equipment and technology can pose challenges. Schools may face budget constraints that hinder the widespread adoption of robotics education. Some educators may feel unprepared or lack confidence in integrating robotics into their teaching practices. Providing ongoing professional development is essential to address this challenge. The demand for covering core curriculum content

*Figure 6. Robotics and automation in education*

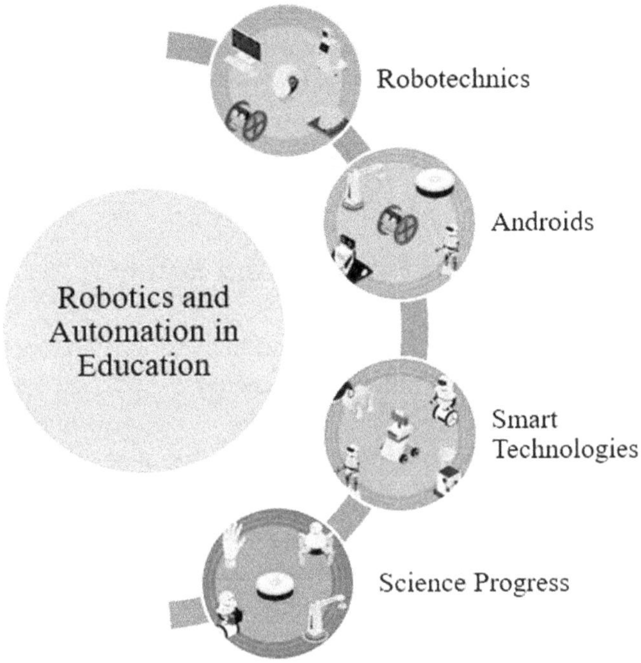


may lead to time constraints. Balancing the integration of robotics with other subjects requires thoughtful planning and collaboration among educators. Ensuring equitable access to robotics education is crucial. Schools should address issues of access and work towards creating an inclusive learning environment that reaches students from diverse backgrounds. The future of robotics in education is likely to witness advancements in educational robotics platforms, virtual simulations and the incorporation of artificial intelligence (Kazemzadeh, K., et al., 2023; Skouby et al., 2022). Additionally, robotics competitions and challenges at local, national and international levels are expected to continue growing, providing pupils with chances to showcase their skills and innovations.

## ETHICAL CONSIDERATIONS IN AI EDUCATION

Fairness and equity are fundamental principles that should underpin every facet of the education system. As educators, policymakers and stakeholders strive to create inclusive learning environments, it is imperative to address and mitigate systemic inequalities that can impede the educational journey of certain groups of students. This article explores the importance of ensuring fairness and equity in education, highlighting key considerations, challenges and actionable strategies to foster an inclusive educational landscape. Promoting fairness and equity involves fostering a learning environment that celebrates diversity and inclusivity. Students from various cultural, ethnic and socio-economic backgrounds should see themselves represented and valued within the curriculum (Sigdel, S., et al., 2021; Wanjale et al., 2023).

Fairness in education means providing every student with equal opportunities to succeed. This includes equitable access to resources, extracurricular activities, advanced coursework and support services that cater to individual needs. Equity efforts focus on identifying and addressing systemic disparities that disproportionately affect certain student groups. This includes acknowledging and rectifying historical and institutional biases that may exist within educational systems. Fair and equitable education considers the social and emotional well-being of students. Creating a supportive and inclusive environment fosters a sense of belonging, reducing the likelihood of disparities in mental health and well-being (Jagers, R. J., et al., 2019). Major components while dealing with ethical considerations in AI education are shown in Figure 7.

## Key Considerations in Promoting Fairness and Equity

Promoting fairness and equity involves careful consideration of various factors to ensure just and inclusive outcomes. Key considerations include following elements:

a) **Culturally Responsive Teaching:** Incorporate teaching practices that are culturally responsive, recognizing and integrating the diverse cultural backgrounds of students. This approach ensures that the curriculum reflects the experiences and perspectives of all learners.
b) **Equitable Resource Allocation:** Fairness involves allocating resources in an equitable manner. This includes ensuring that schools in economically disadvantaged areas have access to the same quality of teachers, facilities, technology and educational materials as more affluent institutions.
c) **Differentiated Instruction:** Adopt differentiated instruction strategies to accommodate diverse learning styles and abilities. Recognize and address individual strengths and challenges, providing additional support when necessary to ensure equitable learning outcomes.

*Figure 7. Ethical considerations in AI education*

d) **Regular Assessment and Monitoring:** Regularly assess and monitor educational practices and outcomes to identify and rectify any disparities. Utilize data to analyze performance, access and opportunities among different student groups, allowing for targeted interventions.
e) **Professional Development on Equity:** Provide ongoing professional development for educators on equity issues. This training should focus on recognizing and mitigating bias, fostering inclusive classrooms and employing strategies to meet the needs of diverse learners.

## Actionable Strategies for Ensuring Fairness and Equity

Implementing fairness and equity requires actionable strategies to address potential biases and create inclusive systems. Here are some key strategies:

a) **Diverse Curriculum Representation:** Ensure that the curriculum reflects the diversity of the student population. Include diverse perspectives, authors and historical narratives to provide a well-rounded and inclusive educational experience.
b) **Affirmative Policies and Practices:** Implement affirmative policies and practices that actively promote fairness and equity. This may include affirmative action programs, mentorship initiatives and targeted support for underrepresented groups.
c) **Accessible Technology and Resources:** Ensure that technology and educational resources are accessible to all students, regardless of their socio-economic background. Provide support for students who may not have reliable access to digital devices or the internet at home.
d) **Culturally Competent Professional Development:** Offer professional development opportunities that enhance educators' cultural competence. This includes understanding the diverse cultural backgrounds of students, incorporating culturally relevant teaching methods and addressing implicit biases.

Challenges in Ensuring Fairness and Equity

a) **Implicit Bias:** Implicit biases, which are unconscious stereotypes or prejudices, can influence decision-making processes. Addressing these biases requires ongoing training and awareness among educators, administrators and stakeholders.
b) **Resource Disparities:** Resource disparities among schools and districts can contribute to inequitable educational outcomes. Advocacy for equitable funding and resource allocation is essential to bridge these gaps.
c) **Standardized Testing Biases:** Standardized testing may introduce biases that disproportionately affect certain student groups. Efforts should be made to explore alternative assessment methods that provide a more accurate representation of students' abilities.
d) **Parental Involvement Disparities:** Disparities in parental involvement can impact a student's educational journey. Strategies to bridge this gap may involve creating welcoming and inclusive school environments and offering resources that support parental engagement.

# THE EVOLVING ROLE OF TEACHERS IN AN AI-AUGMENTED WORLD

## Redefining the Teacher's Role

In the rapidly evolving landscape of education, the role of teachers is undergoing a transformative shift. This article explores the changing nature of the teacher's role in the 21$^{st}$ century, emphasizing the need for adaptability, collaboration and a holistic approach to education.

Instead of being the primary source of information, teachers are becoming facilitators of learning. The emphasis is on guiding students in exploring and discovering knowledge independently, fostering critical thinking and problem-solving skills. The integration of technology into education is reshaping how teachers deliver content and engage with students. Teachers are now required to be proficient in leveraging technology tools to enhance learning experiences and prepare students for a digital future (Kilag, O. K. et al., 2023, Falloon, G., 2020). Beyond academic knowledge, teachers are increasingly focusing on cultivating essential soft skills such as communication, collaboration, creativity and adaptability. These skills are crucial for students to thrive in a rapidly changing and interconnected world.

The modern teacher is an inclusive educator, recognizing and valuing the diverse backgrounds, learning styles and abilities of students. Creating an inclusive classroom environment that accommodates various needs is a fundamental aspect of the redefined role. This involves employing differentiated instruction, personalized learning approaches and embracing flexibility in teaching methods. Beyond imparting knowledge, teachers serve as mentors and guides, providing support and encouragement to students.

## Strategies for Embracing the Redefined Role

Engagement in continuous professional development to stay abreast of educational trends, technology advancements and innovative teaching methodologies leads to professional growth is essential for meeting the evolving needs of students. Collaborative Learning Communities that include Sharing insights, best practices and collaborating on interdisciplinary projects fosters a culture of continuous improvement and innovation (Leigh Smith, B., et al., 2009). The integration of technology into the classroom utilize digital tools to enhance instruction, facilitate collaboration and provides students with opportunities to develop digital literacy skills.

Cultivating mindset among students by embracing various challenges as opportunities for learning, demonstrate resilience and encouraging students to view setbacks as stepping stones toward improvement. Integrating AI education into pre-service teacher education programs can help in promoting future educators enter the profession with a foundation in tech literacy and AI integration.

## Maintaining the Human Element in Education

While technology offers unprecedented opportunities, the essence of education lies in the human connection between educators and students. This article explores the importance of preserving the human element in education, the challenges posed by technological trends and strategies for fostering meaningful connections in the digital age. Human interaction fosters emotional connections between educators and students. These connections create a supportive learning environment where students feel seen, heard and valued. Emotional bonds contribute to a positive educational experience and enhance overall well-being (Jones, S. M., et al., 2017). Realisation of Natural Language Processing while using various Artificial

Intelligence algorithms for education is one of the most important constrain while taking sentiments of teachers and pupils under consideration (Naithani, K., & Raiwani, Y.P., 2022). Human interaction allows educators to guide students in navigating complex emotions, developing empathy and fostering interpersonal relationships. Personalized attention and encouragement from educators play a crucial role in motivating and engaging students. The human element in education enables educators to tailor their approach to individual learning styles, providing targeted support and encouragement. Educators serve as role models, imparting not just academic knowledge but also essential life skills and values. The human connection allows for the transmission of wisdom, ethical values and the development of character traits that extend beyond the academic realm.

Meaningful discussions, debates and collaborative activities are integral to the cultivation of critical thinking skills. The human element in education provides a platform for dynamic and interactive learning experiences that stimulate intellectual curiosity.

### Challenges to the Human Element in Education

The increasing integration of technology in education may lead to an overreliance on digital tools, potentially diminishing the personal connections between educators and students. Balancing technology with human interaction is crucial to prevent the erosion of the human element. The globalization of education and the rise of remote learning, especially in the wake of global events, can pose challenges to fostering meaningful connections. Physical distance may create barriers to the personal interactions that contribute to a sense of belonging and community Social Media Platforms play a major role in both communication as well as distracting while studying (Naithani, K., Raiwani, Y.P., 2023). The emphasis on standardized testing and academic performance metrics can divert attention from holistic education. Educators may feel pressured to prioritize exam results over the development of interpersonal skills and emotional intelligence. Time constraints within academic schedules may limit the opportunities for educators to engage in meaningful one-on-one interactions with students. Balancing administrative tasks, curriculum delivery and personal connections requires intentional time management.

## GLOBAL AND FAIR ACCESS TO EDUCATION THROUGH AI

In the realm of education, Artificial Intelligence (AI) emerges as a powerful ally in the quest to bridge educational gaps and promote inclusive learning environments. This article delves into the transformative potential of AI in addressing educational disparities, exploring the benefits, challenges and strategies for leveraging AI to ensure equitable access to quality education.

Educational disparities often arise from diverse learning needs among students. AI has the capacity to adapt and tailor learning experiences to individual requirements, offering personalized education that caters to varied learning styles. Disparities in educational resources, both physical and human, contribute to gaps in learning outcomes. AI technologies can help optimize resource allocation, ensuring that educational tools and expertise are distributed more equitably across diverse learning environments (Chan, C. K. Y., 2023). Rural or remote areas may face challenges in accessing quality education due to geographical barriers. AI-powered virtual learning platforms can overcome these obstacles, bringing educational opportunities to underserved regions and fostering a more inclusive global education landscape. Language and cultural diversity can pose barriers to effective learning. AI-driven language processing tools and culturally sensitive content can facilitate a more inclusive educational experience, catering to students from various linguistic and cultural backgrounds.

### The Role of AI in Bridging Educational Gaps

AI enables personalized learning experiences by analyzing individual learning patterns and adapting content accordingly. This tailoring of educational content addresses the diverse needs and paces at which students absorb information, fostering a more inclusive approach to education. AI-driven assessments provide adaptive feedback, allowing educators to understand each student's fortes and weak points (Rane, N. et al., 2023). This personalized feedback not only supports individual learning journeys but also aids educators in addressing specific needs within a diverse classroom. AI-powered accessibility tools benefit students with special education needs. From text-to-speech applications to adaptive interfaces, these tools enhance accessibility, enabling a more inclusive educational experience for students with diverse learning abilities. AI facilitates global connectivity and collaboration by breaking down geographical barriers. Virtual classrooms, online collaborations and AI-powered language translation tools enhance communication and cooperation among students from different regions, fostering a more interconnected educational community (Kamalov, F. et al., 2023). AI's analytical capabilities enable data-driven decision-making in education. By analyzing educational data, policymakers can identify areas with significant educational gaps, allowing for targeted interventions and resource allocation to address specific needs.

## THE FUTURE OF HIGHER EDUCATION WITH AI

The landscape of higher education is undergoing a transformative shift with the integration of Artificial Intelligence (AI). As technology continues to advance, educators, administrators and policymakers must proactively navigate this evolving terrain to ensure that AI enhances, rather than hinders, the quality and accessibility of higher education.

An era of unprecedented technological innovation has been evolved with AI emerging as a key driver of change across various sectors. In higher education, AI is poised to revolutionize traditional teaching and learning methods, offering a plethora of possibilities to improve efficiency, accessibility and personalization.

Current State of AI in Higher Education includes AI-driven LMS, Intelligent Tutoring Systems, Automated Grading and Assessment, Virtual and Augmented Reality and many more that provide Enhanced Personalization, Increased Accessibility, Predictive Analytics. This in turn will lead to Engaging educators, industry leaders and policymakers in dialogue, developing ethical guidelines for AI implementation in education.

Continuous adaptation of AI in Education will embrace a growth mindset to navigate evolving technologies, fostering a culture of innovation within educational institutions. Prioritizing accessibility and diversity in AI development the future of AI driven education system will ensure that AI benefits all students, regardless of background. NLP enables the development of automated grading systems, saving educators time and providing quick feedback to students. Blockchain can be used for secure and transparent verification of academic credentials, reducing fraud and streamlining the hiring process for employers. AI-powered social robots can aid in classrooms, helping with tasks and supporting student engagement (Santosh Kumar et al, 2016). Not only this, but AI-driven analytics can help institutions make data-informed decisions related to enrolment management, resource allocation and strategic planning. Analysing data on student engagement and performance can inform educators on effective teaching strategies and interventions. Various educational applications use AI to provide interactive and adaptive learning experiences. In the coming years AI has the ability to enhance the effectiveness of online learning platforms by personalizing content, providing feedback and facilitating collaborative learning experiences.

## CONCLUSION

AI in higher education has prompted a range of initiatives to prepare students for AI-related careers, such as integrating AI into curricula, providing personalized AI tutors, and teaching AI-related skills like data analytics and machine learning. The blend of key findings in this book chapter highlights essential approaches and considerations for institutions aiming to equip students with the skills, knowledge and ethical awareness needed in the dynamic field of Artificial Intelligence (AI).

After analysing this book chapter, it has been observed that dedicated AI courses and majors provide students with a foundational understanding of AI concepts, machine learning and ethical considerations. Combining AI with other fields through interdisciplinary programs helps students develop a holistic skill set, enabling them to apply AI solutions across diverse industries. Tailoring AI education to specific industries prepares students to apply AI solutions to unique sector challenges, bridging educational gaps and evolving the role of teachers in an AI-augmented world. Highlighting AI's role in sustainable development prepares students to address global challenges through AI applications. The future of education is being shaped by AI, with its integration into higher education leading to a range of benefits and considerations. This reflection explores the transformative potential, opportunities and challenges that an AI-augmented world presents to the realm of education.

The integration of AI in higher education holds immense promise for transforming the way we teach and learn. By addressing challenges and embracing opportunities, the future of higher education with AI can be shaped into a dynamic and inclusive ecosystem. As stakeholders work together, they can ensure that AI is harnessed to enhance the educational experience, fostering a new era of innovation and excellence.

In conclusion, a holistic approach to preparing students for AI-related careers in higher education involves a combination of specialized curricula, practical experiences, ethical considerations, global perspectives and strategic partnerships with industry. By embracing these key findings, institutions can empower students to thrive in the rapidly evolving landscape of AI and contribute meaningfully to the advancements in this transformative field.

## REFERENCES

Alam, A. (2021). Should robots replace teachers? Mobilisation of AI and learning analytics in education. In *2021 International Conference on Advances in Computing, Communication, and Control (ICAC3)* (pp. 1-12). IEEE. 10.1109/ICAC353642.2021.9697300

Barua, T., Doshi, R., & Hiran, K. K. (2020). *Mobile Applications Development: With Python in Kivy Framework*. Walter de Gruyter GmbH & Co KG. doi:10.1515/9783110689488

Chan, C. K. Y. (2023). A comprehensive AI policy education framework for university teaching and learning. *International Journal of Educational Technology in Higher Education*, *20*(1), 38. doi:10.1186/s41239-023-00408-3

Doshi, R., Hiran, K. K., Ranolia, R., & Joshi, C. (2023). Monitor Cloud Performance and Data Safety With Artificial Intelligence. In Applications of Artificial Intelligence in Wireless Communication Systems (pp. 92-108). IGI Global. doi:10.4018/978-1-6684-7348-1.ch006

Doshi, R., Hu, Y. C., Garg, L., & Fagbola, T. (2023). Special issue "Towards a Higher Education of the Future: Transformational Roles of Edge Intelligence". *Array (New York, N.Y.)*, 100332. doi:10.1016/j.array.2023.100332

Easwaran, B., Hiran, K. K., Krishnan, S., & Doshi, R. (Eds.). (2022). *Real-Time Applications of Machine Learning in Cyber-Physical Systems*. IGI Global., doi:10.4018/978-1-7998-9308-0

Eguchi, A., & Uribe, L. (2017). Robotics to promote STEM learning: Educational robotics unit for 4th grade science. In *2017 IEEE integrated stem education conference (ISEC)* (pp. 186-194). IEEE.

Falloon, G. (2020). From digital literacy to digital competence: The teacher digital competency (TDC) framework. *Educational Technology Research and Development*, *68*(5), 2449–2472. doi:10.1007/s11423-020-09767-4

Grassini, S. (2023). Shaping the future of education: Exploring the potential and consequences of AI and ChatGPT in educational settings. *Education Sciences*, *13*(7), 692. doi:10.3390/educsci13070692

Harrington, M. C., Bledsoe, Z., Jones, C., Miller, J., & Pring, T. (2021). Designing a virtual arboretum as an immersive, multimodal, interactive, data visualization virtual field trip. *Multimodal Technologies and Interaction*, *5*(4), 18. doi:10.3390/mti5040018

Hiran, K. K., Doshi, R., & Patel, M. (Eds.). (2024). *Applications of Virtual and Augmented Reality for Health and Wellbeing*. IGI Global. doi:10.4018/979-8-3693-1123-3

Hiran, K. K., Hemachandran, K., Pise, A., & Rabi, B. (Eds.). (2023). *Handbook of Research on AI and Knowledge Engineering for Real-Time Business Intelligence*. IGI Global. doi:10.4018/978-1-6684-6519-6

Jagers, R. J., Rivas-Drake, D., & Williams, B. (2019). Transformative social and emotional learning (SEL): Toward SEL in service of educational equity and excellence. *Educational Psychologist*, *54*(3), 162–184. doi:10.1080/00461520.2019.1623032

Jones, S. M., Barnes, S. P., Bailey, R., & Doolittle, E. J. (2017). Promoting social and emotional competencies in elementary school. *The Future of Children*, *27*(1), 49–72. doi:10.1353/foc.2017.0003

Kamalov, F., Santandreu Calonge, D., & Gurrib, I. (2023). New era of artificial intelligence in education: Towards a sustainable multifaceted revolution. *Sustainability (Basel)*, *15*(16), 12451. doi:10.3390/su151612451

Kazemzadeh, K., Akhlaghdoust, M., & Zali, A. (2023). Advances in artificial intelligence, robotics, augmented and virtual reality in neurosurgery. *Frontiers in Surgery*, *10*, 10. doi:10.3389/fsurg.2023.1241923 PMID:37693641

Kilag, O. K., Miñoza, J., Comighud, E., Amontos, C., Damos, M., & Abendan, C. F. (2023). Empowering Teachers: Integrating Technology into Livelihood Education for a Digital Future. *Excellencia: International Multi-disciplinary Journal of Education (2994-9521), 1*(1), 30-41.

Kumar, S., Sharma, R., Singh, V., & Shrikant Tiwari, S. K. (2023). Potential Impact of Data-Centric AI on Society. *IEEE Technology and Society Magazine, 42*(3), 98-107. doi:10.1109/MTS.2023.3306532

Kumar, S., Tiwari, S., & Singh, S. K. (2016). *Face Recognition of Cattle: Can it be done?* Proceedings of the National Academy of Sciences, India. doi:10.1007/s40010-016-0264-2

Lai, J. W., & Cheong, K. H. (2022). Adoption of virtual and augmented reality for mathematics education: A scoping review. *IEEE Access : Practical Innovations, Open Solutions, 10*, 13693–13703. doi:10.1109/ACCESS.2022.3145991

Law, E. L. C., & Heintz, M. (2021). Augmented reality applications for K-12 education: A systematic review from the usability and user experience perspective. *International Journal of Child-Computer Interaction, 30*, 100321. doi:10.1016/j.ijcci.2021.100321

Leigh Smith, B., & MacGregor, J. (2009). Learning communities and the quest for quality. *Quality Assurance in Education, 17*(2), 118–139. doi:10.1108/09684880910951354

Liu, Y. L. E., Lee, T. P., & Huang, Y. M. (2023). Enhancing university students' creative confidence, learning motivation, and team creative performance in design thinking using a digital visual collaborative environment. *Thinking Skills and Creativity, 50*, 101388. doi:10.1016/j.tsc.2023.101388

Mijwil, M. M., Gök, M., Doshi, R., Hiran, K. K., & Kösesoy, I. (2023). Utilizing Artificial Intelligence Techniques to Improve the Performance of Wireless Nodes. In Applications of Artificial Intelligence in Wireless Communication Systems (pp. 150-162). IGI Global. doi:10.4018/978-1-6684-7348-1.ch010

Mijwil, M. M., Hiran, K. K., Doshi, R., Dadhich, M., Al-Mistarehi, A. H., & Bala, I. (2023). ChatGPT and the future of academic integrity in the artificial intelligence era: A new frontier. *Al-Salam Journal for Engineering and Technology*, 2(2), 116–127. doi:10.55145/ajest.2023.02.02.015

Naithani, K., & Raiwani, Y. P. (2022). Realization of natural language processing and machine learning approaches for text-based sentiment analysis. *Expert Systems: International Journal of Knowledge Engineering and Neural Networks, 40*(5), e13114. Advance online publication. doi:10.1111/exsy.13114

Naithani, K., & Raiwani, Y. P. (2023). Sentiment Analysis on Social Media Data: A Survey. In H. S. Saini, R. Sayal, A. Govardhan, & R. Buyya (Eds.), *Innovations in Computer Science and Engineering. ICICSE 2022. Lecture Notes in Networks and Systems* (Vol. 565). Springer., doi:10.1007/978-981-19-7455-7_59

Naithani, K., Raiwani, Y. P., & Sissodia, R. (2022). Text-Based Analysis of COVID-19 Comments Using Natural Language Processing. In A. Dev, S. S. Agrawal, & A. Sharma (Eds.), *Artificial Intelligence and Speech Technology. AIST 2021. Communications in Computer and Information Science* (Vol. 1546). Springer. doi:10.1007/978-3-030-95711-7_17

Patel, K. (2024). Ethical Reflections on Data-Centric AI: Balancing Benefits and Risks. *International Journal of Artificial Intelligence Research and Development*, 2(1), 1–17.

Radianti, J., Majchrzak, T. A., Fromm, J., & Wohlgenannt, I. (2020). A systematic review of immersive virtual reality applications for higher education: Design elements, lessons learned, and research agenda. *Computers & Education*, *147*, 103778. doi:10.1016/j.compedu.2019.103778

RaneN.ChoudharyS.RaneJ. (2023). Education 4.0 and 5.0: Integrating Artificial Intelligence (AI) for personalized and adaptive learning. Available at SSRN 4638365. doi:10.2139/ssrn.4638365

Roslan, F. A. B. M., & Ahmad, N. B. (2023). The Rise of AI-Powered Voice Assistants: Analyzing Their Transformative Impact on Modern Customer Service Paradigms and Consumer Expectations. *Quarterly Journal of Emerging Technologies and Innovations*, *8*(3), 33–64.

Sigdel, S., & Sharma, M. R. (2021). Critical pedagogy and equity promotion in culturally and linguistically diverse classroom. *Journal of English Education and Teaching*, *5*(2), 201–215. doi:10.33369/jeet.5.2.201-215

Singh, S. V., & Hiran, K. K. (2022). The impact of AI on teaching and learning in higher education technology. *Journal of Higher Education Theory and Practice*, *22*(13).

Skouby, K. E., Dhotre, P., Williams, I., & Hiran, K. (Eds.). (2022). *5G, Cybersecurity and Privacy in Developing Countries*. CRC Press. doi:10.1201/9781003374664

Talib, C. A., Aliyu, H., Aliyu, F., Maimun, A., Malik, A., Anggoro, S., & Ali, M. (2020). Integration of robotics into STEM education for facilitating environmental sustainability. *Solid State Technology*, *63*(1s), 767–783.

Tedre, M., Toivonen, T., Kahila, J., Vartiainen, H., Valtonen, T., Jormanainen, I., & Pears, A. (2021). Teaching machine learning in K–12 classroom: Pedagogical and technological trajectories for artificial intelligence education. *IEEE Access : Practical Innovations, Open Solutions*, *9*, 110558–110572. doi:10.1109/ACCESS.2021.3097962

Vignesh, U. M., M., & Doshi, R. (Eds.). (2024). Bio-Inspired Optimization Techniques in Blockchain Systems. IGI Global. doi:10.4018/979-8-3693-1131-8

Wanjale, K., Chitre, A. V., & Doshi, R. (2023). Opting for Industry 4.0: Challenge or Opportunity. In *AI, IoT, Big Data and Cloud Computing for Industry 4.0* (pp. 3–20). Springer International Publishing. doi:10.1007/978-3-031-29713-7_1

# Chapter 19
# Role of Video Content Generation in Education Systems Using Generative AI

**Lalit Kumar**
https://orcid.org/0000-0002-8441-1696
*Motilal Nehru National Institute of Technology, India*

**Dushyant Kumar Singh**
*Motilal Nehru National Institute of Technology, India*

**Mohd Aquib Ansari**
*Bennett University, India*

## ABSTRACT

*This chapter delves into the transformative potential of three cutting-edge models, i.e., CCVS, DreamPose, and Fast Vid2Vid, in reshaping educational video content creation. CCVS, a dynamic framework amalgamating generative and discriminative models, excels in synthesizing high-quality videos from text descriptions. Its versatility in video generation, interpolation, and prediction marks a paradigm shift in educational content development. DreamPose, an advanced AI system leveraging stable diffusion, translates textual descriptions into visually stunning fashion videos. Its user-friendly design caters to diverse fashion styles, making it an ideal tool for educators seeking visually engaging content across disciplines. Fast Vid2Vid, a deep learning model, takes the spotlight for efficiently generating high-quality videos from a single image. Recognized for its realism, it holds promise in dynamic visualizations for educational purposes, spanning virtual and augmented reality experiences. Practical insights and implementation strategies empower educators to seamlessly integrate these models into educational settings, offering a comprehensive guide from planning and scripting to interactive element incorporation. This chapter lays the foundation for educators and content creators to elevate the educational experience through innovative visual storytelling and AI-driven technologies.*

DOI: 10.4018/979-8-3693-2440-0.ch019

## INTRODUCTION

Video content creation using generative AI involves leveraging artificial intelligence algorithms, specifically generative models, to generate, enhance, or manipulate video content. Generative AI, such as Generative Adversarial Networks (GANs) or Variational Autoencoders (VAEs), can be employed to create realistic and novel video sequences (Kumar & Singh, 2023; Kumar et el., 2023). This process typically involves training the model on a large dataset of existing videos, enabling it to learn patterns, styles, and characteristics of the input data. Once trained, the generative AI can produce new video content by generating frames or even entire sequences autonomously. This technology allows for the creation of unique, visually appealing videos, special effects, and animations without the need for extensive manual labour. It has applications in various industries, including entertainment, marketing, and virtual reality, providing a powerful tool for content creators to explore innovative and dynamic visual experiences.

Video plays a crucial role in the education system by providing a dynamic and engaging medium for delivering content (Figure 1). It has become an integral part of modern pedagogy, offering students visual and auditory stimulation that caters to diverse learning styles. Educational videos can bring complex concepts to life, making them more accessible and facilitating better understanding. They also enable educators to create virtual field trips, demonstrations, and simulations, expanding the learning experience beyond traditional classroom boundaries. However, it's important to approach video integration with a mindful awareness of potential pitfalls. One challenge is the risk of passive consumption, where students may become more focused on the entertainment value rather than the educational content. Additionally, issues of accessibility and equity may arise, as not all students may have equal access to high-quality internet or devices. Striking a balance between utilizing videos for enhanced learning experiences and ensuring equitable access requires thoughtful implementation and consideration of individual student needs. By addressing these challenges with empathy and fostering an inclusive learning environment, educators can harness the power of video to enrich the educational journey for all students (Haga, 2002; Aldausari et al., 2022).

To address challenges associated with video content creation using generative AI, several strategies can be implemented. Firstly, to mitigate the risk of passive consumption, educators can design interactive and participatory activities that accompany the generated video content. This encourages students to actively engage with the material, ask questions, and collaborate with their peers. Additionally, incorporating assessments that gauge comprehension and critical thinking skills related to the video content ensures that students are not merely passive viewers but active learners (Wessel et al., 2023).

To tackle issues of accessibility and equity, educators should be mindful of the varying technological resources available to students. Providing alternative means of accessing content, such as transcripts or written summaries, can accommodate different learning preferences and address challenges related to internet access or device availability. Furthermore, schools and institutions can work towards ensuring equitable access to technology, bridging the digital divide and promoting inclusivity in the learning environment. Continuous monitoring and improvement of generative AI models are essential to enhance the accuracy and relevance of the content generated. Regular updates and refinements to the algorithms can help address any biases or limitations that may emerge during the content creation process. Additionally, involving students in the feedback loop by encouraging them to provide insights on the generated content fosters a collaborative and adaptive learning environment.

The aim of video generation for educational content creation is to enhance learning experiences by leveraging multimedia tools to deliver information in engaging and accessible formats. By incorporating

*Figure 1. Benefits of video generation in education sector using generative AI*

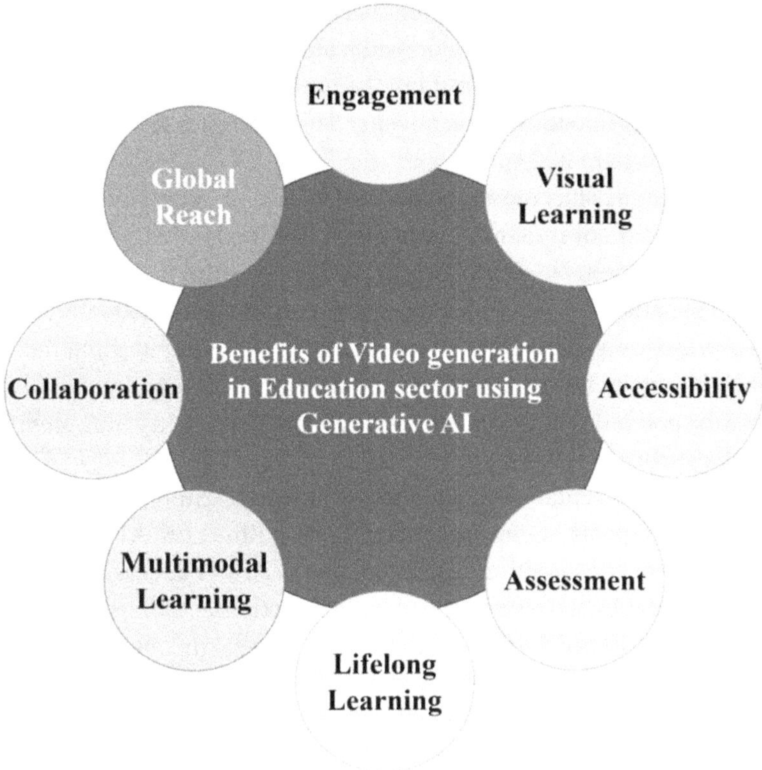


visuals, animations, and demonstrations, educational videos aim to cater to diverse learning styles and capture learners' attention more effectively than traditional text-based materials. The motivation behind this approach lies in its potential to facilitate comprehension, retention, and application of knowledge, ultimately fostering deeper understanding and mastery of subjects. Additionally, videos can transcend geographical barriers, making education more accessible to learners worldwide, and offer flexibility for self-paced learning. Overall, the goal is to empower learners with dynamic, interactive, and immersive educational resources that inspire curiosity and promote lifelong learning.

By incorporating these measures, educators can harness the benefits of video content creation using generative AI while proactively addressing potential challenges, ensuring a more inclusive, engaging, and effective learning experience for all students.

## RELATED WORK

The use of Generative AI (GenAI) in education has garnered attention in the research community, with various studies exploring its applications, benefits, and challenges. Below are some related works that provide insights into the use of generative AI in education:

Leiker et al. explores the use of generative artificial intelligence (AI) in the context of learning videos featuring synthetic virtual instructors. The study aims to assess the potential benefits and challenges associated with incorporating generative AI into educational content creation. The researchers investigate how AI-generated virtual instructors can enhance the learning experience by creating dynamic and engaging videos for educational purposes. The paper likely delves into the impact on student engagement, the effectiveness of AI-generated content in conveying educational concepts, and potential issues related to passive consumption or accessibility. By examining the intersection of generative AI and education, the study likely contributes insights into leveraging advanced technologies for more effective and interactive learning experiences (Leiker et al., 2023).

Safinah Ali and her colleagues has presented a study for use of generative AI in educational system. The study focuses on middle school students, aiming to understand the impact of introducing generative models on their learning experiences. The paper likely explores the pedagogical strategies employed to engage students with generative AI and may discuss the challenges encountered, as well as potential benefits observed. By presenting findings at a prominent human-computer interaction conference, the paper contributes valuable insights into the intersection of education and generative AI technologies, offering a glimpse into the potential future of innovative and interactive learning environments for middle school students (Ali et al., 2021).

The paper explores the implementation of a modified flipped learning approach as a strategy to counteract the potential negative impacts of generative artificial intelligence (AI) on education. Recognizing the challenges such as passive consumption of content and issues of accessibility, the study proposes a pedagogical shift that integrates interactive and participatory activities alongside generative AI-generated video content. The modified flipped learning model encourages students to actively engage with the material, fostering critical thinking and collaboration. The paper also emphasizes the importance of addressing issues related to equity by providing alternative means of accessing content and advocating for equal technological resources. Furthermore, the study highlights the need for ongoing refinement of generative AI algorithms to improve content accuracy and relevance. By adopting this modified flipped learning approach, the paper suggests a proactive and collaborative strategy to enhance the positive impact of generative AI on education while minimizing potential drawbacks (Lawan et al., 2023).

García et al. explores the transformative impact of generative artificial intelligence on the landscape of education. It delves into the novel possibilities that arise from the integration of generative AI in educational settings, particularly focusing on video content creation. The authors highlight the potential for enhanced engagement and comprehension through the use of generative AI in generating dynamic and interactive educational videos. The paper also addresses the challenges associated with this technological shift, emphasizing the importance of mitigating passive consumption, ensuring accessibility, and continuously refining AI models to avoid biases. By examining the new reality of education shaped by advances in generative AI, the paper provides insights into fostering a more inclusive, interactive, and effective learning environment (García et al., 2023).

Chiu et al. explores the transformative effects of Generative AI (GenAI) on the field of education by focusing on two prominent examples, ChatGPT and Mid journey. The study investigates how these AI technologies influence educational practices, shape policies, and guide the trajectory of research in the sector. The research delves into the practical applications of ChatGPT and Mid journey in educational settings, analysing their impact on teaching methods, student engagement, and overall learning outcomes. Additionally, the paper assesses the implications of these AI tools on educational policies, considering issues related to privacy, ethical considerations, and the equitable distribution of AI resources in diverse educational environments. Furthermore, the study examines the influence of GenAI on the direction of research in education. It explores the emerging trends, challenges, and opportunities that arise as a result of incorporating AI technologies into educational research. The paper addresses the potential of GenAI to catalyse innovative approaches in pedagogy and highlights the need for educators, policymakers, and researchers to adapt to this evolving landscape. Ultimately, this paper contributes to a deeper understanding of the profound impact that Generative AI has on education, shedding light on the opportunities and challenges that arise with the integration of advanced technologies like ChatGPT and Mid journey in educational settings (Chiu et al., 2023).

The pandemic's impact on education has underscored the necessity of enhancing pre-service teachers' digital skills training. This quantitative study delved into pre-service teachers' perspectives on how the creation, design, and dissemination of didactic videos can bolster their teaching competencies. Across early childhood, primary, and secondary education, English (as a foreign language) pre-service teachers crafted a diverse array of educational content in video format, ranging from stories and linguistic materials to tutorials and documentaries. These videos, spanning various genres such as news programs and literary reviews, were tailored for school audiences and disseminated through YouTube channels linked to an open-access online TV portal. The findings revealed that the production of educational videos significantly enriched the participating teachers' skill sets. Particularly notable was the positive feedback regarding the development of teamwork abilities, prompting researchers to consider more effective strategies for leveraging didactic video generation to enhance teacher education. This study sheds light on the potential of digital media in teacher training and underscores the importance of collaborative learning experiences in fostering pedagogical expertise (García et al., 2024).

## APPROACHES OF VIDEO CONTENT CREATION

Video content creation involves various approaches and strategies, depending on the goals, target audience, and platform. Here are some key approaches to video content creation:

### CCVS (Context-aware Controllable Video Synthesis Explained)

CCVS (Context-aware Controllable Video Synthesis Explained) (Le et al., 2021) is a novel framework for generating high-quality, temporally coherent videos from text descriptions. It combines the strengths of both generative and discriminative models to achieve state-of-the-art results on a variety of video synthesis tasks.

The CCVS framework consists of two main components: a generator and a discriminator. The generator is responsible for synthesizing videos from text descriptions, while the discriminator is responsible for evaluating the quality of the generated videos. The generator is trained using a combination of adversarial training and perceptual loss, while the discriminator is trained using a cross-entropy loss. The CCVS framework has been shown to achieve state-of-the-art results on a variety of video synthesis tasks, including:

- Video generation from text descriptions: CCVS can generate high-quality, temporally coherent videos from text descriptions of varying complexity.
- Video interpolation: CCVS can generate intermediate frames between two existing video frames, preserving the temporal coherence and visual quality of the original videos.
- Video prediction: CCVS can predict future frames of a video sequence, given a few initial frames.

*Figure 2. Video generation using CCVS approach*

The CCVS framework is a powerful tool for generating high-quality, temporally coherent videos from text descriptions (Figure 2). It has the potential to revolutionize the way we create and interact with videos, and opens up new possibilities for applications such as video editing, video games, and virtual reality.

## DreamPose

Dreampose (Karras et al., 2023) is a cutting-edge AI system that enables the creation of captivating fashion videos using Stable Diffusion, a state-of-the-art text-to-image generation model. With Dreampose, users can unleash their creativity and generate visually stunning fashion content simply by providing text descriptions. The process of using Dreampose is straightforward and user-friendly. Users begin by inputting a textual description of the desired fashion video, specifying elements such as clothing styles, models, backgrounds, and any additional creative details. Dreampose then harnesses the power of Stable Diffusion to transform these text prompts into a series of captivating images, which are subsequently stitched together to form a seamless video.

One of the key advantages of Dreampose is its versatility. It caters to a wide range of fashion styles, from haute couture to streetwear, making it an ideal tool for fashion designers, content creators, and enthusiasts alike. Additionally, Dreampose offers a variety of customization options, allowing users to fine-tune the appearance of their videos by adjusting factors such as lighting, camera angles, and even the movement of the models. Overall, Dreampose represents a significant advancement in the field of AI-generated fashion content. Its ability to produce high-quality fashion videos from mere text descriptions opens up new possibilities for creative expression and storytelling within the fashion industry.

## Fast Vid2Vid

Fast Vid2Vid (Kumar & Singh, 2023) is a deep learning model that can generate high-quality videos from a single image. It was developed by researchers at the University of California, Berkeley, and

*Figure 3. Video generation process of DreamPose model*

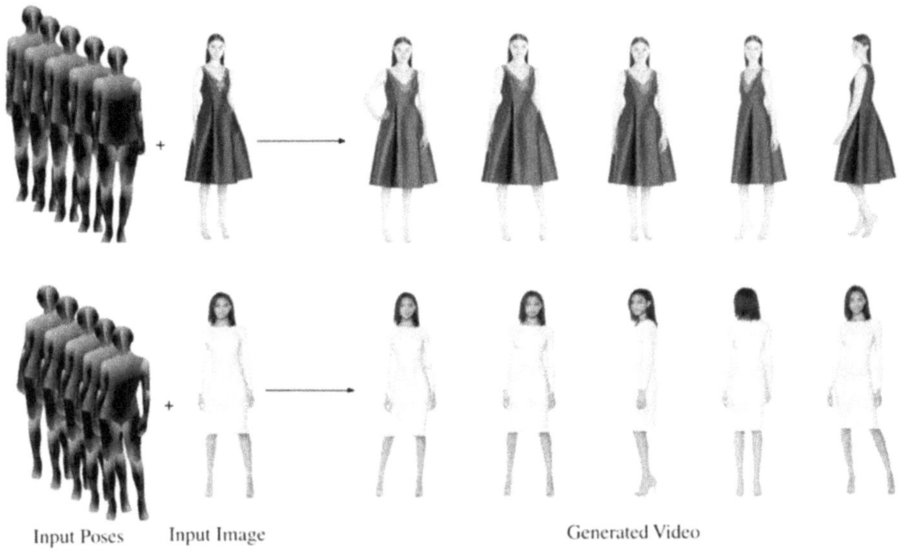


was published in the journal Nature in 2019. The model works by first learning a representation of the input image. This representation is then used to generate a sequence of video frames, which are then combined into a final video. The model is able to generate videos that are both realistic and temporally coherent (Figure 4).

Fast Vid2Vid is a significant improvement over previous video generation models, which were often slow and produced low-quality videos. The model is able to generate videos at a rate of 30 frames per second, and the videos it produces are of high quality. The model has a number of potential applications, including:

*Figure 4. Performance of Fast-Vid2Vid over some approaches*

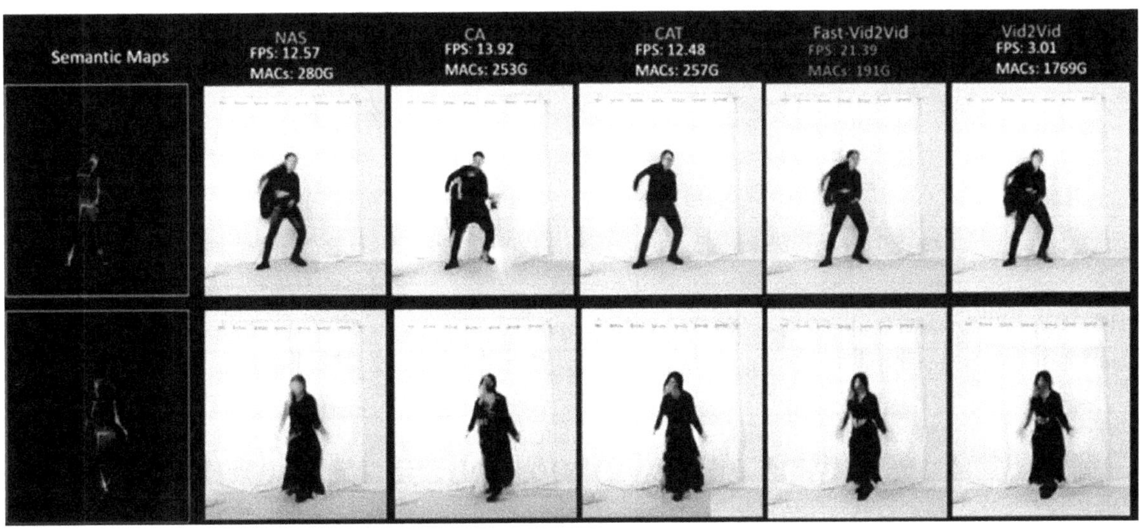

- Generating videos for virtual reality and augmented reality experiences
- Creating visual effects for movies and TV shows
- Generating educational videos
- Generating videos for marketing and advertising

Fast Vid2Vid is a powerful tool that has the potential to revolutionize the way we create videos. Instead of this, we also have created a comparison table between these three approaches.

## Analysis of Video Generation Approach

In the realm of video content creation, three distinct approaches showcase the advancements in AI-driven video synthesis. The first approach, CCVS (Context-aware Controllable Video Synthesis Explained), introduces a groundbreaking framework that amalgamates generative and discriminative models, heralding a new era in video synthesis technology. At its core, CCVS employs a generator responsible for synthesizing videos from text descriptions, coupled with a discriminator evaluating their quality. This dual-model architecture enables CCVS to excel in various video synthesis tasks, ranging from generating high-quality videos based on textual prompts to interpolating frames between existing ones and even predicting future frames. The versatility of CCVS extends across diverse domains, including video editing, video games, and virtual reality experiences, promising a paradigm shift in how we conceive and interact with videos.

Transitioning to the fashion industry, Dreampose emerges as a cutting-edge AI system revolutionizing the creation of fashion-related video content. Leveraging Stable Diffusion, a state-of-the-art text-to-image generation model, Dreampose empowers users to effortlessly translate textual descriptions into visually stunning fashion videos. Its adaptability in accommodating a wide spectrum of fashion styles and offering customization options, such as adjusting lighting and camera angles, makes it an indispensable tool for fashion designers and content creators alike. By seamlessly transforming textual prompts into captivating images and stitching them together into cohesive videos, Dreampose not only streamlines the content creation process but also sparks new dimensions of creativity within the fashion industry.

*Table 1. A short comparison between video generation approaches*

| Feature | CCVS | DreamPose | Fast Vid2Vid |
|---|---|---|---|
| Model Type | Deep learning-based computer vision | Deep learning-based pose estimation | Deep learning-based video generation |
| Application | Video content creation, editing, animation | Pose-based animation, motion capture | Video-to-video synthesis, animation, video enhancement |
| Training Data | Diverse datasets containing various, visual elements (images, videos) | Pose annotated datasets, Human motion datasets | Video datasets with paired frames (input and target) |
| Output Quality | High-quality, realistic videos with customizable elements | Realistic human motion synthesis, animation | Realistic video synthesis with controllable parameters |
| Speed | Moderate to slow depending on the complexity of the task | Real-time or near real-time depending on hardware | Moderate to fast, depending on the hardware and complexity of task |
| Customization | Highly customizable through various | Limited customization options, | Moderate customization options, |

In the third approach, Fast Vid2Vid emerges as a formidable deep learning model poised to revolutionize video generation processes. Developed by researchers at the University of California, Berkeley, Fast Vid2Vid addresses previous limitations by generating high-quality videos from a single image at an unprecedented rate of 30 frames per second. This remarkable speed, coupled with its ability to maintain realism and temporal coherence, unlocks a myriad of applications across various domains. From immersive virtual and augmented reality experiences to seamless integration of visual effects in movies, TV shows, educational videos, and marketing campaigns, Fast Vid2Vid emerges as a versatile and powerful tool reshaping the landscape of video content creation.

Each of these approaches represents a significant leap forward in AI-driven video synthesis, offering unique capabilities and applications that cater to diverse needs and industries. As technology continues to evolve and AI models become increasingly sophisticated, the potential for leveraging video generation in educational contexts becomes even more compelling. By harnessing the power of generative models like CCVS, Dreampose, and Fast Vid2Vid, educators can create engaging and interactive educational content that enhances learning experiences, fosters creativity, and empowers students to explore complex concepts in innovative ways.

## USE OF VIDEO CONTENT CREATION APPROACHES FOR EDUCATIONAL PURPOSE

In this section of the manuscript, we will discuss about how we can use the above discussed approaches in creation of education content.

### CCVS (Context-Aware Controllable Video Synthesis Explained)

Using CCVS (Context-aware Controllable Video Synthesis Explained) for educational content creation can be a groundbreaking approach to enhance the learning experience. Here are several ways in which CCVS can be leveraged for educational purposes:

#### Visualizing Complex Concepts

CCVS can be employed to generate high-quality videos from text descriptions that explain complex concepts in various subjects. For example, it can visualize scientific processes, historical events, or mathematical equations, making educational content more engaging and understandable.

#### Interactive Learning Modules

The ability of CCVS to generate videos from text descriptions allows educators to create interactive learning modules. These modules can include dynamic visualizations, simulations, and demonstrations that cater to different learning styles and enhance comprehension.

### Historical Reenactments

For history lessons, CCVS can generate videos that reenact historical events based on textual descriptions. This immersive approach can provide students with a more vivid understanding of the past, making history lessons more captivating and memorable.

### Language Learning

CCVS can be utilized to create language learning materials by generating videos that depict real-life language scenarios. For instance, it can produce conversational scenarios, pronunciation exercises, and cultural context, facilitating a more immersive language learning experience.

### Science Experiments and Demonstrations

In science education, CCVS can be applied to simulate experiments and demonstrations that might be challenging to conduct in a physical classroom. This allows students to witness scientific phenomena in action, reinforcing theoretical concepts.

### Mathematical Problem Solving

CCVS can visualize step-by-step solutions to mathematical problems, providing a dynamic and interactive learning experience. This can be particularly helpful for complex problem-solving processes, helping students grasp mathematical concepts more effectively.

### Historical Time Travel

By leveraging CCVS's ability to interpolate frames and generate intermediate content, educators can create videos that simulate time travel through historical periods. This innovative approach can make history lessons more immersive and relatable for students.

### Predicting Scientific Phenomena

CCVS's capability for video prediction can be used to simulate the outcomes of scientific experiments or natural phenomena. This predictive aspect can foster critical thinking and hypothesis testing among students.

In summary, CCVS has the potential to transform educational content creation by providing a dynamic, visually engaging, and interactive medium for conveying information. Whether visualizing abstract concepts, demonstrating scientific principles, or creating historical simulations, CCVS can enhance the educational experience and cater to a wide range of subjects and learning styles.

## DreamPose

While Dreampose is primarily designed for fashion video creation, its versatility and user-friendly interface make it an innovative tool that can be creatively adapted for educational content. Here are some ways Dreampose could be utilized in the creation of education content:

### Visualizing Historical Events

Teachers or content creators can input text descriptions of historical events, specifying details like clothing styles, settings, and characters. Dreampose can then transform these descriptions into visually appealing videos, offering students a more engaging and immersive way to learn about historical periods.

### Language Learning Scenarios

Language teachers can use Dreampose to generate videos that depict various language learning scenarios. By inputting text descriptions related to dialogues, cultural settings, or language-specific events, educators can create dynamic and culturally relevant content to enhance language learning experiences.

### Science Experiments and Concepts

Dreampose could be employed to illustrate scientific concepts or experiments. Teachers can describe the experimental setup, scientific phenomena, or historical scientific breakthroughs in text, and Dreampose can then visualize these descriptions, providing students with a visual aid to better understand complex scientific topics.

### Literary Analysis and Storytelling

English and literature teachers can use Dreampose to bring literature to life. By inputting text descriptions of scenes from novels or plays, educators can generate visual representations of literary works, aiding in literary analysis and helping students visualize the settings and characters in the stories they study.

### Geography and Cultural Studies

For geography or cultural studies, educators can describe different regions, cultural practices, or historical events, allowing Dreampose to create videos that visually represent the diversity and uniqueness of various cultures and places around the world.

### Customized Educational Scenarios

Teachers can create customized educational scenarios tailored to their lesson plans. By specifying elements such as characters, settings, and activities, Dreampose can generate videos that align with specific learning objectives, making the educational content more engaging and memorable.

### Student Projects and Presentations

Students can use Dreampose as a creative tool for presenting their research projects or assignments. By describing their topics in text, they can generate visually appealing videos to accompany their presentations, adding a multimedia dimension to their work.

While Dreampose was initially designed for fashion content, its adaptability and customization options make it a promising tool for educators seeking to enhance the visual and creative aspects of their educational content. The ability to transform text descriptions into visually stunning videos can significantly contribute to a more immersive and engaging learning experience for students across various subjects.

## Fast Vid2Vid

Utilizing the Fast Vid2Vid model for educational video content creation involves several steps to ensure the effective and engaging delivery of educational material. Here's a guide on how to leverage the capabilities of Fast Vid2Vid for educational purposes:

### Content Planning

Define the educational objectives and topics you want to cover in the video. Outline the key points and structure of the content to ensure clarity and coherence.

### Scripting

Develop a detailed script that aligns with your educational goals. Break down the content into key segments and consider how the Fast Vid2Vid model can enhance the visual representation of each concept.

### Visual Representation

Identify specific visual elements that can be enhanced through video synthesis. This might include dynamic representations of processes, historical events, scientific phenomena, or any other educational content that benefits from visual storytelling.

### Image Inputs

Gather relevant images or create visual assets that represent the key concepts in your educational video. These images will serve as inputs to the Fast Vid2Vid model for generating dynamic video content.

### Fast Vid2Vid Implementation

Input the selected images into the Fast Vid2Vid model to generate a sequence of video frames. Ensure that the model settings are optimized for educational content, balancing realism and coherence with the speed of video generation.

### Review and Refinement

Review the generated video content to ensure it aligns with the educational objectives. Refine the output as needed, adjusting parameters or incorporating additional elements to enhance clarity.

### Narration and Annotations

Integrate narration or voiceovers to explain the educational content. Use annotations or on-screen text to highlight key points, providing additional context to the visual representation.

### Interactive Elements

Consider incorporating interactive elements within the video, such as quizzes, polls, or clickable annotations, to engage learners actively and assess their understanding.

### Accessibility Considerations

Ensure that the educational video is accessible to a diverse audience. Include subtitles, provide alternative text for visual elements, and consider other accessibility features to accommodate different learning needs.

### Distribution and Engagement

Choose appropriate platforms for distributing your educational videos, such as educational websites, learning management systems, or video-sharing platforms. Encourage learner engagement through discussions, comments, or supplementary materials.

### Feedback and Iteration

Collect feedback from learners and educators to continuously improve the educational content. Use this feedback for future iterations, refining both the script and the use of the Fast Vid2Vid model.

By following these steps, you can harness the capabilities of the Fast Vid2Vid model to create visually compelling and informative educational videos. This approach can enhance the learning experience and cater to different learning styles, making educational content more engaging and effective.

## CONCLUSION

In conclusion, this book chapter has provided an extensive exploration of the revolutionary potential embedded within three cutting-edge models—CCVS, DreamPose, and Fast Vid2Vid—in the context of reshaping educational video content creation. The transformative impact of CCVS was evident as it seamlessly combined generative and discriminative models, presenting a versatile framework capable of synthesizing high-quality videos from text descriptions. Applications ranging from video generation to interpolation and prediction showcased CCVS's adaptability, ushering in a paradigm shift in the development of educational content. DreamPose emerged as a user-friendly and advanced AI system, demonstrating its prowess in translating textual descriptions into visually captivating fashion videos. Its versatility across diverse fashion styles positions DreamPose as an invaluable tool for educators seeking to create engaging content in various disciplines. Fast Vid2Vid, recognized for its efficiency and realism, promises dynamic visualizations for educational purposes. From virtual and augmented reality experiences to visual effects, Fast Vid2Vid offers a transformative approach to enhancing educational videos.

The practical insights and implementation strategies shared throughout the chapter empower educators to seamlessly integrate CCVS, DreamPose, and Fast Vid2Vid into educational settings. From the initial stages of planning and scripting to the incorporation of interactive elements, this comprehensive guide lays the foundation for educators and content creators to elevate the educational experience through innovative visual storytelling and the integration of AI-driven technologies. As the landscape of educational content creation evolves, these models stand as powerful tools, opening new frontiers for engaging and effective learning experiences.

## REFERENCES

Aldausari, N., Sowmya, A., Marcus, N., & Mohammadi, G. (2022). Video generative adversarial networks: A review. *ACM Computing Surveys*, *55*(2), 1–25. doi:10.1145/3487891

Ali, S., DiPaola, D., Lee, I., Hong, J., & Breazeal, C. (2021, May). Exploring generative models with middle school students. In *Proceedings of the 2021 CHI conference on human factors in computing systems* (pp. 1-13). ACM. 10.1145/3411764.3445226

Chiu, T. K. (2023). The impact of Generative AI (GenAI) on practices, policies and research direction in education: A case of ChatGPT and Midjourney. *Interactive Learning Environments*, 1–17. doi:10.1080/10494820.2023.2253861

García-Peñalvo, F. J., Llorens Largo, F., & Vidal, J. (2023). *The new reality of education in the face of advances in generative artificial intelligence.*

García-Sampedro, M., Agudo Prado, S., & Torralba-Burrial, A. (2024). Pre-service teachers' skills development through educational video generation. *European Journal of Teacher Education*, 1–19. doi:10.1080/02619768.2024.2323925

Haga, H. (2002). Combining video and bulletin board systems in distance education systems. *The Internet and Higher Education*, *5*(2), 119–129. doi:10.1016/S1096-7516(02)00084-2

Karras, J., Holynski, A., Wang, T. C., & Kemelmacher-Shlizerman, I. (2023, October). Dreampose: Fashion image-to-video synthesis via stable diffusion. In *2023 IEEE/CVF International Conference on Computer Vision (ICCV)* (pp. 22623-22633). IEEE. 10.1109/ICCV51070.2023.02073

Kumar, L., & Singh, D. K. (2023). A comprehensive survey on generative adversarial networks used for synthesizing multimedia content. *Multimedia Tools and Applications*, *82*(26), 40585–40624. doi:10.1007/s11042-023-15138-x

Kumar, L., & Singh, D. K. (2023, June). Comparative analysis of Vid2Vid and fast Vid2Vid models for video-to-video synthesis on cityscapes dataset. In *2023 International Conference on Computer, Electronics & Electrical Engineering & their Applications (IC2E3)* (pp. 1-5). IEEE. 10.1109/IC2E357697.2023.10262586

Kumar, L., Singh, D. K., & Srivas, A. (2023, July). Performance Evaluation of Video-to-Video Synthesis GAN models on Cityscapes Dataset. In *2023 14th International Conference on Computing Communication and Networking Technologies (ICCCNT)* (pp. 1-6). IEEE. 10.1109/ICCCNT56998.2023.10306535

Lawan, A. A., Muhammad, B. R., Tahir, A. M., Yarima, K. I., Zakari, A., Abdullahi, A. H. II, & Lawan, S. (2023). Modified flipped learning as an approach to mitigate the adverse effects of generative artificial intelligence on education. *Education Journal*, *12*(4), 136–143.

Le Moing, G., Ponce, J., & Schmid, C. (2021). Ccvs: Context-aware controllable video synthesis. *Advances in Neural Information Processing Systems*, *34*, 14042–14055.

Leiker, D., Gyllen, A. R., Eldesouky, I., & Cukurova, M. (2023, June). Generative AI for learning: investigating the potential of learning videos with synthetic virtual instructors. In *International conference on artificial intelligence in education* (pp. 523-529). Cham: Springer Nature Switzerland. 10.1007/978-3-031-36336-8_81

Wessel, M., Adam, M., Benlian, A., & Thies, F. (2023). Generative AI and its transformative value for digital platforms. *Journal of Management Information Systems*.

# Chapter 20
# Script Generation for Silent Speech in E-Learning

**S. M. Emdad Hossain**
*University of Nizwa, Oman*

**Sallam Khairy**
https://orcid.org/0000-0003-2845-5675
*University of Nizwa, Oman*

**Arockiasamy Soosaimanickm**
*University of Nizwa, Oman*

**Rabie Ramadan**
https://orcid.org/0000-0002-0281-9381
*University of Nizwa, Oman*

## ABSTRACT

*This chapter is all about an advanced system by which the speech without sound will be recognized, and the equivalent script will be generated automatically. All the relevant stakeholders, i.e. students, instructors, then collect script and study insight. To develop the proposed system, it is planned to use one of the most prominent and popular datasets called synthetic-speech-commands-dataset-SSCD, which is freely available. The outcome of this research will provide an opportunity to develop community/reason-based database which will be a potential contribution in the field of conventional education, AI based education and bioinformatics for the research community.*

## INTRODUCTION

The speech recognition from muted video will be a challenging task and will provide an opportunity to explore further improvement in the recognition system by the future researchers as well. The most important challenges will be the lack of a well-suited platform and linguistic constraints, especially the pronunciation of languages used. To make it simple, this research will consider English language speaking

DOI: 10.4018/979-8-3693-2440-0.ch020

as a potential dataset to conduct the study using artificial intelligence and machine learning techniques. This research will explore the possibility of identifying a suitable methodology to develop an appropriate recognition system to convert recognized speech into script. The researchers have already completed successful research work related to the proposed topic (Afouras et al., 2018; Easwaran et al., 2022; Anusuya & Katti, 2009; Hiran et al., 2023). However, it is understood that the real-time script generation for the speech recognition from the muted video has not been properly attempted before. Through this research work, we aimed to explore various aspects and possibilities to generate the proposed real-time system for speech recognition. Figure 1 (below) demonstrates the flow of activities to generate the script from the silent voice using both AI and Machine Learning Technique.

However, the main objective of this research work is to establish a dynamic system to recognize speech and automatic script-generation as a result using AI-ML technique with the aim to apply in e-learning. Further, this paves the way for the definition of some of the sub-objectives to be considered in this research.

I. Considering the English language speaking video to measure the lip movement.
II. Feature extraction from the input video o Real-time script generation and reporting
III. Develop a speech recognition dataset for future research work with all possible and common English words along with its Eigenvector.
IV. Develop an efficient system for recognizing muted speech by analyzing the lips movement.
V. It is important to utilize machine learning techniques for accurate and efficient lips recognition.
VI. The project will push the boundaries of speech recognition by exploring script generation based on silent speech.

Moreover, almost all higher education institutions have moved into online teaching; in this instance, it is very important that speech recognition systems add substantial value to people who have hearing inabilities. This research will also contribute to the fields of computer vision and bio-informatics as scientific research contributions for the research community in this area. In addition, it may provide the following benefits or advantages to the community.

- It will address the public sentiments on drawbacks of online teaching and learning.
- It will add value to the physically disabled people with hearing inabilities.

*Figure 1. Flow of Activities to Generate the Script*

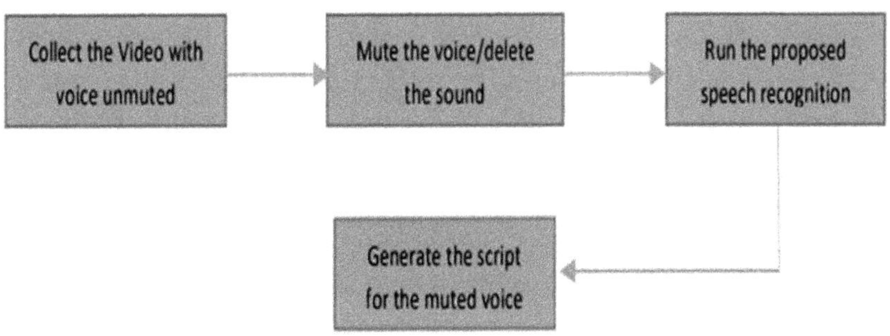

- The scientific contribution in the area of Human Computer Interaction and Machine Learning in combination of AI.

## BACKGROUND

It is very important to derive an idea for the proposed research by referring to research work done on similar or related research topics. The most vital part of this research is the lip reading, which will be the basis for interpreting the lip movement in the generated script. This research work has Collected the Video with the voice unmuted, muted the voice/deleted the sound, and Run the proposed speech recognition. Generate the script for the muted voice in multiple aspects to consider, e.g., identity verification, language proficiency, detecting the word, etc. Amit et al. (Amit, Jnoyola, & Sameep, 2016) use deep learning approaches to provide solutions to the lip-reading task using Convolutional Neural Network (CNN) and LSTM. The features extracted by the CNN layer are then used by LSTM layers to extract temporal information from a sequence. The accuracy rate of the validation set achieves 73% for words, 79% for phrases, and 76% for both words and phrases. The researchers also encountered a serious problem in the speech recognition system, where people use different accents while speaking. In (Ahmad & Hassanat, n.d.), to ensure the human ability to read lip movements, the researchers conducted experiments with a voice sample of two males and two females. The sample dataset used has four videos from PDA Database (Baldwin, 2004), where the speaker has spoken ten digits/characters in each video. The average word recognition rate measured for all the participants was 53%.

Further, Hiran & Doshi (Hiran & Doshi, 2013) focus on automatic lip-reading based on backdrop subtraction and image prediction techniques. Background subtraction is a method in image processing, which extracts the foreground image for further processing. In this situation, the object is a region of interest (ROI). The proposed method consists of four stages: gray-scaling, resizing images from 640×640 pixels into 32×24 pixels, background subtraction to segment the lips, vertical and horizontal projection to extract the features (the result used as input of classifier), and word using artificial neural network. The experiments were conducted to classify three words ('saya,''mau,''makan') in the Malaysian Language. The best result was obtained when using a vertical projection that gives an accuracy of 71.1%. Likewise, in (Achmad & Fadillah, 2015) the cascade classifier method is used to detect the location of the lip. Then, the image area around the lip is cropped. The cropped area is then segmented. Lip segmentation is performed based on the difference in color composition between the lip and the skin. Multiple experiments have been conducted with various individual voice samples and resulted in different accuracies. The accuracy for red lips, pale lips, and pale lips with mustaches are 74%, 68%, and 38%, respectively.

Furthermore, in (Mijwil et al., 2022), the authors used a dynamic feature from lip images to recognize Japanese words. The dynamic features are calculated as first-order regression coefficients gained from several neighboring images. This better represents the time derivative of a basic static image. Dynamic features are processed using convolutional neural networks (CNN) (Yamashita et al., 2018), which are able to reduce the adverse effects caused by subject shocks and blurring of faces that are blurred at the level of feature extraction. Its effectiveness has been confirmed by word recognition experiments that compare the proposed method with conventional static images. The results were obtained using the dynamic feature, which reaches an accuracy of 71%, while the static feature gives 58%, and the combination of both produces 59%. However, after extensive literature review it became very much clear on the gap identified in measuring the stable accuracy along with the script generation in English. The important point noted from the existing research works is that there is significant interest shown by the researchers to identify the lip movement. Even though, the dynamic script generation was missing. Eventually non had the mechanism/deployed AI or Machine Learning Technique which could improve accuracy and robustness of the system. None of them highlighted the potentiality of applying this AI-ML based technique into the education sector especially for e-learning. The definitive objective of this chapter is to cover the identified gap above and to highlight the importance of AI-ML in e-learning. It is also noted that the stable accuracy is an important challenge to be taken care in this chapter. By considering all those shortcomings, in this research we are aiming to design a new speech recognition system with dynamic script generation for future learning arena which is e-learning.

## METHODOLOGY

Due to the limitations of the traditional audio-based speech recognition systems in muted videos, there is a need for new efficient approaches. This project will explore different potential Artificial Intelligence (AI) techniques as hybrid approach for script generation from muted videos, including Deep Learning (Das, 2024), Generative Adversarial Networks (GANs) (Olynick, 2024), Audio-Visual Embeddings (Narasimhan, 2023), and Transfer Learning (Mahrishi et al., 2020), figure 2 shows the overall methodology.

The methodological glimpse of total experiments are follows:

1. **Deep Learning with Lip Reading:**
   A. **Convolutional Neural Networks (CNNs):** This excels at extracting features from images and can be tailored for lip reading. A CNN architecture for this task involves:
      - Preprocessing: this step is used for noise reduction and normalization to ensure consistency across different lighting conditions.
      - Feature Extraction: the convolutional layers are utilized to extract features from each frame, with the focus on areas around the mouth such as lips and jawline. Those features will be able to capture the speaker's mouth shape, position, and movement during speech.
      - Pooling Layers: those layers are usually used to reduce the dimensionality of extracted features. At the same time, it preserves the lip movement essential information.

*Figure 2. Initial Method of Potential Experiments*

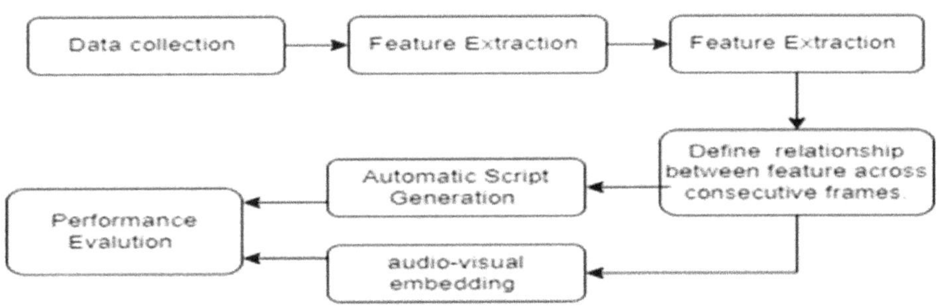

B. **Recurrent Neural Networks (RNNs):** Particularly it is a Long Short-Term Memory (LSTM) networks, will be used to handle the sequential lip movement data. Therefore, CNN output as a sequence of the output from the CNN, each frame sequence of features is fed to the LSTM network. The LSTM network will do the following:
   - It is used to analyze the temporal relationship between features across consecutive frames.
   - It will be used to learn how to recognize lips patterns and interrelate it to specific phonemes.
   - Also, it will be used to predict the likely sequence of phonemes based on the learned patterns.

2. **Generative Adversarial Networks (GANs):** A GAN framework can be employed for script generation where it has two main components:
   - Generator: The GAN network will take the video frames as input and try to generate silent speech scripts. LSTM will be used by the generator to generate the text sequence word by word based on the features extracted from the video by CNN.
   - Discriminator: The main function of the discriminator is to differentiate between scripts generated from human conversations and scripts generated by the generator. It will analyze both the generated scripts and their corresponding video frames, assessing the accuracy and coherence of the generated text.

This adversarial training is expected to continuously refine the script generation process.

3. **Audio-Visual Embeddings**: This approach bridges the gap between missing audio and visual cues (lip movements). Two separate models can be trained:

   - Visual Model: This model analyzes video frames using the CNN approach. It extracts features related to lip movements.
   - Audio Model: While the audio information is limited in muted videos, any residual audio cues (background noise, breathing sounds) can be leveraged. So, this model will be able to extract any relevant auditory features from the available audio data.

These models will be able to learn to create a combination of the embedding that correspond to the speech content. These embedding also will be able to capture the relationship between any visual cues (lip movements) and any available auditory information. The language model will benefit from the combined embedding.

- Language Model: The language model is a model that is trained or pre-trained with huge dataset of text and speech pairs. This model is already learned mapping the text sequences to their corresponding speech representations and vice versa. With audio-visual embedding into the language model, the model will be able to predict the most likely words and sentences spoken in the video.
  **Challenges and Considerations**: Although the proposed machine learning techniques are promising, the accuracy of Lip-Reading models can be affected by several factors as follows:
- Lighting variations: Video poor lighting could be a problem to CNN to capture the features.

- Speaker's facial features: different pip sizes, shapes and other factors could affect the accuracy of the model abilities accurately detect lip movements.
- Head pose: it is the angle of the speaker's head relative to the camera. It also affects lip movement detection.
- Dataset Availability: Training datasets are important for the AI models training. Therefore, we might need to collect the data by ourselves.
- Privacy Concerns: generating the script from muted videos might raise ethical concerns.

However, by considering all possible challenges and potentiality the experiments stated at expected phases next section of this chapter will describe the experiments and result.

## EXPERIMENTS AND RESULTS

To sum-up the experimental mechanism; it is said that lip movement is one key trait has been deployed for this research and the lip reading involves different components including the dataset either audio or visual, feature extraction, and classification networks, and classification schemes, see figure 3.

As given in Figure 3, the first component is the dataset that can be used for training. Due to the importance of lip-reading in various applications, there are many datasets generated by the researchers. Some of these datasets are presented in Table 1. Most of those datasets are in English and others are in Chines, Arabic, and multiple languages.

The second and third components are feature extraction and classification. However, some of those methods can be used for both feature extraction and classification. This could depend on the lip-reading systems or research goals. For instance, Optical Flow could be used in conjunction with CNNs for special and motion features. Also, HMMs could be used in conjunction with neural networks. Moreover, Multimodal Fusion Techniques are mostly relevant to systems with audio data in which it complements visual lip movement information. Therefore, the selection of the method will depend on the nature of the data, complexity of the task, available computational resources, and the goal of the system. Those methods are presented in Table 2 their primary usage.

Table 3 below visually summarizes the performance of lip-reading systems with feature extraction and classification algorithms. The '+' sign in the algorithms names separates the feature extraction method from the classification method. The indicated performance in the figure shows various combinations of algorithms. The accuracy percentage ranges from ~30% to 98.5% in which it shows impact of methodological synergy on performance outcomes.

The provided (Table.3: below) results reveal that traditional feature extraction methods such as Sparse Tensor PCA and Autoencoders when combined with simpler classifiers like feedforward networks, yield modest accuracy. On the other hand, the combination of 3D Convolutional Neural Networks with advanced loss functions, notably contrastive loss gives a significant leap in performance. This is to say

*Figure 3. Lip-Reading Components*

*Table 1. List of Lip-Reading Datasets*

| Dataset Name | Language | Resolution | Description |
|---|---|---|---|
| LRW (Lip Reading in the Wild (LRW) dataset, n.d.) | English | 500x500 pixels | It is a word level lip-reading dataset with over 1000 speakers from BBC television. |
| GRID (Loy, n.d.) | English | 720x576 pixels | It has sentence-level videos with a fixed grammar structure. It could be used for word- and sentence-level lip-reading tasks. |
| LRS2 (Lip Reading Sentences 2 (LRS2) dataset, n.d.) | English | 160x160 pixels | This dataset is used for sentence-level lip-reading; the recording is from BBC programs with a diverse vocabulary. |
| LRS3 (Lip Reading Sentences 3 Dataset, 2024) | English | 1920x1080 pixels | This dataset is related to sentence-level lip-reading. It has wide range of speakers and developed based on TED talks, |
| AVLetters (Tian, 2023) | English | 576x720 pixels | It is a dataset based on letters from A to Z. therefore, it is based on letter-level lip-reading. |
| AVLetters2 (Tian, 2023) | English | 720x576 pixels | An HD version of AVLetters with more repetitions and speakers. |
| CUAVE (Patterson et al., 2002) | English | 720x480 pixels | it has isolated and connected digit utterances. |
| OuluVS2 (Zuwei, 2024) | English | 864x480 pixels | It is phrase-level lip-reading challenges, and it has several phrases uttered by each speaker in controlled conditions. |
| TIMIT (for audio-visual studies) (Harte & Gillen, 2015) | English | Varies | TIMIT is designed for phonetic research and it has been adopted for lip-reading studies. |
| LRW-1000 (Papers with Code - CAS-VSR-W1k (LRW-1000) Dataset, n.d.) | Chinese | 720x1280 pixels | it is one of the large-scale naturally distributed dataset. It consists of 1000 words uttered by a variety of Chinese TV speakers. |
| MIRACL-VC1 (Rekik, Ben-Hamadou, & Mahdi, 2014) | Arabic | 480x640 pixels | it is an Arabic dataset consists of isolated words. |
| AVICAR (Six visual speech recognition data sets and a company about speech recognition, n.d.) | English | 720x480 pixels | AVICAR is recorded by American speaker in a moving vehicle it includes digits and letters. |
| IBM ViaVoice (Potamianos, Luettin, & Neti, 2001) | English | Varies | the dataset is used for speech recognition, but it is also adopted for lip-reading. |
| AVAS (Elrefaei, Alhassan, & Omar, 2019) | Arabic | Varies | An Arabic audio-visual speech dataset which includes several speakers articulating Arabic phonemes and sentences. |
| eNTERFACE (Martin et al., 2006) | Multiple | Varies | eNTERFACE dataset consists of audio-visual expressions produced in six different languages including English, French, German, Turkish, Spanish, and Mandarin. |

that 3D CNN has a superior capability in lip reading systems. Moreover, classifiers like Deep Belief Networks have moderate performance but their combination with feature extractor methods does not exploit their full potential. Furthermore, the combination of bidirectional variants of GRUs and LSTMs with amalgamated with attention mechanisms, delivers exceptionally high accuracy.

Hybrid approaches that encapsulate CNNs for feature extraction combined with LSTM classification give notable performance which indicates their roles in capturing both spatial and temporal dependencies effectively. At the same base, the usage of Autoencoders for dimensionality reduction prior to LSTM-based sequencing could enhance the classification performance.

Therefore, the 3D CNNs with bidirectional LSTMs and a CTC loss function, as well as the fusion of 2D and 3D CNN features with complex classification mechanisms reveals remarkable performance. This result signifies the importance of deep learning applications of visual and sequential data analysis.

*Table 2. Feature Extraction and Classification Methods*

| Method | Primary Use (Feature Extraction, Classification) |
|---|---|
| Convolutional Neural Networks (CNNs) (Exarchos et al., 2024) | Feature Extraction |
| Recurrent Neural Networks (RNNs) (Xing et al., 2023) | Both |
| Long Short-Term Memory (LSTM) (Exarchos et al., 2024) | Both |
| Gated Recurrent Unit (GRU) (Prakash et al., 2024) | Both |
| 3D Convolutional Neural Networks (3D CNNs) (Cai et al., 2023) | Feature Extraction |
| Autoencoders (Yang et al., 2024) | Feature Extraction |
| Variational Autoencoders (VAEs) (Yang et al., 2024) | Feature Extraction |
| Attention Mechanisms (Yang, Wang, & Liew, 2023) | Both |
| Transformers (Yang, Wang, & Liew, 2023) | Both |
| Graph-Based Methods (Thapa, 2023) | Feature Extraction |
| Optical Flow (Lu, Xu, & Fu, 2022) | Feature Extraction |
| Siamese Networks (Ma et al., 2021) | Feature Extraction |
| Temporal Convolutional Networks (TCN) (Atila & Sabaz, 2022) | Both |
| Deep Boltzmann Machines (Pan et al., 2024) | Feature Extraction |
| Hidden Markov Models (HMM) (Liu, Liu, & Li, 2024) | Both |
| Multimodal Fusion Techniques (Ryumin, Ryumina, & Ivanko, 2023) | Feature Extraction |
| Capsule Networks (Vidal & Busso, 2023) | Feature Extraction |
| Generative Adversarial Networks (GAN) (Ngiam et al., 2011) | Both |

However, the performance of the lip reading depends on various parameters including variable lighting, speaker diversity, and background noise.

## CONCLUSION

The potential impact of this research will lead to social benefit and cultural enhancement for the people in connected to the education section which will surely have impact on the society and to the nation. Since the education is the backbone of a nation; the research output directly will have impact on the backbone as the aim of this research is to implement AI and ML based speech generation for silent speech for e-learning. Further, the current economic strategy or modern economy; every single action in the society has impact on the economy. The only thing is to measure is; the size of impact. However, successful implementation of this research outcome; will have impact on long-run for the world community which lead to sustainable economic development. A successful implementation of this research project will provide significant recognition in the field of scientific research conducted in higher education institutions for the development of education system especially for e-learning using AI and ML. This will create an opportunity to explore further on the enhancement of speech recognition system for the future researchers too. Other than these; it will introduce a number of exciting benefits to the society in general.

*Table 3. Combination of Feature Extraction and Classification Algorithms Performance*

| No | Algorithms/Classifier | Accuracy Rate (%) |
|---|---|---|
| 1 | 2D plus 3D CNN + Bidirectional LSTM plus CTC (Lu & Li, 2019) | 98 |
| 3 | 3D CNN plus Highway + Bidirectional GRU plus Attention (Margam et al., 2019) | 97.1 |
| 3 | 3D CNN + Bidirectional LSTM (Lu & Li, 2019) | 87.6 |
| 4 | 3D CNN plus ResNet + Bidirectional LSTM (Xu et al., 2018) | 83 |
| 5 | 3D CNN + Contrastice Loss (Stafylakis & Tzimiropoulos, 2017) | 98.5 |
|  | Autoencoder + Bidirectional LSTM (Tor et al., 2017) | 94.7 |
| 7 | Autoecoder + Bidirectional LSTM (Petridis, Wang, Li, & Pantic, 2017) | 91.8 |
| 8 | Autoencoder + LSTM (Petridis, Wang, Li, & Pantic, 2017) | 84.5 |
| 9 | CNN + LSTM plus Attention (Petridis, Li, & Pantic, 2017) | 97 |
| 10 | Feedforward + LSTM (Son & Zisserman, 2017) | 79.5 |
| 10 | CFI plus VGG + LSTM (Wand, Koutník, & Schmidhuber, 2016) | 76 |
| 12 | CFI + GoogleNet (Garg, Noyola, & Bagadia, 2016) | 85.6 |
| 13 | DBNF plus DCT + LSTM (Saitoh et al., 2016) | 81.8 |
| 14 | CNN + LSTM (Petridis & Pantic, 2016) | 81.1 |
| 15 | CNN + CNN (Fox, O'Mullane, & Reilly, 2005) | 93.2 |
| 16 | SyncNet + LSTM (Chung & Zisserman, 2015) | 94.1 |
| 17 | 3D CNN + Bidirectional GRU plus CTC (Chung & Zisserman, 2016) | 93.4 |
| 18 | LDA plus MLTT plus SAT + Feed Forward (Assael et al., 2016) | 53 |
| 19 | HiLDA + Feed Forward (Almajai et al., 2016) | 84.67 |
| 20 | Scatteing Coefficient plus LDA + Feed Forward (Thangthai et al., 2015) | 30.64 |
| 21 | Deep BeliefNetwork (Mroueh, Marcheret, & Goel, 2015) | 55.3 |
| 22 | DCT plus LDA + Deep BeliefNetwork (Moon, Kim, & Wang, 2015) | 35.7 |
| 23 | Sparse Tensor PCA + Autoencoder (Huang & Kingsbury, 2013) | 64.4 |

- Development of the system will provide cultural and social impacts.
- It will provide an opportunity to promote scientific research culture in the field of machine learning and human computer interaction in combination of AI.
- The potential database creation will support the research community in higher education institutions around the word.
- This research work will provide an opportunity for the research in the education section especially for initial capacity building.

After long discussion and argument, it is certainly can recapitulate that the proposed script generation from silent speech is showing promising result which can be applied for e-learning. Similarly, it is also opening a new window for AI and ML to be applied education.

*Figure 4. Combination of Feature Extraction and Classification Algorithms Performance*

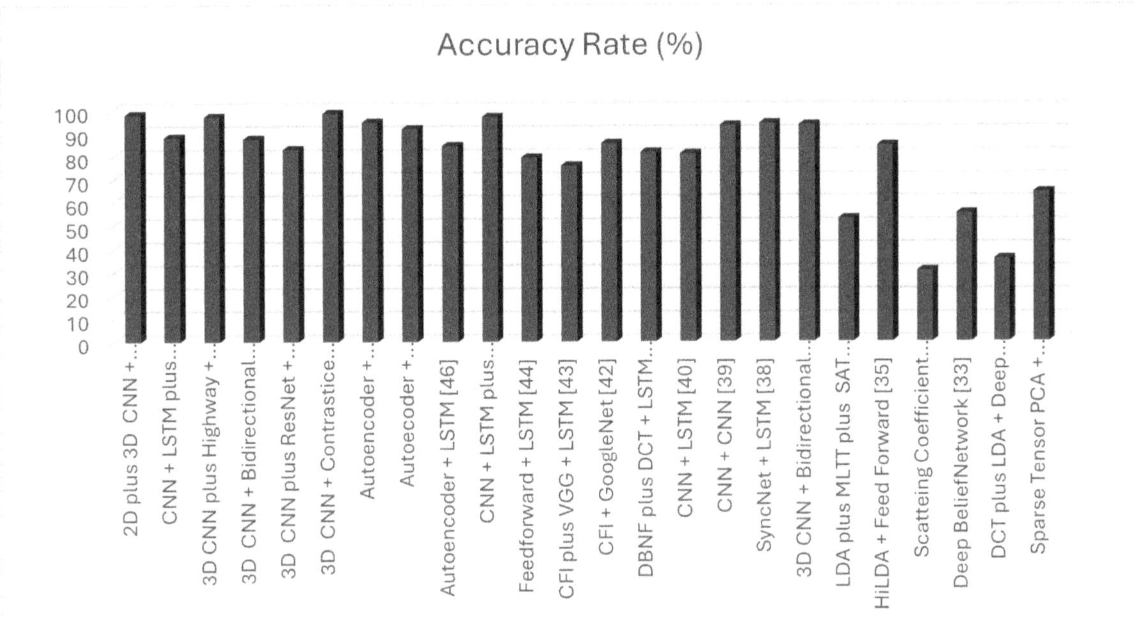


## REFERENCES


Achmad & Fadillah, L. (2015). Lip Motion Pattern Recognition for Indonesian Syllable Pronunciation Utilizing Hidden Markov Model Method. *Telkomnika (Telecommunication Computing Electronics and Control), 13*(1), 173–180.

Afouras, T., Chung, J. S., Senior, A., Vinyals, O., & Zisserman, A. (2018). Deep Audio-Visual Speech Recognition. *arXiv*, 1809.02108v2. https://arxiv.org/pdf/1809.02108.pdf

Ahmad, B. A., & Hassanat, A. (n.d.). *Visual Speech Recognition. IT Department, Mu'tah University.* Speech and Language Technologies. https://www.intechopen.com/chapters/38380

Almajai, S., Cox, S., Harvey, R., & Lan, Y. (2016). Improved speaker independent lip reading using speaker adaptive training and deep neural networks. In *Proceedings of the IEEE International Conference on Acoustics, Speech, and Signal Processing (ICASSP)* (pp. 2722-2726). IEEE.

Amit, G., Jnoyola, J. N., & Sameep, S. B. (2016). *Lip reading using CNN and LSTM*. Stanford University Technical Report.

Anusuya, M. A., & Katti, S. K. (2009). Speech Recognition by Machine: A Review. *International Journal of Computer Science and Information Security*, *6*(3). https://arxiv.org/ftp/arxiv/papers/1001/1001.2267.pdf

Assael, Y. M., Shillingford, B., Whiteson, S., & de Freitas, N. (2016). Lip-Net: End-to-end sentence level lipreading. In *Proceedings of the ICLR Conference* (pp. 1-13). Academic Press.

Atila, Ü., & Sabaz, F. (2022). Turkish lip-reading using Bi-LSTM and deep learning models. *Engineering Science and Technology, an International Journal, 35*, 101206.

Baldwin, P. (2004). PDA Databases. *Journal of Hospital Librarianship, 4*(1), 83–89. doi:10.1300/J186v04n01_08

Berkol, A., Sivri, T. T., & Erdem, H. (2024). Lip Reading Using Various Deep Learning Models with Visual Turkish Data. *Gazi University Journal of Science, 1*(1).

Cai, Z., Ghosh, S., Stefanov, K., Dhall, A., Cai, J., Rezatofighi, H., ... Hayat, M. (2023). Marlin: Masked autoencoder for facial video representation learning. In *Proceedings of the IEEE/CVF Conference on Computer Vision and Pattern Recognition* (pp. 1493-1504). IEEE.

Chung, J. S., & Zisserman, A. (2015). Lip reading in the wild. In *Proceedings of the Asian Conference on Computer Vision* (pp. 87-103). Academic Press.

Chung, J. S., & Zisserman, A. (2016). Out of time: Automated lip sync in the wild. In *Proceedings of the Asian Conference on Computer Vision* (pp. 251-263). Springer.

DasA. (2024). Lip2Text: Sentence-Level Lipreading on English Speakers Using the Deep Learning Approach. Preprint. https://doi.org/ doi:10.21203/rs.3.rs-3852300/v1

Easwaran, B., Hiran, K. K., Krishnan, S., & Doshi, R. (Eds.). (2022). *Real-Time Applications of Machine Learning in Cyber-Physical Systems*. IGI Global. doi:10.4018/978-1-7998-9308-0

Elrefaei, L. A., Alhassan, T. Q., & Omar, S. S. (2019). An Arabic Visual Dataset for Visual Speech Recognition. *Procedia Computer Science, 163*, 163–170. doi:10.1016/j.procs.2019.12.122

Exarchos, T., Dimitrakopoulos, G. N., Vrahatis, A. G., Chrysovitsiotis, G., Zachou, Z., & Kyrodimos, E. (2024). Lip-Reading Advancements: A 3D Convolutional Neural Network/Long Short-Term Memory Fusion for Precise Word Recognition. *BioMedInformatics, 4*(1), 410–422.

Fox, N. A., O'Mullane, B. A., & Reilly, R. B. (2005). VALID: A new practical audio-visual database, and comparative results. In *Proceedings of the International Conference on Audio-Video-Based Biometric Person Authentication* (pp. 777-786). Academic Press.

Garg, J., Noyola, J., & Bagadia, S. (2016). *Lip reading using CNN and LSTM*. Stanford University Technical Report CS231n Project.

Harte, N., & Gillen, E. (2015). TCD-TIMIT: An Audio-Visual Corpus of Continuous Speech. *IEEE Transactions on Multimedia, 17*(5), 603–615. doi:10.1109/TMM.2015.2407694

Hiran, K. K., & Doshi, R. (2013). An artificial neural network approach for brain tumor detection using digital image segmentation. *Brain, 2*(5), 227–231.

Hiran, K. K., Hemachandran, K., Pise, A., & Rabi, B. (Eds.). (2023). *Handbook of Research on AI and Knowledge Engineering for Real-Time Business Intelligence*. IGI Global. doi:10.4018/978-1-6684-6519-6

Huang, J., & Kingsbury, B. (2013). Audio-visual deep learning for noise robust speech recognition. In *Proceedings of the IEEE International Conference on Acoustics, Speech, and Signal Processing* (pp. 7596-7599). IEEE.

Lip Reading in the Wild (LRW) dataset. (n.d.). Retrieved April 4, 2024, from https://www.robots.ox.ac.uk/~vgg/data/lip_reading/lrw1.html

Lip Reading Sentences 2 (LRS2) dataset. (n.d.). Retrieved April 4, 2024, from https://www.robots.ox.ac.uk/~vgg/data/lip_reading/lrs2.html

Lip Reading Sentences 3 Dataset. (2024). Retrieved April 4, 2024, from https://mmai.io/datasets/lip_reading/

Liu, L., Liu, L., & Li, H. (2024). Computation and Parameter Efficient Multi-Modal Fusion Transformer for Cued Speech Recognition. *IEEE/ACM Transactions on Audio, Speech, and Language Processing*.

Loy, C. C. (n.d.). *QMUL underGround Re-IDentification (GRID) Dataset*. Retrieved April 4, 2024, from https://personal.ie.cuhk.edu.hk/~ccloy/downloads_qmul_underground_reid.html

Lu, L., Xu, X., & Fu, J. (2022). Siamese decoupling network for speaker-independent lipreading. *Journal of Electronic Imaging*, *31*(3), 033045–033045.

Lu, Y., & Li, H. (2019). Automatic lip-reading system based on deep convolutional neural network and attention-based long short-term memory. *Applied Sciences (Basel, Switzerland)*, *9*(8), 1599.

Ma, P., Wang, Y., Shen, J., Petridis, S., & Pantic, M. (2021). Lip-reading with densely connected temporal convolutional networks. In *Proceedings of the IEEE/CVF Winter Conference on Applications of Computer Vision* (pp. 2857-2866). IEEE.

Mahrishi, M., Hiran, K. K., Meena, G., & Sharma, P. (Eds.). (2020). Machine Learning and Deep Learning in Real-Time Applications. IGI Global.

MargamK.AralikattiR.SharmaT.ThandaP. A. K.RoyS.VenkatesanS. M. (2019). LipReading with 3D-2D-CNN BLSTM-HMM and word-CTC models. arXiv:1906.12170. http://arxiv.org/abs/1906.12170

Martin, O., Kotsia, I., Macq, B., & Pitas, I. (2006). The eNTERFACE' 05 Audio-Visual Emotion Database. *22nd International Conference on Data Engineering Workshops (ICDEW'06)*. https://doi.org/10.1109/ICDEW.2006.145

Mijwil, M. M., Aggarwal, K., Doshi, R., Hiran, K. K., & Gök, M. (2022). The Distinction between R-CNN and Fast RCNN in Image Analysis: A Performance Comparison. *Asian Journal of Applied Sciences*, *10*(5).

Moon, S., Kim, S., & Wang, H. (2015). Multimodal transfer deep learning with applications in audio-visual recognition. *Proceedings of the MMML Workshop Neural Information Processing Systems*.

Mroueh, Y., Marcheret, E., & Goel, V. (2015). Deep multimodal learning for audio-visual speech recognition. In *Proceedings of the IEEE International Conference on Acoustics, Speech, and Signal Processing (ICASSP)* (pp. 2130-2134). IEEE.

Narasimhan, M. (2023). *Multimodal Long-Term Video Understanding* (Doctoral dissertation, University of California, Berkeley).

Ngiam, J., Khosla, A., Kim, M., Nam, J., Lee, H., & Ng, A. Y. (2011). Multimodal deep learning. In *Proceedings of the 28th International Conference on Machine Learning (ICML)* (pp. 1-8). Academic Press.

Olynick, D. (2024). Exploring Generative AI and Its Transformative Power. In *Interfaceless: Conscious Design for Spatial Computing with Generative AI* (pp. 17–60). Apress.

Pan, W., Li, H., Zhou, X., Jiao, J., Zhu, C., & Zhang, Q. (2024). Research on Pig Sound Recognition Based on Deep Neural Network and Hidden Markov Models. *Sensors (Basel)*, *24*(4), 1269.

Papers with Code - CAS-VSR-W1k (LRW-1000) Dataset. (n.d.). Retrieved April 4, 2024, from https://paperswithcode.com/dataset/lrw-1000

Patterson, E., Gurbuz, S., Tufekci, Z., & Gowdy, J. (2002). Moving-talker speaker-independent feature study and baseline results using the cuave multimodal speech corpus. *EURASIP Journal on Applied Signal Processing*, *2002*, 1189–1201.

Petridis, S., Li, Z., & Pantic, M. (2017). End-to-end visual speech recognition with LSTMS. In *Proceedings of the IEEE International Conference on Acoustics, Speech, and Signal Processing (ICASSP)* (pp. 2592-2596). IEEE.

Petridis, S., & Pantic, M. (2016). Deep complementary bottleneck features for visual speech recognition. In *Proceedings of the IEEE International Conference on Acoustics, Speech, and Signal Processing (ICASSP)* (pp. 2304-2308). IEEE.

Petridis, S., Wang, Y., Li, Z., & Pantic, M. (2017). End-to-end audiovisual fusion with LSTMs. In *Proceedings of the 14th International Conference on Auditory-Visual Speech Processing* (pp. 36-40). Academic Press.

Petridis, S., Wang, Y., Li, Z., & Pantic, M. (2017). End-to-end multi-view lipreading. In *Proceedings of the British Machine Vision Conference* (pp. 1-14). Academic Press.

Potamianos, G., Luettin, J., & Neti, C. (2001). Hierarchical discriminant features for audio-visual LVCSR. *Proceedings of the IEEE International Conference on Acoustics, Speech, and Signal Processing*, *1*, 165-168. https://doi.org/10.1109/ICASSP.2001.940793

Prakash, V., Bhavani, R., Karthik, D., Rajalakshmi, D., Rajeswari, N., & Martinaa, M. (2024). Visual Speech Recognition by Lip Reading Using Deep Learning. In *Advanced Applications in Osmotic Computing* (pp. 290–310). IGI Global.

. Rekik, A., Ben-Hamadou, A., & Mahdi, W. (2014). A New Visual Speech Recognition Approach for RGB-D Cameras. *ICIAR*, 21-28.

Ryumin, D., Ryumina, E., & Ivanko, D. (2023). EMOLIPS: Towards Reliable Emotional Speech Lip-Reading. *Mathematics*, *11*(23), 4787.

Saitoh, T., Zhou, Z., Zhao, G., & Pietikainen, M. (2016). Concatenated frame image based CNN for visual speech recognition. In *Proceedings of the Asian Conference on Computer Vision* (pp. 277-289). Springer.

Six visual speech recognition data sets and a company about speech recognition. (n.d.). Retrieved April 4, 2024, from https://en.speechocean.com/Cy/757.html

Son, J. S., & Zisserman, A. (2017). Lip reading in profile. In *Proceedings of the British Machine Vision Conference* (pp. 1-11). Academic Press.

Stafylakis, T., & Tzimiropoulos, G. (2017). Combining residual networks with LSTMs for lipreading. In Proceedings of Interspeech (pp. 3652-3656). Academic Press.

Thangthai, K., Harvey, R., Cox, S., & Theobald, B. J. (2015). Improving lipreading performance for robust audiovisual speech recognition using DNNs. In *Proceedings of the International Conference on Auditory-Visual Speech Processing* (pp. 127-131). Academic Press.

Thapa, K. (2023). *End-to-end Lip-reading: A Preliminary Study* (Doctoral dissertation, London South Bank University).

Tian, C. (2023, November 17). *foowaa/AVSR-datasets*. GitHub. Retrieved from https://github.com/foowaa/AVSR-datasets

Tor, S. M., Iranmanesh, S., Nasrabadi, N., & Dawson, J. (2017). 3D convolutional neural networks for cross audio-visual matching recognition. *IEEE Access : Practical Innovations, Open Solutions*, *5*, 22081–22091.

Vidal, A., & Busso, C. (2023). Multimodal attention for lip synthesis using conditional generative adversarial networks. *Speech Communication*, *153*, 102959.

Wand, M., Koutník, J., & Schmidhuber, J. (2016). Lipreading with long short-term memory. In *Proceedings of the IEEE International Conference on Acoustics, Speech, and Signal Processing (ICASSP)* (pp. 6115-6119). IEEE.

Xing, G., Han, L., Zheng, Y., & Zhao, M. (2023). Application of deep learning in Mandarin Chinese lip-reading recognition. *EURASIP Journal on Wireless Communications and Networking*, *2023*(1), 90.

Xu, K., Li, D., Cassimatis, N., & Wang, X. (2018). LCANet: End-to-end lipreading with cascaded attention-CTC. In *Proceedings of the 13th IEEE International Conference on Automatic Face and Gesture Recognition (FG)* (pp. 548-555). IEEE.

Yamashita, R., Nishio, M., Do, R. K. G., & Togashi, K. (2018). Convolutional neural networks: An overview and application in radiology. *Insights Into Imaging*, *9*, 611–629. doi:10.1007/s13244-018-0639-9

Yang, L., Wang, S., & Liew, A. W. C. (2023). Fine-Grained Lip Image Segmentation using Fuzzy Logic and Graph Reasoning. *IEEE Transactions on Fuzzy Systems*.

Yang, Q., Bai, Y., Liu, F., & Zhang, W. (2024). Integrated visual transformer and flash attention for lip-to-speech generation GAN. *Scientific Reports*, *14*(1), 4525.

Zuwei, L. (2024, March 31). *lzuwei/end-to-end-multiview-lipreading*. GitHub. Retrieved from https://github.com/lzuwei/end-to-end-multiview-lipreading

# Chapter 21
# Exploring Challenges in Online Higher Education for AI Integration Using MICMAC Analysis

**Ramji Nagariya**
https://orcid.org/0000-0002-2739-9838
*Christ University, India*

**Priyanshu Sharma**
*Birla Institute of Technology, Mesra, India*

**Abhineet Saxena**
https://orcid.org/0000-0003-0467-7900
*Amity University, Jaipur, India*

**Priti Saxena**
*S.P. Mandali's Prin. L.N. Welingkar Institute of Management, Development, and Research, India*

**Garima Pancholi**
https://orcid.org/0000-0002-5039-4998
*Amity University, Jaipur, India*

## ABSTRACT

*The consequence of Covid-19 has affected the traditional higher education system. Acknowledging the significant role of online education in national development for accessibility and quality education, countries around the world have understood its importance in current digital era. Indian policymakers have been giving due importance to enhancing the education quality, however the progress made by the country in higher education is not adequate. Amidst all the inadequacies of traditional education system, artificial intelligence (AI) technologies are bringing new ray of hope to democratize education system. This chapter is subjected to identify the challenges in online education and suggest specific ways to address each of them. The challenges are categorized into internal and external challenges/barriers. These challenges have been modeled with the expertise of educationalist's opinions and interpretive structural modeling to create a hierarchy of the barriers using MICMAC analysis and categorize these barriers into four clusters.*

DOI: 10.4018/979-8-3693-2440-0.ch021

## INTRODUCTION

Sudden Digital Transition of higher education system in India was triggered by Covid 19 pandemic it was so abrupt that many of the universities were not prepared to combat such a global pandemic and they had to make substantial changes in their teaching methods while keeping in mind that it should be convenient and approachable to all levels of students in terms of understanding (Carroll & Conboy, 2020), but the change which was imposed on the academia due to abrupt halt in classroom learning owing to nationwide lockdown has emerged as an important game changer for higher education system and has proved to be a critical enabler for democratizing education. However online education sector faces several challenges like limited interaction between students and faculties through video conferencing, connectivity issues, providing study material digitally, concentration span, digital burn out etc.

The pandemic only exacerbated an already burgeoning problem of slow progress towards quality education worldwide, it is being estimated that in India, almost 300 million people will lack basic literacy and numeracy skills by 2030 if concrete measures are not undertaken to improve the situation. The list of seventeen Sustainable Development Goals as laid out by United nations have duly acknowledged the importance of education to achieve many of the SDGs, education has been recognized as a key measure to reduce several inequalities like gender, income etc., it empowers people to break from the cycle of poverty and help them live a healthy and sustainable life, education also enable more tolerant and cohesive societies. SDG Goal No. 4 is Quality Education, it emphasizes the need for higher education financing to make education free and compulsory for all, increase the number of faculties, improve basic infrastructure, and embrace digital transformation. The AI was developed to execute work that needed human intelligence. The AI helps in problem-solving, decision making, understanding and learning the unorganized data. AI tools such as ChatGPT, Quillbot, Cognii, Dall-E etc., are now part of tech landscape. AI is not just a word meant for the techies but its wide application across the world is making life easier and operationally feasible for people. When it comes to education, a spike is noticed in the use of technology after the Covid period. AI can further ease the operations not just for the teachers but also for the students/learners. Apart from operational ease, use of AI can also assist in identifying the need for skill learning of the learners. Education sector in India a growing rapidly and to reach the acme of its potential, blending AI is important (Hiran et al., 2024; Doshi et al., 2023).

At the end of March'20, when Indian government-imposed lockdown across the country, it had a direct impact on economy especially on education sector of developing countries. Especially when large number of migrant workers were left with no choice except to left their work place and went back to their native place without food and money (Maity et al., 2021a)(Maity et al., 2021b). It was a time when everybody had to accept a new way of learning i.e. digital learning or digital platform. From school level to university level, everyone was encountered with the challenge to cope up with this new way of learning. Somehow it compromised with the quality in learning process. In this chaotic situation, Zoom and Google meet played crucial role in classroom sessions. Study reveals that students in both school and university were drained out by the sudden drift into novel digital teaching and learning modes (Maity et al., 2020a).

Digital Transformation as emphasized by SDGs as an important requirement for enhancing and democratizing higher education system, however while replacing conventional teaching methods with digital method several challenges are faced by everyone i.e. from management, teachers, non-teachings staff to the students. It becomes a challenging task for teachers to keep students logged in and to make them attend classes. On the other hand it is a progressive educational environment for everybody, digital technology also give an opportunity to teachers to refine their skills while enrolling in Faculty Development Programs (FDPs) and webinars etc. (Maity et al., 2021b). This research focuses on the opportunity for the higher education with the help of new age educational technology. Hence aligned with the above, the study addresses following questions:

RQ1- What are the challenges/barriers faced by higher education while implementing Artificial Intelligence in West India?

RQ2- How these challenges/barriers are interrelated?

RQ3- How these barriers can be classified into different segments?

On the basis of these research questions, the following objectives were set for this study;

(i) To understand the important challenges faced by higher education while embracing Artificial Intelligence in West India.
(ii) To find the hierarchy of importance of these challenges/barriers.
(iii) To identify the critical factors requiring special attention and classification into different segments.

Subsequently Section 2 presents the review of related literature, Section 3, presents the research methodology; section 4 discusses the case study. Section 5 comprises of the results and discussion and Section 6 includes the conclusion.

## REVIEW OF RELATED LITERATURE

India is progressing as a developing nation in the field of education and has experienced tremendous growth with the increasing number of universities/higher level institutions and colleges. The toughest challenge for the higher education system while embracing Artificial Intelligence and digital technology to develop courses specifically for online, distance learning and to design policies that attract overseas students (Rastogi, 2020). This study identifies the internal and external barriers and these will be discussed in this section. The internal barriers affecting the higher education sector are identified through rigorous literature review.

### Internal Barriers Affecting the Higher Education

The faculties and staff of the universities face many challenges while adopting Artificial Intelligence for online education. These challenges affect the teaching-learning process at large. These challenges are mentioned in this section and are referred to as barriers in this paper. First and foremost is the Internet or Connectivity issues (IB1) as many of the faculties are not able to connect to classes due to limited internet packs and availability (Radif et al., 2015)(Radif et al., n.d.). Many faculties are not properly trained for these online applications to connect with students and university, hence they struggle while using online apps' (IB2) such as Zoom, MS Team, Google Meet etc. (Goodier et al., 2014).

Several challenges make adoption of digital technology highly stressful, these challenges are communication gap between students & faculties (Kerres, 2020a), absence of classroom atmosphere (IB3) from both students & faculties perspective due to which proper discussion of project work is often missing, lack of incentive plan (IB4) for faculties to upskill themselves (Maity et al., 2020b), limited concentration span (IB5) (Dwivedi et al., 2020), absence of immersive industrial training (IB6), pressure to finish courses on fast pace' (IB7) and lack of designated work place with appropriate time (IB8) (Ågerfalk et al., 2020) . Owing to all these challenges, academia need to redesign the entire course content for better understanding and also to meet future needs (Ponomarenko et al., 2019). Against this background, the faculties should also try to get cordial with the AI tools (Doshi et al., 2023; Hiran et al., 2023).

### External Barriers Affecting Higher Education

Students who are used to traditional way of teaching find it difficult as they cannot interact with faculties because of online teaching methods as it allows very limited time of interactions with the faculties (EB1) i.e. one at a time(Kerres, 2020b). External challenges are the challenges faced by the students that affect their understanding level, placements, trainings and therefore, a lack of social and writing skills (EB2) are observed (Kerres, 2020b). These challenges are categorized as the external challenges/ barriers. Economic challenges in education sector (EB3) includes manpower reductions in universities (EB4), less salary payouts, incentives and promotions (Iivari et al., 2020). Due to inconsistency in classes, students get negatively impacted in daily life, parents worry about fees as few of the online institutes don't offer placement programs (EB5), severe health issues among students like mental disorders and anxiety are observed (Kodama, 2020). Every student has different level of understanding, so most of the students find it difficult to adapt to new method of learning i.e. digital platform for education (Maity et al., 2021b). Indiscipline among students during online classes and change in their behavior are observed (Maity et al., 2020a). Lack of interest for online classes among the students is observed as they miss class atmosphere (EB6). All these challenges might negatively affect the career development of the students and the reputation of the universities (Radif et al., 2015). Students often find the process of choosing the right online course for themselves very onerous, several other health issues among students (EB7) are also observed (Mijwil et al., 2023; Mishra et al., 2021; Easwaran et al., 2022).

## RESEARCH METHODOLOGY

### Interpretive Structural Modeling

Interpretive structural modeling is a technique to extract inter-relationship between the variables and it handles unstructured factors quite satisfactorily (Nagariya et al., 2021a; Warfield, 1974a). ISM facilitates factors related decisions with reference to procedural relationships and structure of complex factors ISM technique is dependent on the opinions of the experts. According to (Warfield, 1974b). ISM involves development of structural self-interaction matrix, construction of initial reach ability matrix involving the rule of V, A, X & O, checking of transitivity, partitioning of enablers in different levels, formation of diagraph, development of ISM model from diagraph and evaluation of model.

## CASE STUDY

As this study focuses on the challenges faced by the universities, faculties, and students while embracing digital transformation in western India, the samples were collected from different universities of Rajasthan, India. Only the dean, directors and faculty members were contacted for the collection of responses. The reason for collecting responses from senior personal was that they are more aware about the system and the challenges faced by the faculties and students as they are required to handle these challenges. Five director, six deans and nine faculties from six different universities agreed to participate in this study. For this kind of study, a sample size of 10 - 20 is recommended by therefore the sample size used in this study is sufficient. Due to the confidentiality clause the names of the universities and the profiles of the experts are not disclosed. The responses were collected from June 2022 to September 2023. The identified barriers were also presented to them and after their consent the barriers were finalized. The aim and purpose of the study was discussed with them. The experts provided their responses for the internal barriers (IBs) and external barriers (EBs) in the ISM sheets. Their responses were aggregated, and final responses are mentioned in the structural self-interaction matrix (SSIM). Further, these responses were analyzed by using ISM method and the results and findings are discussed in the next sections.

For the development of the contextual interaction between internal barriers, the notations were given to the experts to form SSIM based on pair based comparison (Nagariya et al., 2021b). Following are the notations:

i – Column of the table
j – Row of the table
V = internal barriers i supports internal barrier j
A = internal barriers j supports internal barrier i
X = internal barriers i and internal barrier j support each other
O = internal barriers i and internal barrier j do not support each other

## Analysis of Internal Barriers

Following substitution rules (See table 1) were used to develop Initial Reachability Matrix from SSIM (See table 2) depicts SSIM mapping for internal barriers:

Table 3 exhibits the structural self-interaction matrix for the internal barriers and it is based on the inputs of the experts. Initial reachability matrix has been converted into final reachability matrix through transitivity. Table 4 exhibits the Final reachability matrix for internal barriers.

Partitioning has been deployed to extract hierarchical levels of internal barriers through interaction sect of reachability and antecedent sets. The reachability set includes internal barriers and various considered barriers supported by internal barriers (see table 5). The antecedent set includes internal barriers and other barriers which may support internal barriers. Level 1 is assigned to the same internal barriers existing in the intersection set and reachability set. Remaining internal barriers are selected for further leveling. This procedure is iterated until all the internal barriers are leveled. Table 5 and 6 are exhibiting iterations and assigned levels.

*Table 1. Substitution rules (SSIM into initial reachability matrix)*

| SSIM Notation Cell ij | Initial Reachability Matrix Cell ij | Initial Reachability Matrix Cell ji |
|---|---|---|
| V | 1 | 0 |
| A | 0 | 1 |
| X | 1 | 1 |
| O | 0 | 0 |

*Table 2. SSIM for Internal Barriers*

| Internal Barriers | IB8 | IB7 | IB6 | IB5 | IB4 | IB3 | IB2 | IB1 |
|---|---|---|---|---|---|---|---|---|
| Internet or connectivity issues (IB1) | O | O | X | V | V | V | V | O |
| Facing challenges while using online apps (IB2) | O | O | O | X | X | V | O | |
| No classroom atmosphere (IB3) | X | O | O | O | O | O | | |
| No incentive plans (IB4) | O | O | O | O | O | | | |
| Lack of concentration (IB5) | V | O | O | O | | | | |
| No industrial training (IB6) | O | X | O | | | | | |
| Online classes to finish courses at fast pace (IB7) | V | O | | | | | | |
| No designated work place with appropriate time (IB8) | O | | | | | | | |

*Table 3. Initial reachability matrix for internal barriers*

| Internal Barriers | B8 | B7 | B6 | B5 | B4 | B3 | B2 | B1 |
|---|---|---|---|---|---|---|---|---|
| Internet or connectivity issues (B1) | 0 | 0 | 1 | 1 | 1 | 1 | 1 | 0 |
| Facing challenges while using online apps (B2) | 0 | 0 | 0 | 1 | 1 | 1 | 0 | 0 |
| No classroom atmosphere (B3) | 1 | 0 | 0 | 0 | 0 | 0 | 0 | 0 |
| No incentive plans (B4) | 0 | 0 | 0 | 0 | 0 | 1 | 1 | 0 |
| Lack of concentration (B5) | 1 | 0 | 0 | 0 | 0 | 1 | 1 | 0 |
| No industrial training (B6) | 0 | 1 | 0 | 0 | 0 | 0 | 0 | 1 |
| Online classes to finish courses at fast pace (B7) | 1 | 0 | 1 | 1 | 0 | 0 | 0 | 0 |
| No designated work place with appropriate time (B8) | 0 | 0 | 0 | 0 | 0 | 1 | 0 | 0 |

*Table 4. Final reachability matrix for internal barriers*

| Internal Barriers | IB8 | IB7 | IB6 | IB5 | IB4 | IB3 | IB2 | IB1 | Driving power |
|---|---|---|---|---|---|---|---|---|---|
| Internet or connectivity issues (IB1) | 1a | 0 | 1 | 1 | 1 | 1 | 1 | 1a | 7 |
| Facing challenges while using online apps (IB2) | 1a | 0 | 0 | 1 | 1 | 1 | 1a | 0 | 5 |
| No classroom atmosphere (IB3) | 1 | 0 | 0 | 0 | 0 | 1a | 0 | 0 | 2 |
| No incentive plans (IB4) | 1a | 0 | 0 | 1a | 1a | 1 | 1 | 0 | 5 |
| Lack of concentration (IB5) | 1 | 0 | 0 | 1a | 1a | 1 | 1 | 0 | 5 |
| No industrial training (IB6) | 1a | 1 | 1a | 1a | 1a | 1a | 1a | 1 | 8 |
| Online classes to finish courses at fast pace (IB7) | 1 | 1a | 1 | 1 | 0 | 1a | 0 | 1a | 6 |
| No designated work place with appropriate time (IB8) | 1a | 0 | 0 | 0 | 0 | 1 | 0 | 0 | 2 |
| Dependence power | 8 | 2 | 3 | 6 | 5 | 8 | 5 | 3 | 40/40 |

From three iterations, total three levels were assigned to the internal barriers. Based on the levels of internal barriers, a hierarchical model is drawn as shown in Figure 1.

*Table 5. Iteration I*

| Internal Barriers | Reachability set | Antecedent set | Intersection set | Level |
|---|---|---|---|---|
| Internet or connectivity issues (IB1) | 1,2,3,4,5,6,8 | 1,6,7 | 1,6 | |
| Facing challenges while using online apps (IB2) | 2,3,4,5,8 | 1,2,4,5,6 | 2,4,5 | |
| No classroom atmosphere (IB3) | 3,8 | 1,2,3,4,5,6,7,8, | 3,8 | I |
| No incentive plans (IB4) | 2,3,4,5,8 | 1,2,4,5,6 | 2,4,5 | |
| Lack of concentration (IB5) | 2,3,4,5,7 | 1,2,4,5,6,7 | 2,4,5,7 | |
| No industrial training (IB6) | 1,2,3,4,5,6,7,8 | 1,6,7 | 1,6,7 | |
| Online classes to finish courses at fast pace (IB7) | 1,3,5,6,7,8 | 6,7 | 6,7 | |
| No designated work place with appropriate time (IB8) | 3,8 | 1,2,3,4,5,6,7,8 | 3,8 | I |

Note-In first iteration IB3 and IB8 are assigned level I.

*Table 6. Iteration II*

| Internal Barriers | Reachability set | Antecedent set | Intersection set | Level |
|---|---|---|---|---|
| Internet or connectivity issues (IB1) | 1,2,4,5,6 | 1,6,7 | 1,6 | III |
| Facing challenges while using online apps (IB2) | 2,4,5 | 1,2,4,5,6 | 2,4,5 | II |
| No incentive plans (IB4) | 2,4,5 | 1,2,4,5,6 | 2,4,5 | II |
| Lack of concentration (IB5) | 2,4,5,7 | 1,2,4,5,6,7 | 2,4,5,7 | II |
| No industrial training (IB6) | 1,2,4,5,6,7 | 1,6,7 | 1,6,7 | III |
| Online classes to finish courses at fast pace (IB7) | 1,5,6,7 | 6,7 | 6,7 | III |

Note- In second iteration as er table 5, IB2, IB4 and Ib5 are assigned level II. The IB1, IB6 and IB7 are assigned level III.

Out of eight internal barriers "Internet or connectivity issues (IB1)" "no industrial training (IB6)" and "online classes to finish courses on fast pace (IB7)" are identified as most critical and independent enablers. Internet connectivity is the most crucial part of any university that makes sure that the academic activities are conducted properly. Internet or connectivity facility also makes sure that the university is providing best possible services to the students. Due to the 'internet or connectivity issues', the faculties were directed to 'finish the courses at fast pace' (IB7) and therefore, whole learning process were affected at large. Due to Covid-19 protocols, 'industrial trainings' (IB6) could not be arranged by the universities for the students. This affected the real understanding of their professional courses of the students.

## MICMAC Analysis

Internal barriers have been classified in to four quadrants through MICMAC analysis on the basis of driving and dependence power. Figure 2 exhibits four quadrants viz. Autonomous, Driver, Linkage and Dependent. Autonomous region which indicates low driving and dependence powers, there are no internal barriers and it concludes the connection of the barriers to the system. Driver quadrant indicates high driving power and low dependence power; it includes IB1, IB6 and IB7 which are designated as "key barriers" and establish foundation of structural model.

*Figure 1. ISM model for the internal barriers*

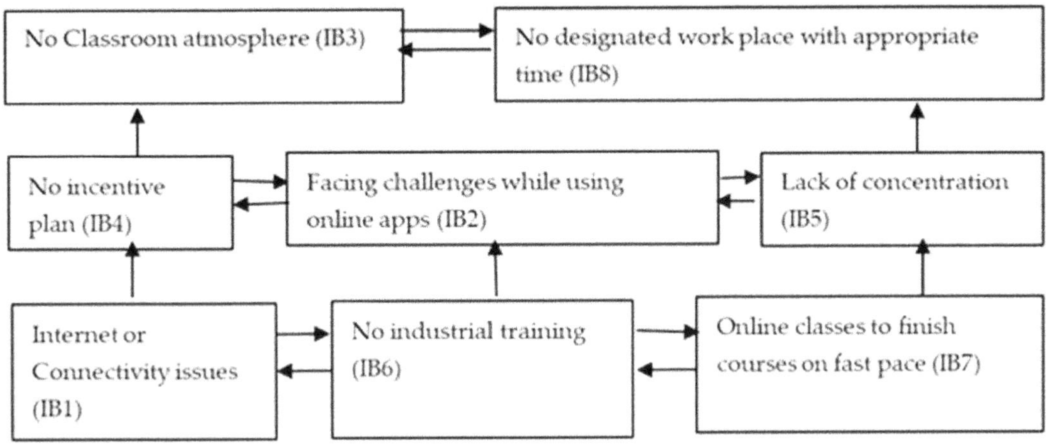


The internal barriers of the linkage region have high driving and dependence power. Generally, these barriers are observed to be unstable in nature as a little change in the barriers of the independent region can bring a huge change in the barriers of the linkage region and have the potential to change the desired outcome. The barriers 'facing challenges while using online apps' IB2, 'no incentive plans' IB4 and 'lack of concentration' IB5 are identified in this region. These internal barriers form a link between the barriers of the independent region and dependent region. A special care from the decision makers is expected for these challenges.

The internal barriers of the dependent region are considered to have low driving power and are strongly dependent on other barriers. In the structural model, these barriers take the top position. In the dependent region 'no classroom atmosphere' (IB3) and 'no designated work place with appropriate time' (IB8) were identified.

*Figure 2. MICMAC analysis of internal barriers*

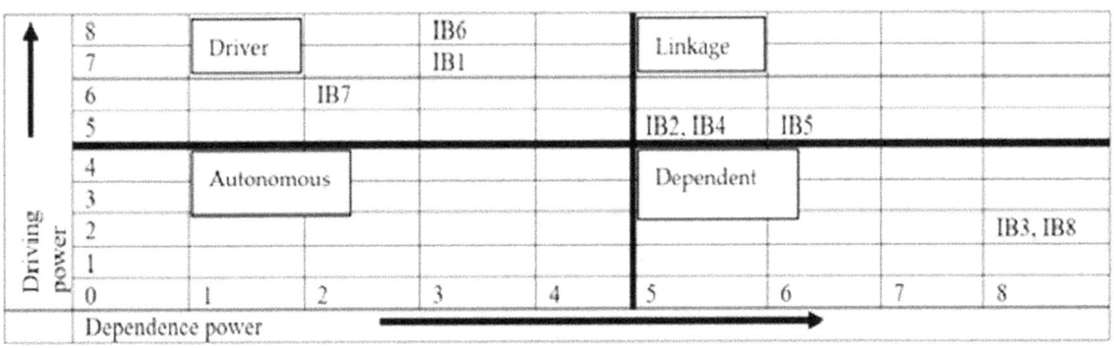

## Analysis of External Barriers

The responses from the experts were collected and after aggregating these responses the SSIM was formed for the external barriers (see table 7 and 8). Table 9 provide the Final reachability matrix for external barriers.

*Table 7. Structural self-interaction matrix for external barriers*

| External Barriers | EB7 | EB6 | EB5 | EB4 | EB3 | EB2 | EB1 |
|---|---|---|---|---|---|---|---|
| Couldn't interact with faculties (EB1) | V | X | V | A | O | O | O |
| Lack of social skill and loss of writing skill (EB2) | X | A | X | O | O | O | |
| Economic challenges in education (EB3) | O | V | V | X | O | | |
| Manpower reduction in colleges (EB4) | O | O | V | O | | | |
| No Placement Programmes (EB5) | X | O | O | | | | |
| Missing class atmosphere (EB6) | O | O | | | | | |
| Several health issues among students (EB7) | O | | | | | | |

*Table 8. Initial reachability matrix for external barriers*

| External Barriers | EB7 | EB6 | EB5 | EB4 | EB3 | EB2 | EB1 |
|---|---|---|---|---|---|---|---|
| Couldn't interact with faculties (EB1) | 1 | 1 | 1 | 0 | 0 | 0 | 0 |
| Lack of social skill and loss of writing skill (EB2) | 1 | 0 | 1 | 0 | 0 | 0 | 0 |
| Economic challenges in education (EB3) | 0 | 1 | 1 | 1 | 0 | 0 | 0 |
| Manpower reduction in colleges (EB4) | 0 | 0 | 1 | 0 | 1 | 0 | 1 |
| No Placement Programmes (EB5) | 1 | 0 | 0 | 0 | 0 | 1 | 0 |
| Missing class atmosphere (EB6) | 0 | 0 | 0 | 0 | 0 | 1 | 1 |
| Several health issues among students (EB7) | 0 | 0 | 1 | 0 | 0 | 1 | 0 |

*Table 9. Final reachability matrix for external barriers*

| External Barriers | EB7 | EB6 | EB5 | EB4 | EB3 | EB2 | EB1 | Driving power |
|---|---|---|---|---|---|---|---|---|
| Couldn't interact with faculties (EB1) | 1 | 1 | 1 | 0 | 0 | 1a | 1a | 5 |
| Lack of social skill and loss of writing skill (EB2) | 1 | 0 | 1 | 0 | 0 | 1a | 0 | 3 |
| Economic challenges in education (EB3) | 1a | 1 | 1 | 1 | 1a | 1a | 1a | 7 |
| Manpower reduction in colleges (EB4) | 1a | 1a | 1a | 1a | 1 | 1a | 1 | 7 |
| No Placement Programmes (EB5) | 1 | 0 | 1a | 0 | 0 | 1 | 0 | 3 |
| Missing class atmosphere (EB6) | 1a | 1a | 1a | 0 | 0 | 1 | 1 | 5 |
| Several health issues among students (EB7) | 1a | 0 | 1 | 0 | 0 | 1 | 0 | 3 |
| Dependence power | 7 | 4 | 7 | 2 | 2 | 7 | 4 | 33/33 |

Table 10 and 11 exhibit iterations and assigned levels for external barriers. Partitioning has been deployed to extract hierarchical levels of external barriers also through intersection set of reachability and antecedent.

## MICMAC Analysis of External Barriers

Linkage region displays external barriers with high driving and dependence power in Figure 4; these are considered unstable because small change in the factors of driver quadrant can trigger high change in the linkage quadrant. Barriers of economic challenges in education sector, manpower reductions in colleges, limited number of interactions with faculties are critical enablers and should be cautiously handled. External barriers falling in the dependent quadrant are seen as the desired results and exhibit low driving power and high dependence on other enablers. External barriers take significant position in the structural model. Dependent quadrant in our study exhibits lack of social skills and loss of writing skills, no placements programs and severe health issues among students (Singh et al., 2022; Rathi et al., 2023).

# DISCUSSION

The massive traction garnered by artificial intelligence and digital technology in higher education was ensued by covid 19 crisis, however use of commercial digital technology has a long history in many education systems across the world (Hogan and Thompson 2020; Williamson 2019). The edtech community had always been advocating the adoption of the same to augment accessibility, collaboration and learning in higher education system, through this study we have identified key barriers that affect

*Table 10. Iteration I for external barriers*

| External Barriers | Reachability set | Antecedent set | Intersection set | Level |
|---|---|---|---|---|
| Couldn't interact with faculties (EB1) | 1,2,5,6,7 | 1,3,4,6 | 1,6 | |
| Lack of social skill and loss of writing skill (EB2) | 2,5,7 | 1,2,3,4,5,6,7 | 2,5,7 | I |
| Economic challenges in education (EB3) | 1,2,3,4,5,6,7 | 3,4 | 3,4 | |
| Manpower reduction in colleges (EB4) | 1,2,3,4,5,6,7 | 3,4 | 3,4 | |
| No Placement Programmes (EB5) | 2,5,7 | 1,2,3,4,5,6,7 | 2,5,7 | I |
| Missing class atmosphere (EB6) | 1,2,5,6,7 | 1,3,4,6 | 1,6 | |
| Several health issues among students (EB7) | 2,5,7 | 1,2,3,4,5,6,7 | 2,5,7 | I |

*Table 11. Iteration II for external barriers*

| External Barriers | Reachability set | Antecedent set | Intersection set | Level |
|---|---|---|---|---|
| Couldn't interact with faculties (EB1) | 1,6, | 1,3,4,6 | 1,6 | II |
| Economic challenges in education (EB3) | 1,3,4,6 | 3,4 | 3,4 | III |
| Manpower reduction in colleges (EB4) | 1,3,4,6 | 3,4 | 3,4 | III |
| Missing class atmosphere (EB6) | 1,6 | 1,3,4,6 | 1,6 | II |

*Figure 3. ISM model for external barriers*
*Note(s): Figure 3 represents the ISM model for the external barriers.*

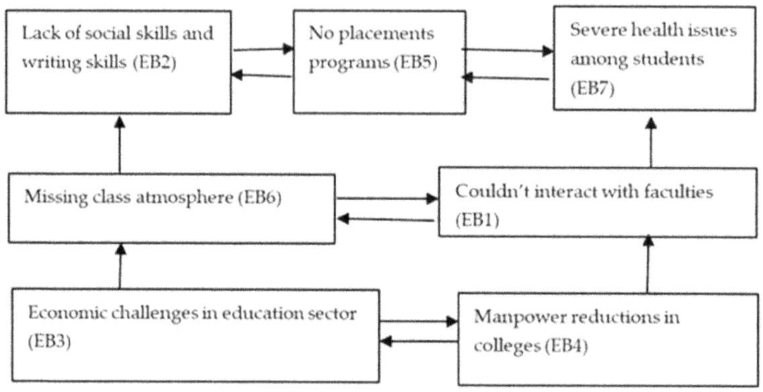


*Figure 4. MICMAC analysis for external barriers*

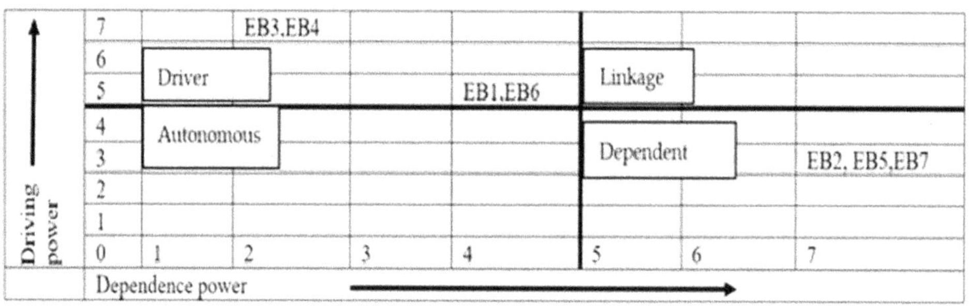


the performance and teaching-learning process of the universities while embracing digital technology. The use of AI transforms the higher education system where education is not limited to learning in classrooms and working in labs, but it creates a breakthrough for knowledge transfer partnership around the globe. Regardless of the opportunities, AI presents some drawbacks as well. Some of the barriers were identified from rigorous literature review and were finalized with the expert's consensus. A total of fifteen barriers were identified. The experts helped in categorizing the barriers into internal and external barriers. A total of twenty senior level experts agreed to participate in this study. Their responses were collected and analyzed by using ISM methodology. ISM created the hierarchical structure of the internal and external barriers. Further MICMAC analysis was carried out to classify the barriers into autonomous region, independent region, linkage region, and dependent region.

Generative artificial intelligence has emerged as a major trend creator for economies worldwide and across sectors, to attain SDG goals as well digitalization of higher education. The system has been heralded as one of the most crucial contributors (Gouvea et al., 2018; Sachs et al., 2019b; Seele and Lock, 2017). The study focuses on the challenges that affect the performance and teaching-learning process of the universities while embracing digital technology, the faculties face the challenge of using online apps. Lack of proper guidance and training emerged as the primary reason behind many faculties finding it difficult to connect with students via apps/online, this specially holds true for new faculties. Due, to the challenge in connecting with students through online apps, faculties cannot concentrate on the teaching activities. In this study also, 'facing challenges while using online apps' and 'lack of concentration' are identified in the linkage region of MICMAC analysis. Other three challenges that affected the performance of the universities are classified in independent region of MICMAC analysis. 'internet/ connectivity issue', 'no industrial training', and 'online classes to finish courses at fast pace' were found at the bottom of the ISM model and in the independent region of MICMAC analysis. Therefore, it can be concluded that these barriers have high driving power and low dependence power. These barriers affect the barriers of linkage region also and the corresponding changes in the barriers of linkage region should be noticed carefully. The study will enable the decision makers of the universities to identify and address the critical challenges that affect the performance of the universities significantly.

In external barriers, the economic challenges in education sector, manpower reduction in universities, missing classroom atmosphere and limited interaction of students with the faculties emerged as the most critical barriers that affect the performance of the universities. Further due to delay in paying fees and difficulty in follow up for the same often, universities face economic challenges to meet their operating expenditures. Due to low interactions with the faculties' members the doubts of the students could not be handled properly. placements programs are not very effective, as no classroom atmosphere can be created social skills and writing skills development among the students is a challenge, due to isolated study spaces and long digital exposure, many students face severe health issues also and cannot concentrate during the regular classes. All these points affected the performance of the universities at large. The decision makers can take a lesson from the findings of the study and take corrective measures to adopt some changes in order to enhance the learning outcomes while embracing digital technology for higher education system. AI also presents certain ethical and pedagogical concerns which results in establishing unreliable and false content, misuse of data.

The study also makes significant theoretical and managerial contributions and these are mentioned in the subsequent subsections.

## Theoretical Contributions

The study identifies the internal and external barriers that affect the teaching-learning process of universities while embracing digital technology. The identification of the barriers and the contextual relationship among these barriers can be considered as the major theoretical contribution.

## Practical Implications

The practical implications of the study are many folds. This research will help the decision makers of the universities in identifying and understanding the real challenges faced by the universities. The understanding of the barriers will enable them to handle them effectively and therefore can produce better quality of teaching-learning experience to the students. The hierarchy of the barriers will enable the decision makers in identifying the critical barriers that majorly affect the teaching-learning process and ultimately affects the reputation of the university. Hence while allocating resources to address these challenges hierarchy can be referred to for prioritizing the efforts. When the new tools are developing every now and then, it is also important to enhance digital literacy as a skill set for students and faculties. Instead of looking at AI as a threat, universities should consider it as a chance to transform and develop. Many institutions are also working on integrating digital literacy to curriculum in order to improve the understanding and skills. This will also help the faculties to master emerging technologies.

## CONCLUSION

The eight internal and seven external barriers were identified through a comprehensive literature review and experts' inputs. The ISM method facilitates establishing contextual associations and hierarchical levels of the identified barriers. 'Internet or connectivity issues' (IB1), 'no industrial training' (IB6) and 'online classes to finish course on fast pace' (IB7) were identified as the most influencing internal barriers as these barriers' were having high driving power. In external barriers 'lack of social skill and writing skill' (EB2), 'no placement programs' (EB5) and 'several health issues among students' (EB7) were identified as the most influencing external barriers as these barriers were having high driving power and low dependency on other barriers. In the realm of Generative Artificial Intelligence, it is important to enhance the scope of learner-teacher interaction in the online learning platforms and this can only be achieved after addressing the barriers of online higher education system. The learner satisfaction level and quality learning can be improved by escalating the student involvement and interaction channels. Just like traditional classroom teaching, AI can offer personalized learning which is tailored according to individual needs, immediate feedback, and adaptive assessment techniques. Furthermore, AI also provides virtual assistance where learners get instant solutions to the problems which not only contribute to achieving satisfaction. AI can play a vital role in achieving the SDG 4 of providing access and equity in education. Some of the students who were deprived of attending traditional brick and mortar school now have the opportunity to attend classes through online learning platforms. This integration works towards achieving greater equality and inclusivity. Hence, unlocking the complexities of leveraging AI into online learning is significant for enhancing its advantages, mitigating the disadvantages, while promising that online learning will give accessibility, fairness and quality.

## REFERENCES

Ågerfalk, P. J., Conboy, K., & Myers, M. D. (2020). Information systems in the age of pandemics: COVID-19 and beyond. *European Journal of Information Systems*, *29*(3), 203–207. doi:10.1080/0960085X.2020.1771968

Carroll, N., & Conboy, K. (2020). Normalising the "new normal": Changing tech-driven work practices under pandemic time pressure. *International Journal of Information Management*, *55*, 102186. doi:10.1016/j.ijinfomgt.2020.102186 PMID:32836643

Doshi, R., Hiran, K. K., Mijwil, M. M., & Anand, D. (2023). To That of Artificial Intelligence, Passing Through Business Intelligence. In Handbook of Research on AI and Knowledge Engineering for Real-Time Business Intelligence (pp. 1-16). IGI Global. doi:10.4018/978-1-6684-6519-6.ch001

Doshi, R., Hu, Y. C., Garg, L., & Fagbola, T. (2023). Towards a Higher Education of the Future: Transformational Roles of Edge Intelligence. *Array (New York, N.Y.)*, 100332. doi:10.1016/j.array.2023.100332

Dwivedi, Y. K., Hughes, D. L., Coombs, C., Constantiou, I., Duan, Y., Edwards, J. S., Gupta, B., Lal, B., Misra, S., Prashant, P., Raman, R., Rana, N. P., Sharma, S. K., & Upadhyay, N. (2020). Impact of COVID-19 pandemic on information management research and practice: Transforming education, work and life. *International Journal of Information Management*, *55*, 102211. doi:10.1016/j.ijinfomgt.2020.102211

Easwaran, B., Hiran, K. K., Krishnan, S., & Doshi, R. (Eds.). (2022). *Real-Time Applications of Machine Learning in Cyber-Physical Systems*. IGI Global., doi:10.4018/978-1-7998-9308-0

Goodier, G. H. G., McCormack, J., Egan, S. J., Watson, H. J., Hoiles, K. J., Todd, G., & Treasure, J. L. (2014). Parent skills training treatment for parents of children and adolescents with eating disorders: A qualitative study: PARENT SKILLS TRAINING TREATMENT. *International Journal of Eating Disorders*, *47*(4), 368–375. doi:10.1002/eat.22224 PMID:24843891

Gouvea, R., Kapelianis, D., & Kassicieh, S. (2018). Assessing the nexus of sustainability and information & communications technology. *Technological Forecasting and Social Change*, *130*, 39–44. doi:10.1016/j.techfore.2017.07.023

Hiran, K. K., Doshi, R., & Patel, M. (Eds.). (2024). *Applications of Virtual and Augmented Reality for Health and Wellbeing*. IGI Global. doi:10.4018/979-8-3693-1123-3

Hiran, K. K., Hemachandran, K., Pise, A., & Rabi, B. (Eds.). (2023). *Handbook of Research on AI and Knowledge Engineering for Real-Time Business Intelligence*. IGI Global. doi:10.4018/978-1-6684-6519-6

Hogan, A., & Thompson, G. (Eds.). (2020). *Privatisation and commercialisation in public education: How the public nature of schooling is changing*. Routledge. doi:10.4324/9780429330025

Iivari, N., Sharma, S., & Ventä-Olkkonen, L. (2020). Digital transformation of everyday life – How COVID-19 pandemic transformed the basic education of the young generation and why information management research should care? *International Journal of Information Management*, *55*, 102183. doi:10.1016/j.ijinfomgt.2020.102183 PMID:32836640

Kerres, M. (2020a). Against All Odds: Education in Germany Coping with Covid-19. *Postdigital Science and Education*, *2*(3), 690–694. doi:10.1007/s42438-020-00130-7

Kerres, M. (2020b). Against All Odds: Education in Germany Coping with Covid-19. *Postdigital Science and Education*, *2*(3), 690–694. doi:10.1007/s42438-020-00130-7

Kodama, M. (2020). Digitally transforming work styles in an era of infectious disease. *International Journal of Information Management*, *55*, 102172. doi:10.1016/j.ijinfomgt.2020.102172 PMID:32836634

Maity, S., Sahu, T. N., & Sen, N. (2021a). Panoramic view of digital education in COVID-19: A new explored avenue. *Review of Education*, *9*(2), 405–423. doi:10.1002/rev3.3250

Maity, S., Sahu, T. N., & Sen, N. (2021b). Panoramic view of digital education in COVID-19: A new explored avenue. *Review of Education*, *9*(2), 405–423. doi:10.1002/rev3.3250

Maity, S., Sen, N., & Sahu, T. N. (2020a). COVID-19: Triggers fear psychosis among private sector employees. *Journal of Labor and Society*, *23*(4), 503–513. doi:10.1111/wusa.12490

Maity, S., Sen, N., & Sahu, T. N. (2020b). COVID-19: Triggers fear psychosis among private sector employees. *Journal of Labor and Society*, *23*(4), 503–513. doi:10.1111/wusa.12490

Mijwil, M. M., Gök, M., Doshi, R., Hiran, K. K., & Kösesoy, I. (2023). Utilizing Artificial Intelligence Techniques to Improve the Performance of Wireless Nodes. In Applications of Artificial Intelligence in Wireless Communication Systems (pp. 150-162). IGI Global. doi:10.4018/978-1-6684-7348-1.ch010

Mishra, A., Tripathi, A., Khazanchi, D., Hiran, K. K., Vyas, A. K., & Padmanaban, S. (2021). A framework for applying artificial intelligence (AI) with Internet of NanoThings (IoNT). In *Machine Learning for Sustainable Development* (pp. 1–16). De Gruyter. doi:10.1515/9783110702514-001

Nagariya, R., Kumar, D., & Kumar, I. (2021a). Enablers to implement sustainable practices in the service only supply chain: A case of an Indian hospital. *Business Process Management Journal*. doi:10.1108/BPMJ-10-2020-0469

Nagariya, R., Kumar, D., & Kumar, I. (2021b). Enablers to implement sustainable practices in the service only supply chain: A case of an Indian hospital. *Business Process Management Journal*. doi:10.1108/BPMJ-10-2020-0469

Ponomarenko, E., Oganesyan, A., & Teslenko, V. (2019). New trends in higher education: Massive open online courses as an innovative tool for increasing university performance. *International Journal of Economic Policy in Emerging Economies*, *12*(4), 391. doi:10.1504/IJEPEE.2019.104635

Radif, M., Fan, D. I., & McLaughln, D. P. (n.d.). INTERNAL AND EXTERNAL BARRIERS INFLUENCING LMS IMPLEMENTATION IN IRAQI. *Higher Education*, 12.

Radif, M., Fan, I., & McLaughln, P. (2015). INTERNAL AND EXTERNAL BARRIERS INFLUENCING LMS IMPLEMENTATION IN IRAQI HIGHER EDUCATION. *ICERI2015: 8th International Conference of Education, Research and Innovation*, 11.

Rastogi, R. (2020). Recent Trends in Indian Higher Education System. *International Journal of Advanced Science and Technology*, *29*(8), 7.

Rathi, S., Hiran, K. K., & Sakhare, S. (2023). Affective state prediction of E-learner using SS-ROA based deep LSTM. *Array (New York, N.Y.)*, *19*, 100315. doi:10.1016/j.array.2023.100315

Sachs, J. D., Schmidt-Traub, G., Mazzucato, M., Messner, D., Nakicenovic, N., & Rockström, J. (2019). Six transformations to achieve the sustainable development goals. *Nature Sustainability*, *2*(9), 805–814. doi:10.1038/s41893-019-0352-9

Seele, P., & Lock, I. (2017). The game-changing potential of digitalization for sustainability: Possibilities, perils, and pathways. *Sustainability Science*, *12*(2), 183–185. doi:10.1007/s11625-017-0426-4

Singh, S. V., & Hiran, K. K. (2022). The impact of AI on teaching and learning in higher education technology. *Journal of Higher Education Theory and Practice*, *22*(13).

Sun, Q.-H., & Su, Y. (2020). Psychological crisis intervention for college students during novel coronavirus infection epidemic. *Psychiatry Research*, *289*, 113043. doi:10.1016/j.psychres.2020.113043 PMID:32387793

Warfield, J. N. (1974a). Developing Interconnection Matrices in Structural Modeling. *IEEE Transactions on Systems, Man, and Cybernetics*, *SMC-4*(1), 81–87. doi:10.1109/TSMC.1974.5408524

Warfield, J. N. (1974b). Developing Interconnection Matrices in Structural Modeling. *IEEE Transactions on Systems, Man, and Cybernetics*, *SMC-4*(1), 81–87. doi:10.1109/TSMC.1974.5408524

Williamson, B. (2019). Policy networks, performance metrics and platform markets: Charting the expanding data infrastructure of higher education. *British Journal of Educational Technology*, *50*(6), 2794–2809. doi:10.1111/bjet.12849

*World Health Statistics 2020: Monitoring Health for the SDGs*. (2020). World Health Organization.

# Chapter 22
# Shaping Tomorrow's Minds:
## The Future of Education in an AI (Artificial Intelligence)-Augmented World

**Meeta Chaudhry**
*KIET Group of Institutions, India*

**Nandini Goswami**
*KIET Group of Institutions*

## ABSTRACT

*The chapter explores the evolution of AI, distinguishing it from generative AI, and examines its current applications in education, spanning from primary to higher education levels. Unveiling the multifaceted landscape of AI technologies, such as machine learning, deep learning, and natural language processing, the narrative delves into personalized learning, smart tutoring systems, and administrative efficiency. The chapter anticipates a future where AI collaborates seamlessly with educators, offering hyper-personalized learning journeys, immersive experiences through augmented and virtual reality, and fostering collaborative and project-based learning. Challenges, including ethical concerns, digital inclusion, and teacher training, are acknowledged, emphasizing the importance of addressing these issues for an inclusive and equitable AI-augmented educational future. As we stand at the brink of this transformative era, the chapter envisions a harmonious fusion of technology and human ingenuity shaping the minds of tomorrow.*

## INTRODUCTION

"Shaping Tomorrow's Minds: The Future of Education in an AI-Augmented World" embarks on a captivating exploration of the evolution, current landscape, and future possibilities of artificial intelligence (AI) in education. This chapter unfolds the historical tapestry of AI, tracing its origins from ancient myths to the formal inception in the mid-20th century, highlighting key milestones and challenges faced along its dynamic journey. Distinguishing between traditional AI and the transformative realm of generative AI, the narrative unfolds the multifaceted nature of AI technologies such as machine learning,

DOI: 10.4018/979-8-3693-2440-0.ch022

deep learning, and natural language processing (Kankanhalli, 2024). The present role of AI in education is illuminated, showcasing its applications from primary to higher education levels, encompassing personalised learning, smart tutoring systems, and administrative efficiency. As the chapter peers into the future, it envisions the role of AI in 2040, foreseeing hyper-personalised learning, immersive experiences, and collaborative educational landscapes. However, the narrative remains grounded, addressing the ethical considerations, data privacy concerns, and the imperative need for teacher training. Through a comprehensive lens, this chapter offers readers a panoramic view of the past, present, and potential future of AI in education, advocating for a balanced approach that harnesses AI's transformative power while navigating the ethical complexities that accompany it.

The journey of Artificial Intelligence (AI) from its inception to its current state is a testament to the relentless pursuit of innovation (Abukmeil et al., 2021). Initially conceived as a concept in the mid-20th century, AI has undergone transformational evolution, transcending its theoretical roots to become an integral part of our daily lives. In recent years, the application of AI in education has garnered significant attention, presenting both opportunities and challenges. This chapter explores the evolution of AI, distinguishing it from generative AI, and delves into the current and future role of AI in education, emphasising the integration of generative AI to achieve Sustainable Development Goals (SDGs).

The goal of the computer science field of artificial intelligence (AI) is to build intelligent machines that can mimic human behavior and cognitive processes. Fundamentally, artificial intelligence (AI) is the creation of algorithms and systems that are able to sense their surroundings, analyze them, and make choices to accomplish particular objectives. Artificial Intelligence comprises several subfields, such as robotics, computer vision, natural language processing, and machine learning. These days, artificial intelligence (AI) is being incorporated into more and more areas of our life, from online shopping sites and streaming platforms to virtual assistants like Siri and Alexa. AI-powered solutions are transforming a number of industries, including manufacturing, healthcare, finance, and transportation. They do this by streamlining workflows, increasing productivity, and fostering creativity. But while AI develops quickly, it also brings with it ethical and cultural issues, such as privacy concerns, job displacement, and biases in algorithmic decision-making. AI is still developing despite these difficulties, offering revolutionary potential in the future (Doshi et al., 2023; Hiran et al.; 2023).

Looking toward the future, the chapter envisions a 2040 educational landscape enriched by hyper-personalised learning, immersive experiences, and collaborative environments. However, a balanced perspective is maintained, addressing ethical considerations, data privacy concerns, and the imperative need for teacher training. The exploration of AI's past, present, and potential future in education offers readers a comprehensive view, advocating for harnessing AI's transformative power while navigating the ethical complexities accompanying it.

This chapter also explores the dynamic evolution of AI and its transformative impact on education. Distinguishing between traditional AI and generative AI, we unravel the current role of AI in education, showcasing its potential to revolutionise learning experiences. Looking forward, we advocate for a future where generative AI collaborates with educators to achieve Sustainable Development Goals. However, we acknowledge the challenges that come with this paradigm shift, emphasising the need for ethical considerations and safeguards. As we stand on the cusp of an AI-augmented educational world, this chapter envisions a future where technology and human ingenuity combine to shape tomorrow's minds (Doshi et al., 2023; Mishra et al., 2021).

## HISTORY AND EVOLUTION OF AI

The history of artificial intelligence (AI) traces its roots back to ancient times, where myths and folklore hinted at the creation of artificial beings with human-like intelligence (Adam et al. 2021). However, the formal inception of AI occurred in the mid-20th century. In 1950, Alan Turing proposed the Turing Test, a benchmark for evaluating machine intelligence, and the term "artificial intelligence" was coined in 1956 at the Dartmouth Conference. The following decades saw the development of early AI programs like the General Problem Solver and the exploration of expert systems in the 1970s and 1980s. Despite initial enthusiasm, the field faced setbacks during the "AI winter" when funding and interest dwindled. The late 20th century witnessed a resurgence in AI, marked by breakthroughs in machine learning and the triumph of IBM's Deep Blue over a chess grandmaster in 1997 (Adams et al., 2017). The 2010s brought about a new era with the rise of deep learning, leading to significant advancements in image and speech recognition. Presently, AI is a pervasive force, impacting diverse sectors like healthcare, finance, and autonomous vehicles, with ongoing research focusing on ethical considerations and responsible AI development. The history of AI reflects a dynamic journey marked by peaks of progress and troughs of challenges, shaping the technology landscape of the modern era (Easwaran et al., 2022; Singh et al., 2022).

The roots of AI can be traced back to the mid-20th century when researchers aimed to create machines that could mimic human intelligence. Over the decades, (Xuesong Zhai et al., 2021) AI has evolved from rule-based systems to machine learning and neural networks, marking a paradigm shift in its capabilities. The emergence of generative AI represents a groundbreaking development, allowing machines not only to learn from data but also to create new content autonomously.

In the bustling realm of modern artificial intelligence, a diverse tapestry of technologies and methodologies come together to weave a narrative of unprecedented capabilities. At its heart lies machine learning, a versatile protagonist that learns from labelled data in supervised fashion, navigates uncharted territories in unsupervised mode, and engages in trial-and-error with reinforcement learning (Mijwil et al., 2023; Al-Shahwani et al., 2024). Deep learning, a close companion, unveils the power of neural networks with multiple layers, a technological odyssey reshaping industries through image and speech recognition, natural language processing, and generative feats. In this landscape, the eloquence of natural language processing enables machines to converse with humans, while computer vision paints a vivid picture, decoding visual data for applications like facial recognition and autonomous navigation. Robotics, embodying the fusion of AI and machines, dances to the tune of autonomous decision-making in manufacturing plants and healthcare corridors. The sage-like expert systems lend their wisdom to domains requiring nuanced decision support, while recommender systems whisper personalised suggestions in the ears of online platforms. As the plot thickens, generative models give birth to new data, and explainable AI seeks to demystify the algorithms' decision-making processes. The narrative extends beyond the cloud, venturing into the edges where devices host their own AI prowess, and ethical considerations take centre stage in the plot, addressing issues of bias and accountability. Quantum computing emerges as a subplot, promising to revolutionise AI's problem-solving prowess. The story of modern AI unfolds with characters like machine learning, deep learning, and ethical considerations playing pivotal roles, guiding technology toward a future yet to be fully imagined.

The timeline illustrates the evolution of AI from its conceptualization in the 1950s to its pervasive integration into various sectors in the 2020s. The chapter distinguishes between traditional AI, relying on predefined algorithms, and generative AI, capable of independent content creation. Current roles of AI in education, from personalised learning to administrative efficiency, are highlighted, laying the groundwork for future possibilities.

Let's take a look at the timeline and compare whether this is the AI era or has been around for way longer than we realise (Ahani et al., 2019; Skouby et al., 2022; Wanjale et al., 2023).

## 1950s-1960s: The Birth of Artificial Intelligence (AI)

- **1950:** The term "Artificial Intelligence" was coined by computer scientist John McCarthy during the Dartmouth Conference, marking the official beginning of AI as a field of study.
- **1956:** The Dartmouth Conference becomes a seminal moment, gathering leading scientists to explore the possibilities of creating machines that can mimic human intelligence.
- **1950s-1960s:** Early AI research focuses on symbolic AI, where computers are programmed with explicit rules to perform tasks. Researchers, including Allen Newell and Herbert A. Simon, develop the Logic Theorist and General Problem Solver.

## 1970s-1980s: Expert Systems and AI Winter

- **1970s:** Research in AI expands to include expert systems, which emulate the decision-making abilities of a human expert. However, limitations in computing power and unrealistic expectations lead to a period known as the "AI Winter," where funding and interest in AI decline.
- **1980s:** Despite challenges, expert systems gain traction in various industries. Japan's Fifth Generation Computer Systems project accelerates AI research.
- MYCIN, a rule-based expert system created at Stanford University to diagnose bacterial infections, is one such example.

## 1990s: The Rise of Machine Learning

- **1997:** IBM's Deep Blue defeats chess world champion Garry Kasparov, showcasing the power of specialised AI in narrow domains.
- **1990s:** Machine learning gains prominence, with algorithms like Support Vector Machines and Decision Trees becoming popular. Research in neural networks continues, though at a slower pace.
- Applications of machine learning include email spam filtering, recommendation systems, and handwriting recognition.

## 2000s: The Big Data Revolution and Deep Learning

- **Mid-2000s:** The availability of massive datasets and increased computing power contribute to the resurgence of interest in neural networks, especially deep learning.
- **2011:** IBM's Watson wins Jeopardy!, showcasing advancements in natural language processing and machine learning.

- Examples include numerous uses of deep learning in autonomous cars and Google's DeepMind AlphaGo, which defeated human champions in the game of Go.

## 2010s: AI Goes Mainstream

- **2012:** The ImageNet competition sees a breakthrough with deep learning, as a convolutional neural network (CNN) achieves significantly improved image classification accuracy.
- **2015:** Generative models like Generative Adversarial Networks (GANs) gain attention, enabling the creation of new content by AI systems.
- **Late 2010s:** AI applications become widespread in industries such as healthcare, finance, and autonomous vehicles. Voice-activated virtual assistants like Siri and Alexa become commonplace.

## 2020s: AI Integration Across Industries

- **2020s:** AI is an integral part of daily life, influencing areas such as recommendation systems, autonomous vehicles, language translation, and more.
- **Ongoing:** Continued advancements in AI, including reinforcement learning, explainable AI, and AI ethics, shape the trajectory of the technology. The integration of AI into various sectors accelerates, with an emphasis on responsible and ethical AI development.
- Developments such chatbots (like OpenAI's GPT models), sentiment analysis tools for social media monitoring, and language translation models (like Google Translate). Robotics has also benefited greatly from AI, which has made it possible to create autonomous systems that can sense their surroundings and act instantly. Autonomous vehicles, drones for a range of tasks including delivery and monitoring, and robotic aides in sectors like manufacturing and healthcare are a few examples.

The figure 1, shows the timeline that provides a broad overview of the evolution of AI, from its conceptualization in the 1950s to its widespread integration into various aspects of modern life in the 2020s. The journey has been marked by breakthroughs, challenges, and a continuous quest for creating intelligent machines.

# AI VS. GENERATIVE AI

Generative AI refers to a category of artificial intelligence that involves systems capable of generating new, original content. (Ahmed et al. 2020) Unlike traditional AI systems that rely on pre-programmed rules or patterns, generative AI has the ability to create novel outputs on its own. This capability is often achieved through the use of neural networks, particularly in the context of deep learning.

There are several types of generative AI models, and they are used for various applications, including text generation, image synthesis, and even creating realistic video or audio content. Two common types of generative models are:

*Figure 1. History and evolution of AI*

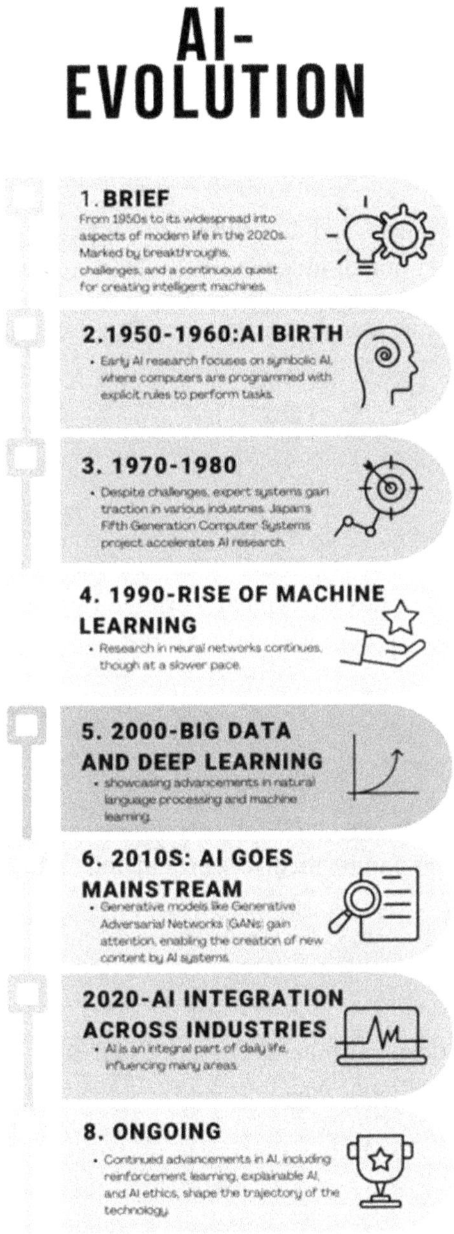


1. Generative Adversarial Networks (GANs):
   - GANs consist of two neural networks, a generator, and a discriminator, which are trained simultaneously through a competitive process. The generator creates new data instances, such as images, while the discriminator evaluates them for authenticity. This adversarial training

process helps the generator improve its ability to create content that is increasingly indistinguishable from real data.

2. Variational Autoencoders (VAEs):
    - VAEs are a type of generative model that works by learning a probabilistic mapping between input data and a latent space. This latent space allows for the generation of new data points similar to those in the training set. VAEs are often used in scenarios where capturing uncertainty and variability in the generated outputs is important.

While traditional AI relies on predefined algorithms to perform specific tasks, generative AI possesses the ability to generate novel content independently. This crucial distinction opens new horizons for creativity and problem-solving, making generative AI a powerful tool in education.

## Traditional AI

### Rule-Based Systems

- Traditional AI relies on rule-based systems where explicit rules and logic are programmed to solve specific problems. These rules are typically crafted by human experts who have a deep understanding of the domain.

### Task-Specific

- Traditional AI systems are often designed for specific tasks or domains. They excel in well-defined problems where the rules can be precisely articulated and programmed.

### Examples

- Expert systems, rule-based decision-making systems, and early natural language processing applications are examples of traditional AI.

## Generative AI

### Learning From Data

- Generative AI, particularly in the context of deep learning, focuses on learning from data. Instead of relying on explicit programming, generative models learn patterns and representations from large datasets.

### Content Creation

- Generative AI is designed to create new content. It can generate realistic and novel outputs, such as images, text, or even audio, by learning the underlying patterns and structures present in the training data.

### Example

- Generative AI finds applications in various creative domains, such as image synthesis, text generation, and content creation. It is also used for tasks like data augmentation, where new data samples are generated to enhance machine learning model training databases.

## BASICS OF NEURAL NETWORKS AND CNN

### Neural Networks

Neural networks are a fundamental concept in artificial intelligence and machine learning inspired by the structure and function of the human brain's interconnected neurons. They consist of layers of interconnected nodes, called neurons or units, organised into an input layer, one or more hidden layers, and an output layer.

- **Input Layer:** This layer receives input data, which could be features extracted from images, text, or other forms of structured or unstructured data.
- **Hidden Layers:** These layers perform computations on the input data through weighted connections between neurons. Each neuron in a hidden layer receives inputs from the previous layer, applies an activation function to the weighted sum of those inputs, and passes the result to the next layer.
- **Output Layer:** This layer produces the final output of the neural network, which could be a classification, regression, or any other prediction based on the problem being solved.

Training Process: Neural networks are trained using a process called backpropagation, where the network learns to adjust the weights of its connections based on the error between predicted and actual outputs. This iterative process involves feeding training data through the network, calculating the error, and updating the weights to minimise the error using optimization algorithms like gradient descent.

Activation Functions: Activation functions introduce non-linearity into the neural network, allowing it to learn complex patterns in the data. Common activation functions include sigmoid, tanh, ReLU (Rectified Linear Unit), and softmax.

Applications: Neural networks have applications in various domains, including image and speech recognition, natural language processing, autonomous vehicles, healthcare, finance, and more.

*Figure 2.*
*Reference Taken from https://www.mckinsey.com/featured-insights/mckinsey-explainers/whats-the-future-of-generative-ai-an-early-view-in-15-charts*

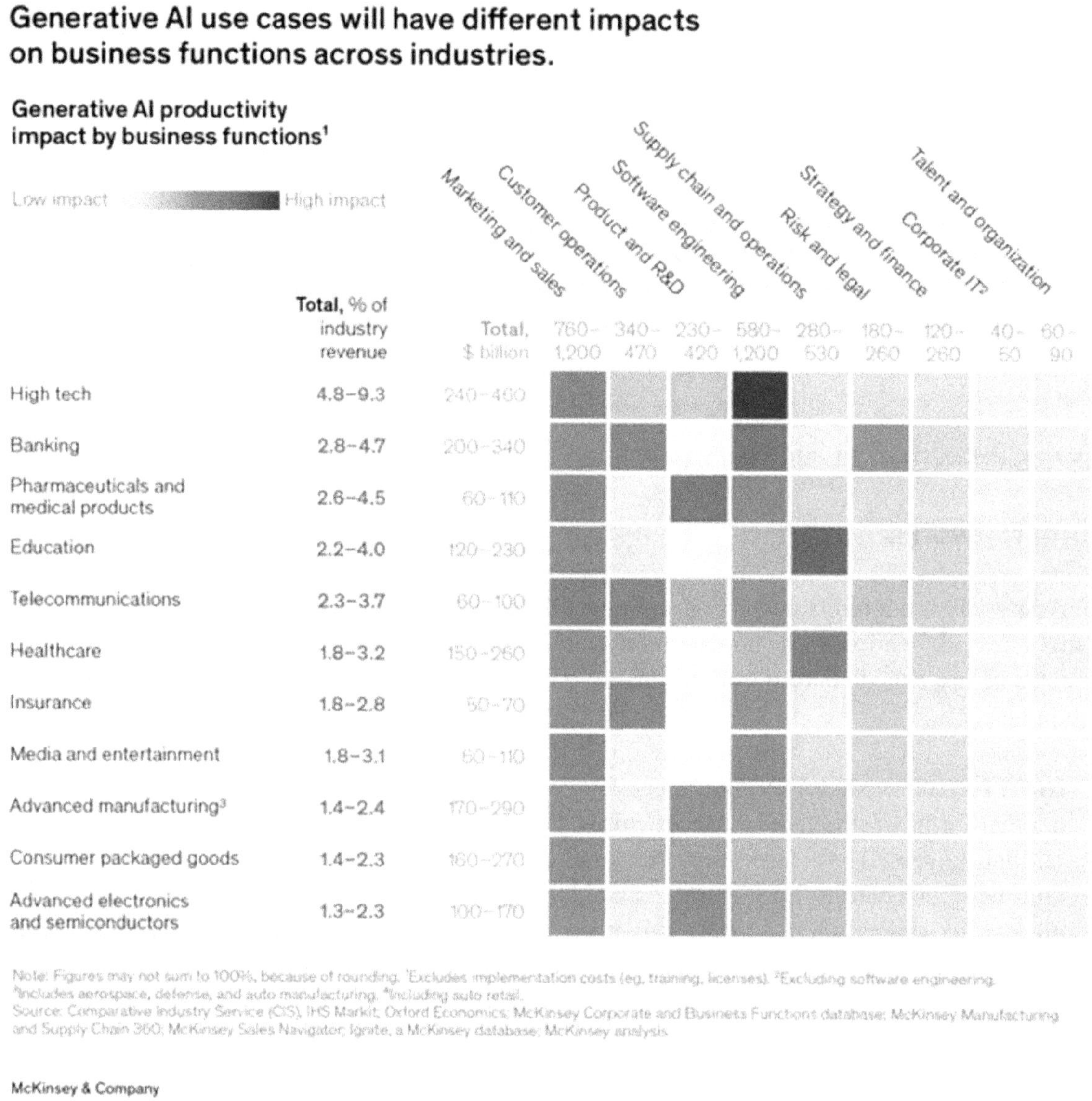


## Convolutional Neural Networks (CNNs)

Convolutional Neural Networks (CNNs) are a specialised type of neural network designed for processing structured grid-like data, such as images or videos. They are particularly effective in tasks involving visual recognition and classification.

## Key Components

- **Convolutional Layers:** These layers consist of filters (also called kernels) that slide over the input image, performing element-wise multiplication and aggregation operations to extract spatial features such as edges, textures, and patterns.
- **Pooling Layers**: Pooling layers downsample the feature maps generated by convolutional layers, reducing the spatial dimensions while retaining important information. Common pooling operations include max pooling and average pooling.
- **Fully Connected Layers:** These layers are similar to those in traditional neural networks and are typically placed at the end of the network. They process the features extracted by convolutional and pooling layers to make predictions or classifications.

## Advantages of CNNs

- Parameter Sharing: CNNs leverage parameter sharing, where the same set of weights (filters) is applied across different spatial locations in the input, allowing the network to learn translation-invariant features.
- Hierarchical Feature Learning: CNNs learn hierarchical representations of visual features, starting from low-level features (e.g., edges) in early layers to high-level abstract features (e.g., object shapes) in later layers.

Training CNNs: Training CNNs involves feeding labelled training images through the network and adjusting the weights using backpropagation and optimization algorithms. CNNs are often pre-trained on large datasets like ImageNet and fine-tuned for specific tasks to improve performance.

Applications: CNNs are widely used in image classification, object detection, facial recognition, medical image analysis, autonomous driving, and many other computer vision tasks.

In summary, neural networks and CNNs are powerful tools in the field of artificial intelligence, enabling machines to learn from data, extract meaningful features, and make accurate predictions or classifications in various domains, particularly in tasks involving complex visual data like images and videos.

The Figure 3, shows the basic working of artificial neural network

# CURRENT ROLE OF AI IN EDUCATION

In the present era, AI has become an integral component of the educational landscape. From personalised learning platforms to intelligent tutoring systems, AI is reshaping the way students engage with educational content. Adaptive learning systems use AI algorithms to tailor educational experiences, catering to individual learning styles and preferences. (Akter et al. 2022). This personalised approach enhances the effectiveness of education by addressing the unique needs of each learner.

AI has been increasingly integrated into education at various levels, from primary schools to higher education institutions. Its applications span a wide range of areas, aiming to enhance the learning experience, personalise education, and streamline administrative tasks. (Guilherme 2019; Biesta 2013). Here's an overview of the current role of AI in education at different levels:

*Figure 3. Artificial neural network basic working*

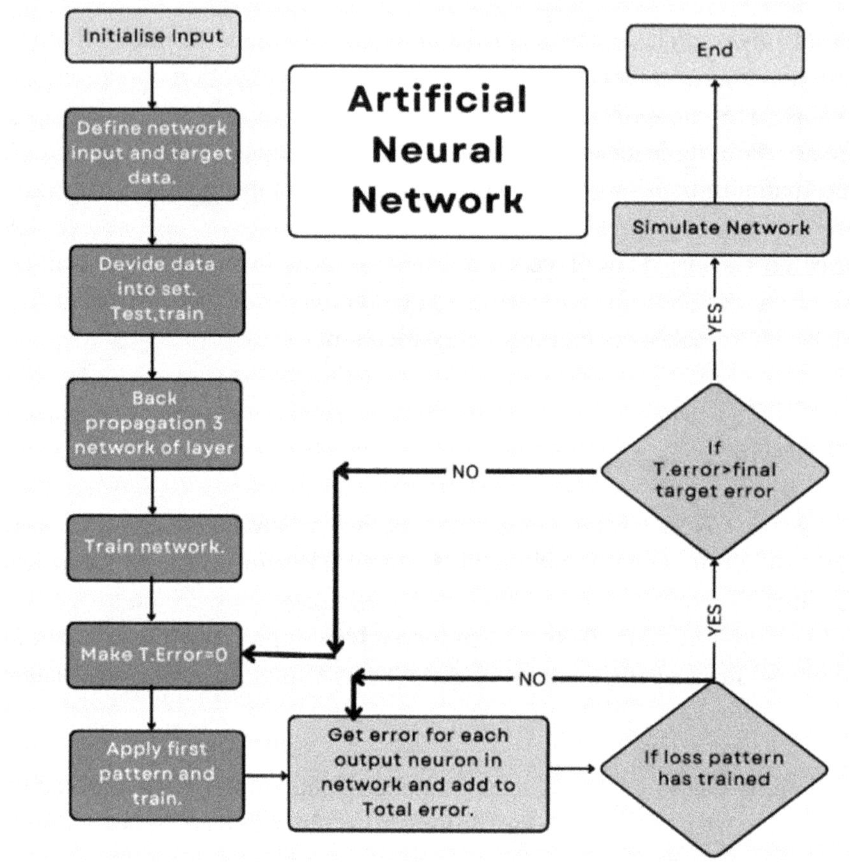


## Primary and Secondary Education

### Personalized Learning

- AI algorithms analyse students' learning patterns and adapt content to their individual needs. This helps in providing customised learning experiences, addressing the unique strengths and weaknesses of each student.
- Example: Adaptive learning platforms like DreamBox and Khan Academy adjust content based on a student's performance, providing targeted exercises to reinforce understanding or challenge them appropriately.

### Smart Tutoring Systems

- AI-powered tutoring systems offer real-time feedback and assistance. These systems can identify areas where students are struggling and provide additional support, helping them grasp concepts more effectively.
- Example: Carnegie Learning offers AI-driven tutoring systems that provide real-time feedback and adapt to students' responses, helping them navigate through maths concepts at their own pace.

### Gamification

- AI is used to develop educational games that make learning more engaging and interactive. Gamification encourages participation, collaboration, and problem-solving skills among students.
- Example: "Prodigy" is an educational game that uses AI to adapt questions to each student's skill level, making learning maths engaging and enjoyable.

### Early Intervention

- AI tools can identify early signs of learning difficulties or developmental issues, enabling teachers and parents to intervene and provide timely support.
- Example: The Waterford Early Learning program employs AI to identify early signs of learning difficulties in young students, allowing educators to provide timely support.

## Higher Education

### Adaptive Learning Platforms

- AI is employed in adaptive learning systems that adjust the curriculum based on students' progress and performance. This helps ensure that each student receives a tailored educational experience.
- Example: Smart Sparrow is an adaptive learning platform used in higher education that tailors content to individual student needs, promoting a more personalised learning experience.

### Automated Grading

- AI can automate the grading of assignments, quizzes, and exams, freeing up educators' time to focus on more interactive and personalised aspects of teaching.
- Example: Gradescope uses AI to streamline the grading process for educators by automating the grading of assignments and exams, providing detailed feedback.

### Learning Analytics

- AI-driven analytics provide insights into student performance and engagement. Educators can use this data to identify areas for improvement in teaching methods and curriculum design.
- Example: Canvas Learning Management System incorporates learning analytics to provide insights into student engagement, performance trends, and participation levels.

### Virtual Classrooms

- AI facilitates virtual classrooms, enabling students to attend classes remotely. Virtual classrooms often include AI-driven tools for collaboration, discussion, and real-time interaction.
- Example: Zoom, Microsoft Teams, and Google Meet utilize AI for features like automatic transcription, virtual backgrounds, and facial recognition to enhance the virtual classroom experience.

## Administrative Tasks

### Chatbots and Virtual Assistants

- AI-powered chatbots assist students and staff with administrative queries, course information, and scheduling. Virtual assistants help streamline administrative processes, enhancing efficiency.
- Example: Ivy, a chatbot developed by Georgia State University, assists students with administrative queries, course information, and scheduling.

### Predictive Analytics

- AI is used for predicting enrollment trends, resource allocation, and identifying areas where additional support or resources may be needed.
- Example: Predictive analytics tools like IBM Watson Analytics are employed to forecast enrollment trends, helping institutions allocate resources efficiently.

## Professional Development

### AI for Educator Training

- AI tools are utilised for professional development, offering educators personalised training modules and resources based on their teaching styles and areas of improvement.
- Example: Squirrel AI provides AI-driven professional development courses for educators, offering personalised training modules based on individual teaching styles and needs.

### Automated Lesson Planning

- AI can assist educators in creating lesson plans by suggesting content, activities, and assessments based on curriculum requirements and student needs.
- Example: AI tools like Quillionz assist educators in generating lesson plans by automatically creating questions, activities, and assessments aligned with curriculum standards.

## FUTURE APPROACHES TO AI IN EDUCATION

Looking ahead, the future of education lies in a seamless integration of AI, with a focus on generative AI to foster creativity and critical thinking. Imagine classrooms where AI collaborates with educators to develop customised learning experiences that not only transmit knowledge but also stimulate innovation. (Alami et al. 2020) AI-powered tools will play a pivotal role in automating administrative tasks, enabling educators to dedicate more time to personalised instruction.

Predicting the exact role of AI in education iis challenging due to the dynamic nature of technological advancements and evolving educational needs. (Preiksaitis, Rose 2023) However, based on current trends and anticipated developments, we can outline some potential roles and contributions of AI in education by 2040:

### Hyper-Personalized Learning

#### AI-Infused Learning Journeys

- AI will play a central role in designing highly personalised learning journeys for each student. Learning platforms will leverage AI to understand individual learning styles, preferences, and progress, tailoring educational content and experiences accordingly.

#### Intelligent Learning Assistants

- Intelligent virtual assistants will provide continuous support to students, offering personalised tutoring, answering questions, and adapting instructional methods based on real-time assessments of individual strengths and weaknesses.

#### Example

- A student, Sarah, engages with an AI-driven learning platform. The platform analyses Sarah's learning history, preferences, and real-time performance data. It adapts the curriculum, providing tailored lessons, interactive exercises, and personalised feedback. Sarah's AI-powered learning companion guides her through challenges and reinforces concepts based on her individual needs.

## Immersive and Interactive Learning

### Augmented and Virtual Reality Integration

- AI-powered augmented and virtual reality will become integral to education, providing immersive simulations and experiences that enhance understanding in subjects ranging from history to complex scientific concepts.

### Natural Language Interaction

- Improved natural language processing will enable students to interact with educational content and AI tutors using conversational interfaces, making the learning process more intuitive and engaging.

### Understand It Like This

- Sarah in a history class use AI-powered augmented reality glasses to explore historical events. The AI guides them through interactive simulations, allowing them to witness key moments firsthand. This immersive experience enhances their understanding and engagement with historical content.

## Collaborative and Project-Based Learning

### AI-Enhanced Collaboration Platforms

- Advanced AI algorithms will facilitate seamless collaboration among students, both locally and globally. AI will contribute to the creation of dynamic project-based learning environments, fostering critical thinking, creativity, and problem-solving skills.

### Automated Project Feedback

- AI will streamline the assessment of collaborative projects, providing automated feedback that evaluates both individual and group contributions. This allows educators to focus on guiding and mentoring students rather than administrative tasks.
- skills and interests. Automated feedback mechanisms assess individual contributions, fostering a sense of shared responsibility.

### Understand It Like This

- Now, Sarah wants to do a global collaborative project, initiated where students from diverse backgrounds work together on solving a real-world problem. AI algorithms facilitate collaboration by matching students based on their skills and interests. Automated feedback mechanisms assess individual contributions, fostering a sense of shared responsibility.

## Lifelong Learning and Continuous Upskilling

### AI-Powered Continuous Skill Assessment

- AI will continuously assess the skills and knowledge of learners, providing real-time feedback and suggesting personalised learning pathways to meet evolving career demands.

### Customised Professional Development

- Professionals will have access to AI-driven platforms offering personalised and relevant professional development opportunities, ensuring ongoing career relevance in rapidly changing industries.

### Example

- Sarah, Now a professional in the technology industry, receives continuous skill assessments from an AI-driven platform. Based on his performance and industry trends, the AI recommends personalised learning paths to help her acquire new skills, ensuring his continuous relevance in a rapidly evolving field.

## CHALLENGES AND DRAWBACKS

However, this transformation is not without challenges. (Kumar,et al. 2023) Ethical considerations, data privacy concerns, and the potential for reinforcing biases are critical issues that demand careful navigation. As we embrace AI in education, (Tahiru, 2021; Ke Zhang et al. 2021; Sallam et al. 2023; Holmes et al., 2022) it is essential to address these drawbacks to ensure an inclusive and equitable learning environment.

## Ethical Concerns and Bias

### Challenge

- AI algorithms can inadvertently perpetuate biases present in training data, leading to unfair outcomes and reinforcing existing inequalities. Ethical considerations related to student privacy, data security, and algorithmic transparency are paramount.

### Consideration

- Developing and enforcing ethical guidelines for the use of AI in education, ensuring transparency in algorithmic decision-making, and regularly auditing AI systems for biases are essential to address these challenges.

## Digital Inclusion and Accessibility

### Challenge

- The digital divide can widen educational inequalities, as not all students have equal access to technology and high-speed internet. Those without access may be left behind, exacerbating educational disparities.

### Consideration

- Efforts should focus on providing equitable access to technology, ensuring that AI-driven educational resources are accessible to all students, regardless of socio-economic background or geographic location.

## Teacher Training and Professional Development

### Challenge

- Many educators may not be adequately prepared to integrate AI tools into their teaching practices. Lack of training and professional development opportunities can hinder the effective use of AI in the classroom.

### Consideration

- Investing in teacher training programs that equip educators with the skills needed to leverage AI tools effectively. This includes ongoing professional development to keep educators abreast of evolving technologies.

## Data Privacy and Security

### Challenge

- The collection and use of student data by AI systems raise concerns about privacy and security. Unauthorised access to sensitive information can have serious consequences for individuals and institutions.

### Consideration

- Implementing robust data privacy policies, ensuring secure storage and transmission of data, and obtaining informed consent from students and parents are critical measures to mitigate data-related risks.

## Overreliance on Technology

### Challenge

- Over Reliance on AI systems might diminish the importance of human interaction and personalised mentorship in education. Students may lose critical social and emotional learning experiences.

### Consideration

- Balancing the use of technology with traditional teaching methods, emphasising the importance of human connection in education, and integrating socio-emotional learning into AI-driven platforms can help address this challenge.

Addressing these challenges requires a coordinated effort from educators, policymakers, technologists, and other stakeholders. Striking the right balance between technological innovation and ethical, inclusive, and equitable education practices is crucial for the successful integration of AI in the educational landscape.

## CONCLUSION

In the exploration of "Shaping Tomorrow's Minds: The Future of Education in an AI-Augmented World," we have journeyed through the historical evolution of artificial intelligence (AI) and witnessed its transformative impact on education. From mythical beginnings to the formal inception in the mid-20th century, AI has become an integral force shaping the educational landscape. The chapter has dissected the nuances of AI technologies, distinguishing traditional AI from the generative realm, and has showcased its present applications across educational levels.

As we cast our gaze toward the future, envisioning the educational landscape of 2040, the narrative paints a picture of hyper-personalised learning, immersive experiences, and collaborative environments. This utopian vision, however, is tempered by a pragmatic approach that addresses ethical considerations, data privacy concerns, and the crucial necessity for teacher training. It is an acknowledgment that while AI holds immense potential to revolutionise education, it requires careful stewardship to ensure it aligns with human values and serves as a tool for empowerment rather than control.

The timeline provided in this chapter underscores the relentless progression of AI from its conceptualization in the 1950s to its widespread integration into diverse sectors in the 2020s. The differentiation between traditional AI and generative AI establishes a foundation for understanding the dynamic capabilities of this evolving technology. The current roles of AI in education, from personalised learning to administrative efficiency, serve as a testament to its versatility and adaptability.

Looking ahead, the chapter anticipates a future where AI collaborates seamlessly with educators, offering hyper-personalised learning journeys, immersive experiences through augmented and virtual reality, and fostering collaborative and project-based learning. However, it is crucial to approach this future with a mindful perspective. The challenges posed by ethical concerns, digital inclusion, and teacher training must be met with proactive solutions to ensure that the benefits of AI are accessible to all and that educators are equipped to harness its potential.

In this transformative era, the chapter serves as a call to action—an urging to control AI and not let AI control us. As we harness the transformative power of AI in education, it is essential to maintain a human-centred approach, placing ethical considerations at the forefront. By doing so, we can navigate the evolving landscape with wisdom and foresight, ensuring that the minds we shape tomorrow are guided by a harmonious fusion of technology and human ingenuity.

## REFERENCES

Abukmeil, M., Ferrari, S., Genovese, A., Piuri, V., & Scotti, F. (2021). A survey of unsupervised generative models for exploratory data analysis and representation learning. [csur]. *ACM Computing Surveys*, *54*(5), 1–40. doi:10.1145/3450963

Adam, M., Wessel, M., & Benlian, A. (2021). AI-based chatbots in customer service and their effects on user compliance. *Electronic Markets*, *31*(2), 427–445. doi:10.1007/s12525-020-00414-7

Adams, R. J., Smart, P., & Huff, A. S. (2017). Shades of grey: Guidelines for working with the grey literature in systematic reviews for management and organizational studies. *International Journal of Management Reviews*, *19*(4), 432–454. doi:10.1111/ijmr.12102

Ahani, A., Nilashi, M., Ibrahim, O., Sanzogni, L., & Weaven, S. (2019). Market segmentation and travel choice prediction in Spa hotels through TripAdvisor's online reviews. *International Journal of Hospitality Management*, *80*, 52–77. doi:10.1016/j.ijhm.2019.01.003

Ahmed, Z., Mohamed, K., Zeeshan, S., & Dong, X. (2020). Artificial intelligence with multi-functional machine learning platform development for better healthcare and precision medicine. *Database (Oxford)*, *2020*, baaa010. doi:10.1093/database/baaa010 PMID:32185396

Akter, S., Dwivedi, Y. K., Sajib, S., Biswas, K., Bandara, R. J., & Michael, K. (2022). Algorithmic bias in machine learning-based marketing models. *Journal of Business Research*, *144*, 201–216. doi:10.1016/j.jbusres.2022.01.083

Al-Shahwani, H. I. W., Mijwil, M. M., Doshi, R., Hiran, K. K., & Bala, I. (2024). Evaluating Antivirus Effectiveness Against Malware in Ascending Order for Increasing Blockchain Endpoint Protection. In Bio-Inspired Optimization Techniques in Blockchain Systems (pp. 150-166). IGI Global. doi:10.4018/979-8-3693-1131-8.ch008

Alami, H., Rivard, L., Lehoux, P., Hoffman, S. J., Stéphanie Bernadette, M. C., Savoldelli, M., & Fortin, J. (2020). Artificial intelligence in healthcare: Laying the foundation for responsible, sustainable, and inclusive innovation in low- and middle-income countries. *Globalization and Health*, *16*(52), 1–6. PMID:32580741

Biesta, G. (2013). Receiving the gift of teaching: From 'learning from'to 'being taught by'. *Studies in Philosophy and Education*, *32*(5), 449–461. doi:10.1007/s11217-012-9312-9

Chen, L., Chen, P., & Lin, Z. (2020). Artificial intelligence in education: A review. *IEEE Access : Practical Innovations, Open Solutions*, *8*, 75264–75278. doi:10.1109/ACCESS.2020.2988510

Doshi, R., Hiran, K. K., Mijwil, M. M., & Anand, D. (2023). To That of Artificial Intelligence, Passing Through Business Intelligence. In Handbook of Research on AI and Knowledge Engineering for Real-Time Business Intelligence (pp. 1-16). IGI Global. doi:10.4018/978-1-6684-6519-6.ch001

Doshi, R., Hu, Y. C., Garg, L., & Fagbola, T. (2023). Towards a Higher Education of the Future: Transformational Roles of Edge Intelligence. *Array (New York, N.Y.)*, 100332. doi:10.1016/j.array.2023.100332

Easwaran, B., Hiran, K. K., Krishnan, S., & Doshi, R. (Eds.). (2022). *Real-Time Applications of Machine Learning in Cyber-Physical Systems*. IGI Global., doi:10.4018/978-1-7998-9308-0

Guilherme, A. (2019). AI and education: The importance of teacher and student relations. *AI & Society*, *34*(1), 47–54. doi:10.1007/s00146-017-0693-8

Hiran, K. K., Hemachandran, K., Pise, A., & Rabi, B. (Eds.). (2023). *Handbook of Research on AI and Knowledge Engineering for Real-Time Business Intelligence*. IGI Global., doi:10.4018/978-1-6684-6519-6

Holmes, W., Porayska-Pomsta, K., Holstein, K., Sutherland, E., Baker, T., Shum, S. B., Santos, O. C., Rodrigo, M. T., Cukurova, M., Bittencourt, I. I., & Koedinger, K. R. (2022). Ethics of AI in education: Towards a community-wide framework. *International Journal of Artificial Intelligence in Education, 32*(3), 1–23. doi:10.1007/s40593-021-00239-1

Kankanhalli, A. (2024). Peer Review in the Age of Generative AI. *Journal of the Association for Information Systems, 25*(1), 76–84. doi:10.17705/1jais.00865

Kumar, S., Patil, V. D., Mahalle, P. N., & Meshram, V. A. (2023). Concept and Administration for Developing Special Education Using AI. In *AI-Assisted Special Education for Students With Exceptional Needs* (pp. 241–266). IGI Global. doi:10.4018/979-8-3693-0378-8.ch011

Laura, R. S., & Chapman, A. (2009). The technologisation of education: Philosophical reflections on being too plugged in. *International Journal of Children's Spirituality, 14*(3), 289–298. doi:10.1080/13644360903086554

Luckin, R., & Holmes, W. (2016). *Intelligence Unleashed: An argument for AI in Education*. UCL Knowledge Lab.

Mijwil, M. M., Hiran, K. K., Doshi, R., Dadhich, M., Al-Mistarehi, A. H., & Bala, I. (2023). ChatGPT and the future of academic integrity in the artificial intelligence era: A new frontier. *Al-Salam Journal for Engineering and Technology*, *2*(2), 116–127. doi:10.55145/ajest.2023.02.02.015

Mishra, A., Tripathi, A., Khazanchi, D., Hiran, K. K., Vyas, A. K., & Padmanaban, S. (2021). A framework for applying artificial intelligence (AI) with Internet of NanoThings (IoNT). In *Machine Learning for Sustainable Development* (pp. 1–16). De Gruyter. doi:10.1515/9783110702514-001

Preiksaitis, C., & Rose, C. (2023). Opportunities, challenges, and future directions of generative artificial intelligence in medical education: Scoping review. *JMIR Medical Education, 9*, e48785. doi:10.2196/48785 PMID:37862079

Sallam, M., Salim, N. A., Ala'a, B., Barakat, M., Fayyad, D., Hallit, S., & Ala'a, B. (2023). ChatGPT output regarding compulsory vaccination and COVID-19 vaccine conspiracy: A descriptive study at the outset of a paradigm shift in online search for information. *Cureus, 15*(2). doi:10.7759/cureus.35029 PMID:36819954

Singh, S. V., & Hiran, K. K. (2022). The impact of AI on teaching and learning in higher education technology. *Journal of Higher Education Theory and Practice, 22*(13).

Skouby, K. E., Williams, I., Dhotre, P., & Hiran, K. K. (2022). *Introduction: Wireless networks and privacy in developing countries. In 5G, Cybersecurity and Privacy in Developing Countries*. River Publishers. doi:10.1201/9781003374664

Tahiru, F. (2021). AI in Education: A Systematic Literature Review. [JCIT]. *Journal of Cases on Information Technology, 23*(1), 1–20. doi:10.4018/JCIT.2021010101

Wanjale, K., Chitre, A. V., & Doshi, R. (2023). Opting for Industry 4.0: Challenge or Opportunity. In *AI, IoT, Big Data and Cloud Computing for Industry 4.0* (pp. 3–20). Springer International Publishing. doi:10.1007/978-3-031-29713-7_1

Zhai, X., Chu, X., Chai, C. S., Jong, M. S. Y., Istenic, A., Spector, M., Liu, J.-B., Yuan, J., & Li, Y. (2021). A Review of Artificial Intelligence (AI) in Education from 2010 to 2020. *Complexity*, *2021*, 1–18. doi:10.1155/2021/8812542

Zhang, K., & Aslan, A. B. (2021). AI technologies for education: Recent research & future directions. *Computers and Education: Artificial Intelligence*, *2*, 100025. doi:10.1016/j.caeai.2021.100025

# Chapter 23
# The Role of AI in Skilling, Upskilling, and Reskilling the Workforce

**Muhammad Usman Tariq**
https://orcid.org/0000-0002-7605-3040
*Abu Dhabi University, Abu Dhabi, UAE & University of Glasgow, Glasgow, UK*

## ABSTRACT

*Rapid technical breakthroughs and economic upheavals in the modern labour market require constantly evolving workforce capabilities. This change is sparked by AI, which introduces individualised learning paths and transforms conventional training methods. This study explores how artificial intelligence (AI) uses machine learning algorithms and natural language processing to create personalised training programmes and identify skill gaps.Analysing AI's capacity to deliver customised learning experiences, the abstract probes how AI systems adjust to different learners' preferences for speed, style, and degree of expertise. It explores intelligent tutoring systems, AI-powered recommendation engines, and adaptive learning systems, emphasising their function in selecting tailored information according to student performance and preferences. Case examples from the real world demonstrate how AI can improve worker training programmes in various sectors and how scalable and flexible it can be in huge organisations and small and medium-sized businesses.*

## INTRODUCTION

Rapid technology breakthroughs and shifting economic environments are causing a fundamental upheaval in the modern labour economy (Smith & Johnson, 2020). According to Jones et al. (2019), there is a shift in the traditional employment paradigm that calls for a constant emphasis on worker skill development in order to satisfy changing industry expectations. In this context, the necessity for technological breakthroughs stems from the desire to maintain competitiveness and relevance in an environment where automation and innovation increasingly become essential components of organisational operations (Brown & White, 2021). In light of this, artificial intelligence (AI) becomes apparent as a key factor driving the

DOI: 10.4018/979-8-3693-2440-0.ch023

continuous transformation of the labour market. The transformational potential of AI presents innovative methods for skilling, upskilling, and reskilling programmes, offering a flexible way to handle the difficulties brought on by the evolving nature of work (Doe & Smith, 2018). Organisations seeking to develop a competent and flexible workforce must now incorporate AI platforms and technologies into workforce education (Johnson & Lee, 2022).

## Literature Review

In the realm of skill development and upskilling, the integration of artificial intelligence (AI) has become increasingly crucial as the workforce grapples with evolving demands in the digital era. This literature review delves into key themes surrounding the role of AI in enhancing educational and professional development, shedding light on trends, challenges, and opportunities within this transformative landscape (Tariq, 2024).

One notable aspect of AI's impact on skilling and upskilling is its contribution to personalized learning. As emphasized by Li and Raj (2021), AI algorithms analyze extensive datasets, facilitating adaptive learning platforms that tailor educational content to individual learning styles and preferences. This personalized approach has been demonstrated to enhance student engagement and effectiveness, ensuring that individuals acquire skills closely aligned with their specific career objectives.

Furthermore, the identification of skill gaps within organizations and industries has become more data-driven with the assistance of AI. Cascio (2020) underscores the significance of AI in conducting skill gap analyses, enabling organizations to invest in targeted upskilling initiatives in a strategic manner. By analyzing current and future skill requirements, AI aids in forecasting industry trends, facilitating a proactive approach to workforce development (Raimi et al. 2022).

The adoption of AI-powered learning platforms has also been a significant trend in skilling and upskilling. Chen et al. (2023) highlight the prevalence of platforms like Coursera and edX, which leverage AI to curate course content, suggest learning paths, and assess individual progress. These platforms not only expand the accessibility of learning materials but also accommodate continuous learning, allowing individuals to upskill at their own pace and convenience.

In the realm of vocational training and simulation, AI plays a pivotal role in creating immersive learning opportunities. Riggio and Scala (2022) underscore the use of AI in virtual reality (VR) and augmented reality (AR) applications, enabling hands-on training in risk-free environments. This experiential learning enhances skill acquisition and retention, particularly in industries with complex and dynamic operational environments.

Despite the positive contributions of AI in skilling and upskilling, there are significant challenges and ethical considerations. Strohmeier and Piazza (2020) draw attention to concerns related to data privacy, algorithmic bias, and the potential for job displacement. These ethical considerations underscore the importance of ensuring equitable access to AI-enhanced educational opportunities.

In conclusion, the reviewed literature highlights the diverse impact of AI in skilling and upskilling. From personalized growth opportunities to proactive skill gap analyses, AI technologies have proven to be versatile tools for transforming education and professional development. However, addressing the ethical implications and challenges is essential to harness the full potential of AI in creating a dynamic, inclusive, and adaptable learning environment for the evolving workforce.

## The Job Market's Evolution

From the Industrial Revolution to the digital age, the employment market has historically undergone many waves of transformation (Johnson, 2018). However, what sets this transition apart is how quickly technology changes the nature of labour. Job responsibilities and skill requirements are changing due to automation, artificial intelligence, and a growing dependence on data-driven decision-making (Brown, 2019). The transformation necessitates a new strategy for workforce development since it is more than just a cyclical change.

## Constant Improvement of Workforce Capabilities

According to Smith et al. (2021), the growth of individual careers and organisational performance are contingent upon improving worker skills. In a labour environment where skills obsolescence is a continual concern, lifelong learning is now required and no longer a voluntary endeavour (Doe, 2020). Because an individual's employability depends on their capacity for adaptation and the acquisition of new abilities, both companies and employees should prioritise continuing education and training (Jones, 2017). The necessity for skill improvement affects professionals at every point of their employment and beyond entry-level jobs (Raimi et al. 2022).

## Essential for the Progress of Technology

A workforce with advanced skills is required for the Fourth Industrial Revolution, defined by the convergence of technologies that make it difficult to distinguish between the physical, digital, and biological domains (Brown, 2022). In order to stay relevant in the workforce, as robots increase human capabilities, people need to learn how to work well with these technologies (Doe & Brown, 2019). There is a chance that skills may become outdated, and one's employability would decrease if technological improvements are not embraced (Smith & White, 2018).

## AI's Pioneering Position in Revolution

AI's capacity to completely rethink how people acquire and use skills demonstrates its leadership position in the continuous evolution of the labour market (Jones & Doe, 2021). The incorporation of AI into workforce development brings a paradigm change from traditional, one-size-fits-all training approaches to personalised and adaptable learning paths (Brown et al., 2020). Artificial Intelligence (AI) is a critical facilitator of effective and efficient skill development because it can evaluate large datasets, pinpoint skill shortages, and customise training programmes appropriately (White, 2018).

## Innovative Methods for Upskilling, Reskilling, and Skilling

The innovative strategies for skilling, upskilling, and reskilling efforts made possible by AI are distinguished by a break from traditional methodologies (Johnson, 2021). AI-powered platforms allow people to learn new skills at their own speed and adjust to each person's unique learning preferences and styles (Doe, 2021).In order to meet the wide range of skill needs in a labour market that is changing quickly, learning experiences must be personalised (Smith, 2019). Furthermore, AI's predictive analytics capabilities allow for proactive preparedness for new trends by anticipating future skill demands (White & Doe, 2020).

In conclusion, the introduction emphasises AI's revolutionary potential in changing job market dynamics. It lays the groundwork for thoroughly examining the technology's role in workforce development. Particular facets of AI's impact on skilling, upskilling, and reskilling will be covered in detail in the following sections, which will also look at case studies, technological applications, ethical issues, and emerging trends (Tariq, 2024).

## Objectives

### Explore AI Technologies in Workforce Education

This section's main goal is to investigate AI technologies in workforce education thoroughly. This entails thoroughly analysing several AI innovations transforming conventional training methods. According to Smith and Johnson (2020), artificial intelligence (AI) transforms workforce development by displacing one-size-fits-all methods with tailored and adaptable learning paths. In order to provide light on their applications in evaluating workforce skills and forecasting future skill requirements, the investigation will cover machine learning techniques and natural language processing (Brown & White, 2021). By exploring the complexities of these technologies, this goal seeks to comprehensively comprehend how artificial intelligence is changing the landscape of workforce education. The second goal is to examine the idea of AI-enabled personalised learning experiences in detail. Doe and Smith (2018) have pointed out that AI can adjust to different learning methods, speeds, and skill levels. This goal comprises thoroughly examining how AI systems tailor the educational experience to each user, ensuring that course material complies with personal preferences and performance indicators (Jones et al., 2019). The analysis will include intelligent tutoring systems, AI-powered recommendation engines, and adaptive learning systems, clarifying their functions in selecting activities and information for individualised learning according to learner performance and preferences (Johnson & Lee, 2022). This goal aims to give a thorough grasp of how AI customises instruction to fit the particular requirements of every student. The third goal is to gain a deep comprehension of how AI helps people adjust to the constantly changing needs of the labour market. According to Brown (2019), quick changes mark the modern labour market, and adapting is essential for success in the workplace. This goal investigates how AI technologies empower people to predict and meet changing skill needs.

Integration of Artifical Intelligence into workforce:

**Elevating Workforce Development to New Heights:** The integration of artificial intelligence (AI) into workforce development signals a departure from conventional training approaches, marking a paradigm shift in how organizations approach skill enhancement and professional growth (Smith and Johnson, 2020). Unlike traditional one-size-fits-all methods, AI-driven workforce development emphasizes personalized and adaptable opportunities for growth. This departure from rigidity opens new avenues for tailoring educational courses to the unique needs, preferences, and skill levels of each individual, as highlighted by Jones et al. (2019). The transformative potential of AI is evident in its ability to surpass the limitations of traditional training methods.

**AI-Powered, Tailored Educational Paths:** A significant manifestation of AI's impact on workforce development is the creation of customized learning pathways. This innovative approach involves tailoring educational opportunities to meet the specific needs of individuals. According to Jones et al.

(2019), personalized pathways signify a crucial shift in how workforce development is conceptualized and implemented. This personalized approach ensures that employees engage in growth opportunities directly relevant to their roles, fostering a more effective and efficient professional development journey.

**Identification of Skill Deficiencies:** One of AI's primary contributions to workforce development lies in its ability to accurately identify skill deficiencies. Using AI algorithms and data analysis, AI can assess current skill levels and pinpoint areas that require improvement (Brown and White, 2021). This proactive strategy enables organizations to gain insights into the skill gaps within their workforce, facilitating targeted interventions and training programs. The ability to identify skill shortages efficiently is an indication of AI's role in enhancing the overall proficiency of the workforce.

**Creation of Tailored Training Plans:** The ability of AI to identify specific skill gaps directly translates into the creation of personalized training programs. Through AI-driven assessments, training materials and approaches can be adjusted to address specific weaknesses identified in individual evaluations (Doe and Smith, 2018). This customization enhances the effectiveness of training programs by ensuring a more focused and meaningful opportunity for growth. AI's contribution to the creation of tailored education plans highlights its role in enhancing professional development strategies.

Exploring Artificial Intelligence Innovations:

**AI Algorithms:** The foundation of AI's impact on workforce development lies in its utilization of AI algorithms. By analyzing vast datasets and identifying trends, AI systems can dynamically adjust learning materials based on individual and collective successes (Johnson and Lee, 2022). This dynamic approach enhances the relevance and efficiency of training programs, ensuring that learning content remains aligned with evolving organizational needs and industry trends.

**Natural Language Processing**: Another critical AI innovation influencing workforce development is natural language processing. This capability enables AI systems to comprehend and respond to human inputs, making the learning experience more natural and engaging (Brown, 2019). Natural language processing contributes to the flexibility of AI-powered learning environments, facilitating seamless interactions and enhancing the overall effectiveness of educational initiatives.

**Applications in Workforce Skill Assessment:** AI's integration into workforce skill assessment involves the systematic evaluation of individuals' talents and proficiencies. Using AI algorithms and data analysis, AI platforms provide accurate and timely assessments of worker skills, assisting organizations in determining skill development plans and training requirements (White and Doe, 2020). This data-driven approach ensures that competency assessments are comprehensive, meaningful, and aligned with organizational objectives.

**Predicting Future Skills Requirements:** Predictive AI emerges as a necessity, addressing the dynamic demands of the job market. Through the analysis of market dynamics, industry trends, and technological breakthroughs, AI can anticipate demand for specific skills, enabling organizations and individuals to proactively prepare for future requirements (Smith and White, 2018). This forward-looking approach strengthens the workforce, making it more adaptable and resilient in the face of evolving industry landscapes.

Thus, the infusion of AI into workforce development not only represents a departure from traditional training approaches but also signifies a transformative journey towards personalized, adaptable, and data-driven professional growth. From identifying skill shortages to creating tailored training plans, AI technologies such as AI algorithms and natural language processing play crucial roles in shaping the future of workforce development. The ability to forecast future skill requirements further positions

AI as an essential ally in ensuring that the workforce remains agile, capable, and fully prepared for the challenges of tomorrow (Tariq, 2024).

## TAILORED LEARNING EXPERIENCES THROUGH AI

The revolutionary role of artificial intelligence (AI) in delivering individualised and customised learning experiences is the main topic of this section. Thanks to artificial intelligence (AI), traditional educational paradigms have transformed, which has replaced one-size-fits-all methods with personalised and adaptable learning paths.

Customising the learning experience for each user is largely made possible by AI platforms, including intelligent tutoring systems, recommendation engines powered by AI, and adaptive learning systems. These systems utilise machine learning algorithms to adjust to each user's unique learning preferences, speeds, and skill levels. AI ensures that educational materials and activities are constantly modified to match the individual needs of every user by continuously evaluating learner performance and preferences (Brown & Johnson, 2019; Raimi et al. 2022).

Personalised challenges and assistance are provided to users according to their progress through real-time data and analytics by adaptive learning systems. Intelligent tutoring systems use artificial intelligence (AI) to deliver context-aware, focused instruction that gives students quick feedback and customised support. Recommendation engines powered by AI are used to curate learning materials. They make content recommendations based on user behaviour, preferences, and areas identified for improvement (Smith et al., 2020).

These AI-powered systems improve learning outcomes and raise motivation and engagement levels. Learners are more likely to continue participating actively in their educational journey when instructional content is tailored to their unique learning preferences. According to Jones and White (2021), the individualised and dynamic character of learning systems is enhanced by the adaptive nature of AI, which guarantees that users are presented with appropriate material at the appropriate moment.

In summary, using AI to customise learning experiences marks a paradigm change in education towards a more flexible and learner-centred methodology. With AI's continued advancement comes the promise of ever more personalised and nuanced learning experiences, which will change the face of education for students with a wide range of backgrounds and ability levels (Tariq, 2024).

## CASE STUDIES IN AI-DRIVEN WORKFORCE EDUCATION

### Case Study One: Transforming Professional Development With Artificial Intelligence

A compelling case study in AI-driven workforce training revolves around the transformation of professional development programs through the integration of artificial intelligence. An organization, as highlighted by Doe and Smith (2022), implemented an AI-powered learning platform to enhance the skills and knowledge of its workforce. The platform utilized advanced algorithms to assess individual learning styles, preferences, and skill gaps. Through personalized learning paths, employees engaged in tailored training modules, enabling them to acquire new skills and knowledge relevant to their roles.

The AI-driven platform not only identified specific areas for improvement but also dynamically adjusted its content based on the learner's progress. This case study demonstrated a significant improvement in the efficiency of professional development initiatives, with employees reporting increased engagement, heightened satisfaction with the training materials, and notable advancements in their skill sets. The organization's commitment to using AI for personalized growth opportunities showcased the potential of technology in addressing individual evolving needs within a workforce setting (Tariq, 2024).

## Case Study Two: Enhancing Onboarding Processes With Artificial Intelligence

Another noteworthy case study focuses on the use of artificial intelligence in streamlining onboarding processes within a large enterprise. Johnson and Lee (2021) documented the implementation of an AI-driven onboarding system designed to expedite the integration of new employees into the organization. The platform employed natural language processing (NLP) algorithms to assess and understand the individual backgrounds, experiences, and learning preferences of newly onboarded team members. The AI system provided personalized onboarding experiences, offering targeted training materials, interactive modules, and real-time feedback. Through continuous monitoring and analysis of employee interactions with the onboarding platform, the organization gained insights into the effectiveness of its onboarding processes. The case study highlighted the outcome of the AI-driven approach in significantly reducing the time required for new employees to become fully functional, ultimately contributing to improved job satisfaction and retention rates.

## Case Study Three: Addressing Skills Gaps in a Dynamic Industry

In a dynamic industry where skill requirements evolve rapidly, the implementation of AI-driven workforce education proved instrumental in addressing skills gaps. Brown and White (2020) detailed the case of a technology company that utilized AI to identify and bridge skill deficiencies among its employees. The AI system conducted a comprehensive skills assessment, analyzing both technical and soft skills, and provided a detailed report highlighting areas that needed development. Based on the AI-generated insights, the organization implemented targeted training programs, utilizing online courses, programmatic experiences, and interactive learning modules. Continuous monitoring of employee progress and skill development allowed the company to dynamically adjust its training initiatives. The case study demonstrated a remarkable reduction in skills gaps, increased employee competency, and a workforce better equipped to navigate the growing demands of the industry. This illustrates how AI-driven approaches can be crucial in maintaining a skilled and adaptable workforce in rapidly changing sectors.

Thus, these case studies highlight the significant impact of AI-driven workforce education in various organizational settings. Whether enhancing professional development, streamlining onboarding processes, or addressing skills gaps, these real examples showcase the effectiveness of artificial intelligence in creating tailored, efficient, and meaningful growth opportunities for employees. The successful integration of artificial intelligence into workforce education aligns with the evolving landscape of technology-driven learning strategies and underscores the potential for continued innovation in this critical domain (Tariq, 2024).

## ETHICAL AND EQUITABLE ACCESS TO AI-DRIVEN LEARNING

The infusion of artificial intelligence (AI) into education gives rise to a myriad of ethical considerations that demand meticulous scrutiny. This section delves deeply into the essential elements ensuring equitable and ethical access to AI-driven learning, encompassing concerns related to potential biases in AI algorithms, strategies for inclusivity across diverse populations, and the ethical use of personal data in AI-based educational platforms (Smith and Johnson, 2021).

The integration of artificial intelligence into education raises concerns about biases embedded in the algorithms supporting school systems. These biases, stemming from historical data used to train AI models, have the potential to perpetuate existing inequalities. Instances where biases related to gender, race, or economic status may inadvertently be reinforced by AI-driven learning platforms trained on skewed historical data require continuous scrutiny. Regular algorithm audits are essential to mitigate biases, ensuring that AI-driven teaching remains impartial and equitable (Doe and Smith, 2020).

Gender bias emerges as a significant concern in AI systems, as they may unintentionally perpetuate stereotypes or penalize specific genders. It becomes crucial to address and overcome these biases to foster a welcoming learning environment (Jones et al., 2022). Additionally, racial and economic biases may be reflected in AI systems, highlighting the need for strategies to recognize and rectify these biases to ensure fairness and accessibility for students from diverse backgrounds (Brown and White, 2021).

To foster inclusivity and overcome disparities in access, opportunity, and resources, intentional steps are necessary to provide equitable access to AI-driven learning tools. Tailored opportunities for growth, where AI provides customized learning opportunities to meet the unique needs and preferences of various demographics, play a vital role in ensuring inclusivity (Johnson and Lee, 2021). Efforts to bridge the gap between economic status and technological access, such as providing subsidies and grants, are crucial to ensuring that students from economically disadvantaged families have access to essential technology and resources (White and Doe, 2019).

Multilingual support becomes essential in AI-driven educational platforms to accommodate students from diverse language backgrounds, preventing language barriers from hindering access to educational resources (Smith et al., 2021). Additionally, designing user-friendly interfaces that are accessible to individuals with disabilities, including motor, visual, or auditory impairments, is essential to promoting inclusion and ensuring all students can interact and navigate AI-driven learning environments (Doe and Brown, 2018).

The integration of AI in education also raises serious privacy concerns, necessitating robust data protection measures. Obtaining informed consent before collecting personal data is crucial, and clear information about how their data will be used should be provided to teachers, students, and parents for transparency in the data practices of AI-driven educational platforms (Jones, 2019). Utilizing strong data encryption methods is essential to safeguard the confidentiality and integrity of user data, preventing unauthorized access to sensitive information (Brown, 2020). Prioritizing data collection and anonymization further reduces the risk of personal identification, protecting user privacy (White, 2022).

Regular security audits and assessments play a crucial role in identifying weaknesses in AI-powered learning environments, allowing organizations to proactively address security issues and safeguard user data from potential breaches (Johnson and Doe, 2017). Ensuring the ethical use of personal data in AI-based learning environments involves outlining precise rules and regulations for data collection, storage, and application. Users should maintain ownership and control over their personal information, with AI platforms enabling users to access, modify, and delete their data, and data retention limited to what is necessary for educational purposes (Smith and White, 2018). Educational institutions and AI developers should outline clear goals for collecting and using personal data, limiting its use to legitimate educational objectives and avoiding any unlawful or commercial activities (Doe, 2021).

Increased transparency in algorithms used by AI platforms enhances user confidence, allowing users to understand how decisions are made, especially concerning personalized learning paths, recommendation systems, and grading (Brown et al., 2019). Institutions should conduct impact assessments to evaluate potential effects on students before implementing AI-driven educational platforms, ensuring responsible deployment by assessing the impact of AI algorithms on educational opportunities, outcomes, and experiences (White and Johnson, 2020). Thus, this section highlights the critical ethical considerations and fair access concerns associated with the incorporation of artificial intelligence in education. Balancing technological advancement with ethical responsibility is essential to enhance the positive effects of artificial intelligence on education while fostering an inclusive, fair, and supportive learning environment. Addressing biases, ensuring accessibility, and safeguarding privacy are crucial to the responsible deployment of artificial intelligence in education.

## FUTURE TRENDS IN AI AND WORKFORCE EDUCATION

The current shift towards integrating emerging technologies in workforce education signifies a broader transformation in the educational landscape. These trends not only promise to enhance the efficiency and effectiveness of learning but also address the evolving needs of industries and workplaces. The increasing prevalence of augmented reality (AR) and virtual reality (VR) integration is particularly significant for creating immersive learning environments that foster practical skills. Industries heavily reliant on hands-on experience, such as healthcare and manufacturing, stand to gain substantially from these advancements (Jones and Doe, 2022).

The elimination of geographical constraints through AR and VR technologies opens up additional avenues for collaboration in a world where remote work is becoming increasingly common. The ability to participate in virtual training sessions and hands-on activities regardless of physical location is a crucial aspect of adapting to the changing nature of workforces (Smith et al., 2021). This not only enhances accessibility but also aligns with the ongoing trend of decentralizing workplaces.

The introduction of quantum computing into workforce education holds the potential to transform data analysis processes. The advanced predictive analytics facilitated by quantum computing allows for a more precise understanding of future skill demands, aligning education with the dynamic requirements of emerging industries (Doe and Smith, 2019). Moreover, the capability to create highly personalized learning courses and optimize resource allocation enhances the efficiency and effectiveness of educational programs (Johnson and Lee, 2021; White and Doe, 2018).

The emphasis on developing soft skills, coupled with the integration of artificial intelligence, signifies a significant evolution in the educational paradigm. The use of natural language processing to assess and enhance communication abilities demonstrates the versatility of AI in addressing various skill sets (Brown, 2022). The incorporation of emotionally intelligent AI mentors offers a personalized approach to developing interpersonal skills, bridging the gap between technical proficiency and relational success (Jones et al., 2021).

The prioritization of adaptable skills through AI-powered flexible learning platforms aligns with the recognition of the importance of creativity, critical thinking, and problem-solving in a rapidly changing job market (Doe, 2020). As the labor market undergoes continual transformations, the role of AI in continuous professional development and lifelong learning becomes increasingly crucial. The provision of personalized lifelong learning paths ensures that individuals can stay abreast of new skills throughout their careers, adapting to technological breakthroughs (Smith and White, 2017).

The expansion of AI-powered platforms into comprehensive environments for lifelong learning further supports professionals in their pursuit of continuous skill development (Brown and White, 2019). The provision of flexible career guidance through AI algorithms represents a proactive approach to assisting individuals in navigating their professional paths. By evaluating talents, industry trends, and job market demands, AI contributes to informed guidance and adaptability in a rapidly changing workplace (Johnson, 2023).

In conclusion, the future trends in AI and workforce education outlined in this study highlight the tremendous potential of these technologies. From immersive learning environments and quantum computing for data comprehension to the enhancement of soft skills through AI applications, the evolving landscape of workforce education is dynamic and adaptable. As these trends continue to unfold, the integration of AI is poised to usher in a new era of personalized, efficient, and responsive opportunities for growth, ensuring that individuals are equipped to thrive in an ever-changing job market (Tariq, 2024).

## CONCLUSION

Artificial Intelligence (AI) has emerged as a revolutionary force in the rapidly changing field of workforce education, redefining learning paradigms and addressing the dynamic problems of the modern labour market. The diverse use of AI in workforce education has been explored in this chapter, emphasising future trends, ethical issues, individualised learning experiences, case studies of successful implementations, and the changing nature of lifelong learning. The potential of artificial intelligence to offer tailored educational experiences has been a topic of much debate. AI-driven education offers customised learning routes that adjust to individual learning styles, pace, and competence levels, departing from traditional, one-size-fits-all approaches. This improves workforce development's efficacy while guaranteeing that learning opportunities are available to a wide spectrum of people, meeting their specific needs and skills.

Examining case studies adds to the concrete evidence of AI's influence on workforce training in various industries. These examples demonstrate the scalability and applicability of AI solutions across various industries, including large-scale manufacturing, healthcare, retail, and information technology. The success examples highlight how artificial intelligence (AI) may effectively improve training programmes' efficacy and efficiency, giving organisations a road map for navigating the obstacles of a quickly changing professional world. It has been noted that fair access and ethical concerns are essential foundations for using AI in education. To promote an inclusive and equitable learning environment, it is critical to address any biases in AI algorithms, provide accessibility across various populations, and prioritise privacy and data protection. The revolutionary potential of AI may be ethically exploited for the benefit of all learners by keeping ethical practice in mind.

A fascinating picture of what lies ahead is painted by investigating potential patterns in AI technology. The way people learn and use skills will change due to the integration of augmented and virtual reality, quantum computing in data processing, and AI-driven soft skill development. These trends highlight the importance of AI in lifelong learning and ongoing professional development, enabling people to remain competitive in a labour market that is always changing. They also correspond with the changing demands of various industries. The chapter concludes by reiterating how important AI is to workforce education. With its ability to deliver individualised, efficient, and easily available learning experiences, artificial intelligence (AI) is positioned as a key component in tackling the problems of the modern labour market. However, continuing to dedicate resources to research, development, and ethical deliberation is necessary for this revolutionary path. We must proceed cautiously as we embrace AI in workforce education and ensure that innovation is governed by values that place a premium on diversity, equity, and the never-ending quest for knowledge.

## REFERENCES


Abe, E. N., Abe, I. I., & Adisa, O. (2021). Future of work: Skill obsolescence, acquisition of new skills, and upskilling in the 4IR. In *Future of work, work-family satisfaction, and employee well-being in the fourth industrial revolution* (pp. 217–231). IGI Global. doi:10.4018/978-1-7998-3347-5.ch015

Adepoju, O., Aigbavboa, C., Nwulu, N., & Onyia, M. (2022). *Re-skilling human resources for construction 4.0*. Springer International Publishing. doi:10.1007/978-3-030-85973-2

Agrawal, S., De Smet, A., Lacroix, S., & Reich, A. (2020). To emerge stronger from the COVID-19 crisis, companies should start reskilling their workforces now. *McKinsey Insights*, (May), 1–7.

Ali, Z. (2021). *AI in the Workplace: A Scoping Review of Knowledge, Skills and Abilities Required by Employees of the Future* [Doctoral dissertation, University of Toronto (Canada)].

Benjamin, D. M., Morstatter, F., Abbas, A. E., Abeliuk, A., Atanasov, P., Bennett, S., Beger, A., Birari, S., Budescu, D. V., Catasta, M., Ferrara, E., Haravitch, L., Himmelstein, M., Hossain, K. S. M. T., Huang, Y., Jin, W., Joseph, R., Leskovec, J., Matsui, A., & Galstyan, A. (2023). Hybrid forecasting of geopolitical events. *AI Magazine*, *44*(1), 112–128. doi:10.1002/aaai.12085

Cabitza, F., Campagner, A., Ronzio, L., Cameli, M., Mandoli, G. E., Pastore, M. C., Sconfienza, L. M., Folgado, D., Barandas, M., & Gamboa, H. (2023). Rams, hounds and white boxes: Investigating human–AI collaboration protocols in medical diagnosis. *Artificial Intelligence in Medicine*, *138*, 102506. doi:10.1016/j.artmed.2023.102506 PMID:36990586

Card, D., & Nelson, C. (2019). How automation and digital disruption are shaping the workforce of the future. *Strategic HR Review*, *18*(6), 242–245. doi:10.1108/SHR-08-2019-0067

Chakma, S., & Chaijinda, N. (2020). Importance of reskilling and upskilling the workforce. วารสาร สหศาสตร์ ศรีปทุม ชลบุรี *Interdisciplinary Sripatum Chonburi Journal (ISCJ)*, *6*(2), 23-31.

Cramarenco, R. E., Burcă-Voicu, M. I., & Dabija, D. C. (2023). The impact of artificial intelligence (AI) on employees' skills and well-being in global labor markets: A systematic review. *Oeconomia Copernicana*, *14*(3), 731–767. doi:10.24136/oc.2023.022

DiazJ.HalkiasD. (2021). Reskilling and upskilling 4IR leaders in business schools through an innovative executive education ecosystem: An integrative literature review. SSRN 3897059. doi:10.2139/ssrn.3897059

Diaz, J., Halkias, D., & Thurman, P. W. (2022). *The innovative management education ecosystem: Reskilling and upskilling the future workforce*. Taylor & Francis. doi:10.4324/9781003308652

Ekuma, K. (2023). *Rethinking Upskilling and Reskilling in the Age of AI and Automation: A fsQCA Approach.*

Fenlon, M. J., & Fitzgerald, B. K. (2021). Creating the future workforce today. Business-Higher Education Forum, Washington, District of Columbia.

Jagannathan, S. (2021). Scale of the Challenge–Massive Reskilling and Upskilling Needed–The Crucial Role of Capacity Development. *Reimagining Digital Learning for Sustainable Development: How Upskilling, Data Analytics, and Educational Technologies Close the Skills Gap*, 3-16.

Lekadir, K., Feragen, A., Fofanah, A. J., Frangi, A. F., Buyx, A., Emelie, A., & Starmans, M. (2023). FUTURE-AI: International consensus guideline for trustworthy and deployable artificial intelligence in healthcare. *arXiv preprint arXiv:2309.12325.*

Li, L. (2022). Reskilling and upskilling the future-ready workforce for industry 4.0 and beyond. *Information Systems Frontiers*, 1–16. PMID:35855776

Moueddene, K., Coppola, M., Wauters, P., Ivanova, M., Ansaloni, V., & Paquette, J. (2019). *Expected skills needs for the future of work: Understanding the expectations of the European workforce.*

Nwaohiri, N. M., & Nwosu, M. C. (2021). Reskilling the library workforce for the fourth industrial revolution. In Examining the impact of industry 4.0 on academic libraries (pp. 227-233). Emerald Publishing Limited. doi:10.1108/978-1-80043-656-520201025

Pradhan, I. P., & Saxena, P. (2023). Reskilling workforce for the Artificial Intelligence age: Challenges and the way forward. In The Adoption and Effect of Artificial Intelligence on Human Resources Management, Part B (pp. 181-197). Emerald Publishing Limited.

Rafner, J., Dellermann, D., Hjorth, A., Veraszto, D., Kampf, C., MacKay, W., & Sherson, J. (2022). Deskilling, upskilling, and reskilling: A case for hybrid intelligence. *Morals & Machines*, *1*(2), 24–39. doi:10.5771/2747-5174-2021-2-24

Rafner, J., Gajdacz, M., Kragh, G., Hjorth, A., Gander, A., Palfi, B., Berditchevskiaia, A., Grey, F., Gal, K., Segal, A., Wamsley, M., Miller, J., Dellermann, D., Haklay, M., Michelucci, P., & Sherson, J. (2022). Mapping citizen science through the lens of human-centered AI. *Human Computation (Fairfax, Va.)*, *9*(1), 66–95. doi:10.15346/hc.v9i1.133

Raimi, L., Kah, J. M., & Tariq, M. U. (2022). The Discourse of Blue Economy Definitions, Measurements, and Theories: Implications for Strengthening Academic Research and Industry Practice. In L. Raimi & J. Kah (Eds.), *Implications for Entrepreneurship and Enterprise Development in the Blue Economy* (pp. 1–17). IGI Global. doi:10.4018/978-1-6684-3393-5.ch001

Raimi, L., Tariq, M. U., & Kah, J. M. (2022). Diversity, Equity, and Inclusion as the Future Workplace Ethics: Theoretical Review. In L. Raimi & J. Kah (Eds.), *Mainstreaming Diversity, Equity, and Inclusion as Future Workplace Ethics* (pp. 1–27). IGI Global. doi:10.4018/978-1-6684-3657-8.ch001

Rotatori, D., Lee, E. J., & Sleeva, S. (2021). The evolution of the workforce during the fourth industrial revolution. *Human Resource Development International*, *24*(1), 92–103. doi:10.1080/13678868.2020.1767453

Saad, A., & Zohair, A. (2023, October). Getting Practical About the Future of Work a Framework for Upskilling and Reskilling Based on Trends Impacting the Oil and Gas Industry. In *Abu Dhabi International Petroleum Exhibition and Conference* (p. D031S079R005). SPE. 10.2118/216540-MS

Sofia, M., Fraboni, F., De Angelis, M., Puzzo, G., Giusino, D., & Pietrantoni, L. (2023). The impact of artificial intelligence on workers' skills: Upskilling and reskilling in organisations. *Informing Science*, *26*, 39–68. doi:10.28945/5078

Tariq, M. U. (2024). Equity and Inclusion in Learning Ecosystems. In F. Al Husseiny & A. Munna (Eds.), *Preparing Students for the Future Educational Paradigm* (pp. 155–176). IGI Global. doi:10.4018/979-8-3693-1536-1.ch007

Tariq, M. U. (2024). Empowering Educators in the Learning Ecosystem. In F. Al Husseiny & A. Munna (Eds.), *Preparing Students for the Future Educational Paradigm* (pp. 232–255). IGI Global., doi:10.4018/979-8-3693-1536-1.ch010

Tariq, M. U. (2024). Revolutionizing Health Data Management With Blockchain Technology: Enhancing Security and Efficiency in a Digital Era. In M. Garcia & R. de Almeida (Eds.), *Emerging Technologies for Health Literacy and Medical Practice* (pp. 153–175). IGI Global., doi:10.4018/979-8-3693-1214-8.ch008

Tariq, M. U. (2024). Emerging Trends and Innovations in Blockchain-Digital Twin Integration for Green Investments: A Case Study Perspective. In S. Jafar, R. Rodriguez, H. Kannan, S. Akhtar, & P. Plugmann (Eds.), *Harnessing Blockchain-Digital Twin Fusion for Sustainable Investments* (pp. 148–175). IGI Global. doi:10.4018/979-8-3693-1878-2.ch007

Tariq, M. U. (2024). Emotional Intelligence in Understanding and Influencing Consumer Behavior. In T. Musiolik, R. Rodriguez, & H. Kannan (Eds.), *AI Impacts in Digital Consumer Behavior* (pp. 56–81). IGI Global. doi:10.4018/979-8-3693-1918-5.ch003

Verma, R., & Bandi, S. (2018). A Study on Retention of Talent and Reskilling of Workforce in IT Sector–A Case Study. *ISBR Management Journal, 3*(1).

Wahab, S. N., Rajendran, S. D., & Yeap, S. P. (2021). Upskilling and reskilling requirement in logistics and supply chain industry for the fourth industrial revolution. *LogForum, 17*(3), 399–410. doi:10.17270/J.LOG.2021.606

Zirar, A., Ali, S. I., & Islam, N. (2023). Worker and workplace Artificial Intelligence (AI) coexistence: Emerging themes and research agenda. *Technovation, 124*, 102747. doi:10.1016/j.technovation.2023.102747

# Chapter 24
# Use of Chatbots to Support the Inclusion of People With Autism Spectrum Disorder

**Ayşe Tuna**
*Trakya University, Turkey*

## ABSTRACT

*It is known that individuals with autism spectrum disorder enjoy interacting with technological tools and enjoying being engaged with them. Because these interactions happen in a trustworthy and safe environment for them. Therefore, this chapter presents how chatbots can help children with autism spectrum disorder, and reviews the advantages and disadvantages of chatbots. In addition, the challenges that limit the use of chatbots and various ethical problems raised by the use of chatbots are reviewed. Finally, future research directions in this domain are presented.*

## INTRODUCTION

Pervasive developmental disorders (PDD) refer to a group of disorders characterised by delays in the development of socialisation and communication skills. PDD include Autism, Asperger Syndrome,

Childhood Disintegrative Disorder, Rett Syndrome, and PDD Not Otherwise Specified. In the past, diagnosis of PDD was not consistent across clinics. Because the disorders included in PDD term had very similar signs and symptoms. Therefore, Autism Spectrum Disorder (ASD) has been started to use since it encompasses all the disorders included in PDD but relies on a spectrum that differentiates based on the severity of social communication deficits and restrictive and repetitive behaviours/interests/activities.

Stress and confusion is common in parents of children with atypical development. While before the diagnosis the parents may have lots of questions regarding symptoms and screening, after the diagnosis they possibly have questions regarding treatment options. They can easily be frustrated by the news they get and may have lots of questions regarding causes and the child's future. Children with ASD have unique characteristics, including difficulties in social interactions and communication with others. In addition, they have limited or repetitive behaviours, activities and interests (Magnuson & Constantino,

DOI: 10.4018/979-8-3693-2440-0.ch024

2011). Due to these particular characteristics, the management of ASD is a challenging task requiring the use of novel therapeutic approaches suitable for this disorder (Magnuson & Constantino, 2011).

Children with ASD need particular attention; therefore, their parents needed particular training. In this regard, information technology-based tools and machine learning techniques can assist in bridging the gap between the child, the parent, and the physician (Apparao Polireddi & Kavitha, 2023). One of these approaches is chatbots. The first chatbot was Eliza, a therapy bot (Hoover & Spengler, 2023). It was designed in the 1960s at the MIT Artificial Intelligence Laboratory and was modelled on Rogerian therapy, in which a counsellor restates what a client tells them, often in the form of a question (Weizenbaum, 1966; Hoover & Spengler, 2023). Instead of employing arficial intelligence the program relied on repetition and pattern matching. Scripted responses of Eliza gave its users the impression that they were talking to something that understood them (Hoover & Spengler, 2023). Therefore, the users engaged in intense and extensive conversations with the program.

In recent years chatbots with artificial intelligence-driven, scripted responses have been available. Woebot (Fitzpatrick, Darcy, & Vierhile, 2017; Mijwil et al., 2023) is one of those chatbots. It was designed to play the role of an actual therapist and based on cognitive behavioural therapy practices (Rathnayaka et al., 2022). Chatbots were highly demanded throughout the pandemic as more people than ever sought out mental health services. In addition to individuals looking for medical advice, chatbots are used by children who seek help with homework and by people who need everyday companionship. But those chatbots only deliver scripted responses and are generally narrower in scope, ChatGPT's richer conversation can be more effective for individuals that try to work out complex social issues (Hoover & Spengler, 2023).

Robots and artificial intelligence can understand emotions and/or feelings and help users feel more comfortable while communicating their true feelings (Chaturvedi et al., 2023). Because the users realise that they will not be judged (Apparao Polireddi & Kavitha, 2023; Boison et al., 2022). In this context, this chapter both reviews chatbots designed to help children with ASD and delves into design issues and approaches used in these chatbots. In addition, as chatbots may cause various ethical problems, such as misunderstanding users' questions, causing emotional harm and being offensive, and failing to provide the benefits and deliver the service promised (Coghlan et al., 2023; Al-Shahwani et al., 2024), in this chapter ethical issues related to their use are also reviewed.

In this chapter it is aimed to try to address some research questions. First, with their customisable language and communication settings, can social chatbots meet the individual needs of each child with ASD? Second, can social chatbots reduce anxiety and stress levels of children with ASD? Finally, can social chatbots help to improve cognitive and social skills of children with ASD? Relying on a scooping study is the main limitation of this chapter.

## AUTISM SPECTRUM DISORDER AND TECHNOLOGY

ASD is a neurological and developmental disorder. Individuals with ASD typically have difficulty with communication and interaction with other people, restricted interests and repetitive behaviours and symptoms that considerably affect their ability to function in school, work, and other areas of life (American Psychiatric Association, DSM-5 Task Force, 2013). Although ASD can be diagnosed at any age, its symptoms generally appear in the first 2 years of life (National Institute of Mental Health, n.d.). Technology can be used to support daily activities, facilitate independence, and provide assistance with occupational skills for individuals with ASD (Khanlou et al., 2021). In recent years, with this goal, various technological tools have been used. Some examples of this are the use of virtual reality for social skills training (Yuan & Ip, 2018), the use of serious games for cognitive and face-processing training (Whyte et al., 2015) and the use of tablets as speech-generating devices (Lorah et al., 2015). However, the ability of these examples to promote interaction is not enough (Aghakhani et al., 2023).

Individuals with ASD like to enjoy themselves and be engaged when interacting with computers, smart phones, tablets, virtual agents and robots. Because these interactions happen in a trustworthy and safe environment (Valencia et al., 2019). Technological tools can help individuals with ASD to work on skills that may not have developed as such tools provide repetitive controlled situations in which users can practice their strengths time after time, improve their weaknesses, enjoying themselves and not causing tension (Aresti-Bartolome & Garcia-Zapirain, 2014; Barua et al., 2020). Nevertheless, ensuring that the content provided by such tools fits the individuals' ages and needs and setting limits for the use of these technologies is essential. Because although technological tools can assist individuals with ASD in practicing strengths and improving weaknesses, such tools can lead to addiction and even to further isolation (Aresti-Bartolome & Garcia-Zapirain, 2014). Robots, mixed reality and software applications offer interaction with inanimate objects with predictable behaviour, this makes users feel both comfortable and secure working with them (Aresti-Bartolome & Garcia-Zapirain, 2014). Different from other technological tools, robots allow reproducing sequences of movements that could be imitated by users. This way the users can work on both motor and imitation skills (Aresti-Bartolome & Garcia-Zapirain, 2014).

## AUTISM SPECTRUM DISORDER AND CHATBOTS

ASD is a broad category of disorders characterised by challenges with social skills, repetitive behaviours/interests/activities, speech, and non-verbal communication (Apparao Polireddi & Kavitha, 2023). The impact of ASD varies from individual to individual due to a number of characteristics and challenges brought on by the spectrum condition (Apparao Polireddi & Kavitha, 2023). Managing children with ASD is complex and challenging because of the symptoms that are related to the disorder affecting their cognitive and behavioural functioning (Magnuson & Constantino, 2011). In this regard, Hadri and Bouramoul (2023a) developed an artificial intelligence-assisted chatbot for assisting and accompanying children with ASD. The chatbot can understand the questions of its users and give them advice and recommendations. This way, it helps prevent depression.

Apparao Polireddi and Kavitha (2023) developed a dashboard supported by a conversational chatbot. The chatbot is simple to customise, discover emotions, and requirements. It is able to present individualised replies dynamically adjusted based on the child's mood, by employing a decision tree architecture based on fuzzy classifier. The chatbot offers empathetic conversational style and provides weekly charts that outline mental condition.

Empathy is often understood as the ability to share and understand another individual's state of mind or emotion (McDonald & Messinger, 2011; Schaaff, Reinig, & Schlippe, 2023). In recent years, it has received significant attention as its importance in human-computer interaction has become more prominent in parallel with increasing use of chatbots in several domains. Therefore, Schaaff et al. (2023) investigated the extent to which ChatGPT based on GPT-3.5 can exhibit emotional expressions and empathetic responses. They tried to find out whether ChatGPT can understand and express emotions, provide parallel emotional response, and show empathic personality. The results in their study proved that in 91.7% of the cases, ChatGPT correctly identified emotions and produced appropriate answers.

In conversations, ChatGPT reacted with a parallel emotion in 70.7% of cases. Om the other hand, the scores of ChatGPT in different aspects of empath are sworse than the average of healthy humans (Schaaff, Reinig, & Schlippe, 2023).

ASD and Achluophobia, fear of darkness, are common neurodevelopment disorders in children. In order to diagnose these disorders Mujeeb et al. (2017) designed a chatbot, called Aquabot. The chatbot can diagnose the severity of the disorder based on user's text based questions. Aquabot relies on Decision Trees and uses natural language processing to extract meaning. From user's chat, NLP unit first extracts meaning of keywords defining intensity of disorder's symptoms and then performs similarity matching of sentences. Depth first search approach is used to traverse Decision Tree and make decision about severity of disorder. Aquabot can achieve an accuracy of 88% in diagnosing these disorders (Mujeeb, Javed, & Arshad, 2017).

It is known that many of individuals with ASD are not verbal. However, using augmentative and alternative communication aids they can communicate (Cooper & Ireland, 2018). Cooper and Ireland (2018) designed an Android application with social agent, called Alex. Alex is able to engage with its users on a number of topics using images and symbols. It does not require any specialised computer skills; therefore, without any training speech and occupational therapists can program it (Cooper & Ireland, 2018).

Non-cooperative tendencies are common during therapy sessions held for children with ASD, because it is difficult for these invidiuals to process information and adapt to new situations. Therefore, Friendy, a contextual chatbot technology-based framework supported by deep learning, was developed to enhance the therapy experience for children with ASD (Hadri & Bouramoul, 2023b). In the performance testing aiming to find out its usability in future therapy processes, it achieved an accuracy rate of 80.5% (Hadri & Bouramoul, 2023b).

Using artificial intelligence as conversational agents is promising especially for individuals with ASD. Therefore, Xygkou et al. (2024) aimed to explore the interactions of 6 adults with ASD and 6 non-ASD adults with a social chatbot over 1-4 weeks. Findings of the research show that although users with ASD were willing to have a conversation with the chatbot, they did not develop relationship with the chatbot. The findings also show that users with ASD expected empathy from the chatbot. Although non-ASD users continuously tried to test the agent's conversational and cognitive skills, users with ASD were content with the agent's conversational skills and expected more in-depth conversations (Xygkou et al., 2024). Therefore, there is a need for human-chatbot interaction focusing on companionship and social connectedness.

Mateos-Sanchez et al. (2022) proposed a chatbot called CapacitaBOT to allow individuals with intellectual disabilities to foster their social skills. CapacitaBOT assist individuals with intellectual disabilities in initiating, maintaining and ending an interaction with others, understanding and responding in different contexts and situations and being able to respond to the others' demands (Mateos-Sanchez et al., 2022). The main challenge encountered by Mateos-Sanchez et al. (2022) was that there was a limited time to conduct a follow-up of each of the selected users. Therefore, it was not possible to collect enough conversational contexts. In addition, the time was limited for the chatbot to learn from the users themselves. As a result, the chatbot was not adequately trained to generate new questions and answers automatically (Mateos-Sanchez et al., 2022). Nevertheless, previously collected information was used to simulate a conversation as real as possible (Mateos-Sanchez et al., 2022).

## ChatGPT

ChatGPT is a chatbot developed by OpenAI. It relies on natural language processing to generate responses to user inputs in a conversational manner (Mijwil et al., 2023; Mishra et al., 2021). Using a large dataset of human conversation allows it to learn and improve its responses over time. Its safe and controlled environment in terms of communication and social interaction is quite promising to help children with ASD. Different from human communication partners, ChatGPT can provide consistent and predictable responses, this way it can reduce anxiety and stress for the child. Importantly, its customisable language and communication settings allows to meet for the individual needs of each child. In addition, ChatGPT can be used to improve cognitive and social skills of children with ASD by provide engaging and educational content.

# DISCUSSION ON USING CHATBOTS FOR INDIVIDUALS WITH ASD

Using chatbots for mental health offers promising clinical outcomes (Daley et al., 2020). In adults, therapies delivered by a chatbot reduces depressive symptoms (Lim et al., 2022). Similarly, in adults, it provides promising improvements in attention-deficit/hyperactivity symptoms (Jang et al., 2021). In college students, chatbot-delivered psychotherapy reduces anxiety symptoms (Klos et al., 2021). Importantly, chatbot utilisation can provide higher retention rates compared to other types of interventions provided by various technological tools (Lim et al., 2022). Beatty et al. (2022) showed that in creating positive relationships with adults chatbots are promising. The reason of this lies in the fact that chatbots are perceived as caring, non-judgmental, open to listening and safe (Dosovitsky & Bunge, 2021).

Artificial intelligence can be described as the ability of a computer system to mimic human cognitive functions (Microsoft, 2023). Nevertheless, such models that can truly mimic human cognitive abilities is quite complex (Williams, 2023). Current artificial intelligence models do not possess human cognitive abilities such as understanding, reasoning, and consciousness (Zhao et al., 2022; Doshi et al., 2023). By using natural language processing, chatbots understand, respond to, and generate human language (Sheth et al., 2019). In the past, mimicking human conversation was the primary function of chatbots, but platforms such as ChatGPT have more abilities (Stokel-Walker & Van Noorden, 2023).

While the use of chatbots is promising for individuals with ASD, it has advantages and disadvantages which need investigating. Because individuals with social deficiencies have a tendency to gravitate towards companionship with chatbots and such chatbots are appealing to a lot of people struggling with face-to-face conversations, this may lead to further social isolation (Gibson & Franze, 2023; Franze et al., 2023). Therefore, there is an urgent need to find out the impact of chatbots on neurodiverse people.

Although chatbots can offer benefits for individuals with intellectual disabilities, they have challenges and may create risks. One of this risks is ethical issues. Ethical issues raised by the use of chatbots are generally due to the replacement of trained professionals and not having an acceptable level of evidence base and appropriate policies for data use and information security.

## Pros

Some chatbots show no opposing view or resistance that characterises human conversations, thereby leaving users the full control of the conversation (Gibson & Franze, 2023). This way the users can pause, delay, or even break off the conversation. However, this approach is not productive to developing essential social skills of the real world.

It is known that it may be better to choose chatbots instead of human contact and conversation in embarrassing or stigmatising circumstances (Nadarzynski et al., 2019; Mijwil et al., 2023; Hiran et al., 2023). Because users may feel more comfortable and disclose factual and emotional information to chatbots easier than to a human (Coghlan et al., 2023). In addition, for socially isolated individuals, chatbots may potentially engender emotional connections. Because one of the vital elements for successful therapy is mutual understanding and trust (Roter, 2000). Therefore, chatbots that facilitate emotional connections promoting trust (Srivastava et al., 2020) and understanding may carry out a key role for a range of user groups. In this regard, the technology must meet the needs of users safely and effectively. This can only be achieved if developers become responsive to user feedbacks and problems (Egger, 2000).

## Cons

Chatbots could lead to perpetuating communication difficulties for individuals with ASD, anxiety and limited social skills (Franze et al., 2023). While chatbots are seen as a safe and reliable means of carrying out social interaction with no or limited risk of negative judgement, this is risky. Because using social chatbots can make users become dependent on them and this may lead them withdraw even further from human interactions This is because ot the fact that most chatbots are unable to carry out a real conversation or display soft emotional skills and empathy and in many neurodiverse people this can reinforce dysfunctional habits (Franze et al., 2023; Doshi et al., 2023; Hiran et al., 2024).

There are some barriers to using chatbots for individuals with intellectual disabilities. Privacy concerns, scepticism, reduced willingness and financial constraints are a few of them (Crutzen et al., 2014). The literature shows that major barriers to the use of chatbots among adolescents are embarrassment, stigma, preferences for self-reliance and poor mental health literacy (Gulliver et al., 2010). An important concern about chatbots use for mental health is that such applications generally tend to over-medicalise distress and over-emphasise 'individual responsibility for mental well-being' (Parker et al., 2018; Hiran et al., 2023).

Although the literature shows that chatbots are generally safe and improve stress, distress, depression, and acrophobia, it is not possible how and up to which limit to draw definitive conclusions regarding their safety and effectiveness (Abd-Alrazaq et al., 2020; Doshi et al., 2023). Because, in most researches, the performance of chatbots on the severity of depression over other interventions was not statistically different (Abd-Alrazaq et al., 2020). In addition, conflicting results for some outcomes were reported (Abd-Alrazaq et al., 2020). Therefore, chatbots should be offered as an adjunct to already available interventions by healthcare providers (Abd-Alrazaq et al., 2020).

## Ethical Principles

Chatbots are a promising educational tool for individuals with various intellectual disabilities, especially mild ones, because by providing personalised and immediate feedbacks they can enhance the learning experience. On the other hand, using chatbots raises several ethical challenges. In this regard, one of the foremost ethical risks is the replacement of human interaction and expertise with the technology and artificial intelligence. This can be quite concerning in some fields such as counselling and mental health, considering that instead of trained professionals, students may try to get emotional support from chatbots (Kooli, 2023). It was shown that college students do not see chatbots as a substitute for human support, they just perceive chatbots as useful and helpful (Pesonen, 2021). Considering the use of chatbots, another ethical risk is the potential for bias. The ability of learning from a diverse set of data sources is one of the prominent attributes of chatbots (Qadir, 2022). Because artificial intelligence based systems can work unbiased if the data they have been trained on is unbiased. Otherwise, their responses may also be biased (Pedro et al., 2019). This may lead to discrimination and inequality in some fields.

Like all artificial intelligence based systems, chatbots typically learn from an extensive set of data obtained from the internet, which mostly represents societal biases. If chatbots are trained using data containing biased attitudes, like other artificial intelligence based systems the chatbots will likely assimilate these biases and reproduce them, even unintentionally (Bolukbasi et al., 2016). It is essential to note that even without artificial intelligence, regulations and policies, such as General Data Protection Regulation (GDPR), also risk reproducing prejudices and societal bias (Baker & Hawn, 2021). Therefore, such potential biases must be recognised and mitigated by developers, therapists, families and policymakers. The first and foremost step in this regard is to make sure that these chatbots should be trained using diverse and representative datasets (Nazer et al., 2023).

The five principles of non-maleficence, beneficence, justice, respect for autonomy and explicability (Floridi & Cowls, 2019; Coghlan et al., 2023) can be used to understand and address ethical issues raised by the use of chatbots. While the first four ones were drawn from medical ethics (Beauchamp & Childress, 2001), explicability was added due to the special nature of emerging approaches such as artificial intelligence (Coghlan et al., 2023).

Explicability is composed of accountability and transparency. Accountability has importance in part as it can be unclear who is legally and ethically liable for adverse outcomes of technological solutions (Floridi & Cowls, 2019). As the ways in which technological solutions work are often unknown to users, transparency is important. Although all of the principles mentioned earlier are non-absolute, they can be used by who design, implement, research or supervise technological solutions (Coghlan et al., 2023).

## Future Research Directions

In recent years chatbots has started to become more and more popular, it is essential to find out the antecedents, contents and consequences of communication with non-human agents (Følstad et al., 2021). This way, the behavioural, affective and cognitive dimensions of engagement with these agents, the extent to which there are systematic differences between individuals, groups or contexts of use, and the individual, group and societal implications of this phenomenon can be explored (Følstad et al., 2021).

It is seen that there is a need for designing and developing abstractions that allows facilitating the design, development, integration and testing of chatbots (Følstad et al., 2021). This way anyone without programming development experience can deliver human-like interactive experiences (Følstad et al., 2021). Visual programming approaches can make this easier. However, this may lead to unintended consequences, such users do not have knowledge about the complexities of modelling proper human-artificial intelligence experiences (Yang et al., 2020). Underlying information about machine learning techniques and algorithms, artificial intelligence based decision-making, and latent bias in the training data that can lead to social biases can be hidden by abstractions (Zou & Schiebinger, 2018).

Taking into consideration the meaningful value of human-chatbot collaboration for productivity and decision making, roles of chatbots in collaborative interactions can have varying degrees of involvement and complexity. Therefore, such automation should be considered as a service design challenge (Brandtzaeg & Følstad, 2017).

Chatbots will not only lead to some ethical challenges but also hold implications for democratisation of technology (Følstad et al., 2021). This should be researched. Natural language processing can be used to allow interacting with chatbots; however, this is possibly a limited way of accessing information and services and promoting inclusion (Følstad et al., 2021). Because of design choices and technological limitations, this can lead to discriminate against some user groups or excluding them, perpetuate and even reinforce existing biases in society, and enshrine or over-represent specific values (Følstad et al., 2021).

There is a need to analyse democratisation of chatbots in practice. Because chatbots should be made widely and easily accessible for various user groups and businesses across the globe in order to offer their conversational interaction capabilities to more people (Følstad et al., 2021). This aspect plays a key role as chatbots can act as agents that operate in social contexts.

Bui et al. (2022) proved that parents of children with neurodevelopmental disorders support the use of gamification elements in chatbots for neurodevelopmental disorders. However, a user-centred design is needed in the medical domain so that a foundation for researchers focusing on the development of chatbots for medically vulnerable populations can be provided. In parallel with this, having wide range of gamification elements with many potential users is essential to find out the effects of gamification elements in increasing knowledge mobilisation (Bui et al., 2022).

## CONCLUSION

Social chatbots may seem attractive to individuals with ASD, anxiety, and limited social skills, because they offer a risk-free environment for interaction. Different from traditional chatbots delivering scripted responses, ChatGPTrelies on a large dataset of human conversation to learn and improve its responses over time. It can help children with ASD by providing a safe and controlled environment with its consistent and predictable responses for communication and social interaction. With its customisable language and communication settings, it can meet the individual needs of each child. Not only it can reduce anxiety and stress for each child but also it can help to improve cognitive and social skills of the child by providing engaging and educational content.

Although social chatbots may be particularly appealing to individuals with ASD, who may view the technology alternative to human interaction, and be helpful to relieve some social anxiety problems of users, this may lead to a form of dependency that has negative impacts on actual relationships. Therefore, there is a need for feedback from therapists, teachers, parents and family members to have a broader understanding of chatbots' impacts. This way, policies and industry practices can be developed to guide both safer and reasonable use of chatbots.

## REFERENCES

Abd-Alrazaq, A. A., Rababeh, A., Alajlani, M., Bewick, B. M., & Househ, M. (2020). Effectiveness and Safety of Using Chatbots to Improve Mental Health: Systematic Review and Meta-Analysis. *Journal of Medical Internet Research*, *22*(7), e16021. doi:10.2196/16021 PMID:32673216

Aghakhani, S., Carre, N., Mostovoy, K., Shafer, R., Baeza-Hernandez, K., Entenberg, G., Testerman, A., & Bunge, E. L. (2023). Qualitative analysis of mental health conversational agents messages about autism spectrum disorder: A call for action. *Frontiers in Digital Health, 5*, 1251016. doi:10.3389/fdgth.2023.1251016 PMID:38116099

Al-Shahwani, H. I. W., Mijwil, M. M., Doshi, R., Hiran, K. K., & Bala, I. (2024). Evaluating Antivirus Effectiveness Against Malware in Ascending Order for Increasing Blockchain Endpoint Protection. In Bio-Inspired Optimization Techniques in Blockchain Systems (pp. 150-166). IGI Global. doi:10.4018/979-8-3693-1131-8.ch008

American Psychiatric Association, DSM-5 Task Force. (2013). *Diagnostic and statistical manual of mental disorders: DSM-5* (5th ed.). American Psychiatric Publishing, Inc., doi:10.1176/appi.books.9780890425596

Apparao Polireddi, N. S., & Kavitha, J. (2023). Effectiveness of automated chatbots for operational support and self-service based on fuzzy classifier for ASD. *Soft Computing*. doi:10.1007/s00500-023-08541-x

Aresti-Bartolome, N., & Garcia-Zapirain, B. (2014). Technologies as support tools for persons with autistic spectrum disorder: A systematic review. *International Journal of Environmental Research and Public Health, 11*(8), 7767–7802. doi:10.3390/ijerph110807767 PMID:25093654

Baker, R. S., & Hawn, A. (2021). Algorithmic bias in education. *International Journal of Artificial Intelligence in Education, 32*(4), 1052–1092. doi:10.1007/s40593-021-00285-9

Barua, T., Doshi, R., & Hiran, K. K. (2020). *Mobile Applications Development: With Python in Kivy Framework*. Walter de Gruyter GmbH & Co KG. doi:10.1515/9783110689488

Beatty, C., Malik, T., Meheli, S., & Sinha, C. (2022). Evaluating the Therapeutic Alliance With a Free-Text CBT Conversational Agent (Wysa): A Mixed-Methods Study. *Frontiers in Digital Health, 4*, 847991. doi:10.3389/fdgth.2022.847991 PMID:35480848

Beauchamp, T. L., & Childress, J. F. (2001). *Principles of biomedical ethics* (5th ed.). Oxford University Press.

Boison, D. K., Malcalm, E., Antwi-Boampong, A., Doumbia, M. O., & Hiran, K. K. (2022). Assessing Factors Affecting the Blockchain Adoption in Public Procurement Delivery in Ghana: A Correlational Study Using UTAUT2 Theoretical Framework. [IJACI]. *International Journal of Ambient Computing and Intelligence, 13*(1), 1–13. doi:10.4018/ijaci.314568

Bolukbasi, T., Chang, K. W., Zou, J. Y., Saligrama, V., & Kalai, A. T. (2016). Man is to computer programmer as woman is to homemaker? debiasing word embeddings. *Proceedings of the 30th International Conference on Neural Information Processing Systems (NIPS'16)* (pp. 4356–4364). Curran Associates Inc., Red Hook, NY, USA.

Brandtzaeg, P. B., & Følstad, A. (2017). Why People Use Chatbots. In I. Kompatsiaris, (Eds.), Lecture Notes in Computer Science: Vol. 10673. *Internet Science. INSCI 2017*. Springer. doi:10.1007/978-3-319-70284-1_30

Bui, T. A., Pohl, M., Rosenfelt, C., Ogourtsova, T., Yousef, M., Whitlock, K., Majnemer, A., Nicholas, D., Demmans Epp, C., Zaiane, O., & Bolduc, F. V. (2022). Identifying Potential Gamification Elements for A New Chatbot for Families with Neurodevelopmental Disorders: User-Centered Design Approach. *JMIR Human Factors*, *9*(3), e31991. doi:10.2196/31991 PMID:35984679

Chaturvedi, R., Verma, S., Das, R., & Dwivedi, Y. K. (2023). Social Companionship with Artificial Intelligence: Recent Trends and future avenues. *Technological Forecasting and Social Change*, *193*, 122634. doi:10.1016/j.techfore.2023.122634

Coghlan, S., Leins, K., Sheldrick, S., Cheong, M., Gooding, P., & D'Alfonso, S. (2023). To chat or bot to chat: Ethical issues with using chatbots in mental health. *Digital Health*, *9*, 20552076231183542. doi:10.1177/20552076231183542 PMID:37377565

Cooper, A., & Ireland, D. (2018). Designing a Chat-Bot for Non-Verbal Children on the Autism Spectrum. *Studies in Health Technology and Informatics*, *252*, 63–68. doi:10.3233/978-1-61499-890-7-63 PMID:30040684

Crutzen, R., Bosma, H., Havas, J., & Feron, F. (2014). What can we learn from a failed trial: Insight into non-participation in a chat-based intervention trial for adolescents with psychosocial problems. *BMC Research Notes*, *7*(1), 824. doi:10.1186/1756-0500-7-824 PMID:25409911

Daley, K., Hungerbuehler, I., Cavanagh, K., Claro, H. G., Swinton, P. A., & Kapps, M. (2020). Preliminary Evaluation of the Engagement and Effectiveness of a Mental Health Chatbot. *Frontiers in Digital Health*, *2*, 576361. doi:10.3389/fdgth.2020.576361 PMID:34713049

Doshi, R., Hiran, K. K., Mijwil, M. M., & Anand, D. (2023). To That of Artificial Intelligence, Passing Through Business Intelligence. In Handbook of Research on AI and Knowledge Engineering for Real-Time Business Intelligence (pp. 1-16). IGI Global. doi:10.4018/978-1-6684-6519-6.ch001

Doshi, R., Hiran, K. K., Ranolia, R., & Joshi, C. (2023). Monitor Cloud Performance and Data Safety With Artificial Intelligence. In Applications of Artificial Intelligence in Wireless Communication Systems (pp. 92-108). IGI Global. doi:10.4018/978-1-6684-7348-1.ch006

Dosovitsky, G., & Bunge, E. L. (2021). Bonding With Bot: User Feedback on a Chatbot for Social Isolation. *Frontiers in Digital Health*, *3*, 735053. doi:10.3389/fdgth.2021.735053 PMID:34713203

Egger, F. N. (2000). 'Trust me, I'm an online vendor': towards a model of trust for e-commerce system design. In *CHI '00 extended abstracts on human factors in computing systems* (pp. 101–102). Association for Computing Machinery. doi:10.1145/633292.633352

Firsanova, V. (2020). Supporting the Inclusion of People with Asperger Syndrome: Building a Customizable Chatbot with Transfer Learning. In *AINL: Artificial Intelligence and Natural Language Conference. Workshop on Human-AI Interaction*.

Fitzpatrick, K. K., Darcy, A., & Vierhile, M. (2017). Delivering Cognitive Behavior Therapy to Young Adults with Symptoms of Depression and Anxiety Using a Fully Automated Conversational Agent (Woebot): A Randomized Controlled Trial. *JMIR Mental Health*, *4*(2), e19. doi:10.2196/mental.7785 PMID:28588005

Floridi, L., & Cowls, J. (2019). A unified framework of five principles for AI in society. Harvard Data Science Review. In S. Carta (Ed.), *Machine Learning and the City*., doi:10.1002/9781119815075.ch45

Følstad, A., Araujo, T., Law, E. L. C., Brandtzaeg, P. B., Papadopoulos, S., Reis, L., Baez, M., Laban, G., McAllister, P., Ischen, C., Wald, R., Catania, F., Meyer von Wolff, R., Hobert, S., & Luger, E. (2021). Future directions for chatbot research: An interdisciplinary research agenda. *Computing*, *103*(12), 2915–2942. doi:10.1007/s00607-021-01016-7

Franze, A., Galanis, C. R., & King, D. L. (2023). Social chatbot use (e.g., ChatGPT) among individuals with social deficits: Risks and opportunities. *Journal of Behavioral Addictions*, *12*(4), 871–872. doi:10.1556/2006.2023.00057 PMID:38141065

Gibson, C., & Franze, A. (2023, December 11). *We need to talk about social chatbots and the impact of AI*. Home. https://www.unisa.edu.au/media-centre/Releases/2023/we-need-to-talk-about-social-chatbots-and-the-impact-of-ai/

Goldkind, L. (2021). Social Work and Artificial Intelligence: Into the Matrix. *Social Work*, *66*(4), 372–374. doi:10.1093/sw/swab028 PMID:34279661

Goldkind, L., Wolf, L., Glennon, A., Rios, J., & Nissen, L. (2024). The End of the World as We Know It? ChatGPT and Social Work. *Social Work*, *69*(1), 103–105. doi:10.1093/sw/swad044 PMID:37972352

Gulliver, A., Griffiths, K. M., & Christensen, H. (2010). Perceived barriers and facilitators to mental health help-seeking in young people: A systematic review. *BMC Psychiatry*, *10*(1), 113. doi:10.1186/1471-244X-10-113 PMID:21192795

Hadri, S. A., & Bouramoul, A. (2023a). Towards a deep learning based contextual chat bot for preventing depression in young children with autistic spectrum disorder. *Smart Health (Amsterdam, Netherlands)*, *27*, 100371. doi:10.1016/j.smhl.2022.100371

Hadri, S. A., & Bouramoul, A. (2023b). Friendy: A Deep Learning based Framework for Assisting in Young Autistic Children Psychotherapy Interventions. *Journal of Communications Software and Systems*, *19*(1), 30–38. doi:10.24138/jcomss-2022-0074

Hiran, K. K., Doshi, R., & Patel, M. (Eds.). (2024). *Applications of Virtual and Augmented Reality for Health and Wellbeing*. IGI Global. doi:10.4018/979-8-3693-1123-3

Hiran, K. K., Hemachandran, K., Pise, A., & Rabi, B. (Eds.). (2023). *Handbook of Research on AI and Knowledge Engineering for Real-Time Business Intelligence*. IGI Global. doi:10.4018/978-1-6684-6519-6

Hoover, A., & Spengler, S. (2023, May 30). *For some autistic people, chatgpt is a Lifeline*. Wired. https://www.wired.com/story/for-some-autistic-people-chatgpt-is-a-lifeline/

Jang, S., Kim, J. J., Kim, S. J., Hong, J., Kim, S., & Kim, E. (2021). Mobile app-based chatbot to deliver cognitive behavioral therapy and psychoeducation for adults with attention deficit: A development and feasibility/usability study. *International Journal of Medical Informatics*, *150*, 104440. doi:10.1016/j.ijmedinf.2021.104440 PMID:33799055

Khanlou, N., Khan, A., Vazquez, L. M., & Zangeneh, M. (2021). Digital literacy, access to technology and inclusion for young adults with developmental disabilities. *Journal of Developmental and Physical Disabilities*, *33*(1), 1–25. doi:10.1007/s10882-020-09738-w PMID:33814873

Klos, M. C., Escoredo, M., Joerin, A., Lemos, V. N., Rauws, M., & Bunge, E. L. (2021). Artificial Intelligence-Based Chatbot for Anxiety and Depression in University Students: Pilot Randomized Controlled Trial. *JMIR Formative Research*, *5*(8), e20678. doi:10.2196/20678 PMID:34092548

Kooli, C. (2023). Chatbots in Education and Research: A Critical Examination of Ethical Implications and Solutions. *Sustainability (Basel)*, *15*(7), 5614. doi:10.3390/su15075614

Lim, S. M., Shiau, C. W. C., Cheng, L. J., & Lau, Y. (2022). Chatbot-Delivered Psychotherapy for Adults With Depressive and Anxiety Symptoms: A Systematic Review and Meta-Regression. *Behavior Therapy*, *53*(2), 334–347. doi:10.1016/j.beth.2021.09.007 PMID:35227408

Lorah, E. R., Parnell, A., Whitby, P. S., & Hantula, D. (2015). A Systematic Review of Tablet Computers and Portable Media Players as Speech Generating Devices for Individuals with Autism Spectrum Disorder. *Journal of Autism and Developmental Disorders*, *45*(12), 3792–3804. doi:10.1007/s10803-014-2314-4 PMID:25413144

Magnuson, K. M., & Constantino, J. N. (2011). Characterization of depression in children with autism spectrum disorders. *Journal of Developmental and Behavioral Pediatrics*, *32*(4), 332–340. doi:10.1097/DBP.0b013e318213f56c PMID:21502871

Mateos-Sanchez, M., Melo, A. C., Blanco, L. S., & García, A. M. F. (2022). Chatbot, as Educational and Inclusive Tool for People with Intellectual Disabilities. *Sustainability (Basel)*, *14*(3), 1520. doi:10.3390/su14031520

McDonald, N. M., & Messinger, D. S. (2011). The Development of Empathy: How, When, and Why. In A. Acerbi, J. A. Lombo, & J. J. Sanguineti (Eds.), *Moral behavior and free will: A neurobiological and philosophical approach* (pp. 333–359). IF Press.

Microsoft. (2023). *What is Microsoft's Approach to AI?* Microsoft. https://news.microsoft.com/source/features/ai/microsoft-approach-to-ai/

Mijwil, M. M., Gök, M., Doshi, R., Hiran, K. K., & Kösesoy, I. (2023). Utilizing Artificial Intelligence Techniques to Improve the Performance of Wireless Nodes. In Applications of Artificial Intelligence in Wireless Communication Systems (pp. 150-162). IGI Global. doi:10.4018/978-1-6684-7348-1.ch010

Mijwil, M. M., Hiran, K. K., Doshi, R., Dadhich, M., Al-Mistarehi, A. H., & Bala, I. (2023). ChatGPT and the future of academic integrity in the artificial intelligence era: A new frontier. *Al-Salam Journal for Engineering and Technology*, *2*(2), 116–127. doi:10.55145/ajest.2023.02.02.015

Mishra, A., Tripathi, A., Khazanchi, D., Hiran, K. K., Vyas, A. K., & Padmanaban, S. (2021). A framework for applying artificial intelligence (AI) with Internet of NanoThings (IoNT). In *Machine Learning for Sustainable Development* (pp. 1–16). De Gruyter. doi:10.1515/9783110702514-001

Mujeeb, S., Javed, M. H., & Arshad, T. (2017). Aquabot: A Diagnostic Chatbot for Achluophobia and Autism. [ijacsa]. *International Journal of Advanced Computer Science and Applications*, *8*(9). doi:10.14569/IJACSA.2017.080930

Nadarzynski, T., Miles, O., Cowie, A., & Ridge, D. (2019). Acceptability of artificial intelligence (AI)-led chatbot services in healthcare: A mixed-methods study. *Digital Health*, *5*, 2055207619871808. doi:10.1177/2055207619871808 PMID:31467682

National Institute of Mental Health. (n.d.). *Autism spectrum disorder*. NIH. https://www.nimh.nih.gov/health/topics/autism-spectrum-disorders-asd

Nazer, L. H., Zatarah, R., Waldrip, S., Ke, J. X. C., Moukheiber, M., Khanna, A. K., Hicklen, R. S., Moukheiber, L., Moukheiber, D., Ma, H., & Mathur, P. (2023). Bias in artificial intelligence algorithms and recommendations for mitigation. *PLOS Digital Health*, *2*(6), e0000278. doi:10.1371/journal.pdig.0000278 PMID:37347721

Parker, L., Bero, L., Gillies, D., Raven, M., Mintzes, B., Jureidini, J., & Grundy, Q. (2018). Mental Health Messages in Prominent Mental Health Apps. *Annals of Family Medicine*, *16*(4), 338–342. doi:10.1370/afm.2260 PMID:29987082

Pedro, F., Subosa, M., Rivas, A., & Valverde, P. (2019). *Artificial Intelligence in Education: Challenges and Opportunities for Sustainable Development*. UNESCO.

Pesonen, J. A. (2021). 'Are You OK?' Students' Trust in a Chatbot Providing Support Opportunities. In *Learning and Collaboration Technologies: Games and Virtual Environments for Learning: 8th International Conference, LCT 2021, Held as Part of the 23rd HCI International Conference, HCII 2021, Virtual Event, Proceedings, Part II* (pp. 199-215). Springer: Cham, Switzerland.

Qadir, J. (2022). Engineering Education in the Era of ChatGPT: Promise and Pitfalls of Generative AI for Education. *2023 IEEE Global Engineering Education Conference (EDUCON),* Kuwait, Kuwait. 10.1109/EDUCON54358.2023.10125121

Rathnayaka, P., Mills, N., Burnett, D., De Silva, D., Alahakoon, D., & Gray, R. (2022). A Mental Health Chatbot with Cognitive Skills for Personalised Behavioural Activation and Remote Health Monitoring. *Sensors (Basel)*, *22*(10), 3653. doi:10.3390/s22103653 PMID:35632061

Roter, D. (2000). The enduring and evolving nature of the patient-physician relationship. *Patient Education and Counseling*, *39*(1), 5–15. doi:10.1016/S0738-3991(99)00086-5 PMID:11013543

Schaaff, K., Reinig, C., & Schlippe, T. (2023). Exploring ChatGPT's Empathic Abilities. In *11th International Conference on Affective Computing and Intelligent Interaction (ACII)* (pp. 1-8). IEEE. 10.1109/ACII59096.2023.10388208

Sheth, A., Yip, H. Y., Iyengar, A., & Tepper, P. (2019). Cognitive Services and Intelligent Chatbots: Current Perspectives and Special Issue Introduction. *IEEE Internet Computing*, *23*(2), 6–12. doi:10.1109/MIC.2018.2889231 PMID:33746506

Srivastava, B., Rossi, F., Usmani, S., & Bernagozzi, M. (2020). Personalized chatbot trustworthiness ratings. *IEEE Transactions on Technology and Society*, *1*(4), 184–192. doi:10.1109/TTS.2020.3023919

Stokel-Walker, C., & Van Noorden, R. (2023). What ChatGPT and generative AI mean for science. *Nature, 614*(7947), 214–216. doi:10.1038/d41586-023-00340-6 PMID:36747115

Valencia, K., Rusu, C., Quiñones, D., & Jamet, E. (2019). The Impact of Technology on People with Autism Spectrum Disorder: A Systematic Literature Review. *Sensors (Basel), 19*(20), 4485. doi:10.3390/s19204485 PMID:31623200

Weizenbaum, J. (1966). ELIZA—A computer program for the study of natural language communication between man and machine. *Communications of the ACM, 9*(1), 36–45. doi:10.1145/365153.365168

Whyte, E. M., Smyth, J. M., & Scherf, K. S. (2014). Designing Serious Game Interventions for Individuals with Autism. *Journal of Autism and Developmental Disorders, 45*(12), 3820–3831. doi:10.1007/s10803-014-2333-1 PMID:25488121

Williams, R. T. (2023). The ethical implications of using generative chatbots in higher education. *Frontiers in Education, 8*, 1331607. doi:10.3389/feduc.2023.1331607

Xygkou, A., Siriaraya, P., She, W.-J., Covaci, A., & Ang, C. S. (2024). "can I be more social with a chatbot?": Social connectedness through interactions of autistic adults with a conversational virtual human. *International Journal of Human-Computer Interaction*, 1–18. doi:10.1080/10447318.2023.2292880

Yang, Q., Steinfeld, A., Rosé, C., & Zimmerman, J. (2020). Re-examining whether, why, and how Human-AI Interaction is uniquely difficult to design. *Proceedings of CHI 2020* (pp. 1-13). ACM, New York. 10.1145/3313831.3376301

Yuan, S. N. V., & Ip, H. H. S. (2018). Using virtual reality to train emotional and social skills in children with autism spectrum disorder. *London Journal of Primary Care, 10*(4), 110–112. doi:10.1080/17571472.2018.1483000 PMID:30083244

Zhao, J., Wu, M., Zhou, L., Wang, X., & Jia, J. (2022). Cognitive psychology-based artificial intelligence review. *Frontiers in Neuroscience, 16*, 1024316. doi:10.3389/fnins.2022.1024316 PMID:36278021

Zou, J., & Schiebinger, L. (2018). AI can be sexist and racist - it's time to make it fair. *Nature, 559*(7714), 324–326. doi:10.1038/d41586-018-05707-8 PMID:30018439

## ADDITIONAL READING

Boser, K. I., Goodwin, M. S., & Wayland, S. C. (Eds.). (2013). *Technology Tools for Students with Autism: Innovations that Enhance Independence and Learning*. Brookes Publishing.

Cardon, T. A. (Ed.). (2016). *Technology and the Treatment of Children with Autism Spectrum Disorder*. Springer. doi:10.1007/978-3-319-20872-5

Chakraborty, U., Banerjee, A., Saha, J. K., Sarkar, N., & Chakraborty, C. (Eds.). (2022). *Artificial Intelligence and the Fourth Industrial Revolution* (1st ed.). Jenny Stanford Publishing. doi:10.1201/9781003159742

Kientz, J. A., Hayes, G. R., Goodwin, M. S., Gelsomini, M., & Abowd, G. D. (2022). *Interactive technologies and autism* (2nd ed.). Springer.

Matson, J. L., & Sturmey, P. (Eds.). (2022). *Handbook of Autism and Pervasive Developmental Disorder: Assessment, Diagnosis, and Treatment*. Springer. doi:10.1007/978-3-030-88538-0

## KEY TERMS AND DEFINITIONS

**Artificial Intelligence:** Artificial intelligence is the simulation of human intelligence processes by machines, especially computer systems. Specific applications of AI include expert systems, natural language processing, speech recognition and machine vision.

**Autism Spectrum Disorder:** A developmental disability that affects how people behave, see and understand the world and interact with others. People with this developmental disability may have special interests, repetitive behaviours and under or overreact to sensory input.

**Chatbot:** A chatbot is a software application or web interface that is designed to mimic human conversation through text or voice interactions.

**ChatGPT:** Based on a large language model, it enables users to refine and steer a conversation towards a desired length, format, style, level of detail, and language.

# Chapter 25
# Impact of Generative AI in Education 2030

**Subhajit Adhikari**
*Institute of Engineering and Management, Kolkata, India*

**Dulal Kumbhakar**
*Vivekananda Mahavidyalaya, Haripal, India*

**Nabanita Indra**
*Dinabandhu Andrew's Institute of Technology and Management, Kolkata, India*

**Sunil Karforma**
*The University of Burdwan, India*

## ABSTRACT

*This book chapter contains the basics of generative AI, evaluation of generative AI, working process of generative AI, and applications of generative AI in Education 2030. In this chapter, the authors will introduce the emerging concept of large language model (LLM), reinforcement learning, response generation, neural network, and tokenization as the building blocks of generative AI. In this context, the authors will analyze the role of AI based ChatGpt technology in Education. The applications of generative AI in educational policy making, infrastructure development, research, innovation, activity building, and content generation for the students at schools and colleges will be discussed. But the contents of above mentioned activities must be guided by a teacher of school and college because such contents have more context wise decision making abilities rather than AI based solutions.*

## INTRODUCTION

Artificial intelligence (AI) is a transformative technology which is increasingly integrated into various industries and sectors, impacting everything from business operations to societal concerns. This may lead various challenges and risks, particularly security. Therefore, the use of AI must be reliable, fair, transparent, and trustworthy. To achieve this, the authority ISO has published ISO/IEC 42001:2023 (De-

DOI: 10.4018/979-8-3693-2440-0.ch025

cember 18, 2023), a comprehensive standard that provides a structured approach to managing the unique challenges and risks associated with AI technologies. It addresses ethical considerations, transparency, and continuous learning challenges in AI. The advantages include transparency, demonstrating responsible AI use, traceability, a framework for managing risk and opportunities, cost savings, reliability, and efficiency gains. Implementing ISO/IEC 42001 ensures responsible AI use, reputation management, AI governance, practical guidance, and innovation (ISO/IEC, 2023).

## BACKGROUND

Despite a huge history of AI research and applications has found in education, it took the fast success of ChatGPT to encourage educators, students, and university administrators all across the world to address its practical implications. A framework has been developed which is applicable for higher education in Australia and tested the tools based on the concept of generative AIto design and access the online tests (Smolansky et al., 2023). Artificial intelligence (AI) serves the essential role in the digitalization of society. The ability of artificial intelligence to automate procedures, handle data in massive volumes, and produce predictive insights will eventually revolutionize many facets of our everyday life (Cooper, 2023).The applications of creative writing in education are demonstrated using the concept of ashing conceptual questions, math questions, story writing, essay writing (outlined), code generation and many more (Qadir, 2022). One new framework titled as IDEE is proposed using ChatGPT tool where IDEE stands with the objectives of (1) Finding of desired outputs (2) Automation level determination (3) Ethical implications (4) Effectiveness evaluation (Su & Yang, 2023).

## INTRODUCTION TO GENERATIVE AI

The generative version of AI concentrates on generating data or content that is new (Chan, 2023). The generative pre-trained transformers which is known as GPT, takes the help of deep learning to create content in natural language. The most recent improvements from GPT, version of GPT 3.5 to version of GPT 4, are models of large language processing trained on a huge text corpus (Chan, 2023). In education, generative AI systems can provide various benefits, like increasing learner involvement in learning activities, generating feedback on time, making collaboration, and enhancing ease of access (Smolansky et al., 2023). In the humanities and arts, ChatGPT has a wide range of functions, including promoting artistic expression and creativity as well as research, teaching, and cultural preservation. In order to stimulate creativity and artistic expression, artists can work together with the model to co-create artwork, try out various writing styles, and brainstorm ideas. Scholars in the humanities frequently sift through vast amounts of textual material in quest of significant discoveries. In this situation, ChatGPT is quite helpful since it can summarize intricate literature, generate theories, and offer a variety of viewpoints on a certain subject. It enhances learning and makes education more approachable and interesting by customizing study materials, essays, and practice questions to each student's needs. In the humanities and arts, ChatGPT plays a transformational and diverse function. It stimulates innovation, advances analysis and research, transforms education, protects cultural heritage, promotes intercultural understanding, and ignites crucial moral and social debates (Rane, 2023).

## THE WORKING PROCESS OF GENERATIVE AI

In this chapter, we are going to present the basic building blocks that are required for understating of the concept of generative AI. Now, in the next section, the large language model is depicted.

## LARGE LANGUAGE MODEL (LLM)

These models come under the generative AI that creates human understandable language. The OpenAI's text generation models are based on the training of vast volumes of text in terms of novels, news stories, websites, and Wikipedia, using machine learning techniques (Cooper, 2023).

From the above figure 1, we can see that prompts are used to take input for large language model and the output is the suggested next tokens as output. Transformer networks, a type of deep learning architecture, are commonly used for large language models. A model of transformer is actually a neural network that derives context and meaning from sequential input, such as the words making a particular sentence. The building blocks of a transformer are many transformer blocks, often termed as layers like layers of self attention mechanism, layers of feed forward, and normalization layers that all work together to decode input and forecast output streams at inference (Nvidia, n.d.).

From the figure 2, it is very clear that LLM can be trained with various types of data and can perform a variety of tasks like in information extraction, Q & A and many more. To act this model as chatBot for question and answering, the model must be fine-tuned as per the diagram in figure 3. Also, reinforcement training is done based on human feedback, depicted in figure 4.

Positional encodings and self-attention are two significant developments creating transformers specifically suitable for large language models. The order in which the input appears inside a specific sequence is encoded using positional encoding. Positional encoding enables them to be fed words in non sequentially into the neural network. While processing the input data, self-attention provides a weight to each component. This weight indicates the significance of that input in comparison with other part

*Figure 1. Prompt engineering for NLP task*
**Source:** (*Cohere, n.d.*)

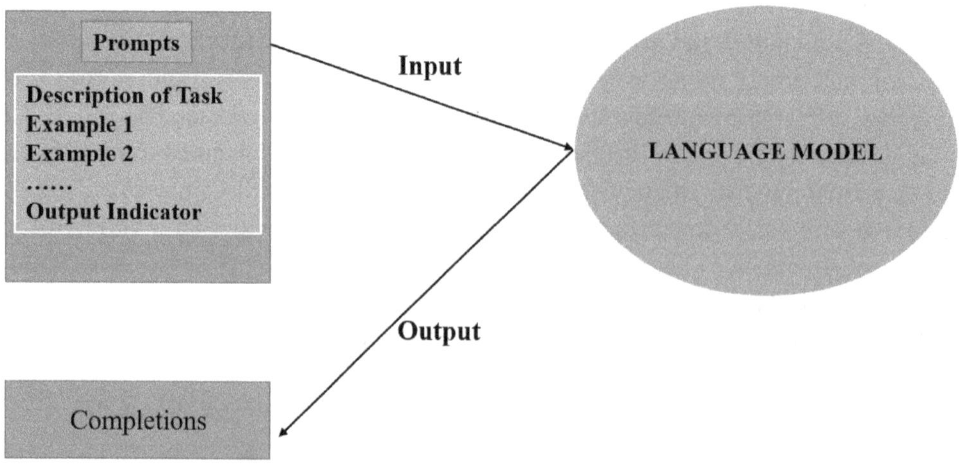

*Figure 2. Large language model as foundation model*
**Source**: *(Bommasani et al. 2022)*

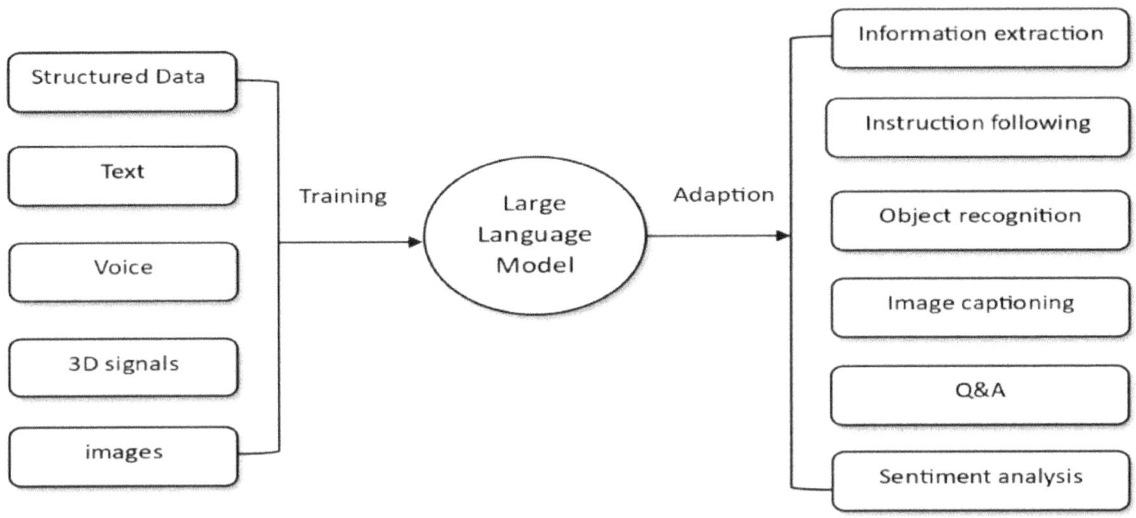


*Figure 3. Representation of fine-tuned model*

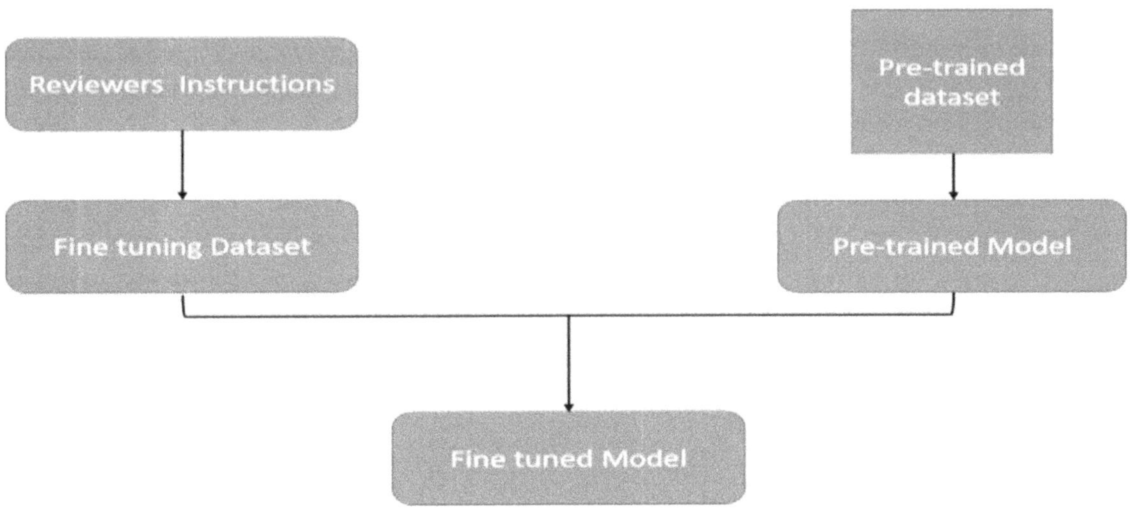


*Figure 4. Adding human feedback to fine-tuned model*

of the input. In this regard, models no longer need to pay equal attention to all inputs and may focus on the most significant input parts. Let's talk about positional encoding.

## POSITIONAL ENCODING

Absolute positional encoding offers a unique label to each place in a series depending on its distance from the beginning of the sequence, resulting in a global coordinate system relative to the sequence's start (Niser, n.d.). Positional encoding is given via functions of sine and cosine with different frequencies.

$$PE(Kpos,2I) = \sin(Kpos/N^{2I/dim})$$

$$PE(Kpos,2I+1) = \cos(Kpos/N^{2I/dim})$$

In the above equation, the variable "Kpos" holds the value of the position of an object in the sequence of input, 0≤Kpos≤Len, **dim** represents as the dimension of the embedding space that is considered as output, the function *PE(m,n)* as depicts the mapping a position "m" in the input sequence to the index (m,n) of the matrix. The variable "N" depicts the user-specified scalar, with the value of"10,000" by the authors of Attention Is All You Need (Vaswani et al., 2017).

The variable "I" is utilized for mapping to column indices values with the range $0 \leq I \leq \frac{dim}{2}$, with a single value mapping of "I" to both functions (Saeed, 2023). Positional encoding represents an entity's placement or position in a sequence, with each position allocated a representation that is unique. To comprehend the aforementioned term, consider the sentence "I am a boy," with N=100 and dim=4. Figure 5 depicts the encoding matrix in terms of positions for this sentence. In reality, this matrix would be identical for every phrase consisting four letters with N=100 and dim=4.

The top 5 rows of positional encoding matrix with the value of dim=5, N=100are given in Table1.

In the next segment, another important concept that is word embedding is outlined with examples.

*Figure 5. Representation of Embedding matrix in terms of position*

| Sequence | Kpos | I=0 | I=1 | I=2 | I=3 |
|---|---|---|---|---|---|
| I | 0 | $PE_{00} = \sin 0 = 0$ | $PE_{01} = \cos 0 = 1$ | $PE_{02} = \sin 0 = 0$ | $PE_{03} = \cos 0 = 0.$ |
| am | 1 | $PE_{10} = \sin(\frac{1}{1}) = 0.84$ | $PE_{11} = \cos(\frac{1}{1}) = 0.54$ | $PE_{12} = \sin\left(\frac{1}{10}\right) = 0.10$ | $PE_{13} = \cos(\frac{1}{10}) = 1.0$ |
| a | 2 | $PE_{20} = \sin\left(\frac{2}{1}\right) = 0.91$ | $PE_{21} = \cos(\frac{2}{1}) = -0.42$ | $PE_{22} = \sin(\frac{2}{10})$=0.20 | $PE_{23} = \cos\left(\frac{2}{10}\right) = 0.98$ |
| boy | 3 | $PE_{30} = \sin\left(\frac{3}{1}\right) = 0.14$ | $PE_{31} = \cos(\frac{3}{1}) = -0.99$ | $PE_{32} = \sin\left(\frac{3}{10}\right) = 0.30$ | $PE_{33} = \cos(\frac{3}{10})$=0.96 |

*Table 1. Representation of positional embedding*

| 0 | 1 | 0 | 1 | 0 |
|---|---|---|---|---|
| 0.841 | 0.54 | 0.158 | 0.987 | 0 |
| 0.909 | -0.416 | 0.312 | 0.95 | 0 |
| 0.141 | -0.99 | 0.458 | 0.889 | 0 |
| -0.757 | -0.654 | 0.592 | 0.806 | 0 |

## WORD EMBEDDING

The concept of word embeddings express words in terms of vectors that consists of numbers real in nature, in that case produced real numbers portrays the underlying text, in a very particular statistical and computational meaning comparing the semantics of various phrases and in efficient data representation leads to reduction in dimension (Bhalerao, 2020). Word embedding can be categorized into two types such as frequency related embedding and prediction related embedding (Worth, 2023). In the figure 6, how textual input is transformed into machines understandable data structures is presented.

So, the using the above steps, the word embedding may capture both the meaning as per specific semantic and syntax of a word. In the year 2013, a Google team under the leadership of Tomas Mikolov designed and released the Word2Vec technique for word embedding, which can be further divided into skip gram and continuous bag of words (CBOW) models (Dharma et al., 2022). To demonstrate, how the input sentences are used to predict the next tokens with some probability values, the python code is given below.

sentences = [['write', 'an', 'essay', 'about', 'dog'],

*Figure 6. How textual input transformed into machines understandable data structures*

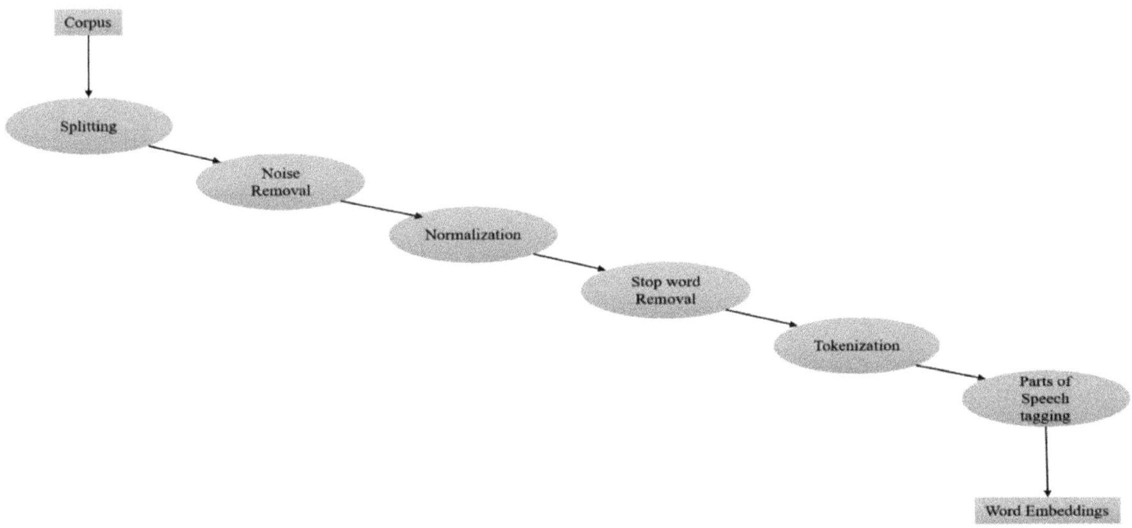

```
['write .', 'an', 'paragraph', 'on', 'lions'],
['write', 'an', 'essay', 'describing', 'ai'],
['what', 'is', 'your', 'favourite', 'pet'],
['my', 'favorite', 'color', 'is', 'black']]
sims = model1.wv.most_similar('write', topn=10)
```

With the help of the above program code that is "model1.wv.most_similar('write', topn=10)", will give the top-10 most similar words of the input "write" using cosine similarity. The output is given in figure 7. The scatter plot of PCA projection of word2vec is given in figure 8.

From the figure 7, it can be concluded that the words like "your", "favorite" can be predicted next, because they have highest probability score. Next, the reinforcement learning is going to be discussed.

*Figure 7. Probability values of predicted next words*

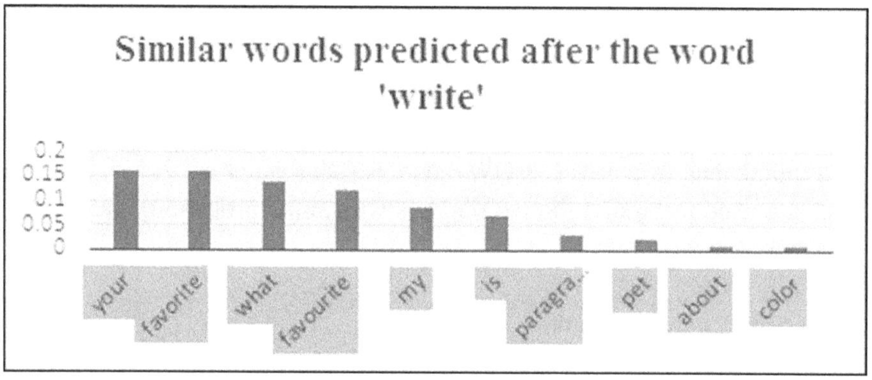


*Figure 8. Representation using scatter plot of PCA projection of Word2vec*

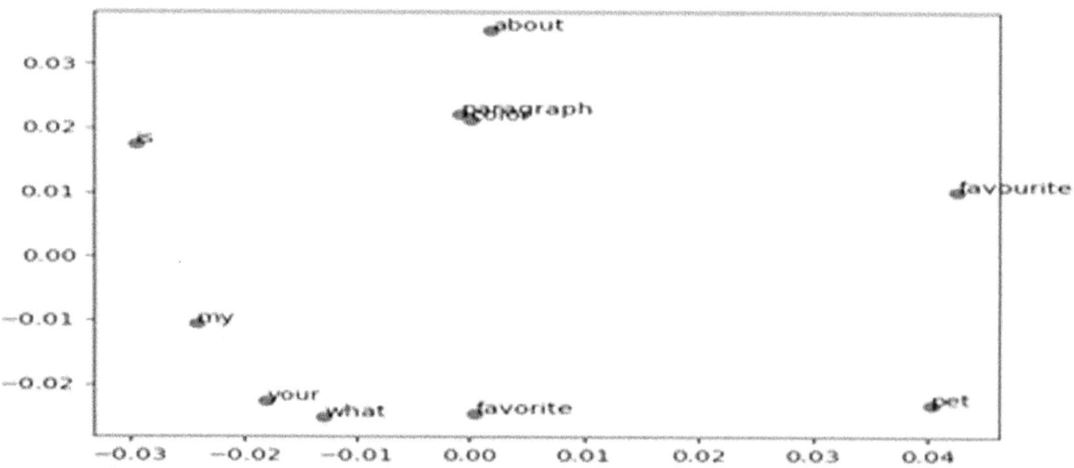

## REINFORCEMENT LEARNING

Reinforcement learning (RL) is primarily concerned with learning an optimal policy to maximize the intended reward or achieve specified goals through the agent- environment interactions (Su & Yang, 2023). A reward function properly defined is essential for the proper training of a reinforcement learning agent. With the comparison with supervised and unsupervised learning, reinforcement learning includes evaluative feedback with the labeling that is unsupervised. Deep RL is a subclass of RL that incorporates deep neural networks for state representation and/or "a value function's approximation", a reward function, policy, and transition model (Li et al., 2023). Diagrammatic view of relationship is given in Figure 9.

Now, with limited sensor information, it is hard to develop a reward function that is precise in nature to evaluate if the job is properly accomplished for varied activities such as cleaning of a table or clothing folding when the goals are complicated and not well defined. In this approach, human expertise or human intuition are further addressed with the aim of knowledge transfer to minimize mismatch between human preferences and the aims of RL agents and to speed efficiency while learning without any prior knowledge or experience. With the rapid growth of deep reinforcement learning, this approach has garnered a great deal of interest and can be referred to the term "Reinforcement Learning with Human Feedback" (known as RLHF), depicted in Figure 10.

The ability of large-scale language models (LMs) to create really "good" texts is heavily influenced by human preferences. The concept of RLHF has been successfully put in with the aim of fine tuning

*Figure 9. Representation of relationship between AI, ML, deep learning and reinforcement learning*

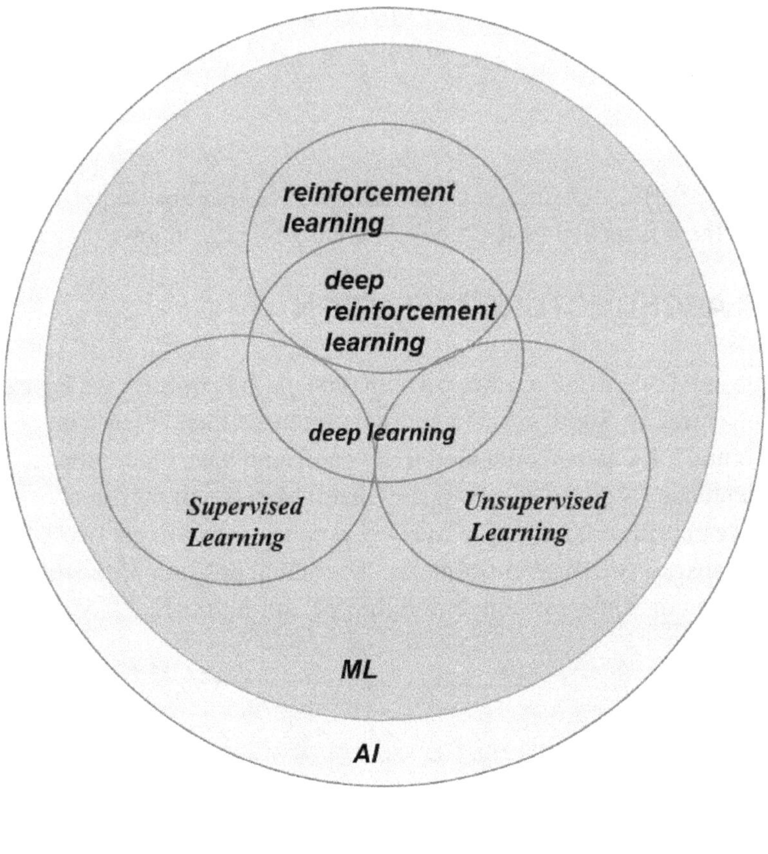

*Figure 10. Representation of human feedback reinforcement learning in NLP*

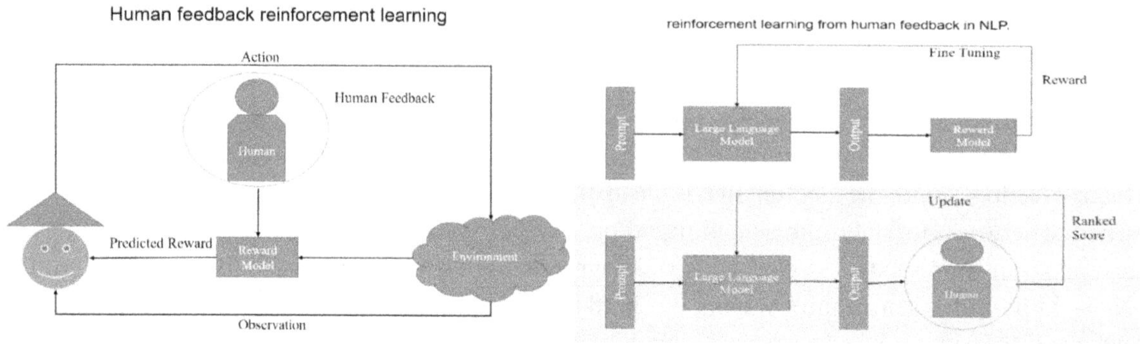


language models in most natural language processing fields like conversation translation, story development, evidence extraction, and semantic parsing. In the next section, the neural network is going to study in detail.

## NEURAL NETWORK

A neural network manipulates information as the working of human brain. It is a network of artificial neurons. An artificial neuron is a computational model with input units, weighted edges connected to a processing unit. Input data is processed to produce the output. Neural network learns from example. We have to train our neural network to do complex tasks. In table 2, we have demonstrated single layer neural network with weights and bias. Also, AND operation is modeled using this type of neural network with appropriate activation function.

## TOKENIZATION

Suppose we have a sentence like "tell me about your hobby". The tokenization process takes this sentence as input and produces the tokens like "tell", "me", "about", "your", "hobby".

## TRANSFORMER ARCHITECTURE ATTENTION

Transformer generates text one word at a time. To understand transformer we have to know the basics of context pulling in sentences. Suppose there are two sentences like, "Please buy a pen and a pencil", "Apsara is a pencil brand". It can be concluded that "pen" and "pensil" are the two objects of similar type. In the second sentence, "Apsara" is a company that makes pensil, "Apsara" is closely related with the word "brand". If we take the embedding of the two sentences, we will get two different arrangements in the embeddings because of two different contexts. The actual position of the token changes rapidly if the context changes. The concept is presented in figure 11 and figure 12.

*Table 2. Basic concept of neural network*

$Y_{\_IN} = \sum X_I \times W_I$

**Activation Function:**
$Y_{\_OUT}$ = 1 IF $Y_{\_IN}$ >threshold
= 0 otherwise

**Artificial Neural network without Bias**

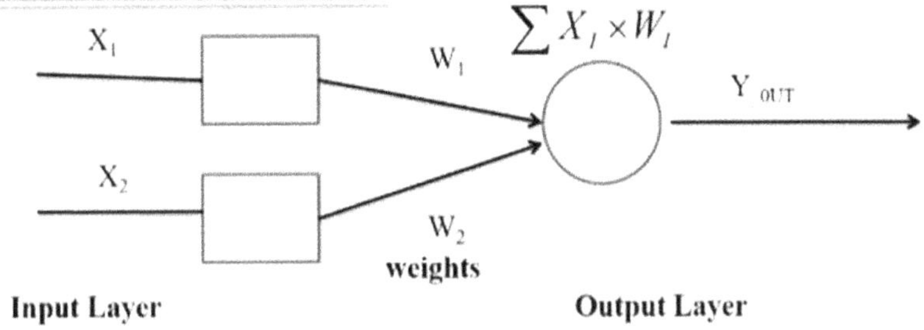


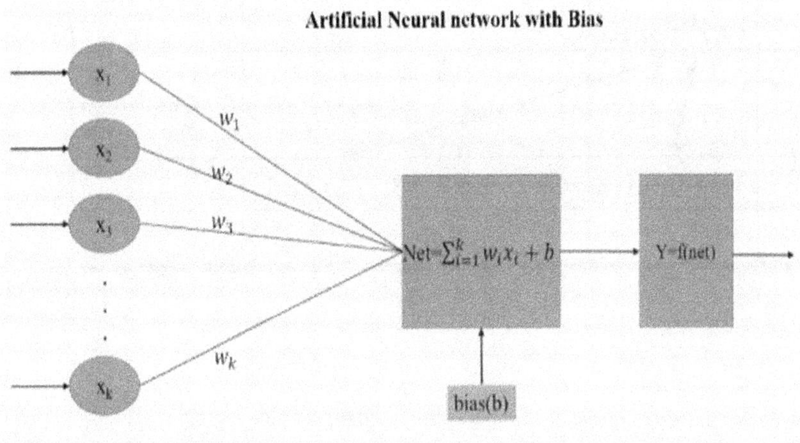


**AND function using Neural Network**

**Step 1:** Initialize the weights
$W_1 = 1$ and $W_2 = 1$

**Step 2:** Calculate the weighted input
$Y_{\_IN} = W_1 \times X_1 + W_2 \times X_2$

**Step 3:** Calculate the value of **Activation Function**

| $X_1$ | $X_2$ | $X_1$ AND $X_2$ | $Y_{\_IN}$ | $Y_{\_OUT}$ |
|---|---|---|---|---|
| 0 | 0 | 0 | 0 | 0 |
| 0 | 1 | 0 | 1 | 0 |
| 1 | 0 | 0 | 1 | 0 |
| 1 | 1 | 1 | 2 | 1 |

**$Y_{\_OUT} = f(Y_{\_IN}) = 1$ IF $Y_{\_IN} >= 2$**
**0 otherwise**

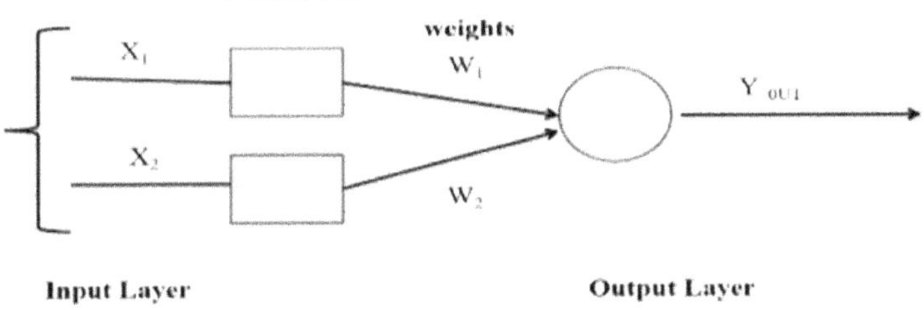

*Figure 11. Context pulling of the sentence "Please buy a pen and a pencil"*

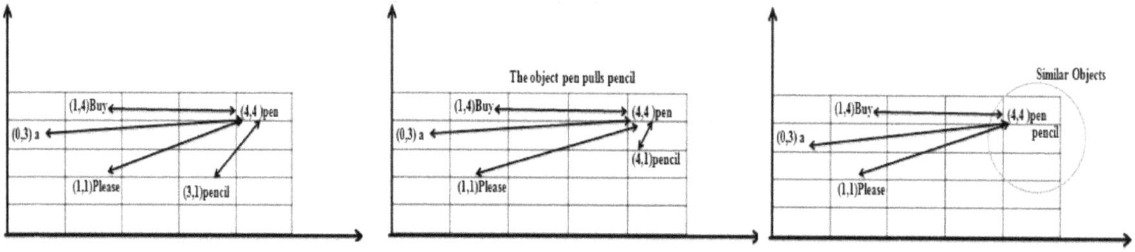


*Figure 12. Context pulling of the tokens from the sentence "Apsara is a pencil brand"*

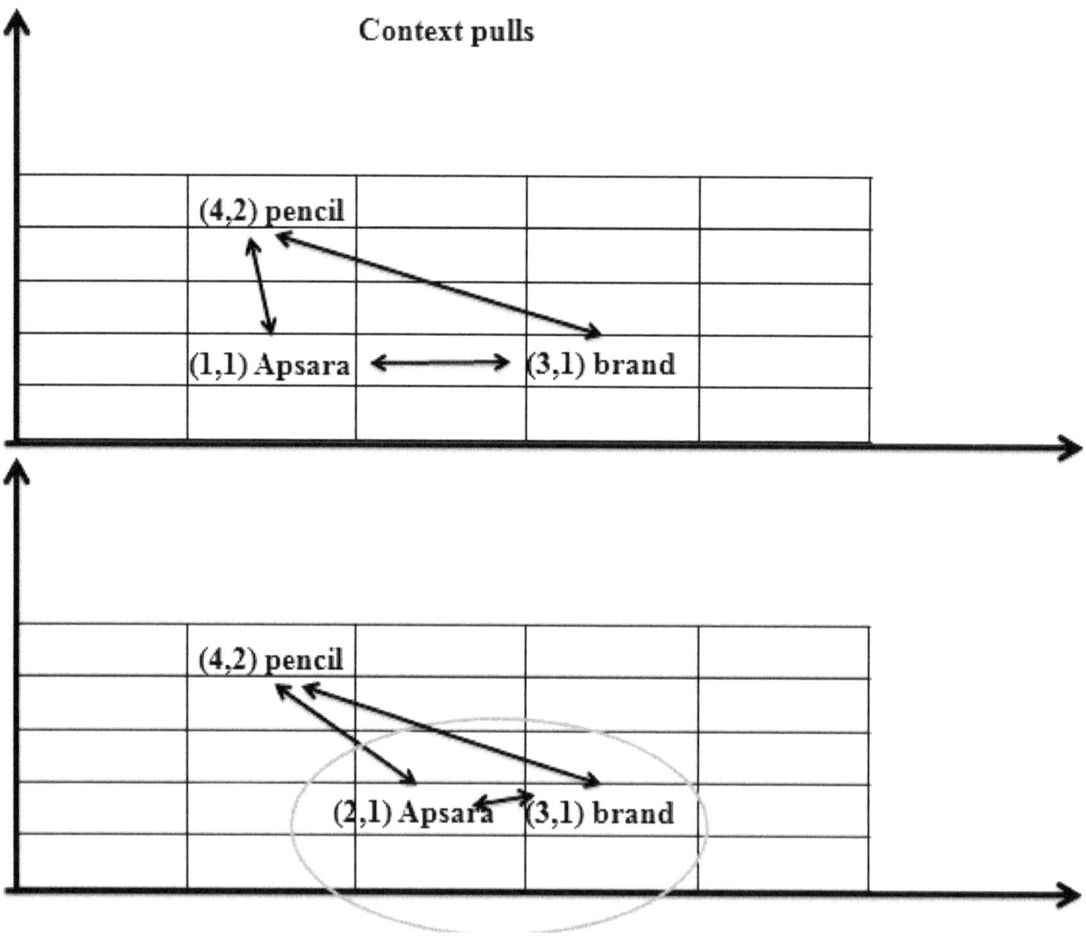


## MULTI HEAD ATTENTION

Mulit-head attention is very much required to get the best embedding of all. We can see that the embedding 2 is better than others.

*Figure 13. Different embedding for the tokens "Pen," "Pencil," and "Eraser"*

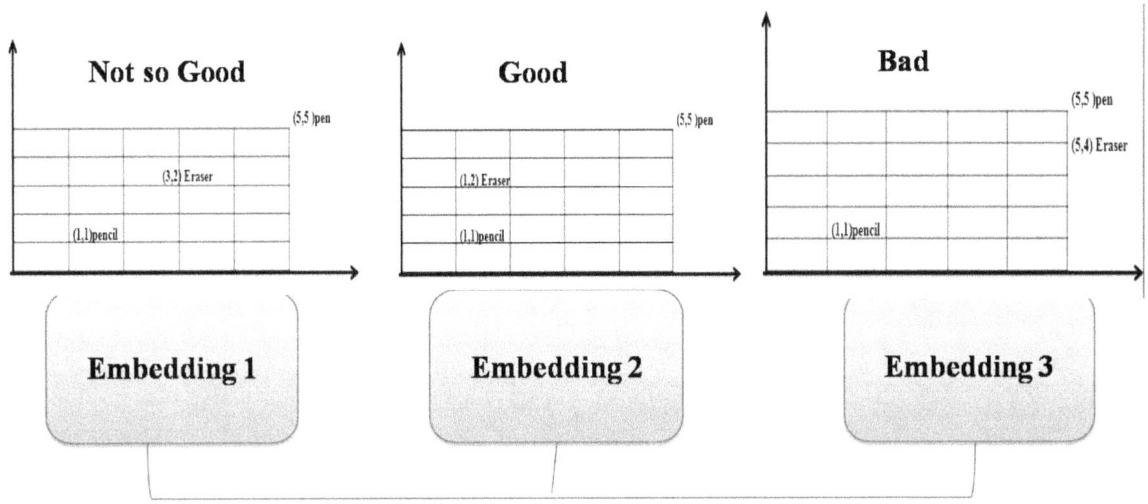


Now to create more embeddings, we often use linear transformations. The process is given in Figure 13, we can use linear transformations like rotating, stretching horizontally and vertically to create the different embeddings from the existing ones. This process is given in Figure 14. The working of Multi-Head attention is given in Figure 15, step by step.

The series of transformer block is given in figure 16, below.

The first step is to take input and then perform tokenization. Then embedding process is performed and then positional encoding is done. The output co-ordinates are given as input into the neural network which is trained to predict the next token with a score to form the sentence. The score is calculated using softmax function, which represents the probability of each tokens. The neural network consists of attention and feed forward layers. In between each feed forward layers there is one attention layer. For training and testing phase the details are given in figure 16 and figure 17.

## AI BASED CHATGPT TOOL

OpenAI developed the ChatGPT model. It's design is built around the model of "GPT" (termed as "Generative Pre-trained Transformer") (Qadir, 2022; Liu et al., 2023; ChatGPT, 2023). It is a variation

*Figure 14. Linear Transformation for Generating New Forms of Embedding*

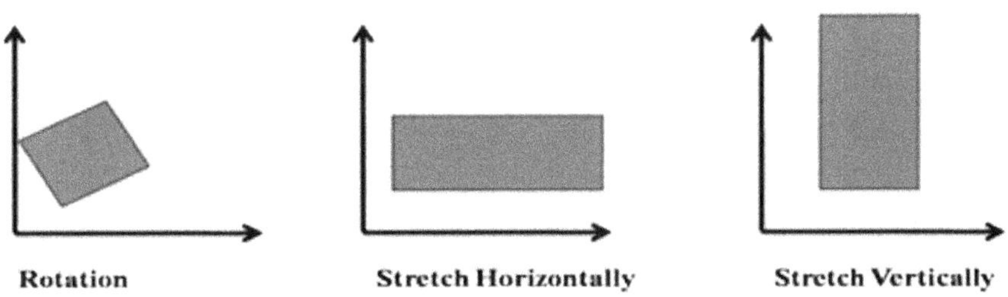

*Figure 15. Working of Multi-Head Attention for the Sentence "Apsara is a pencil brand"*

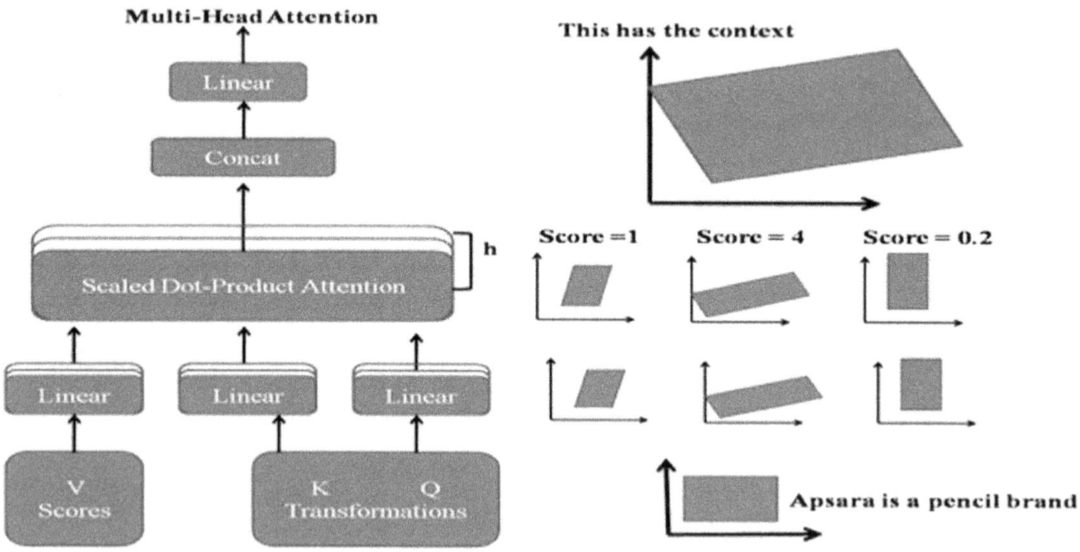


*Figure 16. Representation of Series of Transformer Blocks*

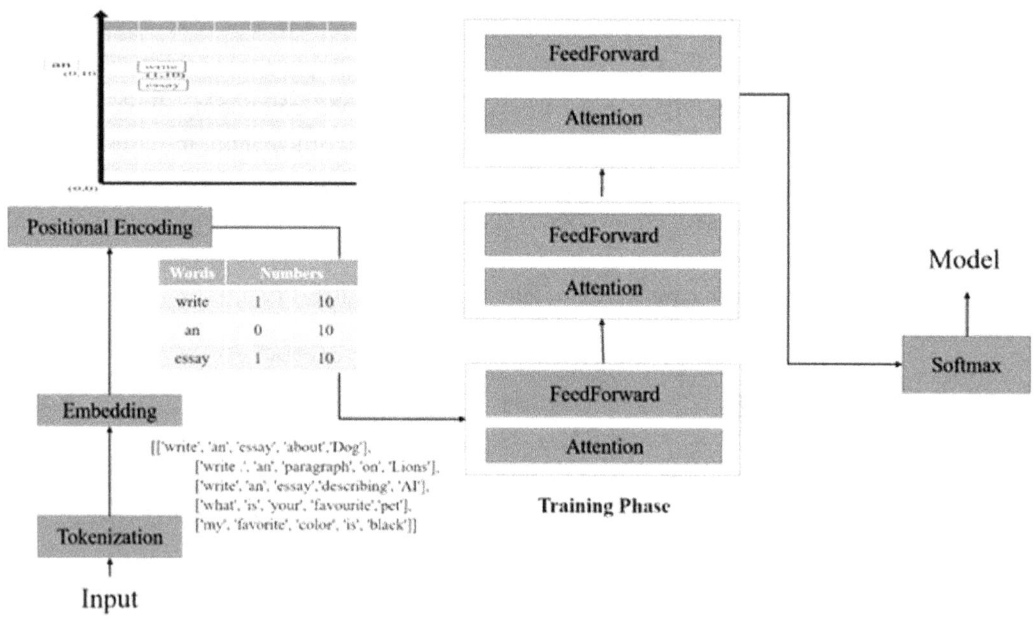


on the "GPT model" to produce human understandable language (Cooper, 2023; Wu et al., 2023). The evolution of the tool is outline in the figure 18. In figure 19, the number of tokens processed and data size for pre training are mentioned.

In the context of AI based ChatGPT tool, we have also compared the ChatGPT application tool with Bard application standard of generative AI. The comparison table is shown below.

*Figure 17. Output generation by transformer architecture*

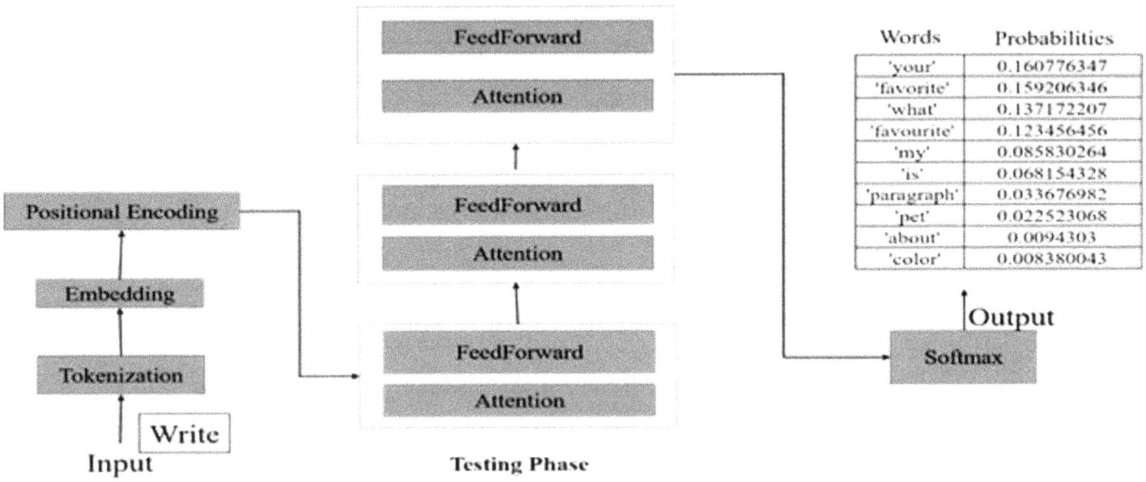


*Figure 18. Evolution of ChatGPT*

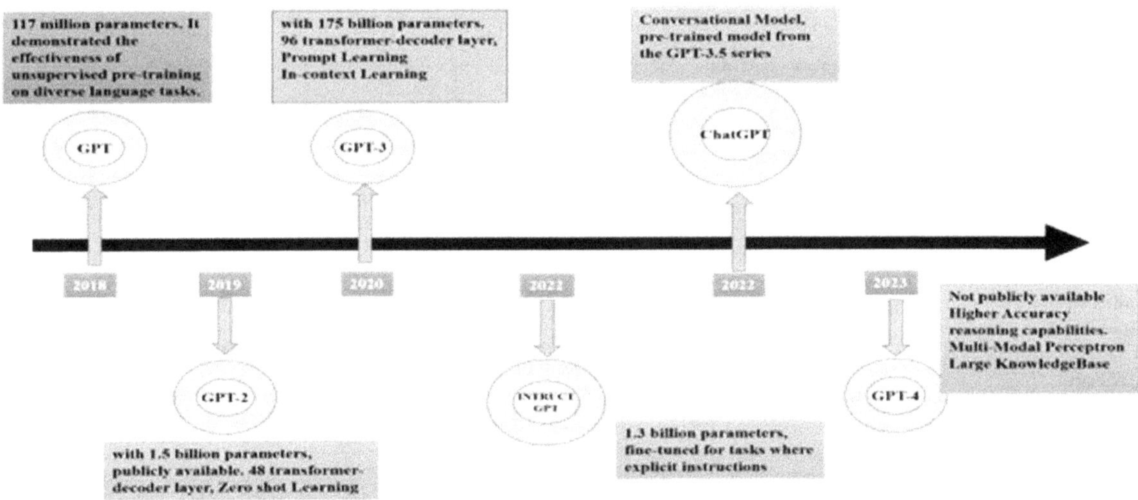


*Figure 19. Context Window (No of tokens), left; and pre-training data size of GPT series, right*

*Table 3. Comparison of ChatGpt Tool with Google Bard (Musiol, 2023; Maya, 2023; Campesato, 2023; Ciesla, 2024; Marquis, 2024)*

| | ChatGpt | Google Bard/Gemini |
|---|---|---|
| **Training** | **Trained on internet data, books, articles, websites and forums** | **language that people use to reflect the human experience** |
| **Backend** | GPT-4 | PaLM2/ LaMDA |
| **Purpose** | Built for conversational and interactive task | Built for creative writing task |
| **Image Generation** | Not Possible | Possible |
| **Latex formula generation** | Not accurate | Accurate |
| **Style of Output and Structure** | It produces informative and coherence responses with the given prompt | detailed answers with visual elements |
| **User Experience And Applications** | Offers a versatile user experience that caters to chatbots, virtual assistants and text based customer support systems | Offers unique user experience that adheres to creative writing, enthusiasts, poets and seeking poetic inspirations. It provides better interface and formatted text |
| **Employs Context** | Collect information from previous conversation and prior interactions with the user in form of a chat | Use the context in the conversations |
| **Summarizing Content** | ChatGpt better than Google Bard | Less efficient than ChatGPT |
| **Mimicking natural language and facilitating open ended questions** | Not very good in this context | Google Bard performs better |
| **Integration** | Plagiarism detection Tool Microsoft's Bing. | Integrated with Google search, Adobe and Spotify |
| **Language Support** | Supports over 10 languages | Supports over 40 languages, making it highly accessible |
| **Access** | Not Free | Free |
| **Multimodal Search Capabilities** | Not Present | Present |
| **Efficiency** | Excellent conversational capabilities for a range of scenarios. | Better operational efficiency with lighter versions of LLMs. It supports larger volume of simultaneous users |
| **Computing power** | High | Less |
| **Rate of adoption** | High across different industries, from education to business, due to its versatility | Expected to be high, especially with integration into Google's ecosystem |

## APPLICATIONS OF CHATGPT TOOL

ChatGPT has been utilized in a range of applications, including developing chatbot answers, story and content ideas, and even music. ChatGPT can be used in the paradigm of education by both students and teachers (Qadir, 2022). ChatGPT is currently employed in many ways including services proved for library, healthcare, and education. In the world of education, ChatGPT may be utilized to construct virtual instructors, reply student inquiries, and give customized experiences for learning (Su & Yang, 2023).

Making with AI motivated teachers to think about the distinctive character of crafts, as well as the tensions and tradeoffs of incorporating generative AI into craft processes. The user may provide a prompt (a written description of what the user wants) that informs the AI to envisage and visualise evening dresses with a description of the chosen colour, materials, style, scenery, lighting, and so on (Vartiainen & Tedre, 2023). To verify the applications of ChatGpt tool, we have carefully designed one questionnaire as a survey form and 535 responses are collected across different domains of undergraduate students, post-graduate students, faculty members and research scholars from different institutions. There are five qualitative features like "Very relevant", "Somewhat relevant", "Informative", "Helpful", "Not relevant" and "Grammatically correct" as answers in the survey form. The analysis is given in this section for each sub headings like "EDUCATIONAL POLICY MAKING". The questions are given in this manuscript. The answers of ChatGPT is included in the "Data Availability" section.

## EDUCATIONAL POLICY MAKING

Some important challenges are noticed by government authorities all around the world like AI discrimination and bias, loss of privacy, violation of human rights, and harmful use of AI (Chan, 2023). The education related to entrepreneurship should equip learners to take use of new chances provided by developing technologies such as generative AI in order to successfully prepare them for future entrepreneurial pursuits. As per the suggestion made, it can supplement and replace duties related to the process idea generating, the process of selling, the process of scaling, the process of content generation, and communication (R. Bell & H. Bell, 2023). In the field of education, AI based ChatGpt tool has appeared as a propitious technology for improving learning processes and supporting teaching skills by providing personalized, real-time feedback. Educational policy makers can suggest ChatGpt tool in a number of ways to improve learning and teaching process (Sifat, 2023).

- **Creating educational materials**: Teachers can use ChatGpt to get ideas for preparing class notes or assignments or assessments. As such, teachers will able to teach the students with high quality. Also, it helps the students to develop their skills by providing customized needs and practice opportunities.
- **Supporting personalized learning:** AI based ChatGpt tool can be used to generate personalised educational learning aspects that can help the students to keep engage and motivate through effective learning experience.
- **Providing remote learning:** Policy makers can use this emerging AI based tool to provide the learning facilities through subject for students who are not able to attend the classes in person.
- **Supporting real-time feedback:** ChatGpt tool supports real-time feedback technique that is more helpful for the students to improve their literacy and numeracy skills based on their efforts.
- **Making a decision:** Educational policy makers can collect information which is generated by AI based tools to analyze and determine the scope of different teaching methods. Hence, it helps to make a decision in selecting appropriate teaching method for improving education outcomes.

What are five educational policy making strategies in schools and colleges?

## INFRASTRUCTURE DEVELOPMENT IN SCHOOLS AND COLLEGES

ChatGpt can assist the various key aspects like planning, budgeting regarding infrastructure development in schools and colleges. Some important keys are listed below (Atlas, 2023).

*Figure 20. Responses collected for the question "What are five educational policy making strategies in schools and colleges?"*

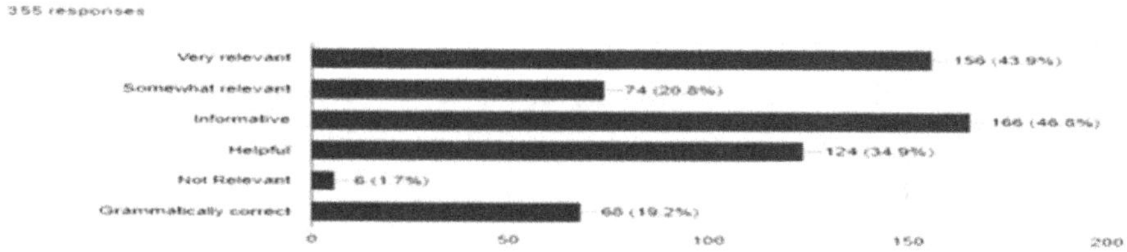


- **Proposal assessment:** ChatGpt tool is helpful to determine school's or college's requirements such as optimal classrooms design, advanced technology, online learning platforms and other related proposals also.
- **Environmental conscious:** ChatGPT can provide the best ideas for environmentally friendly practices of the design planning to make a more eco-friendly and efficient infrastructure in educational premises.
- **Budgeting:** ChatGPT can provide a realistic budget for the project planning including cost-effective solutions, prioritizing essential elements for educational infrastructure.
- **Communication strategy:** Engagement: ChatGpt helps to provide the strategies for involving the communities such as parents, business organization and other stakeholders in the development process.

How teaching learning process can be improved using generative AI?

## RESEARCH AND INNOVATION ACTIVITIES IN SCHOOLS AND COLLEGES

The activities related to research and innovations can be governed by the AI tools. Suppose to set up an innovation lab the required tools can be suggested via the gen AI . But the teachers have to choose the correct ones according to the need.

Write the role of generative AI in the domain of education within 100 words.

Write the demerits of generative AI in the domain of education within 100 words.

*Figure 21. Responses collected for the question "How teaching learning process can be improved using generative AI?"*

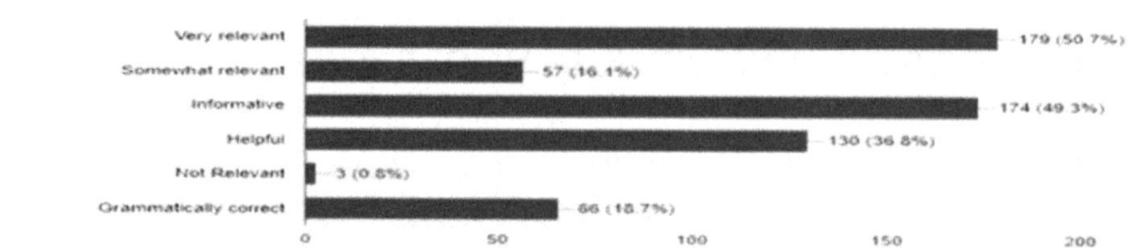

*Figure 22. Responses collected for the question "Write the role of generative AI in the domain of education within 100 words?"*

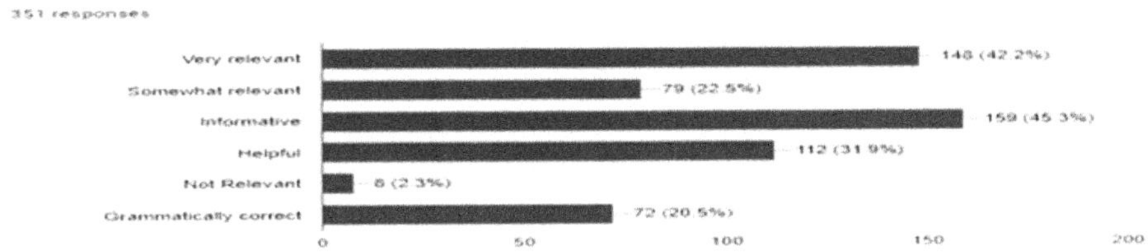


## RESEARCH PROPOSAL WRITING

ChatGpt can assist the research proposal writing by providing various key components such as follows (Rahman et al., 2023):

- **Creating basic ideas:** Research scholars many times struggle with formulating research hypotheses. Regarding this aspect ChatGpt can assist through brainstorming and proper refining process.
- **Literature survey:** ChatGpt tool can provide relevant sources and summarize key facts so that existing research is integrated into research proposal writing.
- **Methodology:** Methodology section comprises of selected research techniques regarding data analysis and collection. Here, ChatGpt tool can assist by providing guidance on selecting research methods.
- **Clarity and consistency:** ChatGpt tool can provide appropriate guidelines in writing research proposals to improve the clarity and consistency so that the research proposals are easy to understand.

Find the most suitable methodology framework suggestions for research within 200 words.

## RESEARCH PAPER WRITING

ChatGpt plays a pivotal role in expediting the research paper writing process for researchers. However, ChatGpt provides some general guidelines for writing an effective research paper. These include (Aly et al., 2023):

*Figure 23. Responses collected for the question "Write the demerits of generative AI in the domain of education within 100 words?"*

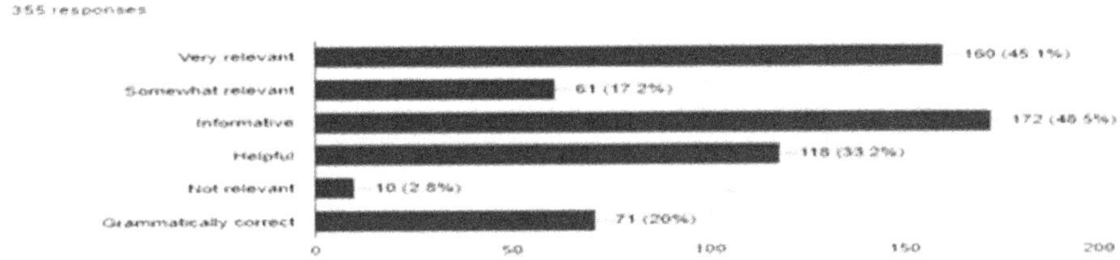

*Figure 24. Responses collected for the request "Find the most suitable methodology framework suggestions for research within 200 words,"*

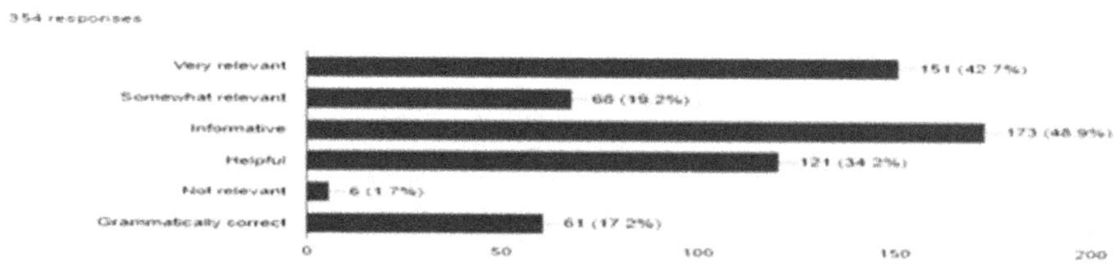


- **Brainstorm ideas:**ChatGpt can help with the brainstorming process by suggesting appropriate ideas based on researcher's interests or requirements.
- **Outline generator:** Once a topic has selected, researchers can use ChatGpt tool to produce an outline with details for selected assignment as possible.
- **Review and clarification:** After outline of research topic, a chatGpt tool helps to find related literature insights and summaries with proper explanations for a specific aspect to support research paper writing.
- **Editing and Proofreading:**ChatGpt can provide the suggestions regarding grammatical and syntax errors and overall formatting styles in writing a research paper.
- **Citations and References:** Creating the citations linked with reference list is a vital work. Regarding this, the use of ChatGpt tool is more helpful to provide the guidance on proper citation styles with references.

## DEVELOPMENT OF INNOVATION LABS

AI based ChatGPT tool has a large potential effect on development of innovation of educational labs in several ways (Fütterer et al., 2023):

- **Module creation& problem solving**: ChatGPT can assist to create a design of innovative curricula or module for the development of educational lab activities or experiments that engage students and fulfill the aim of educational goals. It can also provide the solutions to the issues which may occur in the design and implementation of educational labs.

*Figure 25. Responses collected for the request "Outline how generative AI could improve research paper writing within 5 points,"*

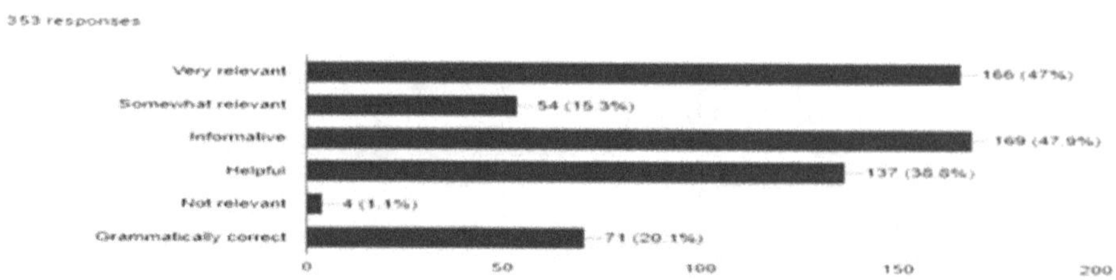

- **Technology Integration**: To achieve modern learning experience, ChatGPT tool can suggest ways to incorporate emerging technologies into educational labs in efficiently.
- **Cross-discipline Approaches**: This AI based tool helps to bring two or more academic disciplines into single approach in educational lab settings.
- **Evaluation and Assessment**: In this context, ChatGPT can develop suitable methods for assessing the effectiveness of educational labs in achieving learning outcomes.

Write a paragraph about AI Innovation Lab within 100 words?

## EDUCATIONAL CONTENT GENERATION

Using ChatGPT for educational content generation refers to make use of the language model to produce brainstorming sessions, lesson plans and learning styles. For example, ChatGPT can assist constructive activities, group projects, or gamified learning practices that make educational content creation more interactive and delightful (Gill et al., 2023). ChatGPT can also be used as a tool for content formulation providing the model with an appropriate topic or a theme and put forward to generate a list of important subtopics or headlines. It is worth for content generation but it cannot replace human content writers. It is a tool that can encourage to generate more content efficiently.

Describe the chemical composition of water in 300 words.

How generative AI can assist in authoring automated content generation in education? Give a brief note.

*Figure 26. Responses collected for the REQUEST "Write a paragraph about AI Innovation Lab within 100 words,"*

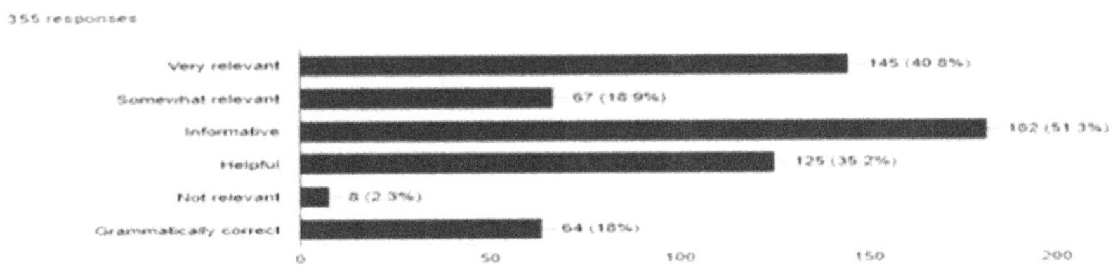


*Figure 27. Responses collected for the REQUEST "Describe the chemical composition of water in 300 words,"*

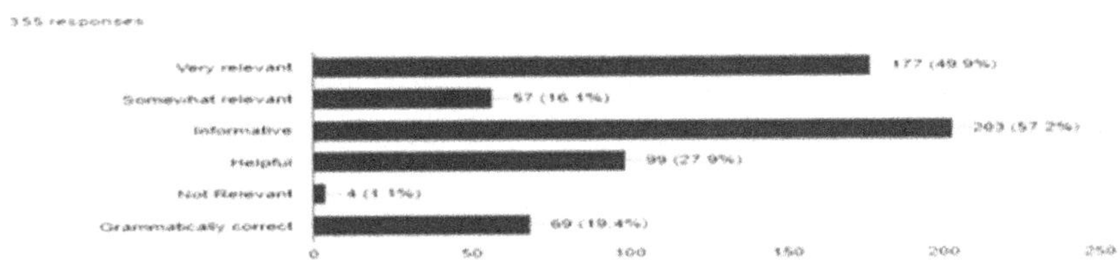

*Figure 28. Responses collected for the question "How can generative AI assist in authoring automated content generation in education? Give a brief note?"*

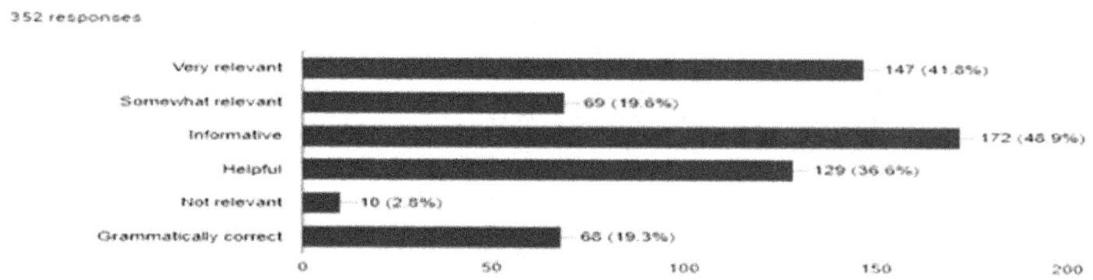


## FUTURE RESEARCH DIRECTIONS

In future the task of policy making, infrastructure development in schools and colleges, research innovation activities development, research paper and proposal writing, innovation lab setup and educational context generation can be done efficiently, precisely and context wise but in a human controlled or human guided framework.

## CONCLUSION

In this chapter, we have discussed very basic and fundamental blocks of large language model, generative AI and its application in education system. From a detailed survey it can be concluded that the generative AI can make significant contribution in the context of education system in 2030. But we have to be very careful at the time of taking help of generative AI, constant human intervention is required.

## DATA AVAILABILITY

The data underlying this study are collected through the conducted survey available at the https://docs.google.com/forms/d/e/1FAIpQLScgdVFIaEKp60O1YNf4QyjF2CUBIxp-dVt2kmzzpfZSBaMeaw/viewform?usp=sf_link

## REFERENCES

Aly, T., & Aly, A. (2023). Chat GPT in Preparation of the Scientific Papers in Spinal Cord Injuries in the Middle East? *International Journal of Clinical Studies & Medical Case Reports, 33*(4). doi:10.46998/IJCMCR.2023.33.000817

Atlas, S. (2023). *ChatGPT for Higher Education and Professional Development: A Guide to Conversational AI.* Research Gate. https://digitalcommons.uri.edu/cba_facpubs/548

Bell, R., & Bell, H. (2023). Entrepreneurship education in the era of generative artificial intelligence. *Entrepreneurship Education, 6*(3), 229–244. doi:10.1007/s41959-023-00099-x

Bhalerao, P. (2020). *Classification using a word embedding techniques*. UMBC.. //https://redirect.cs.umbc.edu/courses/graduate/676/SP2020/SP2020presentations/Bhalerao%20Prachi%20Term%20Paper

Bommasani, R., Hudson, D. A., & Adeli, E. (2022). On the Opportunities and Risks of Foundation Models. *Center for Research on Foundation Models* (CRFM), 1-214.//https://arxiv.org/pdf/2108.07258.pdf

Campesato, O. (2023). *Gpt-4 for Developers*. Walter de Gruyter GmbH & Co KG. doi:10.1515/9781501519024

Chan, C. K. Y. (2023). A comprehensive AI policy education framework for university teaching and learning. *International Journal of Educational Technology in Higher Education*, *20*(38), 1–25. doi:10.1186/s41239-023-00408-3

ChatGPT. (2023). *ChatGPT Evolution Timeline*. Open AI. //https://chat.openai.com/share/a7d038b9-af2b-4049-8762-a2438f672d19

Ciesla, R. (2024). *The Book of Chatbots: From ELIZA to ChatGPT*. Springer Nature. Cohere. https://docs.cohere.com/docs/prompt-engineering

Cooper, G. (2023). Examining Science Education in ChatGPT: An Exploratory Study of Generative Artificial Intelligence. *Journal of Science Education and Technology*, *32*(3), 444–452. doi:10.1007/s10956-023-10039-y

Dharma, E. M., Gaol, F. L., Warnars, H. L. H. S., & Soewito, B. (2022). The Accuracy Comparison among Word2vec, Glove, and Fasttext towards Convolution Neural Network (Cnn) Text Classification. *Journal of Theoretical and Applied Information Technology*, *100*(2), 31.

Fütterer, T., Fischer, C., Alekseeva, A., Chen, X., Tate, T., Warschauer, M., & Gerjets, P. (2023). *ChatGPT in education: global reactions toAIinnovations*. Scientifc Reports., doi:10.1038/s41598-023-42227-6

Gill, S. S., Xu, M., Patros, P., Wu, H., Kaur, R., Kaur, K., Fuller, S., Singh, M., Arora, P., Parlikad, A. K., Stankovski, V., Abraham, A., Ghosh, S. K., Lutfiyya, H., Kanhere, S. S., Bahsoon, R., Rana, O., Dustdar, S., Sakellariou, R., & Buyya, R. (2023). Transformative Effects of ChatGPT on Modern Education: Emerging Era of AI Chatbots. *Internet of Things and Cyber-Physical Systems*, *4*, 19–23. doi:10.1016/j.iotcps.2023.06.002

Li, L., Ma, Z., Fan, L., Lee, S., Yu, H., & Hemphill, L. (2023). ChatGPT in education: A discourse analysis of worries and concerns on social media. *Education and Information Technologies*. doi:10.1007/s10639-023-12256-9

Liu, Y., Yang, Z., Yu, Z., Liu, Z., Liu, D., Lin, H., & Shi, S. (2023). Generative artificial intelligence and its applications in materials science: Current situation and future perspectives. *Journal of Materiomics*.

Marquis, Y., Oladoyinbo, T. O., Olabanji, S. O., Olaniyi, O. O., & Ajayi, S. A. (2024). Proliferation of AI tools: A multifaceted evaluation of user perceptions and emerging trend. *Asian Journal of Advanced Research and Reports*, *18*(1), 30–55. doi:10.9734/ajarr/2024/v18i1596

Maya, L. (2023). *Google Bard AI Expertise: Unlock the Power of "Google Bard AI Expertise" and Transform Your Content*. Estalontech.

Musiol, M. (2023). *Generative AI Navigating the Course to the Artificial General Intelligence Future.* Wiley. Niser. //https://www.niser.ac.in/~smishra/teach/cs461/23cs461/assignment/adhil/CS461_notes_positional_encoding

QadirJ. (2022). Engineering Education in the Era of ChatGPT: Promise and Pitfalls of Generative AI for Education. TechRxiv. // doi:10.36227/techrxiv.21789434.v1

Rahman, M.M. & Watanobe, Y. (2023). ChatGPT for Education and Research: Opportunities, Threats, and Strategies. *Appl. Sci.*, *13*, 5783. /https://doi.org//. doi:10.3390

RaneN. (2023). Role and Challenges of ChatGPT and Similar Generative Artificial Intelligence in Arts and Humanities. // doi:10.2139/ssrn.4603208

Saeed, M. (2023). *A Gentle Introduction to Positional Encoding in Transformer Models. Machine learning mastery*. Machine Learning Mastery. https://machinelearningmastery.com/a-gentle-introduction-to-positional-encoding-in-transformer-models-part-1

Sifat, R.I. (2023). ChatGPT and the Future of Health Policy Analysis: Potential and Pitfalls of Using ChatGPT in Policymaking. *Ann Biomed Eng*, *51*, 1357–1359. //. doi:10.1007/s10439-023-03204-2

Smolansky, A., Cram, A., Raduescu, C., Zeivots, S., Huber, E., & Kizilcec, F. R. (2023). Educator and Student Perspectives on the Impact of Generative AI on Assessments in Higher Education. *In Proceedings of the Tenth ACM Conference on Learning @ Scale (L@S'23)*,1–22.

Su, J., & Yang, W. (2023). Unlocking the Power of ChatGPT: A Framework for Applying Generative AI in Education. *ECNU Review of Education*, *6*(3), 355–366. doi:10.1177/20965311231168423

Vartiainen, H., & Tedre, M. (2023). Using artificial intelligence in craft education: Crafting with text-to-image generative models. *Digital Creativity (Exeter)*, *34*(1), 1–21. doi:10.1080/14626268.2023.2174557

Vaswani, A., Shazeer, N., Parmar, N., Uszkoreit, J., Jones, L., Gomez, A. N., & Polosukhin, I. (2017). Attention is all you need. *Advances in Neural Information Processing Systems*, 30.

Worth, P. J. (2023). Word embeddings and semantic spaces in natural language processing. *International Journal of Intelligence Science*, *13*(1), 1–21. doi:10.4236/ijis.2023.131001

Wu, T., He, S., Liu, J., Sun, S., Liu, K., Han, Q. L., & Tang, Y. (2023). A brief overview of ChatGPT: The history, status quo and potential future development. *IEEE/CAA Journal of AutomaticaSinica*, *10*(5), 1122-1136.

# Chapter 26
# Bridging Data-Driven Learning and Generative AI:
## A Framework for Sustainable Education Through Metacognitive Resource Utilization

**Rajiv Verma**
https://orcid.org/0009-0009-7729-3204
*Sir Padampat Singhania University, India*

**Manish Dadhich**
*Sir Padampat Singhania University, India*

**Arvind Sharma**
*Sir Padampat Singhania University, India*

## ABSTRACT

*This chapter presents a framework to enhance sustainable education by bridging data-driven learning and generative artificial intelligence (AI) with metacognitive resource utilization. The framework offers educators a structured approach to integrate innovative pedagogical strategies grounded in the intersection of educational theory and emerging technologies. Through a comprehensive review of literature, the study identifies gaps and theoretical frameworks relevant to sustainable education. The proposed framework emphasizes the importance of promoting metacognitive skills alongside sustainability principles, empowering students to become active agents in addressing global challenges. However, challenges such as inequalities in access to resources and the need for comprehensive educator support are acknowledged. Although these challenges persist, the framework marks a notable advancement in nurturing critical thinking, problem-solving abilities, and conscientious citizenship among students. Further research and fine-tuning are imperative to guarantee its efficacy and accessibility across varied educational environments.*

DOI: 10.4018/979-8-3693-2440-0.ch026

## INTRODUCTION

In the digital transformation era, the convergence of data-driven methodologies and AI presents a revolutionary opportunity to redefine the landscape of education (Alwahedi et al. 2024). By harnessing the power of data analytics and generative AI, educators can unlock new possibilities for personalized learning, adaptive instruction, and cognitive enhancement. In this context, the synergy between data-driven learning and generative AI offers a promising framework for sustainable education, where using metacognitive resources becomes paramount in shaping the learning experience (Bedington et al. 2024). Data-driven learning, characterized by its reliance on empirical evidence and quantitative analysis, has emerged as a cornerstone of contemporary educational practices. By leveraging data analytics, educators can gain valuable insights into student learning patterns, preferences, and performance metrics, enabling targeted interventions and instructional adjustments. From adaptive learning platforms to predictive modeling of student outcomes, data-driven methodologies empower educators to tailor their pedagogical strategies to meet learners' diverse needs (Chiu 2024) effectively.

Complementing data-driven learning, generative AI represents a paradigm shift in how educational content is created, personalized, and disseminated. Generative AI algorithms, equipped with natural language processing and deep learning capabilities, can simulate human-like reasoning and creativity, generating personalized learning materials, instructional content, and assessment tools. This transformative technology enhances the efficiency and scalability of educational delivery and fosters learner engagement, creativity, and critical thinking skills (Dai, Liu, and Lim 2023).

At the intersection of data-driven learning and generative AI lies the concept of MRU – the strategic deployment of cognitive processes to monitor, control, and optimize one's learning strategies. Metacognition, encompassing self-awareness, self-regulation, and reflective thinking, plays a crucial role in fostering deep learning, knowledge retention, and lifelong learning habits. By integrating metacognitive strategies into data-driven and AI-enabled educational environments, educators can empower learners to take ownership of their learning journeys, adaptively navigate complex tasks, and cultivate higher-order thinking skills (Gupta et al. 2024; Holmström and Carroll 2024).

However, while the fusion of data-driven learning and generative AI holds immense promise for sustainable education, it also poses significant challenges and ethical considerations. Issues such as data privacy, algorithmic bias, and the commodification of education demand careful attention to ensure that technological innovations serve the best interests of learners and educators (Hsu, Tan, and Stantic 2024). Moreover, the democratization of access to AI-driven educational resources must be accompanied by efforts to bridge digital divides and promote equitable educational opportunities for all learners.

The significance of the study in its exploration of cutting-edge educational methodologies to address the evolving needs of learners and educators in a rapidly changing world (Dadhich et al. 2022). By investigating the integration of data-driven learning and generative AI into educational frameworks, this research seeks to revolutionize traditional approaches to teaching and learning. Enhancing metacognitive resource utilization through this integration promises to empower learners to become more self-aware, reflective, and adaptable in their learning journeys. By leveraging the capabilities of AI and data analytics, educators can personalize learning experiences, provide targeted support, and identify areas for improvement, thereby fostering a more sustainable and effective educational ecosystem. Having considered the above prominent studies, the following research question can be formulated.

RQ.1: How can a framework integrating data-driven learning and generative AI be effectively designed and implemented to enhance metacognitive resource utilization in sustainable education practices?

## REVIEW OF LITERATURE

(Liu, Zhang, and Biebricher 2024) explored the opportunities and challenges associated with data-driven learning in education. The paper discussed how data analytics can inform instructional design, personalize learning experiences, and improve student outcomes. They also addressed challenges such as data privacy concerns and the need for ethical guidelines in utilizing student data for educational purposes. (Mizumoto 2023) examined the transformative potential of generative AI in reshaping learning environments in education. The paper discussed how generative AI algorithms can create personalized learning materials, simulate instructional scenarios, and enhance student engagement. He also addressed ethical considerations related to developing and deploying AI-driven educational technologies.

(Moorhouse 2024) focused on the role of MRU in promoting student success in education. The paper discussed strategies for fostering metacognitive skills such as self-regulation, reflection, and goal-setting. The work also explored how educators can integrate metacognitive strategies into instructional practices to empower learners and facilitate deeper learning experiences. (Sands et al. 2024) explored the concept of sustainable education and the role of technology, including data-driven learning and generative AI, in promoting sustainability in educational practices. The paper discussed how technology can support personalized learning, adaptive instruction, and lifelong learning habits while addressing challenges such as digital equity and ethical considerations.

(Stohr et al. 2024) examined the ethical considerations associated with AI-enabled education, including integrating generative AI and data-driven learning approaches. The paper discussed data privacy, algorithmic bias, and the ethical implications of using AI technologies in educational settings. They also explored strategies for promoting responsible AI deployment and safeguarding learner rights and well-being. (Walkowiak 2023) provided guidelines and recommendations for the ethical adoption of AI technologies in education, including data-driven learning and generative AI approaches. The paper argued principles such as transparency, fairness, accountability, and inclusivity in AI deployment. He also examined policy implications and regulatory frameworks to promote responsible AI adoption in educational settings. The study discussed various approaches for fostering metacognitive awareness, self-regulation, and reflection among learners within technology-enhanced educational settings. Nguyen also explores the potential benefits and challenges of combining data-driven methodologies with metacognitive interventions. (Bedington et al. 2024) investigated the professional development and training needs of educators in AI-driven classrooms, including those utilizing data-driven learning and generative AI technologies. The work emphasized strategies for equipping educators with the skills and knowledge necessary to leverage AI tools effectively, promote student engagement and address ethical considerations. The authors examined barriers to adoption and recommendations for supporting educators in integrating AI into their instructional practices in HEIs.

Numerous studies have explored the application of data-driven approaches in education, highlighting the benefits of leveraging educational data to personalize learning experiences and improve student outcomes (Gupta et al. 2024; Holmström and Carroll 2024). Research has shown that data-driven interventions, such as adaptive learning systems and learning analytics platforms, can enhance student engagement, motivation, and academic achievement by providing timely feedback, identifying learning gaps, and adapting instruction to individual learner needs.

## RESEARCH METHOD

The research employs a secondary data analysis approach to develop a conceptual framework. Beginning with a comprehensive literature review, the study examines existing research on data-driven learning, generative AI, metacognition, and sustainable education, identifying gaps and theoretical frameworks. Secondary data from academic journals, reports, and online repositories undergoes qualitative content analysis to extract themes and patterns (Basco et al. 2022). A conceptual framework is proposed through a synthesis of findings, outlining theoretical principles, practical strategies, and implementation guidelines for integrating data-driven learning, generative AI, and MRU in sustainable education. Validation and evaluation involve expert review and stakeholder feedback to assess feasibility and impact, while limitations and avenues for further research are discussed. Ultimately, this methodology aims to contribute to effective and sustainable learning practices in education.

## ANALYSIS AND DISCUSSION

Developing a framework for sustainable education through MRU involves integrating sustainability principles into educational practices while leveraging metacognition to enhance learning outcomes. There's a framework that outlines key components:

Understanding Sustainability: Education on sustainability involves comprehensive instruction on its environmental, social, and economic dimensions, emphasizing the intricate connections between human activities and their impacts on these systems. Through this education, stakeholders gain insight into how issues like climate change, biodiversity loss, and social inequality are interrelated, fostering a holistic understanding of sustainability challenges (Chiu 2024).

Metacognitive Awareness: Metacognitive strategies are taught to empower learners to monitor, regulate, and evaluate their learning processes effectively. By developing skills such as goal-setting, self-assessment, and reflection, students become more self-aware of their learning strengths and weaknesses, enabling them to adapt their approaches to learning tasks accordingly.

Integrated Curriculum: Sustainability concepts are integrated into various subjects and disciplines, ensuring students encounter them throughout their educational experience. This integration fosters interdisciplinary understanding and encourages students to apply sustainability principles to diverse contexts, comprehensively preparing them to address real-world challenges.

Active Learning Strategies: Active learning methodologies such as project-based learning and collaborative problem-solving engage students in hands-on exploration of sustainability issues. Through these approaches, students develop critical thinking skills and gain practical experience in innovatively addressing complex sustainability challenges (M. Dadhich, R. Doshi, S. Mathur, R. Meena 2021).

Utilization of Resources: Educational institutions optimize resource usage by implementing strategies to minimize waste, conserve energy, and reduce environmental impact. By promoting resource conservation practices and incorporating sustainability principles into facilities management, schools contribute to environmental sustainability while providing a model for responsible resource utilization.

Community Engagement: Partnerships with local communities and organizations are fostered to address sustainability challenges collaboratively. By involving community members as resources and mentors, students gain valuable insights into local sustainability issues and develop practical solutions with real-world impact (Manish Dadhich; Himanshu Purohit; Ritesh Tirole; Sumit Mathur; Aman Jain 2023).

Assessment and Feedback: Assessment methods are designed to evaluate both content knowledge and metacognitive skills, providing students with constructive feedback to support their learning process. Educators ensure that learning outcomes align with sustainability goals by assessing students' understanding of sustainability concepts and their ability to apply metacognitive strategies.

Professional Development: Educators receive training and support to integrate sustainability and metacognitive practices into their teaching. Ongoing professional development opportunities enable educators to stay updated on best practices and collaborate with colleagues to enhance sustainability education efforts.

Continuous Improvement: The framework is continuously evaluated and refined based on stakeholder feedback and emerging research. By fostering a culture of constant improvement, educational institutions adapt their practices to meet evolving sustainability challenges and enhance student learning outcomes effectively.

Through values education and fostering a mindset of lifelong learning, students are encouraged to develop a deep appreciation for sustainability and become actively engaged in creating positive change. By cultivating empathy, responsibility, and stewardship, schools instill in students the values and attitudes needed to build a more sustainable future.

Integrating data-driven learning and generative AI into educational frameworks presents a promising educational frontier, offering opportunities to enhance metacognitive resource utilization and foster sustainable learning practices. In this discussion, we delve into this integration's implications and potential, considering its benefits and challenges. Firstly, using data-driven learning methodologies allows educators to leverage vast amounts of educational data to gain insights into learner behavior, preferences, and performance (Gaurav Kumar Singh; Manish Dadhich 2023). By analyzing this data, educators can personalize learning experiences, provide targeted interventions, and adapt teaching strategies to meet the diverse needs of learners. This personalized approach enhances learner engagement and motivation and promotes metacognitive development by encouraging learners to reflect on their learning processes and make informed decisions about their learning strategies (Chiu 2024).

*Figure 1. Metacognitive resource utilization*

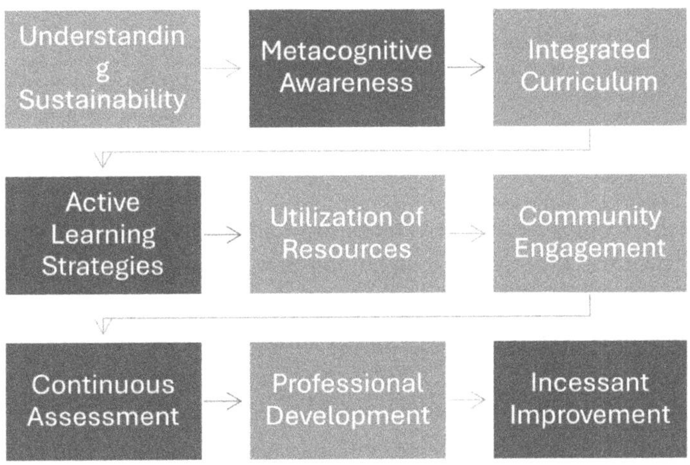

## IMPLICATIONS

The proposed framework for bridging data-driven learning and generative AI with metacognitive resource utilization in sustainable education offers several significant implications. Firstly, it provides educators with a structured approach to integrating emerging technologies and pedagogical strategies into their teaching practices, fostering more effective and engaging student learning experiences. Secondly, by promoting metacognitive skills development alongside sustainability principles, the framework empowers learners to become active agents in addressing complex global challenges. Additionally, integrating data-driven insights and generative AI tools enhances personalized learning opportunities, catering to diverse learner needs and preferences. Thus, the framework has the potential to contribute to the advancement of sustainable education practices and the cultivation of critical thinking and problem-solving skills essential for navigating an increasingly complex world.

## LIMITATIONS AND FUTURE SCOPE

Despite its potential benefits, the framework for sustainable education through MRU may face several limitations. Firstly, the reliance on data-driven approaches and AI technologies may exacerbate existing inequalities in access to resources and digital literacy skills, potentially widening the gap between privileged and marginalized learners. Secondly, the successful implementation of the framework depends on adequate support and training for educators, which may pose logistical and resource challenges for educational institutions. Additionally, the framework's effectiveness in different cultural and socio-economic contexts requires careful consideration and adaptation to ensure its relevance and inclusivity.

There are several avenues for future research and development related to the framework proposed for sustainable education. Firstly, longitudinal studies could investigate the long-term impact of integrating data-driven learning, generative AI, and metacognitive strategies on student learning outcomes and behavior change regarding sustainability practices. Secondly, exploring the role of emerging technologies such as virtual reality, augmented reality, and blockchain in enhancing sustainability education could provide insights into innovative approaches to engage learners and promote real-world application of knowledge. Furthermore, examining the ethical implications of AI-driven educational interventions and ensuring transparency, fairness, and accountability in algorithmic decision-making are crucial for further investigation. Overall, continued research and refinement of the framework will contribute to the evolution of sustainable education practices in the digital age.

## CONCLUSION

The framework proposed for sustainable education by integrating data-driven learning, generative AI, and MRU holds significant promise for advancing teaching and learning practices. By providing educators with a structured approach to leverage emerging technologies and pedagogical strategies, the framework fosters engaging and personalized learning experiences for students while empowering them to address complex global challenges. However, it is essential to acknowledge potential limitations, including inequalities in access to resources and the need for comprehensive educator support and training. Despite these challenges, the framework represents a crucial step toward promoting critical thinking, problem-solving skills, and responsible citizenship among learners. Continued research and refinement will ensure its effectiveness and inclusivity across diverse educational contexts, ultimately advancing sustainable education practices in the digital age.

## REFERENCES

Alwahedi, F., Aldhaheri, A., Ferrag, M. A., Battah, A., & Tihanyi, N. (2024). Machine Learning Techniques for IoT Security: Current Research and Future Vision with Generative AI and Large Language Models. *Internet of Things and Cyber-Physical Systems*, *4*(2), 1–19. doi:10.1016/j.iotcps.2023.12.003

Basco, R., Hair, J. F. Jr, Ringle, C. M., & Sarstedt, M. (2022). Advancing Family Business Research through Modeling Nonlinear Relationships : Comparing PLS-SEM and Multiple Regression. *Journal of Family Business Strategy*, *13*(3), 1–12. doi:10.1016/j.jfbs.2021.100457

Bedington, A., Halcomb, E. F., McKee, H. A., Sargent, T., & Smith, A. (2024). Writing with Generative AI and Human-Machine Teaming: Insights and Recommendations from Faculty and Students. *Computers and Composition*, *71*(2), 1–12. doi:10.1016/j.compcom.2024.102833

Chiu, T. K. F. (2024). Future Research Recommendations for Transforming Higher Education with Generative AI. *Computers and Education: Artificial Intelligence*, *6*(12), 1–15. doi:10.1016/j.caeai.2023.100197

Dadhich, M., Doshi, R., Mathur, S., Meena, R., Gujral, R. K., & Dhotre, P. (2021). *Empirical Study of Awareness towards Blended E-Learning Gateways during Covid-19 Lockdown*. In *2021 International Conference on Computing, Communication and Green Engineering (CCGE)*, Pune, India. 10.1109/CCGE50943.2021.9776386

Dadhich, M., Hiran, K. K., Rao, S. S., & Sharma, R. (2022). Impact of Covid-19 on Teaching-Learning Perception of Faculties and Students of Higher Education in Indian Purview. *Journal of Mobile Multimedia*, *18*(4), 957–980. doi:10.13052/jmm1550-4646.1841

Dadhich, M., Purohit, H., Tirole, R., Mathur, S., & Jain, A. (2023). Industry 4.0 Revolution towards a Future-Ready Society and Manufacturing Excellence. In AIP Conference Proceedings. doi:10.1063/5.0113614

Dai, Y., Liu, A., & Lim, C. P. (2023). Reconceptualizing ChatGPT and Generative AI as a Student-Driven Innovation in Higher Education. *Procedia CIRP*, *119*, 84–90. doi:10.1016/j.procir.2023.05.002

Gupta, P., Ding, B., Guan, C., & Ding, D. (2024). Generative AI: A Systematic Review Using Topic Modelling Techniques. *Data and Information Management*, *3*(2), 1–66. doi:10.1016/j.dim.2024.100066

Holmström, J., & Carroll, N. (2024). How Organizations Can Innovate with Generative AI. *Business Horizons*, *4*(2), 1–25. doi:10.1016/j.bushor.2024.02.010

Hsu, C. H. C., Tan, G., & Stantic, B. (2024). A Fine-Tuned Tourism-Specific Generative AI Concept. *Annals of Tourism Research*, *104*, 1–4. doi:10.1016/j.annals.2023.103723

Liu, M., Zhang, L. J., & Biebricher, C. (2024). Investigating Students' Cognitive Processes in Generative AI-Assisted Digital Multimodal Composing and Traditional Writing. *Computers & Education*, *211*, 1–15. doi:10.1016/j.compedu.2023.104977

Mizumoto, A. (2023). Data-Driven Learning Meets Generative AI: Introducing the Framework of Metacognitive Resource Use. *Applied Corpus Linguistics*, *3*(3), 1–14. doi:10.1016/j.acorp.2023.100074

Moorhouse, B. L. (2024). Beginning and First-Year Language Teachers' Readiness for the Generative AI Age. *Computers and Education: Artificial Intelligence*, *6*(11), 1–9. doi:10.1016/j.caeai.2024.100201

Sands, S., Campbell, C., Ferraro, C., Demsar, V., Rosengren, S., & Farrell, J. (2024). Principles for Advertising Responsibly Using Generative AI. *Organizational Dynamics*, *4*, 1–9. doi:10.1016/j.orgdyn.2024.101042

Singh, G. K., & Dadhich, M. (2023). Supply Chain Management Growth With the Adoption of Blockchain Technology (BoT) and Internet of Things (IoT). In *2023 3rd International Conference on Advance Computing and Innovative Technologies in Engineering (ICACITE)*, (pp. 321–25). IEEE. 10.1109/ICACITE57410.2023.10182619

Stohr, A., Ollig, P., Keller, R., & Rieger, A. (2024). Generative Mechanisms of AI Implementation: A Critical Realist Perspective on Predictive Maintenance. *Information and Organization*, *34*(2), 1–11. doi:10.1016/j.infoandorg.2024.100503

Walkowiak, E. (2023). Task-Interdependencies between Generative AI and Workers. *Economics Letters*, *231*(3), 1–13. doi:10.1016/j.econlet.2023.111315

# Compilation of References


. Rekik, A., Ben-Hamadou, A., & Mahdi, W. (2014). A New Visual Speech Recognition Approach for RGB-D Cameras. *ICIAR*, 21-28.

Guilherme, A. (2019). AI and education: The importance of teacher and student relations. *AI & Society*, *34*(1), 47–54. doi:10.1007/s00146-017-0693-8

Algabri, H. K., Kharade, K. G., & Kamat, R. K. (2021b). Promise, Threats and Personalization in Higher Education with Artificial Intelligence. *Webology*, *18*(6), 2129–2139.

Abd-Alrazaq, A. A., Rababeh, A., Alajlani, M., Bewick, B. M., & Househ, M. (2020). Effectiveness and Safety of Using Chatbots to Improve Mental Health: Systematic Review and Meta-Analysis. *Journal of Medical Internet Research*, *22*(7), e16021. doi:10.2196/16021 PMID:32673216

Abdous, M. (2023). How AI Is Shaping the Future of Higher Ed. *Inside Higher Ed*. https://www.insidehighered.com/views/2023/03/22/how-ai-shaping-future-higher-ed-opinion

Abdullah, M., Madain, A., & Jararweh, Y. (2022). ChatGPT: Fundamentals, applications & social impacts. In *2022 Ninth International Conference on Social Networks Analysis, Management & Security (SNAMS)*. IEEE.

Abe, I. I., & Adisa, O. (2021, January 1). Future of Work. *Advances in Human Resources Management and Organizational Development Book Series*. IGI Global. doi:10.4018/978-1-7998-3347-5.ch015

Abukmeil, M., Ferrari, S., Genovese, A., Piuri, V., & Scotti, F. (2021). A survey of unsupervised generative models for exploratory data analysis and representation learning. [csur]. *ACM Computing Surveys*, *54*(5), 1–40. doi:10.1145/3450963

Acemoglu, D., & Restrepo, P. (2018). Artificial intelligence, automation and work. *NBER Working Paper, (24196)*.

Achmad & Fadillah, L. (2015). Lip Motion Pattern Recognition for Indonesian Syllable Pronunciation Utilizing Hidden Markov Model Method. *Telkomnika (Telecommunication Computing Electronics and Control)*, *13*(1), 173–180.

Adam, M., Wessel, M., & Benlian, A. (2021). AI-based chatbots in customer service and their effects on user compliance. *Electronic Markets*, *31*(2), 427–445. doi:10.1007/s12525-020-00414-7

Adams, R. J., Smart, P., & Huff, A. S. (2017). Shades of grey: Guidelines for working with the grey literature in systematic reviews for management and organizational studies. *International Journal of Management Reviews*, *19*(4), 432–454. doi:10.1111/ijmr.12102

Adepoju, O., Aigbavboa, C., Nwulu, N., & Onyia, M. (2022). *Re-skilling human resources for construction 4.0*. Springer International Publishing. doi:10.1007/978-3-030-85973-2

Adıgüzel, T., Kaya, M. H., & Cansu, F. K. (2023). Revolutionizing education with AI: Exploring the transformative potential of ChatGPT. *Contemporary Educational Technology*, *15*(3), ep429. doi:10.30935/cedtech/13152

Afouras, T., Chung, J. S., Senior, A., Vinyals, O., & Zisserman, A. (2018). Deep Audio-Visual Speech Recognition. *arXiv*, 1809.02108v2. https://arxiv.org/pdf/1809.02108.pdf

Agajanian, S., Alshahrani, M., Bai, F., Tao, P., & Verkhivker, G. M. (2023). Exploring and learning the universe of protein allostery using artificial intelligence augmented biophysical and computational approaches. *Journal of Chemical Information and Modeling*, *63*(5), 1413–1428. doi:10.1021/acs.jcim.2c01634 PMID:36827465

Agarwal, N. (2023). A Study on the teacher's aptitude about managerial skill with respect to training and learners performance. *International Journal of Management and Organizational Research*, *2*(2), 78–84.

Agarwal, N. (2023). Strength of distributed web page management system within the space of online e-learning administration in a contextualized group of science teachers. *European Chemical Bulletin*, *12*(4), 144–155.

Agarwal, S., & Gupta, R. (2019). AI in the informal sector: Opportunities and challenges for Indian workers. *Journal of Informal Economy Studies*, *1*(2), 87–102.

Ågerfalk, P. J., Conboy, K., & Myers, M. D. (2020). Information systems in the age of pandemics: COVID-19 and beyond. *European Journal of Information Systems*, *29*(3), 203–207. doi:10.1080/0960085X.2020.1771968

Aggarwal, D., Sharma, D., & Saxena, A. B. (2023). Exploring the Role of Artificial Intelligence for Augmentation of Adaptable Sustainable Education. *Asian Journal of Advanced Research and Reports*, *17*(11), 179–184. doi:10.9734/ajarr/2023/v17i11563

Aghakhani, S., Carre, N., Mostovoy, K., Shafer, R., Baeza-Hernandez, K., Entenberg, G., Testerman, A., & Bunge, E. L. (2023). Qualitative analysis of mental health conversational agents messages about autism spectrum disorder: A call for action. *Frontiers in Digital Health*, *5*, 1251016. doi:10.3389/fdgth.2023.1251016 PMID:38116099

Agrawal, S., De Smet, A., Lacroix, S., & Reich, A. (2020). To emerge stronger from the COVID-19 crisis, companies should start reskilling their workforces now. *McKinsey Insights*, (May), 1–7.

Ahad, M. A., Paiva, S., Tripathi, G., & Feroz, N. (2020). Enabling technologies and sustainable smart cities. *Sustainable Cities and Society*, *61*, 102301. doi:10.1016/j.scs.2020.102301

Ahani, A., Nilashi, M., Ibrahim, O., Sanzogni, L., & Weaven, S. (2019). Market segmentation and travel choice prediction in Spa hotels through TripAdvisor's online reviews. *International Journal of Hospitality Management*, *80*, 52–77. doi:10.1016/j.ijhm.2019.01.003

Ahmad, B. A., & Hassanat, A. (n.d.). *Visual Speech Recognition. IT Department, Mu'tah University*. Speech and Language Technologies. https://www.intechopen.com/chapters/38380

Ahmad, I., AlQurashi, F., Abozinadah, E., & Mehmood, R. (2021). A novel deep learning-based online proctoring system using face recognition, eye blinking, and object detection techniques. *International Journal of Advanced Computer Science and Applications*, *12*(10). doi:10.14569/IJACSA.2021.0121094

Ahmady, S., & Hosseini, T. M. (2022). Effectiveness of Video-assisted Debriefing Versus Standard Oral Debriefing Following Screen-based Simulation (CyberPatient TM) Training. *Journal of Medical Education*, *21*(1). doi:10.5812/jme-127021

Ahmed, Z., Bhinder, K. K., Tariq, A., Tahir, M. J., Mehmood, Q., Tabassum, M. S., Malik, M., Aslam, S., Asghar, M. S., & Yousaf, Z. (2022). Knowledge, attitude, and practice of artificial intelligence among doctors and medical students in Pakistan: A cross-sectional online survey. *Annals of Medicine and Surgery (London)*, *76*, 103493. doi:10.1016/j.amsu.2022.103493 PMID:35308436

Ahmed, Z., Mohamed, K., Zeeshan, S., & Dong, X. (2020). Artificial intelligence with multi-functional machine learning platform development for better healthcare and precision medicine. *Database (Oxford), 2020*, baaa010. doi:10.1093/database/baaa010 PMID:32185396

Akavova, A., Temirkhanova, Z., & Lorsanova, Z. (2023). Adaptive learning and artificial intelligence in the educational space. *E3S Web of Conferences, 451*. 06011. . doi:10.1051/e3sconf/202345106011

Akgun, S., & Greenhow, C. (2022). Artificial intelligence in education: Addressing ethical challenges in K-12 settings. *AI and Ethics*, *2*(3), 431–440. doi:10.1007/s43681-021-00096-7 PMID:34790956

Aktan, D., & Demirbağ Kaplan, M. (2023). Re-designing higher education for mindfulness: Conceptualization and communication. The Sustainable University of the Future. Research Gate. doi:10.1007/978-3-031-20186-8_4

Akter, S., Dwivedi, Y. K., Sajib, S., Biswas, K., Bandara, R. J., & Michael, K. (2022). Algorithmic bias in machine learning-based marketing models. *Journal of Business Research*, *144*, 201–216. doi:10.1016/j.jbusres.2022.01.083

Alam, A. (2021, December). Should robots replace teachers? Mobilisation of AI and learning analytics in education. In *2021 International Conference on Advances in Computing, Communication, and Control (ICAC3)* (pp. 1-12). IEEE. 10.1109/ICAC353642.2021.9697300

Alami, H., Rivard, L., Lehoux, P., Hoffman, S. J., Stéphanie Bernadette, M. C., Savoldelli, M., & Fortin, J. (2020). Artificial intelligence in healthcare: Laying the foundation for responsible, sustainable, and inclusive innovation in low- and middle-income countries. *Globalization and Health*, *16*(52), 1–6. PMID:32580741

Aldausari, N., Sowmya, A., Marcus, N., & Mohammadi, G. (2022). Video generative adversarial networks: A review. *ACM Computing Surveys*, *55*(2), 1–25. doi:10.1145/3487891

Algabri, H. K., Kharade, K. G., & Kamat, R. K. (2021a). Designing and Implementation of Technology in Higher Education. *Webology*, *18*(5), 1365–1377.

Alharbi, W. (2023). AI in the Foreign Language Classroom: A Pedagogical Overview of Automated Writing Assistance Tools. *Education Research International*, *2023*, 2023. doi:10.1155/2023/4253331

Ali, Z. (2021). *AI in the Workplace: A Scoping Review of Knowledge, Skills and Abilities Required by Employees of the Future* [Doctoral dissertation, University of Toronto (Canada)].

Ali, S., DiPaola, D., Lee, I., Hong, J., & Breazeal, C. (2021, May). Exploring generative models with middle school students. In *Proceedings of the 2021 CHI conference on human factors in computing systems* (pp. 1-13). ACM. 10.1145/3411764.3445226

Almajai, S., Cox, S., Harvey, R., & Lan, Y. (2016). Improved speaker independent lip reading using speaker adaptive training and deep neural networks. In *Proceedings of the IEEE International Conference on Acoustics, Speech, and Signal Processing (ICASSP)* (pp. 2722-2726). IEEE.

Almario, O. (2023). Assessing User Experience Learning Management System for Liberal Arts and Education Programs: Implications for Hybrid Learning. *Cosmos An International Journal of Management, 12*(2), 73-78.

Almario, O. (2023). Assessing User Experience of Learning Management System for Liberal Arts and Education Programs: Implications for Hybrid Learning. *Cosmos An International Journal of Management, 12*(2), 73-78.

Almutawa, A. M., & Sruthi, S. (2022). Students' perspective towards online proctoring in exams during COVID-19. *Journal of Engineering Research*, *10*(no. 4A).

Alonso-Silverio, G. A., Perez-Escamirosa, F., Bruno-Sanchez, R., Ortiz-Simon, J. L., Muñoz-Guerrero, R., Minor-Martinez, A., & Alarcón-Paredes, A. (2018). Development of a laparoscopic box trainer based on open source hardware and artificial intelligence for objective assessment of surgical psychomotor skills. *Surgical Innovation*, *25*(4), 380–388. doi:10.1177/1553350618777045 PMID:29809097

Alqurashi, E. (2019). Predicting student satisfaction and perceived learning within online learning environments. *Distance Education*, *40*(1), 133–148. doi:10.1080/01587919.2018.1553562

Alrassi, J., Katsufrakis, P. J., & Chandran, L. (2021). Technology can augment, but not replace, critical human skills needed for patient care. *Academic Medicine*, *96*(1), 37–43. doi:10.1097/ACM.0000000000003733 PMID:32910005

Al-Shahwani, H. I. W., Mijwil, M. M., Doshi, R., Hiran, K. K., & Bala, I. (2024). Evaluating Antivirus Effectiveness Against Malware in Ascending Order for Increasing Blockchain Endpoint Protection. In *Bio-Inspired Optimization Techniques in Blockchain Systems* (pp. 150–166). IGI Global. doi:10.4018/979-8-3693-1131-8.ch008

AL-Smadi, M. (2023). *ChatGPT and Beyond: The Generative AI Revolution in Education*. Research Gate. doi:10.13140/RG.2.2.11376.23049

Alvarez, J., & Lane, S. (2023). Rising Against the Machine: Appeasing the Educators' Fears of Artificial Intelligence Taking Over Foreign Language Education. *UNC System Learning and Technology Journal, 1*(1).

Alwahedi, F., Aldhaheri, A., Ferrag, M. A., Battah, A., & Tihanyi, N. (2024). Machine Learning Techniques for IoT Security: Current Research and Future Vision with Generative AI and Large Language Models. *Internet of Things and Cyber-Physical Systems*, *4*(2), 1–19. doi:10.1016/j.iotcps.2023.12.003

Aly, T., & Aly, A. (2023). Chat GPT in Preparation of the Scientific Papers in Spinal Cord Injuries in the Middle East? *International Journal of Clinical Studies & Medical Case Reports*, *33*(4). doi:10.46998/IJCMCR.2023.33.000817

American Psychiatric Association, DSM-5 Task Force. (2013). *Diagnostic and statistical manual of mental disorders: DSM-5* (5th ed.). American Psychiatric Publishing, Inc., doi:10.1176/appi.books.9780890425596

Amit, G., Jnoyola, J. N., & Sameep, S. B. (2016). *Lip reading using CNN and LSTM*. Stanford University Technical Report.

Anaya, E. A., Nakano-Miyatake, M., & Perez Meana, H. M. (2019) Network forensics with Neurofuzzy techniques. In: *52nd IEEE international Midwest Symposium on Circuits and Systems (MWSCAS '19)*. IEEE.

Andersen, L. (2019). Artificial Intelligence in International Development: Avoiding Ethical Pitfalls. *Journal of Public & International Affairs*.

Ang, L., Bonifacio, N., Garcia, J. K., Medina, R., & Santiago, J. (2023). The Rise of Artificial Intelligence: A Correlational Study on AI-Powered Bots and Customer Satisfaction in A People-Oriented Industry. *Cosmos Journal of Engineering & Technology*, *13*(1), 81–94. doi:10.46360/cosmos.et.620231008

Antonio, G. C. (2023). Influence of Teachers' Leadership Style Under The New Normal System in Education. *Globus Journal of Progressive Education*, *13*(1), 14–25.

Anusuya, M. A., & Katti, S. K. (2009). Speech Recognition by Machine: A Review. *International Journal of Computer Science and Information Security*, *6*(3). https://arxiv.org/ftp/arxiv/papers/1001/1001.2267.pdf

An, X., Chai, C. S., Li, Y., Zhou, Y., Shen, X., Zheng, C., & Chen, M. (2023). Modeling English teachers' behavioral intention to use artificial intelligence in middle schools. *Education and Information Technologies*, *28*(5), 5187–5208. doi:10.1007/s10639-022-11286-z

Apparao Polireddi, N. S., & Kavitha, J. (2023). Effectiveness of automated chatbots for operational support and self-service based on fuzzy classifier for ASD. *Soft Computing*. doi:10.1007/s00500-023-08541-x

Aresti-Bartolome, N., & Garcia-Zapirain, B. (2014). Technologies as support tools for persons with autistic spectrum disorder: A systematic review. *International Journal of Environmental Research and Public Health*, *11*(8), 7767–7802. doi:10.3390/ijerph110807767 PMID:25093654

Arnold, M. H. (2021). Teasing out artificial intelligence in medicine: An ethical critique of artificial intelligence and machine learning in medicine. *Journal of Bioethical Inquiry*, *18*(1), 121–139. doi:10.1007/s11673-020-10080-1 PMID:33415596

Arntz, M., Gregory, T., & Zierahn, U. (2016). The Risk of Automation for Jobs in OECD Countries: A Comparative Analysis. *OECD Social, Employment and Migration Working Papers, (189).*

Asnani, D., & Agarwal, K. (n.d.). AN EXPERT SYSTEM FOR CAREER COUNSELLING USING CLIPS. *International Journal of Management, Technology, and Engineering*.

Assael, Y. M., Shillingford, B., Whiteson, S., & de Freitas, N. (2016). Lip-Net: End-to-end sentence level lipreading. In *Proceedings of the ICLR Conference* (pp. 1-13). Academic Press.

Atila, Ü., & Sabaz, F. (2022). Turkish lip-reading using Bi-LSTM and deep learning models. *Engineering Science and Technology, an International Journal, 35*, 101206.

Atlas, S. (2023). *ChatGPT for Higher Education and Professional Development: A Guide to Conversational AI*. Research Gate. https://digitalcommons.uri.edu/cba_facpubs/548

Atreides, K. (2021). E-governance with ethical living democracy. *Procedia Computer Science*, *190*, 35–39. doi:10.1016/j.procs.2021.06.004

Aungst, T. D., & Patel, R. (2020). Integrating digital health into the curriculum—Considerations on the current landscape and future developments. *Journal of Medical Education and Curricular Development*, *7*, 2382120519901275. doi:10.1177/2382120519901275 PMID:32010795

Autor, D. H. (2015). Why Are There Still So Many Jobs? The History and Future of Workplace Automation. *The Journal of Economic Perspectives*, *29*(3), 3–30. doi:10.1257/jep.29.3.3

Avaid, M., Haleem, A., Khan, I. H., & Suman, R. (2023). Understanding the potential applications of Artificial Intelligence in Agriculture Sector. *Advanced Agrochem*, *2*(1), 15–30. doi:10.1016/j.aac.2022.10.001

Avella, J. T., Kebritchi, M., Nunn, S. G., & Kanai, T. (2016). Learning analytics methods, benefits, and challenges in higher education: A systematic literature review. *Online Learning : the Official Journal of the Online Learning Consortium*, *20*(2), 13–29.

Badih, H., & Alagrash, Y. (2020). Static Analysis Framework Based on Multi - Agent System. In *Proceedings of International IOT, Electronics and Mechatronics Conference (IEMTRONICS),* (pp. 1-6). IOT. 10.1109/IEMTRONICS51293.2020.9216382

Bahrani, P., & Arshadi Khamseh, A. (2020). Competitive environment between green and non-green products considering disruption and alliance strategy. *Global Journal of Flexible Systems Managment*, *21*(2), 135–161. doi:10.1007/s40171-020-00234-w

Baidoo-Anu, D., & Ansah, L. O. (2023). Education in the era of generative artificial intelligence (AI): Understanding the potential benefits of ChatGPT in promoting teaching and learning. *Journal of AI*, *7*(1), 52–62. doi:10.61969/jai.1337500

Baker, R. S., & Hawn, A. (2021). Algorithmic bias in education. *International Journal of Artificial Intelligence in Education, 32*(4), 1052–1092. doi:10.1007/s40593-021-00285-9

Balash, D. G., Kim, D., Shaibekova, D., Fainchtein, R. A., Sherr, M., & Aviv, A. J. (2021). Examining the examiners: Students' privacy and security perceptions of online proctoring services. In *Seventeenth symposium on usable privacy and security (SOUPS 2021)*, (pp. 633-652). IEEE.

Baldwin, P. (2004). PDA Databases. *Journal of Hospital Librarianship, 4*(1), 83–89. doi:10.1300/J186v04n01_08

BaliB. (2023). Analysis of Emerging Trends in Artificial Intelligence in Education in Nigeria. Research square. Preorint. doi:10.21203/rs.3.rs-3819828/v1

Banerjee, S., & Dasgupta, R. (2021). AI for rural skill development: A case study in India. *Journal of Rural Studies, 82*, 120–135.

Barbour, A. B., Frush, J. M., Gatta, L. A., McManigle, W. C., Keah, N. M., Bejarano-Pineda, L., & Guerrero, E. M. (2019). Artificial intelligence in health care: Insights from an educational forum. *Journal of Medical Education and Curricular Development, 6*, 2382120519889348. doi:10.1177/2382120519889348 PMID:32064356

Barona, R., & Anita, E. A. M. (2017). A survey on data breach challenges in cloud computing security: Issues and threats. *2017 International Conference on Circuit, Power and Computing Technologies (ICCPCT)*, (pp. 1–8). IEEE. 10.1109/ICCPCT.2017.8074287

Barua, T., Doshi, R., & Hiran, K. K. (2020). *Mobile Applications Development: With Python in Kivy Framework*. Walter de Gruyter GmbH & Co KG. doi:10.1515/9783110689488

Başar, T., & Şahin, L. (2021). Technology integration in teaching English as a foreign language: A content analysis study. *Journal of Educational Technology and Online Learning, 5*(1), 204–222. doi:10.31681/jetol.972577

Basco, R., Hair, J. F. Jr, Ringle, C. M., & Sarstedt, M. (2022). Advancing family business research through modeling nonlinear relationships : Comparing PLS-SEM and multiple regression. *Journal of Family Business Strategy, 13*(3), 1–12. doi:10.1016/j.jfbs.2021.100457

Bates, T., Cobo, C., Mariño, O., & Wheeler, S. (2020). Can artificial intelligence transform higher education? *International Journal of Educational Technology in Higher Education, 17*(42), 1–12. doi:10.1186/s41239-020-00218-x

Beatty, C., Malik, T., Meheli, S., & Sinha, C. (2022). Evaluating the Therapeutic Alliance With a Free-Text CBT Conversational Agent (Wysa): A Mixed-Methods Study. *Frontiers in Digital Health, 4*, 847991. doi:10.3389/fdgth.2022.847991 PMID:35480848

Beauchamp, T. L., & Childress, J. F. (2001). *Principles of biomedical ethics*. Oxford University Press.

Becker, J. M., Cheah, J. H., Gholamzade, R., Ringle, C. M., & Sarstedt, M. (2023). PLS-SEM's most wanted guidance. *International Journal of Contemporary Hospitality Management, 35*(1), 321–346. doi:10.1108/IJCHM-04-2022-0474

Bedington, A., Halcomb, E. F., McKee, H. A., Sargent, T., & Smith, A. (2024). Writing with Generative AI and Human-Machine Teaming: Insights and Recommendations from Faculty and Students. *Computers and Composition, 71*(2), 1–12. doi:10.1016/j.compcom.2024.102833

Bell, R., & Bell, H. (2023). Entrepreneurship education in the era of generative artificial intelligence. *Entrepreneurship Education, 6*(3), 229–244. doi:10.1007/s41959-023-00099-x

Benjamin, D. M., Morstatter, F., Abbas, A. E., Abeliuk, A., Atanasov, P., Bennett, S., Beger, A., Birari, S., Budescu, D. V., Catasta, M., Ferrara, E., Haravitch, L., Himmelstein, M., Hossain, K. S. M. T., Huang, Y., Jin, W., Joseph, R., Leskovec, J., Matsui, A., & Galstyan, A. (2023). Hybrid forecasting of geopolitical events. *AI Magazine*, *44*(1), 112–128. doi:10.1002/aaai.12085

Benzaquen, J., & Charles, V. (2020). A stratified bootstrapping approach to assessing the success of TQM implementation in Peruvian companies. *Total Quality Management & Business Excellence*, *0*(0), 1–24. doi:10.1080/14783363.2020.1816165

Berkol, A., Sivri, T. T., & Erdem, H. (2024). Lip Reading Using Various Deep Learning Models with Visual Turkish Data. *Gazi University Journal of Science, 1*(1).

Betancur, J., Commandeur, F., Motlagh, M., Sharir, T., Einstein, A. J., Bokhari, S., Fish, M. B., Ruddy, T. D., Kaufmann, P., Sinusas, A. J., Miller, E. J., Bateman, T. M., Dorbala, S., Di Carli, M., Germano, G., Otaki, Y., Tamarappoo, B. K., Dey, D., Berman, D. S., & Slomka, P. J. (2018). Deep learning for prediction of obstructive disease from fast myocardial perfusion SPECT: A multicenter study. *JACC: Cardiovascular Imaging*, *11*(11), 1654–1663. doi:10.1016/j.jcmg.2018.01.020 PMID:29550305

Bhalerao, P. (2020). *Classification using a word embedding techniques*. UMBC.. //https://redirect.cs.umbc.edu/courses/graduate/676/SP2020/SP2020presentations/Bhalerao%20Prachi%20Term%20Paper

Bhargava, A., Bester, M., & Bolton, L. E. (2020, August 12). Employees' Perceptions of the Implementation of Robotics, Artificial Intelligence, and Automation (RAIA) on Job Satisfaction, Job Security, and Employability. *Journal of Technology in Behavioral Science*. doi:10.1007/s41347-020-00153-8

Bhati, S.; Manish Dadhich; Anand A Bhasker; Kamal Kant Hiran; Roshni Sharma; Anurag. (2023). Quantifying the Contemporary Enablers in Achieving e-Governance for Sustainable Techno-Societal Development: A High Directive SEM Analysis. *2023 International Conference on Emerging Trends in Networks and Computer Communications (ETNCC)*, (pp. 157–162). IEEE. 10.1109/ETNCC59188.2023.10284979

Bhattacharjee, A., & Bansal, V. (2021). The Major Emotional and Economical Drawbacks Derived from the Coronavirus Outbreak from the North Pole to the South Pole. In S. Poddar, B. Kar, S. Samanta, & A. Bhaumik (Eds.), Human resource management and mental health A Psychosocial Aspect, 1-8. Lincoln research and publishing limited, Australia. doi:10.46977/book.2021.hrmmh

Bhattacharjee, A., & Juman, M. K. I. (2020). Does delay or scarcity in working capital increase unexpected financial risk for women entrepreneurs in the developing country? *International Journal of Economics, Commerce and Management, 8*(8), 433-446. http://ijecm.co.uk/wp-content/uploads/2020/08/8827.pdf

Bhattacharjee, A., & Bansal, V. (2023). Sustainable Approaches of Blockchain Tech, Artificial Intelligence, and Climate Finance in the 4&5IR: Low Emission Technologies and Economy. In S. Trivedi, R. Aggarwal, & G. Singh (Eds.), *Perspectives on Blockchain Technology and Responsible Investing* (pp. 85–116). IGI Global. doi:10.4018/978-1-6684-8361-9.ch004

Bhattacharjee, A., Bansal, V., & Juman, M. K. I. (2021). COVID-19 Emergency: Faux Healthcare Service Causes Distress and Life Dissatisfaction. *Asian Journal of Medicine and Health, 18*(12), 53–61. doi:10.9734/ajmah/2020/v18i1230290

Bhattacharjee, A., & Ghosh, A. (2024). Sustainable Green Supply Chain Management for Organizational Performance and Carbon Reduction. In Y. Ramakrishna & B. Srivastava (Eds.), *Strategies for Environmentally Responsible Supply Chain and Production Management* (pp. 128–155). IGI Global. doi:10.4018/979-8-3693-0669-7.ch007

Bhattacharjee, A., & Jahanshahi, A. A. (2021). Artificial landscape strategy: A business growth recovery plan in the post pandemic world. *Academia Letters, 2311.* Advance online publication. doi:10.20935/AL2311

Bhattacharjee, A., Jahanshahi, A. A., Bhuiyan, M., & Sultana, S. (2020). Mental health of cisgender and transgender during COVID-19 pandemic. *International Journal of Medical Research and Review, 8*(5), 344–351. doi:10.17511/ijmrr.2020.i05.02

Bhattacharjee, A., Jahanshahi, A. A., & Chakraborty, S. (2024). Unlocking the link between low emission supply chains, blockchain adoption, and financial success: The payoff of socially responsible practices in supply chains. *Business Strategy & Development, 7*(1), e341. doi:10.1002/bsd2.341

Bhattacharya, S., & Roy, D. (2019). AI and entrepreneurship in India: Opportunities and challenges for startups. *International Journal of Innovation and Technology Management, 16*(5), 1–20.

Bhatt, P., & Muduli, A. (2023). Artificial intelligence in learning and development: A systematic literature review. *European Journal of Training and Development, 47*(7–8), 677–694. doi:10.1108/EJTD-09-2021-0143

Bhnushali, D. M., & Itankar, P. (2020). Online Career Counsellor System based on Artificial Intelligence: An approach. [IORD]. *International Organization of Research & Development, 08*(02). doi:10.5281/zenodo.4699065

Biesta, G. (2013). Receiving the gift of teaching: From 'learning from'to 'being taught by'. *Studies in Philosophy and Education, 32*(5), 449–461. doi:10.1007/s11217-012-9312-9

Bilgram, V., & Laarmann, F. (2023). Accelerating Innovation with Generative AI: AI-augmented Digital Prototyping and Innovation Methods. *IEEE Engineering Management Review, 51*(2), 18–25. doi:10.1109/EMR.2023.3272799

Bilimoria, K., Harish, V., McCoy, L., Mehta, N., Morgado, F., Nagaraj, S., & Zheng, J. (2019). *Training for the future: preparing medical students for the impact of artificial intelligence.*

Biliran, A. (2023). Students' 21st Century Skills: Level of Readiness for Large- Scale Assessments. *Cosmos An International Journal of Art & Higher Education, 12*(1), 85–97. doi:10.46360/cosmos.ahe.520231007

Billionniere, E. (2022, August 23). *Bridging the Gender and Skills Gaps with Emerging Technologies.* ASEE. https://peer.asee.org/41916

Bishop, F., Zagermann, J., Pfeil, U., Sanderson, G., Reiterer, H., & Hinrichs, U. (2019). Construct-a-vis: Exploring the free-form visualization processes of children. *IEEE Transactions on Visualization and Computer Graphics, 26*(1), 451–460. doi:10.1109/TVCG.2019.2934804 PMID:31443024

Bitterman, D. S., Aerts, H. J., & Mak, R. H. (2020). Approaching autonomy in medical artificial intelligence. *The Lancet. Digital Health, 2*(9), e447–e449. doi:10.1016/S2589-7500(20)30187-4 PMID:33328110

Blair, K.P. (2007). *Pedagogical agents for learning by teaching: Teachable agents.*

Bleakley, A. (2014). *Patient-centred medicine in transition: The heart of the matter* (Vol. 3). Springer Science & Business Media. doi:10.1007/978-3-319-02487-5

Boison, D. K., Malcalm, E., Antwi-Boampong, A., Doumbia, M. O., & Hiran, K. K. (2022). Assessing Factors Affecting the Blockchain Adoption in Public Procurement Delivery in Ghana: A Correlational Study Using UTAUT2 Theoretical Framework. [IJACI]. *International Journal of Ambient Computing and Intelligence, 13*(1), 1–13. doi:10.4018/ijaci.314568

Boldea, P. (2019). *Campus study investigates how artificial intelligence can learn metaphorical language.* The Daily Californian.

Bolukbasi, T., Chang, K. W., Zou, J. Y., Saligrama, V., & Kalai, A. T. (2016). Man is to computer programmer as woman is to homemaker? debiasing word embeddings. *Proceedings of the 30th International Conference on Neural Information Processing Systems (NIPS'16)* (pp. 4356–4364). Curran Associates Inc., Red Hook, NY, USA.

Bommasani, R., Hudson, D. A., & Adeli, E. (2022). On the Opportunities and Risks of Foundation Models. *Center for Research on Foundation Models* (CRFM), 1-214.//https://arxiv.org/pdf/2108.07258.pdf

BonawitzK.EichnerH.GrieskampW.HubaD.IngermanA.IvanovV. (2017). Towards Federated Learning At Scale: System Design. arXiv:1902.01046v1.

Bonderud, D. (2021). *What Is Edge Computing, and How Can It Be Leveraged for Higher Ed?* EdTech. https://edtechmagazine.com/higher/article/2021/11/what-edge-computing-and-how-can-it-be-leveraged-higher-ed-perfcon

Borkan, J. M., Stagg Elliott, V., Wolpaw, T., Hassan, I., & Lomis, K. D. (2021). Looking ahead: the dynamic nature of health systems science, future trends, and the role of learners as change agents. *Health Systems Science*, 303-313.

Borromeo, D. (2023). Impact of Educational Technology Tools on the Digital and Information Literacy Skills of Selected Dominican Schools in the Philippines. *Cosmos An International Journal of Management, 12*(2), 01-08.

Borromeo, D., Estrella, N., & Caparas, E.R. (2023). Impact of Educational Technology Tools on the Digital and Information Literacy Skills of Selected Dominican Schools in the Philippines. *Cosmos An International Journal of Management, 12*(2), 01-08.

Borsatto, J. M. L. S., Marcolin, C. B., Abdalla, E. C., & Amaral, F. D. (2024). Aligning community outreach initiatives with SDGs in a higher education institution with artificial intelligence. *Cleaner and Responsible Consumption, 12*, 100160. doi:10.1016/j.clrc.2023.100160

Bouteraa, M., Chekima, B., Thurasamy, R., Bin-Nashwan, S. A., Al-Daihani, M., Baddou, A., Sadallah, M., & Ansar, R. (2024). Open Innovation in the Financial Sector: A Mixed-Methods Approach to Assess Bankers' Willingness to Embrace Open-AI ChatGPT. *Journal of Open Innovation, 10*(1), 1–14. doi:10.1016/j.joitmc.2024.100216

Brandford, S. A. (n.d.). *Investigating Barriers to Effective Career Counseling Services in Taraba State's Secondary Education*. Research Gate. https://www.researchgate.net/publication/373448378

Brandtzaeg, P. B., & Følstad, A. (2017). Why People Use Chatbots. In I. Kompatsiaris, (Eds.), Lecture Notes in Computer Science: Vol. 10673. *Internet Science. INSCI 2017*. Springer. doi:10.1007/978-3-319-70284-1_30

Briganti, G., & Le Moine, O. (2020). Artificial intelligence in medicine: Today and tomorrow. *Frontiers in Medicine, 7*, 27. doi:10.3389/fmed.2020.00027 PMID:32118012

Brynjolfsson, E., & McAfee, A. (2014). *The Second Machine Age: Work, Progress, and Prosperity in a Time of Brilliant Technologies*. W. W. Norton & Company.

Brynjolfsson, E., & McAfee, A. (2014). *The second machine age: Work, progress, and prosperity in a time of brilliant technologies*. WW Norton & Company.

Brynjolfsson, E., & Mitchell, T. (2017). What can machine learning do? Workforce implications. *Science, 358*(6370), 1530–1534. doi:10.1126/science.aap8062 PMID:29269459

Bui, T. A., Pohl, M., Rosenfelt, C., Ogourtsova, T., Yousef, M., Whitlock, K., Majnemer, A., Nicholas, D., Demmans Epp, C., Zaiane, O., & Bolduc, F. V. (2022). Identifying Potential Gamification Elements for A New Chatbot for Families with Neurodevelopmental Disorders: User-Centered Design Approach. *JMIR Human Factors, 9*(3), e31991. doi:10.2196/31991 PMID:35984679

Burgess, M. (2017). The NHS is trialling an AI chatbot to answer your medical questions. *Wired UK (2017, January 5).*

Burgsteiner, H., Kandlhofer, M., & Steinbauer, G. (2016). Irobot: Teaching the basics of artificial intelligence in high schools. *Proceedings of the AAAI Conference on Artificial Intelligence*, *30*(1). doi:10.1609/aaai.v30i1.9864

Burrows, L. (2021). *The present and future of AI.* Harvard John A. Paulson School of Engineering and Applied Sciences. https://seas.harvard.edu/news/2021/10/present-and-future-ai

Busch, F., Adams, L. C., & Bressem, K. K. (2023). Biomedical Ethical Aspects Towards the Implementation of Artificial Intelligence in Medical Education. *Medical Science Educator*, *33*(4), 1–6. doi:10.1007/s40670-023-01815-x PMID:37546190

Butt, P., Kamran, M., Afzal, F., & Mukit, M. M. H. (2021). Being agile in market orientation to enhance firm performance: The role of green supply chain management. *International Journal of Agile Systems and Management*, *14*(4), 517–542. doi:10.1504/IJASM.2021.120237

Cabitza, F., Campagner, A., Ronzio, L., Cameli, M., Mandoli, G. E., Pastore, M. C., Sconfienza, L. M., Folgado, D., Barandas, M., & Gamboa, H. (2023). Rams, hounds and white boxes: Investigating human–AI collaboration protocols in medical diagnosis. *Artificial Intelligence in Medicine*, *138*, 102506. doi:10.1016/j.artmed.2023.102506 PMID:36990586

Cai, Z., Ghosh, S., Stefanov, K., Dhall, A., Cai, J., Rezatofighi, H., ... Hayat, M. (2023). Marlin: Masked autoencoder for facial video representation learning. In *Proceedings of the IEEE/CVF Conference on Computer Vision and Pattern Recognition* (pp. 1493-1504). IEEE.

Campesato, O. (2023). *Gpt-4 for Developers.* Walter de Gruyter GmbH & Co KG. doi:10.1515/9781501519024

Canterbury, R. M. (2000). Higher education marketing: A challenge. *Journal of Marketing for Higher Education*, *9*(3), 15–24. doi:10.1300/J050v09n03_02

Card, D., & Nelson, C. (2019). How automation and digital disruption are shaping the workforce of the future. *Strategic HR Review*, *18*(6), 242–245. doi:10.1108/SHR-08-2019-0067

Carin, L. (2020). On artificial intelligence and deep learning within medical education. *Academic Medicine*, *95*(11S), S10–S11. doi:10.1097/ACM.0000000000003630 PMID:32769462

Carroll, N., & Conboy, K. (2020). Normalising the "new normal": Changing tech-driven work practices under pandemic time pressure. *International Journal of Information Management*, *55*, 102186. doi:10.1016/j.ijinfomgt.2020.102186 PMID:32836643

Carvalho, G., Cabral, B., Pereira, V., & Bernardino, J. (2021). Edge computing: Current trends, research challenges and future directions. *Computing*, *103*(5), 993–1023. doi:10.1007/s00607-020-00896-5

Casas-Rosal, J. C., Segura, M., and Maroto, C. (2023). Food market segmentation based on consumer preferences using outranking multi-criteria approaches. *International Transactions in Operational Research: A Journal of The International Federation of Operational Research Societies, 30*(3), 1537–1566. doi:10.1111/itor.12956

Castelli, M., & Manzoni, L. (2022). Generative models in artificial intelligence and their applications. *Applied Sciences (Basel, Switzerland)*, *12*(9), 4127. doi:10.3390/app12094127

Caudell, T. P., Summers, K. L., Holten, J. IV, Hakamata, T., Mowafi, M., Jacobs, J., Lozanoff, B. K., Lozanoff, S., Wilks, D., Keep, M. F., Saiki, S., & Alverson, D. (2003). Virtual patient simulator for distributed collaborative medical education. *Anatomical Record. Part B, New Anatomist*, *270*(1), 23–29. doi:10.1002/ar.b.10007 PMID:12526063

Celik, I. (2022). Exploring the Determinants of Artificial Intelligence (Ai) Literacy: Digital Divide, Computational Thinking, Cognitive Absorption. SSRN *Electronic Journal, 83*(7), 1–11. doi:10.2139/ssrn.4244763

Celik, I. (2023). Exploring the Determinants of Artificial Intelligence (AI) Literacy: Digital Divide, Computational Thinking, Cognitive Absorption. *Telematics and Informatics*, *83*(7), 1–14. doi:10.1016/j.tele.2023.102026

Chai, C. S., Lin, P. Y., Jong, M. S. Y., Dai, Y., Chiu, T. K., & Qin, J. (2021). Perceptions of and behavioral intentions towards learning artificial intelligence in primary school students. *Journal of Educational Technology & Society*, *24*(3), 89–101.

Chakma, S., & Chaijinda, N. (2020). Importance of reskilling and upskilling the workforce. วารสาร สห ศาสตร์ ศรีปทุม ชลบุรี *Interdisciplinary Sripatum Chonburi Journal (ISCJ), 6*(2), 23-31.

Chan, C. K. Y., & Tsi, L. H. (2023). The AI Revolution in Education: Will AI Replace or Assist Teachers in Higher Education? *arXiv preprint arXiv:2305.01185.*

Chan, C. K. Y. (2023). A comprehensive AI policy education framework for university teaching and learning. *International Journal of Educational Technology in Higher Education*, *20*(1), 38. doi:10.1186/s41239-023-00408-3

Chan, K. S., & Zary, N. (2019). Applications and challenges of implementing artificial intelligence in medical education: Integrative review. *JMIR Medical Education*, *5*(1), e13930. doi:10.2196/13930 PMID:31199295

ChatGPT. (2023). *ChatGPT Evolution Timeline*. Open AI. //https://chat.openai.com/share/a7d038b9-af2b-4049-8762-a2438f672d19

Chatterjee, A., & Das, S. (2019). AI and job redesign: Implications for workplace design in Indian organizations. *Journal of Workplace Design & Management*, *12*(3), 112–127.

Chatterjee, S., & Bhattacharjee, K. K. (2020). Adoption of artificial intelligence in higher education: A quantitative analysis using structural equation modelling. *Education and Information Technologies*, *25*(5), 3443–3463. doi:10.1007/s10639-020-10159-7

Chaturvedi, R., Verma, S., Das, R., & Dwivedi, Y. K. (2023). Social Companionship with Artificial Intelligence: Recent Trends and future avenues. *Technological Forecasting and Social Change*, *193*, 122634. doi:10.1016/j.techfore.2023.122634

Cheah, J. H., Amaro, S., & Roldán, J. L. (2023). Multigroup analysis of more than two groups in PLS-SEM: A review, illustration, and recommendations. *Journal of Business Research*, *156*, 113539. doi:10.1016/j.jbusres.2022.113539

Chen, C. K. (2010). *Curriculum Assessment Using Artificial Neural Network and Support Vector Machine Modeling Approaches: A Case Study. IR Applications*. Association for Institutional Research (NJ1).

Cheng, E. C. K., & Wang, T. (2023). Leading digital transformation and eliminating barriers for teachers to incorporate artificial intelligence in basic education in Hong Kong. *Computers and Education: Artificial Intelligence*, *5*(10), 1–12. doi:10.1016/j.caeai.2023.100171

Chen, J. (2017). Playing to our human strengths to prepare medical students for the future. *Korean Journal of Medical Education*, *29*(3), 193–197. doi:10.3946/kjme.2017.65 PMID:28870022

Chen, J. S. (Ed.). (2023). *Advances in hospitality and leisure*. Advances in Hospitality and Leisure., doi:10.1108/S1745-3542202318

Chen, L., Chen, P., & Lin, Z. (2020). Artificial intelligence in education: A review. *IEEE Access : Practical Innovations, Open Solutions*, *8*, 75264–75278. doi:10.1109/ACCESS.2020.2988510

Chen, X., Zou, D., Cheng, G., & Xie, H. (2021, July). Artificial intelligence-assisted personalized language learning: systematic review and co-citation analysis. *2021 International Conference on Advanced Learning Technologies (ICALT)*. IEEE. 10.1109/ICALT52272.2021.00079

Chen, Y.-F., & Hsiao, C.-H. (2009). Applying market segmentation theory to student behavior in selecting a school or department. *New Horizons in Education*, *57*(2), 32–43. https://files.eric.ed.gov/fulltext/EJ860823.pdf

Chilewa, E. A., & Osaki, K. (2022). The Effectiveness of Guidance and Counselling Practices on Students' Career Development in Secondary Schools in Temeke Municipality. *The Journal of Humanistic Education and Development*, *4*(1), 160–181. doi:10.22161/jhed.4.1.17

Chiong, J. W., & Catipunan-Francisco, J. C. (2023). Life Dynamics as a Behavioral Program for Student Leaders of Jose Rizal University. *Cosmos An International Journal of Art & Higher Education*, *12*(1), 196–204. doi:10.46360/cosmos.ahe.520231017

Chiu, T. K. (2023). The impact of Generative AI (GenAI) on practices, policies and research direction in education: A case of ChatGPT and Midjourney. *Interactive Learning Environments*, 1–17. doi:10.1080/10494820.2023.2253861

Chiu, T. K. F. (2024). Future research recommendations for transforming higher education with generative AI. *Computers and Education: Artificial Intelligence*, *6*(12), 1–15. doi:10.1016/j.caeai.2023.100197

Chiu, T. K. F., & Chai, C. S. (2020). Sustainable curriculum planning for artificial intelligence education: A self-determination theory perspective. *Sustainability (Basel)*, *12*(14), 5568. doi:10.3390/su12145568

Chng, E., Tan, A. L., & Tan, S. C. (2023). Examining the Use of Emerging Technologies in Schools: A Review of Artificial Intelligence and Immersive Technologies in STEM Education. *Journal for STEM Education Research*, *6*(3), 385–407. doi:10.1007/s41979-023-00092-y

Choubisa, M., Doshi, R., Khatri, N., & Hiran, K. K. (2022, May). A simple and robust approach of random forest for intrusion detection system in cyber security. In *2022 International conference on IoT and blockchain technology (ICIBT)* (pp. 1-5). IEEE. 10.1109/ICIBT52874.2022.9807766

Chung, J. S., & Zisserman, A. (2015). Lip reading in the wild. In *Proceedings of the Asian Conference on Computer Vision* (pp. 87-103). Academic Press.

Chung, J. S., & Zisserman, A. (2016). Out of time: Automated lip sync in the wild. In *Proceedings of the Asian Conference on Computer Vision* (pp. 251-263). Springer.

Ciesla, R. (2024). *The Book of Chatbots: From ELIZA to ChatGPT*. Springer Nature. Cohere. https://docs.cohere.com/docs/prompt-engineering

Clarke, A. C. (1980). Electronic tutors. *Omni Magazine*, *2*(9), 77–78.

Coghlan, S., Miller, T., & Paterson, J. (2020). *"Good proctor or" Big Brother"? AI Eth-ics and Online Exam Supervision Technologies*. arXiv preprint arXiv:2011.07647

Coghlan, S., & Coghlan, B. (2018). One Health, bioethics, and nonhuman ethics. *The American Journal of Bioethics*, *18*(11), 3–5. doi:10.1080/15265161.2018.1524224 PMID:30475184

Coghlan, S., Leins, K., Sheldrick, S., Cheong, M., Gooding, P., & D'Alfonso, S. (2023). To chat or bot to chat: Ethical issues with using chatbots in mental health. *Digital Health*, *9*, 20552076231183542. doi:10.1177/20552076231183542 PMID:37377565

Coghlan, S., Miller, T., & Paterson, J. (2021). Good proctor or "big brother"? Ethics of online exam supervision technologies. *Philosophy & Technology*, *34*(4), 1581–1606. doi:10.1007/s13347-021-00476-1 PMID:34485025

Cohen, I. G., & Mello, M. M. (2019). Big data, big tech, and protecting patient privacy. *Journal of the American Medical Association*, *322*(12), 1141–1142. doi:10.1001/jama.2019.11365 PMID:31397838

Collado, R. (2023). Hyping Personal Engagement (HYPE): Upgrading Research Writing Skills Among Students Using Hyperdocs. *Globus An International Journal of Management & IT, 14*(2), 01-05.

Cooper, A., & Ireland, D. (2018). Designing a Chat-Bot for Non-Verbal Children on the Autism Spectrum. *Studies in Health Technology and Informatics*, *252*, 63–68. doi:10.3233/978-1-61499-890-7-63 PMID:30040684

Cooper, G. (2023). Examining Science Education in ChatGPT: An Exploratory Study of Generative Artificial Intelligence. *Journal of Science Education and Technology*, *32*(3), 444–452. doi:10.1007/s10956-023-10039-y

Cramarenco, R. E., Burcă-Voicu, M. I., & Dabija, D. C. (2023). The impact of artificial intelligence (AI) on employees' skills and well-being in global labor markets: A systematic review. *Oeconomia Copernicana*, *14*(3), 731–767. doi:10.24136/oc.2023.022

Crutzen, R., Bosma, H., Havas, J., & Feron, F. (2014). What can we learn from a failed trial: Insight into non-participation in a chat-based intervention trial for adolescents with psychosocial problems. *BMC Research Notes*, *7*(1), 824. doi:10.1186/1756-0500-7-824 PMID:25409911

Cui, K. (2023). Artificial intelligence and creativity: Piano teaching with augmented reality applications. *Interactive Learning Environments*, *31*(10), 7017–7028. doi:10.1080/10494820.2022.2059520

Curtis, B., Hefley, B., & Miller, S. (2002). *People Capability Maturity Model (P-CMM) version 2.0*. Software Engineering Institute.

Dadhich, M., & Tiwari, H. (2022). Quantum Blockchain for Smart Society: Applications, Challenges, and Opportunities. In Advancements in Quantum Blockchain With Real-Time Applications. IGI Global. doi:10.4018/978-1-6684-5072-7.ch009

Dadhich, M., Purohit, H., Tirole, R., Mathur, S., & Jain, A. (2023). Industry 4.0 Revolution towards a Future-Ready Society and Manufacturing Excellence. In AIP Conference Proceedings. doi:10.1063/5.0113614

Dadhich, M., Doshi, R., Mathur, S., Meena, R., Gujral, R. K., & Dhotre, P. (2021). *Empirical Study of Awareness towards Blended E-Learning Gateways during Covid-19 Lockdown*. In *2021 International Conference on Computing, Communication and Green Engineering (CCGE)*, Pune, India. 10.1109/CCGE50943.2021.9776386

Dadhich, M., Hiran, K. K., Rao, S. S., & Sharma, R. (2022). Impact of Covid-19 on Teaching-Learning Perception of Faculties and Students of Higher Education in Indian Purview. *Journal of Mobile Multimedia*, *18*(4), 957–980. doi:10.13052/jmm1550-4646.1841

Dadhich, M., Rathore, S., Akwasi, B., Ajibade, S. M., & Agozie, D. Q. (2023). Quantifying the Dynamic Factors Influencing New-Age Users' Adoption of 5G Using TAM and UTAUT Models in Emerging Country : A Multistage PLS-SEM Approach. *Education Research International*, *1*, 1–15. doi:10.1155/2023/5452563

Dadhich, M., Yadav, P., Saxena, A., Birda, R. K., Mathur, S., & Hiran, K. K. (2023). Dynamic Determinants of AI-Based Innovation Management Practices and Sustainable FinTech: Application Preferences of AI-Innovators. *2023 IEEE International Conference on Contemporary Computing and Communications (InC4)*, (pp. 1–5). IEEE. 10.1109/InC457730.2023.10263140

Dadhich, Manish, Rao, Shalendra Singh, & Sharma, Renu, R. M. (2023). Emerging Determinants and Analyatics of Off-balance Sheet Activities (OBSA) of Commercial Banks. *Finance India*, *XXXVII*(2), 383–400.

Dahlan, S., Idris, E., & Susanto, E. (2020). Improve student career certainty using self-information: A career counseling in the school. *Cypriot Journal of Educational Sciences*, *15*(6), 1480–1494. doi:10.18844/cjes.v15i6.5292

Dai, J., Wang, J., Huang, W., Shi, J., & Zhu, Z. (2020). Machinery health monitoring based on unsupervised feature learning via generative adversarial networks. *IEEE/ASME Transactions on Mechatronics*, *25*(5), 2252–2263. doi:10.1109/TMECH.2020.3012179

Dai, Y., Liu, A., & Lim, C. P. (2023). Reconceptualizing ChatGPT and Generative AI as a Student-Driven Innovation in Higher Education. *Procedia CIRP*, *119*, 84–90. doi:10.1016/j.procir.2023.05.002

Daley, K., Hungerbuehler, I., Cavanagh, K., Claro, H. G., Swinton, P. A., & Kapps, M. (2020). Preliminary Evaluation of the Engagement and Effectiveness of a Mental Health Chatbot. *Frontiers in Digital Health*, *2*, 576361. doi:10.3389/fdgth.2020.576361 PMID:34713049

Dang Truong Ho Chi, H. (2020). Development of an AI Chatbot to Support Admissions and Career Guidance for Universities. *International Journal of Emerging Multidisciplinary Research*, *4*(2), 13–20. doi:10.22662/IJEMR.2020.4.2.013

DasA. (2024). Lip2Text: Sentence-Level Lipreading on English Speakers Using the Deep Learning Approach. Preprint. https://doi.org/ doi:10.21203/rs.3.rs-3852300/v1

Davari, M., Noursalehi, P., & Keramati, A. (2019). Data mining approach to professional education market segmentation: A case study. *Journal of Marketing for Higher Education*, *29*(1), 45–66. doi:10.1080/08841241.2018.1545724

Dave, D. M., Mandvikar, S., & Engineer, P. A. (2023). Augmented intelligence: Human-ai collaboration in the era of digital transformation. *International Journal of Engineering Applied Sciences and Technology*, *8*(6), 24–33. doi:10.33564/IJEAST.2023.v08i06.003

Davenport, T., & Kalakota, R. (2019). The potential for artificial intelligence in healthcare. *Future Healthcare Journal*, *6*(2), 94–98. doi:10.7861/futurehosp.6-2-94 PMID:31363513

De Fauw, J., Ledsam, J. R., Romera-Paredes, B., Nikolov, S., Tomasev, N., Blackwell, S., Askham, H., Glorot, X., O'Donoghue, B., Visentin, D., van den Driessche, G., Lakshminarayanan, B., Meyer, C., Mackinder, F., Bouton, S., Ayoub, K., Chopra, R., King, D., Karthikesalingam, A., & Ronneberger, O. (2018). Clinically applicable deep learning for diagnosis and referral in retinal disease. *Nature Medicine*, *24*(9), 1342–1350. doi:10.1038/s41591-018-0107-6 PMID:30104768

De Oliveira Silva, A., & Dos Santos Janes, D. (2020). Exploring the Role of Artificial Intelligence in Education: A Comprehensive Perspective. *Review of Artificial Intelligence in Education*, *1*(00), e05–e05. doi:10.37497/rev.artif.intell.education.v1i00.5

Demestichas, K., & Daskalakis, E. (2020). Information and communication technology solutions for the circular economy. In Sustainability (Switzerland) (Vol. 12, Issue 18, pp. 1–19). MDPI. doi:10.3390/su12187272

Dhamija, P., & Bag, S. (2020). Role of artificial intelligence in operations environment: a review and bibliometric analysis. In TQM Journal (Vol. 32, Issue 4, pp. 869–896). Emerald Group Holdings Ltd. doi:10.1108/TQM-10-2019-0243

Dhanabalan, T., Sathish, A., & Tamilnadu, K. (2018). *TRANSFORMING INDIAN INDUSTRIES THROUGH ARTIFICIAL INTELLIGENCE AND.*, *9*(10), 835–845.

Dharma, E. M., Gaol, F. L., Warnars, H. L. H. S., & Soewito, B. (2022). The Accuracy Comparison among Word2vec, Glove, and Fasttext towards Convolution Neural Network (Cnn) Text Classification. *Journal of Theoretical and Applied Information Technology*, *100*(2), 31.

DiazJ.HalkiasD. (2021). Reskilling and upskilling 4IR leaders in business schools through an innovative executive education ecosystem: An integrative literature review. SSRN 3897059. doi:10.2139/ssrn.3897059

Diaz, J., Halkias, D., & Thurman, P. W. (2022). *The innovative management education ecosystem: Reskilling and upskilling the future workforce*. Taylor & Francis. doi:10.4324/9781003308652

Dongre, G., Vadraiwala, F., Upadhyaya, J., & Ghosal, D. (n.d.). WEB-BASED CAREER COUNSELLING SYSTEM WITH CHATBOT. *International Research Journal of Modernization in Engineering Technology and Science.*

Doroudi, S. (2023). The intertwined histories of artificial intelligence and education. *International Journal of Artificial Intelligence in Education, 33*(4), 885–928. doi:10.1007/s40593-022-00313-2

Doshi, R., Hiran, K. K., Mijwil, M. M., & Anand, D. (2023). To That of Artificial Intelligence, Passing Through Business Intelligence. In Handbook of Research on AI and Knowledge Engineering for Real-Time Business Intelligence (pp. 1-16). IGI Global.

Doshi, R., Hiran, K. K., Ranolia, R., & Joshi, C. (2023). Monitor Cloud Performance and Data Safety With Artificial Intelligence. In Applications of Artificial Intelligence in Wireless Communication Systems (pp. 92-108). IGI Global. doi:10.4018/978-1-6684-7348-1.ch006

Doshi, R., Hiran, K. K., Mijwil, M. M., & Anand, D. (2023). To That of Artificial Intelligence, Passing Through Business Intelligence. In *Handbook of Research on AI and Knowledge Engineering for Real-Time Business Intelligence* (pp. 1–16). IGI Global. doi:10.4018/978-1-6684-6519-6.ch001

Doshi, R., Hu, Y. C., Garg, L., & Fagbola, T. (2023). Towards a Higher Education of the Future: Transformational Roles of Edge Intelligence. *Array (New York, N.Y.)*, 100332. doi:10.1016/j.array.2023.100332

Dosovitsky, G., & Bunge, E. L. (2021). Bonding With Bot: User Feedback on a Chatbot for Social Isolation. *Frontiers in Digital Health, 3*, 735053. doi:10.3389/fdgth.2021.735053 PMID:34713203

Dreyer, K. J., & Geis, J. R. (2017). When machines think: Radiology's next frontier. *Radiology, 285*(3), 713–718. doi:10.1148/radiol.2017171183 PMID:29155639

Du, B. (2023). Research on the factors influencing the learner satisfaction of MOOCs. *Education and Information Technologies, 28*(2), 1935–1955. doi:10.1007/s10639-022-11269-0

Dumford, A. D., & Miller, A. L. (2018). Online learning in higher education: Exploring advantages and disadvantages for engagement. *Journal of Computing in Higher Education, 30*(3), 452–465. doi:10.1007/s12528-018-9179-z

Dumić-Čule, I., Orešković, T., Brkljačić, B., Kujundžić Tiljak, M., & Orešković, S. (2020). The importance of introducing artificial intelligence to the medical curriculum–assessing practitioners' perspectives. *Croatian Medical Journal, 61*(5), 457–464. doi:10.3325/cmj.2020.61.457 PMID:33150764

Dwivedi, Y. K., Hughes, D. L., Coombs, C., Constantiou, I., Duan, Y., Edwards, J. S., Gupta, B., Lal, B., Misra, S., Prashant, P., Raman, R., Rana, N. P., Sharma, S. K., & Upadhyay, N. (2020). Impact of COVID-19 pandemic on information management research and practice: Transforming education, work and life. *International Journal of Information Management, 55*, 102211. doi:10.1016/j.ijinfomgt.2020.102211

Easwaran, B., Hiran, K. K., Krishnan, S., & Doshi, R. (Eds.). (2022). *Real-time applications of machine learning in cyber-physical systems*. IGI global. doi:10.4018/978-1-7998-9308-0

Edgar, F., & Workman, J. (2018). Developing the Career Agility of the Contemporary Worker: A Framework for Research and Practice. *Journal of Vocational Behavior, 106*, 73–84.

Egger, F. N. (2000). 'Trust me, I'm an online vendor': towards a model of trust for e-commerce system design. In *CHI '00 extended abstracts on human factors in computing systems* (pp. 101–102). Association for Computing Machinery. doi:10.1145/633292.633352

Eglash, R., Bennett, A., Babbitt, W., Lachney, M., Reinhardt, M., & Hammond-Sowah, D. (2020). Decolonizing posthumanism: Indigenous material agency in generative STEM. *British Journal of Educational Technology*, *51*(4), 1334–1353. doi:10.1111/bjet.12963

Eguchi, A., & Uribe, L. (2017). Robotics to promote STEM learning: Educational robotics unit for 4th grade science. In *2017 IEEE integrated stem education conference (ISEC)* (pp. 186-194). IEEE.

Ekuma, K. (2023). *Rethinking Upskilling and Reskilling in the Age of AI and Automation: A fsQCA Approach.*

Ellaway, R. H. (2014). Medical education and the war with the machines. *Medical Teacher*, *36*(10), 917–918. doi:10.3109/0142159X.2014.955088 PMID:25216159

Elrefaei, L. A., Alhassan, T. Q., & Omar, S. S. (2019). An Arabic Visual Dataset for Visual Speech Recognition. *Procedia Computer Science*, *163*, 163–170. doi:10.1016/j.procs.2019.12.122

Eminaga, O., Laurie, M., Lee, T., Jia, X., Xing, L., & Liao, J. C. (2023). Potential of educational cystoscopy atlas for augmented intelligence. In Advanced Biomedical and Clinical Diagnostic and Surgical Guidance Systems XXI, 12368, 141-147. doi:10.1117/12.2650920

Estevez, J., Garate, G., & Graña, M. (2019). Gentle introduction to artificial intelligence for high-school students using scratch. *IEEE Access : Practical Innovations, Open Solutions*, *7*, 179027–179036. doi:10.1109/ACCESS.2019.2956136

Exarchos, T., Dimitrakopoulos, G. N., Vrahatis, A. G., Chrysovitsiotis, G., Zachou, Z., & Kyrodimos, E. (2024). Lip-Reading Advancements: A 3D Convolutional Neural Network/Long Short-Term Memory Fusion for Precise Word Recognition. *BioMedInformatics*, *4*(1), 410–422.

Fagbola, T. M., Fagbola, F. I., Aroba, O. J., Doshi, R., Hiran, K. K., & Thakur, S. C. (2022). Smart face masks for Covid-19 pandemic management: A concise review of emerging architectures, challenges and future research directions. *IEEE Sensors Journal*, *23*(2), 877–888. doi:10.1109/JSEN.2022.3225067

Faiz, M., Sandhu, R., Akbar, M., Shaikh, A. A., Bhasin, C., & Fatima, N. (2023). Machine Learning Techniques in Wireless Sensor Networks: Algorithms, Strategies, and Applications. *International Journal of Intelligent Systems and Applications in Engineering*, *11*(9s), 685–694.

Falloon, G. (2020). From digital literacy to digital competence: The teacher digital competency (TDC) framework. *Educational Technology Research and Development*, *68*(5), 2449–2472. doi:10.1007/s11423-020-09767-4

Fan, K. Y., Hu, R., & Singla, R. (2020). Introductory machine learning for medical students: A pilot. *Medical Education*, *54*(11), 1042–1043. doi:10.1111/medu.14318 PMID:32862464

Fan, S., Guo, J., Ma, S., Li, L., Wang, G., Xu, H., & Zhao, Z. (2023). Framework and key technologies of human-machine hybrid-augmented intelligence system for large-scale power grid dispatching and control. *CSEE Journal of Power and Energy Systems*, *10*(1), 1–12. doi:10.17775/CSEEJPES.2023.00940

Farahmand, S. (2022). *CyberPatient™-an innovative approach to medical education* [Doctoral dissertation, University of British Columbia].

Fariani, R. I., Junus, K., & Santoso, H. B. (2022). A Systematic Literature Review on Personalised Learning in the Higher Education Context. Technology. *Knowledge and Learning*, *28*(2), 449–476. doi:10.1007/s10758-022-09628-4

Fazlollahi, A. M., Bakhaidar, M., Alsayegh, A., Yilmaz, R., Winkler-Schwartz, A., Mirchi, N., Langleben, I., Ledwos, N., Sabbagh, A. J., Bajunaid, K., Harley, J. M., & Del Maestro, R. F. (2022). Effect of artificial intelligence tutoring vs expert instruction on learning simulated surgical skills among medical students: A randomized clinical trial. *JAMA Network Open*, *5*(2), e2149008–e2149008. doi:10.1001/jamanetworkopen.2021.49008 PMID:35191972

Feng, Y., Vanam, S., Cherukupally, M., Zheng, W., Qiu, M., & Chen, H. (2023). Investigating code generation performance of ChatGPT with crowdsourcing social data. In *2023 IEEE 47th Annual Computers, Software, and Applications Conference (COMPSAC)* (pp. 876-885). IEEE. 10.1109/COMPSAC57700.2023.00117

Fenlon, M. J., & Fitzgerald, B. K. (2021). Creating the future workforce today. Business-Higher Education Forum, Washington, District of Columbia.

Fernández-Caramés, T. M., & Fraga-Lamas, P. (2019). Towards Next Generation Teaching, Learning, and Context-Aware Applications for Higher Education: A Review on Blockchain, IoT, Fog and Edge Computing Enabled Smart Campuses and Universities. *Applied Sciences (Basel, Switzerland)*, *9*(21), 4479. doi:10.3390/app9214479

Ferrara, E. (2024). GenAI against humanity: Nefarious applications of generative artificial intelligence and large language models. *Journal of Computational Social Science*, 1–21. doi:10.1007/s42001-024-00250-1

Filippi, C. G., Stein, J. M., Wang, Z., Bakas, S., Liu, Y., Chang, P. D., Lui, Y., Hess, C., Barboriak, D. P., Flanders, A. E., Wintermark, M., Zaharchuk, G., & Wu, O. (2023). Ethical Considerations and Fairness in the Use of Artificial Intelligence for Neuroradiology. *AJNR. American Journal of Neuroradiology*, *44*(11), 1242–1248. doi:10.3174/ajnr.A7963 PMID:37652578

Firsanova, V. (2020). Supporting the Inclusion of People with Asperger Syndrome: Building a Customizable Chatbot with Transfer Learning. In *AINL: Artificial Intelligence and Natural Language Conference. Workshop on Human-AI Interaction*.

Fitzpatrick, K. K., Darcy, A., & Vierhile, M. (2017). Delivering Cognitive Behavior Therapy to Young Adults with Symptoms of Depression and Anxiety Using a Fully Automated Conversational Agent (Woebot): A Randomized Controlled Trial. *JMIR Mental Health*, *4*(2), e19. doi:10.2196/mental.7785 PMID:28588005

Floridi, L., & Cowls, J. (2022). A unified framework of five principles for AI in society. *Machine Learning and the City: Applications in Architecture and Urban Design*, (pp. 535–545). Wiley. doi:10.1002/9781119815075.ch45

Floridi, L. (2019). Establishing the rules for building trustworthy AI. *Nature Machine Intelligence*, *1*(6), 261–262. doi:10.1038/s42256-019-0055-y

Floridi, L., Cowls, J., Beltrametti, M., Chatila, R., Chazerand, P., Dignum, V., Luetge, C., Madelin, R., Pagallo, U., Rossi, F., Schafer, B., Valcke, P., & Vayena, E. (2018). AI4People—An Ethical Framework for a Good AI Society: Opportunities, Risks, Principles, and Recommendations. *Minds and Machines*, *28*(4), 689–707. doi:10.1007/s11023-018-9482-5 PMID:30930541

Følstad, A., Araujo, T., Law, E. L. C., Brandtzaeg, P. B., Papadopoulos, S., Reis, L., Baez, M., Laban, G., McAllister, P., Ischen, C., Wald, R., Catania, F., Meyer von Wolff, R., Hobert, S., & Luger, E. (2021). Future directions for chatbot research: An interdisciplinary research agenda. *Computing*, *103*(12), 2915–2942. doi:10.1007/s00607-021-01016-7

Formosa, P., Wilson, M., & Richards, D. (2021). A principlist framework for cybersecurity ethics. *Computers & Security*, *109*, 102382. doi:10.1016/j.cose.2021.102382

Fox, N. A., O'Mullane, B. A., & Reilly, R. B. (2005). VALID: A new practical audio-visual database, and comparative results. In *Proceedings of the International Conference on Audio-Video-Based Biometric Person Authentication* (pp. 777-786). Academic Press.

Frank, M. R., Autor, D., Bessen, J. E., Brynjolfsson, E., Cebrian, M., Deming, D. J., Feldman, M., Groh, M., Lobo, J., Moro, E., Wang, D., Youn, H., & Rahwan, I. (2019). Toward understanding the impact of artificial intelligence on labour. *Proceedings of the National Academy of Sciences of the United States of America, 116*(14), 6531–6539. doi:10.1073/pnas.1900949116 PMID:30910965

Franze, A., Galanis, C. R., & King, D. L. (2023). Social chatbot use (e.g., ChatGPT) among individuals with social deficits: Risks and opportunities. *Journal of Behavioral Addictions, 12*(4), 871–872. doi:10.1556/2006.2023.00057 PMID:38141065

Furey, H., & Martin, F. (2019). AI education matters: A modular approach to AI ethics education. *AI Matters, 4*(4), 13–15. doi:10.1145/3299758.3299764

Fütterer, T., Fischer, C., Alekseeva, A., Chen, X., Tate, T., Warschauer, M., & Gerjets, P. (2023). *ChatGPT in education: global reactions toAIinnovations.* Scientifc Reports., doi:10.1038/s41598-023-42227-6

Galindo-Domínguez, H., Delgado, N., Losada, D., & Etxabe, J. M. (2023). An analysis of the use of artificial intelligence in education in Spain: The in-service teacher's perspective. *Journal of Digital Learning in Teacher Education*, 1–16.

Gallix, B., & Chong, J. (2019). Artificial intelligence in radiology: Who's afraid of the big bad wolf? *European Radiology, 29*(4), 1637–1639. doi:10.1007/s00330-018-5995-9 PMID:30734848

Galvex, S. (2023). The Effects of Students' Resiliency on Academic Performance Amidst Pandemic. *Globus An International Journal of Medical Science, Engineering and Technology, 9*(1), 01-04.

Gandedkar, N. H., Wong, M. T., & Darendeliler, M. A. (2021). Role of virtual reality (VR), augmented reality (AR) and artificial intelligence (AI) in tertiary education and research of orthodontics: An insight. *Seminars in Orthodontics, 27*(2), 69–77. doi:10.1053/j.sodo.2021.05.003

Gandhi, A., & Kapoor, V. (2020). AI and skill development policy in India: A critical appraisal. *Journal of Policy Research in Higher Education, 6*(2), 98–115.

Gangal, R., Johri, P., & Kumar, A. (2023). A Systematic Review of Artificial Intelligence Techniques in Lung Cancer Detection and Accurate Diagnosis. *Cosmos Journal of Engineering & Technology, 13*(1), 51–56. doi:10.46360/cosmos.et.620231005

Ganjam, S. V., P S, P., & Vinayak, H. (2023). Conversational AI Whatsapp Chatbot. [IJERT]. *International Journal of Engineering Research & Technology (Ahmedabad), 11*(05).

Gao, P., Li, J., & Liu, S. (2021). An introduction to key technology in artificial intelligence and big data driven e-learning and e-education. *Mobile Networks and Applications, 26*(5), 2123–2126. doi:10.1007/s11036-021-01777-7

García-Peñalvo, F. J., Llorens Largo, F., & Vidal, J. (2023). *The new reality of education in the face of advances in generative artificial intelligence.*

García-Sampedro, M., Agudo Prado, S., & Torralba-Burrial, A. (2024). Pre-service teachers' skills development through educational video generation. *European Journal of Teacher Education*, 1–19. doi:10.1080/02619768.2024.2323925

Garg, J., Noyola, J., & Bagadia, S. (2016). *Lip reading using CNN and LSTM.* Stanford University Technical Report CS231n Project.

Gaurav, K. (2023). Empirical investigation of industry 4.0 for sustainable growth and implication for future-ready compatibility for cement industry of India. *AIP Conference Proceedings, 2521*(040026), 1–12. 978-0-7354-4650-2/$30.00

Gentile, M., Città, G., Perna, S., & Allegra, M. (2023, March). Do we still need teachers? Navigating the paradigm shift of the teacher's role in the AI era. []. Frontiers.]. *Frontiers in Education*, *8*, 1161777. doi:10.3389/feduc.2023.1161777

Gevaert, C. M., Carman, M., Rosman, B., Georgiadou, Y., & Soden, R. (2021). Fairness and accountability of AI in disaster risk management: Opportunities and challenges. *Patterns (New York, N.Y.)*, *2*(11), 100363. doi:10.1016/j.patter.2021.100363 PMID:34820647

Ghai, D., Tripathi, S. L., Saxena, S., Chanda, M., & Alazab, M. (Eds.). (2022). *Machine Learning Algorithms for Signal and Image Processing*. John Wiley & Sons. doi:10.1002/9781119861850

Gibson, C., & Franze, A. (2023, December 11). *We need to talk about social chatbots and the impact of AI*. Home. https://www.unisa.edu.au/media-centre/Releases/2023/we-need-to-talk-about-social-chatbots-and-the-impact-of-ai/

Gill, S. S., Xu, M., Patros, P., Wu, H., Kaur, R., Kaur, K., Fuller, S., Singh, M., Arora, P., Parlikad, A. K., Stankovski, V., Abraham, A., Ghosh, S. K., Lutfiyya, H., Kanhere, S. S., Bahsoon, R., Rana, O., Dustdar, S., Sakellariou, R., & Buyya, R. (2023). Transformative Effects of ChatGPT on Modern Education: Emerging Era of AI Chatbots. *Internet of Things and Cyber-Physical Systems*, *4*, 19–23. doi:10.1016/j.iotcps.2023.06.002

Gilson, A., Safranek, C., Huang, T., Socrates, V., Chi, L., Taylor, R. A., & Chartash, D. (2022). How well does ChatGPT do when taking the medical licensing exams? The implications of large language models for medical education and knowledge assessment. medRxiv, 2022-12.

Gligorea, I., Cioca, M., Oancea, R., Gorski, A.-T., Gorski, H., & Tudorache, P. (2023). Adaptive Learning Using Artificial Intelligence in e-Learning: A Literature Review. *Education Sciences*, *13*(12), 1216. doi:10.3390/educsci13121216

Goddard, K., Roudsari, A., & Wyatt, J. C. (2012). Automation bias: A systematic review of frequency, effect mediators, and mitigators. *Journal of the American Medical Informatics Association : JAMIA*, *19*(1), 121–127. doi:10.1136/amiajnl-2011-000089 PMID:21685142

Golab-Andrzejak, E. (2022). Enhancing Customer Engagement in Social Media with AI - a Higher Education case study. *Procedia Computer Science*, *207*, 3022–3031. doi:10.1016/j.procs.2022.09.361

Goldkind, L. (2021). Social Work and Artificial Intelligence: Into the Matrix. *Social Work*, *66*(4), 372–374. doi:10.1093/sw/swab028 PMID:34279661

Goldkind, L., Wolf, L., Glennon, A., Rios, J., & Nissen, L. (2024). The End of the World as We Know It? ChatGPT and Social Work. *Social Work*, *69*(1), 103–105. doi:10.1093/sw/swad044 PMID:37972352

González-González, C. S., Infante-Moro, A., & Infante-Moro, J. C. (2020). Implemen-tation of e-proctoring in online teaching: A study about motivational factors. *Sustainability (Basel)*, *12*(8), 3488. doi:10.3390/su12083488

Goodier, G. H. G., McCormack, J., Egan, S. J., Watson, H. J., Hoiles, K. J., Todd, G., & Treasure, J. L. (2014). Parent skills training treatment for parents of children and adolescents with eating disorders: A qualitative study: PARENT SKILLS TRAINING TREATMENT. *International Journal of Eating Disorders*, *47*(4), 368–375. doi:10.1002/eat.22224 PMID:24843891

Goralski, M. A., & Tan, T. K. (2020). Artificial intelligence and sustainable development. *International Journal of Management Education*, *18*(1), 100330. doi:10.1016/j.ijme.2019.100330

Gorski, A.-T., Gligorea, I., Gorski, H., & Oancea, R. (2022). Workforce and Workplace Ecosystem - Challenges and Opportunities in the Age of Digital Transformation and 4IR. *International Conference of Knowledge-Based Organization, 28*, 187-194. 10.2478/kbo-2022-0028

Gouvea, R., Kapelianis, D., & Kassicieh, S. (2018). Assessing the nexus of sustainability and information & communications technology. *Technological Forecasting and Social Change*, *130*, 39–44. doi:10.1016/j.techfore.2017.07.023

Grassini, S. (2023). Shaping the future of education: Exploring the potential and consequences of AI and ChatGPT in educational settings. *Education Sciences*, *13*(7), 692. doi:10.3390/educsci13070692

Graßmann, C., Schölmerich, F., & Schermuly, C. C. (2020). The relationship between working alliance and client outcomes in coaching: A meta-analysis. *Human Relations*, *73*(1), 35–58. doi:10.1177/0018726718819725

Gresse von Wangenheim, C., Hauck, J. C., Pacheco, F. S., & Bertonceli Bueno, M. F. (2021). Visual tools for teaching machine learning in K-12: A ten-year systematic mapping. *Education and Information Technologies*, *26*(5), 5733–5778. doi:10.1007/s10639-021-10570-8 PMID:33967587

Grunhut, J., Wyatt, A. T., & Marques, O. (2021). Educating future physicians in artificial intelligence (AI): An integrative review and proposed changes. *Journal of Medical Education and Curricular Development*, *8*, 23821205211036836. doi:10.1177/23821205211036836 PMID:34778562

Guidance, W. H. O. (2021). *Ethics and governance of artificial intelligence for health.* World Health Organization.

Gulliver, A., Griffiths, K. M., & Christensen, H. (2010). Perceived barriers and facilitators to mental health help-seeking in young people: A systematic review. *BMC Psychiatry*, *10*(1), 113. doi:10.1186/1471-244X-10-113 PMID:21192795

Guo, J., & Li, B. (2018). The application of medical artificial intelligence technology in rural areas of developing countries. *Health Equity*, *2*(1), 174–181. doi:10.1089/heq.2018.0037 PMID:30283865

Gupta, R., Singh, S., Verma, S., & Singhal, S. (2008). Intrusion detection system using SNORT. *IRJET.* https://www.irjet.net/archives/V4/i4/IRJET-V4I4439.pdf



Gupta, R., Singh, S., Verma, S., & Singhal, S. (2008). Intrusion detection system using SNORT. *IRJET.* https://www.irjet.net/archives/V4/i4/IRJET-V4I4439.pdf



Gupta, A., & Singh, B. (2019). AI-driven transformation in the Indian manufacturing sector. *International Journal of Advanced Manufacturing Technology*, *102*, 1397–1412.

Gupta, M., & Kapoor, A. (2021). AI and skill development in the Indian IT industry: A case study of software engineers. *International Journal of Information Management*, *57*, 1–12.

Gupta, P., Ding, B., Guan, C., & Ding, D. (2024). Generative AI: A Systematic Review Using Topic Modelling Techniques. *Data and Information Management*, *3*(2), 1–66. doi:10.1016/j.dim.2024.100066

Gupta, T., & Khan, S. (2023). Education and International Collaboration in the Digital Age. *Globus Journal of Progressive Education*, *13*(1), 79–87.

Hadri, S. A., & Bouramoul, A. (2023a). Towards a deep learning based contextual chat bot for preventing depression in young children with autistic spectrum disorder. *Smart Health (Amsterdam, Netherlands)*, *27*, 100371. doi:10.1016/j.smhl.2022.100371

Hadri, S. A., & Bouramoul, A. (2023b). Friendy: A Deep Learning based Framework for Assisting in Young Autistic Children Psychotherapy Interventions. *Journal of Communications Software and Systems*, *19*(1), 30–38. doi:10.24138/jcomss-2022-0074

Haenssle, H. A., Fink, C., Schneiderbauer, R., Toberer, F., Buhl, T., Blum, A., Kalloo, A., Hassen, A. B. H., Thomas, L., Enk, A., Uhlmann, L., Alt, C., Arenbergerova, M., Bakos, R., Baltzer, A., Bertlich, I., Blum, A., Bokor-Billmann, T., Bowling, J., & Zalaudek, I. (2018). Man against machine: Diagnostic performance of a deep learning convolutional neural network for dermoscopic melanoma recognition in comparison to 58 dermatologists. *Annals of Oncology : Official Journal of the European Society for Medical Oncology*, *29*(8), 1836–1842. doi:10.1093/annonc/mdy166 PMID:29846502

Haga, H. (2002). Combining video and bulletin board systems in distance education systems. *The Internet and Higher Education*, *5*(2), 119–129. doi:10.1016/S1096-7516(02)00084-2

Hair, J. F., Risher, J. J., & Ringle, C. M. (2018). When to use and how to report the results of PLS-SEM. *European Business Review*, *31*(1), 2–24. doi:10.1108/EBR-11-2018-0203

Hammer, A., & Karmakar, S. (2021, April 29). Automation, AI and the Future of Work in India. *Employee Relations*, *43*(6), 1327–1341. doi:10.1108/ER-12-2019-0452

Han, E. R., Yeo, S., Kim, M. J., Lee, Y. H., Park, K. H., & Roh, H. (2019). Medical education trends for future physicians in the era of advanced technology and artificial intelligence: An integrative review. *BMC Medical Education*, *19*(1), 1–15. doi:10.1186/s12909-019-1891-5 PMID:31829208

Han, X., Hu, F., Xiong, G., Liu, X., Gong, X., Niu, X., & Wang, X. (2018). Design of AI+ curriculum for primary and secondary schools in Qingdao. In *2018 Chinese Automation Congress (CAC),* (pp. 4135-4140). IEEE. 10.1109/CAC.2018.8623310

Harfouche, A., Quinio, B., Saba, M., & Saba, P. B. (2023). The Recursive Theory of Knowledge Augmentation: Integrating human intuition and knowledge in Artificial Intelligence to augment organizational knowledge. *Information Systems Frontiers*, *25*(1), 55–70. doi:10.1007/s10796-022-10352-8

Harrington, M. C., Bledsoe, Z., Jones, C., Miller, J., & Pring, T. (2021). Designing a virtual arboretum as an immersive, multimodal, interactive, data visualization virtual field trip. *Multimodal Technologies and Interaction*, *5*(4), 18. doi:10.3390/mti5040018

Harte, N., & Gillen, E. (2015). TCD-TIMIT: An Audio-Visual Corpus of Continuous Speech. *IEEE Transactions on Multimedia*, *17*(5), 603–615. doi:10.1109/TMM.2015.2407694

Hasoon, J. N., Almtrf, A., Alagrash, Y., & Althubiti, M. (2023). A Hybrid Approach of Image Retrieving In Biometric ID. In *Proceedings of International Conference on Computing and Information Technology*, (pp. 1-6). IEEE. 10.1109/ICCIT58132.2023.10273904

Hastin, M., Naqiyah, N., & Darminto, E. (2022). Guidance and Counseling Services to Develop Student Career Maturity. IJORER. *International Journal of Recent Educational Research*, *3*(6), 688–700. doi:10.46245/ijorer.v3i6.261

Hemsley-Brown, J. (2020). Higher education market segmentation. In The International Encyclopedia of Higher education Systems and Institutions (pp. 711–713). Springer. doi:10.1007/978-94-017-8905-9_33

Hiran, K. K., & Dadhich, M. (2024). Predicting the core determinants of cloud-edge computing adoption (CECA) for sustainable development in the higher education institutions of Africa: A high order SEM-ANN analytical approach. *Technological Forecasting and Social Change*, *199*, 122979. doi:10.1016/j.techfore.2023.122979

Hiran, K. K., & Doshi, R. (2013). An artificial neural network approach for brain tumor detection using digital image segmentation. *Brain*, *2*(5), 227–231.

Hiran, K. K., Doshi, R., & Patel, M. (Eds.). (2024). *Applications of Virtual and Augmented Reality for Health and Wellbeing*. IGI Global. doi:10.4018/979-8-3693-1123-3

Hiran, K. K., Hemachandran, K., Pise, A., & Rabi, B. (Eds.). (2023). *Handbook of Research on AI and Knowledge Engineering for Real-Time Business Intelligence*. IGI Global. doi:10.4018/978-1-6684-6519-6

Hiran, K. K., & Henten, A. (2020). An integrated TOE-DoI framework for cloud computing adoption in higher education: The case of Sub-Saharan Africa, Ethiopia. In Soft Computing: Theories and Applications [Springer Singapore.]. *Proceedings of SoCTA, 2018*, 1281–1290.

Hiran, K. K., Khazanchi, D., Vyas, A. K., & Padmanaban, S. (Eds.). (2021). *Machine learning for sustainable development* (Vol. 9). Walter de Gruyter GmbH & Co KG. doi:10.1515/9783110702514

Hitron, T., Wald, I., Erel, H., & Zuckerman, O. (2018). Introducing children to machine learning concepts through hands-on experience. In *Proceedings of the 17th ACM conference on interaction design and children,* (pp. 563-568). ACM. 10.1145/3202185.3210776

Hogan, A., & Thompson, G. (Eds.). (2020). *Privatisation and commercialisation in public education: How the public nature of schooling is changing*. Routledge. doi:10.4324/9780429330025

Holden, O. L., Norris, M. E., & Kuhlmeier, V. A. (2021). Academic integrity in online assessment: A research review. In Frontiers in Education, 6. Frontiers Media SA.

Holmes, W., Porayska-Pomsta, K., Holstein, K., Sutherland, E., Baker, T., Shum, S. B., Santos, O. C., Rodrigo, M. T., Cukurova, M., Bittencourt, I. I., & Koedinger, K. R. (2022). Ethics of AI in education: Towards a community-wide framework. *International Journal of Artificial Intelligence in Education, 32*(3), 1–23. doi:10.1007/s40593-021-00239-1

Holmström, J., & Carroll, N. (2024). How Organizations Can Innovate with Generative AI. *Business Horizons, 4*(2), 1–25. doi:10.1016/j.bushor.2024.02.010

Hoover, A., & Spengler, S. (2023, May 30). *For some autistic people, chatgpt is a Lifeline*. Wired. https://www.wired.com/story/for-some-autistic-people-chatgpt-is-a-lifeline/

Horvath, A. O., & Greenberg, L. S. (1989). Development and validation of the Working Alliance Inventory. *Journal of Counseling Psychology, 36*(2), 223–233. doi:10.1037/0022-0167.36.2.223

Hosseini, M. M., Hosseini, S. T. M., Qayumi, K., Ahmady, S., & Koohestani, H. R. (2023). The Aspects of Running Artificial Intelligence in Emergency Care; a Scoping Review. *Archives of Academic Emergency Medicine, 11*(1). PMID:37215232

Hsu, C. H. C., Tan, G., & Stantic, B. (2024). A Fine-Tuned Tourism-Specific Generative AI Concept. *Annals of Tourism Research, 104*, 1–4. doi:10.1016/j.annals.2023.103723

Huang, J., & Kingsbury, B. (2013). Audio-visual deep learning for noise robust speech recognition. In *Proceedings of the IEEE International Conference on Acoustics, Speech, and Signal Processing* (pp. 7596-7599). IEEE.

Huang, X. (2021). Aims for cultivating students' key competencies based on artificial intelligence education in China. *Education and Information Technologies, 26*(5), 5127–5147. doi:10.1007/s10639-021-10530-2

Huang, X., Zou, D., Cheng, G., Chen, X., & Xie, H. (2023). Trends, research issues and applications of artificial intelligence in language education. *Journal of Educational Technology & Society, 26*(1), 112–131.

Huddar, R., Kharade, K., & Kamat, R. (2023). *Designing of AI-Based Teaching-Learning Model for Revitalizing Education. International Conference on The Future Global Business and Technology*, Kolhapur, India.

Hughes, R. T., Zhu, L., & Bednarz, T. (2021). Generative adversarial networks–enabled human–artificial intelligence collaborative applications for creative and design industries: A systematic review of current approaches and trends. *Frontiers in Artificial Intelligence, 4*, 604234. doi:10.3389/frai.2021.604234 PMID:33997773

Humble, N., & Mozelius, P. (2022). The threat, hype, and promise of artificial intelligence in education. *Discover Artificial Intelligence*, *2*(1), 22. doi:10.1007/s44163-022-00039-z

Hunt, R., & Zeadally, S. (2012, December). Network Forensics: An Analysis of Techniques, Tools, and Trends. *Computer*, *45*(12), 36–43. doi:10.1109/MC.2012.252

Hussain, B., Du, Q., Zhang, S., Imran, A., & Imran, M. A. (2019). Mobile Edge Computing-Based Data-Driven Deep Learning Framework for Anomaly Detection. *IEEE Access : Practical Innovations, Open Solutions*, *7*, 137656–137667. doi:10.1109/ACCESS.2019.2942485

Hussein, M. J., Yusuf, J., Deb, A. S., Fong, L., & Nai-du, S. (2020). An evaluation of online proctoring tools. *Open Praxis*, *12*(4), 509–525. doi:10.5944/openpraxis.12.4.1113

Hutson, J., Jeevanjee, T., Vander Graaf, V., Lively, J., Weber, J., Weir, G., & Edele, S. (2022). Artificial Intelligence and the Disruption of Higher Education: Strategies for Integrations across Disciplines. *Creative Education*, *13*(12), 3953–3980. doi:10.4236/ce.2022.1312253

Ifejiofor, A. P. (2023). Effect of counseling services on career choice of secondary school students in Anambra state, Nigeria. International Journal of Education. *Training and Learning*, *7*(1), 1–6. doi:10.33094/ijetl.v7i1.1152

Iivari, N., Sharma, S., & Ventä-Olkkonen, L. (2020). Digital transformation of everyday life – How COVID-19 pandemic transformed the basic education of the young generation and why information management research should care? *International Journal of Information Management*, *55*, 102183. doi:10.1016/j.ijinfomgt.2020.102183 PMID:32836640

Imran, N., & Jawaid, M. (2020). Artificial intelligence in medical education: Are we ready for it? *Pakistan Journal of Medical Sciences*, *36*(5), 857. doi:10.12669/pjms.36.5.3042 PMID:32704252

Iqbal, A. (2021). Innovation speed and quality in higher education institutions: The role of knowledge management enablers and knowledge sharing process. *Journal of Knowledge Management*, *25*(9), 2334–2360. doi:10.1108/JKM-07-2020-0546

Jadi, A. (2021). New detection cheating method of online-exams during COVID-19 pandemic. *Int. J. Comput. Sci. Netw. Secur*, *21*(4), 123–130.

Jagannathan, S. (2021). Scale of the Challenge–Massive Reskilling and Upskilling Needed–The Crucial Role of Capacity Development. *Reimagining Digital Learning for Sustainable Development: How Upskilling, Data Analytics, and Educational Technologies Close the Skills Gap*, 3-16.

Jagers, R. J., Rivas-Drake, D., & Williams, B. (2019). Transformative social and emotional learning (SEL): Toward SEL in service of educational equity and excellence. *Educational Psychologist*, *54*(3), 162–184. doi:10.1080/00461520.2019.1623032

Jahanshahi, A. A., & Bhattacharjee, A. (2020). Competitiveness improvement in public sector organizations: What they need? *Journal of Public Affairs*, *20*(2), e2011. doi:10.1002/pa.2011

Jahanshahi, A. A., Bhattacharjee, A., & Maghsoudi, T. (2021). Internal capabilities as the source of achieving competitive advantage in small-sized businesses. *International Journal of Business Innovation and Research*, *26*(2), 141–162. doi:10.1504/IJBIR.2021.118446

Jahanshahi, A. A., Bhattacharjee, A., & Polas, M. R. H. (2023). The micro-foundations of sustainable entrepreneurship: The role of individuals' pro-social identity and organisational pro-social identity. *International Journal of Productivity and Quality Management*, *40*(2), 149–170. doi:10.1504/IJPQM.2023.134270

Jahanshahi, A. A., Brem, A., & Bhattacharjee, A. (2017). Who takes more sustainability-oriented entrepreneurial actions? The role of entrepreneurs' values, beliefs and orientations. *Sustainability (Basel)*, *9*(10), 1636. doi:10.3390/su9101636

Jain, S., & Singh, M. (2020). Artificial intelligence in Indian education: Enhancing workforce readiness. *International Journal of Educational Technology in Higher Education, 17*(1), 1–18.

Jaiswal, A., Arun, C. J., & Varma, A. (2021). Rebooting employees: Upskilling for artificial intelligence in multinational corporations. *International Journal of Human Resource Management, 33*(6), 1179–1208. doi:10.1080/09585192.2021.1891114

James, C. A., Wheelock, K. M., & Woolliscroft, J. O. (2021). Machine learning: The next paradigm shift in medical education. *Academic Medicine, 96*(7), 954–957. doi:10.1097/ACM.0000000000003943 PMID:33496428

Jang, C., Song, B. Y., Jeong, Y. S., & Park, H. S. (2023). A Framework for Model-Sharing of Augmented Intelligence in Container-based Modular Robot Using Cloud System. In *2023 20th International Conference on Ubiquitous Robots (UR)*, (pp. 993-996). IEEE. 10.1109/UR57808.2023.10202258

Jang, S., Kim, J. J., Kim, S. J., Hong, J., Kim, S., & Kim, E. (2021). Mobile app-based chatbot to deliver cognitive behavioral therapy and psychoeducation for adults with attention deficit: A development and feasibility/usability study. *International Journal of Medical Informatics, 150*, 104440. doi:10.1016/j.ijmedinf.2021.104440 PMID:33799055

Jaramillo, R. N., Liezl Mae, G. M., Bucao, T. P., Bueno, B. J., Bulatao, L. R., Cabrera, S., & Cacho, L. C. (2022). A Systematic Review of Simulation-Based Learning Versus Traditional Learning. *Cosmos An International Journal of Art & Higher Education, 11*(2), 24–28.

Jia, J., & He, Y. (2021). The design, implementation and pilot application of an intelligent online proctoring system for online exams. *Interactive Technology and Smart Education, 19*(1), 112–120. doi:10.1108/ITSE-12-2020-0246

Jia, J., Yan, J., Jahanshahi, A. A., Lin, W., & Bhattacharjee, A. (2020). What makes employees more proactive? Roles of job embeddedness, the perceived strength of the HRM system and empowering leadership. *Asia Pacific Journal of Human Resources, 58*(1), 107–127. doi:10.1111/1744-7941.12249

Jing, Y. N., Tu, P., Wang, X. P., & Zhang, G. D. (2015). *Distributed-log-based scheme for IP traceback*. The fifth international conference on Computer and Information Technology (CIT' 15), Shanghai, China.

Ji, Y., Bai, Y., Liu, X., & Jia, K. (2020). Progress of liquid crystal polyester (LCP) for 5G application. *Advanced Industrial and Engineering Polymer Research, 3*(4), 160–174. doi:10.1016/j.aiepr.2020.10.005

Jobin, A., Ienca, M., & Vayena, E. (2019). *Artificial Intelligence: the global landscape of ethics guidelines.*

Jobin, A., Ienca, M., & Vayena, E. (2019). The global landscape of AI ethics guidelines. *Nature Machine Intelligence, 1*(9), 389–399. doi:10.1038/s42256-019-0088-2

Johnson, K. B., Wei, W., Weeraratne, D., Frisse, M. E., Misulis, K., Rhee, K., Zhao, J., & Snowdon, J. L. (2021). Precision Medicine, AI, and the Future of Personalized Health Care. doi:10.1111/cts.12884

Johnson, R. D., Ke, F., & Lin, L. (2021). Investigating the Effectiveness of a Personalized Learning Intervention on Improving Middle School Students' Scientific Inquiry Skills. *Journal of Educational Psychology, 113*(4), 683–703.

Jones, S. M., Barnes, S. P., Bailey, R., & Doolittle, E. J. (2017). Promoting social and emotional competencies in elementary school. *The Future of Children, 27*(1), 49–72. doi:10.1353/foc.2017.0003

Jordan, K., Carlile, O., & Stack, J. (2019). Fostering Deep Learning in Online Learning Environments. *EDUCAUSE Review, 54*(2), 46–58.

Jordan, M. I., & Mitchell, T. M. (2015). Machine learning: Trends, perspectives, and prospects. *Science, 349*(6245), 255–260. doi:10.1126/science.aaa8415 PMID:26185243

Joshi, K., Goel, A. K., & Kumar, T. (2020). *Online Career Counsellor System based on Artificial Intelligence: An approach. IEEE 7th International Conference on Smart Structures and Systems ICSSS 2020*. IEEE.

Joshi, M. A. Adaptive Learning through Artificial Intelligence (July 19, 2023). Joshi, M.A. (2024). Adaptive Learning through Artificial Intelligence. *International Journal on Integrated Education. 7*(2), 41-43. https://ssrn.com/abstract=4514887 or doi:10.2139/ssrn.4514887

Joshi, V., & Patel, A. (2022). AI-driven skill development in emerging technology sectors in India. *International Journal of Technology and Human Interaction, 18*(3), 1–18.

Kahraman, H. T., Sagiroglu, S., & Colak, I. (2010, October). Development of adaptive and intelligent web-based educational systems. In *2010 4th international conference on application of information and communication technologies* (pp. 1-5). IEEE. 10.1109/ICAICT.2010.5612054

Kamalov, F., Santandreu Calonge, D., & Gurrib, I. (2023). New Era of Artificial Intelligence in Education: Towards a Sustainable Multifaceted Revolution. *Sustainability (Basel), 15*(16), 1–27. doi:10.3390/su151612451

Kamila, M.K. & Jasrotia, S.S. (2023). Ethical issues in the development of artificial intelligence: Recognizing the risks. *International Journal of Ethics and Systems.*

Kang, J., Thompson, R. F., Aneja, S., Lehman, C., Trister, A., Zou, J., Obcemea, C., & El Naqa, I. (2021). National cancer institute workshop on artificial intelligence in radiation oncology: Training the next generation. *Practical Radiation Oncology, 11*(1), 74–83. doi:10.1016/j.prro.2020.06.001 PMID:32544635

Kankanhalli, A. (2024). Peer Review in the Age of Generative AI. *Journal of the Association for Information Systems, 25*(1), 76–84. doi:10.17705/1jais.00865

Kar, A. K., Choudhary, S. K., & Singh, V. K. (2022). How can artificial intelligence impact sustainability: A systematic literature review. *Journal of Cleaner Production, 376*(5), 1–15. doi:10.1016/j.jclepro.2022.134120

Karras, J., Holynski, A., Wang, T. C., & Kemelmacher-Shlizerman, I. (2023, October). Dreampose: Fashion image-to-video synthesis via stable diffusion. In *2023 IEEE/CVF International Conference on Computer Vision (ICCV)* (pp. 22623-22633). IEEE. 10.1109/ICCV51070.2023.02073

Karras, T., Laine, S., & Aila, T. (2019). A style-based generator architecture for generative adversarial networks. In *Proceedings of the IEEE/CVF conference on computer vision and pattern recognition* (pp. 4401-4410). IEEE. 10.1109/CVPR.2019.00453

Katre, M., Manchanda, S., & Agarwal, R. (2021). Chatbot for Career Counselling. [IJRASET]. *International Journal for Research in Applied Science and Engineering Technology, 9*(7).

Kazemzadeh, K., Akhlaghdoust, M., & Zali, A. (2023). Advances in artificial intelligence, robotics, augmented and virtual reality in neurosurgery. *Frontiers in Surgery, 10*, 10. doi:10.3389/fsurg.2023.1241923 PMID:37693641

Kerres, M. (2020a). Against All Odds: Education in Germany Coping with Covid-19. *Postdigital Science and Education, 2*(3), 690–694. doi:10.1007/s42438-020-00130-7

Khanlou, N., Khan, A., Vazquez, L. M., & Zangeneh, M. (2021). Digital literacy, access to technology and inclusion for young adults with developmental disabilities. *Journal of Developmental and Physical Disabilities, 33*(1), 1–25. doi:10.1007/s10882-020-09738-w PMID:33814873

Khazaal, S. M., & Maarouf, H. (2023). Predicting Coronary Artery Disease Utilizing Support Vector Machines: Optimizing Predictive Model. *Mesopotamian Journal of Artificial Intelligence in Healthcare, 2023*, 21–26. doi:10.58496/MJAIH/2023/004

Kholis, A. (2021). Elsa speak app: automatic speech recognition (ASR) for supplementing English pronunciation skills. *Pedagogy: Journal of English Language Teaching, 9*(1), 01-14.

Khurana, M. (2020). Keeping pace: The need for digital health education in medical schools. *Academic Medicine, 95*(11), 1629–1630. doi:10.1097/ACM.0000000000003672 PMID:33109967

Kiener, M. (2021). Artificial intelligence in medicine and the disclosure of risks. *AI & Society, 36*(3), 705–713. doi:10.1007/s00146-020-01085-w PMID:33110296

Kilag, O. K., Miñoza, J., Comighud, E., Amontos, C., Damos, M., & Abendan, C. F. (2023). Empowering Teachers: Integrating Technology into Livelihood Education for a Digital Future. *Excellencia: International Multi-disciplinary Journal of Education (2994-9521), 1*(1), 30-41.

Kim, D. H., & Irakoze, A. (2022). Identifying market segment for the assessment of a price premium for green certified housing: A Cluster analysis approach. *Sustainability (Basel), 15*(1), 507. doi:10.3390/su15010507

Kim, J. S., Kim, M., & Noh, B. N. (2014). A fuzzy expert system for network forensics. In *Computational science and its applications* (Vol. 3043, pp. 175–182). Springer.

Kim, M. O., Coiera, E., & Magrabi, F. (2017). Problems with health information technology and their effects on care delivery and patient outcomes: A systematic review. *Journal of the American Medical Informatics Association : JAMIA, 24*(2), 246–250. doi:10.1093/jamia/ocw154 PMID:28011595

Kim, W. (2021). A Design-Based Research on Application of Artificial Intelligence AI) Teaching-Learning Model in Elementary School. *International Journal of Advanced Smart Convergence, 10*(2), 201–208. doi:10.7236/IJASC.2021.10.2.201

Kim, Y., Soyata, T., & Behnagh, R. F. (2018). Towards emotionally aware AI smart classroom: Current issues and directions for engineering and education. *IEEE Access : Practical Innovations, Open Solutions, 6*, 5308–5331. doi:10.1109/ACCESS.2018.2791861

Kingma, D.P., & Welling, M. (2019). An introduction to variational autoencoders. *Foundations and Trends® in Machine Learning, 12*(4), 307-392.

Kintsch, W. (2002). The potential of latent semantic analysis for machine grading of clinical case summaries. *Journal of Biomedical Informatics, 35*(1), 3–7. doi:10.1016/S1532-0464(02)00004-7 PMID:12415721

Kizilcec, R. F., Piech, C., & Schneider, E. (2020). Deconstructing Disengagement: Analyzing Learner Subpopulations in Massive Open Online Courses. *EDUCAUSE Review, 55*(5), 52–67.

Klekovkina, V., & Denié-Higney, L. (2022). Machine translation: Friend or foe in the language classroom? *Journal of Linguistics and Language Teaching, 14*(1). doi:10.5070/L214151723

Klos, M. C., Escoredo, M., Joerin, A., Lemos, V. N., Rauws, M., & Bunge, E. L. (2021). Artificial Intelligence-Based Chatbot for Anxiety and Depression in University Students: Pilot Randomized Controlled Trial. *JMIR Formative Research, 5*(8), e20678. doi:10.2196/20678 PMID:34092548

Kodama, M. (2020). Digitally transforming work styles in an era of infectious disease. *International Journal of Information Management, 55*, 102172. doi:10.1016/j.ijinfomgt.2020.102172 PMID:32836634

Kolachalama, V. B., & Garg, P. S. (2018). Machine learning and medical education. *NPJ Digital Medicine, 1*(1), 54. doi:10.1038/s41746-018-0061-1 PMID:31304333

Kong, S. C., Abelson, H., Sheldon, J., Lao, A., Tissenbaum, M., Lai, M., & Lao, N. (2017). Curriculum activities to foster primary school students' computational practices in block-based programming environments. In *Conference Proceedings of International Conference on Computational Thinking Education,* (pp. 84-89). IEEE.

Kooli, C. (2023). Chatbots in Education and Research: A Critical Examination of Ethical Implications and Solutions. *Sustainability (Basel), 15*(7), 5614. doi:10.3390/su15075614

Kristian Vieri, J., Munandar, T. A., & Srisulistiowati, D. B. (2023). Exclusive Clustering technique for customer segmentation in national telecommunications companies. *International Journal of Information Technology and Computer Science Applications, 1*(1), 51–57. doi:10.58776/ijitcsa.v1i1.19

Kuddus, K. (2022). Artificial intelligence in language learning: Practices and prospects. *Advanced Analytics and Deep Learning Models*, 1-17.

Kuleto, V., Ilić, M., Dumangiu, M., Ranković, M., Martins, O. M. D., Păun, D., & Mihoreanu, L. (2021). Exploring Opportunities and Challenges of Artificial Intelligence and Machine Learning in Higher Education Institutions. *Sustainability (Basel), 13*(18), 10424. doi:10.3390/su131810424

Kumar, A. (2022). Customer segmentation of shopping mall users using K-means clustering. In Advancing SMEs Toward E-Commerce Policies for Sustainability (pp. 248–270). Research Gate. doi:10.4018/978-1-6684-5727-6.ch013

Kumar, L., Singh, D. K., & Srivas, A. (2023, July). Performance Evaluation of Video-to-Video Synthesis GAN models on Cityscapes Dataset. In *2023 14th International Conference on Computing Communication and Networking Technologies (ICCCNT)* (pp. 1-6). IEEE. 10.1109/ICCCNT56998.2023.10306535

Kumar, S., Sharma, R., Singh, V., & Shrikant Tiwari, S. K. (2023). Potential Impact of Data-Centric AI on Society. *IEEE Technology and Society Magazine, 42*(3), 98-107. doi:10.1109/MTS.2023.3306532

Kumar, S., Tiwari, S., & Singh, S. K. (2016). *Face Recognition of Cattle: Can it be done?* Proceedings of the National Academy of Sciences, India. doi:10.1007/s40010-016-0264-2

Kumar, A., & Sharma, R. (2021). Impact of artificial intelligence on the labour market in India: Challenges and opportunities. *Journal of Economic Studies (Glasgow, Scotland), 48*(7), 1689–1706. doi:10.1108/JES-08-2020-0431

Kumar, L., & Singh, D. K. (2023). A comprehensive survey on generative adversarial networks used for synthesizing multimedia content. *Multimedia Tools and Applications, 82*(26), 40585–40624. doi:10.1007/s11042-023-15138-x

Kumar, L., & Singh, D. K. (2023, June). Comparative analysis of Vid2Vid and fast Vid2Vid models for video-to-video synthesis on cityscapes dataset. In *2023 International Conference on Computer, Electronics & Electrical Engineering & their Applications (IC2E3)* (pp. 1-5). IEEE. 10.1109/IC2E357697.2023.10262586

Kumar, P., & Nidhi, A. (2009). *Reflections on The Impact of ICT on Teacher Education.* Paradigm Shift in Teacher Education, Vayu Education of India.

Kumar, S. V., Dubey, S., & Sahu, V. (2023). Career Counseling In the Digital Age: A Research on online Personal counseling. *International Journal of Research Publication and Reviews, 4*(5), 3110–3115.

Kumar, S., Patil, V. D., Mahalle, P. N., & Meshram, V. A. (2023). Concept and Administration for Developing Special Education Using AI. In *AI-Assisted Special Education for Students With Exceptional Needs* (pp. 241–266). IGI Global. doi:10.4018/979-8-3693-0378-8.ch011

Laacke, S., Mueller, R., Schomerus, G., & Salloch, S. (2021). Artificial intelligence, social media and depression. A new concept of health-related digital autonomy. *The American Journal of Bioethics, 21*(7), 4–20. doi:10.1080/15265161.2020.1863515 PMID:33393864

Labayen, M., Vea, R., Flórez, J., Aginako, N., & Sierra, B. (2021). Online student authentication and proctoring system based on multimodal biometrics technology. *IEEE Access : Practical Innovations, Open Solutions*, *9*, 72398–72411. doi:10.1109/ACCESS.2021.3079375

Lai, J. W., & Cheong, K. H. (2022). Adoption of virtual and augmented reality for mathematics education: A scoping review. *IEEE Access : Practical Innovations, Open Solutions*, *10*, 13693–13703. doi:10.1109/ACCESS.2022.3145991

Lambert, T. E. (2023). The great resignation in the United States: A study of labor market segmentation. *The Forum for Social Economics*, *52*(4), 373–386. doi:10.1080/07360932.2022.2164599

Lanza, F., Seidita, V., & Chella, A. (2020). Agents and robots for collaborating and supporting physicians in healthcare scenarios. *Journal of Biomedical Informatics*, *108*, 103483. doi:10.1016/j.jbi.2020.103483 PMID:32603793

Latifi, S., Gierl, M. J., Boulais, A. P., & De Champlain, A. F. (2016). Using automated scoring to evaluate written responses in English and French on a high-stakes clinical competency examination. *Evaluation & the Health Professions*, *39*(1), 100–113. doi:10.1177/0163278715605358 PMID:26377072

Laupichler, M. C., Aster, A., Schirch, J., & Raupach, T. (2022). Artificial intelligence literacy in higher and adult education: A scoping literature review. *Computers and Education: Artificial Intelligence*, *3*, 100101. doi:10.1016/j.caeai.2022.100101

Laura, R. S., & Chapman, A. (2009). The technologisation of education: Philosophical reflections on being too plugged in. *International Journal of Children's Spirituality*, *14*(3), 289–298. doi:10.1080/13644360903086554

Lawan, A. A., Muhammad, B. R., Tahir, A. M., Yarima, K. I., Zakari, A., Abdullahi, A. H. II, & Lawan, S. (2023). Modified flipped learning as an approach to mitigate the adverse effects of generative artificial intelligence on education. *Education Journal*, *12*(4), 136–143.

Law, E. L. C., & Heintz, M. (2021). Augmented reality applications for K-12 education: A systematic review from the usability and user experience perspective. *International Journal of Child-Computer Interaction*, *30*, 100321. doi:10.1016/j.ijcci.2021.100321

Le Moing, G., Ponce, J., & Schmid, C. (2021). Ccvs: Context-aware controllable video synthesis. *Advances in Neural Information Processing Systems*, *34*, 14042–14055.

Lee, J. W. (2020). Impact of Proctoring Environments on Student Performance: Online vs Offline Proctored Exams. *Journal of Asian Finance Economics and Business*, *7*(8), 653–660. doi:10.13106/jafeb.2020.vol7.no8.653

Lee, K., & Fanguy, M. (2022). Online exam proctoring technologies: Educational innovation or deterioration? *British Journal of Educational Technology*, *53*(3), 475–490. doi:10.1111/bjet.13182

Leenes, R., Palmerini, E., Koops, B., Bertolini, A., Lucivero, F., Leenes, R., Palmerini, E., Koops, B., & Bertolini, A. (2017). *Regulatory challenges of robotics: some guidelines for addressing legal and ethical issues.* doi:10.1080/17579961.2017.1304921

Lehmann, F., & Buschek, D. (2021). Examining autocompletion as a basic concept for interaction with generative AI. *i-com, 19*(3), 251-264.

Leigh Smith, B., & MacGregor, J. (2009). Learning communities and the quest for quality. *Quality Assurance in Education*, *17*(2), 118–139. doi:10.1108/09684880910951354

Leiker, D., Gyllen, A. R., Eldesouky, I., & Cukurova, M. (2023, June). Generative AI for learning: investigating the potential of learning videos with synthetic virtual instructors. In *International conference on artificial intelligence in education* (pp. 523-529). Cham: Springer Nature Switzerland. 10.1007/978-3-031-36336-8_81

Lekadir, K., Feragen, A., Fofanah, A. J., Frangi, A. F., Buyx, A., Emelie, A., & Starmans, M. (2023). FUTURE-AI: International consensus guideline for trustworthy and deployable artificial intelligence in healthcare. *arXiv preprint arXiv:2309.12325*.

Lewis, T. (1998). The new economics of information. *IEEE Internet Computing*, *2*(5), 93–94. doi:10.1109/4236.722237

Liang, J. C., Hwang, G. J., Chen, M. R. A., & Darmawansah, D. (2023). Roles and research foci of artificial intelligence in language education: An integrated bibliographic analysis and systematic review approach. *Interactive Learning Environments*, *31*(7), 4270–4296. doi:10.1080/10494820.2021.1958348

Li, D., Kulasegaram, K., & Hodges, B. D. (2019). Why we needn't fear the machines: Opportunities for medicine in a machine learning world. *Academic Medicine*, *94*(5), 623–625. doi:10.1097/ACM.0000000000002661 PMID:30768470

Li, L. (2022). Reskilling and upskilling the future-ready workforce for industry 4.0 and beyond. *Information Systems Frontiers*, 1–16. PMID:35855776

Li, L., Ma, Z., Fan, L., Lee, S., Yu, H., & Hemphill, L. (2023). ChatGPT in education: A discourse analysis of worries and concerns on social media. *Education and Information Technologies*. doi:10.1007/s10639-023-12256-9

Limna, P., Kraiwanit, T., Jangjarat, K., Klayklung, P., & Chocksathaporn, P. (2023). The use of ChatGPT in the digital era: Perspectives on chatbot implementation. *Journal of Applied Learning and Teaching*, *6*(1), 64–74. doi:10.37074/jalt.2023.6.1.32

Lim, S. M., Shiau, C. W. C., Cheng, L. J., & Lau, Y. (2022). Chatbot-Delivered Psychotherapy for Adults With Depressive and Anxiety Symptoms: A Systematic Review and Meta-Regression. *Behavior Therapy*, *53*(2), 334–347. doi:10.1016/j.beth.2021.09.007 PMID:35227408

Lim, W. M., Gunasekara, A., Pallant, J. L., Pallant, J. I., & Pechenkina, E. (2023). Generative AI and the future of education: Ragnarök or reformation? A paradoxical perspective from management educators. *International Journal of Management Education*, *21*(2), 100790. doi:10.1016/j.ijme.2023.100790

Lin, C., Zhitang, L., Cuixia, G., & Yingshu, L. (2019) Modeling and analyzing dynamic forensics system based on intrusion tolerance. In: *Ninth IEEE international conference on computer and information technology*, (pp 230–235). IEEE.

Lin, P., & Van Brummelen, J. (2021). Engaging teachers to co-design integrated AI curriculum for K-12 classrooms. In *Proceedings of the 2021 CHI conference on human factors in computing systems*, (pp. 1-12). ACM. 10.1145/3411764.3445377

Lip Reading in the Wild (LRW) dataset. (n.d.). Retrieved April 4, 2024, from https://www.robots.ox.ac.uk/~vgg/data/lip_reading/lrw1.html

Lip Reading Sentences 2 (LRS2) dataset. (n.d.). Retrieved April 4, 2024, from https://www.robots.ox.ac.uk/~vgg/data/lip_reading/lrs2.html

Lip Reading Sentences 3 Dataset. (2024). Retrieved April 4, 2024, from https://mmai.io/datasets/lip_reading/

Liu, Y., Yang, Z., Yu, Z., Liu, Z., Liu, D., Lin, H., & Shi, S. (2023). Generative artificial intelligence and its applications in materials science: Current situation and future perspectives. *Journal of Materiomics*.

Liu, J., Kong, X., Xia, F., Bai, X., Wang, L., Qing, Q., & Lee, I. (2018). Artificial Intelligence in the 21st Century. *IEEE Access : Practical Innovations, Open Solutions*, *6*, 34403–34421. doi:10.1109/ACCESS.2018.2819688

Liu, L., Liu, L., & Li, H. (2024). Computation and Parameter Efficient Multi-Modal Fusion Transformer for Cued Speech Recognition. *IEEE/ACM Transactions on Audio, Speech, and Language Processing*.

Liu, M., Zhang, L. J., & Biebricher, C. (2024). Investigating Students' Cognitive Processes in Generative AI-Assisted Digital Multimodal Composing and Traditional Writing. *Computers & Education, 211*, 1–15. doi:10.1016/j.compedu.2023.104977

Liu, Y. L. E., Lee, T. P., & Huang, Y. M. (2023). Enhancing university students' creative confidence, learning motivation, and team creative performance in design thinking using a digital visual collaborative environment. *Thinking Skills and Creativity, 50*, 101388. doi:10.1016/j.tsc.2023.101388

Liu, Z., & Feng, D. (2015). Incremental fuzzy decision tree-based network forensic system. In Y. Hao, J. Liu, Y. P. Wang, Y. M. Cheung, H. Yin, L. Jiao, J. Ma, & Y. C. Jiao (Eds.), *Computational intelligence and security* (Vol. 3802, pp. 995–1002). Springer. doi:10.1007/11596981_148

Lo Piano, S. (2020). Ethical principles in machine learning and artificial intelligence: Cases from the field and possible ways forward. *Humanities & Social Sciences Communications, 7*(1), 1–7. doi:10.1057/s41599-020-0501-9

Logan, C. (2021). Toward abolishing online proctoring: Counter-narratives, deep change, and pedagogies of educational dignity. *Journal of Interactive Technology and Pedagogy, 20.*

Lohr, A., Stadler, M., Schultz-Pernice, F., Chernikova, O., Sailer, M., Fischer, F., & Sailer, M. (2021). On powerpointers, clickerers, and digital pros: Investigating the initiation of digital learning activities by teachers in higher education. *Computers in Human Behavior, 119*(October 2020), 106715. doi:10.1016/j.chb.2021.106715

López-Belmonte, J., Moreno-Guerrero, A. J., López-Núñez, J. A., & Hinojo-Lucena, F. J. (2023). Augmented reality in education. A scientific mapping in Web of Science. *Interactive Learning Environments, 31*(4), 1860–1874. doi:10.1080/10494820.2020.1859546

Lorah, E. R., Parnell, A., Whitby, P. S., & Hantula, D. (2015). A Systematic Review of Tablet Computers and Portable Media Players as Speech Generating Devices for Individuals with Autism Spectrum Disorder. *Journal of Autism and Developmental Disorders, 45*(12), 3792–3804. doi:10.1007/s10803-014-2314-4 PMID:25413144

Loy, C. C. (n.d.). *QMUL underGround Re-IDentification (GRID) Dataset*. Retrieved April 4, 2024, from https://personal.ie.cuhk.edu.hk/~ccloy/downloads_qmul_underground_reid.html

Lozano, F. A. M., Cruz Pulido, J. M., & García Rodríguez, J. F. (2021). The market segmentation of higher education in Colombia reveals social inequalities. *Cogent Education, 8*(1), 1877885. doi:10.1080/2331186X.2021.1877885

Luan, H., Geczy, P., Lai, H., Gobert, J., Yang, S. J. H., Ogata, H., Baltes, J., Guerra, R., Li, P., & Tsai, C.-C. (2020). Challenges and Future Directions of Big Data and Artificial Intelligence in Education. *Frontiers in Psychology, 11*, 1–11. doi:10.3389/fpsyg.2020.580820 PMID:33192896

Luckin, R., & Holmes, W. (2016). *Intelligence Unleashed: An argument for AI in Education.* UCL Knowledge Lab.

Lu, L., Xu, X., & Fu, J. (2022). Siamese decoupling network for speaker-independent lipreading. *Journal of Electronic Imaging, 31*(3), 033045–033045.

Lüthi, N., Matt, C., Myrach, T., & Junglas, I. (2023). Augmented Intelligence, Augmented Responsibility? *Business & Information Systems Engineering, 65*(4), 391–401. doi:10.1007/s12599-023-00789-9

Lu, Y., & Li, H. (2019). Automatic lip-reading system based on deep convolutional neural network and attention-based long short-term memory. *Applied Sciences (Basel, Switzerland), 9*(8), 1599.

Lyons, A. C., Kass-Hanna, J., & Fava, A. (2022). Fintech development and savings, borrowing, and remittances: A comparative study of emerging economies. *Emerging Markets Review, 51*, 100842. doi:10.1016/j.ememar.2021.100842

Macapagal, P. (2023). Digital Self-Identity in the Age of Technology of the New Normal Learning. *Globus An International Journal of Management & IT, 15*(1), 37-46.

Macpherson, T., Churchland, A., Sejnowski, T., DiCarlo, J., Kamitani, Y., Takahashi, H., & Hikida, T. (2021). Natural and Artificial Intelligence: A brief introduction to the interplay between AI and neuroscience research. *Neural Networks, 144*, 603–613. doi:10.1016/j.neunet.2021.09.018 PMID:34649035

Madry, A., Markelov, A., Schmidt, L., Tsipras, D., & Vladu, A. (2018). Towards deep learning models resistant to adversarial attacks. *6th International Conference on Learning Representations, ICLR 2018 - Conference Track Proceedings,* 1–28.

Maglonzo, M. L., De Luna, J. M., Caparas, L. A., & Manuel, M. J. (2023). A Comparative Analysis of The Decision-Making Styles of Filipino Teachers and South East Asian Teachers. *Globus An International Journal of Management & IT, 14*(2), 26–35. doi:10.46360/globus.mgt.120231003

Magnuson, K. M., & Constantino, J. N. (2011). Characterization of depression in children with autism spectrum disorders. *Journal of Developmental and Behavioral Pediatrics, 32*(4), 332–340. doi:10.1097/DBP.0b013e318213f56c PMID:21502871

Mahrishi, M., Hiran, K. K., Meena, G., & Sharma, P. (Eds.). (2020). Machine Learning and Deep Learning in Real-Time Applications. IGI Global.

Mahrishi, M., Hiran, K. K., Meena, G., & Sharma, P. (Eds.). (2020). *Machine learning and deep learning in real-time applications*. IGI global. doi:10.4018/978-1-7998-3095-5

Mai, J. E. (2016). Big data privacy: The datafication of personal information. *The Information Society, 32*(3), 192–199. doi:10.1080/01972243.2016.1153010

Maity, S., Sahu, T. N., & Sen, N. (2021a). Panoramic view of digital education in COVID-19: A new explored avenue. *Review of Education, 9*(2), 405–423. doi:10.1002/rev3.3250

Maity, S., Sen, N., & Sahu, T. N. (2020a). COVID-19: Triggers fear psychosis among private sector employees. *Journal of Labor and Society, 23*(4), 503–513. doi:10.1111/wusa.12490

Makeleni, S., Mutongoza, B. H., & Linake, M. A. (2023). Language education and Artificial Intelligence: An exploration of challenges confronting academics in global south universities. *Journal of Culture and Values in Education, 6*(2), 158–171. doi:10.46303/jcve.2023.14

Mangano, F. G., Admakin, O., Lerner, H., & Mangano, C. (2023). Artificial intelligence and augmented reality for guided implant surgery planning: A proof of concept. *Journal of Dentistry, 133*, 104485. doi:10.1016/j.jdent.2023.104485 PMID:36965859

Manyika, J., Lund, S., Bughin, J., Woetzel, J., Manyika, J., Lund, S., & Woetzel, J. (2017). *Jobs lost; jobs gained: Workforce transitions in a time of automation*. McKinsey Global Institute.

Ma, P., Wang, Y., Shen, J., Petridis, S., & Pantic, M. (2021). Lip-reading with densely connected temporal convolutional networks. In *Proceedings of the IEEE/CVF Winter Conference on Applications of Computer Vision* (pp. 2857-2866). IEEE.

Maquiling, E. E. (2023). Critical Thinking Skills as Predictors of Students' Performance in A Problem-Based Learning Environment. *Globus Journal of Progressive Education, 13*(1), 107–111.

MargamK.AralikattiR.SharmaT.ThandaP. A. K.RoyS.VenkatesanS. M. (2019). LipReading with 3D-2D-CNN BLSTM-HMM and word-CTC models. arXiv:1906.12170. http://arxiv.org/abs/1906.12170

Marquis, Y., Oladoyinbo, T. O., Olabanji, S. O., Olaniyi, O. O., & Ajayi, S. A. (2024). Proliferation of AI tools: A multifaceted evaluation of user perceptions and emerging trend. *Asian Journal of Advanced Research and Reports*, *18*(1), 30–55. doi:10.9734/ajarr/2024/v18i1596

Martínez-Ramón, J. P., Morales-Rodríguez, F. M., Pérez-López, S., Méndez, I., & Ruiz-Esteban, C. (2023). Predicción de la resiliencia docente mediante redes neuronales artificiales: Influencia del burnout y del estrés por COVID-19. *Anales de Psicología*, *39*(1), 100–111.

Martin, O., Kotsia, I., Macq, B., & Pitas, I. (2006). The eNTERFACE' 05 Audio-Visual Emotion Database. *22nd International Conference on Data Engineering Workshops (ICDEW'06)*. https://doi.org/10.1109/ICDEW.2006.145

Masoumian Hosseini, M., Masoumian Hosseini, S. T., Qayumi, K., Hosseinzadeh, S., & Sajadi Tabar, S. S. (2023). Smartwatches in healthcare medicine: Assistance and monitoring; a scoping review. *BMC Medical Informatics and Decision Making*, *23*(1), 248. doi:10.1186/s12911-023-02350-w PMID:37924029

Masters, K. (2019). Artificial intelligence in medical education. *Medical Teacher*, *41*(9), 976–980. doi:10.1080/0142159X.2019.1595557 PMID:31007106

Masters, K. (2020). Artificial intelligence developments in medical education: A conceptual and practical framework. *MedEdPublish*, *9*(239), 239. doi:10.15694/mep.2020.000239.1 PMID:38058891

Mate, M. H., & Kapse, S. R. (2015). Network Forensic Tool — Concept and Architecture. *2015 Fifth International Conference on Communication Systems and Network Technologies*. IEEE. 10.1109/CSNT.2015.204

Mateos-Sanchez, M., Melo, A. C., Blanco, L. S., & García, A. M. F. (2022). Chatbot, as Educational and Inclusive Tool for People with Intellectual Disabilities. *Sustainability (Basel)*, *14*(3), 1520. doi:10.3390/su14031520

Mathur, T., Dattatray, P. S., Singh, M., Kumar, P., & Student, B. E. (n.d.). Intelligent Career Guidance System using Machine Learning. *IJARIIE*. Retrieved from www.ijariie.com647

Maťová, H., & Triznova, M. (n.d.). *Responsible consumer in the context of circular economy*. Research Gate. https://www.researchgate.net/publication/335882971

Maya, L. (2023). *Google Bard AI Expertise: Unlock the Power of "Google Bard AI Expertise" and Transform Your Content*. Estalontech.

McCarthy, J., & Hayes, P. J. (1981). Some philosophical problems from the standpoint of artificial intelligence. In *Readings in artificial intelligence* (pp. 431–450). Morgan Kaufmann. doi:10.1016/B978-0-934613-03-3.50033-7

McCorduck, P., & Cfe, C. (2004). *Machines who think: A personal inquiry into the history and prospects of artificial intelligence*. CRC Press. doi:10.1201/9780429258985

McDonald, N. M., & Messinger, D. S. (2011). The Development of Empathy: How, When, and Why. In A. Acerbi, J. A. Lombo, & J. J. Sanguineti (Eds.), *Moral behavior and free will: A neurobiological and philosophical approach* (pp. 333–359). IF Press.

McDougall, R. J. (2018). Computer knows best? The need for value-flexibility in medical AI. *Journal of Medical Ethics*. PMID:30467198

McShane, M. K., Nanda, S., & Bagheri, R. (2017). The Promise and Challenge of Artificial Intelligence for Workforce Development. *International Journal of Adult Vocational Education and Technology*, *8*(4), 56–70.

Megahed, F. M., Chen, Y. J., Ferris, J. A., Knoth, S., & Jones-Farmer, L. A. (2024). How generative AI models such as ChatGPT can be (mis) used in SPC practice, education, and research? An exploratory study. *Quality Engineering*, *36*(2), 287–315. doi:10.1080/08982112.2023.2206479

Merlette, D., & Pruthi, D. P. (2013). *Network security; NetDetector: identifying real threats and securing your network.* Niksun. https://www.niksun.com/, 09 Dec 2013.

Meskó, B., Hetényi, G., & Győrffy, Z. (2018). Will artificial intelligence solve the human resource crisis in healthcare? *BMC Health Services Research*, *18*(1), 1–4. doi:10.1186/s12913-018-3359-4 PMID:30001717

Meulmeester, F. L., Dubois, E. A., Krommenhoek-van Es, C., de Jong, P. G. M., & Langers, A. M. J. (2021). Medical students' perspectives on online proctoring during remote digital progress test. *Medical Science Educator*, *31*(6), 1773–1777. doi:10.1007/s40670-021-01420-w PMID:34611498

Mhlanga, D. (2021). Artificial intelligence in the industry 4.0, and its impact on poverty, innovation, infrastructure development, and the sustainable development goals: Lessons from emerging economies? *Sustainability (Basel)*, *13*(11), 5788. doi:10.3390/su13115788

Mhlanga, D., & Moloi, T. (2020). COVID-19 and the digital transformation of education: What are we learning on 4ir in South Africa? *Education Sciences*, *10*(7), 1–11. doi:10.3390/educsci10070180

Microsoft. (2023). *What is Microsoft's Approach to AI?* Microsoft. https://news.microsoft.com/source/features/ai/microsoft-approach-to-ai/

Mijwil, M. M., Doshi, R., Hiran, K. K., Al-Mistarehi, A. H., & Gök, M. (2022). Cybersecurity Challenges in Smart Cities: An Overview and Future Prospects. *Mesopotamian journal of cybersecurity,* 1-4.

Mijwil, M. M., Aggarwal, K., Doshi, R., Hiran, K. K., & Gök, M. (2022). The Distinction between R-CNN and Fast RCNN in Image Analysis: A Performance Comparison. *Asian Journal of Applied Sciences*, *10*(5).

Mijwil, M. M., Gök, M., Doshi, R., Hiran, K. K., & Kösesoy, I. (2023). Utilizing Artificial Intelligence Techniques to Improve the Performance of Wireless Nodes. In *Applications of Artificial Intelligence in Wireless Communication Systems* (pp. 150–162). IGI Global. doi:10.4018/978-1-6684-7348-1.ch010

Mijwil, M. M., Hiran, K. K., Doshi, R., Dadhich, M., & Bala, I. (2023). ChatGPT and the Future of Academic Integrity in the Artificial Intelligence Era: A New Frontier. *Al-Salam Journal for Engineering and Technology*, *2*(2), 116–127. doi:10.55145/ajest.2023.02.02.015

Miller, T., Howe, P., & Sonenberg, L. (2017). Explainable AI: Beware of inmates running the asylum or: How I learnt to stop worrying and love the social and behavioural sciences. *arXiv preprint arXiv:1712.00547.*

Mishra, A., & Das, P. (2022). AI and skill development policy in India: A comparative analysis of state initiatives. *Journal of Comparative Policy Analysis*, *24*(1), 89–107.

Mishra, A., Tripathi, A., Khazanchi, D., Hiran, K. K., Vyas, A. K., & Padmanaban, S. (2021). A framework for applying artificial intelligence (AI) with Internet of NanoThings (IoNT). In *Machine Learning for Sustainable Development* (pp. 1–16). De Gruyter. doi:10.1515/9783110702514-001

Mishra, R., & Verma, S. (2020). AI in higher education: A case study of Indian institutions. *International Journal of Educational Technology in Higher Education*, *17*(1), 1–17.

Mittal, R., Pathak, V., Gandhi, G. C., & Mishra, N. (2020). *Effect of Curve Algorithms on Standard SLAM algorithm for Prediction of Path.*

Mittal, R., Mishra, D. N., & Pathak, D. V. (2019, October 30). Exploration of Designed Robot in Non Linear Movement Using EKF SLAM and Its Stability on Loose Concrete Surface. *International Journal of Engineering and Advanced Technology*, *9*(1), 875–878. doi:10.35940/ijeat.A9398.109119

Mittal, R., Mishra, N., Pathak, V., & Gandhi, G. C. (2020, January 30). An Exploration of Force Exerted on Moving Robot in Arcuated Path on Different Surface using Standard SLAM Algorithm. [IJRTE]. *International Journal of Recent Technology and Engineering*, *8*(5), 4080–4083. doi:10.35940/ijrte.E6685.018520

Mittal, R., Rani, G., Pathak, V., Chhikara, S., Dhaka, V. S., Vocaturo, E., & Zumpano, E. (2023, December 1). Low-Cost Multisensory Robot for Optimized Path Planning in Diverse Environments. *Computers*, *12*(12), 250. doi:10.3390/computers12120250

Mizumoto, A. (2023). Data-Driven Learning Meets Generative AI: Introducing the Framework of Metacognitive Resource Use. *Applied Corpus Linguistics*, *3*(3), 1–14. doi:10.1016/j.acorp.2023.100074

Mnguni, L. (2023). A critical reflection on the affordances of web 3.0 and artificial intelligence in life sciences education. *Journal of Pedagogical Sociology and Psychology*, *5*(2), 1–9. doi:10.33902/jpsp.202322298

Mogavi, R. H., Deng, C., Kim, J. J., Zhou, P., Kwon, Y. D., Metwally, A. H. S., & Hui, P. (2023). *Exploring user perspectives on chatgpt: Applications, perceptions, and implications for ai-integrated education.* arXiv preprint arXiv:2305.13114.

Mon, B. F., Wasfi, A., Hayajneh, M., & Slim, A. (2023, August). A Study on Role of Artificial Intelligence in Education. In *2023 International Conference on Computing, Electronics & Communications Engineering (iCCECE)* (pp. 133-138). IEEE. 10.1109/iCCECE59400.2023.10238613

Moon, S., Kim, S., & Wang, H. (2015). Multimodal transfer deep learning with applications in audio-visual recognition. *Proceedings of the MMML Workshop Neural Information Processing Systems.*

Moorhouse, B. L. (2024). Beginning and First-Year Language Teachers' Readiness for the Generative AI Age. *Computers and Education: Artificial Intelligence*, *6*(11), 1–9. doi:10.1016/j.caeai.2024.100201

Morandini, S., Fraboni, F., De Angelis, M., Puzzo, G., Giusino, D., & Pietrantoni, L. (2023). The Impact of Artificial Intelligence on Workers' Skills: Upskilling and Reskilling in Organisations. *Informing Science: The International Journal of an Emerging Transdiscipline, 26*, 039–068.

Morandini, S., Fraboni, F., De Angelis, M., Puzzo, G., Giusino, D., & Pietrantoni, L. (2023). The Impact of Artificial Intelligence on Workers' Skills: Upskilling and Reskilling in Organisations. *Informing Science*, *26*, 39–68. doi:10.28945/5078

Motwani, S., Nagpal, C., Motwani, M., Nagdev, N., & Yeole, A. (2021). AI-based proctoring system for online tests. In *Proceedings of the 4th International Conference on Advances in Science & Technology (ICAST2021).* IEEE.

Moueddene, K., Coppola, M., Wauters, P., Ivanova, M., Ansaloni, V., & Paquette, J. (2019). *Expected skills needs for the future of work: Understanding the expectations of the European workforce.*

Mroueh, Y., Marcheret, E., & Goel, V. (2015). Deep multimodal learning for audio-visual speech recognition. In *Proceedings of the IEEE International Conference on Acoustics, Speech, and Signal Processing (ICASSP)* (pp. 2130-2134). IEEE.

Mubarak, M. A. (2022, June 28). Sustainably Developing in a Digital World: Harnessing artificial intelligence to meet the imperatives of work-based learning in Industry 5.0. *Development and Learning in Organizations.* doi:10.1108/DLO-04-2022-0063

Mughal, A. A. (2017). *Artificial Intelligence in Information Security: Exploring the Advantages, Challenges, and Future Directions.*

Mujeeb, S., Javed, M. H., & Arshad, T. (2017). Aquabot: A Diagnostic Chatbot for Achluophobia and Autism. [ijacsa]. *International Journal of Advanced Computer Science and Applications*, *8*(9). doi:10.14569/IJACSA.2017.080930

Mukherjee, S., & Das, A. (2021). AI and gender disparities in workforce development: A case study of India. *Gender, Work and Organization*, *28*(6), 235–253.

Munir, H., Vogel, B., & Jacobsson, A. (2022). Artificial intelligence and machine learning approaches in digital education: A systematic revision. *Information (Basel)*, *13*(4), 203. doi:10.3390/info13040203

Muñoz-Basols, J., Neville, C., Lafford, B. A., & Godev, C. (2023). Potentialities of Applied Translation for Language Learning in the Era of Artificial Intelligence. *Hispania*, *106*(2), 171–194. doi:10.1353/hpn.2023.a899427

Musiol, M. (2023). *Generative AI Navigating the Course to the Artificial General Intelligence Future*. Wiley. Niser. // https://www.niser.ac.in/~smishra/teach/cs461/23cs461/assignment/adhil/CS461_notes_positional_encoding

Nadarzynski, T., Miles, O., Cowie, A., & Ridge, D. (2019). Acceptability of artificial intelligence (AI)-led chatbot services in healthcare: A mixed-methods study. *Digital Health*, *5*, 2055207619871808. doi:10.1177/2055207619871808 PMID:31467682

Nagariya, R., Kumar, D., & Kumar, I. (2021a). Enablers to implement sustainable practices in the service only supply chain: A case of an Indian hospital. *Business Process Management Journal*. doi:10.1108/BPMJ-10-2020-0469

Naithani, K., & Raiwani, Y. P. (2022). Realization of natural language processing and machine learning approaches for text-based sentiment analysis. *Expert Systems: International Journal of Knowledge Engineering and Neural Networks*, *40*(5), e13114. Advance online publication. doi:10.1111/exsy.13114

Naithani, K., & Raiwani, Y. P. (2023). Sentiment Analysis on Social Media Data: A Survey. In H. S. Saini, R. Sayal, A. Govardhan, & R. Buyya (Eds.), *Innovations in Computer Science and Engineering. ICICSE 2022. Lecture Notes in Networks and Systems* (Vol. 565). Springer., doi:10.1007/978-981-19-7455-7_59

Naithani, K., Raiwani, Y. P., & Sissodia, R. (2022). Text-Based Analysis of COVID-19 Comments Using Natural Language Processing. In A. Dev, S. S. Agrawal, & A. Sharma (Eds.), *Artificial Intelligence and Speech Technology. AIST 2021. Communications in Computer and Information Science* (Vol. 1546). Springer. doi:10.1007/978-3-030-95711-7_17

Nalbant, K. (2021). The Importance of Artificial Intelligence in Education: A short review. *Journal of Review in Science and Engineering*, 1-15.

Naqvi, S. G., Iqbal, F., Yousaf, J., & Tariq, R. (2023). The Impact of Artificial Intelligence (AI) and Robotics on Higher Education. Journal of Management Practices. *Humanities and Social Sciences*, *7*(3), 11–17. doi:10.33152/jmphss-7.3.2

Narasimhan, M. (2023). *Multimodal Long-Term Video Understanding* (Doctoral dissertation, University of California, Berkeley).

National Institute of Mental Health. (n.d.). *Autism spectrum disorder*. NIH. https://www.nimh.nih.gov/health/topics/autism-spectrum-disorders-asd

Nazer, L. H., Zatarah, R., Waldrip, S., Ke, J. X. C., Moukheiber, M., Khanna, A. K., Hicklen, R. S., Moukheiber, L., Moukheiber, D., Ma, H., & Mathur, P. (2023). Bias in artificial intelligence algorithms and recommendations for mitigation. *PLOS Digital Health*, *2*(6), e0000278. doi:10.1371/journal.pdig.0000278 PMID:37347721

Neha, K. (2020). Role of Artificial Intelligence in Education. *Alochana Chakra Journal*, *IX*(IX), 305–309.

Ngiam, J., Khosla, A., Kim, M., Nam, J., Lee, H., & Ng, A. Y. (2011). Multimodal deep learning. In *Proceedings of the 28th International Conference on Machine Learning (ICML)* (pp. 1-8). Academic Press.

Nguyen, J. G., Keuseman, K. J., & Humston, J. J. (2020). Minimize online cheating for online assessments during COVID-19 pandemic. *Journal of Chemical Education*, *97*(9), 3429–3435. doi:10.1021/acs.jchemed.0c00790

Nigam, A., Pasricha, R., Singh, T., & Churi, P. (2021). A systematic review on AI-based proctoring systems: Past, present and future. *Education and Information Technologies*, *26*(5), 6421–6445. doi:10.1007/s10639-021-10597-x PMID:34177348

Nilsson, N. J. (1998). *Artificial intelligence: a new synthesis*. Morgan Kaufmann.

Noorbehbahani, F., Mohammadi, A., & Aminazadeh, M. (2022). A systematic review of research on cheating in online exams from 2010 to 2021. *Education and Information Technologies*, *27*(6), 8413–8460. doi:10.1007/s10639-022-10927-7 PMID:35283658

Nwaohiri, N. M., & Nwosu, M. C. (2021). Reskilling the library workforce for the fourth industrial revolution. In Examining the impact of industry 4.0 on academic libraries (pp. 227-233). Emerald Publishing Limited. doi:10.1108/978-1-80043-656-520201025

Obermeyer, Z., & Emanuel, E. J. (2016). Predicting the future—Big data, machine learning, and clinical medicine. *The New England Journal of Medicine*, *375*(13), 1216–1219. doi:10.1056/NEJMp1606181 PMID:27682033

Oesch, T. (2018). *Using Artificial Intelligence to Augment Coaching*.

Ohm, A., & K, B. (2019). Chatbot for Career Guidance Using AI. *International Journal on Computer Science and Engineering*, *7*(6), 856–860. doi:10.26438/ijcse/v7i6.856860

Olynick, D. (2024). Exploring Generative AI and Its Transformative Power. In *Interfaceless: Conscious Design for Spatial Computing with Generative AI* (pp. 17–60). Apress.

Ovalle, A. (2023). *Decoding The Digital Fuk\'u: Deciphering Colonial Legacies to Critically Assess ChatGPT in Dominican Education*. arXiv preprint arXiv:2310.17533.

Pallavi, A. & Vishal, S. (2013). Network Monitoring and Analysis by Packet Sniffing Method. *International Journal of Engineering Trends and Technology (IJETT)*.

Palmares, M. (2023). Technological, Pedagogical, Content Knowledge (TPACK) of Science Teachers: Basis of in-Service Training Design Development. *Cosmos Journal of Engineering & Technology, 13*(1), 01-15.

Pangarso, A., & Setyorini, R. (2023). The drivers of e-learning satisfaction during the early COVID-19 pandemic: Empirical evidence from an Indonesian private university. *Cogent Education*, *10*(1), 2149226. doi:10.1080/2331186X.2022.2149226

Pan, W., Li, H., Zhou, X., Jiao, J., Zhu, C., & Zhang, Q. (2024). Research on Pig Sound Recognition Based on Deep Neural Network and Hidden Markov Models. *Sensors (Basel)*, *24*(4), 1269.

Papachristou, I., & Bosanquet, N. (2020). Improving the prevention and diagnosis of melanoma on a national scale: A comparative study of performance in the United Kingdom and Australia. *Journal of Public Health Policy*, *41*(1), 28–38. doi:10.1057/s41271-019-00187-0 PMID:31477796

Papaspyridis, A. (2020). *AI in Higher Education: opportunities and considerations*. Microsoft. https://news.microsoft.com/apac/2020/03/26/ai-in-higher-education-opportunities-and-considerations/

Papers with Code - CAS-VSR-W1k (LRW-1000) Dataset. (n.d.). Retrieved April 4, 2024, from https://paperswithcode.com/dataset/lrw-1000

Parab, A., Palkar, S., Maurya, S., & Balpande, S. (2017). An Intelligent Career Counselling Bot: A System for counseling. *International Research Journal of Engineering and Technology (IRJET), 4*(03).

Paranjape, K., Schinkel, M., Panday, R. N., Car, J., & Nanayakkara, P. (2019). Introducing artificial intelligence training in medical education. *JMIR Medical Education*, *5*(2), e16048. doi:10.2196/16048 PMID:31793895

Parker, L., Bero, L., Gillies, D., Raven, M., Mintzes, B., Jureidini, J., & Grundy, Q. (2018). Mental Health Messages in Prominent Mental Health Apps. *Annals of Family Medicine*, *16*(4), 338–342. doi:10.1370/afm.2260 PMID:29987082

Park, S. H., Do, K. H., Kim, S., Park, J. H., & Lim, Y. S. (2019). What should medical students know about artificial intelligence in medicine? *Journal of Educational Evaluation for Health Professions*, *16*, 16. doi:10.3352/jeehp.2019.16.18 PMID:31319450

Patel, H., Sanghavi, J., Shah, S., Thacker, S., & Mishra, S. (2021). CAREER GUIDANCE SYSTEM USING MACHINE LEARNING. *IJCRT*, *9*(5).

Patel, K. (2024). Ethical Reflections on Data-Centric AI: Balancing Benefits and Risks. *International Journal of Artificial Intelligence Research and Development*, *2*(1), 1–17.

Patel, N., & Mehta, K. (2021). Ethical dimensions of AI in workforce development: A case study in India. *Journal of Business Ethics*, *169*, 629–645.

Patel, S., Vyas, A. K., & Hiran, K. K. (2022). Infrastructure health monitoring using signal processing based on an industry 4.0 System. *Cyber-Physical Systems and Industry*, *4*, 249–260.

Pathak, N., & Singhal, S. (2023, January 27). *Fraud detection in financial domain using Machine learning.* Presented at the 2023 International Conference on Artificial Intelligence and Smart Communication (AISC), Greater Noida, India. 10.1109/AISC56616.2023.10085181

Pathak, N., Singhal, S., Naruka, M. S., Awasthi, S., & Chamoli, S. (2023, May 11). *Detection of Weed by using Hybrid Technique.* Presented at the 2023 International Conference on Disruptive Technologies (ICDT), Greater Noida, India. 10.1109/ICDT57929.2023.10151283

Patterson, E., Gurbuz, S., Tufekci, Z., & Gowdy, J. (2002). Moving-talker speaker-independent feature study and baseline results using the cuave multimodal speech corpus. *EURASIP Journal on Applied Signal Processing*, *2002*, 1189–1201.

Paulk, M. C., Weber, C. V., Curtis, B., & Chrissis, M. B. (1995). *The Capability Maturity Model: Guidelines for Improving the Software Process.* Addison-Wesley Professional.

Pedro, F., Subosa, M., Rivas, A., & Valverde, P. (2019). *Artificial Intelligence in Education: Challenges and Opportunities for Sustainable Development.* UNESCO.

Pesonen, J. A. (2021). 'Are You OK?' Students' Trust in a Chatbot Providing Support Opportunities. In *Learning and Collaboration Technologies: Games and Virtual Environments for Learning: 8th International Conference, LCT 2021, Held as Part of the 23rd HCI International Conference, HCII 2021, Virtual Event, Proceedings, Part II* (pp. 199-215). Springer: Cham, Switzerland.

Petridis, S., Wang, Y., Li, Z., & Pantic, M. (2017). End-to-end audiovisual fusion with LSTMs. In *Proceedings of the 14th International Conference on Auditory-Visual Speech Processing* (pp. 36-40). Academic Press.

Petridis, S., Wang, Y., Li, Z., & Pantic, M. (2017). End-to-end multi-view lipreading. In *Proceedings of the British Machine Vision Conference* (pp. 1-14). Academic Press.

Petridis, S., Li, Z., & Pantic, M. (2017). End-to-end visual speech recognition with LSTMS. In *Proceedings of the IEEE International Conference on Acoustics, Speech, and Signal Processing (ICASSP)* (pp. 2592-2596). IEEE.

Petridis, S., & Pantic, M. (2016). Deep complementary bottleneck features for visual speech recognition. In *Proceedings of the IEEE International Conference on Acoustics, Speech, and Signal Processing (ICASSP)* (pp. 2304-2308). IEEE.

Pokrivcakova, S. (2019). Preparing teachers for the application of AI-powered technologies in foreign language education. *Journal of Language and Cultural Education, 7*(3), 135–153. doi:10.2478/jolace-2019-0025

Polas, M. R. H., Tabash, M. I., Bhattacharjee, A., & Dávila, G. A. (2023). Knowledge management practices and green innovation in SMES: The role of environmental awareness towards environmental sustainability. *The International Journal of Organizational Analysis, 31*(5), 1601–1622. doi:10.1108/IJOA-03-2021-2671

Ponomarenko, E., Oganesyan, A., & Teslenko, V. (2019). New trends in higher education: Massive open online courses as an innovative tool for increasing university performance. *International Journal of Economic Policy in Emerging Economies, 12*(4), 391. doi:10.1504/IJEPEE.2019.104635

Potamianos, G., Luettin, J., & Neti, C. (2001). Hierarchical discriminant features for audio-visual LVCSR. *Proceedings of the IEEE International Conference on Acoustics, Speech, and Signal Processing, 1*, 165-168. https://doi.org/10.1109/ICASSP.2001.940793

Pradhan, I. P., & Saxena, P. (2023). Reskilling workforce for the Artificial Intelligence age: Challenges and the way forward. In The Adoption and Effect of Artificial Intelligence on Human Resources Management, Part B (pp. 181-197). Emerald Publishing Limited.

Prajapati, R. K., Bhardwaj, Y., Jain, R. K., & Hiran, K. K. (2023, April). A Review Paper on Automatic Number Plate Recognition using Machine Learning: An In-Depth Analysis of Machine Learning Techniques in Automatic Number Plate Recognition: Opportunities and Limitations. In *2023 International Conference on Computational Intelligence, Communication Technology and Networking* (CICTN) (pp. 527-532). IEEE. 10.1109/CICTN57981.2023.10141318

Prakash, V., Bhavani, R., Karthik, D., Rajalakshmi, D., Rajeswari, N., & Martinaa, M. (2024). Visual Speech Recognition by Lip Reading Using Deep Learning. In *Advanced Applications in Osmotic Computing* (pp. 290–310). IGI Global.

Prasanna, L. (2019). Smart Career Guidance and Recommendation System. *IJEDR, 7*(3).

Preiksaitis, C., & Rose, C. (2023). Opportunities, challenges, and future directions of generative artificial intelligence in medical education: Scoping review. *JMIR Medical Education, 9*, e48785. doi:10.2196/48785 PMID:37862079

Priyadarshi, N., Padmanaban, S., Hiran, K. K., Holm-Nielson, J. B., & Bansal, R. C. (Eds.). (2021). *Artificial intelligence and internet of things for renewable energy systems* (Vol. 12). Walter de Gruyter GmbH & Co KG. doi:10.1515/9783110714043

Pugliese, R., Regondi, S., & Marini, R. (2021). Machine learning-based approach: Global trends, research directions, and regulatory standpoints. *Data Science and Management, 4*, 19–29. doi:10.1016/j.dsm.2021.12.002

Pujari, A. M., Dalvi, R. M., Gawde, K. S., & Nagarhalli, T. P. (2019). SCCAI-A Student Career Counselling Artificial Intelligence. *International Journal for Research and Innovation, 1*(2). www.viva-technology.org/New/IJRI

Purohit, H., Dadhich, M., & Ajmera, P. K. (2022). Analytical study on users' awareness and acceptability towards adoption of multimodal biometrics (MMB) mechanism in online transactions : A two-stage SEM-ANN approach. *Multimedia Tools and Applications, 1*, 1–25. doi:10.1007/s11042-022-13786-z PMID:36157357

Qadir, J. (2022). Engineering Education in the Era of ChatGPT: Promise and Pitfalls of Generative AI for Education. *2023 IEEE Global Engineering Education Conference (EDUCON)*, Kuwait, Kuwait. 10.1109/EDUCON54358.2023.10125121

QadirJ. (2022). Engineering Education in the Era of ChatGPT: Promise and Pitfalls of Generative AI for Education. TechRxiv. // doi:10.36227/techrxiv.21789434.v1

Quinn, T. P., & Coghlan, S. (2021). Readying medical students for medical AI: The need to embed AI ethics education. *arXiv preprint arXiv:2109.02866*.

Quinn, T. P., Senadeera, M., Jacobs, S., Coghlan, S., & Le, V. (2021). Trust and medical AI: The challenges we face and the expertise needed to overcome them. *Journal of the American Medical Informatics Association : JAMIA*, *28*(4), 890–894. doi:10.1093/jamia/ocaa268 PMID:33340404

Radianti, J., Majchrzak, T. A., Fromm, J., & Wohlgenannt, I. (2020). A systematic review of immersive virtual reality applications for higher education: Design elements, lessons learned, and research agenda. *Computers & Education*, *147*, 103778. doi:10.1016/j.compedu.2019.103778

Radif, M., Fan, D. I., & McLaughln, D. P. (n.d.). INTERNAL AND EXTERNAL BARRIERS INFLUENCING LMS IMPLEMENTATION IN IRAQI. *Higher Education*, 12.

Radif, M., Fan, I., & McLaughln, P. (2015). INTERNAL AND EXTERNAL BARRIERS INFLUENCING LMS IMPLEMENTATION IN IRAQI HIGHER EDUCATION. *ICERI2015: 8th International Conference of Education, Research and Innovation*, 11.

Rafner, J., Dellermann, D., Hjorth, A., Verasztó, D., Kampf, C., Mackay, W., & Sherson, J. (2021). Deskilling, Upskilling, and Reskilling: A Case for Hybrid Intelligence. *Morals & Machines*, *1*(2), 24–39. doi:10.5771/2747-5174-2021-2-24

Rafner, J., Gajdacz, M., Kragh, G., Hjorth, A., Gander, A., Palfi, B., Berditchevskiaia, A., Grey, F., Gal, K., Segal, A., Wamsley, M., Miller, J., Dellermann, D., Haklay, M., Michelucci, P., & Sherson, J. (2022). Mapping citizen science through the lens of human-centered AI. *Human Computation (Fairfax, Va.)*, *9*(1), 66–95. doi:10.15346/hc.v9i1.133

Raghu, H. V., & Nedungadi, P. (2021). Adoption of online proctored examinations by university students during COVID-19: Innovation diffusion study. *Education and Information Technologies*, *26*(6), 7339–7358. doi:10.1007/s10639-021-10581-5 PMID:34093065

Rahman, M.M. & Watanobe, Y. (2023). ChatGPT for Education and Research: Opportunities, Threats, and Strategies. *Appl. Sci.*, *13*, 5783. /https://doi.org//. doi:10.3390

RahmanM. (2023). Artificial Intelligence in Career Counseling: A Test Case with ResumAI. http://arxiv.org/abs/2308.14301

Rai, A., Constantinides, P., & Sarker, S. (2019). Editor's comments: Next-generation digital platforms: Toward human-AI hybrids. *Management Information Systems Quarterly*, *43*, iii–ix.

Raimi, L., Kah, J. M., & Tariq, M. U. (2022). The Discourse of Blue Economy Definitions, Measurements, and Theories: Implications for Strengthening Academic Research and Industry Practice. In L. Raimi & J. Kah (Eds.), *Implications for Entrepreneurship and Enterprise Development in the Blue Economy* (pp. 1–17). IGI Global. doi:10.4018/978-1-6684-3393-5.ch001

Raimi, L., Tariq, M. U., & Kah, J. M. (2022). Diversity, Equity, and Inclusion as the Future Workplace Ethics: Theoretical Review. In L. Raimi & J. Kah (Eds.), *Mainstreaming Diversity, Equity, and Inclusion as Future Workplace Ethics* (pp. 1–27). IGI Global. doi:10.4018/978-1-6684-3657-8.ch001

Rajput, S., & Sharma, P. (2021). AI and skill development in the Indian healthcare sector: A case study of medical professionals. *International Journal of Healthcare Management*, *14*(3), 321–335.

Ramasamy, J., & Doshi, R. (2022). Machine learning in cyber physical systems for healthcare: brain tumor classification from MRI using transfer learning framework. In *Real-Time Applications of Machine Learning in Cyber-Physical Systems* (pp. 65–76). IGI global. doi:10.4018/978-1-7998-9308-0.ch005

RamirezM. A.KimS.-K.Al HamadiH.DamianiE.ByonY.-J.KimT.-Y.ChoC.-S.YeunC. Y. (2022). Poisoning Attacks and Defenses on Artificial Intelligence: A Survey. http://arxiv.org/abs/2202.10276

Randhawa, G. K., & Jackson, M. (2020, January). The role of artificial intelligence in learning and professional development for healthcare professionals. [). Sage CA: Los Angeles, CA: SAGE Publications.]. *Healthcare Management Forum*, *33*(1), 19–24. doi:10.1177/0840470419869032 PMID:31802725

RaneN. (2023). Role and Challenges of ChatGPT and Similar Generative Artificial Intelligence in Arts and Humanities. // doi:10.2139/ssrn.4603208

RaneN.ChoudharyS.RaneJ. (2023). Education 4.0 and 5.0: Integrating Artificial Intelligence (AI) for personalized and adaptive learning. Available at SSRN 4638365. doi:10.2139/ssrn.4638365

Rao, S., & Deshmukh, P. (2021). Harnessing AI for inclusive skilling: Insights from Indian social enterprises. *Journal of Social Entrepreneurship*, *13*(2), 245–264.

Rastogi, R. (2020). Recent Trends in Indian Higher Education System. *International Journal of Advanced Science and Technology*, *29*(8), 7.

Rathi, S., Hiran, K. K., & Sakhare, S. (2023). Affective state prediction of E-learner using SS-ROA based deep LSTM. *Array (New York, N.Y.)*, *19*, 100315. doi:10.1016/j.array.2023.100315

Rathnayaka, P., Mills, N., Burnett, D., De Silva, D., Alahakoon, D., & Gray, R. (2022). A Mental Health Chatbot with Cognitive Skills for Personalised Behavioural Activation and Remote Health Monitoring. *Sensors (Basel)*, *22*(10), 3653. doi:10.3390/s22103653 PMID:35632061

Rauen, C. (2018). Quo vadis, Business Coaching? Presentation at the DBVC Coaching Kongress in Berlin/Potsdam, Germany.

Rausch, T., & Dustdar, S. (2019). Edge Intelligence: The Convergence of Humans, Things, and AI. In *Proceedings of International Conference on Cloud Engineering*, (pp. 1-6). IEEE. 10.1109/IC2E.2019.00022

Reddy, S., Allan, S., Coghlan, S., & Cooper, P. (2020). A governance model for the application of AI in health care. *Journal of the American Medical Informatics Association : JAMIA*, *27*(3), 491–497. doi:10.1093/jamia/ocz192 PMID:31682262

Reisenwitz, T. H. (2020). Examining the necessity of proctoring online exams. *Journal of Higher Education Theory and Practice*, *20*(1), 118–124.

Rejeb, A., Rejeb, K., Appolloni, A., Treiblmaier, H., & Iranmanesh, M. (2024). Exploring the impact of ChatGPT on education: A web mining and machine learaning approach. *International Journal of Management Education*, *22*(1), 1–14. doi:10.1016/j.ijme.2024.100932

Rekhis, S., Krichene, J., & Boudriga, N. (2018) DigForNet: digital forensic in networking. In: Jajodia S, Samarati P, Cimato S (eds) IFIP TC-11 *23rd international information security conference*, *278*. Springer, Boston.

Ren, W. (2004) On a network forensics model for information security. *3rd international conference on Information Systems Technology and its Applications (ISTA 2004)*, Utah, USA.

Reyes, V.,, Camara, M.,, Bantigue, A., & Caling, M. (2023). The Role of Learning Action Cell Session in Research Self-Efficacy Level: Basis for the Development of an Action Plan. *Globus An International Journal of Medical Science, Engineering and Technology*, *9*(1), 01-04.

Reyes, V., Camara, M., Bantigue, A., & Caling, M. A. (2023). The Role of Learning Action Cell Session in Research Self-Efficacy Level: Basis for the Development of An Action Plan. Globus An International Journal of Medical Science. *Engineering and Technology*, *11*(1), 80–86.

Rizvi, F. (2023). Internationalization of higher education and the advantage of diaspora. *International Higher Education,* (113), 16–17. https://ejournals.bc.edu/index.php/ihe/article/view/16099

Robert, L., Cheung, C., Matt, C., & Trenz, M. (2018). Int ne t R es ea rch Int ern et Re se. *Internet Research*, *28*, 829–850.

Robeznieks, A. (2018). ways medical AI can improve workflow for physicians. American Medical Association.

Robles-Carrillo, M. (2021). European Union policy on 5G: Context, scope and limits. *Telecommunications Policy*, *45*(8), 102216. doi:10.1016/j.telpol.2021.102216

Rohde, F., Wagner, J., Meyer, A., Reinhard, P., Voss, M., Petschow, U., & Mollen, A. (2024). Broadening the perspective for sustainable artificial intelligence: Sustainability criteria and indicators for Artificial Intelligence systems. *Current Opinion in Environmental Sustainability*, *66*, 1–12. doi:10.1016/j.cosust.2023.101411

Roslan, F. A. B. M., & Ahmad, N. B. (2023). The Rise of AI-Powered Voice Assistants: Analyzing Their Transformative Impact on Modern Customer Service Paradigms and Consumer Expectations. *Quarterly Journal of Emerging Technologies and Innovations*, *8*(3), 33–64.

Rotatori, D., Lee, E. J., & Sleeva, S. (2021). The evolution of the workforce during the fourth industrial revolution. *Human Resource Development International*, *24*(1), 92–103. doi:10.1080/13678868.2020.1767453

Roter, D. (2000). The enduring and evolving nature of the patient-physician relationship. *Patient Education and Counseling*, *39*(1), 5–15. doi:10.1016/S0738-3991(99)00086-5 PMID:11013543

Rudin, C. (2019). Stop explaining black box machine learning models for high stakes decisions and use interpretable models instead. *Nature Machine Intelligence*, *1*(5), 206–215. doi:10.1038/s42256-019-0048-x PMID:35603010

Russell, S. J., & Norvig, P. (2010). *Artificial intelligence a modern approach.*

Rus, V., D'Mello, S., Hu, X., & Graesser, A. (2013). Recent advances in conversational intelligent tutoring systems. *AI Magazine*, *34*(3), 42–54. doi:10.1609/aimag.v34i3.2485

Ryan, M. (2020). In AI We Trust: Ethics, Artificial Intelligence, and Reliability. *Science and Engineering Ethics*, *26*(5), 2749–2767. doi:10.1007/s11948-020-00228-y PMID:32524425

Ryumin, D., Ryumina, E., & Ivanko, D. (2023). EMOLIPS: Towards Reliable Emotional Speech Lip-Reading. *Mathematics*, *11*(23), 4787.

Saad, A., & Zohair, A. (2023, October). Getting Practical About the Future of Work a Framework for Upskilling and Reskilling Based on Trends Impacting the Oil and Gas Industry. In *Abu Dhabi International Petroleum Exhibition and Conference* (p. D031S079R005). SPE. 10.2118/216540-MS

Sachs, J. D., Schmidt-Traub, G., Mazzucato, M., Messner, D., Nakicenovic, N., & Rockström, J. (2019). Six transformations to achieve the sustainable development goals. *Nature Sustainability*, *2*(9), 805–814. doi:10.1038/s41893-019-0352-9

Sadanand, V. S., Guruvyas, K. R. R., Patil, P. P., Acharya, J. J., & Suryakanth, S. G. (2022). An automated essay evaluation system using natural language processing and sentiment analysi. *Iranian Journal of Electrical and Computer Engineering*, *12*(6), 6585–6593. doi:10.11591/ijece.v12i6.pp6585-6593

Saeed, M. (2023). *A Gentle Introduction to Positional Encoding in Transformer Models. Machine learning mastery.* Machine Learning Mastery. https://machinelearningmastery.com/a-gentle-introduction-to-positional-encoding-in-transformer-models-part-1

Saitoh, T., Zhou, Z., Zhao, G., & Pietikainen, M. (2016). Concatenated frame image based CNN for visual speech recognition. In *Proceedings of the Asian Conference on Computer Vision* (pp. 277-289). Springer.

Salas-Pilco, S. Z., & Yang, Y. (2022). Artificial intelligence applications in Latin American higher education: A systematic review. *International Journal of Educational Technology in Higher Education, 19*(1), 21. doi:10.1186/s41239-022-00326-w

Sallam, M., & Mousa, D. (2024). Evaluating ChatGPT performance in Arabic dialects: A comparative study showing defects in responding to Jordanian and Tunisian general health prompts. *Mesopotamian Journal of Artificial Intelligence in Healthcare, 2024*, 1–7. doi:10.58496/MJAIH/2024/001

Sallam, M., Salim, N. A., Ala'a, B., Barakat, M., Fayyad, D., Hallit, S., & Ala'a, B. (2023). ChatGPT output regarding compulsory vaccination and COVID-19 vaccine conspiracy: A descriptive study at the outset of a paradigm shift in online search for information. *Cureus, 15*(2). doi:10.7759/cureus.35029 PMID:36819954

Sands, S., Campbell, C., Ferraro, C., Demsar, V., Rosengren, S., & Farrell, J. (2024). Principles for Advertising Responsibly Using Generative AI. *Organizational Dynamics, 4*, 1–9. doi:10.1016/j.orgdyn.2024.101042

Santos, R. P. D. (2023). *Enhancing chemistry learning with chatgpt and bing chat as agents to think with: A comparative case study.* arXiv preprint arXiv:2305.11890.

Sarstedt, M., Hair, J. F. Jr, Cheah, J., Becker, J., & Ringle, C. M. (2019). How to specify, estimate, and validate higher-order constructs in. [AMJ]. *Australasian Marketing Journal, 27*(3), 197–211. doi:10.1016/j.ausmj.2019.05.003

Sarstedt, M., Hair, J. F., Ringle, C. M., Thiele, K. O., & Gudergan, S. P. (2016). Estimation issues with PLS and CBSEM : Where the bias lies. *Journal of Business Research, 69*(10), 3998–4010. doi:10.1016/j.jbusres.2016.06.007

Sayyed, F., Sanghani, R., Vora, A., & Lemos, N. (2020). AI-based Career Guidance. *International Research Journal of Engineering and Technology (IRJET), 07*(05).

Scantlebury, A., Sheard, L., Watt, I., Cairns, P., Wright, J., & Adamson, J. (2017). Exploring the implementation of an electronic record into a maternity unit: A qualitative study using Normalisation Process Theory. *BMC Medical Informatics and Decision Making, 17*(1), 1–10. doi:10.1186/s12911-016-0406-0 PMID:28061781

Schaaff, K., Reinig, C., & Schlippe, T. (2023). Exploring ChatGPT's Empathic Abilities. In *11th International Conference on Affective Computing and Intelligent Interaction (ACII)* (pp. 1-8). IEEE. 10.1109/ACII59096.2023.10388208

Schroeder, R. (2022). Artificial Intelligence to Assist, Tutor, Teach and Assess in Higher Ed. *Inside Higher Ed.* https://www.insidehighered.com/digital-learning/blogs/online-trending-now/artificial-intelligence-assist-tutor-teach-and-assess

Schwartz, W. B., Patil, R. S., & Szolovits, P. (1987). Artificial intelligence in medicine. *The New England Journal of Medicine, 316*(11), 685–688. doi:10.1056/NEJM198703123161109 PMID:3821801

Seele, P., & Lock, I. (2017). The game-changing potential of digitalization for sustainability: Possibilities, perils, and pathways. *Sustainability Science, 12*(2), 183–185. doi:10.1007/s11625-017-0426-4

Segbenya, M., Bervell, B., Frimpong-Manso, E., Otoo, I. C., Andzie, T. A., & Achina, S. (2023). Artificial intelligence in higher education: Modelling the antecedents of artificial intelligence usage and effects on 21st century employability skills among postgraduate students in Ghana. *Computers and Education: Artificial Intelligence, 5*, 1–12. doi:10.1016/j.caeai.2023.100188

Selwyn, N. (2022). The future of AI and education: Some cautionary notes. *European Journal of Education*, *57*(4), 620–631. doi:10.1111/ejed.12532

Senados, J. (2023). Positive Reinforcement and Its Effect on Students' Classroom Behavior and Classroom Work-Related Values. *Globus Journal of Progressive Education, 13*(1), 69-78.

Shah, S., Mishra, A., Shaikh, I., Yadav, A., & Ambekar, R. (2022). Career Guidance Chatbot. [IJAEM]. *International Journal of Advances in Engineering and Management*, *4*, 661. doi:10.35629/5252-0404661665

Shal, T., Ghamrawi, N., & Naccache, H. (2024). Leadership styles and AI acceptance in academic libraries in higher education. *Journal of Academic Librarianship*, *50*(2), 1–16. doi:10.1016/j.acalib.2024.102849

Shang, H., Sivaparthipan, C. B., & ThanjaiVadivel. (2022). Interactive teaching using human-machine interaction for higher education systems. *Computers & Electrical Engineering*, *100*, 107811. doi:10.1016/j.compeleceng.2022.107811

Shanmugasundaram, K., Memon, N., Savant, A., & Bronnimann, H. (2003). ForNet: a distributed forensics network. In V. Gorodetsky, L. Popyack, & V. Skormin (Eds.), *Computer network security* (Vol. 2776, pp. 1–16). Springer. doi:10.1007/978-3-540-45215-7_1

Sharma, L. (2023). Leadership and Governance in Hospital Management: Best Practices and Challenges. Globus An International Journal of Medical Science. *Engineering and Technology*, *12*(1), 89–93.

Sharma, P., Sharma, I., Pamecha, S., & Hiran, K. K. (2022). Green Currency Based on Blockchain Technology for Sustainable Development. In *Advancements in Quantum Blockchain With Real-Time Applications* (pp. 102–118). IGI Global. doi:10.4018/978-1-6684-5072-7.ch005

Sharma, R., & Verma, S. (2020). AI-driven workforce transformations: Implications for talent management in Indian organizations. *Journal of Human Resource Management in Emerging Economies*, *2*(1), 45–60.

Sharma, S., & Gupta, N. (2022). Comparative analysis of AI-driven skilling initiatives in emerging economies. *International Journal of Comparative Education and Development*, *24*(1), 45–64.

Sheth, A., Yip, H. Y., Iyengar, A., & Tepper, P. (2019). Cognitive Services and Intelligent Chatbots: Current Perspectives and Special Issue Introduction. *IEEE Internet Computing*, *23*(2), 6–12. doi:10.1109/MIC.2018.2889231 PMID:33746506

Shrivas, M. K., Hiran, K. K., Bhansali, A., & Doshi, R. (Eds.). (2022). *Advancements in Quantum Blockchain with Real-time Applications*. IGI global. doi:10.4018/978-1-6684-5072-7

Shrivastava, G., & Gupta, B. B. (2014). An Encapsulated Approach of Forensic Model for digital investigation. *2014 IEEE 3rd Global Conference on Consumer Electronics (GCCE)*, (pp. 280–284). IEEE. 10.1109/GCCE.2014.7031241

Shukla, A., Dadhich, M., Vaya, D., & Goel, A. (2024). Impact of Behavioral Biases on Investors' Stock Trading Decisions : A Comparehensive Quantitative Analysis. *Indian Journal of Science and Technology*, *17*(8), 670–678. doi:10.17485/IJST/v17i8.2845

Shukur, B. S., & Mijwil, M. M. (2023). Involving machine learning techniques in heart disease diagnosis: A performance analysis. *Iranian Journal of Electrical and Computer Engineering*, *13*(2), 2177–2185. doi:10.11591/ijece.v13i2.pp2177-2185

Shukur, B. S., Yaacob, N. M., & Doheir, M. (2023). Diabetes at a Glance: Assessing AI Strategies for Early Diabetes Detection and Intervention. *Mesopotamian Journal of Artificial Intelligence in Healthcare*, *85–89*, 85–89. doi:10.58496/MJAIH/2023/017

Siau, K. (2017). *Impact of Artificial Intelligence, Robotics, and Automation on Higher Education. Americas Conference on Information Systems (AMCIS 2017)*, Boston, MA.

Siau, K. (2018). Education in the Age of Artificial Intelligence: How will Technology Shape Learning? *The Global Analyst*, *7*(3), 22–24.

Siemens, G., & Long, P. (2011). Penetrating the Fog: Analytics in Learning and Education. *EDUCAUSE Review*, *46*(5), 30–32.

Sifat, R.I. (2023). ChatGPT and the Future of Health Policy Analysis: Potential and Pitfalls of Using ChatGPT in Policymaking. *Ann Biomed Eng*, *51*, 1357–1359. //. doi:10.1007/s10439-023-03204-2

Sigdel, S., & Sharma, M. R. (2021). Critical pedagogy and equity promotion in culturally and linguistically diverse classroom. *Journal of English Education and Teaching*, *5*(2), 201–215. doi:10.33369/jeet.5.2.201-215

Singh, B., & Singhal, S. (2020). Automated personality classification using Data mining techniques. SSRN Electronic Journal. doi:10.2139/ssrn.3602540

Singh, G. K., & Dadhich, M. (2023). Supply Chain Management Growth With the Adoption of Blockchain Technology (BoT) and Internet of Things (IoT). In *2023 3rd International Conference on Advance Computing and Innovative Technologies in Engineering (ICACITE)*, (pp. 321–25). IEEE. 10.1109/ICACITE57410.2023.10182619

Singh, J., Jaiswal, K., Singh, M., Sama, M., & Singhal, S. (2023, May 11). *Market segmentation using ML*. Presented at the 2023 International Conference on Disruptive Technologies (ICDT), Greater Noida, India. 10.1109/ICDT57929.2023.10150639

Singhal, S., & Pathak, N. (2023, January 27). *The future era of computing: Automatic computing*. Presented at the 2023 International Conference on Artificial Intelligence and Smart Communication (AISC), Greater Noida, India. 10.1109/AISC56616.2023.10085022

Singhal, S., Ahuja, L., & Monga, H. (2020, December 18). *State of the art of Machine learning for product sustainability*. Presented at the 2020 2nd International Conference on Advances in Computing, Communication Control and Networking (ICACCCN), Greater Noida, India. 10.1109/ICACCCN51052.2020.9362746

Singhal, S., Ahuja, L., & Monga, H. (2023, January 27). *Sustainable manufacturing integrated into cloud-based data analytics for e-commerce SMEs*. Presented at the 2023 International Conference on Artificial Intelligence and Smart Communication (AISC), Greater Noida, India. 10.1109/AISC56616.2023.10085046

Singhal, S., Sharma, R., Ahuja, L., & Rana, A. (2020, October 9). *Approach in web application for regression testing using crawlers*. Presented at the 2020 International Conference on Smart Technologies in Computing, Electrical and Electronics (ICSTCEE), Bengaluru, India. 10.1109/ICSTCEE49637.2020.9277186

Singh, N., & Sharma, A. (2022). AI and rural employment generation in India: Prospects and challenges. *Journal of Rural Development*, *41*(1), 45–60.

Singh, P., & Reddy, A. R. (2020). Socio-economic implications of AI-driven workforce transformations in India. *The Indian Journal of Social Work*, *81*(4), 531–548. doi:10.1177/0018726720961507

Singh, R., & Pandey, A. (2020). AI and entrepreneurship development in India: Opportunities and challenges for startups. *International Journal of Entrepreneurial Behaviour & Research*, *26*(5), 987–1005.

Singh, S. V., & Hiran, K. K. (2022). The impact of AI on teaching and learning in higher education technology. *Journal of Higher Education Theory and Practice*, *22*(13).

Sinha, R., & Chatterjee, S. (2020). AI and the future of work in India: A qualitative study of employee perceptions. *Journal of Organizational Change Management*, *33*(4), 789–805.

Sit, C., Srinivasan, R., Amlani, A., Muthuswamy, K., Azam, A., Monzon, L., & Poon, D. S. (2020). Attitudes and perceptions of UK medical students towards artificial intelligence and radiology: A multicentre survey. *Insights Into Imaging*, *11*(1), 1–6. doi:10.1186/s13244-019-0830-7 PMID:32025951

Six visual speech recognition data sets and a company about speech recognition. (n.d.). Retrieved April 4, 2024, from https://en.speechocean.com/Cy/757.html

Skouby, K. E., Williams, I., Dhotre, P., & Hiran, K. K. (2022). Introduction: Wireless networks and privacy in developing countries. In 5G, Cybersecurity and Privacy in Developing Countries (pp. 1-18). River Publishers. doi:10.1201/9781003374664

Smolansky, A., Cram, A., Raduescu, C., Zeivots, S., Huber, E., & Kizilcec, F. R. (2023). Educator and Student Perspectives on the Impact of Generative AI on Assessments in Higher Education. *In Proceedings of the Tenth ACM Conference on Learning @ Scale (L@S'23)*,1–22.

Son, J. B., Ružić, N. K., & Philpott, A. (2023). Artificial intelligence technologies and applications for language learning and teaching. *Journal of China Computer-Assisted Language Learning*, (0).

Son, J. S., & Zisserman, A. (2017). Lip reading in profile. In *Proceedings of the British Machine Vision Conference* (pp. 1-11). Academic Press.

Sotomayor-Vidal, A., Mini-Cuadros, D. A., & Carlos Quiroz-Flores, J. (n.d.). *The influence of digital marketing on the student recruitment process in the private higher education sector in Perú*. IEOM Society. from https://ieomsociety.org/proceedings/2022malaysia/424.pdf

Sotomayor-Vidal, A., Mini-Cuadros, D. A., & Carlos Quiroz-Flores, J. (n.d.). *The influence of digital marketing on the student recruitment process in the private higher education sector in Perú*. IEOM Society. https://ieomsociety.org/proceedings/2022malaysia/424.pdf

Soudi, M. (2024). Robotics Education in Africa: Africa Compete. In Impacts of the Knowledge Society on Economic and Social Growth in Africa, 1-16. doi:10.4018/978-1-4666-5844-8.ch012

Srikant, S., & Aggarwal, V. (2017h). Introducing data science to school kids. In *Proceedings of the 2017 ACM SIGCSE technical symposium on computer science education*, (pp. 561-566). ACM. 10.1145/3017680.3017717

Srivastava, B., Rossi, F., Usmani, S., & Bernagozzi, M. (2020). Personalized chatbot trustworthiness ratings. *IEEE Transactions on Technology and Society*, *1*(4), 184–192. doi:10.1109/TTS.2020.3023919

Srivastava, T. K., & Waghmare, L. (2020). Implications of artificial intelligence (AI) on dynamics of medical education and care: A perspective. *Journal of Clinical and Diagnostic Research : JCDR*, *14*(3), 1–2. doi:10.7860/JCDR/2020/43293.13565

Stafylakis, T., & Tzimiropoulos, G. (2017). Combining residual networks with LSTMs for lipreading. In Proceedings of Interspeech (pp. 3652-3656). Academic Press.

Stahl, B. C., & Wright, D. (2018). Ethics and Privacy in AI and Big Data: Implementing Responsible Research and Innovation. *IEEE Security and Privacy*, *16*(3), 26–33. doi:10.1109/MSP.2018.2701164

Stohr, A., Ollig, P., Keller, R., & Rieger, A. (2024). Generative Mechanisms of AI Implementation: A Critical Realist Perspective on Predictive Maintenance. *Information and Organization*, *34*(2), 1–11. doi:10.1016/j.infoandorg.2024.100503

Stokel-Walker, C., & Van Noorden, R. (2023). What ChatGPT and generative AI mean for science. *Nature*, *614*(7947), 214–216. doi:10.1038/d41586-023-00340-6 PMID:36747115

Stone, P., Brooks, R., Brynjolfsson, E., Calo, R., Etzioni, O., Hager, G., & Teller, A. (2022). Artificial intelligence and life in 2030: the one hundred year study on artificial intelligence. *arXiv preprint arXiv:2211.06318.*

Stone, P., Brooks, R., Brynjolfsson, E., Calo, R., Etzioni, O., Hager, G., & Teller, A. (2022). *Artificial intelligence and life in 2030: the one-hundred-year study on artificial intelligence*. arXiv preprint arXiv:2211.06318.

Stravodimos, K., Katafigiotis, I., Pournaras, C., Dimitroulis, D., Kousournas, G., Fragkiadis, E., & Constantinides, C. (2019). Combined robot assisted right partial nephrectomy and cholecystectomy with single docking. *Journal of Robotic Surgery, 13*(1), 167–169. doi:10.1007/s11701-018-0805-6 PMID:29600421

Street, V. (2005). *Indian Institute of Technology Gandhinagar., 14*(3), 13210003.

Sue-Chan, C., & Latham, G. P. (2004). The relative effectiveness of external, peer, and self-coaches. *Applied Psychology, 53*(2), 260–278. doi:10.1111/j.1464-0597.2004.00171.x

Su, J., & Yang, W. (2023). Unlocking the Power of ChatGPT: A Framework for Applying Generative AI in Education. *ECNU Review of Education, 6*(3), 355–366. doi:10.1177/20965311231168423

Suleimenov, I. E., Vitulyova, Y. S., Bakirov, A. S., & Gabrielyan, O. A. (2020, April). Artificial Intelligence: what is it? In *Proceedings of the 2020 6th International Conference on Computer and Technology Applications* (pp. 22-25). ACM. 10.1145/3397125.3397141

Sun, Q.-H., & Su, Y. (2020). Psychological crisis intervention for college students during novel coronavirus infection epidemic. *Psychiatry Research, 289*, 113043. doi:10.1016/j.psychres.2020.113043 PMID:32387793

Suresh, N., Mukabe, N., Hashiyana, V., Limbo, A., & Hauwanga, A. (2021). Career Counseling Chatbot on Facebook Messenger using AI. *ACM International Conference Proceeding Series*, (pp. 65–73). ACM. 10.1145/3484824.3484875

Sutton, H. (2019). Minimize online cheating through proctoring, consequences. *Recruiting & Retaining Adult Learners, 21*(5), 1–5. doi:10.1002/nsr.30434

Szolovits, P. (Ed.). (2019). *Artificial intelligence in medicine*. Routledge. doi:10.4324/9780429052071

Tahiru, F. (2021). AI in Education: A Systematic Literature Review. [JCIT]. *Journal of Cases on Information Technology, 23*(1), 1–20. doi:10.4018/JCIT.2021010101

Talib, C. A., Aliyu, H., Aliyu, F., Maimun, A., Malik, A., Anggoro, S., & Ali, M. (2020). Integration of robotics into STEM education for facilitating environmental sustainability. *Solid State Technology, 63*(1s), 767–783.

Tang, Y., & Daniels, T. E. (2015) A simple framework for distributed forensics. In: *25th IEEE International Conference on Distributed Computing Systems Workshops (ICDCS 15),* (pp. 163–169). IEEE.

Tapalova, O., & Zhiyenbayeva, N. (2022). Artificial Intelligence in Education: AIEd for Personalised Learning Pathways. *Electronic Journal of e-Learning, 20*(5), 639–653. doi:10.34190/ejel.20.5.2597

Tariq, M. U. (2024). Emerging Trends and Innovations in Blockchain-Digital Twin Integration for Green Investments: A Case Study Perspective. In S. Jafar, R. Rodriguez, H. Kannan, S. Akhtar, & P. Plugmann (Eds.), *Harnessing Blockchain-Digital Twin Fusion for Sustainable Investments* (pp. 148–175). IGI Global. doi:10.4018/979-8-3693-1878-2.ch007

Tariq, M. U. (2024). Emotional Intelligence in Understanding and Influencing Consumer Behavior. In T. Musiolik, R. Rodriguez, & H. Kannan (Eds.), *AI Impacts in Digital Consumer Behavior* (pp. 56–81). IGI Global. doi:10.4018/979-8-3693-1918-5.ch003

Tariq, M. U. (2024). Empowering Educators in the Learning Ecosystem. In F. Al Husseiny & A. Munna (Eds.), *Preparing Students for the Future Educational Paradigm* (pp. 232–255). IGI Global. doi:10.4018/979-8-3693-1536-1.ch010

Tariq, M. U. (2024). Equity and Inclusion in Learning Ecosystems. In F. Al Husseiny & A. Munna (Eds.), *Preparing Students for the Future Educational Paradigm* (pp. 155–176). IGI Global. doi:10.4018/979-8-3693-1536-1.ch007

Tariq, M. U. (2024). Revolutionizing Health Data Management With Blockchain Technology: Enhancing Security and Efficiency in a Digital Era. In M. Garcia & R. de Almeida (Eds.), *Emerging Technologies for Health Literacy and Medical Practice* (pp. 153–175). IGI Global. doi:10.4018/979-8-3693-1214-8.ch008

Tedre, M., Toivonen, T., Kahila, J., Vartiainen, H., Valtonen, T., Jormanainen, I., & Pears, A. (2021). Teaching machine learning in K–12 classroom: Pedagogical and technological trajectories for artificial intelligence education. *IEEE Access : Practical Innovations, Open Solutions*, *9*, 110558–110572. doi:10.1109/ACCESS.2021.3097962

Terwiesch, C. (2023). Would chat GPT3 get a Wharton MBA. A prediction based on its performance in the operations management course. [Mack Institute for Innovation Management at the Wharton School, University of Pennsylvania].

Thangthai, K., Harvey, R., Cox, S., & Theobald, B. J. (2015). Improving lipreading performance for robust audiovisual speech recognition using DNNs. In *Proceedings of the International Conference on Auditory-Visual Speech Processing* (pp. 127-131). Academic Press.

Thapa, K. (2023). *End-to-end Lip-reading: A Preliminary Study* (Doctoral dissertation, London South Bank University).

Tian, C. (2023, November 17). *foowaa/AVSR-datasets*. GitHub. Retrieved from https://github.com/foowaa/AVSR-datasets

Timms, M. J. (2016). Letting artificial intelligence in education out of the box: Educational cobots and smart classrooms. *International Journal of Artificial Intelligence in Education*, *26*(2), 701–712. doi:10.1007/s40593-016-0095-y

Topol, E. J. (2019). High-performance medicine: The convergence of human and artificial intelligence. *Nature Medicine*, *25*(1), 44–56. doi:10.1038/s41591-018-0300-7 PMID:30617339

Torrance, S. (2013). *Artificial agents and the expanding ethical circle*. doi:10.1007/s00146-012-0422-2

Tor, S. M., Iranmanesh, S., Nasrabadi, N., & Dawson, J. (2017). 3D convolutional neural networks for cross audio-visual matching recognition. *IEEE Access : Practical Innovations, Open Solutions*, *5*, 22081–22091.

Touretzky, D., Gardner-McCune, C., Breazeal, C., Martin, F., & Seehorn, D. (2019). A year in K-12 AI education. *AI Magazine*, *40*(4), 88–90. doi:10.1609/aimag.v40i4.5289

Trappey, A. J. C., Lin, A. P. C., Hsu, K. Y. K., Trappey, C. V., & Tu, K. L. K. (2022). Development of an Empathy-Centric Counseling Chatbot System Capable of Sentimental Dialogue Analysis. *Processes (Basel, Switzerland)*, *10*(5), 930. doi:10.3390/pr10050930

Tsai, Y. S., & Gasevic, D. (2017, March). Learning analytics in higher education---challenges and policies: a review of eight learning analytics policies. In *Proceedings of the seventh international learning analytics & knowledge conference* (pp. 233-242).

Turing, A. M. (2009). *Computing machinery and intelligence*. Springer Netherlands. doi:10.1007/978-1-4020-6710-5_3

Tynan, A. C., & Drayton, J. (1987). Market segmentation. *Journal of Marketing Management*, *2*(3), 301–335. doi:10.1080/0267257X.1987.9964020

Udvaros, J., & Forman, N. (2023). Artificial Intelligence and Education 4.0. In *INTED2023 Proceedings*, 6309-6317. 10.21125/inted.2023.1670

Unogwu, O. J., Hiran, K. K., Doshi, R., & Dadhich, M. (2022). Integrating InSAR, GNSS, IoT, 5G, and Cybersecurity for Earthquakes/Tremor Monitoring and Forecasting in Abuja, Nigeria. In 5G, Cybersecurity and Privacy in Developing Countries (pp. 195-209). River Publishers.

Urlaub, P., & Dessein, E. (2022). From disrupted classrooms to human-machine collaboration? The Pocket Calculator, Google Translate, and the future of language education. *Journal of Linguistics and Language Teaching*, *14*(1), x. doi:10.5070/L214151790

Valencia, K., Rusu, C., Quiñones, D., & Jamet, E. (2019). The Impact of Technology on People with Autism Spectrum Disorder: A Systematic Literature Review. *Sensors (Basel)*, *19*(20), 4485. doi:10.3390/s19204485 PMID:31623200

Valledor, A., Olmedo, A., Hellín, C. J., Tayebi, A., Otón-Tortosa, S., & Gómez, J. (2023). The Eclectic Approach in English Language Teaching Applications: A Qualitative Synthesis of the Literature. *Sustainability (Basel)*, *15*(15), 11978. doi:10.3390/su151511978

van der Niet, A. G., & Bleakley, A. (2021). Where medical education meets artificial intelligence:'Does technology care?'. *Medical Education*, *55*(1), 30–36. doi:10.1111/medu.14131 PMID:32078175

Van Der Vleuten, C. P., Schuwirth, L. W. T., Driessen, E. W., Govaerts, M. J. B., & Heeneman, S. (2015). Twelve tips for programmatic assessment. *Medical Teacher*, *37*(7), 641–646. doi:10.3109/0142159X.2014.973388 PMID:25410481

Van Wynsberghe, A. (2021). Sustainable AI: AI for sustainability and the sustainability of AI. *AI and Ethics*, *1*(3), 213–218. doi:10.1007/s43681-021-00043-6

VanLehn, K. (2011). The relative effectiveness of human tutoring, intelligent tutoring systems, and other tutoring systems. *Educational Psychologist*, *46*(4), 197–221. doi:10.1080/00461520.2011.611369

Varma, J. R., Fernando, S., Ting, B. Y., Aamir, S., Sivaprakasam, R., & Ting, B. Y. Z. (2023). The Global Use of Artificial Intelligence in the Undergraduate Medical Curriculum: A Systematic Review. *Cureus*, *15*(5). doi:10.7759/cureus.39701 PMID:37398823

Vartiainen, H., & Tedre, M. (2023). Using artificial intelligence in craft education: Crafting with text-to-image generative models. *Digital Creativity (Exeter)*, *34*(1), 1–21. doi:10.1080/14626268.2023.2174557

Vasiliu, L. A., Roman, D., & Prodan, R. (2023). Extreme and Sustainable Graph Processing for Green Finance Investment and Trading. *Companion of the 2023 ACM/SPEC International Conference on Performance Engineering*, (pp. 249–250). ACM. 10.1145/3578245.3585337

Vaswani, A., Shazeer, N., Parmar, N., Uszkoreit, J., Jones, L., Gomez, A. N., & Polosukhin, I. (2017). Attention is all you need. *Advances in Neural Information Processing Systems*, 30.

Verma, R., & Bandi, S. (2018). A Study on Retention of Talent and Reskilling of Workforce in IT Sector–A Case Study. *ISBR Management Journal, 3*(1).

Vidal, A., & Busso, C. (2023). Multimodal attention for lip synthesis using conditional generative adversarial networks. *Speech Communication*, *153*, 102959.

Vignesh, U. M., M., & Doshi, R. (Eds.). (2024). Bio-Inspired Optimization Techniques in Blockchain Systems. IGI Global. doi:10.4018/979-8-3693-1131-8

Vinuesa, R., Balaam, M., & Dignum, V. (n.d.). *The role of artificial intelligence in achieving the Sustainable Development Goals*. Research Gate. https://www.researchgate.net/publication/332831993

Vogt, K., & Flindt, N. (2023). Artificial Intelligence and the Future of Language Teacher Education: A Critical Review of the Use of AI Tools in the Foreign Language Classroom. *The Future of Teacher Education*, 179-199.

Vogt, H., Green, S., Ekstrøm, C. T., & Brodersen, J. (2019). How precision medicine and screening with big data could increase overdiagnosis. *BMJ (Clinical Research Ed.)*, 366. doi:10.1136/bmj.l5270 PMID:31519649 von Krogh, G. (2018). Artificial intelligence in organizations: New opportunities for phenomenon-based theorizing. *Academy of Management Discoveries*, *4*(4), 404–409. doi:10.5465/amd.2018.0084

Wachter, S., Mittelstadt, B., & Russell, C. (2020). *Why Fairness Cannot Be Automated: B Ridging The Gap Between Eu Non - Discrimination Law And AI*. 1–72.

Wagan, A. A., Khan, A. A., Chen, Y. L., Yee, P. L., Yang, J., & Laghari, A. A. (2023). Artificial Intelligence-Enabled Game-Based Learning and Quality of Experience: A Novel and Secure Framework (B-AIQoE). *Sustainability (Basel)*, *15*(6), 5362. doi:10.3390/su15065362

Wahab, S. N., Rajendran, S. D., & Yeap, S. P. (2021). Upskilling and reskilling requirement in logistics and supply chain industry for the fourth industrial revolution. *LogForum*, *17*(3), 399–410. doi:10.17270/J.LOG.2021.606

Walkowiak, E. (2023). Task-Interdependencies between Generative AI and Workers. *Economics Letters*, *231*(3), 1–13. doi:10.1016/j.econlet.2023.111315

Walsh, K. (2020). Artificial intelligence and healthcare professional education: Superhuman resources for health? *Postgraduate Medical Journal*, *96*(1133), 121–122. doi:10.1136/postgradmedj-2019-137132 PMID:31771964

Wand, M., Koutník, J., & Schmidhuber, J. (2016). Lipreading with long short-term memory. In *Proceedings of the IEEE International Conference on Acoustics, Speech, and Signal Processing (ICASSP)* (pp. 6115-6119). IEEE.

Wang, X., Han, Y., Leung, V. C. M., Niyato, D., Yan, X., & Chen, X. (2020). *Edge AI: Convergence of Edge Computing and Artificial Intelligence*. Springer. https://link.springer.com/book/10.1007/978-981-15-6186-3

Wang, D., Li, T., Liu, S., Zhang, J., & Liu, C. (2017). *Dynamical network forensics based on immune agent. Third International Conference on Natural Computation (ICNC 2017)*, Haikou, Hainan, China.

Wang, Z., & Majewicz Fey, A. (2018). Deep learning with convolutional neural network for objective skill evaluation in robot-assisted surgery. *International Journal of Computer Assisted Radiology and Surgery*, *13*(12), 1959–1970. doi:10.1007/s11548-018-1860-1 PMID:30255463

Wanjale, K., Chitre, A. V., & Doshi, R. (2023). Opting for Industry 4.0: Challenge or Opportunity. In *AI, IoT, Big Data and Cloud Computing for Industry 4.0* (pp. 3–20). Springer International Publishing. doi:10.1007/978-3-031-29713-7_1

Waqar, A., Andri, Qureshi, A. H., Almujibah, H. R., Tanjung, L. E., & Utami, C. (2023). Evaluation of success factors of utilizing AI in digital transformation of health and safety management systems in modern construction projects. *Ain Shams Engineering Journal*, *14*(11), 1–17. doi:10.1016/j.asej.2023.102551

Ward, J. P., Gordon, J., Field, M. J., & Lehmann, H. P. (2001). Communication and information technology in medical education. *Lancet*, *357*(9258), 792–796. doi:10.1016/S0140-6736(00)04173-8 PMID:11253986

Warfield, J. N. (1974a). Developing Interconnection Matrices in Structural Modeling. *IEEE Transactions on Systems, Man, and Cybernetics*, *SMC-4*(1), 81–87. doi:10.1109/TSMC.1974.5408524

Wartman, S. A., & Combs, C. D. (2018). Medical education must move from the information age to the age of artificial intelligence. *Academic Medicine*, *93*(8), 1107–1109. doi:10.1097/ACM.0000000000002044 PMID:29095704

Wartman, S. A., & Combs, C. D. (2019). Reimagining medical education in the age of AI. *AMA Journal of Ethics*, *21*(2), 146–152. doi:10.1001/amajethics.2019.146 PMID:30794124

Weidenbach, M., Trochim, S., Kreutter, S., Richter, C., Berlage, T., & Grunst, G. (2004). Intelligent training system integrated in an echocardiography simulator. *Computers in Biology and Medicine*, *34*(5), 407–425. doi:10.1016/S0010-4825(03)00084-2 PMID:15145712

Weizenbaum, J. (1966). ELIZA—A computer program for the study of natural language communication between man and machine. *Communications of the ACM*, *9*(1), 36–45. doi:10.1145/365153.365168

Weng, S. F., Vaz, L., Qureshi, N., & Kai, J. (2019). Prediction of premature all-cause mortality: A prospective general population cohort study comparing machine-learning and standard epidemiological approaches. *PLoS One*, *14*(3), e0214365. doi:10.1371/journal.pone.0214365 PMID:30917171

Wessel, M., Adam, M., Benlian, A., & Thies, F. (2023). Generative AI and its transformative value for digital platforms. *Journal of Management Information Systems.*

Westman, S., & Mononen, A. (n.d.). Artificial Intelligence for Career Guidance-Current Requirements and Prospects for the Future. In IAFOR Journal of Education: Technology in Education, 9. doi:10.22492/ije.9.4.03

Whyte, E. M., Smyth, J. M., & Scherf, K. S. (2014). Designing Serious Game Interventions for Individuals with Autism. *Journal of Autism and Developmental Disorders*, *45*(12), 3820–3831. doi:10.1007/s10803-014-2333-1 PMID:25488121

Wibowo, A., Narmaditya, B. S., Suparno, Sebayang, K. D. A., Mukhtar, S., & Shafiai, M. H. M. (2023). How does digital entrepreneurship education promote entrepreneurial intention? The role of social media and entrepreneurial intuition. *Social Sciences & Humanities Open*, *8*(1), 100681. doi:10.1016/j.ssaho.2023.100681

Wiljer, D., & Hakim, Z. (2019). Developing an artificial intelligence–enabled health care practice: Rewiring health care professions for better care. *Journal of Medical Imaging and Radiation Sciences*, *50*(4), S8–S14. doi:10.1016/j.jmir.2019.09.010 PMID:31791914

Williamson, B. (2019). Policy networks, performance metrics and platform markets: Charting the expanding data infrastructure of higher education. *British Journal of Educational Technology*, *50*(6), 2794–2809. doi:10.1111/bjet.12849

Williams, P. (2019). Does competency-based education with blockchain signal a new mission for universities? *Journal of Higher Education Policy and Management*, *41*(1), 104–117. doi:10.1080/1360080X.2018.1520491

Williams, R. T. (2023). The ethical implications of using generative chatbots in higher education. *Frontiers in Education*, *8*, 1331607. doi:10.3389/feduc.2023.1331607

Woo, J. H., & Choi, H. (2021). *Systematic review for AI-based language learning tools*. arXiv preprint arXiv:2111.04455.

Wood, E. A., Ange, B. L., & Miller, D. D. (2021). Are we ready to integrate artificial intelligence literacy into medical school curriculum: Students and faculty survey. *Journal of Medical Education and Curricular Development*, *8*, 23821205211024078. doi:10.1177/23821205211024078 PMID:34250242

*World Health Statistics 2020: Monitoring Health for the SDGs*. (2020). World Health Organization.

Worth, P. J. (2023). Word embeddings and semantic spaces in natural language processing. *International Journal of Intelligence Science*, *13*(1), 1–21. doi:10.4236/ijis.2023.131001

Wu, T., He, S., Liu, J., Sun, S., Liu, K., Han, Q. L., & Tang, Y. (2023). A brief overview of ChatGPT: The history, status quo and potential future development. *IEEE/CAA Journal of AutomaticaSinica*, *10*(5), 1122-1136.

Xing, G., Han, L., Zheng, Y., & Zhao, M. (2023). Application of deep learning in Mandarin Chinese lip-reading recognition. *EURASIP Journal on Wireless Communications and Networking*, *2023*(1), 90.

Xu, K., Li, D., Cassimatis, N., & Wang, X. (2018). LCANet: End-to-end lipreading with cascaded attention-CTC. In *Proceedings of the 13th IEEE International Conference on Automatic Face and Gesture Recognition (FG)* (pp. 548-555). IEEE.

Xu, Y., Liu, X., Cao, X., Huang, C., Liu, E., Qian, S., Liu, X., Wu, Y., Dong, F., Qiu, C.-W., Qiu, J., Hua, K., Su, W., Wu, J., Xu, H., Han, Y., Fu, C., Yin, Z., Liu, M., & Zhang, J. (2021). Artificial intelligence: A powerful paradigm for scientific research. *Innovation (Cambridge (Mass.))*, *2*(4), 1–20. doi:10.1016/j.xinn.2021.100179 PMID:34877560

Xygkou, A., Siriaraya, P., She, W.-J., Covaci, A., & Ang, C. S. (2024). "can I be more social with a chatbot?": Social connectedness through interactions of autistic adults with a conversational virtual human. *International Journal of Human-Computer Interaction*, 1–18. doi:10.1080/10447318.2023.2292880

Yahuza, M., Idris, M. Y. I. B., Wahab, A. W. B. A., Ho, A. T. S., Khan, S., Musa, S. N. B., & Taha, A. Z. B. (2020). Systematic Review on Security and Privacy Requirements in Edge Computing: State of the Art and Future Research Opportunities. *IEEE Access : Practical Innovations, Open Solutions*, *8*, 76541–76567. doi:10.1109/ACCESS.2020.2989456

Yamashita, R., Nishio, M., Do, R. K. G., & Togashi, K. (2018). Convolutional neural networks: An overview and application in radiology. *Insights Into Imaging*, *9*, 611–629. doi:10.1007/s13244-018-0639-9

Yang, S. J. H. (2021). *Education Technology and Society*. International Forum of Educational Technology & Society, National Taiwan Normal University.

Yang, H., & Kyun, S. (2022). The current research trend of artificial intelligence in language learning: A systematic empirical literature review from an activity theory perspective. *Australasian Journal of Educational Technology*, *38*(5), 180–210. doi:10.14742/ajet.7492

Yang, L., Wang, S., & Liew, A. W. C. (2023). Fine-Grained Lip Image Segmentation using Fuzzy Logic and Graph Reasoning. *IEEE Transactions on Fuzzy Systems*.

Yang, Q., Bai, Y., Liu, F., & Zhang, W. (2024). Integrated visual transformer and flash attention for lip-to-speech generation GAN. *Scientific Reports*, *14*(1), 4525.

Yang, Q., Steinfeld, A., Rosé, C., & Zimmerman, J. (2020). Re-examining whether, why, and how Human-AI Interaction is uniquely difficult to design. *Proceedings of CHI 2020* (pp. 1-13). ACM, New York. 10.1145/3313831.3376301

Yang, S. J. H., Ogata, H., Matsui, T., & Chen, N. S. (2021). Human-centered artificial intelligence in education: Seeing the invisible through the visible. *Computers and Education: Artificial Intelligence*, *2*, 100008. doi:10.1016/j.caeai.2021.100008

Yuan, S. N. V., & Ip, H. H. S. (2018). Using virtual reality to train emotional and social skills in children with autism spectrum disorder. *London Journal of Primary Care*, *10*(4), 110–112. doi:10.1080/17571472.2018.1483000 PMID:30083244

Yu, H., & Guo, Y. (2023). Generative artificial intelligence empowers educational reform: Current status, issues, and prospects. Frontiers in Education, 8, p. 1183162. *Frontiers*, 2023.

Yu, K. H., Beam, A. L., & Kohane, I. S. (2018). Artificial intelligence in healthcare. *Nature Biomedical Engineering*, *2*(10), 719–731. doi:10.1038/s41551-018-0305-z PMID:31015651

Yu, Z. (2023). Meta-analyses of effects of augmented reality on educational outcomes over a decade. *Interactive Learning Environments*, 1–15. doi:10.1080/10494820.2023.2205899

Zaidi, D., Raza, S., & Sharma, L. (2021). *Artificial Intelligence Based Career Counselling Chatbot: A System for counseling*. RSCB. http://annalsofrscb.ro

Zastudil, C., Rogalska, M., Kapp, C., Vaughn, J., & MacNeil, S. (2023). Generative ai in computing education: Perspectives of students and instructors. In *2023 IEEE Frontiers in Education Conference (FIE)* (pp. 1-9). IEEE.

Zawacki-Richter, O., Marín, V. I., Bond, M., & Gouverneur, F. (2019). A systematic review of research on artificial intelligence applications in higher education where are the educators? *International Journal of Educational Technology in Higher Education*, *16*(1), 39. doi:10.1186/s41239-019-0171-0

Zeb, A., Ali, A., & Ullah, D. A. (n.d.). The Role of Teachers in Career Guidance of Students at Secondary Level in Pakistan. In *Journal of Social Sciences Review* (Vol. 1). JSSR.

Zeide, E. (2019). Artificial Intelligence in Higher Education: Applications, Promise and Perils, and Ethical Questions. *EDUCAUSE Review*.

Zeniakin, O. (2023). Use of the Artificial Intelligence in Education: Opportunities, Prospects, and Risks. Conference: Psychological And Pedagogical Problems of Higher and Secondary Education in the Conditions of Modern Challenges: Theory and Practice, Kharkiv, Ukraine.

Zhai, X., Chu, X., Chai, C. S., Jong, M. S. Y., Istenic, A., Spector, M., Liu, J. B., Yuan, J., & Li, Y. (2021). A Review of Artificial Intelligence (AI) in Education from 2010 to 2020. *Complexity*, *2021*, 1–18. doi:10.1155/2021/8812542

Zhang, K., & Aslan, A. B. (2021). AI technologies for education: Recent research & future directions. *Computers and Education: Artificial Intelligence*, *2*, 100025. doi:10.1016/j.caeai.2021.100025

Zhang, Y., & Wang, H. (2022). Influence of Voice Interactive Educational Robot Combined with Artificial Intelligence for the Development of Adolescents. *Computational Intelligence and Neuroscience*, *2022*, 2022. doi:10.1155/2022/7655001 PMID:36248952

Zhao, J., Shen, J., Yan, J., Yang, X., Hao, Y., & Ran, Q. (2023). Corruption, market segmentation and haze pollution: Empirical evidence from China. *Journal of Environmental Planning and Management*, *66*(3), 642–664. doi:10.1080/09640568.2021.2001316

Zhao, J., Wu, M., Zhou, L., Wang, X., & Jia, J. (2022). Cognitive psychology-based artificial intelligence review. *Frontiers in Neuroscience*, *16*, 1024316. doi:10.3389/fnins.2022.1024316 PMID:36278021

Zhao, X. (2022). Leveraging artificial intelligence (AI) technology for English writing: Introducing Wordtune as a digital writing assistant for EFL writers. *RELC Journal*, 00336882221094089.

Zhou, C., Liu, X., Yu, C., Tao, Y., & Shao, Y. (2024). Trust in AI-augmented design: Applying structural equation modeling to AI-augmented design acceptance. *Heliyon*, *10*(1), 1–15. doi:10.1016/j.heliyon.2023.e23305 PMID:38192792

Zhu, T., & Liu, Y. (2023). Learning personalized preference: A segmentation strategy under consumer sparse data. *Expert Systems with Applications*, *215*(119333), 119333. doi:10.1016/j.eswa.2022.119333

Zimmerman, M. (2018). *Teaching AI: exploring new frontiers for learning*. International Society for Technology in Education.

Zirar, A., Ali, S. I., & Islam, N. (2023). Worker and workplace Artificial Intelligence (AI) coexistence: Emerging themes and research agenda. *Technovation*, *124*, 102747. doi:10.1016/j.technovation.2023.102747

Zou, J., & Schiebinger, L. (2018). AI can be sexist and racist - it's time to make it fair. *Nature*, *559*(7714), 324–326. doi:10.1038/d41586-018-05707-8 PMID:30018439

Zuwei, L. (2024, March 31). *lzuwei/end-to-end-multiview-lipreading*. GitHub. Retrieved from https://github.com/lzuwei/end-to-end-multiview-lipreading

# About the Contributors

**Ruchi Doshi** has more than 16 years of academic, research and software development experience in Asia and Africa. Currently she is working as research supervisor at the Azteca University, Mexico and Adjunct Professor at the Jyoti Vidyapeeth Women's University, Jaipur, Rajasthan, India. She worked in the BlueCrest University College, Liberia,West Africa as Registrar and Head, Examination; BlueCrest University College, Ghana, Africa; Amity University, Rajasthan, India; Trimax IT Infrastructure & Services, Udaipur, India. She worked as a Founder Chair, Women in Engineering (WIE) and Secretary Position in the IEEE Liberia Subsection. She worked with Ministry of Higher Education (MoHE) in Liberia and Ghana for the Degree approvals and accreditations processes. She is interested in the field of Machine Learning and Cloud computing framework development. She has published numerous research papers in peer-reviewed international journals and conferences. She is a Reviewer, Advisor, Ambassador and Editorial board member of various reputed International Journals and Conferences.

**Sandeep Poddar**, Deputy Vice Chancellor (Research & Innovation), Member of Board of Studies, Lincoln University College, Malaysia, has been graduated from University of Calcutta in 1993 with Honours in Zoology, he has obtained Post Graduate Diploma in Dietetics from All India Institute of Hygiene and Public Health 1995, Master of Science in Zoology with specialization in Biochemical Genetics from Dayalbagh Educational Institute 1998 with distinction. He has completed PhD in Zoology from Vivekananda Institute of Medical Sciences on Cytotoxicity in 2004. After completing PhD he pursued Post Doctoral Research in different projects on Hemoglobinopathies and Oral Cancer mutation. He has published several research papers, filed patent and organized international conferences, and also edited books in Malaysia, Australia and India. Dr Sandeep is Fellow member of Indian Academic Research Association, and World Researchers Associations and Life members of Different associations including Indian Science Congress Association. Dr Sandeep is founder Assistant Secretary of Dr Tarak Nath Podder Memorial Foundation, Kolkata, India

***

**Sbhajit Adhikari** is presently working as an Assistant Professor of Basic Science and Humanities Department, Institute of Engineering & Management (UEM) Kolkata. He had worked in BCA department in DAITM Kolkata for 7 years 6 months. He did his MSC Computer Science from St. Xavier's College, Kolkata and completed MTECH Software Engineering from MAKAUT,WB. He is a gold medallist(First Class First) in MTECH Software Engineering in 2016. He has qualified UGC-NET and WBSET in 2018 and 2019 respectively. He is doing PhD(Registered) in Computer Science from The University Of Burdwan. He has published several research papers in the domain of network security and cryptography. He received

"Young Scientist Award" in the field of Computer Science in 2023 from Dr. Ram Avatar Shiksha Samiti (DRASS) registered under the Societies Act 21, 1860 (Reg. No. 265, 2007-08) since July, 2007. He is teaching "java programming" to undergraduate students for approximately 6 years. The class notes of java programming have converted as E-modules for spreading the knowledge among students through online learning platform. He also teaches "Artificial Intelligence" to the post graduate students.

**Mhd Aquib Ansari** is an esteemed Assistant Professor at Bennett University, located in Noida, India. With a passion for academia and a dedication to excellence, Dr. Ansari brings a wealth of knowledge and experience to his role. His areas of expertise likely include computer vision, Image Processing, and he is committed to nurturing the intellectual growth of his students. With a strong academic background and a penchant for research, Dr. Ansari undoubtedly plays a pivotal role in shaping the minds of future generations at Bennett University.

**Aitab Bhattacharjee**, MBA, has been serving as a lecturer and research associate since 2016. He also holds an affiliate researcher position at Instituto de Investigación, Universidad Católica de Los Ángeles de Chimbote, in Latin America. He has successfully coordinated several international research projects in collaboration with the USA, Japan, India, and Malaysia. He is the author of several books and numerous publications. Mr. Bhattacharjee integrates low-emission technological concepts to investigate issues within eco-friendly industrial management and green economic development. His research work encompasses themes such as green technologies, renewable energy, and artificial/augmented intelligence in sustainable business practices and learning processes, green supply chain management, green entrepreneurship, and sustainability.

**Amiya Bhaumik** is the Founder President of Lincoln University College and is purely from the field of education. He is an Executive Vice President of the International Education Consulting Group, St. Louis, USA since 1999. Dr. Amiya Bhaumik was Research Fellow of UNESCO, Paris during this tenure, Dr. Bhaumik has traveled extensively to Europe, Africa, Asia and Latin America. He has served as professor of Business Administration in University of Lucknow, India and in University of Malaya and many other countries.

**Niket Bhoye** is a third-year student of the Information Technology department at Vishwakarma Institute of Information Technology, Pune. His research interests include Machine Learning.

**Sarvesh Bodakhe** is a third-year student of the Information Technology department at Vishwakarma Institute of Information Technology, Pune. His research interests include Machine Learning, Deep Learning.

**Aok Singh Chauhan** is currently working as an Associate Professor in the School of Computer Applications and Technology, Galgotias University, Greater Noida, Uttar Pradesh, India. He is a researcher, academician and technologist, who wants to do innovative research, share and impart knowledge in the area of Data Mining, Big Data, AI, Machine Learning and Deep Learning. He has done MCA, M.Tech (Information Technology), Executive PGDM (Information Systems Management), and Ph.D. He received a Ph.D. degree in Computer Application from Bundelkhand University, Jhansi, India. He has more than 17 years of experience in academia and research. He is a lifetime member of the International Association of Engineers (IAENG). He was honored as session chair and reviewer in various International conferences and journals. He has published more than 40 research papers in National/International Journals of repute. He has published various book chapters and patents. He presented more than 25 papers at various National/International Conferences and received outstanding paper as well as best paper awards also.

**Gagandeep Singh Cheema** is immersed in a part-time Ph.D. program in Commerce within the Finance domain at Lovely Professional University, where his research is concentrated on the fascinating landscape of Cryptocurrency. Gagandeep is not only deeply engaged in the financial realm but also exhibits a keen enthusiasm for learning about cutting-edge technologies, notably in the fields of AI and Blockchain. His multidisciplinary approach is further highlighted by his role as a co-author in a significant book "Unchaining the Future: A Comprehensive Guide to Blockchain and Economic Perspective of Cryptocurrencies", showcasing his ability to collaborate and contribute to diverse areas of expertise.

**Chaitravee Dusane** is a third-year student of the Information Technology department at Vishwakarma Institute of Information Technology, Pune. Her research interests include Artificial Intelligence.

**Ahijit Ghosh** is a dean of Faculty of Business & Accountancy and permanent professor of strategic management and green entrepreneurship at Lincoln University College in Malaysia. He has a Ph.D in management. Dr. Ghosh has published various articles on strategic management and technology entrepreneurship with a strong focus on technology innovation management.

**Dankan Gowda V**. is currently working as an Assistant Professor in the Department of Electronics and Communication Engineering at BMS Institute of Technology and Management in Bangalore. Previously, he worked as a Research Fellow at ADA DRDO and as a Software Engineer at Robert Bosch. With a total experience of 14 years, including teaching and industry, Dr. Gowda has made significant contributions to both academia and research. He has published over 100 research papers in renowned international journals and conferences. In recognition of his innovative work, Dr. Gowda has been granted six patents, including four from Indian authorities and two international patents. His research interests primarily lie in the fields of IoT and Signal Processing, where he has conducted workshops and handled industry projects. Dr. Gowda is passionate about teaching and strives to create an engaging and effective learning environment for his students. He consistently seeks opportunities to enhance his knowledge and stay updated with the latest advancements in his field.

**Kamal Kant Hiran** has over 19 years of experience in academia, research, and administration in Asia, Africa, and Europe. Currently working with Department of CSE at the Sir Padampat Singhania University, Udaipur, India. He has published 21 International books with repute publishers like BPB Publications, IGI Global, De Gruyter, Wiley from India, USA, Germany, UK. He has made significant contributions to our society's technological transformation. He has several awards to his credit such as International travel grant for attending the IEEE Region 8 Committee Meeting at Warsaw, Poland; International travel grant for Germany from ITS Europe, Passau, Germany; Best Research Paper Award at the University of Gondar, Ethiopia; IEEE Liberia Subsection Founder Award; Gold Medal Award in MTech (Hons.); IEEE Ghana Section Award-Technical and Professional Activity Chair; IEEE Senior Member Recognition, Best IEEE Student Branch Award, Elsevier Reviewer Recognition Award. He has published 75 scientific research papers in SCI/Scopus/Web of Science and IEEE Journals, conferences, 4 Indian Patents, 1 Australian Patent Grants. He has made several international visits to Denmark, Sweden, Germany,

**Mnir Hossen** is an academic researcher at Binary University of Management & Entrepreneurship, Malaysia. Currently, he also holds the position of Assistant Professor and Chairman in the Department of English at CCN University of Science & Technology, Cumilla, Bangladesh. His research interests include green education, global knowledge sharing, and virtual education.

**Naziya Hussain** is an Associate Professor in the department of School of Computers IPS Academy Indore. She obtained her B.E. (CSE) and M.E. (CSE) from RGPV University Bhopal and PhD Computer Science & Engineering from Department of CSE, Rabindranath Tagore University (Formerly AISECT University), Bhopal in Design and Development of Mobility Models Based Attacks Resilient and Efficient Protocol for Vehicular Ad hoc Network. She is having more than 16 years of teaching experience in computer science engineering field. She is the author of more than 25 Research Publication in different International Journals & Conferences. Her interests include Computer Network, Wireless Network, Ad-hoc Network and VANET Internet of Things(IoT), Machine Learning, Mobile Networks, WSN, Information Security, Cyber Security, Cloud Computing and Data Structure.

**Nabanita Indra** completed her graduation (BCA) in 2010 and post graduation(MCA) in 2013 from the Maulana Abul Kalam Azad University Of Technology (MAKAUT)West Bengal. After that she joined the BCA department in Dinabandhu Andrews Institute Of Technology and Management Kolkata in the year 2015. She has more than 8 years of teaching experience for both the undergraduate and post graduate students. She teaches Operating System, Object Oriented Programming using C++ and Java. She also did MTECH(CSE) in the year 2019 from the Maulana Abul Kalam Azad University Of Technology (MAKAUT)West Bengal.

**Mhammad Khairul Islam Juman** is a researcher at Malaysia University of Science and Technology, Malaysia. He also holds the position of Assistant Professor in the Faculty of Business Administration at CCN University of Science & Technology, Bangladesh. He received his Ph.D. in Management from Malaysia University of Science & Technology in 2022. His research interests include financial management, technological management, green management, and information management in education.

**KR. Swetha** is currently working as Assistant Professor, Department of Computer Science and Engineering, BGS Institute of Technology, Adichunchanagiri University, BG Nagara, Nagamangala Tq., Mandya, Karnataka. She obtained her Master of Engineering in Computer Science from UVCE, Bangalore University, Bangalore. She is perusing PhD at Adichunchanagiri University. Qualified GATE-2009 with 3 rd state Rank and 484 th all over India rank. Having 12+ years teaching experience in both undergraduate and postgraduate streams. She has published 5 full length papers in IEEE conferences and 1 Paper published in Q1 journal and 3 more papers published in scopus indexed journals.

**Sunil Karforma** has completed BE (Computer Science and Engineering) and ME (Computer Science and Engineering) from Jadavpur University. He has completed Ph. D. in the field of Computer Science. He is presently holding the post of Dean(Science) faculty The University of Burdwan. Network security and e-commerce are his fields of research interest. He has published approximately 150 research papers in reputed National and International journals and proceedings. Also, He has published many patents. He has guided many PhD scholars also.

**Mndeep Kaur** has completed her PhD in 2021 from lovely professional university, Jalandhar. She has completed her M.Tech in CSE in 2015 from DIET, Kharar under PTU, Jalandhar. She has completed B.Tech in CSE in 2011 from G.G.S.C.M.T. Kharar under PTU, Jalandhar. She is currently working as Assistant Professor in Department of Computer Science and Engineering, Chitkara University, Punjab, India. Previously she has worked in Chandigarh University, Gharuan, Punjab India. She have also worked in SBSSM Govt. College(Girls), Guru Ka, Khuh, Munne. Before that, she was working in GCET, Kahnpur Khuhi, Anandpur Sahib, Punjab. Her area of interest is Fog computing and Cloud computing.

**Llit Kumar** was born in Barabanki, Uttar Pradesh, India in 1996. He received B. Tech. and M.Tech. in Computer Science and Engineering from Dr. A. P. J. Abdul Kalam Technical University, Lucknow. Now, He is Pursuing PhD in Computer Science and Engineering from MNNIT Allahabad. His area of research is Computer Vision. He has more than five Journal and Conference papers.

**Dlal Kumbhakar** is state aided college teacher in the Department of BCA at Vivekananda Mahavidyalaya, Haripal. Hooghly, West Bengal, India.He received his Ph.D. degree in Computer science with an emphasis on Data Security in E Commerce from the University of Burdwan. His research interests lie in the areas of data security, hybrid model, machine learning in respect of e commerce as well as e learning. Dr. Kumbhakar published one book chapter and 13 research papers in reputed International journals.

**Maad M. Mijwil** is an Iraqi Academician; he is born in Baghdad, Iraq, in 1987. He received his B.Sc. degree in software engineering from Baghdad college of economic sciences university, Iraq, in 2009. He received a M.Sc. degree in 2015 from the computer science department, university of Baghdad in the field of wireless sensor networks, Iraq. Currently, he is working as a Lecturer and an academic member of staff in the computer techniques engineering department at Baghdad college of economic sciences university, Iraq. He has over ten years of experience in teaching and guiding projects for undergraduates. He has authored more than 100 publications, including papers/ chapters(published 88 peer reviewed papers in national/international conferences and journals), preprints, presentations, and posters. He is also an editor in more than 10 international/national journals and a reviewer in more than 100 international/ national journals. He has served on technical program committees for many prestigious conferences. Also, he graduated from Publons academy as a peer reviewer. His Google citations are over 1600 mark.

**Tangavel Murugan** serving as an Assistant Professor in the Department of Information Systems and Security, College of Information Technology, United Arab Emirates University. He received Doctorate from Madras Institute of Technology (MIT) Campus, Anna University, Chennai. He received Post Graduate degree as M.E. Computer Science and Engineering from J.J. College of Engineering and Technology, Trichy under Anna University, Chennai (University First Rank Holder & Gold Medalist) and Bachelor's degree as B.E. Computer Science and Engineering from M.A.M College of Engineering, Trichy under Anna University, Chennai (College First Rank Holder & Gold Medalist). He presently holds 10+ years of Teaching and Research experience from various academic institutions. He has published 10+ articles in Journals, 15+ Book Chapters, 25+ in the proceedings of Conferences and 1 Edited Book. He has been actively participating as reviewers in the international journals and conferences. He has been a technical speaker in various Workshops/Conferences. His research specialization is Information Security, High Performance Computing, Cybersecurity Intelligence and Educational Technology.

**Ramji Nagariya** is an Assistant Professor in the School of Business and Management, CHRIST (Deemed to be University), Bangaluru, India. He holds a Ph.D. in area of sustainable service supply chain from the Department of Management Studies, Malaviya National Institute of Technology, Jaipur, India. He holds a M. Tech in Industrial Management from Indian Institute of Technology (BHU), Varanasi and bachelor's degree in Aeronautical Engineering. His research papers are published in Business Process Management Journal, Benchmarking: An International Journal, Journal of Humanitarian Logistics and Supply Chain Management, Decision, International Journal of Services & Operations Management, and International Journal of Productivity & Performance Management. He has published several Scopus indexed book chapters also. His research interest includes service supply chain, buyer-supplier relationship and sustainability in supply chain.

**Kanchan Naithani** is a Research Scholar in the department of Computer Science and Engineering at H.N.B. Garhwal University (A Central University) Srinagar Garhwal, Uttarakhand, India. She completed B. Tech in Computer Science and Engineering from Graphic Era Hill University, Dehradun India (2016). She completed M. Tech in Computer Science and Engineering from G. B. Pant Engineering Institute of Technology, Ghurdauri, Pauri, Uttarakhand, India (2018). Her research interests focus on Artificial Intelligence, Machine Learning, Sentiment Analysis and Natural Language Processing.

**Garima Pancholi** is currently pursuing a PhD from Amity Business School, Amity University Rajasthan. She has also qualified the UGC-NET exam twice. She has completed her Graduation and Post-Graduation from Mohanlal Sukhadia University, specializing in Accountancy and Business Statistics as well as Business Administration. Her areas of focus in her research involve exploring topics such as Organizational Behavior, Organizational Resilience and Sustainability.

**Swati Patil** received a M.Tech degree in Computer Engineering from Vishwakarma Institute of Technology, Pune. She is presently working as an assistant professor in the Information Technology department at Vishwakarma Institute of Information Technology, Pune. She has 18 years of teaching experience. She has taught multiple subjects, including Data Structures, Data Management System and Machine Learning. Her research interest includes Machine Learning, Deep Learning.

**Riya R** is an MBA student at CMS Business School, Jain Deemed-to-be University, Bengaluru, India

**Y. P. Raiwani** is a Professor and Head in the Department of Computer Science and Engineering, and EX-Dean, School of Engineering & Technology at H.N.B. Garhwal University (A Central University) Srinagar Garhwal, Uttarakhand, India. Having teaching experience of all most Thirty three years in the field of Computer Science & Applications in University, He is actively engaged in research work and has published more than 38 research papers in reputed journals. His areas of interests include Data Mining, Machine Learning, Networking, Big data, Pattern Recognition and Signal Processing and Cloud Computing. He holds several administrative posts in university such as Head and Convener Computer Science, Deputy Controller Examination, Assistant Proctor, Programme Officer NSS and Academic In-charge of various courses. He is also associated with reputed academic bodies such as senior life member of Computer Society of India (CSI), and International Association of Engineers (IAENG) etc.

**Rajaprabakaran Rajendran** is an incisive medical communication professional with over 23 years of experience in CME/CPD, medico-marketing/medical communication, client servicing, and KOL management; managing medcom programmes for healthcare professionals in Asia Pacific and the Middle East and North Africa regions. He has extensive experience in the planning and delivery of key innovative medcom programmes through multi-channel platforms for leading pharmaceutical companies in order to facilitate effective engagement with their target audiences across medical specialties. Raja is mainly responsible for designing medical communication/education strategies and delivering high quality medical communication/education programmes in collaboration with national and international medical associations, universities and hospitals, and key opinion leaders across medical specialties. Now he is a research scholar at CMS Business School, Jain Deemed To-Be University, Bangalore.

**Rajaprabakaran Rajendran** is an incisive medical

**Sehal Rathi** received a Ph.D. degree in Computer Engineering from Vishwakarma University, Pune in 2022. She is presently working as an assistant professor in the Computer Engineering department at Vishwakarma Institute of Information Technology, Pune. She has 20 years of teaching experience. She has taught multiple subjects, including Data Structures, Data Mining and Machine Learning. Her research interest includes machine learning, deep learning, soft computing and human-computer interaction.

**Rmandeep Sandhu** is working as an Associate Professor in the School of Computer Science and Engineering, Lovely Professional University, Phagwara, Punjab, India. She received her Ph.D. degree from Lovely Professional University, Phagwara, Punjab, India in the year 2021. She has more than 14 years of teaching experience of reputed institutes. Her general research are areas such as Artificial Intelligence, Cloud Computing, Machine Learning, and Opinion Mining/Sentiment Analysis. She has published 2 books. First one is named "OOPs Awareness with C++", ISBN: 978-93-5300-939-7. Another one is "A Start to C++ Programming with Object Oriented Concepts", ISBN: 978-93-955819-3-6. Now she is writing Book on "Practicing Programming using Python". She has various research publications in Scopus Indexed Journals as well as UGC-approved Journals. She has presented more than 15 research papers in various International/National conferences. She is currently guiding 3 PhD Scholars. She organized National Conference in the year 2014 at CGC Campus Jhanjeri, Mohali. She was honored with Best Teacher Award in the year 2013, 2014, and 2015. Apart from this, she has been honored with Best Communication Skills Award in the year 2019. She has also received Best Paper presentation award in conference held at Baba Farid Group of Institutions in the year 2011.

**Ahineet Saxena** is an incisive professional with 12 years of experience spanning diversified areas such as Corporate Training, Research, and Teaching. He received an MBA degree in Finance and Marketing from Rajasthan technical university, in 2010 and a Ph.D. degree in Microfinance from the University of Rajasthan in 2016. He is NET qualified and currently working as an Assistant professor (AP-3) at the Amity Business School, Amity University Rajasthan. Currently, he is also in charge of Yunus social business Centre – AUR Jaipur. His current research interests include Banking and Finance, corporate finance, Impact assessment of social security schemes, and Holistic rural development. He also received a post-Doctorate fellowship and award from ICSSR New Delhi in the year 2017. He is an experienced professional and has been guiding individuals and Research scholars in eminent educational Institutions. He has worked in various capacities such as Research Project Principal investigator, Educational Consultant, Data analytics Trainer, Examiner, etc., and has honed his professional training and management skills working with globally reputed organizations.

**Piyanshu Sharma** is Associate Lecturer in the Department of Management, Birla Institute of Technology Mesra, Jaipur Campus and has been teaching Finance Management and Taxation since 2009. He is a post graduate in Commerce and also in Business Administration. He holds Ph. D. in Commerce and Management Studies. His current research interests are in Blockchain Technology, Goods and services tax (GST) and Digital Finance. He has published many research papers Scopus, National, International journals and Conference proceedings.

**Chaitali Shewale** received an M.Tech degree in Computer Engineering. She is presently working as an assistant professor in the Information Technology department at Vishwakarma Institute of Information Technology, Pune. She has taught multiple subjects, including Data Structures, Artificial Intelligence.

**Dshyant Kumar Singh** is affiliated with the Department of Computer Science & Engineering, Motilal Nehru National Institute of Technology, where Dr. Dushyant Kumar Singh is currently working as Associate Professor. Dr. Dushyant Kumar Singh has authored and co-authored several national and international publications and is also working as a reviewer for reputed professional journals. Dr. Dushyant Kumar Singh has an active association with different societies and academies around the world. Dr. Dushyant Kumar Singh made his mark in the scientific community with the contributions and widely recognition from Honourable subject experts around the world. Dr. Dushyant Kumar Singh has received several awards for his contributions to the scientific community. Dr. Dushyant Kumar Singh's major research interest involves Computer Vision, Image processing, Embedded Design, Machine Learning & mining in Computer vision.

**Sasti Singhal** is working as a Professor in the Department of Computer Science & Information Technology at KIET Group of Institutions, Ghaziabad- NCR . Her areas of interest includes sustainability manufacturing, Machine Learning techniques, Data Anlaytics and many more .She had published number of research paper in the field of ML.

**Heena Siroya**, a dedicated Research Scholar hailing from the esteemed School of Management at Sir Padampat Singhania University in Udaipur, holds an MBA degree from Jaipur National University and an M.COM from Jai Narain Vyas University, Jodhpur. With over half a decade of rich teaching experience, she has imparted knowledge at various educational institutions, ranging from colleges and universities to schools. Currently, she is pursuing her research at the School of Management, Sir Padampat Singhania University, Udaipur, where she is deeply engrossed in her scholarly pursuits. Her academic contributions include the publication of 2 research papers in internationally acclaimed journals indexed in Scopus and IEEE. In addition, she has presented more than 3 research papers and Faculty Development Programs (FDPs) at both national and international conferences, showcasing her commitment to continuous learning and knowledge sharing. She has partnered with Social Entrepreneurs and Eco-Friendly Product Companies, leveraging her expertise to contribute to these diverse sectors. Her research primarily zeroes in on Social Entrepreneurs and the development of Sustainable Products, reflecting her commitment to social responsibility and environmental sustainability.

**Kirti Siroya** is a distinguished scholar and practitioner in the fields of public health and dental surgery. She holds a Master's degree in Public Health (MPH) from the prestigious School of Public Health, AIIMS Jodhpur, and a Bachelor's degree in Dental Surgery (BDS) from Rajasthan University of Health Sciences, Jaipur, where she was honored as a Gold Medalist. Currently, she is further broadening her academic horizons by pursuing a Postgraduate Diploma in Rural Development from IGNOU. Her professional experience spans across various domains, including a year of clinical dental practice and two years of teaching. In addition to her academic and professional achievements, she has been an integral part of various projects across several departments. She has collaborated with the Department of Pediatrics, the Dental Department, and the Department of Psychiatry, contributing her expertise and knowledge to these diverse fields. She has made contributions to the field of research with two published research articles and has presented her findings at two national conferences. Her research primarily focuses on AI & telemedicine, public health research, health economics and finance, tribal & rural health, and public policy & programs. During her Master's program, she was actively involved in various research projects, further enhancing her understanding and skills in public health. This hands-on experience has equipped her with a comprehensive understanding of the field, enabling her to approach public health issues with a unique perspective.

**S. Yavana Rani**, Professor of MBA in the Decision Science area at CMS Business School, Jain Deemed-to-be University, Bangalore. Since receiving her MBA and Ph.D. in Management, she has devoted her career to Research and Teaching. She also has a Master's degree in Structural Engineering. She is the University rank holder in MBA. She has 16 years of teaching experience. Dr. Rani has received Young Scientist Fellowship Award from Tamilnadu State Council for Science and Technology (TNSCST). She has completed her fellowship from Indian Institute of Science (IISc), Bangalore. She is the life time member in Indian Society for Technical Education (ISTE). Dr. Yavana Rani has done two research projects sponsored by Indian Council for Social Science and Research (ICSSR). She has published more than 10 research articles in Scopus indexed and Springer journals. She has presented papers in National and International conferences in India and abroad. She is the editor for many reputed journals. She has delivered key note address in countries like Egypt, Malaysia. Prof. Rani holds many administrative roles such as Dean Student Affairs, Director Coordination for various activities. She has been project Director for Entrepreneurship Cell (EDC) sponsored by Department of Science and Technology (DST). She also coordinated many programmes. Professor has got funding for conducting conferences, International visit from various funding agencies like DST and ICSSR.

**Snjay Taneja** is currently an Associate Professor in Research at Graphic Era University, Dehradun, India and affiliate professor, Department of finance and banking, University of Usak, turkey. His significant thrust areas are Banking Regulations, Banking and Finance (Fin Tech, Green Finance), Risks, Insurance Management, Green Economics and Management of Innovation in Insurance. He holds a double master's degree (MBA &M.Com.) in management with a specialization in Finance and Marketing. He received his PG degrees in Management (Gold Medalist) from Chaudhary Devi University, Sirsa, India in 2012. He earned his Doctor of Philosophy (Sponsored By ICSSR) in Banking and Finance entitled "An Appraisal of financial performance of Indian Banking Sector: A Comparative study of Public, Private and Foreign banks in 2016 from Chaudhary Devi University, Sirsa, India. He received his Post Doctoral Degree from faculty of Social Sciences, Department of Banking and Insurance, Usak University, Turkey entitled on "Impact of the European Green Deal on Carbon (CO2) Emission in Turkey" in 2023. He has published research papers in reputed SCOPUS/Web of Science/SCI/ABDC/UGC Care Journals. Prof. Taneja has more than fifty publications in total (Scopus/ABDC/Web of Science- 27)

**Muhammad Usman Tariq** has more than 16+ year's experience in industry and academia. He has been working as a consultant and trainer for industries representing six sigma, quality, health and safety, environmental systems, project management, and information security standards. His work has encompassed sectors in aviation, manufacturing, food, hospitality, education, finance, research, software and transportation. He has diverse and significant experience working with accreditation agencies of ABET, ACBSP, AACSB, WASC, CAA, EFQM and NCEAC. Additionally, Dr. Tariq has operational experience in incubators, research labs, government research projects, private sector startups, program creation and management at various industrial and academic levels. He is Certified Higher Education Teacher from Harvard University, USA, Certified Online Educator from HMBSU, Certified Six Sigma Master Black Belt, Lead Auditor ISO 9001 Certified, ISO 14001, IOSH MS, OSHA 30, and OSHA 48. He is member of Harvard Business Review Advisory Council.

**Shrikant Tiwari** (Senior Member, IEEE) received his Ph.D. in the Department of Computer Science & Engineering (CSE) from the Indian Institute of Technology (Banaras Hindu University), Varanasi (India) in 2012 and M. Tech. in Computer Science and Technology from University of Mysore (India) in 2009. Currently, he is working as an Associate Professor in the Department of Computer Science & Engineering (CSE) School of Computing Science and Engineering (SCSE) at Galgotias University, Greater Noida, Uttar Pradesh (India). He has authored or co-authored more than 35 national and international journal publications, book chapters, and conference articles. He has five patents filed to his credit. His research interests include machine learning, deep learning, computer vision, medical image analysis, pattern recognition, and biometrics. Dr. Tiwari is a member of ACM, IET, FIETE, CSI, ISTE, IAENG, SCIEI. He is also a guest editorial board member and a reviewer for many international journals of repute.

**Ayşe Tuna** is a lecturer at Trakya University, Turkey since 2005. She has authored papers in international conference proceedings, and has been actively serving as a reviewer for international conferences and journals. Her research interests are support services for the elderly and disabled, education of autistic and related communication handicapped children, human-robot interaction, human-computer interaction, and data management methodologies.

**Getha V** is an Assistant Professor at PG & Research Department of Commerce, Mannar Thirumalai Naicker College, Madurai.

**W Jaisingh** is an associate professor in the School of CSE abd Information Science at Presidency University, Bangalore, India. He received a doctorate from Anna University, Chennai, in 2013 and a Master of Philosophy in Computer Science from Alagappa University in 2005. He has 22 years of teaching and research experience. He has published more than 20 papers in international refereed journals, 30 papers in international conferences, and contributed chapters to books. He has received the "Indian Book of Records" and the "Asia Book of Records" for contributing as an author to the book titled "Covid 19 and its Impact". The book has been selected for the record "maximum authors contributing to a book". He is a Lead Editor in Maximum Authors Contributing for a Book on "Covid 19 and its Impact,", 2021. His areas of research interest include data science, machine learning, data mining, data analytics, image processing, and deep learning. He is a lifetime member of professional societies such as the International Association of Computer Science and Information Technology (IACSIT), the Computer Science Teachers Association, and the Indian Society for Technical Education (ISTE).

# Index

## D



## E



## F



## G



## H



## I

## J



## K



## L



## M



## N



## O



## P



## R



## S

## T



## U



## V



## W

www.ingramcontent.com/pod-product-compliance
Lightning Source LLC
LaVergne TN
LVHW080620300926
849162LV00005B/1214